COMMUNICATION

Dr. C.S. RAYUDU

B.Com., (Hons.), m.Com., L.L.B., M.A. (Econs.).
Ph.D., FUWAI, CIC, LITT (U.S.A.),

Professor and Head
Department of Commerce
Sri Krishnadevaraya University
Anantpur, A.P.

Himalaya Publishing House

ISO 9001:2015 CERTIFIED

First Edition	:	1997
Second Edition	:	1998
Third Edition	:	2000
Fourth Edition	:	2001
Fifth Revised Edition	:	2004
Sixth Edition	:	2005
Seventh Edition	:	2006
Eight Revised Edition	:	2007
Edition	:	2008, 2009
Ninth Edition	:	2010
Edition	:	2012, 2015, 2016,
Edition	:	2018, 2019, 2022
Edition	:	2023
Edition	**:**	**2025**

Published by : Mrs. Meena Pandey
for **HIMALAYA PUBLISHING HOUSE PVT. LTD.,**
"Ramdoot", Dr. Bhalerao Marg, Girgaon, Mumbai - 400 004.
Phone: 022-23860170, 23863863; **Fax:** 022-23877178
E-mail: himpub@bharatmail.co.in; **Website:** www.himpub.com

Branch Offices :

New Delhi : "Pooja Apartments", 4-B, Murari Lal Street, Ansari Road, Darya Ganj, New Delhi - 110 002. Phone: 011-23270392, 23278631; Fax: 011-23256286

Nagpur : Kundanlal Chandak Industrial Estate, Ghat Road, Nagpur - 440 018. Phone: 0712-2721215, 2721216

Bengaluru : Plot No. 91-33, 2nd Main Road, Seshadripuram, Behind Nataraja Theatre, Bengaluru - 560 020. Phone: 080-41138821; Mobile: 09379847017, 09379847005

Hyderabad : No. 3-4-184, Lingampally, Besides Raghavendra Swamy Matham, Kachiguda, Hyderabad - 500 027. Phone: 040-27560041, 27550139

Chennai : No. 34/44, Motilal Street, T. Nagar, Chennai - 600 017. Mobile: 09380460419

Pune : "Laksha" Apartment, First Floor, No. 527, Mehunpura, Shaniwarpeth (Near Prabhat Theatre), Pune - 411 030. Phone: 020-24496323, 24496333; Mobile: 09370579333

Cuttack : Plot No 5F-755/4, Sector-9, CDA Markat Nagar, Cuttack - 753 014, Odisha. Mobile: 09338746007

Kolkata : 3, S.M. Bose Road, Near Gate No. 5, Agarpara Railway Station, North 24 Parganas, West Bengal - 700109. Mobile: 09674536325

Printed by : Geetanjali Press Pvt. Ltd., Ghat Road, Nagpur - 440 018. On behalf of HPH.

PREFACE

Communication is an exciting and truly challenging field of human interaction. Communication skills, a fascinating study, consists of five segments: speaking, listening, writing, readability and readable writing and non-verbal cues, which are completely neglected in formal education. Communication can be a fun, as we are interacting with others by exchanging facts, feelings, figures, emotions, ideas, opinions etc.

Fast changes in the society demand that people be proficient in all segments of communication. The body of knowledge of communication in all the five segments is just as essential as developing skills in any other disciplines.

In this competitive world, students are now being challenged to exhibit the ability to think, write, observe and speak effectively. Their communication problem is about right perception, use of information, analysis of situation, creation of impulses and finding ways to put across and handle messages.

Presently, this subject is taught in many places in the country at different levels such as undergraduate and post-graduate courses like mass communication, management, commerce, public relations and journalism. In recent years, distance courses have begun to appear on the scene. Such a unique situation has created the need to provide a textbook, and that too, with a set of principles, practice, and oriented to the syllabus. Hence, this kind of a textbook, giving, therefore, the kind consideration to that fact, that this book has been compiled to survive the cause of communication education.

Time is now ripe to recognise the importance of this interesting and multi-disciplinary subject to be introduced to all the students. Whatever their academic discipline, students or any reader would gain much benefit from the subject. Believe that an effective communication is indispensable for effective human relations.

In writing this book, I originally intended to cover only the basic aspects on speaking and writing in five chapters. But I found that the work would be incomplete unless all segments of communication are dealt with. So I was led to include additional chapters on listening, readability, non-verbal cues, feedback, management communication etc., and I included for good measure, chapters on elementary language skills, letter and report writing as well as recent trends and communication technologies. Thus, the book contains fifteen chapters. But still it is a mode of attempt.

My intention to produce this volume is to help explore the methodology of communication process. A cookbook of solutions to the human problems of communication, which are not so simple, but complex and dynamic. Some of its problems are not even amenable to cookbook guidelines because of dynamic intricacies of human interaction and behaviour. Thus, this book provides useful concepts, principles, techniques, guidelines for developing awareness of and competence in the fascinating subject. It is novel in reinforcing that study with modern insights to "Communication Age", in which communication is inseparable from human relations, which directly or indirectly affects every person.

Thus, in many significant ways, this book is different from most communication books because of its integrated approach and comprehensive coverage.

My aim in this book has been to devise a form which is readable, rereadable, and make up interesting, thought provoking, funny and enjoyable and applicable to practical situations. This is what I have tried to accomplish.

Managers, executives, trainees, public relation officers, personal assistants, associates, employees, advocates, journalists, media personnel, teachers, students, politicians, sales force, researchers and host of others will find this book to be of immense practical help to improve their performance.

As to the shape and content of the book I dare say that no individual credit is claimed. Therefore, I cannot do better than to quote the following and every word in the quotations apply fully to the originality or otherwise of this book.

"I gather the flowers by the wayside, by the brooks and in the meadows, and only the string with which I bind them together is my own."

Montaigne

" A book which hath been culled from the flowers of all books."

George Eliot

"I have made here merely a nosegay of other peoples' flowers, and have provided nothing of my own except the thread which holds them together."

Montaigne

"Nothing is said now-a-days that has not been said before."

I may be forgiven if any copyright material is found included for which prior permission has not been obtained owing to the inability to trace the copyright owner and also for similar or other omissions.

You are ultimately right judges of whether I have delivered the goods. I hope after reading this book you will share your responses of this book. This book is truly yours.

I heartly invite any comments and suggestions concerning this book and your recommendations to improve the quality of the book in its next edition.

Subject Arrangement

This book, which runs into fifteen chapters, is for the sake of convenience divided to cover several areas of communication. These chapters provide a logical presentation and development of the subject matter in sequencing. Suggestions, guidelines, hints have been included in each chapter for improving skills and to make speaking, writing, listening, readability and readable writing and non-verbal cues effective. Thus, I have presented the whole of the subject systematically classifying it under the following heads:

To know the elements of communication first, read Chapter 1. It is designed to provide the theoretical and conceptual framework for a foundation to understand the communication process.

Next, look through Chapter 2 which helps you to make good, competent, and effective public speech on any occasion. It helps you to become a successful orator. Chapter 3 discusses how the former is different from the latter and the barriers to listening and offers essentials for good listening.

Then turn to Chapter 4 which contains a detailed discussion on the principles and techniques of writing skills. The subject has been presented in such a form that it can help you to almost any kind of effective writing which are required for it.

If you want to know about readability and readable writing, please look up Chapter 5. This deals with the principles, readability formulae and systematic reading.

Chapter 6 of this book presents detailed instructions on non-verbal cues and skills. It covers cues of facial expression, bodily movement, eye contact, gestures, postures, objectives, language, paralanguage etc.

The last and the important element in the communication process is feedback. Chapter 7 is devoted to the subject dealing with its importance, types, principles and guidelines and shows how to make effective feedback.

Management communication is arranged in Chapter 8. It deals with leadership behaviour and communication, conflict resolution, impression management, cross culture communication etc.

Chapter 9 explains about organisations and formal communication and its various forms, channels, media which every executive is expected to know.

Formation of informal groups in a formal organisation is a natural characteristic. Informal communication is more powerful than formal which no executive is expected to ignore. Thus, Chapter 10 emphasises the dimensions of informal relations and communication implication.

The subject of small group formation, group decision-making, group conflict and communication implications are discussed in Chapter 11.

Report-writing and letter-writing are an art as well as craft. Chapter 12 covers types of reports and ingredients to be followed to make a good report. Similarly, Chapter 13 presents the art of impressive letter writing.

A remarkable transformation has taken place in communication with the development of sophisticated communication technologies. Chapter 14 gives elaborate details of communication technologies and recent trends.

Effective communication is not possible unless language skills are acquired. Chapter 15 reviews and presents preliminaries like grammar, vocabulary, semantics, words and word choice, punctuations etc.

Dr. C. S. Rayudu

28/3/393
Nagavihar.
Saradanagar,
Anantpur (post).

ACKNOWLEDGEMENTS

A great many people have participated, directly or indirectly, in the preparation of this book, but I would like to express my deep sense of gratitude to a few for their valuable contributions.

I am grateful to Prof. K. R. Balan, my mentor, who has been a constant source of inspiration for the intellectual stimulation and guidance. His timely advice and very illuminating discourses on the subject of this book and related areas made this book possible.

No author can write in vacuum and I am certainly no exception. Vast reading of several books and discussions with experts concerned enabled me to write this book. I am greatly indebted to all the authors and publishers of standard books of communication, management and other related texts.

I owe a special debt to my teacher, Prof. R.K. Bharti, Professor of Commerce, Dean and Head of the Department of Commerce, Doctor Harisingh Gour Vishwavidyalaya, Sagar, for his guidance and encouragement.

My family has also an important role in the completion of this book. I am also appreciative of my wife's help in editing and proof-reading and for bearing with me during troublesome periods of preparation of this book. I owe to my wife C. Rathna for maintaining domestic order and comfort which facilitated labours of writing this book.

And also C. Divya and C.S. Chaitanya, my young daughter and son who have provided a pleasurable source of distraction and inspiration. I would be failing in my duty if I do not record my gratitude at a personal level to my paternal uncles Choudem Balaiah and Choudem Subbaiah who brought me up to the present academic position.

I am beholden to Dr. N. Narayana, Professor of Economics, Sri Krishnadevaraya University, Anantpur, the spirit behind the scene, to bring the book in the present shape.

I am also thankful to C. Ramprasada Rao, Head, the Sri Krishnadevaraya Institute of Management, Sri Krishnadevaraya University, Anantpur, for his valuable timely suggestions and advice to shape the contents.

I am equally grateful to Dr. C.R. Reddy, Professor of Commerce, and Head, Department of Commerce, Sri Krishnadevaraya University, Anantpur and H. Lajipathi Roy, Professor of Commerce and Chairman, Board of Studies, Department of Commerce, Sri Krishnadevaraya University, Anantpur, for all their co-operation and advice.

I also thank several others who contributed in their own way to make this book possible.

Dr. C. S. Rayudu

CONTENTS

CHAPTER 1

Fundamentals of Communication

Earliest Efforts — Adam and Eve

One of the earliest examples of interpersonal communication obeying Denis McQuail's linear model, must be the one between Adam and Eve after chewing the forbidden fruit.

Juxtaposing a piece of conversational imagery from John Maria's article "Battle of the Sexes", one may effectively portray how the curtain raises for the first verbal dual between man and woman and how she stoops to conquer.

After eating the apple, the excited Adam, covering himself with fig leaves, looks at Eve in anguish and says, "This is all your fault, I mean who would listen to a snake for Pete's sake?"

Eve Reports

"Who is Pete? And anyway it takes two to a Tango, buster, you did your share of the chewing when it came to the apple."

Adam, losing his ground, looks at Eve in all innocence and asks, "What is a Tango anyway?"[1]

What happened further in the garden of Eden, how Adam, the first male of the homosapien species, got his beating is not our slice of apple.

Pre-Historic Communication

Two million years ago, man made his first appearance on earth, heralding the down of an era yet unborn — the era of Communication. He produced sounds and made gestures to convey his feelings of joy, fear and sorrow.

Time passed by. Man multiplied. His families expanded and coalesced into tribes Soon, a need for communication arose.

Lighting a fire, he sent smoke signals to convey messages over long distances.

Meaning of Communication

The word "communication" is derived from the Latin word *communist,* which means common. In its application, it means a common ground of understanding. It is a process of exchange of facts, ideas, opinions and as a means that individuals or organisations share meaning and understanding with one another. In other words, it is the transmission and interacting of facts, ideas, opinions, feelings or attitudes. Communication is an interdisciplinary concept because theoretically, it is approached from various disciplines such as mathematics, accounting, psychology, ecology, linguistic, systems analysis, etymology, cybernetics, auditing etc.

Communication is a process involving the sorting, selecting and sending of symbols in such a way as to help the listener perceive and recreate in his own mind the meaning contained in the mind of the communicator. Communication involves the creation of meaning in the listener, the transfer of information and thousands of potential stimuli. Communication enables us to do important things, to grow, to learn to be aware of ourselves and to adjust to our environment.

To communicate with one another is a compulsive urge of human beings. There can be no mutual understanding without communication; mutual understanding is the core of human relations. Communication is like birth, death, breath and wanting to be loved as a part of life itself. Man is a communicating animal; he alone has the power to express in words. Sight, sound, touch, smell and taste are the modes of exchange of messages. Communication is the story of man and his efforts to communicate effectively. Civilisation and culture progress to the extent communication has made these possible.

Definitions of Communication

American Society of Training Directors: "The interchange of thought or information to bring about mutual understanding and confidence or good human relation."

Newman and Summer: "Communication is an exchange of facts, ideas, opinions, or emotions by two or more persons. Communication is also defined as intercourse by words, letters, symbols, or messages and as a way that one organisation member shares meaning and understanding with another."

Leland Brown: "Communication is the transmission and interchange of facts, ideas, feelings, or course of action."

Allen Louis A.: "Communication is the sum of all the things one person does when he wants to create understanding in the mind of another. It involves a systematic and continuous process of telling, listening and understanding."

Ordway Tead: "Communicating is a composite of information given and received, of a learning experience in which certain attitudes, knowledge, and skills change, carving with them alterations of behaviour, of listening effort by all involved, of a sympathetic fresh examination of issues by the communicator himself, of a sensitive interacting points of view, leading to a higher level of shared understanding and common intention."

Bellows, Gilson and Odiorne: "Communication is defined as intercourse by words, letters, symbols or messages and a way that one organisation member shares meaning and understanding with another."

Charles E. Redfield: "Communication is the broad field of human interchange of facts and opinions and not the technologies of telephone, telegraph, radio and the like."

Theo Haiemann: "Communication is the process of passing information and understanding from one person to another. It is the process of imparting ideas and making oneself understood by others."

M.T. Myers and G.E. Myers: "Communication refers to a special kind of patterning: patterning which is expressed in symbolic form. For communication to take place between or among people, two requirements must be met: (I) a symbolic system must be shared by the people involved (we need to speak the same language or jargon or dialects) and (2) the associations between the symbols and their referents must be shared."

Katz and Kahn: "Communication — the exchange of information and the transmission of meaning - is the very essence of a social system or an organisation."

Davis: "Process of passing information and understanding from one person to another...." "The only way that management can be achieved in an organisation is through the process of communication."

Chester Barnard: "In exhaustive theory of organisation, communication would occupy a central place because the structure, extensiveness, and scope of organisations are almost entirely determined by communication techniques."

Simon: "The question to be asked of any administrative process is: How does it influence the decisions of the individuals without communication, the answer must always be: It does not influence them at all."

Edwin B. Flippo and Gary M. Munsinger: "Communication is the act of intercourse by words, letters, symbols or messages and is a way that one organisation member shares meaning and understanding with another."

Scope of Communication

The scope of communication is very wide and comprehensive. It is a subject of almost unlimited dimensions and is a interdisciplinary one. It is a two-way process involving both transmission as well as reception. It is a continuous process of exchange of facts, ideas, feelings, attitudes, opinions, figures, and interactions with others. In the process, it uses a set of symbols; symbols may be words, action, pictures or figures. Communication, however, does not mean downward movement of sending directions, orders, instructions etc. It is only one-way communication.

Two-way communication represents movement of communication upward. Internal communication flows in different directions — vertical, horizontal, diagonal and across the organisational structure. Internal communication may be formal and informal. External communication is concerned with transmission of messages outside the organisation with Government, its departments, customers, dealers, intercorporate bodies, general public, investors, etc. External communication promotes goodwill with the public. Internal communication helps in discharge of managerial functions like planning, direction, co-ordination, motivation etc.

The broad policies and objectives flow downward from top management to a lower level. Both written and oral or verbal media can be used to transmit messages. Written media consist of instructions, orders, letters, memos, house journals, posters, bulletins, boards, information racks, handbooks, manuals, annual reports, union publications, etc. Verbal media may consist of face-to-face conversation, lectures, conferences, meetings, interviews, counselling, public address system, telephone, grapevine, etc. Recently, a number of sophisticated communication technologies have emerged, both in oral and written communication on account of technological advancement.

Nature of Communication

Organisations are represented as communication systems. It is a formal process to accomplish the desired common goals. It is an exchange of information between individuals, groups, departments, etc. Every organisation has its own sub-systems and there is always infraction "and interface between sub-systems to achieve goals. Communication transmits information and data to the sub-systems as well as to the total system. Management information system operates effectively through communication. It involves information gathering, storage, processing and monitoring.

It includes both present and past information. Communication is a tool and a vital aspect of management process. As a matter of fact, superior-subordinate relationship can exist only with effective and meaningful communication. There must be two parties to the process of communication. The communicator or sender or transmitter of message and the receiver or recipient or listener or reader is another party at the end. The nature of communication is exchange of message and interaction. Communication may be through written or verbal, action, figures or pictures.

The purpose of communication is to make others to understand and act upon it accordingly in the same sense. Communication is effective when the message is shared and understood with one another. There can be no communication if the information is not understood by the receiver in the same sense as it was intended to be by the communicator. It need not be necessary in effective communication that the receiver must agree or accept the information. It is sufficient if the information is understood even though information is rejected or disagreement exists.

IS COMMUNICATION AN ART OR A SCIENCE?

The concept of communication is universal and is as old as human beings. That is why different views have been expressed about the nature of communication. The nature of communication becomes clearer if an attempt is made to examine the following important issues:

1. Is communication an inborn quality?
2. Is communication a science or an art?
3. Are the principles of communication of universal application?

These question are often raised. For answers to these questions, it is necessary to understand the exact meaning of the terms, science and art.

1. Communication, an Inborn Quality

Communication is an inborn quality. To communicate with one another is a compulsive urge of human beings. Communication is like birth, death, breath and wanting to be loved as an art or of life itself. Man is a communication animal because he alone has the power to express in words. Sight, sound, touch, smell and taste are the modes of exchange of messages.

No doubt, communication is an inborn quality but not an inborn quality without scientific base. In the pre-scientific management of communication period, prior to 1880, there had been a leading concept that communication was an inborn quality. Many people believed that it is not necessary to study any organised body of knowledge of communication concepts, principles, as managers were born and not made. There may be some people who are so efficient and talented in making effective communication since their birth, they lead and are successful in effective exchange of ideas, feelings, facts etc. But, as we see today, this concept has become obsolete by the development of the faculty of communication as a separate discipline.

Therefore, to communicate effectively, it is necessary that one should acquire skills of communication like speaking skills, listening skills, writing skills and reading skills. This is the reason why successful and effective communicators are made but not born. Therefore, this subject is the story of man and his efforts to achieve effective communication. Pre-historic man produced sounds and sent smoke-signals, gestures to convey his feelings. Civilization and cultural progress was possible through communication. It was within the family and very closely living people helped the primitive communities to achieve this.

The last century witnessed the rapid transmission of communication by electronic media which became possible due to the rapid advancement of sophisticated communication technologies. In this "age of communication" the most significant technologies are based on silicon chips, the lesser, fiber optics and a set of technologies known as biotechnologies. The information technology revolution has transformed the communication conscious human society into a global village.

What is Science?

Science may be defined as an organised and systematised body of knowledge based on proper findings and exact principles, pertaining to an area of study and contain some general truths explaining the past events or phenomena. The body of knowledge has been systematised through the application of scientific methods. Thus, we may speak of the science of astronomy, physical sciences, biological science, chemistry and social sciences like sociology, political science, economics etc.

We speak about these sciences to indicate accumulated knowledge with reference to the discovery of general truths. Science explains phenomena because it establishes relationship between cause and effect and its principles are universally applicable. The hypotheses, which are generally called generalisations are tested for their accuracy. Science may be classified into two groups, namely, positive science and normative science. Positive science deals with "what is" and normative science deals with "what to be."

The principles are universal and truthful. For instance, water is formed with two volumes of hydrogen mixed with one volume of oxygen. According to the law of gravitation, if anything is thrown towards the sky, it will come down to the earth. On the other hand, water turns into vapour when it is boiled.

What is Art?

Art is the ability or skill which is due to more practice than learning. In other words, art refers to the best way of doing things. It guides how an objective is to be achieved. The art of management deals with the application of skill and effort for accomplishing desirable results. It is knowing how the application part of a body of knowledge is required. On the other hand, under science, one usually understands the knowing "why."

According to Chester I. Barnard it is the function of the art to accomplish concrete ends, effect results, produce situations that would not come about without the deliberate effort to secure them. It is the application of the body of knowledge acquired. Every art is practical, in that the proof of the practitioner's competence lies in the tangible results.

Communication is an Art and a Science

It is obvious that communication contains both the elements those of a science and those of an art. Then, communication is both an art and science. The science of communication provides a body of principles which can guide the managers to find a solution to the specific problems and objective evaluation of results. Like any art, communication is also creative. It develops new situations, new designs and new systems needed for further improvement.

It is true that there is no one best way of communicating. Everyone has his individual approach, skill, behaviour and techniques in dealing with a particular situation. So, communication is the oldest of the arts and the youngest of the sciences. The process of communication is very much related with the behavioural aspects of the people at work and their dynamics cannot be predicted in exact manner.

The limitation of social sciences are there with the science of communication. But, with the introduction of sophisticated communication technologies in the field, communication is fast growing as a science. The subject has an organised and systematised body of knowledge having its own theories, principles, concepts and nature.

The knowledge of communication can be imparted to newcomers also through formal training. Though communication is an inborn quality, it cannot be effective without proper training. So, managers can be made effective communicators but they are not born.

To illustrate, a doctor knows the body of knowledge of science of anatomy. But, he also practices by applying the principles of science of anatomy. It is similar in a chemist, a physicist, an engineer etc. That is why theoretical knowledge is accompanied with practical work also. Similarly, the skills of communication should be theoretically acquired and practised as an art. The art of communication deals with the application of skill and effort for producing desirable results. So, as a conclusion, we can say that communication is a science as well as a social science, having its own approach, dynamics in different work situations.

Both — the theoretical knowledge and the practical knowledge are necessary. They are complementary to each other and are not mutually exclusive. With the increase in the technique and knowledge of communication, the art is to be improved. Communication science and communication art are indeed interwoven and overlapping in nature. It may be true to say that the art of communication is as old as human history, but the science of communication is an event of the recent past. The emergence of communication as a distinct and leading technology is a pivotal event in a social history. In recent years. considerable attention has been given to communication, resulting in the emergence of sophisticated communication technologies.

Communication is a Social Process

The above discussion establishes that communication process involves the sender of the message and the receiver of the message. In between, encoding and decoding of symbols takes place; reception, listening and knowledge represent the reception stage. Communication is also a special process because there is interpersonal communication process in which two or more people are involved. In case of a written communication, the sender is a writer and receiver is a reader. In case of oral communication the speaker transmits the message and the receiver is the listener. In the case of visual communication, the function of the receiver is observation.

Communication as a social process affects the entire society. It is a tool that enables everyone in society to satisfy his basic needs and desires and to get along with other people. As a social process, it is a means of recording and preserving knowledge by way of writing, symbols or by some other device to pass it on to the next generation. Thus, communication is not only a means of individual and group progress and social advancement, society as a whole interacts in the communication process to influence the society.

Communication is a Human Process

Basically, communication is a human process — an art and craft of transmitting information. Communication is indeed an activity process, consisting of some basic techniques and models for getting information and transmitting of information on the activities or the enterprise for accomplishment of broad objectives. Whatever the broad objectives formulated by the management to be accomplished through organised efforts and co-operative endeavour of individuals and groups, communication becomes a necessity for informing, directing, co-ordinating and unifying the efforts of managerial people towards a common goal. It is the informing, collecting information and activating element in a business enterprise.

The art of getting things done through and with the people in a formally organised group cannot be achieved without a proper communication network. The job of management is to disseminate as much detailed information by various networks and media so as to enable the management groups to understand objectives, policies, procedures and rules to accomplish organisational objectives. On the other hand, it is the function of the management to gather detailed information from appropriate channels which helps managers in making sound decisions and in turn to communicate. Thus, communication is a function of management by means of which the purposes and objectives of an individual or group are determined, communicated, directed, co-ordinated and achieved.

Communication is a human process because two or more people are involved. In an oral communication, every word spoken requires a listener, every letter in a written communication requires a reader, every visual communication requires an observer. The receiver may respond by reporting to someone or by taking some action that will influence others. The recipient of the message in an organisation may try to tell it to someone else or respond by taking some action. Communication, as an organisational process, affects all. It enables us to satisfy our basic needs and desires and to get along with other people. This human and organisational process is also the means of recording knowledge and passing it on to the succeeding generations. Without it, business enterprise cannot operate. Communication is the means of individual and group progress.

Communication is a Universal Process

The principles of communication are in the nature of universal application. The principle of universality of communication is one of the characteristics pertaining to the nature of communication. Truly speaking, the problem of effective communication is present in all interpersonal, group and organisational activities. The problems are present everywhere whether it be a family, a school, State and Central Government departments, undertakings, corporations, trade unions and in all joint activities.

The principles and techniques of communication are universal in application but not necessarily and exclusively applicable to only business. They are applicable to social, religious, charitable, formal, non-formal, non-profit organisations also. Communication is a universal process. The chairman, managing director, heads of various functional areas and subordinates have necessarily, to use the same communication skills and principles in their inter-personal group and organisational situations. The fundamental principles of scientific communication are applicable to all human activities, from the simplest small groups to great corporations and the public.

There are a number of elements fundamental in the process of communication which are common to the process of communication in different walks of life. It is on the basis of these elements that theory of communication can be evolved. The principles and theory of communication are useful because they provide a broad basis for approaching communication problems. Universality of communication principles also means that they are transferable, newcomers can know and be made as effective communicators. Universality of principles also means that all people have to follow the same principles and skills regardless of their position. Thus, communication seeks to harmonise individual efforts with the organisational goals.

The Process of Communication

Communication is a process of exchange of ideas, facts, opinions and manner by which the receiver of the message shares meaning and understanding with another. It is the whole sequence of transmission and interchange of facts, ideas, feelings etc. Process is a course of action. Communication as an organisational process affects all. It enables us to transfer information from one person to another, from one department to another, from outside to the organisation, no matter whether the organisation is an individual, firm, society or a body corporate. The ultimate object is that information transferred must be understandable by the receiver.

It is organisational process because a group of people and group activities are involved. Every information transmission involves a reader or a listener who responds to the message. This organisational process is also the means of preparing information and circulating it to others in the organisation. Without this process, organisational activities do not progress. Communication is the vehicle of individuals and group in the organisation. In this process, the transmitter uses a set of media to convey ideas, opinions, facts or feelings to another. The media may be written media, or oral media, visual or audio-visual media. Visual or communication media carry slides, neon-hoardings, posters, etc. Television and films are audio-visual communication media.

Communication is a process that uses a set of media to transmit ideas, facts and feelings from one person to another. Media challenge the communicator to select them with an awareness of their purpose to the listener or reader. So, a good communicator must understand the receiving and understanding capabilities of the recipient not only of the transmitting message but also their effect.

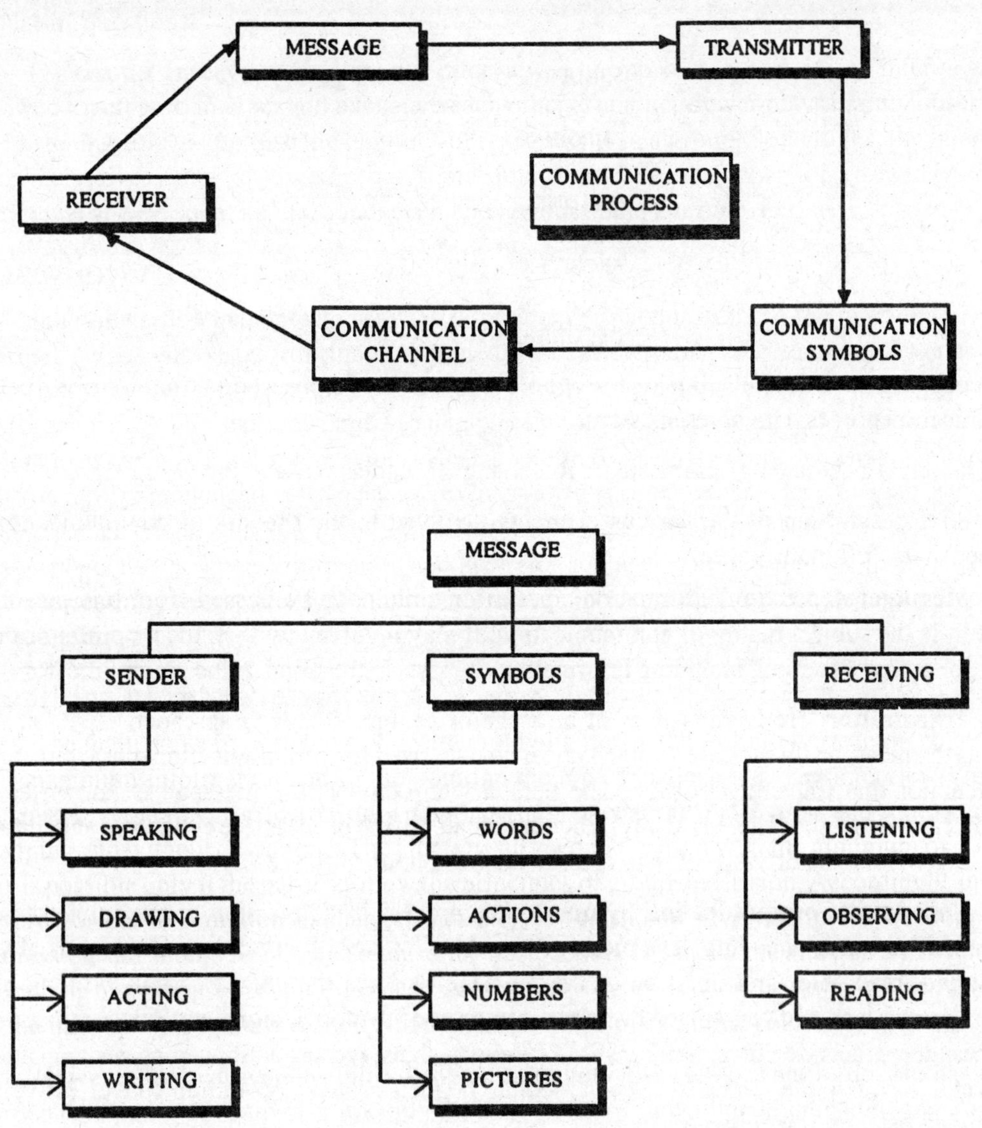

Fig.1.1 Communication Process

In the process of various media, the organisation's mission is accomplished and activised. The transmitter selects when and what to communicate and determines their medium for transmission. The receiver or recipient takes the message, interprets, perceives and responds to it. The whole sequence is the communication process. As a process, it is routine and continues forever. Every time a person transmits the facts, ideas, opinions or feelings, another person responds in turn communicating facts, ideas, feelings or attitudes. It is a never ending process cycle. The cycle, in brief, broadly covers the following elements shown in the figure.

Elements of Communication Process

The whole process of communication involves the following elements:

According to David K. Berlo, the whole sequence of communicating with B (called communication process) involves six steps.

Ideation→Encoding→Transmission→Receiving→(Sender)→Decoding→Acting

A brief description of the various elements involved in the process of communication is described in the following pages.

1. Message: A piece of information, spoken or written, to be passed from one person to another. It is the subject matter of communication. It may involve any fact, idea, opinion, figure, attitude, or course of action, including information. It exists in the mind of the communicator.

2. Transmitter: He is the sender of message or communicator or spreader, a person who transmits the message. In the case of mechanical devices used for communication, para transmitter is an operator that transmit message. The person who conveys the message is known as the communicator or sender. There is always a communicator in the process. He conceives and initiates the message. He is the driving force to change the behaviour of the receiver.

3. Encoding (Communication Symbol): The process of conversion of the subject matter into symbols is called encoding. The message or subject matter of any communication is always abstract and intangible. Transmission of the message requires the use of certain symbols. The communicator plans and organises his ideas into a set of symbols, signs etc. Encoding process translates ideas, facts, feelings, opinions into symbols, signs, words, actions, pictures, and audio-visuals etc. It is up to the sender to select a medium he feels proper to communicate effectively to the intended listener or receiver.

4. Communication Channel: Later, the transmitter has to select the channel for sending the information. Communication channel means the medium or media through which the message passes. The words, symbols or signs selected should be transmitted to the receiver or listener through certain channel or medium. Media in plural represent vehicles to transmit message. The communicator has to decide how best he can pass the message, what he has to convey. Media may be written media or oral media. Again, there are various forms of written media like letters, reports, manuals, circulars, notes, questionnaires etc. The forms of oral media include face-to-face conversation, dictaphone, telephone, recording, radio meeting, conference etc. The channel may be a visual channel like slides, neon hoardings, posters etc. Television and documentary films represent audio-visual channels.

5. Receiver: There is always a receiver in the process of communication. Receiver is the person to whom the message is meant for by the sender. A person who receives the message is called the receiver. Effective communication process is not complete without the existence of a receiver of the message. Responding or acting to the message is done by the receiver only. It is the receiver who receives and tries to interpret, perceive, understand and act upon the message.

6. Decoding: Decoding is the process of translation of an encoded message into ordinary understandable language. Receiver converts the symbols, words or signs received from the sender to get the meaning of the message.

7. Acting: According to the understanding of the message, the receiver acts or implements the message.

8. Feedback: Feedback is though the last element and an important one in the communication process. As it has been explained, communication is an exchange process. For the exchange to be complete the information must go back to the communicator, so that he can know the reaction of the receiver. The sending back of the knowledge about the message to the transmitter is known as feedback. It ensures that the receiver has received the message and understood in the same sense as the sender meant. Feedback enables the communicator to carry out corrections or amendments or change the message to be effective.

The entire sequence described above is the complete communication process or cycle having eight components.

COMMUNICATION PROCESS: MODELS AND THEORIES

There are many communication process models and theories to understand the process involved in it as developed by different people. It is practically very tedious, time and space consuming to consider all the communication models. It is, therefore, desirable to become acquainted with some significant and important models which serve the purpose of understanding the process of communication.

1. LINEAR MODEL

1. Aristotle's Model

The first step towards development of a communication model had been taken by Aristotle. He had developed an easy, simple and elementary model of the communication process. According to Aristotle, in a communication event, there are three main ingredients, such as:

The Speaker,

The Speech, and

The Audience.

Subsequently, a number of experts have developed modern models of communication which are more complex and dynamic.

2. Mathematical Theory

The Mathematical Theory of Communication developed by C. E. Shannon and W. Weaver, popularly called Shannon-Weaver Model, was developed in 1949 as a model in the electronic communication. They considered the theory as strictly mathematical and has been identified with technology and technical aspects of communication. It created an impact on such concepts as measuring the unit of the information transmitted over technical channel.

3. Information Theory

In 1950 the information theory developed separately from the communication theory. Computer science, data processing, cybernetics and so on are the only segments of the information theory. Every discipline has contributed to the communication theory. The behavioural scientists have adopted very successfully the mathematical theory to explain human communication.

Shannon was an engineer, concerned himself with the technical problems of transmitting signals from the one point to another. He considered communication as a mechanistic system consisting of the following five basic elements. They are:

1. Information — source
2. Transmitter — to convert a message into transmittable sign
3. A Channel
4. A receiver — who reconstructs the message from the sign
5. Destination — the person or machine to whom it is intended.

The other four components he introduced in the system, are:

1. The Message;
2. Transmitted Signals;
3. Received Signals;
4. Noise Source.

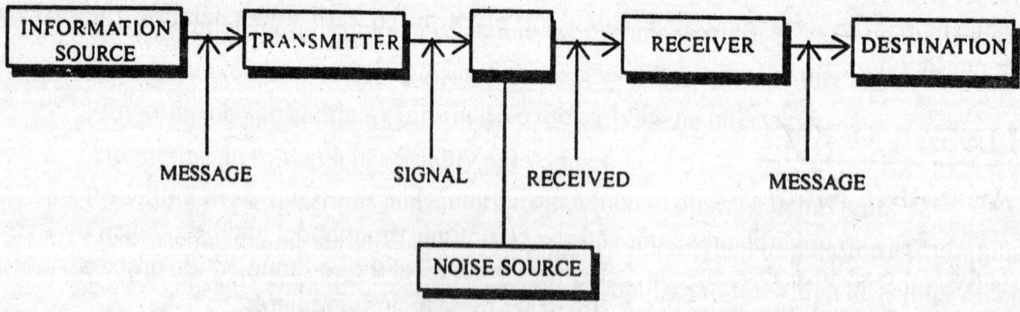

Fig. 1.2 Shannon and Weaver Model

Technological aspects of communication have a direct bearing on measuring the units of information transmitted over the technical channel which led to the development of information theory. The components of information theory are the computer science, data processing, cybernetics etc. Each of these areas have been contributing to communication theory. Communication system and its problems are being tried to be explained by the mathematical model developed by Shannon-Weaver model.

Their model contains the essential elements for explaining the human communication process. They identify the element of semantics — that meaning lies in people. The degree of difference in meaning between the sender and the receiver is accounted for by noise. The mathematical theory of communication is also used in developing the information and computer science.

4. David K. Berlo's Model

David Berlo's process theory is one of the basic theories for all communication theorists. The various theories of process models indicate the idea persuasively to another person. Berlo's model is of basic importance in developing other communication models and for identifying elements of communication. Berlo's process theory has contributed a great deal to the subject of communication. In this model, he identified essential elements and also other factors affecting them such as the five senses. One thing, however, we have to mention here is that the model does not consider verbal and non-verbal stimuli.

The following nine components are included in his model:

A Source
A Encoder
A Message
A Channel
A Receiver
A Decoder
A Meaning
A Feedback and
A Noise

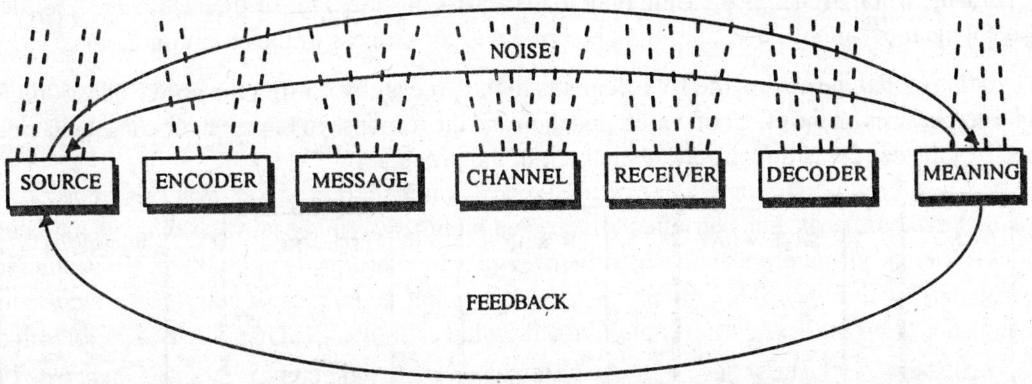

Fig. 1.3 David k. Berlo's Model

5. Harold D. Lasswell Model

The communication process of Lasswell, in its broader analysis, gives rise to four basic and important questions. They are Who? What? Whom? Which? The behavioural aspects of the sender in the communication process is well- established by Lasswell. But his model ignores the essential elements of the communication process. But Lasswell's model indicates the major elements in the process by posing some questions dealing with the act of communication. They are:

Who?

Says What?

In What Channel?

To Whom?

With What Effect?

1. Why?

Why do we want to communicate? What is the purpose of the communication? Is it to persuade or to inform? Is any particular action required?

2. What?

What is it we want to communicate? An order, an idea, an attitude or a feeling? What form of words or possible actions best meets the situation?

3. How?

How are we going to communicate? In what form will the communication get home the message fastest? What impact will a particular form have on the recipient?

4. Who?

Is there a key to the communication situation? How does he feel about me, about this situation?

5. When?

Finally, when? When is the right time to get across this message? When is the receiver likely to give it the most attention? Can timing be critical to the success of the communication?

In this model, he covers the five elements in the process by putting the above questions. The model emphasises on the effect of communication and the response of the receivers. The behavioural aspects of the sender is the important element in the process.

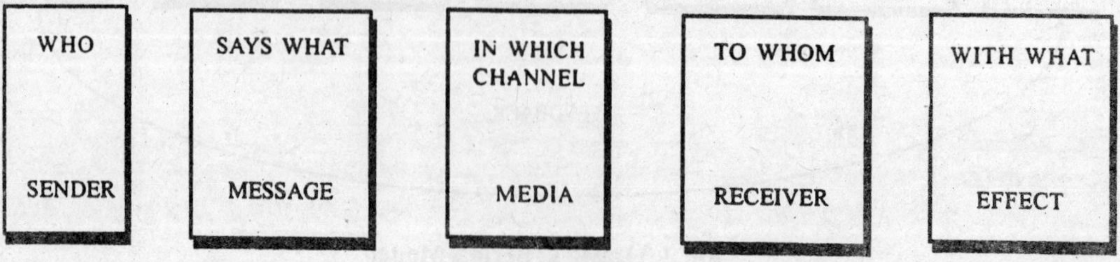

Fig. 1.4 Lasswell Model

6. Wilbur L. Schramm Model

His theory is concerned with mass communication. His model 'How Communication Works' is represented in Fig. 1.5. In this model, the focus is on the signal from the two sides of the source and receiver. The encoder which is the source has to encode and the same is to be decoded towards destination. The model is very simple to understand.

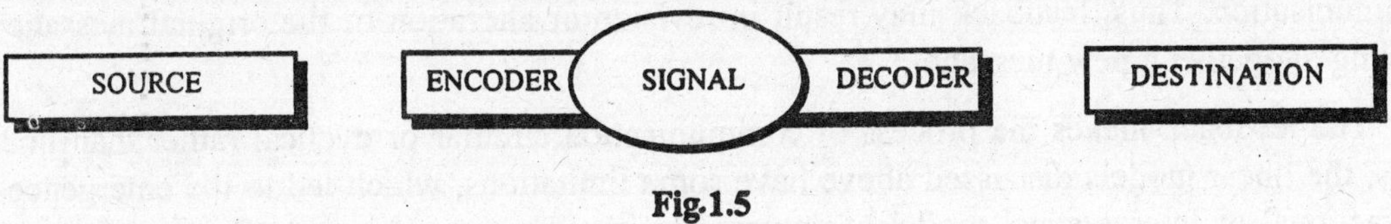

Fig.1.5

7. U.S. Rai and S.M. Rai Model

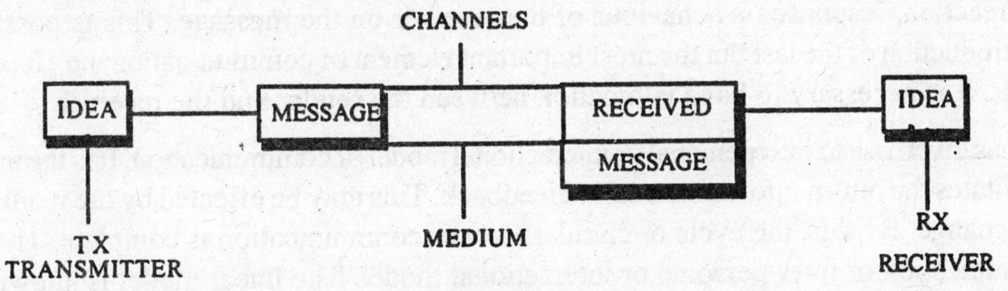

Fig.1.6

8. Roger A. Vogel & William D. Brooks Model

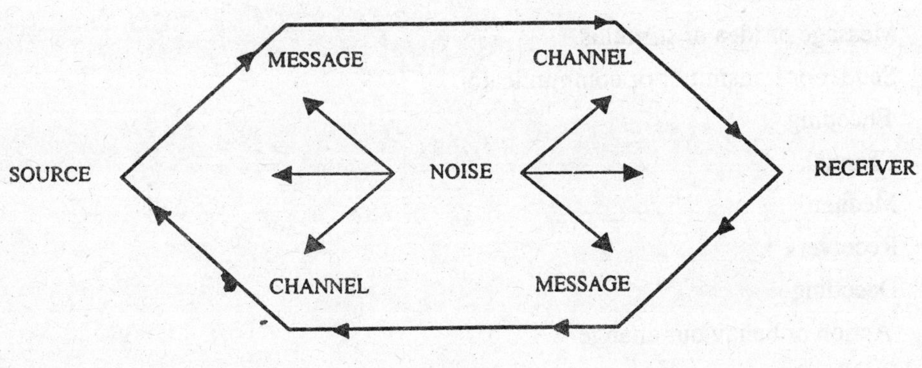

Fig.1.7

2. INTERPERSONAL OR INTERACTIONAL MODEL

The interpersonal or interactional model of communication is also called "circular" or "cyclical" model. The various models discussed above are linear models, which do not consider the response or reply from the receiver of the message. Linear models have some limitations because they contain almost some common elements of communication process. But actually effective communication is cyclical or circular in nature. In the circular system of communication process, the element of feedback is introduced. All linear models may undergo change if the element of feedback is introduced.

Feedback with reference to the communication process means interaction or interface or face-to-face communication with another person who is the receiver of the message. The purpose of feedback is to measure and evaluate the message received by the receiver and to plan for future communication. Thus, feedback may result in revision or alteration of the original message or sending altogether a new message.

The feedback makes the process of communication circular or cyclical rather than linear. Thus, the linear models discussed above have some limitations, which led to the emergence of interactional or interpersonal model of communication. The interpersonal effective process of communication demands that the sender of the message has to ascertain whether the message has been understood by the receiver or acted upon it or behaviour is changed. He must know the receiver's reaction, response or behaviour of the receiver on the message. This is possible only with the introduction of the last but the most important element of communication, i.e., feedback. In other words, it is necessary to have interaction between the sender and the receiver.

This has given rise to interpersonal or interactional model of communication. It is the interaction which facilitates the return information called feedback. This may be effected by the words, sign or behaviour change. By this, the cycle or circular flow of communication is complete. This is two-way communication or inter-personal or interactional model. The linear model is known as one-way communication. This is the reason why effective communication is called interpersonal or interactional communication.

The interpersonal model of communication demands the presence of the following elements in the process of communication:

1. Message or idea or stimulus
2. Sender or transmitter or communicator
3. Encoding
4. Channel
5. Medium
6. Receiver
7. Decoding
8. Action or behaviour change
9. Feedback

The circular model of communication expects response from the receiver, action on the message or behaviour change. It may take the form of action or reply or behaviour in a particular way. Thus, interaction or face-to-face communication facilitates revision or alteration of original message or planning for future communication. Thus, linear models can be changed by introducing the element of feedback for interaction for the purpose of measurement, evaluation and planning future communication.

In this direction, Level and Galle have introduced an element of interaction between the sender and the receiver. In their model called "new model", they call it *The Communication Process.* This model is based on interaction between the sender and the receiver. Hence, it is known as interpersonal communication or interactional model. Accordingly, interpersonal communication is face-to-face communication between individuals. Both oral and non-verbal clues can be used. "There are no media or channel or we can think of the media as oral and the voice as the channel." Two-way process of communication ensures feedback.

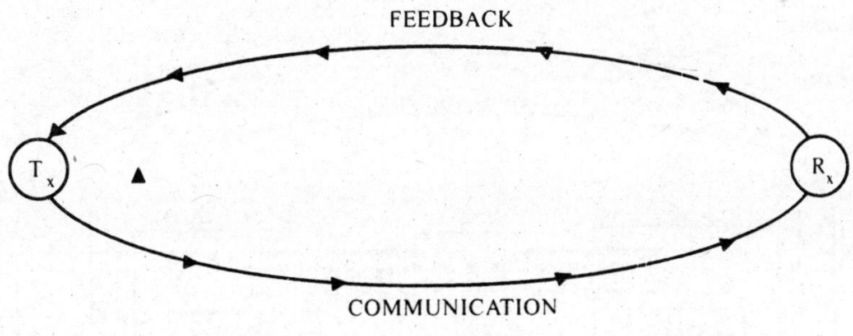

Fig.1.8

The model of Level and Galle greatly helps to identify internal and external variables and the behavioural aspects of the transmitter and the receiver in handling the message.

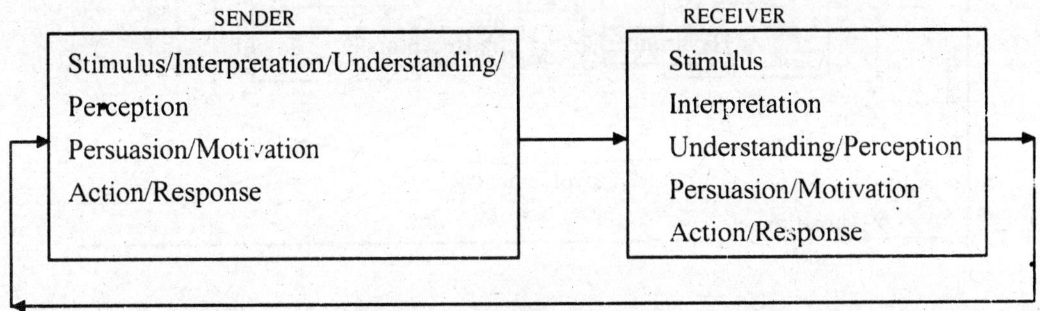

Fig. 1.9

(***Source:*** L. Brow, *Communicating Facts and Ideas in Business*, 1982, p. 12.)

A Composite Model — Relationship

Several elements comprising the communication process have been examined in the above models. Some of the elements are common to all models. The common elements mentioned earlier include the source, message, encoding transmission, receiver, decoding, channel, noise and feedback All the models of human communication contain some common elements

But now we proceed to examine another important factor, i.e., the relationship between the participants. In other words, we emphasise relational aspects of interpersonal behaviour Timothy Learny and his associates have developed a paradigm of interpersonal behaviour. According to them, relationship develops along two dimensions. They are:

1. Dominance, and
2. Affection or Attraction.

Schutz in his research work added another dimension, as a third dimension. It is called "Inclusion" or "Involvement." Baird has added two more dimensions. They are:

1. Time
2. Situation

Thus, the composite model of interpersonal includes the following dimensions:

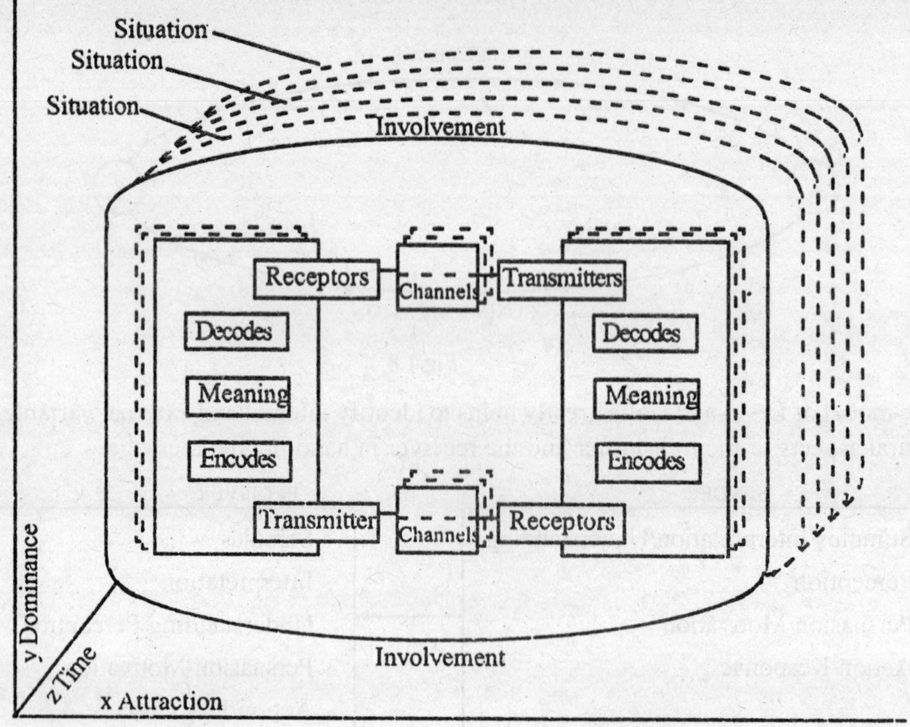

Fig. 1.10 A Composite Model of Interpersonal Relationship

(*Source:* adapted from J. E. Baird, *The Dynamics of Organisational Communication*. 1977, p. 9.)

1. Attraction;
2. Dominance;
3. Involvement;
4. Time; and
5. Situation.

A brief description of these dimensions is given below:

1. Attraction

The dimension of attraction or affection indicates the degree of intimacy by which the participants are positively or negatively attracted to each other. It reveals the likes and dislikes of one another. The more positively the individuals are down towards each other, the closer they are.

Persons are attracted to one another on the basis of similar attitudes, interest towards commonly relevant objects and goals. An individual will interact and form a relationship with other individuals because of common attitudes and values. Interpersonal attraction and relationships are dynamic in nature but not static and subject to change. Time factor introduces changes in attraction.

Relationships are of three types:

1. Convergence
2. Divergence
3. Parallelism.

1. **Convergence:** An individual moves towards each other as they pass through time.
2. **Divergence:** It indicates a step away from other individual because of development of disaffected relationship.
3. **Parallelism:** Under this, individuals neither converge nor diverge, it is a case of parallel relationship.

These relationships are shown in Fig. 1.11.

2. Dominance

The dominance dimension takes into account the ability of the individual to control the behaviour of the other to some extent. It is possible because of the function of one's position within the organisational hierarchy. For instance, an executive is able to exert some control over the behaviour of his subordinates, vice versanal is unreal and does not exist in real life in an hierarchical relationship. Similarly, a foreman is able to exercise more control over the behaviour of the workers. Dominance dimension may exist even otherwise than into hierarchical position. There are a number of factors which influence one`s capacity to dominate others, such as size, intelligence, strategies etc.

These three dimensions of relationships are shown in Fig 1.12.

3. Involvement

Interpersonal involvement is an important dimension of interpersonal relationship and behaviour. According to Patton & Giffin, interpersonal involvement has two components. They are:

1. The amount of interaction between participants.
2. The importance of that interaction to each individual.

4. Time

Baird has introduced the time dimension in interaction and inter-relationship. The other two dimensions like dominance and attraction are quite different. He says that time is somewhat unlike the first three dimensions in that it is constant – it occurs without variation throughout the relationship. The time dimension is an important factor because he argues that "without this dimension, relationship could not develop; changes could not occur in affection, dominance or involvement unless a relationship is allowed to exist across time." (Fig. 1.10)

5. Situation

Baird's second dimension is a situation. It is an important dimension in interpersonal relationship. In other words, situation is an environment in which the communication event occurs (Fig. 1.10). Communicative situations are shown in the figure as parts of the time dimensions. The area within each part or segment indicates the situation in which individuals communicate. On the other hand, the area between segments indicate passage of time between encounters.

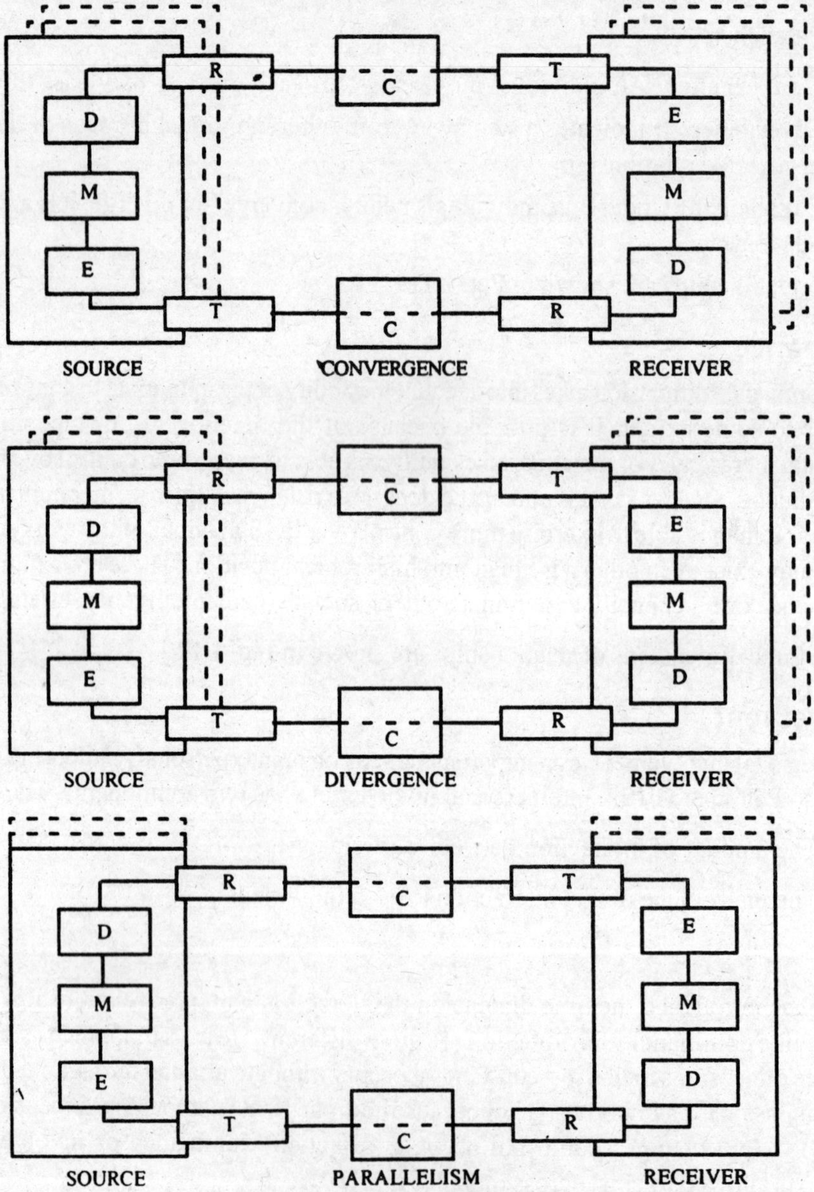

R C T
D E
M M
E D
T C R
SOURCE CONVERGENCE RECEIVER

R C T
D E
M M
E D
T C R
SOURCE DIVERGENCE RECEIVER

R C T
D E
M M
E D
T C R
SOURCE PARALLELISM RECEIVER

Fig. 1.11 Attraction Relationship

(*Source:* Adapted from J. E. Baird, *op. cit.*, p.11.)

Dominance has three general relationship patterns; they arc:

1. Superior-Subordinate : Higher Placement
2. Subordinate-Superior : Lower Placement
3. Peer : Evenly Placed

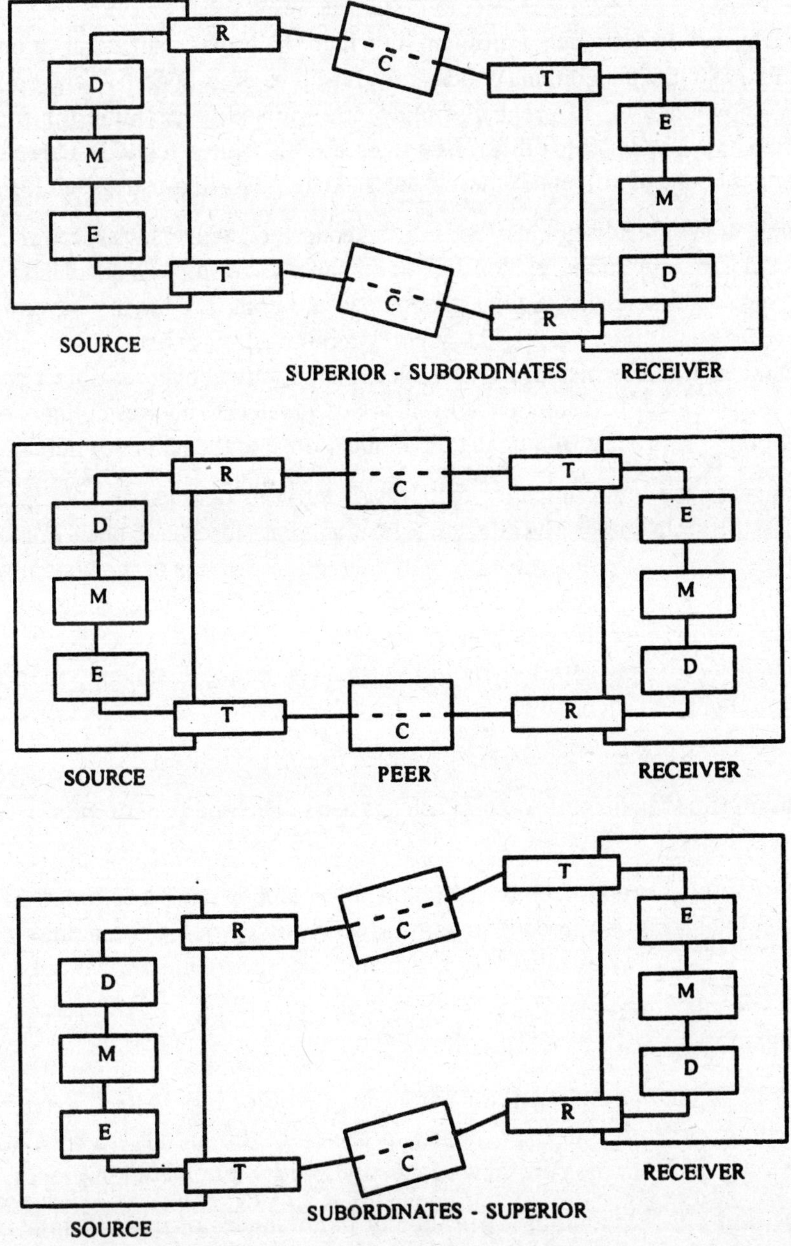

Fig. 1.12

(***Source:*** Adapted from J. E. Baird, *op. cit.*, p.12.)

Communication — An Interdisciplinary Subject

Communication is concerned with behavioural aspects of social relationships or human relationships. These human relationships have multiple aspects like social, linguistic and psychological. A man is studied from different points of social sciences like economics, politics, sociology, psychology etc. The study of communication, therefore, requires the use of various methods peculiar to the social sciences. This is known as Interdisciplinary approach.

It is a technique to approach a problem by which the tools of different sciences are used to find an explanation to the phenomena under study. It is, thus, a co-operative and co-ordinated effort in which the knowledge of different disciplines are utilised to examine the problem. Though communication is independent, other disciplines are also inter-related. Therefore, a study of communication is bound to influence other sciences like English, linguistic, sociology, semantics etc.

Communication is interdisciplinary because it is concerned with many aspects of human relations. Therefore, in order to study social relationships or human relationships, one will have to take recourse to several other social sciences. Social phenomena are complex having several aspects which influence another social phenomena. As such, communication cannot be completely free from external influences. It is interdisciplinary which explains fully about the subject because no single discipline is complete in itself. Communication thus largely refers to interdisciplinary and behavioural-oriented, involving the process of human communication, and the nature of human interaction.

In recent years, the communication theory has been considered as an interdisciplinary theory. As such, it is still in an integrative stage of development, for it has been drawn from various disciplines. By definition, communication is an interaction-process or the way in which one mind influences another. This process is in itself integrative. After recognising communication as interdisciplinary, there is a need to draw from various disciplines of different viewpoints like psychology, mathematics, linguistics, etymology, semantics, management, speech, English, sociology, psychology, psychiatry etc.

Martin K. Starr has identified the following disciplines. They are[3]:

1. Mathematics: Mathematical approach has been developed out of interest in the switching networks of telephony.

2. Psychology: This approach to communication theory examines a person's potential for communication, including his perception abilities, cognitive process and memory. As a matter of fact, psychology is the study of science of a human mind, the mental process of a person.

3. Ecology: The subject of ecology deals with living things and organisms considered in relation to their environment.

4. Ethology: Science of the moral nature and set of ideas or beliefs of a person or a group. The field of ethology deals with the origins and causes of the individual behaviour of animals. Ethology also contributes to the new views concerning the communication process.

5. Accounting: Accounting is also one of the branches of interdisciplinary approach of communication. Accounting is a language of business, a written medium serves as a means of communication. It has a role to play to communicate the results of the business operations to the owners, creditors, investors etc. Accounting is the art of recording, classifying and summarising in a significant manner. There are financial accounting, cost accounting, management accounting and its branches. "Related areas include file maintenance, information indexing and information theory."[4]

6. Auditing: Auditing is the process of detailed examination and scrutiny of books of accounts and vouchers of a business, which enables one to report on the views presented by the accounts, statements prepared by the clients. Martin K. Starr writes that the ultimate method of obtaining specific data for systems analysis is auditing.

7. Linguistics: The word 'linguistics' deals with the science of language. The linguistics also contribute to the communication process.

8. Philology: Philology deals with the study of ancient or medieval literary texts, a comparison and study of the development of related languages. Philology also contributes to communication as it establishes the relation of a language to literature and culture.

9. Etymology: Etymology is the study of the origin and development of words and their meanings, an explanation of the history of a particular word. The subject of etymology concerning the derivation and origin of words contributes to the communication theory at various levels.

10. Semantics: The field of Semantics which deals with the science of meanings of words. Martin writes that, "Semantics is certainly one of the most apparent of these levels." Symbol analysis and content analysis approach the logical and mathematical basis of the communication theory. Content analysis, sometimes, called 'quantitative semantics', deals with the frequency and measurable usage characteristics of letter, word and sentence sets. Sociology and applied anthropology have made use of quantitative interaction analysis."[5]

11. Systems Analysis: Systems analysis " has a strong engineering base and accent logical relations of parts to one another, has developed two strong contributory branches"[6] which are accounting and auditing as one branch and another as work analysis.

12. Work Analysis: According to Martin K. Starr, the second branch of systems analysis is work analysis. He describes it as "Credit analytic detail has emerged in flow charts, micromotion studies" etc.

13. Cybernetics: This theory has "explored machine characteristics based on a strong physiological orientation... cybernetics has contributed in tune with theories of automato."[7] N. Wiener has first adopted the word cybernetics from Greek word Kubernetes, means 'steersman,' He emphasises on control and communication etc., the concept of feedback. It is a scientific study of the way in which information is moved about and control in machines with the brain and the nervous system.

Thus, communication is an interdisciplinary and an independent body of knowledge like the other disciplines — medicine, engineering, accounting etc.

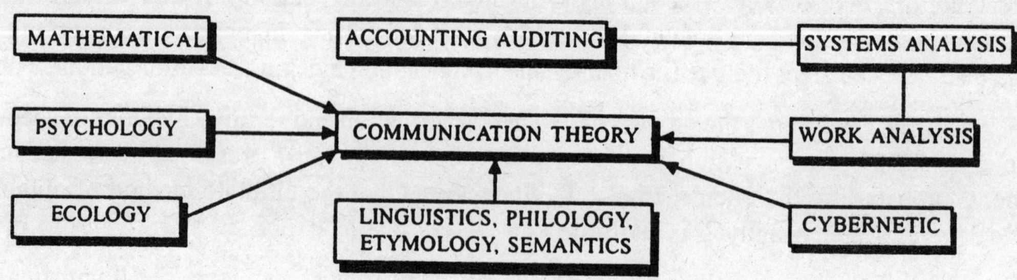

Fig. 1.13 Interdisciplinary Approach

THEORIES OF COMMUNICATION

1. Bull's Eye Theory

Action view is the basis for the theory of communication. The whole process of communication is based on one-way action doing something to someone. The sender plays an important role who encodes the message with the help of arbitrary symbols. The demonstration or doing skills of the sender is for the purpose to change the behaviour of someone or the receiver, to be persuasive, sell or help. The action view believes that words have a meaning and there would be no misunderstanding which is the core of effective communication, provided the right words are used to convey the right message. Misperceptions or misunderstandings are bound to occur, but according to information theory, the sender has to play effectively and adequately.

2. Ping-Pong Theory

This theory is also called as interaction or interpersonal view. This approach to the study of human communication is the ping-pong theory of communication. Ping-Pong is a game of table tennis, represents the interaction theory of communication. It is compared with turns at a table-tennis match. In the process of communication, the turns take place between the sender and the receiver. It is a complex theory of human communication than the Bull's theory which recognises the concept of linear feedback. In this theory there is linear cause and effect.

3. Spiral Theory

The Spiral theory of communication represents and called as transactions view of communication. It recognises more than one interaction between the sender and the receiver. A transaction implies independence, mutual and reciprocal causality. Myers and Myers say that human communication is best understood as a system in which senders are simultaneously receivers and senders. Communication is not a static but dynamic and life-time experience. It is not like a still photograph but continuous flow of motion pictures. The authors say that "Communication in its process view is characterised less by the actions of the sender and the subsequent reactions of a receiver than by the simultaneity of their reciprocal responses, or more simply, by things going on at the same time which affect each other."

PRINCIPLES OR CHARACTERISTICS OF COMMUNICATION

1. An Integral Part of Organisational Process

Decisions of the Managers are conveyed to the subordinates of different rank and file by the superiors. Communication control co-ordinates them for proper work performance. Thus, communication is a part and parcel of organisational function and so an integral and inseparable part of the process. That is the reason why Chester I. Barnard remarked that "the first executive function is to develop and maintain a system of communication."

2. Direct Supervision

Direct supervision is a principle of organisation which facilitates immediate feedback to know the responses or reply of the receiver of the communication. Managers are personally involved in the entire process of communication. Interaction helps the managers to listen to the subordinates' suggestions, work related problems and helps in solving them. Successful managers encourage feedback which offers opportunity to the managers to know how far their instructions and directions have been understood, followed and acted upon by the subordinates. Thus, the managers perform the management functions through communication, and managerial positions become the communication centres to receive information from various sources.

3. Two-way Communication

In the early days of development of the subject, it was considered that communication is concerned with only giving orders and instruction. In this, it is the function of the manager to direct the thing. It is only one-way communication. Communication process is not complete and effective if it is simply downward movement of messages from superiors to subordinates. But it should be a two-way traffic which implies both transmission and reception. It is the managerial function not only to convey any information but also know the reactions and responses from the receivers. Communication should be upward, downward and diagonal-flow so that the managerial task of guiding and directing will be achieved. Two-way communication insists not only to speak, inform, issue orders and instructions but the sender should be ready to listen, accept suggestions and to solve the work-related problems.

4. Informal Communication

The existence of informal organisation should be recognised which is a powerful media of communication. In every organisation there exists good network of informal groups. It is also called "grapevine" which indicates informal means of circulating information or gossip. It is called "informal communication", because it grows up spontaneously from personal and group interest. It does not maintain superior-subordinate relationships. It has no authority and official backing. Under the network of communication, different workers communicate with each other. It is direct, spontaneous and flexible.

5. Listening

Listening is a process of receiving message in the form of symbols, interpreting, and responding to the messages received. The essence of communication is listening. Communication is not effective unless the person at the receiving end listens effectively. Listening is an art which requires much patience and mental effort. The principle of effective communication is listening which improves the information output. Effective listening involves more than hearing the words. It demands to look beyond the words for meaning, and sentiments which the speaker is exhibiting.

6. Result and Cause

Efficiency and effectiveness are the results; it is result-oriented. Sound communication is the result of efficient management but not the cause of it. Communication is only a means to an end but not an end itself. It is a tool of the management towards the end. The competent managers use the tool of communication towards the accomplishment of managerial goals. Communication serves as a lubricant, fostering the smooth operation of management.

7. Clarity

The basic principle in communication is clarity. Clarity in communication implies that messages transmitted should be capable of being understood by the recipient rather than misunderstood. Unfamiliar and superfluous words should not be used. Simple and familiar words are to be selected to present the message. If the principle of precision and clarity are not followed, they may stand as barrier to effective communication.

8. Internal and External

Internal communication is a process of transmitting matters to the people working inside the organisation. It is giving orders, instructions, directions, suggestions or public notice. Public address system constitutes internal system of communication. It may include upward, downward or diagonal communication. External communication is also equally important to provide link between the organisation and the external world. Externally, an organisation has to communicate with outside public like customers, shareholders, dealers, government departments, investors, complaints etc.

9. Specific

Communication should be specific and each specified piece of message should deal with a single subject at a time. This principle is necessary for effective communication. Multiplicity of subject creates a problem of confusion and misunderstanding which is dangerous and unproductive to the organisation. So, when communication is issued, it must be specific in regard to information intended to be conveyed or received.

10. Honesty in Communication

The principle of uprightness and honesty of purpose in communication is very essential. Honest communication involves a sense of obligation to one's self. to other people and to the absolute. Rightness is known by the intuition in the mind. Respect for it gives one an experience in living. All managerial communications should lend to a true and correct understanding in information or message to ensure effective co-ordination among various organisational activities for smooth working.

Communication Getting Information from A into B

Communication is a primary tool for effecting behaviour. We can isolate at least four independent dimensions of the communication process: (1) content (2) noise (3) network characteristics, and (4) direction.

One-way communication has some advantages in speed over two-way. It also has the advantage of protecting the sender from having to recognise his own faults. Two-way communication has the advantages of the greater feelings of certainty for the receiver. But two-way communication involves some psychological risks to the defences of the sender.

Man: A Communicating Animal

Communication like birth, death, breathing and wanting to be loved is part of life itseif; it is a common experience as well. We all have to communicate; we all will communicate. It might even be said that communication is what distinguishes man from the rest of the creation. 'Man', the only animal who can express himself, has the power to express in words. So he can be identified as a 'communicating animal.'

It would be hard to find the president of a nation, the chief executive of a corporate body, a manager, a supervisor, a salesman, a scientist, a technician or anyone else in a business or in any other agency who is not at least concerned with the problem of communication in his own organisation. Even in the case of husband-wife, teacher-taught, parent-child, government-public, communications are not that easy as used to be in the past.

The problems of communication are really the problems of understanding people. Words are tools for achieving effective exchange of information, attitudes and understanding. The problem is that a person is likely to listen through filters. He tends to hear what he wants to hear and disregards what he considers trivial or unimportant.

The snag is that what appears to be trivial to one man may seem positively earth-shattering to another. Another snag is that unless he is very usual, a man listens defensively explaining a way or justifying what he should understand and if he is to increase his own capacity for being effective.

Very often, if the person receiving communication does listen to the message, he may find reasons for disregarding what is being said as unimportant or incorrect.

Man perceives, as a rule, what he expects to see or perceive; he sees largely what he expects to see and hears largely what he expects to hear. The unexpected is usually not received at all; it is neither seen nor heard, but is ignored or misunderstood.

What to Communicate?

The purpose of communicators are numerous and varied. Here are some examples:

To buy	To get information from buyers
To sell	To prevent
To inform	To affirm
To misinform	To clarify

To reveal
To conceal
To teach
To learn
To send information to buyers
To cause
To confuse
To feature sellers
To feature buyers
To compliment
To criticise
To influence, persuade, motivate or actuate

Planning for Communicating

Why?

Why do we want to communicate? What is the purpose of communication? Is it to persuade or to inform? Is any particular action required?

What?

What is it we want to communicate? An order, an idea, an attitude or a feeling? What form of words or possibly actions best meet the situation?

How?

How are we going to communicate? On what form will the communication get home the message fastest? What impact will a particular form have on the recipient?

Sometimes, people have to see you to understand. Others understand perfectly a written communication. Yet others find the telephone completely incomprehensible. So you have to keep choosing, bearing in mind always the person with whom you are communicating, what are his needs?

Who?

Who is the key to the communication situation? How does he feel about me; about this situation? What are his likely reactions to my proposals?

When?

Finally, when? When is the right time to get across this message, when is the receiver likely to give it the most attention? When is he most likely to be influenced? Often, timing can be critical to the success of the communication.

Where?

It implies where does the message reinforce relationships between the sender and the receiver.

Essentials of Communication

The essential basis of all public relations work is the communication process. Reduced to the simplest formula, communication is the transfer of information from one person to another or more recently to an apparatus which stores or process on news. This process almost always takes place between four or five factors:

1. Initiator

The organisation or initiator (e.g., a business corporation or trade association).

2. Communicator

The communicator (e.g., media person or a public relations agency).

3. Message

The message (e.g., a press release or a lecture).

4. Medium

The medium may he newspaper or radio or television or a book or a letter.

5. Addressee

Finally, the addressee (e.g., the newspaper reader or the owner of a telephone or teleprinter or the viewer of a television).

The message is transmitted by spoken or written word, or by image, or a combination of these or other media such as music, colour, mimicry, design, odour and sense of touch.[10]

Other Factors of Importance

And, of course, there are other obvious and important factors that must be taken into consideration wherever or whenever any communication is made, the receiver's level of education (for people with an elementary level of education, for instance, once seen is better than a hundred times heard), the technical possibilities of communication, the address is financial means, the influence of prejudices and biased opinion etc.

There can be no 'mutual understanding' without communication and 'mutual understanding' is the core of public relations.

There are a few problems in life that real communication cannot resolve. If that notion sounds far-fetched, perhaps that is because what we normally call communication is not real communication. We generally think of communication in terms of exchanging information, public speaking, expressing our feelings honestly or being sincere or persuasive. So, we think effective communication depends on having special talent, a good vocabulary, the right circumstances, and especially on the receptivity of other people. Effective and true communication does not depend on any of these things; but rather on uncovering within ourselves the ability to communicate.

Real communication is that experience of being totally understood by another person.

Real communication is a profound understanding, not merely of the words being said, but of the experience and the meaning behind the words.

Real communication produces results. In relationships real communication produces harmony, resolves problems, and dissolves feeling of separateness. It is a mutual experience of being "known", and results in partnership and a sense of well-being.

In families, when communication occurs, gaps are bridged; misunderstandings, conflicts, the resentment disappear.

In organisations, effective communication transforms a group into a team. It reduces effort, fatigue and struggle. Work is accomplished more accurately, and efficiently as conflict and tension give way to co-operation and comradery.

For most of us, experiences of real communication seem to "happen" without our knowing how or why. Regardless of what we do, it often seems difficult, and sometimes impossible to really communicate.

While we may not always know how to make real communication happen, we know we feel when it does occur.

In some,

— True communication is creation.

— It generates experience in others.

— It moves people.

— It not only delivers information to others, it actually transforms their ability to hear.

The Benefits of Communication are

(a) A better understanding of co-worker and customer behaviour.

(b) Increased recognition and ability to change ineffective communication styles.

(c) New skills for resolving interpersonal conflicts.

(d) Higher performance standards established through mutual alignment of management and employees.

(e) Increased productivity even under adverse conditions.

(f) Improved interviewing and consulting techniques.

(g) The ability to create an organisational climate of support and trust.

(h) The flexibility to understand co-workers from different cultures.

(i) Active, accurate listening habits.

(j) The enthusiasm to create team spirit, company pride and goal congruence.

(k) The versatility to communicate across information boundaries, as between, say, R and D marketing departments.

(l) Enhanced powers of interpersonal motivation.

The great value in such communication:

(1) A willingness to participate in group activities.

(2) A greater ease and clarity in writing.

(3) Confidence in presenting briefings.

(4) Improving the effectiveness of committees and groups to accomplish tasks.

(5) To speak effectively before people and to face people with confidence.

The Cabinet of Ministers, the Board of Directors or the Governing Body of an Institution which is responsible for national, and international, corporate or Institutional reputation' must learn how to improve its communication techniques, if it is to create a suitable environment in which reputation may flourish. The government will have to learn how to improve communications with its States and as also improve communications with the staff, and also improve communication with the staff structure itself. Similarly, the "institution" should improve its communication with its own members and others who stand by it.

The speaker does not control communication. It is the listener. The speaker can mouth words all day and every day, as all participants do. Obviously no one listens though one hears him speak. So, no communication has taken place.

COMMUNICATION: A TRANSACTIONAL PROCESS

TRANSACTIONAL ANALYSIS

The concept'on which CTA is based is that life itself is a process of continuous pooling and receiving information. The communication information in turn is measured, evaluated and used in decision-making to approve a problem.

How people communicate will depend, to a great extent, upon the way in which they perceive and think about communication. The process of communication involves selection of symbols, exchange of symbols, attributing meanings to symbols and develop expectation. Stimulus or idea or message has communication value provided, information is translated into symbols or patterned. Patterning means expressing ideas in a symbolic form. Symbols are arbitrary, they have no meanings. Words and meanings are in people, they never occur in a vacuum.

Communication is a transactional process. It implies that one cannot learn without the presence of others, use of symbols and construct meanings. In this process, one may learn many meanings to by observing, watching and listening others. As a result, it is possible to develop a pool of communication information, knowledge and intelligence. Communication is like birth, death and breath; a person is regularly and continuously involved to communicate and share meanings. As a matter of fact, it is a way of life. It is a transactional process wherein the sender and the receiver are continuously involved to construct meanings, develop expectations and exchange symbols. These are the result of their life-time experience, perception and previous communication. The way in which people construct meaning and develop expectation at present is based on the way in which people constructed meaning and developed expectation in the past.

Exchange of symbols by the sender and the receiver is a continuous process involving simultaneously constructing, sharing meaning, and developing expectation of each other. Naturally, the meanings and expectations may change when communication continues, wholly or partly. This forms the basis for a new understanding between the sender and the receiver. "Communication is a transactional process in which you are both cause and effect of whatever is happening."[13]

Definition of Transactional Analysis

Eric Bern has introduced the concept of transactional analysis in his book, *Games People Play.* TA is a common abbreviation for Transactional Analysis. Thomas A. Harris, in his book *I'M OK You're OK,* has given full treatment to all the concepts of transactional analysis. The following are the three definitions on TA given by Harris:

(1) Method of examining one transaction: 'I do something and you do something back."

(2) Method of determining which part of a person is "coming on."

(3) Method of systematising the information derived from analysis of transactions in words with the same meaning for everyone using them.[14]

Analysis of Definition

(1) The first definition is based on the two important elements of theory of communication. They are: stimuli or ideas and response or reply. The sender of the message is concerned with stimuli or ideas and receiver is concerned with response or reply for stimuli. On the other hand, response will, in turn, become a stimulus for the sender. The basic elements in stimulus-response theory of communication are stimulus, interpretation, meaning and behaviour.

The interpersonal and interactional model of communication contains these elements in the transaction between the sender and the receiver. By definition, interpersonal communication is face-to-face or oral. TA, thus, provides a basis for analysis of interaction that takes place. Fig. 1.14 shows the model of interpersonal communication with stimuli-response elements in the transaction between the sender and the receiver.

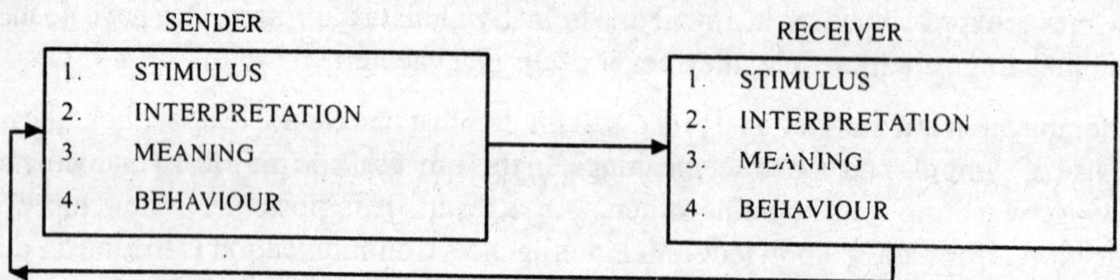

Fig. 1.14 Interpersonal Communication

(***Source:*** Adapted from L. Brown, *Communicating Facts and Ideas in Business,* p. 316.)

(2) The second definition is concerned with the determination of which part of a person is 'coming on.' There are three parts to our personality. They are three egos or parts of personality. They are the parent, adult and child.

Transactional analysis will help to determine which part of a person or which ego is 'coming on' from the other person and thus adjust our own ego or part to be effective in our relationship with that person.[15] The variables like message, behaviour of the speaker, verbal and non-verbal clues etc. will determine the ego of a person. The following are the characteristics of three egos:

1. Parent

Self-righteous, caring, knowledgeable, instructs, tells how, makes pronouncements, points a finger, furrows brow, wags head, signs and clears throat.

2. Adult

Reasoning, logical, receives and processes information, sticks to facts. Feels free in making choices in decision-making and problem-solving and respects freedom and rights of others.

3. Child

Dominated by feelings of dependency, inferiority, and helplessness. Uses tears, lips, temper, and so forth to get what he or she wants.[16]

The third definition is concerned with the systematisation of information resulting from an analysis of the transaction. It implies the use of information derived from the analysis of the transaction. For instance, a superior tells his subordinate to do something he does not want to do and see no reason for doing. But the superior is the authority, and what he says goes. The analysis implies that the subordinate has to fall in his line and respond like an obedient child.

What he tells must be done. The parent and child relationship exists and continues with the superior and the subordinate. The subordinate might, however, respond as an adult and point out to the superior the reason, subordinate does not think it should be done and why his way is better. This gives an opportunity to the superior to change to the adult role in responding to his view. But both the superior and the subordinate should relate as adult-to-adult on their ongoing communication and relationship.

All of us grow and develop from the baby to an adult, involving, in the process a continuous gathering and receiving information, changing attitudes, changing behaviour towards others. The decisions which we have to make are unlimited. There is no end to decision-making, multiplicity of organisational decisions. When one decision is taken, another pops up. This never-ending cycle of decisions goes on and on. A problem is solved; there is another problem to be solved. Stimulus and response are required which help to grow and develop as an individual person and also in our ongoing communication and relationship with other people.

Transactional analysis prescribed four life positions in the developmental process. The positions are expressed in four statements which indicate self concept and attitude in relation to other persons:

"I'm not OK". "You're OK."

"I'm not OK". "You're not OK."

"I'm OK". "You're not OK."

"I'm OK". "You're OK."

Structure of Transactions

A transaction is a basic unit of study in communication; it involves two or more people who mutually and simultaneously take one another into account, differentiate their role, relationship and conduct their interaction by a set of rules. Since they use symbols to pass on the message, it is symbolic interaction.

Every individual in the process has to pay attention to each other at the same time. Mutual awareness is a mutual ingredient which communication transactions take into account because it is mutual awareness that exerts mutual influence. A transaction takes place when the sender perceives himself being perceived by the receiver. There is no need to have physical interdependence in a transaction. For instance, there is no physical interdependence in the case ot communication. The core of transactional analysis is the perception of other person's perception. Both play their respective roles called 'mutual roles.' The situation in which an interpersonal communication occurs is a powerful guidance in determining the appropriate role.

ESSENTIALS OF GOOD COMMUNICATION

The primary purpose of communication is to keep people informal. Communication is a reciprocal, two-way and continuous social process. It should serve the organisational objects. To accomplish this, the management adopts an effective media and network of communication. To make it effective, the communicator must possess certain qualities, understand the receiver, convey the message and to see that he acts on it. Practical experience in the field makes both the sender and receiver to reach perfection. Communication translates organisational information into the language commonly understood in the organisation. Lack of feedback, interaction and effective decoding of signs or words into receiver's capability are the important problems in communication. But they do not alter the basic essentials for successful communication. Wilbur Schramm has suggested for any communication to be transmitted effectively from source to receiver whether the source is personal or non-personal, the message must meet the following three requirements:

(1) It must be so designed and delivered as to gain the all attention of the receiver.

(2) It must use signals that are understood in the same way by both the source and the receiver.

(3) must arouse needs in the receiver and suggest some way of satisfying these needs that is appropriate to the receiver's group-situation when moved to make the desired response.

Knowing audience or receiver in the case of written communication is important.

However, the important principles of communication are discussed under the following paragraphs. These are essentials or factors to be considered while initiating communication to achieve the purpose of communication.

1. Clarity: In the communication process, message is the very subject matter of communication. Clarity of ideas, facts, opinion in the mind of communicator should be clear before communicating. It is a thinking process to conceive the subject. The message is always subject to the test of principle of clarity. It is to be encoded in common, in the direct and simple and easily understandable language, so that the receiver is able to understand it without doubt and difficulty. According to Koontz and Donnell, "A communication possesses clarity when it is expressed in a language and transmitted in a way that can be comprehended by the receiver."[17]

2. Information: Information is different from communication. All communications contain information while all information cannot communicate a message. The word 'information' is comprehensive in which communication is a special kind of transmitting message in symbolic form. The sender first collects and keeps before him the relevant information concerning a particular individual or group of people. The principle of effective communication is to have information and communicate it in symbolic form.

3. Completeness: The subject matter to be communicated must be adequate and full, which enables the receiver to understand the central theme or idea of the message. Incompleteness of a message may result in misunderstanding the subject by the receiver. The decision-making process would be delayed and action may be delayed when the message is incomplete.

4. Emphasis on Attention: The purpose of communication is to draw the attention of the receiver. An effective communication changes the behaviour of the receiver. The process is not complete just by transmitting ideas, facts or opinions. Effective communication is one which we must create interest and pay proper attention to the message and to act accordingly. Action speaks louder than words. This is the underlying principle of attention.

5. Consistency: The message transmitted should not be contradictory. The subject matter of communication is said to be consistent when it is in agreement with the objectives and policies of the organisation. The thinking, action of happenings should be according to the same organisational rules and principles. Communication is said to be most effective when it is consistent than when it varies or is contradicted. Consistency can be achieved if the communicator keeps in his mind the broad objectives, policies and programmes of the enterprise. There should be some linkage and compromise between communications. One communication should not conflict with the previous communication. Conflict and inconsistency create confusion, chaos ultimately resulting in delay in decision-making and action.

6. Integration: Achieving common goals of the enterprise is the objective of group activities. Communication as a tool of management should strengthen the enterprise. Communication is only a means rather than end. The transmitter and receiver has to use communication tool as a means to an end, not an end in itself, so that it promotes integrated efforts of the organisation. On the principle of integrity, Koontz and Donnell observe: "The purpose of managerial communication is to support understanding by individuals as they achieve and maintain the co-operation needed to meet enterprise goals. All communications should be framed and transmitted in such a way as to support the integrity of the formal organisation."

7. Use of Informal Organisation: Informal communication is called grapevine. It is a type of communication which occurs on account of informal relationship between persons. This relationship grows up spontaneously from personal interest, group interest, social and other non-formal relations. Informal channel is the most effective one and transmits information with surprising speed. Informal organisation should be utilised properly to communicate message. It supplements the formal communication channel. Koontz and Donnell observe: "The most effective communication results when managers utilise the informal organisation to supplement the communication channels of the formal organisation."

8. Two-way Communication: An effective communication demands two-way communication, i.e., vertical, upward and downward. It should not always be downward movement from the superior to the subordinates. In such a case, communication cannot produce desired goods. The reaction and response of the receiver are equally needed to achieve the purpose of communication. A manager should thus not only to speak, inform, instruct, and order but should also be prepared to listen, understand, answer, amend and interpret. Thus, it involves a two-way traffic or process and the process is complete. G. Terry states that the sender must get through the receiver, if the communication is to be complete and satisfactory. Thus, it is not the transmission of ideas, facts from one person to another but must be two-way to be effective communication.

9. To know the Receiver: In the communication process, after transmission of the message, the receiver is the kingpin who has to act on the message. The receiver must understand the subject, that is the main purpose of communication. The sender must use such language which may easily be understood by the receiver. The message should be simple, clear and short. Killian suggested "communicate with an awareness of the total and physical and human setting in which the information will be received. Picture the place of work; determine the receptivity and understanding levels of the receivers; be aware of social climate and customs; question the information's timeliness. Ask what, when and in what manner you would like to be communicated with if you were in a similar environment and position."

10. Time: The principal aim of communication is to make the message reach at the appropriate time. It is not just the transmission of ideas, opinions etc. by the superior to the subordinate for the sake of communication. They should be conveyed at the right and proper time. Sending before time or after would not serve the purpose of communication. A delayed message is stale or historical and has no importance.

11. Simplicity: Simplicity in communication produces the best and quickest understanding and response. So, the communicator must try to achieve this principle for effectiveness. Avoid using superfluous words, unnecessary prepositions, jargon; using familiar words is preferable. The language used should be simple and only common words be used, which does not mean using colloquial English. There is no set-rule for using familiar words. The transmitter must know the receiver's vocabulary, knowledge and understanding capacity. Simplicity is always preferable to meet all situations, because the object of any communication is to make others understand and act.

12. Communication Network: Yet another principle of effective communication is the communication network. It is the channel or route through which exchange of transmission or ideas, facts etc. flow to and from the officially designated positions in the organisational structure. Formal communication has a set network which determines the fixed route for information movement. The network covers downward, upward, horizontal line of communication. In a downward line, the message moves from top to bottom and *vice versa* in the case of upward line. Horizontal line is for personnel in one department and personnel of equal, lower or superior position in other departments. Both vertical and horizontal lines should be used for effective communication but the distance should be less as far as possible.

13. Use of Media: There are two media for transmitting message. They are oral and written media. Both have their own merits and demerits. Oral communication is more effective for certain messages and similarly written communication for other circumstances. The principle of strategic use of media is to be adopted. The need, objective and the receiver are the factors that should be kept in mind in selecting a medium.

14. Feedback: Though the last but yet the most important key or principle to effective communication is to obtain feedback from the receiver. Knowing acceptance or rejection as to the messages transmitted is probably the most important method of improving communication. The principle of feedback promotes a two-way communication. Feedback is a process to ascertain whether or not the receiver properly understood the message. It helps to listen, answer, interpret and amend the message. Interface and interaction are possible in feedback. It avoids errors in the transmission of message and invoking effective participation of the subordinates. Thus, feedback enables the communicator to take initiative in order to know the reactions regarding the effectiveness of communication.

TEN COMMANDMENTS OF GOOD COMMUNICATION

We have discussed above some essentials of good communication to improve communication. The American Management Association has given excellent essentials of good communication. They are popularly called Ten Commandments of good communication, they are as follows:"[18]

1. Clarify ideas before communicating: By systematically thinking through the message and considering who will be receiving and/or affected by it, the manager overcomes one of the basic pitfalls of communication—failure to properly plan the communiqué. The more systematically a message is analysed, the more clearly it can be communicated.

2. Examine the true purposes of communication: The manager has to determine what he or she really wants to accomplish with the message. Once this objective is identified, the communiqué can be properly designed.

3. Take the entire environment, physical and human into consideration: Questions such as what is said, to whom, and when will all affect the success of communication. The physical setting, the social climate, and past communication practices should be examined in adapting the message to the environment.

4. When valuable, obtain advice from others in planning communiques: Consulting with others can be a useful method of obtaining additional insights regarding how to handle the communication. In addition, those who help to formulate it usually give it active support.

5. Beware of the overtones as well as the basic content of the message: The listener will be affected by not only what is said but also how it is said. Voice, tone, facial expression, and choice of language, all influence the listener's reaction to the communiqué.

6. When possible, convey useful information: People remember things that are beneficial to them. If the manager wants subordinates to read the message, he or she should phrase it so that it takes into consideration their interests as well as the company's.

7. Follow up on communication: The manager must solicit feedback in ascertaining whether the subordinate understands the communiqué, is willing to comply with it, and then takes appropriate action.

8. Communicate with the future as well as the present in mind: Most communications are designed to meet the demands of the current situation, However, they should be in accord with the long-range goals as well. For example, communiqués designed to improve performance or morale are valuable in handling present problems. Yet, they also serve a useful future purpose promoting long-run organisational efficiency.

9. **Support words with deeds:** When managers contradict themselves by saying one thing and doing another, they undermine their own directives. For example, an executive who issues a notice reminding everyone to be in the building by 8.30 A.M. while he or she continues to show up at 9.15 A.M. should not expect anyone to take the notice seriously. Subordinates, are always cognizant of such managerial behaviour and quickly discount such directions.

10. **Be a good listener:** By concentrating on the speaker's explicit and implicit meanings, the manager can obtain a much better understanding of what is being said.

The essentials of effective communication are more useful in personnel management.

THE SEVEN C's OF COMMUNICATION

1. **Credibility:** Communication starts with the climate of belief. This climate is built by performance on the part of the practitioner. The performance reflects an earnest desire to serve the receiver. The receiver must have confidence in the sender. He must have a high regard for the source's competence on the subject.

2. **Context:** A communication programme must square with the realities of its environment. Mechanical media are only a supplementary to the word and the need that takes place in daily living. The context must provide for participation and playback: the context must confirm, not contradict the message.

3. **Content:** The message must have meaning for the receiver, and it must be compatible with his value system. It must have relevance for him. In general, people select those items of information which promise them the greatest rewards. The content determines the audience.

4. **Clarity:** The message must have meaning put in simple terms. Words must mean the same thing to the receiver as they do to the sender. Complex issues must be compressed into themes, slogans or stereotypes that have simplicity and clarity.

5. **Continuity and consistency:** Communication is an unending process. It requires reception and achieve penetration. Repetition with variation contributes to both factual and attitude learning. The story must be consistent.

6. **Channels:** The established channels of communication should be used, channels that the receiver uses and respects. Creating new ones is difficult. Different channels have different effects and serve effectively in different stages of the diffusion process.

7. **Capability:** Communication must take into account the capability of the audience. Communication are most effective when they require the least effort on the part of the recipient. This includes factors of availability, habit, reading ability and receiver's knowledge.[19]

OBJECTIVES OF COMMUNICATION

1. **Human Relations:** Communication's job is to help and promote human relations, making use of it among other things, in the medium or media. There can be no mutual understanding without communication and mutual understanding in human relations is possible through communication.

2. Empathy: Empathy is feeling with the other person expressed by speech. Sympathy is feeling sorry for him expressed by words.

3. Persuasion: Persuasion is a process of convincing and motivating to get things done. Speech is one of the methods to persuade a person. A sense of human interest on the person who is being persuaded will understand and appreciate the cause and effect of his action.

4. Dialogue: Dialogue is a process of conversation or speech with the purpose. It involves exchange of ideas. It is for influencing behaviour. Conciliation and compromise are generally involved. Dialogue is a democratic, civilised and constructive weapon. It takes the form of discussion, criticism and deliberation. Others viewpoints should be considered and there is no place for monopoly of the conversation in dialogue.

5. Information: In the new information order of the world, information transmission is the process of getting things done. In complex business organisations, effective decisions depend upon collection, storage and supply of information. Information-taking and information-giving is a continuous process in organisations.

6. To influence: The object of transmitting information is to change the behaviour of the recipient. Communication is aimed at influencing, persuading, motivating or activating towards desired goals.

7. Understanding: The main cause for conflict in interpersonal situation is lack of mutual understanding. The problems of communication are really the problems of understanding people. The most important managerial function to bridge the gap is possibly communication, without it mutual understanding cannot be achieved.

8. To Discourage Mis-information: The object of communication is not only to pass and exchange policies, rules, orders, procedures and objectives but also to avoid distortions in communication. Communication is used to discourage the spread of mis-information, rumours, gossip and release of emotional tensions of the workers.

9. Suggestions and Complaints: Another objective is to encourage ideas, suggestions from subordinates for an improvement in the product and work conditions for the reduction in that time or cost involved and for avoidance of the waste or raw material.

10. Free exchange: The two-way communication model ensures free exchange of information and ideas which gives an opportunity to all the employees in understanding and accepting the messages, acting and feedback.

11. Better Relations: Communication improves employees' and management's relations by keeping both in contact with each other. House journal and other labour union publications promote good understanding by mutual exchange of ideas.

12. Fostering Attitude: Motivation, co-operation and job satisfaction are more essential to achieve organisational objective. The purpose of communication is to foster an attitude which is necessary for motivation, co-operation and job satisfaction.

PURPOSE OF COMMUNICATION (FUNCTIONS)

1. Instructive Function: The instructive function invariably and importantly deals with the commanding nature. It is more or less of directive nature. Under this, the communicator transmits with the necessary directives and guidance so as to enable them to accomplish his tasks. In this, instructions flow downwards from top to the lower level.

2. Integration Function: It is a unifying function under which integration of activities is endeavoured. The integration function of communication mainly involves to bringing about inter-relationship among the various functions. It helps in the unification of management functions.

3. Informing Function: The purpose or function of communication in an organisation is to inform the individual or group about the subject. Top management informs policies to the lower level through the middle level. In turn, the lower level informs the top level the reaction through the middle level. Information exchange flow vertically, horizontally and diagonally across the organisation. Becoming informed or informing others is the main purpose of communication.

4. Evaluation Function: Examination of activities to form an idea or judgement of the worth of task is achieved through communication. Communication is a tool to appraise the individual, his contribution to the organisation. Evaluating one's own inputs or another's outputs or some ideological scheme demands an adequate and effective communication process.

5. Directive Function: Communication is necessary to issue directions by the top management or managers to the lower level. Directing others or being directed or instructed cannot take place without a complete communication process. The managerial function of directing involves giving orders to employees immediately subordinate to do a task, stop it or modify it. Directing others may be communicated either orally or in writing. An order may be a common order, request order or implied order.

6. Influencing Function: A complete communication process is necessary in influencing others or being influenced. It implies the provision of feedback which tells the effect of communication. Motivational forces in an individual are to be provided and then stimulated through communication. Motivation is a behavioural concept through which one may try to understand why people behave as they do. Motivation is the result of interaction among three groups of factors such as (*a*) Influences working within the individual, (*b*) Influences working within the organisation, (*c*) Influences working in the external environment.

7. Incidental Neutral Function: Communication discharges several incidental and neutral functions. Many pieces of communication are not directly connected with the accomplishment of the objectives of an organisation. Communication sometimes may contribute indirectly to the organisational goals. For instance, communication has to provide social contact within the organisation.[20]

8. Teaching Function: The importance of personal safety on the job has been greatly recognised. A complete communication process is required to teach and educate workers about personal safety on the jobs. This communication helps the workers to avert accidents, risks etc. and avoid cost, procedures etc.

9. Image Projecting Function: A business enterprise cannot survive by remaining aloof from the rest of the society. There is interrelationship and interdepence between the society and an enterprise operating in the society. Public goodwill and confidence are necessarily created among the public. It is the communication with its multi-media approach which has to project the image of the firm in the society. Through an effective external communication system, an enterprise has to inform the society about its goals, activities, progress, and social responsibilities.

10. Orientation Function: The employees of the organisation are to be oriented with the organisational structure. Communication helps to make people acquainted with the co-employees, superiors and with the policies, objectives, rules and regulations of the organisation.

11. Interview Function: Interview as a medium of communication has been discussed in detail in the chapter on 'Oral Communication.' It is through interviewing people, the interviewer selects qualified and worthy people for the enterprise. Recruitment process implies face-to-face or oral communication.

12. Other Functions: Effective decision-making is possible when required and adequate information is supplied to the decision-maker. Communication, either verbal or written, helps the process of decision-making. In general, everyone in the organisation has to provide with necessary information so as to enable to discharge tasks effectively and efficiently.

FACTORS RESPONSIBLE FOR GROWING IMPORTANCE OF COMMUNICATION

We have emphasised above the importance of communication in different areas: In the preceding paragraphs we tried to identify the areas where communication plays an important role and the need for an effective system of communication. The purpose of this paragraph has been to present factors responsible for the growing importance of communication. Thus, under this paragraph, we will be looking for various factors for the importance of communication.

1. Large-size Organisation: Modern forms of business organisations are larger in size, both in terms of installed capacity and in terms of a large number of people working. The existing organisations have grown in size by the process of expansion, modernisation etc. Large-size organisations have a large number of personnel working within the organisation and outside. It has created several levels of hierarchy in the organisation. Direction and co-ordination among all creates problems. It is an important factor mainly responsible for growing importance of communication. It is only with the multi-media and multi-channel communication, direction, co-ordination and motivation is possible. Thus, communication is a vital aspect in the management process.

2. Technological Improvements: Another important factor responsible for the growing importance is technological advancement or development. A number of mechanical devices, both in oral and written communication, have emerged on account of technical improvements. We have witnessed rapid changes in communication technology, known as 'communication age' or 'communication revolution.' So, a complex modern business organisation should adjust itself to the latest technology available if it is to succeed in this competitive world. Sophisticated communication technologies have been discussed in detail in subsequent chapters. The installation of new technologies ensures speed, accuracy, message load, and avoids frauds. An effective system of mechanical communication network can help the management to overcome communication barriers. A number of audio, visual, audio-visual and electronic media have occupied an important role in communication. Telelecturing or teletutorial, tele-conferencing, computer-aided design, computer-aided manufacturing, television short circuit, and new devices of telecommunication services, computer mail message services, management technological developments are advancements in communication.

3. Growth of Trade Union Activities: Today, trade union activities occupy an important place in the organisation-structure. Management cannot ignore or neglect the existence of trade unions as they survive inspite of many factors. Workers and employees have organised trade unions in all types of organisation, irrespective of small, big, medium, private, public, co-operative, productive and service industries. Union publications ventilate the voice of the union. They are effective media of communication. Management can use trade unions and their media for effective communication. There must be always good relations between the management and trade unions which promote industrial peace and harmony. The executives have to interact with unions and exchange views, share viewpoints to transmit open and frank information to them to create confidence. Importance of communication has arisen in the industry with the growth of trade union movement. Building of a good mutual understanding and developing a friendly and amicable atmosphere of co-operation in the enterprise etc. are possible through an effective system of communication in the industry.

4. Emphasis on Human Relations: In modern days, the emphasis is on recognition of dignity of labour and authority. Workers are not to be treated as a commodity. They are part and parcel of the organisation having a partnership relationship. The concept of master-servant relationship has lost its significance. They are co-partners of the enterprise. A successful management is one which must understand the needs, attitudes and feelings of the workers. As such, the emphasis is on human relations, which implies better understanding of workers. This emphasises, at the same time, the significance of the two-way traffic in communication. Therefore, the growing recognition of human relations and to maintain good human relations with workers and a host of other factors have necessitated to have an effective communication.

5. Public Relations: The social responsibility of management cannot be ignored. The responsibilities imply the obligations which a business house owes to the society. There are four important groups such as owners of the business, i.e., the shareholders, customers, employees and the society at large. These people must be kept informed always about the steps taken in the discharge of their social responsibilities. Public relations emphasise a proper understanding of the nature of the public and the social environment in which an industry is operating and the changes that are constantly taking place. The word 'public' refers to any group of people who share a common interest. Employees are public, known as internal public. Relation is the outcome of mutual understanding derived from the process of sharing of the common interest. The integration of these two elements gives us public relations which is today a specialised management function.

IMPORTANCE OF COMMUNICATION

The world of modern day is often called the "Age of communication and information." The importance of communication has been greatly emphasised by all management experts.

Communication like birth, death, growth and decay is a part of individual life as well as organisational existence. Its importance is self-explanatory and is a common experience of all as well.

A person is a communicating animal. He is the only animal who can express and has the power to express in words. In these days, communication is business; it would be very hard to find the managers, subordinates, salesmen, technicians, foremen, lawyers, auditors, consultants, teachers, doctors, or anyone else who is not at least concerned with the problem of communication.

It is the process of understanding people. Communication is an important aspect of management. No one can overlook its importance. The main cause of misunderstanding is lack of effective communication. In an inter-dependent set-up, the importance of communication in management cannot be overemphasised. Its importance has been widely recognised in recent years.

It has been rightly remarked that "The No. 1 management probiem today is communication." Group activities in the case of common goals cannot be accomplished without communication. The entire organisation, control, co-ordination and motivation cannot be discharged without communication. It is our practical experience to see organisations fully involved in moving messages vertically, horizontally and diagonally between various officially designated positions. The growth and survival of modern industrial organisations is greatly dependent on communication. George R. Terry states: "Communication serves as the lubricant, fostering for the smooth operations of the management process."

The reasons for the growing importance of communication can be judged from the following paragraphs:

1. Co-ordination: The modern complex organistions are large in size having a large number of people working in the organisation to achieve common goals. The organisational structure shows many levels of organisational hierarchy, both tall network and flat network. This always leads to the problem of co-ordination. An effective system of communication promotes better co-ordination. It helps a lot in co-ordination. Co-ordination is necessary between groups; channels are essential for the efficient functioning of the entire organisation. It is the communication which promotes better co-ordination.

2. Smooth Working: Smooth and uninterrupted working of an enterprise is to a great extent dependent on good communication network. Communication assumes a greater role in this direction. Corrective decision-making and efficiency of the organisation is based on information supply. If the messages are not flowing freely across the organisation, smooth functioning and unrestricted working of the organisation are not possible. According to Herbert G. Hicks, "communication is basic to an organisation's existence from birth of the organisation on through its continuing life."

3. Effective Decision-Making: Facts and figures of past and present, are to be provided for quick and effective decision-making. The primary basis is communication through which an effective network which supplies information helps in arriving at quick decisions. Problem-defining, alternative courses of action, selecting the best course of action are all possible only with necessary information supplied to the decision-maker. In its absence, it may not be possible even for the top management to take meaningful decisions. On the other hand, objectives and goals cannot be achieved unless the top management can effectively communicate to the lower levels.

4. Managerial Efficiency: As pointed out earlier, the remark of George R. Terry that communication serves as the lubricant fostering the smooth operation of the management process. Communication promotes managerial efficiency. Efficiency lies in the way in which an individual or group is informed towards the common goals. Managerial functions like planning, control, co-ordination, motivation cannot be discharged without communication. As the management is an art of getting things done through other people, it is communication that educates personnel working in the organisation with the desires of the management. Management conveys goals, policies, targets by issuing orders, instructions orally as well as in written form. The yardstick for measuring managerial efficiency is communication.

5. Co-operation: Co-operation among workers, collective or joint efforts, are possible only with the exchange of information between individuals and groups and between the management and the employees promote industrial peace and maximum production. The two-way communication network develops co-operation between people. There can be no mutual understanding and co-operation without communication. The flow of communication would be smooth and receptive with co-operation and with confidence, messages flow vertically, horizontally and across the organisation. Faith and confidence would be promoted, in short, communication promotes co-operation and understanding among employees.

6. Effective Leadership: Leadership implies the presence of a leader and followers. There is always a continuous process of communication between them. Communication is the basis for direction, motivation, as well as establishment of effective leadership. The followers have to follow him through conveying ideas, opinions, feelings, facts and decisions transmitted to them. It is through the medium of communication that the followers convey their opinions, ideas, feelings, facts etc. to their leader. Thus, transmission and reception ensure a two-way traffic, the *sine qua non* for effective leadership. A manager with good communication can become a successful leader of his subordinates.

7. Job Satisfaction: Communication is essential for achieving job satisfaction. Management conveys messages which promote mutual understanding. Reception and recognition provide job satisfaction to employees. Two-way communication creates confidence which leads to job satisfaction among employees. Openness, frank expression of opinions are necessary in this direction.

8. Increases Productivity: Communication helps the management in achieving maximum productivity with the minimum cost and eliminates waste.

These are all the main objectives of the management. It is remarked that "the great enemy of communication is the illusion of it." This illusion can be avoided only with an effective system of communication. It is through communication that the workers can be well informed about the process of production, new methods of production and the activities of the workers in a similar organisation. Thus, a good system of communication helps the management to achieve maximum productivity with minimum cost, elimination of waste, reduction of cost etc. Inter-firm comparison, to know one's operational efficiency, is not possible without effective communication.

9. Morale Building: Morale and good human relations in the organisation are essential to achieve goals of the organisation and to promote its goodwill in the public. An effective system of communication builds good morale and improve human relations. Participatory communication is the best technique of morale building and motivation. S. Khanwala remarked that "Most of the conflicts in business are not basic but are caused by misunderstood motives and ignorance of facts. Proper communication between the interested parties reduces the points of friction and minimize those that inevitably arise. Management, at every work level, is primarily charged with the responsibility of seeing that proper procedures are established for sympathetic interchange of information between all the two parties concerned."

10. Achieving Managerial Roles: Henry Mintzberg has described a manager's job by assigning three roles. They are inter-personal roles, informational roles and decisional role. Communication plays a vital role in these three types of role. In the case of inter-personal role a manager has to interact always with subordinates. In the information role, a manager has to collect information from various people and supply the necessary information to others both inside and outside the organisation. A manager in a decisional role or written media of communication discharges interpersonal, informational and decisional roles as well.

The importance of communication may be concluded with the remark of Chester I. Barnard, "The first executive function is to develop and maintain a system of communication."

COMMUNICATION, INFORMATION AND DATA

Communication and Information

So far we have discussed the term "communication." Communication is the basis for organising things which takes place in an organisation. In this context, it is necessary to understand and distinguish the words "communication", "information" and "data" and how communication is different from information. A thorough discussion of communication has been presented. At this juncture, it is important to mention the process so as to enable us to distinguish between information and communication.

Patterning is the basic process by which one can transform energy into information. Patterning is the basis for information. The undifferentiated background noise are unpatterned. Patterning is the only one of the aspects of information. Another important aspect is uncertainty which is something predictable. When uncertainty is reduced, it is through the process and function of communication.

Every communication contains information but all informations may not have communicative value. In the words of M. J. Myers and G. E. Myers, "Information is like an enormous umbrella, a broad concept which covers communication as one particular type of information. Information is a global concept referring to any pattern of energy input you are exposed to."[21]

Communication is a process, patterning expressed in symbols. Every information is to be translated into symbols, then only information has communicative value. A message may have information value which the communicator may have, unless he translates it into commonly understandable codes or symbols, it may not have communication value. An Indian and a German are able to communicate with each other only when they use arbitrary symbols which both can understand. Communication is a tool with which a proper transmission of information is possible. Information is to be transmitted to the receiver by translating into a shared symbolic code.

According to Myers and Myers, communication is information because it allows us to reduce uncertainty and to develop expectations. It is more specific than information because while information broadly deals with the recognition of patterns, communication only deals with patterns which can be put into symbols or words.

By definition, "communication" is a process of transmitting information. For this, a variety of media may be selected and information should be well planned accordingly. The best and popular medium of communication should be used, useful for the sender and the receiver. The communicator should keep always in mind the ability of the receiver. The media and information both should be acceptable to the receiver. Accepted information ensures action, while rejected information ensures behaviour based on rejection. Therefore, the information should be put into transmission in an acceptable manner.

Gellermans' remark is relevant in this context: "The sender to be certain that his message will be accepted by the receiver, must be prepared to let the receiver influence him. He must even be prepared to let the receiver alter or modify the message in ways that make it more acceptable to the receiver. Otherwise, it may not be understood, or it may not be accepted, or it may simply be given lip service and ignored."

In organisational communication, information is needed always on various aspects like social, cultural, economic, government control, regulations, raw material, marketing, transport facilities, labour and taxation. The information required may be gathered from two important sources such as internal source and external source.

Data and Information

The word "data" is the plural of singular word "datum." "Datum" means fact; data are facts — a quantitative or numerical information. Common usage of the word data refers to statistical data. Yule and Kendall defined statistics as quantitative data affected, to a marked extent, by multiplicity of causes. Thus, data are numerical expressions. Data are raw materials, subject to processing to obtain information for transmission. Data are not directly an information except in a limited sense, and data are presented by symbols and other techniques of presentation of numerical figures. The data processing converts raw data to get information. Thus, all information consists of data but not all data consist of information. Some data may not produce specific and meaningful information.

As used in data processing, information is data arranged in an order and form useful to the people who receive it, that is, information is relevant knowledge, produced as the output of data processing operations and acquired by people to enhance understanding and to achieve specific purposes.[22]

Additional data may add new dimensions to existing information. But the interpretation of data generally requires human judgement and this varies from person to person. Thus, what's information to one person may only be raw data to another.[23]

Data, therefore, are facts. The data may be processed either by humans or by machines. Thus, data are facts or observations, a representation of facts, concepts or instructions suitable for communication and interpretation. It is the data which are facts from which other facts may be worked out. A data-bank is a large amount of facts which are stored in a computer and from which particular pieces of information can be acquired when needed. Statistics are numerical data.

Some other definitions give us opportunity to understand the concept clearly. In the words of Horace Secriat, statistics are "aggregates of facts, affected to a marked extent by multiplicity of causes numerically expressed, enumerated or estimated according to a reasonable standard of accuracy, collected in a systematic manner for a predetermined purpose and placed in relation to each other."

Webster: "Statistics are the classified facts representing the conditions of the people in a state, specially those facts which can be stated in numbers or in tables of numbers or in any tabular or classified arrangement."

Bowely: "Statistics are numerical statement of facts in any department of enquiry placed in relation to each other."

Yuke and Kendall: "By statistics, we mean quantitative data affected to a marked extent by multiplicity of causes."

'INFORMATION CULTURE' FOR MEANINGFUL COMMUNICATION[24]

In the famous words of U. Than, "It is no longer resources that limit decisions but it is the decisions that make resources. In today's complex world, decision depends upon collection, selection, and correlation of "information" into shortest time. The "New Information Order" which calls the redistribution of the international power of the purse. "The new information order" is a demand for redress of perceived inequities, this time over the "power of the world." It is "the free and balanced flow of information"; not creating and perpetuating an imbalance in the world's flow of information under the guise of maintaining freedom, resulting in a vast and insidious cultural imperialism built on Western monopoly of the means of international communication.

Four Hypotheses

(1) There is an event identifiable in time and place, called a "Decision", which results in the occurrence of derivative events.

(2) Information represents truth — It's a good thing. The more information you have access to, the better. The more people who have access to an item of information, the better. People have a right to information.

(3) Information should be provided to decision-making to aid them.

(4) The more information brought to bear on a decision, the better is the resultant decision.

Information is More than mere Data

Information has complex attributes:

Correctness	Timeliness	Value
Ownership	Language	

Legal rights and Responsibilities of the Buyer, Seller, Carrier, Public.

Utility, and hence value of information derives from its use in decision-making.

What happens as the number of people have access to information increases:

Good: Unit cost of information decreases; improvement in management; liberation of mind and increased social responsibility.

Bad: Decreased quality, loss of privacy; vulnerability to malicious actions and vulnerability to accident.

The Communication of Uncertainty

Telling the truth, the whole truth and nothing but the truth. But what about the usual situation where you do not know the whole truth? You do not know how much of the whole truth do you know? You do not know the importance (e.g., relevance) of what you do not know?

Thus, apart from the substantial difficulty of communicating, what do you know, how do you estimate the size of what you do not know. Express its relative importance.

Towards Effective Information

For satisfactory information in certain fields the following points must be observed:

(1) The volume of information must be adequate.

(2) The density or frequency of the information must be in accordance with practical experience.

(3) The information must be clear and readily understandable.

(4) The information must be objective.

(5) The information must be up-to-date; it must be presented without unnecessary delay, i.e., immediately or at the most only a short time after the event.

(6) The information must be aimed at proper direction and must make use of the proper media to reach the sector of the public for which it is intended.[25]

Types of Information

(1) Pre-emptive Messages

(2) Informative Messages

(3) Evaluative Messages

(4) Imperative Messages

(5) Fidelity Messages

(6) Distortion Messages

CLASSIFICATION OF COMMUNICATION

Communication is broadly classified into the following groups:

(1) Intrapersonal Communication

(2) Interpersonal Communication

(3) Group Communication;
  (a) Small-Group Communication
  (b) Large-Group Communication
(4) Organisational Communication
  (a) Small-Group Communication
  (b) Informal Communication
(5) Mass Communication.

The word "small group" is used to make distinction from a large group like seminars, conferences, workshops, symposium and other large group gatherings.

Plan of the Study

The subject matter and discussion on organisation communication have been presented in detail in Chapter 8 under Management Communication, in Chapter 9, under Formal Communication, in Chapter 10 under Informal Communication. The subject matter of Group Communication has been discussed in Chapter 11, under Group Dynamics and Communication.

The other aspects of interpersonal communication like interpersonal foundation, interpersonal variables, communication models for understanding interpersonal relations have been covered in other chapters in appropriate places.

CLASSIFICATION OF COMMUNICATION

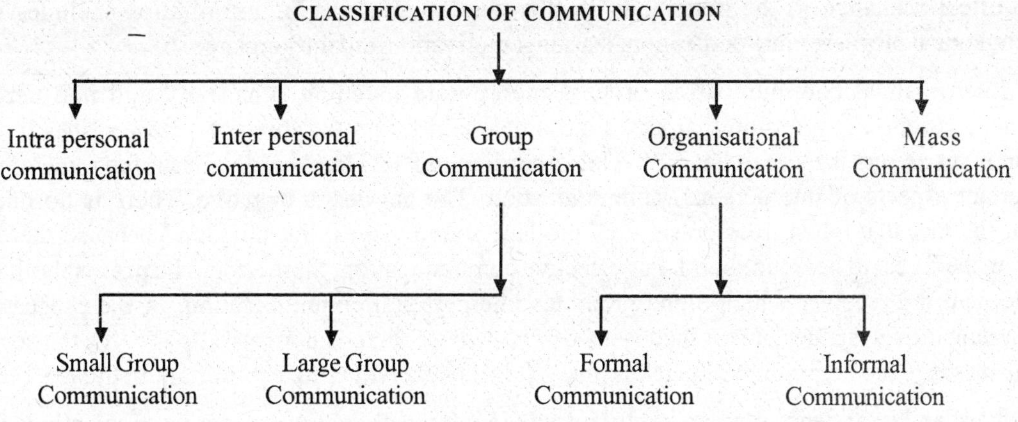

Fig. 1.15

Inter and Intrapersonal Communication

Exchange of information between one-to-one is called "interpersonal communication." Dialogue is a powerful medium of communication. Interaction with people gives rise to interpersonal communication. One of the earliest media of exchange of information between two persons is known as the "interpersonal communication." The basic characteristic feature of interpersonal communication is oral and face-to-face communication. It is quite different from other media, like written, mass or group communication.

Communication is a transaction process where people relate meanings, select arbitary symbols and exchange of symbols. Transactions have an important role in the interpersonal communication. This helps to improve interpersonal skills in communication with other people in one or another situation. Communication is the process of life-time experiences, perceptions and previous communication. Two people contact simultaneously and share the symbols and develop expectations of each other. Interpersonal communication is behaviour-oriented.

Intrapersonal Communication

Interpersonal communication does not include intrapersonal communication. Intrapersonal communication implies communication within the self or inside of oneself. Managers play interpersonal roles. Interview is the best method of interpersonal communication. It may be formal or informal meeting and discussion with someone on a particular subject.

Interpersonal Communication: Behaviour-oriented

There are two important theories known as:

1. Information Theory and
2. Interpersonal Theory

The mathematical orientation to communicate is known as information theory. The interpersonal communication is behaviour oriented. Interpersonal orientation to communication is mainly concerned with transmitting information from one person to another. The object of interpersonal communication is to effect a change in the behaviour. In this way, the passing of information includes the psychological processes like perception, learning, motivation and the language.

Interpersonal communication process incorporate listening sensitivity and non-verbal communication. The question that arises is "is there a noise in the forest if a tree crashes to the ground, but no one is there to hear it?" This according to P. F. Drucker, demonstrates some of the important aspects of interpersonal communication. The answer is negative. There is no doubt about the fact that when trees crash, they produce sound waves, but no sound because there is none in the forest to hear the sound. For effective communication, there should be present both the sender and the receiver which alone promotes interpersonal communication. In the process of communication, a sender of message is necessary. Unless there is a receiver to receive the sound or the message, no communication takes place. It is the receiver who is important in the feedback.

Trust and confidence play an important role in interpersonal aspects of communication. The research study of Glen Mellinger indicates that people who do not trust one another do not communicate effectively with one another. It is of great significance for superior-subordinate relations in an organisation.

There would always be ineffective communication, if the subordinates do not trust the boss or manager. Fred Luthans says that people perceive only what they expect to perceive; the other expected may not be perceived at all. The growing generation gap can play havoc with interpersonal communication; so can status differentiate incompatability of any sort. Given attention to and doing something above these interpersonal variables can spell the difference between effective and ineffective communication. Interpersonal communication plays crucial role in the organisational communication.

COMMUNICATION NOISE

The literary meaning of the word "noise" is sound, an unpleasantly loud sound. Communication noise is one of the elements contained in every communication process. Noise with reference to communication refers to any distortion or destruction, preventing the correctness and effective transmission of impulse or an idea in the mind or the source or sender to the mind of the listener. It has been defined as anything present in the perceived signal or code which was not present in the original message. The word "noise" has an origin from the phraseology of electronic communication. It is an element of communication very important for effective transmission. It is an interfering element; it is a noise in communication.

It seems it is a major element that prevails and surrounds the various stages of communication. Noise is any disruption in the communication system which results in the message received by the receiver quite different from the perceived and intended meaning. In simple words, it is anything that reduces the accuracy or fidelity of communication. It prevails like a cloud over the system and present at all other elements.

It is any where in the entire communication system. "The three mile island of Nuclear Disaster was caused partly by the noise of human failing to correctly decode the instrument message." Noise is unwanted symbols or signals of messages which interfere and disturb the reception of wanted signals. Generally, the distortion is in the form of sound, but it also includes various other non-sound distortions. The element of noise in communication includes non-sound distortions. For instance, a noise can also be in the form of visual, audio-visual, written, physical or psychological in respect of some pieces or bits of information transmission may contain little wanted signals and more noise.

C. F. Shannon who developed the information theory viewed communication as mechanistic. He introduced various basic components in his communication models. Among them, noise is one. The other elements are message, transmitted signals and received signals. Noise may be anything that affect the signal. The noise source may occur at any stage when signals travel through the channels and which prevents the received signal from being identical to the transmitted signals. The communication model of Shannon-Weaver which contains noise element is given below.

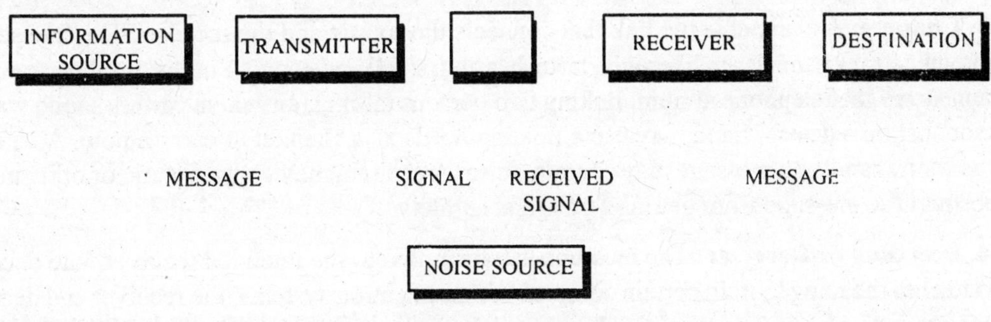

Fig. 1.16 Communication Noise

The communication model of David K. Berlo contains the noise element which forms like a cloud over the entire system of a communication and can be present in all other elements. Here the noise component hangs like a cloud over the system, his model is as follows:

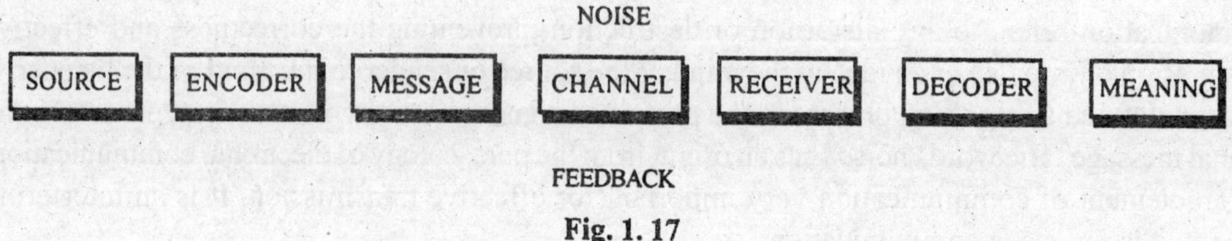

Fig. 1. 17

The important task in the communication process is to see that the information message should reach the destination without distortion or with a minimum of distortion. The noise source should not cause the source of message different from received message at destination. The basic idea of communication model of Shannon is that the information message transmitted represents selected or patterned by the sender from the various alternative possible messages/effectively transmittable. Thus, noise is a physical or technical barrier and an extraneous distracting signal in the way of effective communication.

Sources of Noise

1. Source: Source is the first and basic element of communication that has some thought, need, idea or information to transmit. It is the source where human element translates mental perceptions into a code that represents the message wished to be transmitted. It is the subject matter of any communication.It may involve any fact, idea or impulse, that exists in the mind of the communicator. A sender may create noise if he is unable to understand the message or describe inaccurately something.

2. Encoding: Mental perception is to be encoded into signals or symbols– Language is the most popular code used to express such mental perceptions, the source itself is often encoder of the original message. The process of translating the message into arbitrary symbols may contain noise, if the meaning is not effectively represented by symbols, the idea is subject to transcription and other mistakes.

3. Channel: A channel is the link that connects the source and the receiver. The five senses of communication channels are like sight, taste, hearing, smell and touch. Similarly, other examples of channels are the telephone system, linking two persons talking, air which carries sound waves. A person lost on a desert island may use a floating bottle as a channel to carry a note. A channel adopted for transmitting message may contain noise. A channel may contain static or other noises that obstruct the message from getting through accurately.

4. Decoding or Receiver: The message is transmitted to the intended receiver who decodes it and attaches meaning to it. In certain complex communication systems, the receiver and decoder are separate individuals. The receiver decodes and attaches meaning to understand the intended impulses of the sender. Decoding process also contains noise by way that the receiver may decode the message incorrectly or attach a wrong message to it or understand it in a sense quite different from that of the source meaning. There are many factors on which it depends upon whether the receiver attaches the intended meaning to the message like communication skills, attitudes, experience, environmental, and socio-cultural factors.

Types of Noise

1. Static, Tone or Buzz: Noise is anything that present in the perceived signal which was not present in the original message. So more sounds like static, tone, or buzz may cause noise in the communication.

2. Cultural Differences etc.: Noise may also result from cultural differences, physical sounds, non-verbal distortions, physical defects etc. Physical form of noise creates obstructions in hearing the speaker's message and disturbs one's concentration. For instance, a band practice nearby the place of speaking or hearing, talking to others while a radio is on, playing with loud music or foreman attempts to give orders or instructions to the workers in a noisy machine shop.

3. Different Outlooks: A noise problem arises when two persons with different outlooks.

4. Technical Noise: Poor telephone connections which interrupt conversations, weather and other broadcast systems which interrupt quiet listening; similarly, mudged transcripts and bad handwriting are also some examples of technical noise.

5. Visual Noise: Visual noise can be experienced when a student arrives late to the classroom and all the students are distracted by his late arrival.

6. Social Noise: Myers and Myers say: In the human systems, noise is not simply physical but refers to internal distractions experienced by people. Noise in a social sense is whether it interferes with accurate transmission of messages. Headaches, worries, lack of confidence, defensiveness, lack of motivation, and inadequate training are all examples of noise in human communication.

Redundancy in Transmission

In order to overcome 'noise' and to make the information source get a message to a destination with a minimum amount of distortions, the redundancy in transmission is to be established. The concept of redundancy is to be built up to solve the problem of noise. The principle of redundancy originates from information, and its adoption to the organisational communication is of special interest. Actually, redundancy means expressing an idea which is already conveyed by another word which is also used. In simple words, it means repetition of a message to help prevent noise from occurring in a channel or an exchange. To build redundancy means saying there are enough ways to avoid error.

Myers and Myers say: "It has been estimated that only about half of what we say to each other is really needed to reconstruct a message, and the other half is a sort of noise insurance." Channel redundancy is the best solution in the case of channel noise.

For instance, re-dialing a telephone because of disrupted conversation. It involves the need of a back up channel. In many cases, people try to reduce redundancy, particularly when the charge for the transmission of message is based on the number of words. For example, telegram words. Similarly, in the case of channels, where time is basis of charging a message, for instance, long-distance telephone calls, computer time, radio or television commercials, noise has an adverse consequence and as such redundancy should be used which acts as noise insurance. Redundancy insists on repeating an important point to the listeners, to spell out the key words in the message.

Myers and Myers say that information theory played a vital role in solving the technical problem of signal transmission through noisy channels. However, these principles cannot be literally applied to human communication. For one thing, human beings are generally interested in more than the mere occurrence of a message.

An effective communication system should provide a minimum of noise and a maximum of continuous feedback and sufficient redundancy to eliminate noise in reception.

Examples

1. The air conducting the sound, the voice carries other sounds.
2. The typing work of a secretary.
3. The telephone ringing down the hall, side rooms, reading room.
4. Flying aeroplanes overhead.
5. Disgruntled workers rioting outside.
6. Television programmes may be distorted by video and audio interference.
7. Telephone lines may be affected by static.
8. Resound effects.
9. Erasure, overwriting, striking off of a written or typed matter.
10. Printed words may be obscured by lack of lighting.
11. Every channel is associated with some sort of noise.
12. Any minimal intensity of noise unnoticeable.

Communication Load

The importance of message load or information load cannot be overemphasised and needs no elucidation. The value of the subject matter to be handled is called 'communication load'. In other words, message load means the quantity and the complexity of the message received by the receiver. In communication between an individual or an authority relationship who are expected to handle the message in flow, so that the work can be accomplished. In a formal organisation, message flow is to be handled to achieve the objectives to be achieved, the message flows through different channels to the appropriate users and time. Communication load is also one of the basic barriers to effective communication.

Message load may be underload or overload. Message which is too little is called as underload of message. The word "underload of message" may be defined as the amount of information load which is less than the handling ability of the receiver. On the other hand, "overload of the message" means the amount of information load which exceeds the handling ability of the receiver.

Both underload and overload are barriers to communication. The underload of message means the people get bored, without work involvement, resulting in gossip, rumours, chit-chat, under use of channels, irregular relationship etc., unproductive to the organisation. Optimum load of message flow, formally prescribed is good for the organisational growth which is right load for the communication system. On the other hand, it is difficult to prescribe the correct message load.

The following factors affect a high volume of messages, according to M. T. Myers and G. E. Myers:

1. High structure of communication network will create too much information.
2. When more sub-systems are linked to the major systems, it is the span of management.
3. Organisational rules about who communicates with whom.
4. The incidence of ambiguous orders and questions.
5. The extent of expertness among those attempting to develop messages.
6. The speed with which changes are taking place within the organisation.
7. Rapidity of change and organisational sensitivity to change by the outside environment.
8. The availability of hardware and software to store and process information.[26]

A rapid increase in message load is a costly matter because an organisation may have to create additional systems and personnel to handle the message load. Sometimes it may be necessary to replace personnel or re-organise the sub-systems to cope with the overload.

Regarding responses to overload from the personnel, the study of J.C. Miller in "Information Input Overload and Psycopathology," indicates the following:

1. Omission : Omission of some of the messages which they consider inconsequential or less important, when they think that messages are not needed.

2. Committing Errors: Committing errors of transmission of message. Errors in the process may take place when handling an overload message.

3. Approximation: It means giving partial answers to questions. It may take the form of giving stock replies to questions.

4. Queuing: It implies delaying processing of messages during the peak- periods.

5. Escaping: Escaping may be a psychological or physical response.

6. Multiple Channels: Response to overload is the result of formation of many channels, when the overload is only taking place in a part of the system.

7. Filtering: Filtering is the process of selecting messages on a priority basis.

The responses of the topmost level communication intermediaries and its analysis to system message overload has revealed some interesting features. The results are contained in the report of A. Downs, *Inside Bureaucracy* of a Rand Corporation study.

The following are the responses and predicted reactions in bureaus:

1. "Slowdown of message handling without changing the network structure or rules of transmission." This, writes Downs, is the most common response to overloads because:

(a) Until it is known whether or not the situation is temporary or permanent, the best response is to do as little as possible;

(b) Overload often occurs because of the peaks or crisis, so it is best to respond by delaying reactions; and

(c) Economy in the bureau may be more important than the fast processing of messages, so no changes in message handling are called for.

2. Change rules so that the lower echelons screen out more information or have different "thresholds" of message importance.

3. Add more levels and channels to the existing network.

4. Group the message.

5. Improving the message.[27]

PERCEPTION IN COMMUNICATION

Definition

S.P. Robbins defines perception "As a process by which individuals organise and interpret their sensory impressions in order to give meaning to their environment."

James J. Gibson defines it as, "the process by which an individual maintains contact with his environment."

David T. Kollat *et al,* state that "the process whereby an individual receives stimuli through the various senses and interprets them."

Meaning and Nature

Perception is a mental process to get sensory impression and attributing meaning. What one perceives is generally different from objective reality. It is possible that a person may view a thing or a situation, but as in most of the cases, it is very unusual to find such a situation.

Perception is the ability to see, understand and read clearly. This is an act and process of becoming aware. In other words, it is an interpretation that makes a person to understand. The perceivers have to understand the message of the information. A person's perception is the clear picture of reality of what is and what is not. A correct perception gives meaning correctly through the interpretation of a message and needs understanding. Basically, the message must first enter the mind of the receiver. This stage in communication process is referred to as "perception."

A person may perceive people, events, environments, spoken, written and visual messages. People see things differently. Even 'facts' may be seen quite differently by different people. Relevance to one's needs is the most important determinants of one's personal view of the world. Things that seem to aid one's need, satisfaction are seen quickly. But things that look like obstacles, if they are not critically threatening, may be seen quickly, only then to be denied so that they may appear not to have been there at all. By denying them, people 'protect' themselves temporarily from them. If they really become dangerous, however people drop the blindness and face them.

To ignore differences in perception is to ignore a major determinant of behaviour. Yet it is easy to assume unwarrantedly that everyone views the world from the same perception as the viewer and that time spent trying to reach a common view is wasted time.

Why is the perception important in the study of communication? it is simply because people's understanding the ideas, facts, impulses is based on their perception. What reality is not reality itself. We can explain that individuals may read and listen to things, yet understanding it differently. A number of factors operate to shape and sometimes, filter and distort understanding. These factors can reside in the receiver and, to some extent, in the speaker of the message. The receiver or reader is important in the process of communication.

When a receiver, listeners or readers interpret what he listens or reads, the interpretation is heavily influenced by personal characteristics of the individual receiver. Receivers' attitudes, motives, past experience, interest, confidence on superiors and the extent of trust are the relevant personal characteristics affecting understanding and interpretation.

A meaning may be the same but it can be interpreted differently. The reasons for, the different interpretations are divergent attitudes concerning the multiple meanings of words. Unsatisfied needs or motives stimulate individuals and may exert a strong influence on their understanding. Expectations can distort one's ability of understanding in that one will see what he expects to see. If a subordinate expects a manager to be autocratic, dictatorial or authoritative they may perceive and understand them in that way only.

PERCEPTION PROCESS

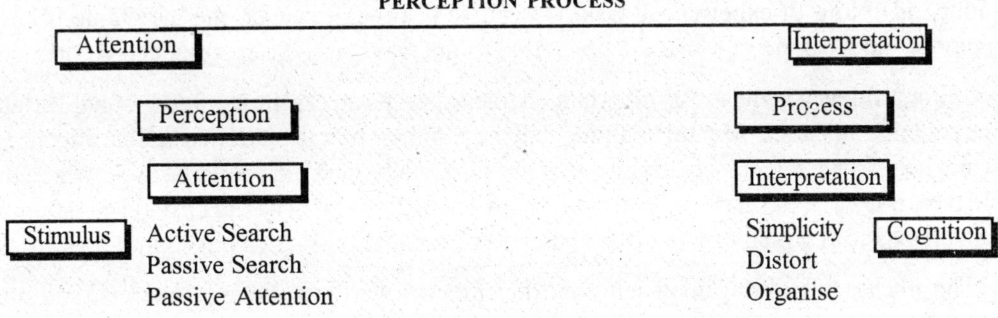

Fig. 1.18

Some Suggestive Determinants of the Perception Process

Stimulus Conditions	Audience Condition
Intensity	Information Needs
Size	Attitudes
Message	Values
Novelty	Interests
Position	Confidence
Context	Social Context
	Cognitive Style

Source: Adapted from David A. Aaker, John G. Myers: *Advertising Management,* Prentice Hall of India Private Limited, New Delhi, 1986, p. 237.

SELF-CONFIDENCE FOR EFFECTIVE COMMUNICATION

Self-confidence is an essential interpersonal variable for effective communication. The literary meaning of the word "self-confidence' is trust or belief in one's confidence. It is a belief and faith in one's own ability to speak. The manager when he is communicating a piece of information gives in the belief that he is transmitting messages in such a way that the receiver receives it and understands the message. In other words, the communicator must have a great deal of trust in oneself or in one's own power of communication. Oral communication is more than a physical process. It has also psychological aspects like establishing justification, developing confidence, etc.

Self-confidence is one thing to speak about the message and quite another thing to have confidence and preserve the same throughout the communication process with the greatest of vigilance and care. One has to be self-trusted and strong mind to exchange one's message in an understandable manner. There are so many temptations around us and it is always possible that the cares and worries of the organisational problems continuously haunts a person and opportunities go astray.

It is, therefore, far simpler to follow a crooked way than stay assiduously in the right course. The weak and the vacillating will hardly make the grade of the man with a good conduct as they are to fall victims to some alluring situations. The weak-minded managers are generally dazzled by the glamour and colour of experienced tasks. In course of time, however, the inevitable is bound to happen and the weak people become converted to the ways of their experienced comparisons.

Self-confidence is the most important characteristic as an essential interpersonal variable for effective communication. Mental qualities find their highest manifestation in self-confidence. With trust and belief a person can communicate more effectively. The old proverb says, "where there is a will, there is a way." Similarly, where there is self-confidence, there would be good communication. It is an art and craft which can be perfected by experience and practice but cannot be fully taught.

The process of building up of self-confidence consists efforts of mental exercise and situation dealings that have to be undergone before a person may hope to acquire the full control over his self or over his will. If the self and the will are strong fanned by the desired goals, the way is generally open to him, the way of all the tenacity and preservance that a person has. It is, therefore, not easy to have a determined belief or trust outright. One has to experience in various interpersonal situations of communication and work for it with all efforts availing opportunities and one has to develop and grow self-confidence gradually and steadily. Analysis of interpersonal communication situations reveals that one good interaction everyday adds to his self-confidence, as one every work will eat into it and hamper its development.

It is not always easy to cultivate one's self-confidence without proper feedback. Managers just occupying positions or beginners may have temperamental capabilities and in these formative periods of interactions, one can make or unmake one's self-confidence. Experience, practical situations are not yet fully set and there is enormous scope for improvement of self-confidence.

One has to develop justifiable self-confidence for this purpose. M.P. Wolf etc, have suggested to maintain a personal achievement journal. They suggested to record particulars of success, failures, experiences which can help to learn, improve and achieve. "From those summaries, write quarterly and yearly accounting for yourself. By reviewing your achievement journal, you will give yourself an ongoing personal inventory of self-insight, performance, and future direction. You will have relevant data for documenting the development of your career. And you will have a communication aid for constantly developing justifiable confidence in yourself."

A communicator cannot establish self-confidence and rise to the occasion all of a sudden. The speakers are otherwise the first to rehearse. M.P. Wolf and others, have suggested the following fundamental steps for self-confidence:

(1) First rehearse alone; and

(2) Rehearse in front of try-out group.

Self-confidence is related to interpersonal communication. One can experience trust when his relationship with another person is characterised by various situational contexts. According to Rossiter and Pearce, the following are such situational context:

(1) Contingency.

(2) Predictability.

(3) Alternative Options.

(1) Contingency: "Contingency" means a situation in which the results of another person's actions significantly affect.

(2) Predictability: "Predictability" means the degree of confidence that one may have in his expectations about the other person's behaviour or intentions.

Establishing self-confidence neither happens by magic nor there is technical, manual or readymade guide which specifies the steps to be followed to make self-confidence. In fact, there is no sure way to make self-confidence. Developing self-confidence sometimes encourages to convince others in interpersonal communication. Thus, trusting one's own strength, however, almost always will make others to distrust the speaker.

Another technique for building goodwill among an audience is to make the listeners to feel important. Due importance should be given to the listeners. The purpose of speech is to make them to understand the message. This can be achieved by showing appreciation for listeners and by taking a personal interest in listening to them and clarifying their doubts. It is an art and tact of the speaker to make them feel important. Speaking from their point of view and mentioning of various practical instances also make them feel important.

Goodwill is friendly and kindly attitude. Listeners' goodwill is a major object of oral communication. Indicating acceptance of suggestions by the listeners will go a long way towards achieving a successful speech. Indicating attention and acknowledgement of what is being suggested will produce positive and favourable reaction from listeners. It will create a friendly confident feeling towards the communicator. Much of interpersonal communication depends on how one is definite in dealing with a situation.

One must appraise his interaction with others' in terms of his self-esteem. One of the most dangerous barriers for interpersonal effective communication is lack of self-confidence. Unless a person has self-confidence, he cannot transmit his achievement, his personal abilities, and his future prospects. The communicator indispensably has to build and develop in himself a justifiable confidence. The exhibition of feelings of anxiety and problems by facial expression are indications of lack of a or low-self-confidence. A person who is closely associated with the qualities of low self-confidence is unable to communicate and put across to a quite different cross-sections of people and in different situations. In real life situations, communicators feel it is difficult to face different faces of audience.

Every person communicating has to endeavour to overcome stage fright. Stage fright is a misdirected awareness on the part of the communicator. When the sender of a message or speaker lacks self-confidence, one may sense a nervousness, a tensing of muscles, a quivering voice, etc. In any case, self-confidence is more important which creates a positive outlook in the person.

A successful manager always endeavours to establish self-confidence among the subordinates. Stanley Coppersmith has suggested three conditions relating to self-confidence. They are:

(1) Managers have to make total acceptance of his subordinates.
(2) To have clearly defined and enforced limits.
(3) To have managerial respect for individual action within the defined limits.

It is the motivation and encouragement of his subordinates which promotes free flow of communication within the organisation in turn building up a right self-confidence among the people working in the organisation. This not only establishes good formal relations but also informal relationships, which are conducive to effective communication.

Leland Brown has suggested the following eight steps. If followed logically, one can achieve self-confidence:

(1) Message preparation. Avoid forgetfulness, which results in stage fright.
(2) Practise aloud, rehearse more times, imagine audience.
(3) To hear one's own voice by tape recorder. Not to memorise talk.
(4) Appropriate dress and appearance for the occasion.
(5) Think about your audience, but not about yourself.
(6) Begin slowly; stage fright disappears after starting.
(7) Speak louder than ordinarily.
(8) Speak as often as you can. The more the practice, the easier it is to speak with confidence.

FILTERING AND DISTORTION OF MESSAGE

Filtering with reference to communication refers to a part of interpretation proces. of communication. When a message is transmitted through translation, explanation, simplification some part of it goes distorted or filtered. Soon after receiving the message, the receiver has to interpret the impulse or idea of the sender. The accurate interpretation will depend upon the past knowledge, experience, beliefs, attitudes, etc.

It is in the interpretation process, a person may filter some bits of information. When the idea passes through the mind, some pieces of information are ignored or filtered out and others are added. In the words of Leland Brown, certain beliefs, likes and dislikes, have programmed certain behaviour pattern that serve as the basis for an individual's *cognitive structure.* The expression "cognitive structure" refers to a "set of values, attitudes, knowledge and expectations that in turn causes rejection or acceptance of the bits of information." This is what exactly the process of filteration describes.

There are three types of filtering. They are:

(1) Levelling: It means knocking down bits of the message. Levelling of filtering takes place when the contents of the message is one incompatible with the contents of the message of the receiver. Thus, it distorts the original idea.

(2) Sharpening: Sharpening is also a type of filtering which distorts the message. In this case, the listener or receiver magnifies and exaggerates the information being disproportionate to the intended or perceived by the sender.

(3) Assimilation: The mind of a reader is preconditioned for being programmed to a particular interpretation and behaviour. In the case of reading into a message which is not there, or the receiver attaches a different meaning that the sender has not perceived or intended, such bits of information are added to the messages and deletion is also possible.

Filtering results at the interpretation stage of communication. The received message from one source may sometimes be selected, edited and transmitted to others. For instance, abstracts from reports, review reports on books, news summaries result in distortion. A manager who receives bits of information from the top management, decides and selects what to pass on to the people who are subordinates to him.

Filtering takes place in the case of preparation of an advertising copy describing only those facts that will create a favourable image of the product or goodwill of a concern. Filtering is a common characteristic feature in which we perceive, what we see, hear and read. It cannot be eliminated totally because it is a natural phenomenon that helps interpretation and perception.

Leland Brown states that, "These factors are everchanging and communicators need to be aware of them to plan and communicate message in language symbols that will help the receiver perceive without distorting the message and thus accomplish the sender's purpose."

In organisational communication, the upward channel, downward channel, diagonal channel and grapevine are all subject of filterations. The message in grapevine receives fresh filteration with every repetition until it gets worst.

The practice of filtering would not achieve the object of communication. A favourable effect of communication can be achieved only when the message is heard, understood, believed and acted upon as perceived and intended by the sender. To achieve it, care must be taken that the message is truly and reliably transmitted. In actual practice, there are more filter points through which the message has to pass. Filtration of some bits of information, therefore, is partly a function, when a span of communication is wider. It is irrespective of whether or not the structure of the organisation is tall or low.

Filteration may take place intentionally in the organisation because of the needs and ambitions of certain members in relation to others in the span or chain. The preconceived idea will have an effect on filteration and multiplied when it passes through successive stages and judgement of various members in the process of communication. Sometimes, an individual position makes guesses on what bits of information actually the next receiver would like to have. Slanting, interpretating, condensing, precise, summaries, abstracts are the possible ways to filter messages (Fig. 1.19).

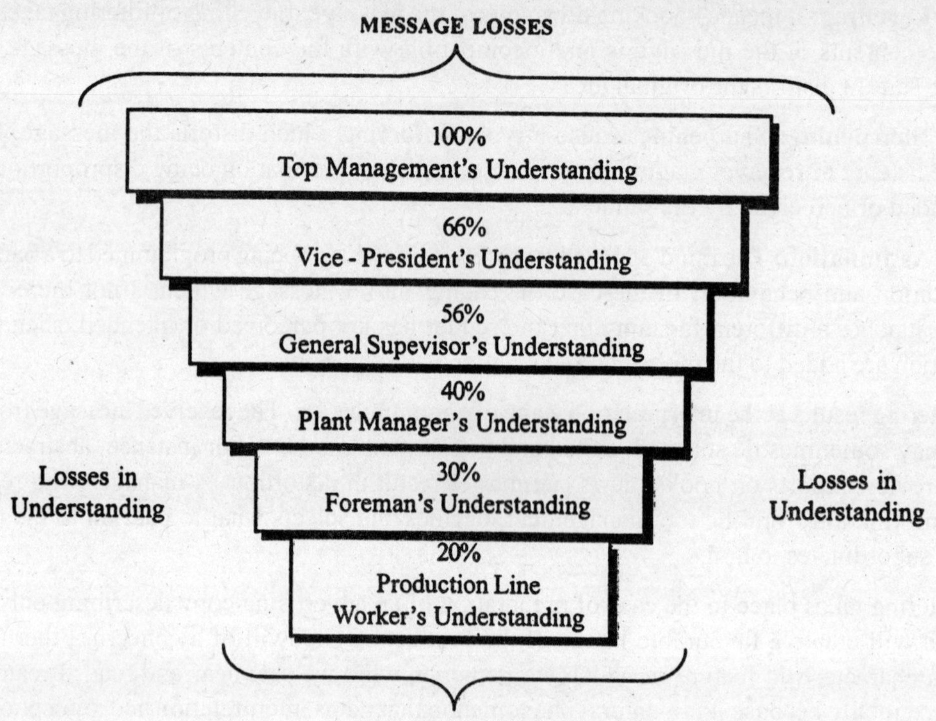

Fig. 1.19 Final Message

(***Source:*** Adapted from Management, Hellreigel.D., *et. al.*, Addison-Wesley Publishing Co., 1982 p. 579.)

HONESTY IN COMMUNICATION

Honest communication involves a sense of obligation to one's self, to other people, and to the absolute. Rightness is known by intuition in the mind. Respect for it gives one an expertness in living.

One of the noblest words among the social virtues is "honesty." It is an essential quality in binding people together in the family, in the community, and in society. It has been esteemed in the lives of people in all civilizations, even though, the standards have been different from time to time and from place to place. It would be difficult to imagine what life would be like if we give up such a fundamental rule of conduct.

In our dealings with other people, honesty may be taken as coming under the cordial virtue "justice." This does not mean merely being faithful to contracts and carrying out the duties required by the laws of the community, but also fidelity in all one's relationships with others, including the obligation to speak honestly.

Honest communication is for everyone. There is a tendency to apply the rigorous ideal of honesty in communication to a few classes like the clergy and teachers. To others, we grant the privilege of being second-best and having that accounted as virtue. Their faults are overlooked when their self-interest proves too strong for their social interest and overrules in their minds the principle of the obligation to speak honestly.

It is useful in considering the need for honest communication in our political society, to realise that every proposed law is in the nature of an alternative. It is not to be judged good or bad except as it is better or worse than some other equally definite course of proceeding which might be adopted instead of it.

PERSUASION

There are two forms of intercourse between individuals and between groups. They are force and persuasion. If one party compels another to do something instead of persuading him, it is despotism, and it transgresses the principles of proper conduct sanctioned by an intelligent and spiritually refined society. It is usually a weakling who runs away from persuasion, he does not want to risk being persuaded against his prejudices. A person with strength of character can listen to persuasion, weigh what is said and arrive at informed conclusions.

Before engaging in persuasion, take time to settle a few questions in your mind. What do I wish to accomplish? What are the interests of the people to whom I shall be talking? What are the facts I wish to tell them?

When a speaker wishes to bring about change in belief or conduct, the heart must not only understand and approve but also he must accept. The speaker needs to minimize misunderstandings and difficulties by giving adequate explanations. "Because I say so" is not an acceptable or effective reason to give in dialogue, debate or persuasion when recommending some action. A sense of human interest is a valuable asset to anyone indulging in persuasion. Human interest is necessary in the person to whom you are presenting your case. Consider what will appeal to him. Whatever your objectives, you must start with his present state of knowledge and belief.

Here is a skeleton upon which you may erect a structure for persuasion:

(1) Show that a problem exists or a situation needs correction.

(2) Explain the essential elements of the problem or the various aspect of the situations.

(3) Tell about the reasons for failure of previous attempts.

(4) Show why your solution is the best one.

(5) Picture your solution in operation, including the benefits it would give to those who join in reaching it.

Don't forget to include a specific suggestion in your conclusion. Tell in definite terms the nature, place, time and method of the response you desire from the participants.

To accomplish an attitude change, suggestion for change must first be received and accepted. "Acceptance of the message" is a critical factor in persuasive communication.

The suggestion is more likely to be accepted if it means existing personality needs and drives.

The suggestion is more likely to be accepted if it is in harmony with group norms and loyalties.

The suggestion is more likely to be accepted if the source is perceived as trustworthy and expert.

Sometimes, emotional appeals are more influential; sometimes, factual ones are. It depends on the kind of message and the kind of audience.

A strong but tactful, threat is generally effective in inducing a desired opinion change.

DIALOGUE

Dialogue is sharing: It is the participation of people in the search for common values and ideas as they deal with problems of joint concern. It is a conversation between two or more persons with a view to reaching an amicable agreement. Tossing an idea around in dialogue gets rid of a lot of chaff and makes the seed viable.

The way to prepare yourself is to participate in question and answer in the proposal and counter-proposal and so find areas of agreement and build upon them. It seems to enlightened persons that this is a better way to solve problems than raising an argument or fighting a battle.

Dialogue offers full scope for both good sense and good personality. The emotions you express should be intrinsically responsible, subject to amendment and yielding to improvement. The smile with which you present your point of view should show your personality. It springs from knowledge of your subject, belief in the integrity of what you sponsor, and a feeling of pleasure in being given the opportunity to speak. Personality is made up of many qualities of the mind and the knowledge and developed skill.

Just as a little discomfort is accepted as one of the occupational hazards of almost every job, so there are difficult periods in any dialogue. All people have not bumped their heads against the same obstacles, so in a group there is bound to be diversity of experience described, variety of beliefs affirmed, and many opinions expressed. Some will be annoying and many will be frustrating or may be infuriating. If then, there is one virtue more than another that should be emphasised as an essential requirement in the person engaged in dialogue and persuasion, it is a patient tact.

REFERENCES

1. Narayana, H., *Yogakshema,* Nov. 1991, pp. 5-9.
2. David, K. Berlo, *The Process of Communication,* New York, Quoted in *Personnel Management,* P.C. Tripathi, Sultan Chand & Sons, 1978, p. 80.
3. The discussion is based on *Management: A Modern Approach by* M.K. Starr, New York, Harcourt Brace Jovanovich, 1971.
4. *Ibid.*

5. *Ibid.*
6. *Ibid.*
7. *Ibid.*
8. The discussion is based on *Managing by Communication by* M.T. Myers and G. E. Myers, McGraw-Hill International Book Company, 1982, pp. 74-77.
9. Balan, K.R. and Rayudu, *C.S., Handbook of Public Relations and Communication,* Castle Books Limited, New Delhi, 1994, p. 19.
10. Balan, K.R. and Rayudu, C.S., *Principles of Public Relations.* Himalaya Publishing House.
11. *Ibid.*
12. Myers and Myers, *op.cit.,* p. 21.
13. *Ibid.*
14. Thomas A. Harris, *I'am OK—You are OK,* New York, Harper & Row, 1969.
15. Brown, L , *Communicating Facts and Ideas in Business,* Prentice Hall, Englewood Cliffs, New Jersey, 1982, p. 317.
16. Quoted in Brown, L., *Ibid.,* p. 317.
17. Knootz, H., and Donnell, O., *Management, A Systems and Contingency Analysis of Managerial Functions,* McGraw-Hill, Kogakush Ltd., 1976 p. 622.
18. Adapted, American Management Association, *Ten Commandments of Good Communication* as Quoted in *Management Theory, Process and Practice,* Richard M. Hodgetls. Holt-Saunders International Editions, 1982, pp. 304-305.
19. Balan, K.R., and Rayudu, C.S., *Handbook of Public Relations and Communication, op. cit.,* pp. 26-27.
20. The discussion from point three to seven are based on the five functions suggested by Lee O. Thayer, *Administrative Communication*, Richard, D. Irwin. Homewood, Hill, 1961, p.283.
21. Myers and Myers, *op. cit.*, p.15.
22. Donald H. Sanders, *Computer Concepts and Applications*, McGraw - Hill International Edition, 1987, p.14.
23. *Ibid.*
24. Balan, K.R., & Rayudu, C.S., Principles of Public Relations.
25. *Ibid.*
26. Myers and Myers, *op. cit.*, p.129.
27. *Ibid*, p.134.

****

CHAPTER 2

Effective Speaking: Verbal or Oral Communication

Introduction

Among the various forms of communication, oral communication is considered to be the earliest and common medium of communication. In oral communication, speech is a widely adopted tool of communication. The sender, the medium, the receiver and the message are the four basic factors associated with communication. Socrates, and Demosthenes were great and renowned speakers. The world is full of speeches. Everyday, in educational institutions, the students and the teachers come into contact; they converse and communicate. In offices, the superiors talk to the subordinates, the subordinates to superiors and among themselves. In productive and service organisations, the customers carry on conversation with the suppliers, lawyers, doctors, auditors, consultants with their clients, so on and so forth.

Whether it is business communication or otherwise, oral communication should be clear and effective to achieve the objects of communication. Speech is an art; for this there are no fixed rules which can be uniformly followed always and in all circumstances. There are a number of factors which influence effective oral communication. Factors like conversation style of the speaker, language, medium, the temperament of the receiver and speaker, size of audience, importance of message, fear of superiors etc., are important. For instance, an important person, appearing on the TV, words if wrongly selected and used, may damage his image.

Human relations are the fundamental elements of public relations. It is with speech, one gets along well with the public, both internal and external. The public are of three categories: *(a)* there are those who know you and like you; *(b)* there are those who know you and do not like you; *(c)* there are those who neither know you nor care for.

Fig. 2.1 Public Speaking

The technique involved in the process of communication is through speech to do business with all types of people. The essential basis of all cross-sections is the communication process. It is the transfer of information from one to another. The message is transmitted by spoken or written words or by image or a combination of these or other media, such as music, colour, mimicry, design, odour, and sense of touch.

In competitive and dynamic market economy, there are information gaps which cannot be filled up by the interaction of supply and demand through prices and costs. This is where communication activity steps in.

PRINCIPLES OF EFFECTIVE ORAL COMMUNICATION

The capacity to communicate effectively and clearly is an important skill. The speakers have to make the message clear and easily understandable, both at work and outside. In any profession, it is not possible to get through without communication. Communication is a valuable asset for all the people in modern days of a busy world, particularly to lawyers, teachers, auditors, consultants, admininistrators, politicians, business executives, parents and children. Thus, speech or talk is basic and indispensable in any group facilities in a civilised society. Speech is for others to understand. The confusion and misunderstanding in conversation are due to ineffective, faulty and vague speech.

There are no standard rules to be followed in making oral communication effective once and for all times to come. However, effective oral communication calls for certain principles to be followed. Whatever the circumstances, the following are the essential ingredients of good oral communication.

(1) Brevity: A message to be delivered should be brief. It should neither be too short nor too long. In real life quite often audience comments about a speech, as too long or too short. Time factor is important because not only the speaker's time is wasted but also that of the audience. So, a message must be brief. Lengthy sentences confuse and may lead to misunderstanding. It should be a short one. One can achieve brevity by taking pains and framing short sentences rather than lengthy and complex sentences. We do come across people who start speech with short sentences. Conversation in short sentences gives the listener time and opportunity to follow what the speaker endeavours to put across. Using precise words, simple and familiar words, and avoiding superfluous words are important factors in effective communication.

(2) Clarity: The essential of good oral communication is clarity. Clarity of message is the first and foremost important among principles. The three most important qualities of oral communication style are: first, clarity, then clarity and last clarity. Before you start talking, think and rethink ideas till they are clear. Then only can one put ideas in conversation in a clear-cut terms. Clarity can be achieved with simple words, short sentences and common words. Daniel Defoe, the author of Robinson Crusoe, said that clarity is a matter of style in which a man speaking to five hundred people of all common and various capacities, idiots and lunatics excepted, should be understood by them all.

(3) Choosing Precise Words: Precision is the most important principle in effective communication. Using the precise words means speaking in exact detail using the right words at right place to the context alone will convey the meaning intended by the speaker. In oral communication, the precise words which are often the concrete words express the real and correct meaning. As far as possible, using vague words should be avoided. But in practice, it is difficult to replace one word with another. No two words give exactly the same meaning. It is better to have full knowledge of synonyms and antonyms of words.

(4) Cliche: Cliche means a phrase which is used often, and has no meaning. The cliches are now stale in oral communication. An effective good communicator avoids cliches. A speaker may use them unconsciously when he is involved in a serious mood of conversation. Examples of cliches are 'I mean', 'oh, really- 'quite fine', 'yes' etc.

A cliche is generally used to express indirectly a simple idea, when it suddenly strikes the speaker. The strongest objection to its use is that, as it is too frequently used and in the wrong context, that it is hackneyed. They are used like catch phrases, faulty in English, because it irritates the listeners, particularly in public speech. Some of the cliches are:

The supreme sacrifice.

The order of the day.

Conspicuous by his absence.

Slowly but steadily.

Cruel to be kind.

(5) Sequences: Presentation of matter in a logical sequence is yet another important principle of effective communication. The speaker should not jump points or change the sequence. Consistency, continuity, and logical development of the subject matter should be there. The manner in which a speaker says something is important than the something itself that matters in communication

(6) Avoid Jargon: In our conversation, we must be conscious to avoid jargon. Jargon is a field, applicable or relating to a particular section of profession. It means language or terminology relating to law, commerce, sports, defence etc. It may be called as legal jargon, military jargon, commercial jargon etc. Only people who are well-versed in a particular subject can understand. But in general conversation, the words used must be clear to other people as well.

(7) Avoid Verbosity: To convey meaning is more important than using superfluous words. Verbosity in oral communication is a great danger. Using more words does not assure greater clarity. Using more words will take more time and the time of the audience is wasted. The listener may tire and may misunderstand the meaning.

(8) Seven C's of Communication: Francis J. Betgin advocates that there are seven C's to remember in spoken communication. They are:

1. Candid
2. Clear
3. Complete
4. Concise
5. Concrete
6. Correct
7. Courteous.

(9) Prepositions: Use of unnecessary prepositions should be avoided. For instance, all employees must follow the safety regulations in regard to work. Here the word 'about' can be used in place of "in regard to." Some other examples are: in connection with, with reference to, in relation to, with regard to.

(10) Adjectives and Adverbs: Adjectives and adverbs should be used where necessary. They emphasise the meaning with the degree of importance, for instance, the problem is under active consideration; a positive decision will be taken; definite results; comparatively, the results are poor.

SPEECH PREPARATION — USEFUL HINTS[1]

Advance preparation and careful planning will prove very helpful in making effective speeches. A check list of the following steps should be kept in view:

(1) Select a Topic: Selection of a subject matter for a speech is the first and the most important task on the part of the speaker. The topic should be specific in content and in scope.

(2) Narrow Down the Scope: For example, environmental pollution is too general, bus noise pollution or air pollution are specific themes. Similarly, in a speech like communication skills, it should be specified as speaking skills, writing skills or listening skills. However, in some cases, narrowing the focus may not be practical.

(3) State the Object: It may be one or the combination of two or more like to inform, to persuade or influence and to entertain.

(4) Prepare an Outline: Make a rough blue print like introduction, body copy, major thrust and conclusion.

(5) Locate Material and Data: Collect information and organise it from books, documents, speeches, magazines, reports etc.

(6) Rough Draft: Attempt the rough draft and refine it. It includes introduction, quotation, anecdotes, body, examples, references and conclusions.

(7) Aids: Consider and procure visual, audio-visual aids like charts, overhead projector, T.V. etc.

(8) Rehearse: Rehearsal and practice should be recognised as advantageous for improvement in speech delivery. Rehearsal gives self-confidence. It is desirable to rehearse in front of try-out group. Invite good points or bad points of the speech, indicating verbal and non-verbal behaviour of the speaker. This will help to infuse confidence. Do retouching of draft where necessary.

A speaker steadily gains confidence, is able to anticipate question from the listeners and answer the queries, use transitional phrases to establish relationship between ideas and concepts.

VOCAL CONTROL PRONUNCIATION AND PHYSICAL BEHAVIOUR[2]

The use and co-ordination of the above attributes enhance the effectiveness of a speaker's message.

1. Vocal Control: (a) Pitch: It is a listener's interpretation of frequency of sound. The high pitch is, in many cases, the result of emotional and physical tension. Through practice and experience, it is possible to adjust the pitch and use different levels and give information to enhance the effect. Two irritating features of the quality of voice must be avoided like:

(i) Muffled effect.

(ii) Breathlessness or whispering effect.

(b) Rate: An average speaker can deliver 120-150 words per minute. About 90-120 words per minute is considered ideal. Uniformity in rate is considered boring. Avoid continuous word delivery. Generally, All-India Radio news reading pattern keeps high range but, in practice, it is not suited to speech- making. Reading at a speed of 120-150 words per minute is acceptable for a short or brief speech or announcement.

(c) Volume: It refers to loudness or softness of a speaker's voice. The simple rule is to accent syllables and important phrases which you think should orally stand out. The volume should match the contents of the various parts of the speech.

2. Pronunciation: Inaccurate and faulty pronunciation reduce the credibility of communication. There are great variations of pronunciation based on national and regional characteristics. But with practice and effort, pronunciation can be improved and stabilised.

3. Physical Behaviour: There are four levels of physical activities that a speaker can utilise to improve the transmission of his message:

(a) **Eye Contact:** This helps to generate a feeling of directness and every member in the audience feels the speaker is talking to him.

(b) **Facial Expressions:** This is the second level of physical reinforcement. The speaker shows his interest, enthusiasm and belief in his ideas, reflecting a sincere effort to share them with his listeners.

(c) **Movement:** Taking a few steps during speech delivery suggest transition, enhances emphasis and helps to overcome nervousness. Adopt a posture in which you feel comfortable but avoid clumsy movements.

(d) **Gestures:** The verbal expressions should be reinforced with graceful movements of head, shoulders, arms or hands. The effect of your ideas is enhanced with gestures and co-ordination.

TECHNIQUES OF EFFECTIVE SPEECH

There are several ways in which speech may be considered 'good' or 'bad' by different people and this is usually because it may be used for many different purposes. These various angles on speech will be discussed in this chapter and we shall deal later with the ways in which each may be improved.

First, why do we speak at all? In fact, is speaking really necessary? We are sure, we all agree that it is. We realize this very forcibly when we go to a country where we do not speak the language. Of course, if one is good at mime, one can get along to a certain extent with gestures. This is fun on a holiday and when there is plenty of time; but we all know that it does not get one far in the end. We may say then that the first and foremost use of speech is to convey our ideas to other people. It is when our speech does not do this, immediately and clearly that it may truly be said to be "bad."

Certain techniques should be followed to be a successful communicator. He must build into his speech an element of goodwill to which the listener will react favourably. A speech creates goodwill provided a message produces a favourable reaction among the listeners. A positive favourable reaction from the listeners can be achieved by promoting a friendly, kind attitude, cheerful towards listeners. Listeners are many and human, of all common and various capacities. They should be treated as such and the message is capable of being understood by them all. A favourable effect of a message is important. One principle is being courteous, which is fundamental in all oral communication and good relations.

However, the following are the important techniques in oral communication to be successful:

(1) Audibility of Voice: Different people speak in different situations; speech which may be perfectly adequate in some circumstances may be inadequate in others. For instance, a soft voice is usually quite satisfactory at home but the same voice might not be heard at the back of a classroom, while a competent teacher, who is clearly audible in the class room may not be heard in a large lecture room, a court of law, a theatre or church. So, the first requirement of good speech is that in any given circumstance, "the voice should be audible."

Here a warning note should be sounded: one should fill, not overfill, the space occupied by one's hearers. It is unpleasant to be shouted at, so unpleasant indeed that anyone with sensitive ears will stop listening to an overloud voice and, then, of course, whatever speaker had to say will not have been taken in and for the effect he has laid on his hearers, he might have not spoken as well. At first, this presents, for the speaker, a real difficulty: how to speak loudly enough not too loudly. There is also another difficulty which comes into this category, how to avoid letting an audible voice fade into inaudibility at the end of phrases[3].

(2) Audibility of Words: The voices of most speakers are in fact usually well audible but quite often, their 'words' are not, and, in cases of this kind, though the speaker is heard, his meaning is not conveyed to us and so again, his speaking is without effect. As with the voice, the amount of clarity required in the articulation of words depends on where one is speaking; it is obviously much easier to make words carry in a small room than in a large one and it is especially difficult if there is a slow "reverberation time" (usually called erroneously, an 'echo') as in most of our lovely stone churches.

(3) The Part Fashion Plays in Speech: Whether we find it pleasant or unpleasant may depend on mere prejudice but it often depends on "fashion." What is called "Standard English" is really just the most fashionable way of speaking at this particular period in time. It is, we think, one of the many pleasant ways of speaking our language but what gives it a very real value is the fact that it is accepted, without comment, in any type of society all over the English speaking world. The moment a speaker of Southern Standard English opens his mouth, he is comprehensible to other speakers in England. Also he sounds educated. In fact, a person with a different accent may be and often is much more highly educated than the speaker with a standard accent but some people feel that they must make sure of his attainments before they accept him. This sounds foolish, but it is a fact. Let us not under-rate the importance of fashion; we all subscribe to it in several ways, in our clothes, of course, but also in the way we spend our holidays, the books we read, in the food we eat and in a thousand other ways. In the choice we make in these matters, we express a good deal about ourselves; show much more than we tell people when they speak. Let us then become aware of how we sound to others and if this is not how we would choose to wound, then let us alter our way of speech[5].

(4) Bringing Out the Meaning: Even when voice and words are easily and suitably audible, the meaning of what we say may still not be conveyed. For instance, if, after a lecture or a sermon, someone who was not there asks what was all about, a person who was present and heard the talk may find that he does not really know. He heard it all clearly at the time but was not made to understand it. This happens, frequently. After hearing a talk, it is a good test to ask your friends, or yourself to recapitulate the points and arguments that were put forward. If this cannot be done, it is best for everyone to blame himself for not speaking well and the listeners should blame themselves for not concentrating properly.[6]

In fact, if we have not listened to what it is being said, this may have been the fault of the speaker since he may have failed to interest us. Apart from the subject, the choice of words, illustrations and so on, what makes a speaker interesting? It is not only the quality of his voice and the clear way in which he expresses his ideas; it is also the variety in his voice and speech and gestures. We all get bored if we have to keep on doing the same thing day after day, if we have to stay always, however, beautiful or if we meet new people, however, much we like our old friends. It is the same with speech: variety is the essence of interest. We must remember that an interesting subject may be made boring by a dull speaker and a dull subject made interesting by a good speaker.

(5) Sincerity: All speech, if it is to sound sincere, must be stimulated by thought, feeling and imagination. Sometimes, one or another of these may predominate. For instance, when one is hurt, the ejaculation "Ow" expresses the feeling of pain while the sighing "Oh" at the sight of something beautiful expresses a feeling of pleasure. On many occasions, thought is predominant and often in poetry, for example, imagination is more important than feeling or thought. All the three elements, however, should be present and we must always think, feel and imagine before we speak if we are to bring out the full meaning.

(6) Tone: Tone is the quality of sound or voice. Tone indicates the speakers' attitude towards a message as well as the response of the listeners. The word choice, paragraphs, structure and the punctuations are the evidence of tone. These factors may influence listener's judgement and response. Tone helps to persuade, to influence, to gain goodwill and inspire confidence. Selection of words affect tone. Therefore, the speaker has to choose the words with due care for context and audience, denotation and connotation. Pronouns demand special attention because they indicate the sender's self-concern with receiver's needs. For instance, using words like "me", "I", "my or "mine" often in a sentence may result in losing rapport with the listeners. Tone of this style indicates exposing and boasting about one's sense of self-importance, as a result, alienates patient listeners. On the other hand, the use of words, like "we", "ours", "ourselves" can bring the speaker and listeners closer together. Though occasional use of words like "you", "your", "yourself are tolerable, but "you - one" can be reinforced by the use of listener's name. Technical tone should be avoided as far as possible; constructive tone is accepted for constructive criticism.

(7) Opening and Closing Words: The opening message should carefully be framed for the situation, audience, subject with appropriate words and sentences to draw the attention of the listeners. The message should be like key-note, to signal core-thought or prepare the listeners for what follows. The effect is adverse when the message is with unnecessary wordiness. Concise and right words would attract attention. The speaker must select that kind of opener which attracts listeners' attention and interest by using relevant and neutral statements.

Developing suitable closing sentence is also equally important. The selection of closing of sentence must reinforce goodwill and good impression or simulate action. For instance, the use of words like "thank you" is discourteous, because it implies taking listeners for granted. Thank the listeners for their patient and effective listening. But do so after the completion of the speech.

(8) Simplicity: Be sincere in delivering a speech in simple sentences. It is easier to understand, keep in mind, memorise, refresh and grasp. When a speech is delivered in long sentences, the position of a speaker is so pathetic when the thread is lost. Simple sentences with subject and predicate makes the speech effective. It is better to split long sentences.

(9) Avoid Long Words: Always, use only short words and avoid using long words. Use of long words is not a good style from literature's point-of view. When there is a shorter word to mean the same meaning, it is a good practice to use only short words.

For example:

Begin	Commence
Request	Instead of ask
True	Veracious

(10) Use of Slang: "Slang" means words and phrases used very informally in a speech, and not for formal and polite use. Appropriate occasion is important for its use but should always be used with restraint. Generally, they are used in the relation of a humorous anecdote. Such words are used mainly by, and typical of, a particular group. For instance, to speak rudely and angrily, vulgarly to or about someone or something. It is equivalent to abusing. Examples are:

Teenage slang

Army slang

(11) Use of Quotations: Every speaker should be cautious in using quotations. Referring a quotation in a speech no doubt gives effectiveness to the subject but it must be apt. Avoid using too much as well as long, foreign or Latin quotations. When it is used, it should be correct and full. A little knowledge and learning is a dangerous thing.

(12) Humour: The technique of being amusing is a very important characteristic that most good communicators possess. The ability to amuse people when speaking means that pleasantness and friendliness will permeate what is spoken. Especially when taking any decision, or action, let the speaker's humorous attitude be apparent from the very beginning, opening with a smile. It is the most desirable feature of oral communication. Being humorous in conversation and speech not only puts the speaker at ease but also relaxes his listeners. Understanding, the right situation and using a technique of humour to deliver message whenever an opportunity arises will increase his speaking ability.

Making a speech humorous or witty is a technique to build a goodwill provided the wit is relevant to the context and effective. Jokes or anecdotes are recommended when used carefully; otherwise the image of the speaker goes down. Corwin's Law: "Never make people laugh. If you could succeed in life, you must be solemn, solemn as an ass. All the great monuments are built over solemn asses." "Never try to make people laugh, teach a point." Markel says "Humour is okay, wit can be dangerous, wisecracking is disastrous."

In most speeches, the use of humour is necessary but it must be in good taste and amusing. The safest joke is against the speaker. An original joke is better which the audience never heard before. Again do not repeat the same; it must be being on the subject of the speech.

(13) Stage Fright: It refers to the place of actual delivery of the message before audience, and is concerned with controlling nerves. Fear of forgetting may result in stage fright. It is a misdirected awareness of the speaker. A speaker who feels stage fright may experience nervousness, tensing of muscles and a quivering of voice. A speaker with a stage fright concentrates his mood excessively on himself than on the listeners or the message.

Stage fright and nervousness can be overcome by constant practice and developing self-confidence. The following guidelines may help to overcome stage fright.

(i) The best method is dress rehearsals addressing before a tryout group.

(ii) To obtain comments from judges of different points of view, like praising, positive features, negative features and areas need improvement.

(iii) Try to increase the supply of oxygen to blood and thus steady nerves. It is good to deflate lungs and then take in a full breath of air and expel it slowly.

(iv) Constant preparation of the subject.

(v) Concentration on the ideas.

(vi) Constantly thinking, rethinking, memorising, rememorising and refreshing the ideas.

(vii) Build, reinforce self-confidence.

(viii) Do sufficient home-work.

(ix) Know about the listeners, their traits, needs, types, desires, attitudes, belief etc.

(14) Accent: Accent is another important factor to be achieved in good speech. It is a thing which may prevent meaning from being clear. If a person is speaking in an accent which is not familiar to the hearers, they may be worrying about the meaning of a word which he has used while he is saying the next phrase and so they do not even listen to the second phrase. The word "accent" covers two separate meanings. It is used in some contexts to mean extra breath-force on a word or syllable (stress): it is also used to indicate the differences of pronounciations heard in different parts of our own country.

If the speaker has a different accent, it is advisable not to try to cancel it. There is nothing to be ashamed of, it gives character to the delivery. The safest accent is that which permits the audience to understand what you say. Use of natural accent is better than artificial foreign or different accent. For example, do not adopt a Latin or Chinese accent in the mistaken belief that it is more refined; by doing so, you will neither convince nor please your audience.

Not firmly stretching over a letter, dropping the initial letter of a word or two, common errors in pronunciation, should be avoided.

Example: Slackness over the letter "h" and dropping the initial letter "h".

House	Ouse
Holiday	Oliday
Hobby	Obby
Holder	Older
Holland	Olland
Home	Ome

Error also arises when adding "h" in certain common words like what, when, where and who.

Running over the words is also another common fault.

Example:	That is	T'is
	Is he	Easy or Izzee

Errors in spelling may also result in pronunciation.

Illusion	Allusion
Fermentation	Fomentation
Complaisant	Complacent
Ingenious	Ingenuous

(15) Friendly Atmosphere: It is the responsibility of the speaker to create a friendly or kindly attitude, benevolent atmosphere at the place. A sincere speech should be in a conversational manner. The message should be capable of putting into writing. A cheerful consent, feeling of warmth to the listener are necessary.

(16) Personal Greeting: The speaker must use a personal greeting while starting the speech, the salutation in oral communication to the listener.

It is always desirable to call the person by name, say "Dear Mr. Saxene" but not "Dear Sir." Use the person's name once or twice during oral conversation.

(17) Appreciation: Showing appreciation towards listeners is a technique for building goodwill. It involves to be grateful to the audience. The speaker must show his personal appreciation for what they have listened. It means giving thanks to an appreciative audience. Every listener likes to be appreciated. The success of speech depends entirely on his satisfaction with his listeners. The listener likes to be treated as an individual and to feel recognised as a person.

(18) Personal Interest: Showing awareness and interest in the listeners as an individual is the desirable quality of successful communication. He can say: It gives me a great pleasure to inform you. I am happy to learn that you are joining the organisation. He must make honest efforts to make the other person feel better or more important.

(19) Smile: The communicator has to open his speech with a smile. It involves showing pleasure. It is an act of a smiling speech or the resulting facial expression. It gives clues to feelings and meanings. In the process, a happy frame of mind when speaking means that pleasantness and friendliness will pass through what is spoken. This is particularly necessary when taking favourable action. It demands for a happy attitude to be apparent from the very beginning.

(20) Listeners to Feel Important: Another technique for building goodwill among the audience is to make the listeners to feel important. Due importance should be given to the listeners. The purpose of speech is to make them to understand the message. This can be achieved by showing appreciation for listeners and by taking a personal interest in listening to them and clarifying their doubts. It is an art and tact of the speaker to make them feel important. Speaking from their point of view and mentioning of various practical instances also make them feel important.

(21) Listener's Goodwill: Goodwill is a friendly and a kindly attitude. Listener's goodwill is a major object of oral communication. Indicating acceptance of suggestions by the listeners will go a long way towards achieving a successful speech. Indicating attention and acknowledgement of what is being suggested will produce positive and favourable reactions from listeners. It will create a friendly, confident feeling towards the communicator. Creating impression is a very difficult task. It is reciprocal and can be applied in all speeches. Speech can be given, but, however, one must remember, listener's goodwill.

(22) Empathy: Empathy is important to a group of audience. Empathy means ability to understand and share the feelings, experiences, opinions etc., of listeners. A certain empathy must exist between the speaker and the listener. It is necessary to show every consideration for the listener that will create interest and persuade the listener. Empathizing with the listeners is the projection of one's personality into the listeners in order to understand the listeners better.

(23) Language: Language is very essential in a good communication. He can adapt his own language but should speak at the listener's level. This will make the message pleasing and interesting. An individual listener is interested in listening anything which satisfies the purpose and desire. A pleasing message not only puts the speaker at ease but also relaxes his listeners.

(24) Honesty: If the speaker is genuinely interested in the listener's view point, then the speaker should be honest in his response. Honesty in speech promotes confidence among the listeners.

(25) Personal Appearance: The style in which a speaker dresses communicates something to listeners. Communicating with an acceptable and modest dress is the one of the most direct and silent way of communication.

John Molloy, a dress consultant with major corporations, believes that the way a person dresses communicates something to others. In his interview with a series of questions of more than hundred top Company Executives revealed many interesting features on communicating with good personal appearance. Some of his findings in his book *Dress for Success* are as follows:

(i) He showed executives, five pictures of men, each wearing expensive, tailored, but high-fashion clothing. He asked the executives if this was a proper dress for a junior business executive. Ninety-two said 'no', eight said 'yes.'

(ii) He showed them five additional pictures of the same people neatly dressed in conservative clothing and asked if they were dressed properly for a young executive. All said "yes."

(iii) He showed them five additional pictures of the same people obviously dressed in lower-middle class attire and asked if these people were dressed properly for a young executive. Forty-six said "yes", fifty four said "no."

(iv) He then asked the executives if they thought that the people dressed in the middle-class suit would succeed better in corporate life than those dressed in the lower middle-class suit. Eight-eight said "yes", twelve said "no."

(26) Action: How physical movements or "still" stand in relation to the audience one is communicating with has a real impact on communication. Message or idea is often communicated through action. A person's gestures also communicates meaning. The movements give us close to a person's self-confidence or interest in the topic. If one is not interested in a subject, he may more likely to lean towards.

(27) Use of Aids: Sometimes, it may be necessary to use aids, visual or audio-visual, in support of speech. Their use is recommended for effective presentation of the matter. It is practically possible to use electrical or electronic tools. The speech is nearly always combined with media. Charts, graphs, tables, TV, visual projections form equipment etc. The speaker must see where they can be used rightly, and use only those aids which will carry message.

(28) Handouts: Prepare a brief note of the subject matter of speech and distribute to the audience. Handouts serve the audience to keep with them which acts as permanent reminders of the speaker's message. Whatever is heard in the meeting may go out of mind soon after the speech is over.

(29) Hearing Ourselves: Now we all hear our own voice and speech from inside ourselves while other people hear us only from the outside, so it is difficult to know, without mechanical aid, how we actually do sound to others. Now that so many people own tape-recorders, it is good idea to listen to ourselves through one of these useful instruments. Listening to a record does not, in itself, make speech better. It only makes one aware of good and bad points in our own voice and speech and in our use of speech, mumbling, hesitation, dullness, repetitions are noticeable on a record, especially in a prepared conversation. When we have become aware of our faults, hard and concentrated work is usually required in order to alter our habits.

(30) Beauty of Speech: A point about speech, which is beyond the very practical points raised above, is the actual quality of the voice itself. Some people are more sensitive to this than others or, perhaps, it would be truer to say that they are more consciously so. A beautiful voice in itself is interesting and pleasant to listen to but here again, another warning must be given: The owner of the lovely voice often takes great pleasure in listening to it himself and anyone who does this is apt to go off the track. Another point is that he may be talking of something ugly or unpleasant and then the unsuitability of lovely tone makes him sound insincere.

(31) Style in Speaking: In fact, suitability of voice and speech to the subject is even more important than the acoustics of the room. In addition, the style should be suited to the audience and to the situation; a good speaker uses different styles when he is speaking, for instance, to small children, to adult students interested in his subject or to the guests at a wedding reception.

(32) Thought Dressing: Addressing by people differ from place to place and from country to country like the address of army men, naval personnel, airport, personnel dressing by religious heads, political leaders, lawyers, doctors, sports people etc. Likewise, thoughts are so dressed by speakers as to gain attention and interest of the audience. Swami Vivekananda began his address to the parliament of religions in Chicago as "Brothers and Sisters" — Not "distinguished Ladies and Gentlemen", as others did before Swamiji's turn had come. Similarly, it is more appropriate to quote the speech of the great Congress leader, Chittaranjan Das, to a vast audience "I feel the weight of iron chains over my body, the handcuffs on my wrist; it is the agony of bondage; the whole of India is a vast prison...."

(33) Build a Vocabulary: We do not inherit words and tales they tell. Many a times, as the story of Aladdin and his Wonderful Lamp has been told, it must be told again for every child as new generation come upon the stage.

When building a vocabulary fit to express all our thoughts, hopes and emotions, we need to remember that words are symbols, standing for things. If we do not have fit words, we should be condemned to carrying around large bundles of things instead, like the professors in Gulliver's satire, *Laputa*.

(34) Voice Segregation: "Ums" and "ahs" and other punctuations in a speech are common features. Sometimes, it may irritate the audience and may cause discomfort. The two main reasons for punctuate speech are insufficient preparation and lack of concentration. Generally, used to buy time, to think, rethink or refresh. Punctuation in a speech divides sentences by voice segregation. When used repeatedly, it interrupts the concentration. If a speaker needs time or pause to think, then it should be a silent pause.

(35) Deciding the Purpose of Speech: A speaker has to deliberately determine the purpose which will not only economise but also enhance speaking task. He must justify the audience. The audience will listen effectively when the message meets their needs. To speak to them about themselves and their needs is the best way to make the people listen. The purpose of the speech is to determine, in terms of a just transmitting message, stimulate, create awareness, educate, affect attitude and behaviour change.

(36) Analyse Audience: A good speaker first proceeds to analyse the characteristics of the composition of audience, nature, size, interest, traits, etc., which will determine the message purpose. The nature of the audience, purpose of listeners would play an important role in planning and presentation of the message. Awareness and knowledge of the traits of the listeners, such as one person or hundreds or thousands, group tasks etc., to whom the message is addressed are necessary. An analysis of audience includes detailed examination of their educational background, experience, occupations, social and political backgrounds, age, sex, etc., will help on effective communication process.

(37) Evaluation of Situation: A critical examination of the circumstances of a communication event is termed as an evaluation of the situation of the speaker, context, arrangements, facilities, lighting, furniture, shape and location of the hall or auditorium, environment etc., which will influence effective speech and effective listening. Evaluation of a situation also includes the need and availability of audio-visual equipment, overhead projector, charts, tables, maps, diagrams, models, public address system, microphones, lectern etc. Evaluation of these factors will help the speaker to familiarise, psychological and physical setting to face and deliver the message.

(38) Organising the Message: Effective and efficient delivery of message require organising the subject systematically. It is to be arranged and organised taking into consideration the purpose, type of audience and nature, and need of the audience. There are no hard and fast rules uniformly applicable to all situations governing organising the message because it may differ from situation to situation like objectives, audience and circumstances. However, factors like drawing attention of the audience, developing audience interest, making listener- oriented discussion and stimulating audience action would generally help to make effective speech.

(39) Attention Creation[7]: A speaker seeks attention at two levels:

1. The physical level and
2. The psychological level.

The contents of your message furnish the psychological input and the physical composition of your message furnishes the other input.

Remember to make use of some of the attention getting stimuli:

(i) Intensity: A loud voice is a reliable stimulus and is a momentary attention-getter.

(ii) Repetition: Repetition is quite helpful in reinforcing a stimulus.

(iii) Movement: Movement, coupled with gestures of the speaker is likely to attract and strengthen the attention of the listeners.

(iv) Contrast: Tactful variation in rate, loudness and pitch help to maintain attention of the listeners.

(40) Delivery of Speech: The subject matter of a message can be presented by various methods. The five major modes of speech delivery are as follows:

(i) Impromptu Delivery: A speech is said to be impromptu delivery when the speaker makes it on the spur of the movement. It is a delivery without a text, notes, or script. A speaker's or participant's comments may be invited following a debate or discussion. It is said, many successful speakers, including the legendary British Prime Minister, Winston Churchill, used to rehearse these speeches at home. His great talent lay in delivering them as if they were on the spur, reactions and observations and not a pre-rehearsed presentation. An intelligent speaker makes prompt changes and modifications to suit the situation and never sounds mechanical. It requires experience and practice to be a successful speaker of the mode. Politicians, parliamentarians etc., are good examples to observe and follow.

(ii) Extemporaneous Delivery: Extemporaneous is a type of speech without previous thought or preparation. Message is delivered spontaneously. Notes are used by establishing and maintaining eye-contact. The speaker takes the help of notes or outline. It is effective in establishing report with the audience and permits more eye contact with them. Their reactions and responses can be assessed instantly and the speaker can modify the contents of the presentation or summarise the main points.

(iii) Textual or Manuscript Delivery: Textual delivery is like an oral report reading aloud full sentence from a prepared manuscript or typed script. The written text is read out verbatim. It is a less effective mode as it prevents frequent eye contact with the audience. The technique is helpful in presenting complex statistics or technical data. Looking at the audience in between the sentences can make this method more effective. The physical possession of typed sheets infuse confidence in the speaker.

(iv) Memorising Delivery: Memorised speech delivery is an oral presentation of a subject learned by memory. When a speaker adopts memorised delivery, he repeats in his mind what he told, word by word, paragraph by paragraph, sentence by sentence. This requires considerable practice to give the effect as the delivery is spontaneous. The method works well with short speeches. A more sensible approach is to avoid word for word memorisation. Attention to ideas and sequence of the speech are important, to avoid embarrassing spells of long pauses of silence if memory fails.

(v) *Combination of all the Above.*

GUIDELINES FOR EFFECTIVE COMMUNICATION

(1) Audience: The communicator should know his audience and accordingly put ideas across. If the audience or listeners are not able to understand, it is an ineffective communication.

(2) Ideas: The transmitter should have clear information to be communicated. One must be clear about ideas, opinions and facts to be communicated, otherwise he cannot make the ideas clear.

(3) Ambiguity: Using words in current use is important and to avoid words which convey vague meaning. A vague communication gives way to confusion in communication.

(4) Conditions: Necessary physical conditions, facilities and environment are to be provided to both the speaker and the listeners.

(5) Not to Talk and Talk: Speak only that much sufficient to convey the central idea of the subject matter. A verbal communication should be short, clear and simple to pass the message.

(6) Gestures and Tone: The style in which the message is conveyed is as important as what is being said. There must be integration between facial expression, voice, gestures, mood to the action of what is said about.

(7) Not to Talk to Impress: The purpose of communication is not to impress but to express, to inspire confidence and make them understand. Expressing and conveying a better message creates an impression. It is not communication if the speaker tries to conceal, intimidate and to impress.

(8) Feedback: Feedback is probably the most important method of improving communication. Two-way process ensures feedback. The communicator has to obtain feedback from the receiver.

(9) Emphasis on Purpose: The subject matter and its theme should be greatly emphasised to draw the attention of the listener.

(10) Avoid Extremes: Some subject matters are too good or too bad. It is desirable to avoid extremes in speaking.

(11) Cultivate Speaking: Listening is different from hearing. Listening and understanding require a lot of reasoning and attitude. The reasons of non- listening are boredom, bias, fear, interruption, etc.

(12) Clarify Ideas: The communicator first has to clarify his ideas himself before; think on the message clearly and clarify ideas to ensure effective communication.

(13) Purpose: The purpose of communication is to make others understand the subject matter. The communication is ineffective if the purpose is not achieved.

(14) Physical and Human Setting: An atmosphere of mutual trust is to be created in the process of communication. It is mainly the responsibility of the superiors. The informal relations is the best weapon to promote physical and human setting in the organisation.

INTERPERSONAL COMMUNICATION

INTERVIEWS

Interview is another medium of communication. It is a formal meeting and discussion with someone on a particular subject. A person applying for a job may have to save interview or a person with information to broadcast on radio or television. It involves another in an interview. The members of interview committee may interview several applicants for the job. A politician or a public servant or chief of an organisation may be interviewed by press reporters about their activities, programmes etc. In an interview, there must be more than one to have effective communication. Two parties are involved in an interview broadly classified as the interviewer and interviewee. Interviewee is a respondent who gives information and facts to questions put by the interviewer. The interviewer is a person who puts questions to the interviewee and on a questionnaire or schedule. In other words, a person who seeks information for media, use a newspaper reporter, or a television or radio panel show moderator etc. An investigator who puts questions and solicits answers, information, facts etc., is a person appointed to carry out interviews.

The object of an interview is to sit face to face and to obtain information from the interviewee. It is the best opportunity to assess correctly on a particular matter for which the interview is proposed. A good interview depends on proper planning. The interviewer must be clear before he talks to the interviewee as to what information he wants and what questions will help to bring out that information. Interview is a personal appraisal method of evaluating the persons interviewed.

Definition of Interview

Myers and *Myers* have defined interviewing: "It is simply a highly specialised form of communication, but one which affects how people are hired for jobs, how they are appraised and told about it, and how they are able to work with others on the job."

James M. Black: "An interview is a conversation, usually between two people, that is confined to a specific subject. The role of the interviewer is to seek information; that of the interviewee is to provide it."

L. Brown: "It is a conversation between two people. It is a conversation, yet, but directed to a purpose other than personal, social satisfaction."

Art of Interviewing

S.G.Ginsburg: "The interviewer's questions must explore viewpoints as well as experiences; they must be as tough as the problems that will face the person who gets the job."

Interviewing is an art which demands training and experience just as any other profession does. Much of the difficulty stems from inadequate appreciation of this art. No intelligent businessman would ever purchase an expensive piece of equipment without making a thorough evaluation of its construction, cost, durability and ability to frequently hire a man for an important job on the flimsiest evidence. He often makes such a personal decision after talking with the applicant for twenty or thirty minutes, basing his evaluation primarily on such surface impressions as appearance, general manners and apparent relevance of experience and training.

However, it is encouraging to note a growing awareness of the importance of the human factor in industry. More and more business leaders are beginning to recognise the tremendous cost of poor selection. Many important selection decisions are being made by untrained employment interviewers.

Fig. 2.2 Inter-personal Communication

The most complicated problem of business today is people. Technical processes may be mastered, plans and offices may be built to exacting specifications, and intricate machines are devised for performing work with fine accuracy, but if the human element in business is disregarded, trouble is ahead.

Successful interviewing presupposes a fair dealing with people drawing them out, analysing and evaluating their strengths and weaknesses. An unselective habit of linking people on sight may distort our judgement. Sympathy is an excellent quality. If we engage an applicant through sympathy, we may have to regret it because our judgement has been so clouded by our attention to the man's needs that we were not alert in estimating his qualifications. The applicant, too, has a very real stake in this business of selection. He is like a commodity or a piece of machinery that can be purchased on an entirely impersonal basis. In many cases, his whole future may be involved. When any assessor of men makes the decision whether or not a given person should be engaged for an important job or upgraded to a higher level position, he is assuming a grave responsibility. He had better be right in his decision, equally for the good of the company and for the good of the man.

Types of Interview

There are many different ways of classifying interviews. Robert Goyer and others give as many as ten separate categories of interviews. They are:[8]

(1) Information getting
(2) Information giving
(3) Advocating
(4) Problem-solving
(5) Counselling
(6) Application for a job
(7) Taking complaints
(8) Giving reprimands
(9) Conducting appraisals
(10) Stress interviewing.

Similarly, Harold Zelko etc., have given two categories of interviews. They are:[9]

(1) Problem solving and counselling
(2) Informative.

While Myers and Myers proposed three general types:

(1) Information interviews
(2) Problem-solving interviews
(3) Professional interviews.

However, the interviews which are in most use which the management most frequently used in communication are discussed as under:

(1) Information Giving Interview: As the name indicates the object of this interview is to provide or supply information. This interview supplies facts, ideas, opinions, feelings, figures and other matters to the interviewer or to the interviewee. It takes the form of telling how, orientation and for giving instructions. Information giving interview is meant either to collect information or giving information. The interviewer and the interviewee probably already have some information for exchange.

(2) Information Collecting Interview: On the basis of function of interview, another type of interview is information seeking interviews. The interview focusses on receiving information. It is a process of getting information. The techniques involved in getting information are asking, questioning, clarifying, investigating and finding out reasons. Two people interact with each other when one seeks information and the other is giving information.

(3) Employment Interview: Employment interview is conducted when the organisation wants to recruit new people. It is an interview-intake, if a person is entering the organisation. The interview should open by putting the applicant at ease and proceed by direct conversation. Interviewer and interviewee interact with each other, in which, the interviewer attempts to determine the suitability of the applicant for the post. Focus is on collecting information to assess, to evaluate and to take decision for selection of the employee.

(4) Appraisal Interview: Another familiar type of organisational interview is conducting an appraisal interview. It is performance appraisal interview which did with job effectiveness. The emphasis is on evaluation of performance of job, need for training, time for promotion, fixing salary etc.

(5) Counselling Interview: Counselling interview is an advisory type, including interviewing as much as providing services. Management counselling promotes good employer-employee relations and brings about a change in the attitude of the interviewee. A two-way process of communication gives participation satisfaction and improves job performance. It takes place out of, on the job interface and interaction that may occur between superiors and subordinates. It covers many areas such as instructing, encouraging, motivating, advice and guiding in their problem-solving. There are many psychological problems which cannot be successfully handled by counselling interviews. Psychiatrists, psychologists, physicians and counselling personnel can conduct counselling interviews effectively. They render professional services. To tackle the problem, managers use some principles. They are suggested by L. Brown:

(a) **Empathy:** looking at problems from the worker's point of view.

(b) **Positive attitude:** showing respect, accepting the worker as a personal showing warmth and a clear feeling.

(c) **Sincerity:** being genuinely interested, honest, and true about feelings and reactions.

(d) **Concreteness:** being direct, accurate, and specific in facts and suggestions.

(e) **Listening:** hearing the other person, giving the other person a chance to express his feelings, often helps to create an awareness and recognition of what should be done about the problem.

(f) **Problem Resolution:** clarifying the problem, suggesting and evaluating alternatives, modifying and implementing the solution.[10]

(6) Complaint or Grievance Interview: Grievance interviews occur because something remedial has to be done. Employees may seek interview to see to find out a solution to their problem. When the employees are not satisfied, they lodge a complaint and sometimes confront in an interview situation. The interview focusses on coming to an agreement, settling a dispute, difference and find a remedy for the problem. This interview is convened to give the employee a hearing opportunity to come to a solution. The grievances, policies and procedures are laid down in the company's manual or handbook.

(7) Disciplinary Interview: When employees who fail to perform according to tasks, they are subject to disciplinary action. Any employee who commits costly mistakes or undesirable behaviour are expected to be involved in a disciplinary interview. In this interview, the causes are identified for changing the behaviour of the person into right direction. Through joint exploration of objectives, the interview finally leads to the settlement of the problem, improving the situation and remedy the problem. A person may be given a chance or warning to improve. In disciplinary interview, which is generally confidential and private between a committee and the person involved, counselling, instructing, correcting, reprimanding and problem-solving steps may take place.

(8) Discussion Interview: A type of interview where a discussion between people takes place. It is also called as exploratory interview. It is interview between a small group or large group engaged in interaction with one another in a face-to-face interview. In this interview, members of the group are in interaction with one another. Group reaches to a decision after thorough deliberations. It is a place where exchange of ideas, data, facts, figures, opinions and feelings etc., are openly expressed, opposed, through discussion, to arrive at a solution to the problem.

(9) Correction Interview: This follows the disciplinary interview. This interview gives a clear statement, identifying disciplinary areas as undesirable or costly errors or alleged violation. Steps are taken to rectify the behaviour and may be put on the line of desirable behaviour. Corrective steps are generally formulated to meet different situations for their implementation.

(10) Evaluation Interview: Evaluation interviews are conducted to form an idea of judgement on a particular subject matter. The members evaluate any functional areas of the organisation, personal and general issues. For instance, evaluation of worthiness, results, performance, events, persons, policies, goals etc.

(11) Exit Interview: Another familiar type of interview is exit interview, i.e., when a person leaves the organisation. This is an interaction between the interviewer and the person leaving the organisation. A face-to-face conversation to review job satisfaction, future prospects in the new organisation and to create a goodwill.

(12) Goal-setting Interview: In this type of interview, particular type of goal-setting is the main activity. The interviewer concentrates on the determination of goals. It is a process which was a beginning of identification of goals, interaction and conclusion. This interview has content; they are about goal- setting, particularly in goal-setting in an area of management by objectives. Here people exchange information. There is clearly defined problem or goal. Both parties exchange information and finally set goals.

(13) Persuading Interview: Also called "Sales Interview." It is an interview between the seller and the buyer. The interaction is either as a seller or a buyer in a persuading interview. It is a highly skilled system. It focuses on convincing or persuading a person to action.

(14) Telephone Interview: Telephone can be used effectively to conduct an interview. It is a type of interview over the telephone. In this mechanical oral communication, views, ideas, opinions, and facts are exchanged. It can be used to form a conclusion on the subject under consideration.

(15) Preliminary Interview: This type of interview is used in the case of employment interview. It is very simple and brief. It is with a view to eliminating unqualified and unsuitable candidates. Some quick evaluation techniques are followed in this type, like test, communication skills, impression etc.

(16) Formal Interview: An official interview which is conducted according to the prescribed rules, procedures laid down. Interview procedures are generally laid down in organizational manuals. In this type of interview, the interviewer puts a set of well-defined questions and takes notes according to the requirements. A common interview is a social research.

(17) Informal Interview: It is in contrast to the formal interview, again a social research interview. In this, the interviewer has full freedom to make suitable alternation in questions. In formal interview, there is no freedom to alter the question.

(18) Personal Interview: The process of interview is only between two individuals; one is the interviewer and the other is the interviewee. The interview enables one to establish a closer personal contact between the interviewer and the interviewee.

(19) Research Interview: The research interview is held to collect certain information relating to the research problem under study. The interviewer prepares a set of well-structured questionnaire in advance and by interviewing people, he gathers the desired information, facts, figures, data etc. It is called research-interview, as the information is gathered for the purpose of research into a problem.

(20) Dummy Interview: An interview is conducted in the usual way with a respondent, the data from which are not intended for use in survey results. Used as training device for interviewers. A type of interview from which the information and data are not intended for use or utility in survey findings. This method is used in order to impart training to the interviewers or investigators.

(21) Other Types of Interviews: (1) Group Interview (2) Diagnostic Interview (3) Treatment Interview (4) Short-contact Interview (5) Prolonged Contact Interview (6) Qualitative Interview (7) Quantitative Interview (8) Mixed Interview (9) Focussed Interview and (10) Repeated Interview.

Techniques of Interview

Interview is a conversation between two people called "the interviewer" and "the interviewee. They interact with each other. They involve in the exchange of facts, figures, ideas, etc. There must be a technique to apply in interview to make the interview more effective. The techniques used usually by both interviewer and interviewee are:

(1) Questioning: Putting questions only ensures collection of information but also results in interaction. A question may be an open-end question, direct question, indirect question, mirror-type question or a loaded question.

(2) Observation and Listening: Listening and observation are the best methods to obtain information and assess the matter. It is a process necessary for understanding and interaction for results. Observation and listening are the simplest forms in seeing and looking into the problem. Observation may be controlled observation or uncontrolled observation. Under this, both the interviewer and the interviewee are involved in observation and listening. Listening to an answer to a question and observing the information obtained. Listening is different from hearing and in listening process, one has to keep his mind open and attuned to the speaker. From the observer's and listener's point of view, it is one-sided communication till they react. In observation, the observer pays attention to the thinking process like what, why, how? etc.

(3) Evaluating: Evaluation is a process to form an idea or judgement on a particular matter. It evaluates qualifications, performance, objectives, policies, persons, events, etc. Evaluating techniques ensures conceiving and understanding, perspective and logical reasoning. Both the interviewer and interviewee evaluate each other on their respective questions and answers.

Evaluation helps perspective on the subject matters, relative to logical reasoning. In this, ideas, facts, figures, opinions are exchanged. The technique of evaluation as applied in interviews increases perceptions and understanding.

(4) Controlling: The essential quality of an interviewer is to keep control of interview. It is a management function in which generally both parties are involved. Leland Brown on the technique of controlling and involvement says: "Controlling on the part of the interviewer is a management function, but in exercising control, both parties become involved. Thus, controlling assures direction, periodic summaries and restatements often provide control of the situation, for they assure direction by stating the main point is crystallize.[11] Involvement means participation that leads to results."

INTERVIEW STYLE

Interview is a common method in communication which helps the management for gathering as well as giving information. This exchange of information is useful in the decision-making process and problem-solving. There is an element of participation, which satisfies employees and as a result, a good employer-employee relation. An effective interview depends largely on the style, among other things. Interview style means "the degree or level of patterning of the interactions between interviewer and interviewee. The style can be informal or formal or any modification or combining of the two. The degree of formality is dependent largely on the relationship of the interviewer and interviewee."[12]

Interview style may be direct interview, indirect interview, stress interview, depth interview etc. As given in the definition by L. Brown, "a modification or combination of two or more styles involves elements of all the styles employed."

On the basis of practice, the styles of communication are:

(1) Direct Interview: It is called a direct planned interview. It is a face- to-face observational method. In this method, with the help of questions and answers, one measures the attitudes, knowledge and suitability of the interviewee. It helps the interviewer to assess personal qualities.

(2) Indirect Interview: It is also called "indirect non-directive interview." It is not a straight-forward question and answer method. Interviewee is given an opportunity and conducive atmosphere to feel free to talk. Interviewee plays a role of speaking on a particular issue and the interviewer plays mainly a listening role.

(3) Patterned Interview: In this, interview questions to the interviewee are standardized in advance.

(4) Stress Interview: In the stress type of interview, the worry or pressure experienced by an interview in a particular circumstance, or the state of anxiety caused by the stress are created deliberately by the interviewer. Under the stress atmosphere, the interviewer obtains information to assess the applicant's action or response under it. Stress is created with anger, silence, criticism, etc.

(5) Depth Interview: In this type of interview, a number of questions on a particular area are put to the interviewee. An answer to any one question does not cover full information. A number of follow-up questions are put by the interviewer.

(6) Board Interview: When a group of people propose to interview respondents, it is called "panel" or "board" interview or interview committee. The board collectively is called "interviewer." An interviewee has to face more than one person interviewing. Each interviewer has his own area of putting questions.

(7) Group Interview: In a group interview, a group of respondents or interviewees are allowed together to interact and exchange each other. The interviewer plays mainly observational and listening role to appraise the qualities of respondents in a group. Sometimes, the interviewers and interviewees may sit together for some time or may live together for a few days to know individual and personal habits, conduct and behaviour of the interviewees.

Interviewer

Interviewer is a person who asks the respondent or put questions to the interviewee. In other words, a person who seeks information for media use, a newspaper reporter, or a television or radio panel show moderator. He puts questions and solicits answers, information, facts, figures, ideas and opinions etc. The interviewer plays an important role in interviewing and, as such, is a common part of management's routine activities. He has a definite role in the process. He is the person who has to control communication in an interview. Interviewer has some data or facts on which information is to be gathered interacting the interviewee. Interviewee is another party in the interview. Interviewee is a respondent who gives information and facts etc., to the questions put to the interviewee by the interviewer. Interviewer seeks maximum information possible and, for that, he has to prepare well for the event.

Qualities of Interviewer

The main concern of the interviewer employing the method of interviewing is to get correct and maximum information and to the point on the topics under issue. The interview can be less expensive, economical, effective only if both parties concentrate on the topic and complete without dragging and without deviations. The aim is to succeed interaction with the minimum of efforts and this is possible only if the parties follow the principles of group discussion. Accordingly, in order to ensure correct information exchange, the interviewer should give maximum freedom of self-expression and should be allowed to describe his reaction. He should be allowed a free hand while describing his response. Usually, the variety of responses depends upon the skills and tactful approach of the interviewer. Therefore, there are no hard and fast rules in this connection.

However, a great responsibility rests on the interviewer as to what to do. He has to make correct decisions which involve not only the interviewee's career but other matters too. As regards the characteristics of good interviewer, there are different views. Some people have suggested traits which a good interviewer should have. The broad categories of traits are generally intellectual abilities, communication skills and psychological traits. In any type of interview, the interviewer occupies a pivotal role. He gathers information and supplies it. The success of interview depends largely on the joint exploration or exchange of information. A personal relationship and personal contact emerges between the interviewer and the interviewee, both interact each other. As such, the personality and the abilities of the interviewer are of crucial significance. A man of integrity, honesty, confidence and with skills of logical thinking can successfully conduct the interview.

However, an interviewer should keep in mind the following points while conducting interview to be an effective interview:

(1) Thorough Knowledge: An interviewer should be thoroughly familiar with the subject and object of the interview. The exchange of ideas, facts and opinions etc., should be given with the full knowledge on the subject.

(2) Narrative: The interviewer should give maximum opportunity of self- expression to the interviewee. He may be allowed to express freely about his experience, hobbies and on informal issues.

(3) Background Information: The interviewer should have knowledge in advance of the kind of facts, ideas, opinions and figures to be obtained from the interviewee in the interview. This helps to avoid confusion and non-important matters are overlooked.

(4) Time Factor: Time as an equally important factor should be considered by the interviewer. It is valuable both to the interviewer and interviewee. But questions should not be put in a hurried manner. The schedule of questions should be prepared in advance to be completed within an adequate time. Sufficient time should also be given to the interviewee so as to enable him to reply to questions.

(5) Freedom: He should be given full freedom to describe whatever he thinks relevant and reasonable. The interviewer should not interfere in his description, if he slightly deviates from the main point and if he gives some irrelevant facts. The interviewee should not be discouraged by imposing checks. So long as he remains with the subject relevant, he should be questioned.

(6) Interview Place: An interview should not be conducted in an open place, in a disturbed atmosphere in respect of certain interview. The interviewer should conduct the interview in a separate room. The face-to-face conversational flow should not be disturbed by holding interview in an open place. A private room is to be selected to avoid disturbances and interruptions.

(7) To Keep Interviewee at Ease: The interviewer should not keep the interviewee in a difficult position. He should not be discouraged with annoying questions and other questions psychologically not good. So, the interviewer should create a friendly and informal atmosphere throughout, at the commencement of interview, during the interview and at the end.

(8) Patience in Listening: Another quality that an interviewer must possess is patience in listening to the interviewee. The interviewer must hear the interviewee with full interest. He should give maximum time and opportunity to the interviewee to speak and express his ideas freely. Therefore, he should not go on speaking but he should be a very good listener and observer. His interference should be limited in order to let the interviewee express himself as far as time allows. He should not give an opportunity to others to guess from his expression that he is bored or his mind is somewhere else.

(9) Understanding the Level: The interviewer should understand the level, vocabulary and other personal background like educational, attitude etc. Not only that, he must adjust and come down to the level of the interviewee so as to assess the abilities and for measuring the ability of the respondent.

(10) No Harshness: It is accepted principle that the interviewee should be allowed freedom of self-expression. If the interviewee is on some irrelevant facts, he must be politely reminded to keep himself within the bounds. Alert direction should not be abrupt and harsh. Under no circumstances can an interviewer afford to offend the interviewee.

(11) Control: In an interview, both the parties should be under control. The success of an interview would depend on planning, and one should plan the interview beforehand. Though interview is a joint-exploration, the interviewer has to keep control of the interview.

(12) To Win the Confidence: Winning the confidence of the interviewee is the essence of successful interviewing. Basically, he must gain the confidence of the interviewer. If there is no confidence in the interviewer, the interviewee may not give information fully, freely and frankly.

(13) No Confrontation: When results are not according to their expectation, they may confront in an interview. As far as possible, the interviewer should not confront an interviewee. Confrontation is needed when incorrect, poor data and weak information are given. It may be a direct confrontation or indirect confrontation.

(14) Training: Interviewing is an art and a special skill and a form of communication. This requires some training and considerable experience to be perfect.

(15) Content: Interview errors occur because of inappropriate content. Interviewer has to plan the questions or the information to be gathered and the sequence. During the interview, he should not wander around with questions. Questions should not be on the subject of his own interest, choice, irrespective of subject of the interview. Uniformity in asking the same type of questions is necessary to make a comparison.

(16) No Jumping to Conclusion: The interviewer should not jump to conclusion without gathering full information. Conclusions should be arrived only after full interaction and satisfaction of both parties.

(17) No Discrimination: The interviewer should be impartial and should not show any discrimination. Equal opportunity should be given, no bias is to be expressed. He should hear in the same spirit. No place for race, religion and politics.

(18) Appreciation of Interviewee: Listening and appreciation of an interviewee is another quality that he should keep in mind. Appreciation of interviewee has a salutary effect on the interviewee who will give them full and correct information.

(19) Closing Interview: The interviewer should have a good sense of time and situation to close an interview. He should learn how and when to close the interview. He should use it with mutual understanding and good relations. Before conclusion of the interview, he should give a brief account of matters not concluded. Thanking the interviewee is a good closing.

(20) Recording: Soon after closing of interview, the interviewer should record the facts and observations made during the process of interview, as well as his impression and judgement. Recording the proceedings of the interview is good for both the parties; it serves as a record for future reference. Recording facts ensures confidence and goodwill among the interviewees.

Richard A. Fears has suggested the following qualities for a good interviewer:

(1) A warm engaging manner
(2) Sensitivity in social situations
(3) Reasonable intelligence
(4) Critical and analytical judgement
(5) Adaptability and
(6) Maturity.

Myers and Myers have suggested how to train for those qualities which include the standard sequence of:

(1) Telling
(2) Demonstrating
(3) Supervised practice and
(4) Evaluation and critique.

Errors of Interviewer: The employment interview should be properly planned; when it is unplanned and unpatterned, it would not achieve the objectives and purpose of the interview. In such a case, it can be equated to a causal or social conversation or chatting or pleasure talk. It should be concentrated on the purpose and objects of the interview. Both the interviewer and interviewee must get as much relevant information as possible from the process. The interviewer must have good knowledge, capacity of listening and making best judgement. Generally, the interviewer in the case of employment interview, commits a number of mistakes, resulting in the interview becoming ineffective.

Robert Minter gives a number of sins of the employment interviewer. The common sins of the employment interviewer are:

1. "Too much talking and too little listening, resulting in sketchy information.
2. Not indicating purpose of interview.
3. Asking irrelevant questions or questions whose answers are already on the resume.
4. Having vague objectives and discussing whatever comes up at the movement.
5. Providing job and company information too early in the interview.
6. Attempting an in-depth personality assessment.
7. Providing stress questions and situations in which to observe behaviour.
8. Overreacting to non-verbal clauses, resulting in a stereotyped impression of the applicant.
9. Not having sufficient information about the particular job for which he is interviewing.
10. Becoming fatigued by interviewing too many applicants in a short- time period.
11. Over emphasising or misusing test results.
12. Attempting a thorough interview in a limited ten or fifteen minutes.
13. Misinterpreting reference letters.
14. Overselling the job and company, resulting in false hopes and expectations."[13]

Interview Shortcomings

Myers and Myers have suggested the following shortcomings of interviews:

(1) Using Untrained Interviewers: The first interview error suggested by them is using untrained interviewers unprepared to take on the situation.

(2) Lack of Interviewer Preparation: An interview plan should be prepared in advance and questions to be put for the purpose of interview, covering the contents.

(3) Inappropriate Content: There is always insufficient or inappropriate content of the subject for interview. Advance interview plan along with questions and sequence should be there. The questions not relating to the object and of his own personal taste and interest should be avoided.

(4) Unwillingness to Confront: In the case of weak answers or poor information, the interviewer has to confront. Unwillingness to confront an interviewee is a serious error in the process of effective interview.

(5) Guiding Answers: Showing discrimination or bias in the interview by the interviewer is a very serious problem which defeats the object of the interview. He gives answers to the interviewee by sign language, cues, facial expressions etc.

(6) Doing All Talk: One of the serious shortcomings of the interview is to talk and talk without giving a chance to the interviewee to give his information. Talking too much by the interviewer should be avoided.

(7) Jumping to Conclusions: Drawing conclusions based on preconceived ideas, anticipating answers, sudden decisions to conclude the interview are the defects of the interview.

(8) Poor Listening: Listening is an art, requires a lot of patience, thinking and understanding. This is the most common error often committed by the interviewer.

(9) Inadequate Setting: Lack of general/good atmosphere for the interview is termed as inadequate setting. Noise, telephone calls, visitors, lack of privacy, inadequate time, and lack of other facilities are the defects of an interview.

(10) Recording and Reporting: Failing to follow a form or a logical sequence can produce a weak report. An interviewer has much to do and much to pay attention to during the session and is handicapped by having to take extensive notes.

Planning Interview

A good interview depends on planning. The interviewer must be clear before he goes to the place about events and order. Interview should be properly patterned and structured as a two-way communication process. Planning the interview involves a process of determining the major objectives of interview and policies and strategies that will govern conducting of the interview. An interview plan provides a possible range of activities before the interview, during the interview and after the interview.

The interviewer has to evaluate the internal and external environment to help, to identify strengths and weaknesses. Various factors involved in the interview to be considered to contribute solutions to the problems. A part of the planning process for the interview is to have full knowledge, to know exact information, facts to be gathered. It involves to find out something about the persons to be interviewed, such as interviewees' background, interest, expertise, the style of rapport, the questions to be asked, sequence etc. This interviewing is to be carefully planned and structured. The rules for the interviewer and the interviewee are carefully prescribed. It is a daydic planning.

Steps in Planning

Richard Huseman and others have suggested the following seven steps in planning an interview:

1. Establishing purpose or purposes to be achieved.
2. Collecting preliminary information on the subject and/or the interviewee.
3. Determining the amount of structure to impose.
4. Identifying and perhaps, recording, the strategic questions or responses that seem to possess potential for fulfilling the interview purpose.
5. Determining the time, place and length of time for the interview.
6. Communicating the purpose, place, time and length of time to the interviewee.
7. Personal preparation, e.g., knowing where one stands on crucial issues and attitudes and predicting points of conflict and resistance.[14]

Leland Brown has suggested the following five steps:

1. To keep objectives in mind.
2. To plan, to adapt to the personality and needs of the interviewee.
3. To bring together needed information and to decide how it will be used.
4. To develop lead-questions and key questions into a sequential list.
5. To explore the possible alternatives and solutions to a course of action or problem.[15]

In many cases, interviewing is a daydic process. It means two persons' activity. Both the interviewer and the interviewee get together and pool their information and interact. The pattern of reflective thinking proposed by John Dewey include the following sequence:

(1) Defining the Problem: A definite problem for discussion and exchange of information should be clearly defined. Both the interviewer and the interviewee should agree to the definition of the problem. A successful interview cannot be expected unless there is mutual solution to the problem which is not possible without clearly defining the problem.

(2) Analysis of the Problem: Interview is a joint exploration of both the interviewer and the interviewee. As such, analysis of the problem also should jointly be attempted.

"If one person is (either interviewer or interviewee) goes fast, off-the-cuff analysis without consultation, then the other should object or at least have the analysis explained."[16]

(3) Alternative Solutions: There may be number of alternative courses of action to a given and defined problem. Selecting the best alternative is the objective in interaction with others. Alternatives can be suggested by the interviewer or interviewee in the exchange process. Both have equal opportunities and chances to suggest solutions and discuss over them to arrive at a solution.

(4) Evaluation: The solution so arrived at out of alternative solutions as the best possible one should be subject to evaluation. It means to review. Solutions should be evaluated by both persons. There is no domination by any person that one is the boss or superior.

(5) Preferred Solution: The preferred solution should be chosen, relating to the problem.

THE PROCESS OF INTERVIEW

Interview as a oral communication device is used to collect information and exchange it between interviewer and interviewee. The process of interview is a direct one, of face-to-face conversation on a clearly defined mutual problem. One interviews someone because he has the message to collect and exchange. Executives interview subordinates, equals or top because they have the subject for interaction with the concerned people. The process may involve exchange of facts, events, opinions, conditions etc. The interview process may also involve to gather subjective data, feelings, reactions, preference etc. Sometimes, their purpose is for problem-solving, panel decision, goal-setting, evaluation, investigation, to take corrective action etc. In brief, it may be said, that it may help in defining the problem and in planning, investigating and finding solutions. Public relation officers, advocates, consultants, teachers, salesmen, counsellers etc. are seen always involved in interviewing several people. Personal and social interaction do not contain problems, solutions, and purposes, and hence do not possess essentials of greeting.

However, the process of interview contain the following stages:

(1) Opening: The first phase is introduction. In this, the parties involve in exchange of greetings.

(2) Object of Interview: Once the formality of introduction is over the interviewer should explain to the interviewee the object of the interview, the nature of the interview and in clear and integlligible terms what is expected to be achieved.

(3) Beginning of Interview: In the commencement of an interview, the atmosphere should be easy and non-stressful. Both the interviewer and interviewee in a light-hearted manner follow the sequence of questions and topic of the question and answer business will continue.

(4) Free Conversation Atmosphere: Free atmosphere is desirable in the process of interview. A moment of relaxation and easy feeling may be allowed to the interviewee. He should be encouraged to express his ideas freely without any fear.

(5) Recalling Time: The interviewer, after observing his facial expressions and feelings, may give time to help him to recall. Sometimes the interviewer, can give a hint or clue to break the silence which encourages the interviewee to speak.

(6) Objective Questions: It has been found from actual experience that the interviewer puts irrelevant questions and questions of his own choice and interest not relating to the objective. Sometimes, interviewee does not expect such questions. So the interviewer should put such questions which will help to achieve the object of interview.

(7) Encouragement: The interviewer should not create a situation to feel discouraged on account of certain incoherences in talk. The interviewee should be encouraged in order to maintain sustained interest in the interview.

(8) Directions: It has been already mentioned that interview is a joint exploration of both the interviewer and the interviewee. Sometimes, they may indulge in an orgy of non-stop talking. It is really a delicate task to bring it to normality. However, the interviewer should politely and patiently, with confidence, exercise direction of talk in the desired course.

(9) Note Taking: Recording of interview proceeding is very important as it may create confidence that their opinions have been considered in arriving at a decision and at the same time. It is not desirable to rely upon memory, write up of notes is very essential which must be done simultaneously with the process of interview. Generally, it takes the form of black and white of certain jottings.

(10) Conclusion: As far as possible, the object of interview should be completed in one sitting. However, on certain matters, several sittings may be necessary to complete an interview. Concluding the interview takes place with the mutual consent of both the parties. The close should be appropriate to the kind of interview. Both must check before concluding.

(11) Report: Report writing is like a minutes-writing of a meeting proceeding. Soon after the conclusions of the interview or each sitting, a report of it should be put in writing. Taking a long period of time to write a report is not good as it may lead to errors, omission, forgetting events in writing the-report.

L. Brown has suggested a structure of interview process into three parts. They are opening, body and closing.[17]

Myers and Myers have given suggestions on how to conduct an interview. The checklist for an interview consists of:

(a) Deciding and clarifying the purpose of the interview.
(b) Plan for the interview.
(c) Prepare the environment.
(d) Prepare the opening.
(e) Carrying out the interview sequence.
(f) The close should be appropriate to the kind of interview.[18]
(g) Write-up your notes or report.

HOW INTERVIEWS HELP GAIN INSIGHTS[19]

(1) Employment Interview

Objective: Induction of the right talent into the organisation.

Psychological premise: It is possible to assess the ability and suitability of people in a face-to-face interaction.

Role of Interviewer: Recommendation maker.

Skills of the Interviewer: Judging the suitability of job applicants by questioning, probing and exploring their minds and expectations.

Response of Interviewee: Projecting himself as the most suitable candidate for the postition or promotion.

Likely Outcome: The right candidate is usually offered a job but rarely the wrong one.

(2) Performance Interview

Objective: Evaluation of work done, with the motive of further improvement.

Psychological Premise: People possess the urge to improve. You have to encourage them by expressing confidence in them.

Role of Interviewer: Encourager.

Skills of Interviewer: Energising people in upward mobility. Reflecting feelings and identifying areas of weakness and suggest solutions.

Response of Interviewee: Accepts suggestions if he is appreciated, not blamed.

Likely Outcome: Individual and collective growth.

(3) Exit Interview

Objective: Sharing perceptions about the organisation from outgoing employees.

Psychological Premise: People will state their frank and honest opinion in a warm and friendly environment.

Role of Interviewer: Listener.

Skills of the Interviewer: Stimulating frank and open talk, without entering into argument or debate.

Response of Interviewee: Overcome traces of resentment or bitterness. Doesn't want to cause offence. Gives guarded opinion. Occasionally unpredictable.

Likely Outcome: Beneficial if you know how to read between the lines.

(4) Counselling Interview

Objective: Inspiring and encouraging employees to improve.

Psychological Premise: People will accept helpful advice, if you don't hurt their self-esteem.

Role of Interviewer: Sympathiser — guide.

Skills of Interviewer: To offer an opportunity to the interviewee to express himself and offer him useful constructive advice.

Response of Interviewee: Perceives you as a well-wisher, usually accepts friendly advice.

Likely Outcome: Mostly encouraging. Possibility of occasional misunderstanding not ruled out.

(5) Reprimand Interview

Objective: Conveying management's concern and dissatisfaction about an employee's actions and performance.

Psychological Premise: People try to avoid situations that repeatedly bring them face-to-face with rejection or disapproval.

Role of the Interviewer: Disciplinarian and censurer.

Skills of the Interviewer: Transmitting negative opinion of the management to an employee, without sounding apologetic. Implying that his future will be monitored carefully. Maintaining a stiff upper lip.

Response to Interviewee: Avoids eye contact. Feels uncomfortable. Remains silent implying he is unconvinced. An understanding employee assures the interviewer that he won't repeat the mistake.

Likely Outcome: Success possible if employee respects the interviewer.

(6) Complaint-redressal Interview

Objective: To promote understanding and goodwill between management and employees.

Pscyhological Premise: Disgruntled people are always keen to be heard and seek redressal of their grievances.

Role of Interviewer: Listener.

Skills of Interviewer: Listening and reflecting feelings. Appreciating employee's grouses. Asking polite exploratory questions and carefully avoiding aggravation or rancour. Displaying the problem-solving behaviour.

Response of Interviewee

Feels assured momentarily. Wait-and-watch attitude.

Likely Outcome: Temporary peace with ceasefire. May become lasting if assurances are fulfilled.

(7) Order-giving-Interview

Objective: Conveying management's directions and seeking their compliance.

Psychological Premise: People resist change but feel re-assured if directions/orders are given to them personally by senior executives. Impersonal treatment provokes protest and resentment, even disobedience.

Role of Interviewer: Explaining the details of new guidelines against the backdrop of overall policy. Appreciating the contribution made by the interviewee.

Skills of Interviewer: Ability to infuse confidence in the employee about new assignment/ increased or new responsibilities. Acknowledge his worth and assure him of continuous support.

Response of the Interviewee: Resists change. Entertains misgivings if incentives or rewards are absent. Seeks assurance of review of orders, after a definite interval.

Likely Outcome: Range from reluctant to willing compliance.

(8) Induction Interview

Objective: Familiarising the new entrant to the overall structure and working of the organisation and his specific duties and functions.

Psychological Premises: People appreciate cordiality and personal introduction. They welcome polite interest in their present one and responsibilities.

Role of Interviewer: Fellow traveller.

Skills of Interviewer: Civil and well-mannered. Displays genuine warmth. Greets and introduces himself as a valuable addition to the organisation. Friendly, helpful and co-operative.

Response of Interviewee: Responds to friendly gestures, with smile and warm handshakes. Tries to make others comfortable. Expresses the hope of making his contribution to the progress of the organisation.

Likely Outcome: Growth and development of the organisation. Cordial inter-personal relationship.

MEDIA OF ORAL COMMUNICATION

In oral communication, important question that arise is as to what are the different forms of tools of oral communication. Media of oral communication means tools or vehicles of communication. The instrument or instruments used or applied in conversation, speech, talk to convey message is/are termed as medium/media of communication. The problem of misunderstanding in group activities or improper implementation of business objectives or broad policies laid down by the top management arises from poor communication. The aims of an organisation can be achieved with effective communication. Transfer of message by any medium available is essential in any organisation like private, public, productive, service, educational institutions, Government departments, undertakings, assembly, etc.

However, it needs to be emphasised at this point the important and popular media of oral communication.

To make communication effective, appropriate medium or media may be selected to meet a particular situation to which the speaker endeavours to put across. All media may not be useful to all circumstances. A particular medium or instrument may be more useful as a conveyor belt carrying the message to a particular group. Any medium may be considered good only when the listener receives, understands, and responds to that or acts accordingly. Diverse educational backgrounds, mental attitude, position occupied, responsibilities, importance of the message, urgency etc., call for different media of oral communication. As such, a particular medium of communication cannot be applied to all the cases.

The chief executive's medium of communication is different from a medium applied by a foreman. Similarly, the medium of communication would certainly vary when the politician wants to convey his ideas. Similarly, the medium of communication would also vary when the Government wants to get the public informed about the welfare and development programmes and achievements during a particular period. Again the medium of communication would definitely vary when a teacher wants to convey or to educate about the subject.

In this connection, it is, therefore, very much necessary to choose an approrpiate medium because the success of communication would depend upon the selection of appropriate instrument or instruments to make for effective communication. Oral communication has mostly and primarily been adopted as a medium for many purposes. The forms of oral communication are many and varied which may be briefly discussed below.

(1) Face-to-Face Conversation: Face-to-face conversation is the most effective type of communication. It has certain advantage. Certain things can be done orally most effectively than written communication. Though modern scientific machines like telephone is used as a device for verbal communication, it is not a face-to-face communication. There are many media in oral communication in which there is no personal contact. It is only in the face-to-face communication that information can statisfactorily be conveyed. Explanations, notes etc., as used in written communication need not necessarily be used in this method, because the necessary clarifications, explanations and doubts can be exchanged orally without loss of time.

A face-to-face communication gives an opportunity of observing facial expressions, reactions and gives effective feedback on the matter. When the communicator and the recipient are talking together, sitting face-to-face there is a definite understanding. Opinions can be expressed freely, opposed, offers and counter-offers and clarifications take place then and there only, which are the most essential for effective decision-making. The verbal words are more direct and personal. Words of mouth expose feelings and actions. The acceptance or rejection can be better understood and necessary clarifications can be given. But the communicator must choose words so that the receiver will be sure to understand them correctly. The following are some of the important principles of effective face-to-face communication:

(1) To avoid waste of time and thought or both.

(2) The message must reveal the necessary facts.

(3) The vocabularly level of the receiver must be considered.

(4) To convey the message in the way we feel towards the receiver.

(5) The manner and style and temperaments are equally important.

(6) Appropriate fitting words to be chosen to convey the central message.

(7) Short sentences, clear words, words currently in use should be used.

Benjamin Balinsky puts it: "If there is any short-cut to executive effectiveness, it is the mastery of the art of face-to-face communication."

(2) Telephoning: A telecommunication device. A communication device for speaking directly to someone at a distant place. The instrument may use either an electric current or radio wave.

Telephone is an instrument for speaking to someone from a distance. Message is transmitted using either an electric current which passes along a wire or radio waves. One speaks to another by means of telephone switchboard at a telephone exchange. Telephone exchange is a central control through which telephone calls are directed. Under direct dial system, one can speak to someone from a distance directly without the assistance of a telephone exchange. Telephonic communication is very essential to create a good impression. It has a good potential for providing two-way interaction when people are scattered over a vast area in an organisation or otherwise. Telephone has, thus, in recent years come to be used for direct contact. Under this, one can hear the natural voice and which is more clear in telephonic communication. It is recognised that telephone is one of the oral communication devices to save time and get the things done quickly.

But in telephonic communication, one should be precise, clear in presenting the message. Similarly, it is not desirable to allow the telephone to ring long because it leads to annoying. In recent years, in many organisations, intercom system has been introduced. Intercom is a system of communication within an organisation, usually by means of microphones and loud speakers. Telephone directory is a book containing the list of names, addresses and telephone numbers of all the subscribers in a particular area who have telephone facilities, quick reference of a particular number to whom to be talked. The directory may be complied covering limited local area, a taluk, district, state and may be a national telephone directory.

(3) Conference: Another medium of oral communication is conference. "Conference" means a meeting for discussion. A conference is the pooling of thoughts of two or more individuals to assist in solving the problems. The conference of political leaders, conference of chief executives, conference of press reporters, conference of scientists etc. meet together to discuss and find a solution to the problem of their interest. In conference, mutual problems constitute the subject of discussion. Eminent and expert participants contribute their thoughts and experience in solving the problem. It is a joint-effort of the people gathered. They interact, exchange with others, teach each other and learn from each other.

Thus, a conference is an assembly of a group of persons gathered to exchange information for some particular purpose. The words "conference" and "meeting" are generally used interchangeably. The group may be small or large. Similarly, there is no difference between speaking in conference and meeting. A conference is also called "convention", when it is attended by a large number of people. In a conference, the speaker speaks his own ideas and opinions on the subject on which the conference is conducted. All the speakers present their own solutions or opinions and the leader of the conference summarises the proceedings. In this type of oral communication, the success is based on the thought process and how well the members are stimulated.

(4) Press Conference: It is a gathering of journalists and press reporters. In a press conference, journalists and reporters from various news agencies are invited to participate, to listen and cover the same in the press. A press conference may be with politicians, Government, corporate executives, local bodies, educational institutions, voluntary agencies etc. The purpose of a press conference is to appraise a situation, problems, achievements, progress, public matters etc. Press reporters are supplied pamphlets covering information and statistical data so as to enable them to cover in the press. The conference enables to carry message to the public. The press is entitled to raise questions and solicit replies or explanation. In a democratic set up press conference is a powerful medium of mass communication.

(5) Demonstration: Action and message is a communication medium called "demonstration". This medium is mostly adopted by corporate marketing strategy. Demonstration is also used to educate the voters as to how to exercise his franchise. The demonstration is a part of the sales presentation where a salesman proves that his company's product will do all. The purpose of the demonstration is to maintain the interest that was aroused on the previous occasions and to build a desire in the mind of the prospect.

The salesman shows and states the benefits that the prospect will receive, supported by facts. He places the product in the hands of the prospect for his examination. The demonstration gives the prospect the opportunity to experience for himself the benefits to be obtained from using particular product. Everyone would rather enjoy a pleasant experience than just be told about it by another person.

(6) Radio: Radio is a vehicle of mass medium. It is a type of communication technology. Radio is extensively used for broadcasting many programmes mainly because of its wide accessibility and relatively low cost. It is one-way communication system. But some institutions in the advanced countries like New Zealand and Australia have evolved radio tutorials and radio conferences. It is only an audio medium. Nassif suggested that audio-visual electronics programme used must be complemented by other media.[20] The effective use of radio to correspondence course began in Japan in 1976.[21]

(7) Recording: Recording is a process which involves recording a programme at a particular place. The process of making a record of something like message, talk, interview especially on a record or on a tape. Record-player is an electrical instrument which reproduces the sounds recorded on records. The information or statements recorded or intended to be repeated are made public. It is written down or recorded for future reference. Recording make it possible to capture a speech or radio programme and replay it by radio before an audience or over a public address system anywhere. Some recordings are made on the spot, special occasions or events. In other cases, special programmes are deliberately produced at a recording studio.

(8) Dictaphone: In oral communication, a mechanical dictating machine is called "dictaphone." Dictating machines by a combination of electronics and mechanical means record the voice. The transcriber reproduces the voice. The machines are most popular and used for dictation of correspondence, recording of proceedings, conferences, recording of interview and are used for the market research. The advantages of using dictating machine are: (1) They save time. (2) Reduce the cost involved in corresponding work. (3) The mistakes in hearing by typist are avoided. (4) Speed and accuracy can be achieved. (5) Personal presence of the typist or stenographer is avoided. (7) The advantage of centralisation can be achieved.

Thus, there are many types and models of dictaphones.

The main function is to record the dictation and transcribe the dictation by switching on the machine which is recorded on a magnetic tape or plastic disc. Making use of a dictaphone to be effective in communication demands and calls for certain norms. They are: (1) clarity in pronunciation;

(2) clarity; (3) simple; (4) short sentences; (5) stop when interruptions take place; (6) avoid a pipe, gum, cigar in mouth while dictating; (7) dictation should be read back.

(9) Meetings: In the real world situation, meetings are yet another medium of oral communication. In a democratic set-up, meetings are a common method. In a restless age of communication, meetings are business. Message can be easily and understandably communicated through the medium of meetings. Message is carried in family meetings, street gatherings, samiti meetings, panchayat meetings, parishad meetings, municipal corporation meetings, Assembly and Parliamentary meetings. Meetings may be convened regularly and in extraordinary circumstances. In corporate management, we frequently come across company meetings.

A company may conduct several types of meetings to convey the matters of the company for the purpose of taking decisions. The usual company meetings are statutory meetings, annual general meetings, extraordinary general meetings, Board of Directors' meetings, shareholders' debentureholders' meetings, creditors' meetings etc. Meetings are gatherings which comprise groups of persons belonging to a particular interest to whom, as groups, some common matters or issues are entrusted. At this place, information is communicated orally, discussed, deliberated and debated to come to a solution or decision. Meetings are supposed to be of democratic origin.

Sometimes, special invitees, *ex-officio* Government nominees, institutional representatives are invited to have their specialised and technical advice for consideration. Meetings ensure collective decisions or team decisions. Collective decisions are taken with oral discussion sitting in meetings and hence fear of authority being concentrated in one perosn is avoided. A meeting may be informational, advisory or problem solving. In information-meeting, the object is to present ideas, data to the members. In advisory type of meetings, the purpose is to gather and seek advise, information and suggestion relating to a problem. The object of problem-solving meeting is to seek a solution out of collective discussion and mutual understanding of a problem. Thus in meetings, communication flows both ways. Discussion is an important object of a meeting. In this verbal form of communication, the group acts as a team with responsibility since they help in arriving at a collective decision.

(10) Rumour: A rumour is an oral information circulating something. It passes from person to person sometimes unfounded news. In rumour communication, a piece of news or story is passed from one person to another person, which may not be true. A verbal general talk or gossip, or a loud untrue sound. It is a talk or report of a person or thing in some way noted or distinguished. The fact of being generally talked about reputation and renown. A rumour is a verbal statement or report circulating in a group, of the truth of which there is no clear evidence.

A rumour once spread is not soon removed. A rumour spreads like a wildfire and may create wonders and miracles as a channel of informal communication. The two persons involved in a rumour are: rumour spreader or a rumour breaker and the receiver. The originator of a rumour is also called "rumour-monger." In grapevine, the leader of a group passes the message to each person in that group. A communication leader recognises rumours. The leader must be trustworthy and should have credibility.

The management can use them for effective communication. The information can be fed into the informal channel to dispel rumours and to provide quick and easy access to the information.

Model Rumours

(1) A rumour circulating that the managing director is going abroad.

(2) Rumour passing from one person to another about the change in holiday arrangements.

(3) A news that secretary got a new job.

(4) A person spread a rumour that a colleague has left the country.

(5) It is rumoured that they are getting transferred.

(11) Demonstration and Dramatization Method: It is a method in which 'doing' skills may be shown, explained and applied. Demonstration is made and dramatized as a means of giving emphasis to the subject under consideration.

(12) Public Address System (PA): In oral communication, public address system is another important dimension. It is a mechanical system. It is a system adopted at meetings, shows, carnivals, melas, exhibitions, gatherings of employees or mass audience. Through a public address system, it is possible mechnically to project the human voice among a large gathering. Mounted on a mini-truck or any other mobile auto, the PA system can be transported from place to place, presenting speakers and programmes as it goes, and reaching a widely distributed audience. Sound tracks can also be rigged up at stationery locations, providing facilities for meetings and special programmes in lieu of a permanently installed PA system. Portable bull horns afford greater mobility wherever amplified sound is needed.[22]

(13) Grapevine: Informal communication is termed as "grapevine." So, the informal medium in oral communication, as the very name implies, is based on informal relationship of the people in the organisation. A successful management must recognise and give importance to the grapevine. It is also known as grapevine communication which means an information communication network constituted to pass message speedily. When an informal channel is used to communicate, it is termed as "grapevine" or "informal communication." it is not a deliberately created and officially prescribed channel for the flow of information and hence free from all sorts of formalities. The network is formed out of personal relationship, social and group relations, but not out of position of line and authority, superior and subordinate, or based on organisational hierarchy. It is a quick vehicle for message.

Informal communication may be conveyed by a simple glance, gesture, smile or mere silence. It is composed of a series of small groups of people linked to one another covering everyone in the organisation. One person in the group passes a message to another person in a particular group. The individuals of the group in turn pass the message to someone in another group. Because of intergroup links and chains, the message quickly passes to all the persons. There are communication leaders in the grapevine and the management can make use of them to communicate. On the other hand, management may create its own grapevine. L. Brown clearly describes the advantages of grapevine to the management in words — "advantages to management include expediency — it saves time, gets immediate response; provides a useful feedback for decision-making; generates ideas and suggestions that may prove helpful; disseminates accurate, factual information that needs to be relayed. In using the grapevine, the management must be able to pinpoint the leaders and work through them, must feed them factual information, listen to the feedback response, and be discerning in not overloading the system and using it inappropriately."[23]

(14) Group Discussion: In the context of group discussion, it is more appropriate to quote Robert Bales who defines: "A small group is defined as any number of persons engaged in interaction with one another in a single face-to- face meeting or series of such meetings in which each member receives some impression or perception of each other member distinctive enough so that he can, either at the time, or in later questioning, give some reaction to each of the others as an individual person, even though it be only to recall that the other was present."

In a group discussion, members of the group are in interaction with one another. A group may be small or large. There are no fixed norms as to the right size for a group; it all depends upon the circumstances of a particular case. A group is headed by a leader generally called "chairman", controller of group discussion. A group may be a causal group, permanent group, learning group, policy-making group and action group. For certain reasons, groups are formed to take decision or to carry out some activities. Communication in the group takes place in the form of deliberations among the leaders and group members. Group reaches decisions after discussion. Group discussions are collective opinions. Group decisions through discussions are superior and better to individual decision which is one-sided. Group discussion is a process of decision-making where communication exchange on validity, reasonability, practicability, time and cost factors are interacted. Thus, group discussion involves defining a problem, generating solutions, analysing alternative solutions, the solution and evaluating the results.

(15) Oral Report: Oral report means presentation of written matter before a group. One must have an oral communication skill for oral report presentation. This method is used in every business activity and at every level. The originator of oral report presents informational and analytical message. The essentials of good speaking will equally apply to oral reports. According to L. Brown, "The function of an oral report is to furnish the facts necessary to expedite action or to persuade someone or any number of persons to take the action the group decided on or to implement the group's solution."[24]

Like in oral message, an oral report to be effective must be carefully planned and developed. When a report is orally read before a gathering, it is similar to an oral presentation and should be written in such a manner. An oral report is generally drafted for a particular group of people. For instance, oral report to the executives of all departments. Like a speech, oral reports have an introduction, body and ending. With a view to clarify certain things or to create interest, audio visual aids may be used.

A successful and effective oral report must follow certain essential principles. Some of the principles are:

(1) A report should be complete, clear and short.

(2) To practise report reading by imagining an audience.

(3) To set a gentle style and tone.

(4) To know the audience.

(5) To fix time limit to read.

(6) To divide a report into paragraphs, each paragraph should give a separate central idea.
(7) Other principles of good oral communication and written communication are equally applicable.

The following are logical steps to acquire self-confidence to present an oral report as suggested by Leland Brown.[25]

(1) Preparing your talk carefully. Fear of forgetting result in stage fright.
(2) Practising aloud. You will know your talk better after rehearsing. Practise alone, going over it again and again, imagining your audience before you, or viewing yourself in a mirror.
(3) By not memorizing your talk; a tape recorder can be helpful for it allows you to hear yourself.
(4) Checking your appearance. Dress appropriately for the occasion and your audience.
(5) When you face your group, waiting a few minutes before you start to talk, think of your audience as your friends. They want you to do well. Do not think about yourself.
(6) Begin slowly; do not give up once you have begun. Stage fright disappears before you start.
(7) Speaking louder than ordinarily, at least at the outset.
(8) Speaking as often as you can. The more practice you get, the easier it is to speak with confidence.

(16) Closed Circuit Television: Closed circuit television means live pictures and sounds can be piped from the originating point at one or more receiving locations for viewing by a selected audience. The programmes of this TV are not transmitted to stations for broadcasting to general home viewers. TV programmes are designed for specifically invited audience. It is as private as a telephone conversation. Tele-lectures are being used quite widely, in education technique widely adopted now-a-days and less expensive in comparison to broadcast.

The medium of oral communication operates by using a television set. Television camera is connected to the receiving set. The camera scans the picture to be transmitted. The camera converts the picture into electrical signals, i.e., video signals. The video-amplifier applies the range of frequencies. Amplitude modulated picture transmitter is a circuit which places the visual information on a career wave. The microphones convert audio signals into electrical signals. The complete process gives us continuous viewing of the pictures and listening of sound.

(17) Dictation: Dictation is a communication process in which something is read or spoken to by the sender to another to write it down. Dictation of message is also another medium of oral communication. It is one of the multi media communications. It is writing with a voice. It involves an effective message dictation and effective listening to write down. It is a work of team task consisting of messages, stenographers, transcribers, typists and professional secretaries. They have to follow a set of dictation procedure and practice.

In the pre-dictation stage, the speaker has to collect, organise the data or material and has to plan to dictate. The person giving dictation has to write notes or cues of the proposed message.

Then he has to visualise the listeners or the person to whom the actual dictation of message is to be given. The actual dictation stage should consider some important factors like classifying the message, delivery in a positive way, constructive tone, speaking clearly, use even-rate of delivery, use conventional language etc.

There are two methods of dictation. First, face-to-face dictation. It is dictation to a personal assistant or secretary or stenographer in person. It facilitates instant interaction. Secondly, machine dictation. The speaker uses the recording element and the typist uses transcribing listening element. A microphone, tape, volume control, playback control, on and off switch etc., constitute the dictation machine system.

(18) Conversing: Conversation is a special category of communication or colloquial. It is opposed to dialogue which has a purpose and is formal, while conversation is without a purpose. Some persons are fond of or good in conversation. This category includes relatively formal and informal speaking that may range from friendly to casual discussion. It is common in social gathering and informal groups. One uses one's speaking skills, listening skills, reciprocal discussion, talks on mutual affairs, friends, sports, travel, entertainment etc.

Advantages of Oral Communication

Thus, the most important and the earliest form of communication is verbal or word, everything is oral and there is no question of black and white. Face-to-face discussion, telephone talks, lectures, conferences, interviews, public speeches are the forms of media of oral communication. The most important merits of verbal communication are outlined as under:

(1) Time Saving: Considerable amount of time is saved in verbal communication. Time is the most important factor to be productively and profitably utilised. It reduces the time of one person. It reduces duplication and errors in saving of time.

(2) Saving in Cost: In oral communication, nothing is reduced to writing. There is no work to put in black and white. There is no need to have qualified and technical personnel like stenographers and typists. The whole of the typing and stenographic work is avoided in verbal communication; ultimately resulting in saving of cost. It results in saving of stationery and other incidental cost in various departments.

(3) Effective Media: Oral communication is comparatively more effective than the others. Communication between persons in the departments is always by way of face-to-face or through mechanical devices. Convincing impression can be created immediately. The action, reaction and the attitude of the persons can be understood by observing facial expression.

(4) Easy Understanding: Easy understandibility of message is important in oral communication so that the receiver can respond quickly and correctly. This advantage of easy understandability can be achieved in oral communication. In a face-to-face conversation, there are no chances of misunderstanding or inability to understand the message. Doubts and clarifications can be sought and the correct idea and meaning of the speaker can be understood. Intentions and objectives can immediately be interacted and confusion can be removed.

(5) To Meausure the Effect of Communication: To measure the effect of communication is difficult in written communication. But, in oral communication, it is easier to understand the listener whether he is understanding or not the speaker's message, so that it is possible to clarify and explain immediately his viewpoint to the other party. In the case of oral communication, immediate changes and amendments are possible on the spot. The recipient's attitude as to acceptance or rejection of communications can be studied.

(6) Emergency Needs: Oral communication is the best media to send messages during an emergency or urgency or extraordinary circumstances, when you need quick and speedy communication.

(7) Not a Costly System: Since in each department, communication takes place without the use of any tool or tools like pen, paper, typewriter and other requirements which are necessary in the case of a written communication.

(8) Mechanical Devices: In large organisations, modern mechanical devices are used for oral communication. These devices do not disturb the work of others; quietness is created in the office. For instance, signals are simple devices used for calling a person.

(9) Decentralisation: Oral communication ensures decentralisation in communication, because everyone can speak to others in a language known to the speaker and the listener. In a pool system, the typist has to type out the messages and circulate to all concerned. There is no secrecy in oral communication and there is nothing behind the screen.

(10) Effective Co-ordination: The importance of co-ordination in management cannot be overemphasised. The problem of management today is co-ordination in all group activities. As there is close personal touch and contact in oral communication, effective co-ordination is achieved, an organisation's relationship can be better promoted largely through communication. Written communication is impersonal and indirect.

(11) Accuracy and Speed: Verbal media carry messages accurately and speedily. The twin advantages of accuracy and speed are possible in this system.

(12) Use of Labour-saving Devices: Labour-saving devices can be used in oral communication. They are mostly mechanical devices such as signals, speaking tubes, dictaphones, telephones, inter-com-system, house exchange system, private automatic branch exchanges etc.

(13) Proper Control and Supervision: Oral communication ensures proper control over implementation. Supervising the effects of communication can be achieved effectively and effficiently.

(14) Follow-up of Message: The success of effective communication is that the receiver must be dealt with and must respond in time. Therefore, the speaker should see that the message received is accepted. If rejected, follow-up action is quite possible without loss of time in oral communication.

(15) Others: Thus, effective oral communication in management ensures smooth and uninterrupted running of the business, quick decisions and implementation, proper planning and co-ordination, informal relations and morale building.

Disadvantages of Oral Communication

The merits of verbal communication for effective information in management or otherwise has been widely recognised in recent years. The importance of this form of communication has been judged point-wise in detail under the above paragraphs. In all forms of oral communication, the speaker and the listener must keep in view the limitations associated with oral communication. There are some inherent demerits in this form. The disadvantages of oral communication may be enumerated as under:

(1) External Communication: The need of typists and stenographers cannot be avoided for the sake of cost saving. In the case of external communication, correspondence with several people in different places is difficult with verbal media. In non-mechanical devices, oral communication is most suitable for internal communication.

(2) Noise: Again, conversation always disturbs the work of others on account of the noise it creates. Written communication is less noisy and gentle and all typing work is done in a typing pool. Thus, there is less disturbance to the other staff.

(3) No Secrecy: Secrecy of official matters cannot be maintained in oral communication. In oral communication, there are chances of secret matters being leaked out. When one is speaking to another openly, there is every possibility of it being overhead by others. There are always certain official matters which are strictly secret.

(4) Problem of Language: Personnel with a diverse educational, literacy and language background are working in an organisation. People with different linguistic backgrounds may not derive the benefits of oral communication. In such a situation, a common medium like English or Hindi, as the case may be, be adopted and the information must go to them through typing.

(5) Drawback of Machine: The mechanical devices used for oral communication create a lot of disturbance to work like calling bell, buzzer, etc. In many cases, they may be misused for personal work.

(6) Problems in Technical Work: A typist or stenogapher is well-versed in technicalities and ensures better communication. All people may not be familiar with the technicalities and legalities of the subject matter to be communicated. Thus, when there is a typing pool, the typist or steno is familiar with the work of all departments. So written communication helps in a greater way in such circumstances.

(7) Absence Creates Problem: The essential requirement of non-mechanical oral communication is the timely presence of both the speaker and the listener. It is normal that subordinates or superiors may go on leave which creates a problem for timely communication of information. Sometimes, they may be absent, or they may not be on their seats. This type of problem does not arise in the case of written communication because the written message can be sent to the desk of the person concerned. Face-to-face communication presupposes the presence of the speaker and the listener.

(8) No Evidence: In verbal communication, there is no work of black and white. Everything is oral and there is no record of matter for future reference. Poor memory, lack of understanding, forgetful nature and absentmindedness, may create a lot of problems. There is no documentary proof or evidence. In a scientific communication in big organisation, filing of communication is essential for successful office organisation.

(9) Place of Work: Oral communication is not possible effectively when the communicator and the recipients are far off. It takes a lct of time to meet each other. It is a problem particularly with field workers and others who are at different work places within the premises but located at distant places.

(10) Costly Devices: Introduction of mechanical devices for oral communication involves a lot of capital investment and recurring expenditure. Since each department or section is to be equipped with mechanical devices for effective communication, it amounts to a costly system. The small organisations cannot afford to go in for such system.

STYLES OF ORAL COMMUNICATION

The word "style" with reference to communication means the manner or way of speaking or writing the subject matter of communication. It may include a formal or informal style of writing or speaking. We find in practical life several different styles of communication. No two people communicate exactly in the same manner. On the other hand, we do not communicate the same way all the time and to all the persons. A person may converse in a variety of manners. Traditional way or fashionable way of communication may be followed. Some people adopt their own way for communication. So, the various ways and features in interpersonal communication is termed as styles in communication.

Different styles may be adopted in different situations, depending upon time, person, place, situation etc. A particular style may be useful in some specific interpersonal situation or group situations. Not everybody communicates as well as everybody else. Much of this difference is related to personal qualities and language used. A particular style should not be used for all interpersonal situations. For instance, using aggressive style in communication in a particular interpersonal situation or group situation is unfit in another interpersonal situation. However, the following are five basic communication styles suggested by Virginia Satir on styles of communication.[26]

(1) Blaming or Aggressive Style: "Blame" means to consider the responsibility for something bad as belonging to a particular person. It means finding fault with a person. Some people communicate in a blaming style to find faults with others. They transmit messages which imply that everybody is foolish and slow at understanding. They exhibit this quality when speaking to a person. The speaker tries to win and dominate the other person, even sometimes, with force. Fault-finders do not recognise the dignity, right and the role of the recipient of the message. Aggressive style of communication always opposes the other person and behaves in the attacking and quarrelsome manner. Some short-tempered persons behave in an imbalanced way sometimes exhibit aggresive tone and fight with others. Blamers always like to order others. The blaming or aggressive style of communication is not a good quality of the communicator. Managers or Executives with this style of communication may not succeed in their informational, interpersonal and decision roles. The responses from subordinates may be negative in conflict and dispute. They cannot establish harmonious and co-operative relationship with others. Myers and Myers have described the nature of blamers in the words: "Blamers usually fail to establish close relationships and feel they have to be constantly vigilant against other peoples' attack and possible retaliation. They tend to feel alienated from other people, misunderstood and unloved. They are usually lonely people."[27]

(2) Placating or Non-Assertive Style: The word "placate" means "to stop a person who is not in his usual mood or feeling otherwise." The persons who placate are called "Placates." People of convincing nature often attempt to get oneself liked by others. A manager may try to ingratiate himself with the top management. They are polite, neutral, sympathetic and do not hurt other person's feeling. They always exhibit pleasing and appeasing behaviour, always keep friendly relations and avoid conflict. "Yes" men, non-controversial people, are opposed to say "no." Accommodating, adaptability, and adjustability — these qualities are found in placates. They easily yield to others and try to please everyone.

(3) Computing or Intellectual Style: Computers or intelligentsia are people who are clever and having ability to understand. People of this type in their interpersonal situations and relations apply intelligence. This style of communication represents the quality of being intelligent. These people appear gentle, polite, calm, with hidden feelings. Myers and Myers have emphasised the qualities of this type of people in these words: "Intellectual often feel quite vulnerable and simply deal with their fears of inadequacy by presenting a distant and aloof front, so that no one can really get too close to them. They choose professions which do not put them in much contact with other people whom they find unpredictable or irrational."[28]

(4) Distracting or Manipulative Style: Persons using distracting or manipulative style act in a quite distinctive way. They tend to act in such a way as to draw aside the mind or attention. In an organisation, a person may be often distracted from his work out of unpleasant things. They always try to handle interpersonal situation skilfully or by manipulating other person's feelings. It involves to manage or influence, cleverness and dishonesty. The people adapting this style while dealing with other people exhibit violent, bitter feelings against someone or something, causing injury or pain to the other people. Other manipulative techniques applied are guilt, i.e., a sense of shame, because he knows that he has done wrong.

(5) Levelling or Assertive Style: The levelling or assertive style of communication can well be understood with the help of the following observation suggested by Myers and Myers. "Levellers are able to stand up for their rights and express feelings, thoughts, or needs in a direct, honest, straight forward manner. Messages are all congruent. Tone of voice, gestures, eye- contact, and stance all fit the words that are spoken. Actions also match words, and the assertive people follow through on what they say will do. The basic point about assertive communication is that it is style which, in our opinion, is most likely to foster mutual trust, self-respect and respect from others. These are all vital ingredients for effective communication transmission on the job."[29]

Other Styles: This part of description of communication styles is based on M.P. Wolf, D.F.Keyser and R.R. Aurner's discussion on effective communication in business. The ten sterotyped miscommunicators they describe include information hog, chatterbox, vague referencer, twister, thunderer, mumbler, scarecrows, laughters, chronologists, and wanderers." [30]

(6) Information Hog: A communicator is one who hoards the message or subject matter unnecessarily. Information hoarders are miscommunicators. Information hoarders retain information and thereby attract the attention of others on the ground that the communicator may have a secret message. In other words, it is called information hog. Hog means selfish or greedy like a miser. It is nothing but a verbal tease.

(7) Chatterbox: A chatterbox is a common communicator, whom we may come across in interpersonal situations. Chatterbox is a person who is talkative. Chatterbox speaks or talks quickly and noisily. He is a person who talks about unnecessary and unimportant things. He conveys needless information to too many people. A chatterbox generally does not maintain secrecy or confidentiality of the subject matter.

(8) Twister: "Twist" means to turn round and round. Twisting with reference to communication refers to transmitting information to others by twisting words and the theme. A twister in conversation tries to change direction of information transmission. The twister in communication is a dishonest or deceiving and unreliable person.

(9) Laughter: Laughter is a person who is addicted to laughing. A laughtering communicator is very fond of making sounds while in conversation and showing happiness and amusement. This communicator laughs in transmitting information, speech with full of happiness and fond of making irrelevant merriment. While speaking, this type of communicator cuts jokes needlessly or inappropriately while message to be transferred is a serious matter, and the listener or the listeners are in a serious mood. It has been rightly remarked by learned people that:

(i) "Never try to make people laugh at the wrong time or just for the sake of being entertaining — make the joke to teach a point." (Corwin's Law)

(ii) "Humour is okay; wit can be dangerous, wisecracking is disastrous." (Markel's Law)

(10) Vague Referencer: "Vague" means not clear, distinct, definite: and imprecise. "Reference" means to mention and the act of referring to someone. "Vague referencer" in communication is a person who acts or speaks or writes "as if to avoid a noun is to earn a fee." A man or woman either in singular or plural or about something in the message to which a speaker is referring used for reference. He uses ""they", or "it", "he", or "she" when a communicator of this type names certain person (s) or object (s). He makes reference to others without clarity or definite and not clear.

(11) Mumbler: "Mumbler" is a person who speaks indistinctly or in muffled tone. This communicator speaks words in such a way that it is difficult to hear. It appears that one is articulating sound with closed lips, indicating inability to speak or to utter a faint sound. It lacks strength, a mumbled indistinct utterance or sound or broken voices. The listener listens to the old man mumbling quietly to himself. The speech of a mumbler is inaudible. By speaking inaudibly, this type of communication compels the listeners to be careful and attentive to understand the message.

(12) Scarecrow: The literal meaning of the word "scarecrow" is a person employed for scaring birds, A device used for frightening birds from growing crops, usually a figure of a man dressed in old and ragged cloth. It is a figure set up in a field to create scare, to drive away birds and prevent them eating the seeds. With reference to communication, scarecrow communicator distracts the attention of the listeners from the message. He may use needless or inappropriate words, facts, body movements, gestures etc. "Scarecrow occasionally amuses, often exasperates, but rarely informs."[31]

(13) Wanderer: Scarecrow does impose at least a distraction upon a message. This communicator who specialises in transmission of messages to move about without a fixed course, aim or goal in conversation. This communicator while communicating move quickly from one subject matter to another and returns to the original theme, further jumps to another message and backtracks to another. Wanderer seems to roam over or across something. A wanderer transmits message without any fixed plan or purpose; without any clear idea about the message to be transmitted. A wanderer has a mental deviation with no definite destination or subject matter in mind. He does not transmit information to achieve the very purpose of communication. So, the speech is not organised and listeners sometimes get involved in confusion and cannot understand the message.

(14) Thunderer: Thunderers are addicted to give greater emphasis for thought and express feelings. "Thunder" literally means the deep rumbling sound heard in the sky after a flash of lighting. Tone of voice along with action all fit the words that are spoken. Sometimes, words also match actions of the thunderer. He makes a speech like a thunder. A thunderer exihibits greater emphasis on thought. Communicator of this type is likely to be ignored and singled out.

(15) Chronologist: The chronologist style is based on not directly with the importance of the message. This communicator is fond of or addicted to report facts according to the order or time. For instance, a manager asks his subordinate "What happened while I was away? This communicator habitually replies that at 11 A.M. he had a regular tea-break, at 1 P.M. he had a usual rest, at 2 P.M. an accident took place in the workshop etc.

OTHER COMMUNICATION TYPES

(1) Intra-management Communication

The expression "intra-management communication" refers to information exchange among the people who are on the same line "of authority. The word 'intra' refers to within or inside a particular channel, while the term "management" includes Executives or Managers. They are generally superiors to operation-level employees and subordinates to top-level strategic management. It is a system of communication which provides opportunities for the horizontal flow of communication. It is because of this horizontal travel, it is known as "horizontal communication." It facilitates exchange of information between Managers or Executives. Intra-management communication flows between functional heads like Sales Manager, Advertisement Manager, Production Manager, Marketing Manager, Personnel Manager etc.

Information exchange between them is necessary to take effective decisions in an integrated manner. The decision of one department may depend on the messages supplied by the other departments. Functional departments are inter-related to each other. Inter-departmental knowledge is necessarily to be possessed by the departmental Heads. Thus, management communicates with management or manager communicates with another manager. For instance, advertisement departments and sales department are inter-related. One function may be influenced by the other. There must be close relationship between sales planning and advertisement planning. The absence of intra-management communication may lead to contrary decisions, it creates confusion, effective decision is not possible, planned physical and financial taragets cannot be achieved. Thus, each department must have enough information and data which help them to formulate an integrated plan and to make correct decisions. Therefore, intra-management communication is very, necessary. Similarly, plant manager needs information about stores manager's information and *vice versa.*

(2) Anonymous Communication

The word "anonymous" with reference to communication means and used instead of the name of the person transmitting the message. A method of communication in which the name or identity of the communicator is not known. "Anon" is a short form of anonymous, without disclosing the name of the transmitter, the subject matter or information is communicated. The sender of the message wishes to remain anonymous. Anoynmous communication is possible both in written as well as verbal communication. An anonoymous author, an anonymous letter, an anoynmous telephone call etc. Pseudonymous letters are without signature or unsigned or without names which are false or ficitious or assumed.

Though it is a way of communication, it is reliable and dependable. Psudonymous letters are common to the editors of a press, in which the names of real authors may not be found. Sometimes, these letters may give useful and correct information or clues most common to Government agencies, like police, customs, tax-authorities etc. The policitical people even receive daily anonymous telephone calls or letters, giving valuable information, sometimes even false or threatening calls. People sometimes resort to this means informing an alleged attack, dacoity, planting a bomb, hijacking, kidnapping, abduction etc., because they think revealing their identity may endanger their lives.

The management should not ignore or neglect the anonymous information, it prevails in spite of its anonymity. It needs tact and intelligence to deal with such communication. It is not always good to treat pieces of anonymous messages as false or incorrect. Though not based on any proof or evidence or identity, such information supplies valuable clues for further processing of messages to find cut their reality or otherwise. In many cases, it is always true that some anonymous letters or calls are to be considered and weightage should be assigned.

(3) Communication in Offer and Acceptance (Negotiating Communication)

The concept of silence as a mode of communication has some legal significance, particularly in the law of contract. Legal doctrines speak on silence. The law of contract — particularly in the stage of acceptance of an offer, the element of silence on communication occurs. The effect of silence on acceptance has been greatly held. The acceptance of an offer cannot be implied from the silence of the offeree or his failure to answer, unless the offeror has by his previous conduct indicated that his silence means that he accepts. Communication of acceptance can be waived by the offeror. An offer sent through post may be accepted by post, unless the offeror indicates some other mode of communication.

Communicating silence as to facts has legal significance in fraud. Section 17 of the Indian Contract Act, 1872, defines the term "fraud." The explanation Section 17 reads: "Mere silence as to facts likely to affect the willingness, of person to enter into a contract is not fraud, unless the circumstances of the case are such that, regard being had to them, it is the duty of the person keeping silence to speak, or unless his silence is, in itself, equivalent to speech."

This means mere silence is not a fraud. A person before entering into a contract need not disclose to the other party the material facts which he knows but he must refrain from active misstatements. There are two exceptions to the explanation to Section 17.

(1) When the circumstances of the case are such that, regard being had to them, it is the duty of the person keeping silence to speak.

Example: F sells by auction to D, his daughter, who has just come to age, a horse F knows to be unsound. Here, the relation between the parties would make it F's duty to tell D that the horse is unsound. If F does not do so, it will amount to a fraud.

(2) When the silence is, in itself, equivalent to speech.

Example: A says to B, "if you do not deny it, I shall assume that the horse is sound." B says nothing. Here, B's silence is equivalent to speech.

Dr. Saul W. Gellerman who has emphasised on silent communication in the words "Motivation and Productivity", says: "The real communication between the manager and his men includes much more than the bald text of their conversation and correspondence. More importantly, it includes what is not said; it also includes shades of meaning and emphasis; and it even includes ambiguities into which the men can read whatever fits their pre-conception best. This subject form of communication between the leader and the led is all the more persuassive because it is largely unconscious, and therefore, neither edited nor analysed by either party, the leader is, therefore, likely to communicate a great deal more than he intends."[32]

(A) Offer: One of the essential elements of a valid contract is communication between the contracting parties. In order to become a contract, the elements of offer and acceptance must be communicated between the parties. According to the Indian Contract Act, a person is said to have made an offer or proposal when he signifies to another his willingness to do or to abstain from doing anything with a view to obtaining the assent of that other to such act or abstinence. An offer may be made by express words, spoken or written. This is known as an express offer. An offer may also be implied from the conduct of the parties or the circumstances of the case. This is known as implied offer. An offer may be a specific offer or general offer. A specific offer is one made to a definite person or class of persons. A general offer is made to the world at large. The legal rule, in so far as communication is concerned, is that an offer to be complete must be communicated to the person or classes of persons to whom it is made or in the case of a general offer to the world at large. Unless an offer is communicated, there can be no acceptance consent to make it a valid contract

The object of communication of an offer is to obtain in return response as the assert of the recipient of offer communication.

(B) Acceptance: Just communication of offer does not constitute a valid and effective communication, legally-binding and enforceable valid contract. The recipient of the offer communication must interact or respond as to its acceptance or rejection. An understanding emerges from the acceptance of an offer. Acceptance is an expression given by the offeree of his willingness to be bound by the subject matter of the offer so communicated. Where a person to whom the offer is transmitted signifies his assent, the offer is said to be accepted. Again acceptance may be express or implied. An acceptance is said to be express when it is communicated by words spoken or written or by doing some required act. It is implied when it is to be gathered from the surrounding circumstances or the conduct of the parties. The legal rule as to acceptance, to create a valid contract, to conclude a contract between the parties, the acceptance must be communicated in some perceptible form. There must be an external manifestation of the intention to be communicated. But, it is not sufficient a mere resolve on the part of the offeree to accept an offer.

Thus, an offer and its acceptance to be complete must be communicated. Unless an offer is communicated, it cannot be accepted. Similarly, an acceptance is to be communicated. An acceptance in ignorance of the offer is not acceptance and does not confer any right on the acceptor. The communication of an offer is complete when it comes to the knowledge of the person to whom it is transmitted. The communication is complete as against the proposer when it is put in the course of transmission to him.

Illustration (A): A proposes, by a letter, to sell a house to B at a certain price. The letter is posted on 10th instant. It reaches B on 12th instant. The communication of the offer is complete when B receives the letter, i.e., on the 12th.

Illustration (B): B accepts A's proposal, in the above case, by a letter sent by post on the 13th instant. The letter reaches A on the 15th instant. The communication of the acceptance is complete, as against A, when the letter is posted, i.e., on the 13th; as against B, when the letter is received by A, i.e., on the 15th.

Like communication of offer and acceptance, revocation (taking back) of an offer and acceptance must also be communicated. The communication of a revocation is complete as against the person who makes it when it is put into a course of transmission to the person to whom it is made.

(4) Honest Communication

Openness and frankness in the subject matter of communication is of utmost importance to create confidence among the readers or the listeners. The message should have characters of truthfulness, not cheating, stealing etc. The message should not cheat others. Honest communication involves a sense of obligation to one's self. Rightness is known by intuition in the mind. One of the noblest words among the social virtues is honesty. It is useful in considering the need for honest communication in every field of message transmission. Honesty in business communication reaches its most visible public-testing point in advertising, labelling and selling. The conviction has grown in recent years that business not only might but must enhance its reputation for trustworthiness in its public statements. The style of writing and speaking is important because gracefulness in the telling of facts makes them more pleasant to read or to hear. Communication of any effective sort needs to keep its purpose in mind. The message of what is said or written should be in harmony with subject and the occasion. The communicator must be careful of stating half-truths as whole truths. A remark has been in circulation that half a loaf is better than no bread but half a truth is not only not better than no truth, it is worse than some lies. Exaggeration which is either with form of ignorance or of dishonesty, weakens what we say and destroys confidence in our opinion. Bias is an enemy to honest communication, often in an insidious and unrecognised way. Honesty can be maintained only by the submission of individual judgements to general rules. Honesty in communication has three basic requirements and one's sensitivity; knowledge, facts, accuracy, and the desire to be honest.

Some of the rules of honest communication of ideas are: *(i)* When the speaker uses a sentence to make a statement, it is implied that he believes it to be true; *(ii)* He implies that he has what he himself believes to be good reasons for his statement; *(iii)* He implies that what he is saying is relevant to the interests and problems of his audience.

(5) Complementary Communication

A characteristic of communication is based upon the position difference or designation difference. In an organisation, all outside people may have different positions and accordingly different inter-personal relationships. Superior-subordinate, auditor-client, lawyer-client, captain-crew, teacher-taught, principal-agent, parent-children etc., are in complementary relationships. Because there is a difference and distance in position and interpersonal relationship, as a result the information, exchange between them is termed as complementary communication. In exchange between these combinations of inter-personal relationship, one is in a dominant position and another is in obedient and humble position. One has authority to exercise and another has to obey the other. In this relationship, one is more influential to command and to be more strong. Myers and Myers state that "one person is up, dominant and has authority; the other person is down, submissive, and has less or no authority"[33]

The relationship is equated as dominant submission. According to Watzlawick, complementary relationship may be implied by social and cultural context. Submission elicits authority; directing provokes obedience.[34]

(6) Symmetrical Communication

Symmetric means the state in which two parts are in equal size, shape, and position. The characteristic of symmetrical communication is that such communication takes place between persons who are equal. Friends and colleagues conversation is a symmetrical communication. "Symmetrical communication is based on similarities between people involved in relationships who tend to mirror each other's behaviour. Symmetrical communication provokes similar behaviour, generally love provokes love, hostility provokes hostility."[35]

(7) Public Communication

Public communication is opposed to private communication. A type of communication with the people in general, including a particular section of people. A way of transmitting message to the public. As the name suggests, a piece of public information, is the subject matter of which concerns the public and is, therefore, of public interest or importance. Written or verbal communication to the editor of newspapers on various current problems or grievance of the day. Dailies and periodicals generally reserve space for public opinion to ventilate grievances, suggestions etc. The subject matter of a public communication may cover public transport, railway safety, sanitation, hygiene tax matters, population problem, unemployment, pollution, politics and corruption. Public address system is generally used in oral public communication of public address, messages, appeals, welcome address, farewell speech, vote of thanks, appeals etc.

(8) Personal Communication (Private)

Information exchange between persons either inside the organisation or outside on personal or private matters is called "private" or "personal communication." Several informal matters may figure in private communication. Domestic matters, wedding, funeral, memorial, betrothal, upanayanam, dinner invitation, cradle ceremony, birthday and other messages on social matters. Personal communication may take place between the superiors, and subordinates and the communicators as well as between equals. There is no channel for the flow of information. It may be one-way or two-way personal communication. The personal communication can be effected through several methods such as spoken words, written words, physical expressions or significant gestures. To be effective, both transmission and reception of message must be there.

REFERENCES

1. The *Week*, Nov. 21, 1993, pp. 18-20.
2. *Ibid.*, pp. 20-21.
3. Balan, K.R., Rayudu, C.S., *Effective Communication*, Castle Books Pvt., Ltd., New Delhi, 1994. p. 149.
4. *Ibid.*, p. 149.
5. *Ibid.*, pp. 150-151.
6. *Ibid.*, pp. 151-152.
7. *The Week*, *op. cit.*, p. 21.
8. Robert Goyer, Charles Redding and James Rickey in their book, *Interviewing Principles and Techniques*, Kendall-Hunt Publishing Company, Dubuque, Iowa, 1986, pp. 7-8.
9. Zelko H., and Dance, F., *Business Professional Speech Communication*, p. 148.
10. Brown, L., *Communication Facts and Ideas in Business*, Prentice Hall, INC, Englewood, Cliffs, New Jersey, 1982, p. 406.
11. *Ibid.*, p. 396.
12. *Ibid*, p. 397.
13. Robert Minter, *The Hiring Interview, Supervisory Management*, 1974, p. 166. Quoted in *Communicating Facts and Ideas in Business*, Brown, L., p. 399.
14. Richard Huseman and Others, *Interpersonal Communication in Organisations*, 1976, p. 179.
15. Brown, L., *op. cit.*, p. 393.
16. Myers, M.T., G.E. Myers, *Management by Communication, An Organisational Approach*; McGraw Hill International Book Company, 1982, p. 283.
17. Brown, L., *op. cit.*, p. 40.
18. Myers and Myers, *op. cit.*, p. 281.
19. Adapted from the *Week*, *op. cit.*, pp. 30-34.

20. Nashif, A.M., 1981, *Communication Media — An Integral Part of a Distance Education Curriculum*. Paper presented to RSDTA, Penang, Malaysia. As reported in *Studies in Distance Education*, 1988, p. 102.
21. Sakamoto, Takash, *Use of Communication Technology in Distance Teaching at the University and College Level in Japan*. Paper presented to RSDTA, Penang, Malaysia. As reported in *Studies in Distance Education*, 1988, p. 102.
22. Balan, K.R., *Lectures on Applied Public Relations*, Sultan Chand & Company, New Delhi, 1984, p. 351.
23. Brown, L., *op. cit.*, p. 428.
24. *Ibid*, p. 361.
25. *Ibid*, p. 361.
26. Myers and Myers, *op. cit.*, pp. 171-174.
27. *Ibid*, p. 172.
28. *Ibid.*, p. 173.
29. *Ibid*, p. 174.
30. Wolf Keyser and Aurner, *Effective Communication in Business*, South Western Publishing Co., Cincinnati, Ohio, pp. 50-52.
31. *Ibid.*, p. 51.
32. Pradhan H., and Others, *Business Communication*, Himalaya Publishing House, 1978, p. 23.
33. Myers and Myers, *op. cit.*, p. 99.
34. *Ibid.*, p. 100.
35. *Ibid.*

*****

CHAPTER 3

Art of Listening

Fig. 3.1

Introduction

1. "Nature gave person two ears but only one tongue, which is a gentle hint that they should listen more than they talk.
2. Listening requires two ears, one for meaning and one for feeling.
3. Decision-makers who do not listen have less information for making sound decisions."[1]

"To listen actively to another human being may be the greatest gift you can give a person. The power to listen is a remarkably sensitive skill, perhaps we greatest tallenst of the human race. It is certainly a skill that makes interpersonal communication truly effective and rewarding for all concerns."[2]

Robert Frost says: "Half the world is composed of people who have something to say and can't, and the other half who have nothing to say and keep on saying it." There are four communication skills:

1. Reading
2. Writing
3. Speaking
4. Listening

The Art of Listening — It's not an easy talk".

"No one really listens to anyone else."

"Try it for a while, and you'll see why."

A poor listener can destroy the speaker's desire to talk or his confidence in his ability to communicate.

An interested listener can sway the direction of the "talk." Watching some speak is a real opportunity to understand that person.

Go on listening, however, prosaic or dull the speech may be. You may get at least one point from him — really valuable.[3]

GOOD LISTENING FOR IMPROVED COMMUNICATION

The Art of Listening

Listening is a very difficult thing to do. A cardinal mistake is to be so anxious to say what we want to say, that we are not really listening to what is being said. Very often when we are speaking to someone, we notice that he is not really listening, he is just waiting for us to finish so that he can say his piece. If neither person is listening to the other, there is a complete breakdown in communication. "We hear ourselves say something, the other person heard us say something, but interpreted what he heard in the light of his own experience and what we said in the light of our experience."

There is the simplest test of effective communication. When a serious impasse is reached in a dispute or an argument, the opponents in the argument should pause and then each in turn should try and repeat exactly the point of view of the other person. It will soon be discovered where the breakdown of communication really is.

Summing

If a company wishes to communicate with its public, staff, customers, shareholders, government, and the public at large, it must create an acceptable attitude in the mind of its public by planning and creating a favourable reputation. A favourable reputation will help establish an acceptable environment, in which acceptable communication can take place.

Rules

1. Perceive your power as a "listener."
2. A poor listener can destroy the speaker's desire to talk or his confidence in his ability to communicate.
3. An interested listener can sway the direction of his talk.

4. Ask questions: do not ask questions just to be polite but rather to clarify what is going on.
5. Reflect feelings that will show you understand what is spoken.
6. Do not be swayed by personal attitudes. Some of the biggest barriers to effective listening are the personal attitudes and prejudices that destroy what we hear.
7. Do not react subjectively. When you hear of government offices, you may immediately think of bureaucratic inefficiencies, for example. It is a subjective reaction that clouds the issue and damages the power of an otherwise perspective listener.
8. " Listen, or thy tongue will keep thee deaf."

And finally a simple example:

Ram : Shyam, is the message clear?

Shyam : Yes, Mr. Ram, the message was clear but I could't comprehend.

Ram : Shyam you said "the message was clear" and in the same breath you say that you couldn't fully comprehend. That means you have been only 'hearing' but not 'listening.'

"I shall now repeat the exercise...." "Please appreciate that the time I have up to communicate to and you to listen', has not achieved the expected result".[4]

Not, Not, Not Listening! Somehow No One is Listening

One of the major problems in the communication process is lack of or ineffective or inactive listening. Everyone is involved in listening, but everyone is not listening to as seriously as required.

Somehow everyone is not listening![5]

Supervisors complain that subordinates do not listen!

Subordinates complain that their bosses do not listen!

Parents complain that their children do not listen!

Children complain that their parents do not listen!

Teachers complain that students do not listen!

Students complain that teachers do not listen!

Somehow everyone is not listening.

Not listening to a speaker may lead to adverse consequences and make interpersonal communication truly ineffective and unproductive.

What do you hear most people complain about? Not being listened to:[6]

"I can't talk to my parents, they never listen."

"I can't talk" to my son, he just won't listen."

"I am quitting this job, my boss never listens to anything I say, it's as if I did not exist."

Managers and subordinates often complain about not listening or being poor listeners which results from various kinds of communication barriers, in addition to the educational system in which there is no lesson on "how to listen."

Workers are known to remark quite often that:

"The boss does not listen to me."

"No good feedback comes from the boss."

DO YOU KNOW THE OTHER SIDE OF THE COIN?

Effective speech is only one side of the coin of communication process. Communication process does not complete by mere transmission of messages. It is only one side of the coin. What about the other side of the coin? The other side of the coin is listening, and the skills for effective listening. Truly speaking, listening is the most neglected part and skill of communication process. But, actually, most people think that they are good listeners, just as they think they are good speakers. Both are different. An effective speaker need not always necessarily be an effective listener. Both speaking and listening have their own special features and specialised skills.

"The problem is not one of getting men to talk. The problem is one of getting leaders to listen." A good listener's mind is alert. His style of observation, his facial expressions and sitting postures usually reflect this fact. He may further show his interest by putting questions and comments. Putting questions, seeking clarifications, clearing doubts and other responses would encourage the speaker to speak effectively and express ideas fully.

Be a Good Listener [7]

The most subtle way to make a man feel important is to listen. Unless a salesman listens, he won't know which of the many features of his product to emphasise. It is very discouraging to tell a prospect all about our new state-of-the-art instrument only to have him say "I do not believe in buying the new products — come back after you have it in the field for two years."

Definitions and Views on Listening

K. Davis: "Listening is a conscious, positive act, requiring will power. It is not a simple, passive exposure to sound."

In a two-way communication, listening is the weak link. Many employees wear "listening ear-muffs."

Holy Bible: "Listen to counsel and receive instruction.

That you may be wise in your latter days."

"Cease listening to instructions, my son,

And you will stray from the words of Knowledge."

M.T. Myers and **G.E. Myers:** Active listening is "to listen to a person without passing judgement on what is being said, and to mirror back what has been said to indicate that you understood, what feelings the speaker was putting across."

Wendell Johnson: Wendell Johnson, a leading authority on communications, has said; "Our lives would be no longer and richer if we were to spend a greater share of them in the tranquil hush of thoughtful listening. We are a noisy lot and of what gets said among us, far more goes unheard and unhealed than seems possible. We have yet to learn on a grand scale how to use the wonders of speaking and listening in our own best interests and for the good of all our fellows. It is the finest art still to be mastered by men.

Rogers: Rogers states that listening reflects a whole orientation to life and people. This orientation implies that to listen is to have the creative power to imagine how it would make sense to say what the other person is saying.

Leland Brown: Listening is an activity that can be turned on and off consciously and unconsciously. It starts with the receiver's becoming aware that they should listen and become attentive to what is being said.

M.V. Rodriques: Listening is a process of receiving, interpreting and reacting to the messages received from the communication sender.

MEANING, NATURE AND IMPORTANCE OF LISTENING

The purpose of this topic is to present principles and techniques that will enable us to improve the art of listening skills. The following brief description will help us to improve our own listening abilities.

Listening is an art, a fine art. The art of listening is a very difficult thing in reality. It has far great importance. A manager spends approximately 50 percent of the day in communication. H. Nelson and others estimate that most of us spend nearly 60 per cent of our workday in listening.

A patient and attentive listening is a compliment to a speaker. Listener is the kingpin in the entire process of communication to whom actually the message is meant to understand, interpret correctly and to act accordingly. Hence, listening is one of the most difficult aspects of communication.

It has been happening that most of us are listening with no better than 35 to 55 per cent efficiency. Listening is a very hard task. In corporate management, managers are not good listeners. Nichols has estimated that when people listen to a ten minute talk, they operate at only 25 per cent efficiency. The process is really unfortunate but listening to the speaker's talk is one of the most important duty. It is the best method to learn about or evaluate the people.

There can be no mutual understanding without listening which is but the core of communication. In day-to-day life, most of us are involved in listening. We generally think of communication, particularly in the case of verbal communication, in terms of transmitting ideas, facts, opinions, exchange of information, expressing feelings honestly or being sincere or persuasive. But it is not so. Effective communication depends on having special talent, patience in listening. Effective and true communication is greatly dependent on the receptive side. The purpose of communication is to make others listen, understand and act accordingly.

There occurs misunderstanding when listening is not good and effective. In an organisation where group activities are involved, clear listening is necessary when information is transmitted. Poor listening may lead to gaps, conflicts, and resentment while in a family, communication gaps are bridged, conflicts disappear but in formal group activities, it is not so. Effective listening requires patience, presence of mind, interest and attitude. It is not an inborn trait or quality, but a skill to be acquired by practice, experience and training. The main reasons for poor listening are lack of clarity, jargon, lack of unity, speed, distractions etc.

One has to pay sufficient attention to listening and to listening comprehensively. The Royal Bank of Canada, Monthly Letter 1979, states that it has been estimated that the listening efficiency of people working in industry is less than fifty per cent, meaning that only about half of the oral messages passed around in the course of the day are fully understood.

Oral communication whether by word of mouth or oral or oral mechanical media, play a key role in all organisations and ways of life. The Monthly Letter also remarks that senior officers of major North American Corporations spend up to 80 per cent of their working time having meetings, discussions, face-to-face conversations or talking over telephone and, at the same time, listening is the most important function.

Listening is a process involving awareness, reception and perception. A common mistake is to anxious to say what we want to say, that we are not really listening to what is being said. It commonly happens when we are talking to someone, we observe that he is not really listening but only hearing. It appears that the listener is just waiting for the speaker to complete his speech so that the listening work is over or he can say his piece. Alternatively, if neither person is listening to the other, there is a complete breakdown in communication.

The listening ability of many people is not effective and active. There may be a variety of reasons for ineffective listening, which may vary from person to person and from region to region. There are people who are compulsive talkers. When a speech is monopolised, it blocks effective listening and feedback. As a matter of fact, communication is a process of exchange of information, it is the listening attitude that meets the end. Remember, after all, communication is a transactional process. Interpersonal communication involves negotiation of mutual meanings.

If interaction is one sided or if it is a one-way communication truly effective and rewarding exchange is not possible. People ego-centric or self-centred, usually monopolise and prefer always monologing constantly rather than exchange of information and sharing of mutual ideas through arbitrary symbols. Such type of people prefer only to speak and do not show interest to hear. While some others listen selectively, matters what interest them and disregard every other thing. Successful executives learn techniques how to hear their subordinates. When they allow subordinates to speak, they may listen about their jobs, their problems, feelings and suggestions related to their job-oriented problems.

But acquiring skills of effective listening is not an easy task. But it is crucial, Carl Rogers states that listening reflects a basic attitude about people rather than just a set of skills. So listening is a skill, not a trait, which can be taught, trained, and improved. Active listening according to them, should be firmly based on the basic attitudes of the listeners.

Listening is a fine art, it can be mastered by cultivation, consciously, carefully and systematically. Poor listening is one of the barriers to effective communication. According to one of the definitions given above, listening demands conscious efforts of interpretation of sounds received by the audio organs, grasping the meaning of the words. It requires attitude and attention to available sound signals and to interpret sound signals cognitively.

Unless conscious efforts are put in, the meaning of arbitrary words or symbols cannot be understood. Listening to a song sung by a girl or a television broadcast is quite an official routine business communication which requires much attention.

There are also some people who both listen and speak effectively. Such people facilitate better listening. One can improve his speaking by listening intently. The best listener may become a good speaker, too.

The real listening is that experience of being totally understood by another person. Real listening is a profound understanding, not merely of words being said, but of the experience and the meaning behind the words. Real listening produces results. In real listening, communication produces harmony resolves problems and dissolves feelings of separateness and promotes mutual understanding and public relations. It is a mutual experience of being known and results in partnership and a sense of well-being.

In families, when communication occurs, gaps are bridged; misunderstandings, conflicts and resentments disappear. In organisations, effective communication transforms a group into a team. It reduces effort, fatigue, boredom, and struggle. Work is accomplished more accurately and effectively as conflict and tension give way to co-operation and comradery.

TEST YOURSELF

Are you an active listener or a poor listener? To find out, give yourself this test.

As a person strikes conversation with you, pose this question to yourself:

"Am I really listening or am I thinking of what I wish to say next?"

Get down to self-examination and analyse your mental process.

Are you,

"Acting polite and faking attention?"

"Interrupting frequently?"

"Straying from the speaker's message?"

"Tuning out uninteresting subjects?"

"Drawing hasty conclusions?"

"Disapproving the speaker's views?"

"Thinking of your work schedule for the remaining part of the day?"

"Trying to put an end to the speaker's chatter by day-dreaming?"

"Thinking of what you want to say?"

If your responses comprise many of the above, you cannot be rated as an active listener. A random survey revealed that 85 per cent of those asked to assess themselves as listeners rated themselves as average or worse. Fewer than five per cent rated themselves as 'excellent' or 'superior'.[9]

HOW TO BE AN ACTIVE LISTENER

A listener receives message, decodes and interprets them. Business communications comprise purposive interchanges of opinions, ideas, reactions and information and the like to fulfil the goals of an organisation.

Communication — a combination of oral, written, visual and non-verbal — is used by the managers for conveying the information and influencing the workers. Influencing also involves motivating and persuading. In a progressive organisation, feedback from workers receives equal weightage and importance.

Ineffective listening comes from hearing only with our ears and not with our minds. Managers often complain about workers being poor listeners. Poor listening results from various kinds of communication barriers, in addition to the faulty educational system in which there is no lesson on *how to listen*.[10]

Are Managers Poor Listeners?

In many cases, managers are known to be poor, and ineffective listeners. Reasons are many such as they are faced with two extra barriers that impede listening. They are:

1. Managers, because of the authority pattern in an organisation, are used to give orders (workers as listeners are the subordinates). When they are expected to listen, and experience a feeling of being demoted or other punishments. Listening hurts their ego.
2. Listening requires managers to reverse the usual role of authority and initiative. Hence, they try to turn a deaf ear, thinking they are battling the threat of erosion of authority.

In an interesting survey conducted in the US in 1991 by the Council for National Register of Health Service Providers of Psychology, consumers were asked to score (on a scale of 1 to 10) a variety of health professionals on their willingness to listen.

The results are that health professionals scored relatively high because of their job entailed listening to people's feelings and problems.

Psychologists — 8.4

Clinical Psychologists — 7.5

Family Practitioners — 7.4

Pediatricians and physical therapists — 2.9

The willingness to listen or not can have tremendous implications on job performance.

One survey revealed that partially "human factors" were the cause of 8 out of 10 commercial airline accidents. A major cause was the inability to listen.

Studies conducted by communication experts show that bosses (managers and above) are terrible listeners. They are fond of listening to their own voices rather than to the grievances and problems of their juniors. Workers are known to remark quite often: "The boss does not listen to me" or "No good feedback comes from the boss".[11]

Who is a Good Listener?

This question was posed by a communication teacher. Here are the attributes people felt a person with good listening habits should have:[12]

He looks at me while I am speaking.

He seeks clarifications by asking questions.

He repeats some of the things I said.

He does not rush me.

He has poise and is emotionally controlled.

He reacts responsible with a nod, a frown or a smile.

He does not interrupt.

He pays close attention.

He keeps on the subject until I have finished my thoughts.

Modifying the Listening Style

There are four stages best understood as overlapping steps involving varying intervals of time, depending on the individual and such factors as personal motivation, learning experience and feedback. They are:

1. **Awareness:** Developing heightened awareness of one's listening habits, along with the desire to change.
2. **Internalising:** The action springs from a decision to modify one's listening behaviour and acquire more effective listening skills.
3. **Practising:** This is marked by the regular practice of effective listening skills, aided by self-evaluation and feedback from others.
4. **Integrating:** Habitual and unconscious use of effective listening skills, accompanied by life-long improvement in listening.[13]

Why Should One Listen to You?

If we are to improve our communication, we must try to learn what it is that makes the person with whom we wish to communicate, listen, if you want to tell him something, he will listen only if what you say interests him, is relevant to him and means something to him.

This is the basic premise of any communication activity: "What is in it for the listener?" It is absolutely no use making a statement or a speech or writing a notice or even a book if you do not take notice of what is in it for the listener or the reader.

What one wants to say is not important. What he wants to hear is all important. If you want some action to result from your communication, if you want the recipient to do something, then communication will stimulate the desired action only if it is couched in a language which can be understood and which give some benefit or satisfaction. If it does not take note of these two simple factors, then the communication will fail.

Make the Recipient Understand it was Important to Him

It is no good blaming the other man if he does not understand your message. The onus is on you to make sure that he does understand.

Managers talking to workers, trade union leaders, management, politician talking to voters, journalists talking to readers, students trying to communicate with the rest of us, and advertisers talking to customers, it is up to the speaker to make sure that the listener understands, accepts and perceives the importance of the message.

We must, therefore, base our speech not only on what we have to say but on what the listener wants to hear. We must try to learn not to show how clever we are by using words that the other man does not understand, he just switches off, he does not bother to listen. Avoid jargon, abbreviations or complex technical phrases.[14]

LISTENING BY SUPERIORS AND SUBORDINATES

Nearly half of the working time of people in business is spent in listening to:

1. The boss discussing instructions, information, goals, or performance.
2. Associates presenting ideas in a conference.
3. A manager, engineer, or associate giving a formal talk.
4. Associates passing information and expressing ideas in two-way verbal exchanges.
5. Salesman promoting products, services, systems, or ideas.
6. Telephone conversation.[15]

Subordinates are expected to listen from superiors on several matters relating to working aspects. In addition to the above areas and subjects for listening, the following are also some messages to be heard by the subordinates from superiors.

1. Listening to task directions or instructions on how to do the job.
2. Listening to messages, which produce an understanding of the task and its relationship to other organisational tasks.
3. Listening to information about policies, procedures, and practices of the organisation.
4. Listening in feedback on performance.
5. To listen to the managers to the suggestions, advice, for the improvement of work.
6. To listen philosophical information regarding the organisation's mission or orientation towards goals of the organisation.
7. To listen to get things done to specification.
8. To listen to prepare for changes.
9. To listen and understand correctly to discourage misinformation and suspicion.
10. To listen means making the people feel the pride of being relatively well-informed.
11. To listen to job instructions, job rationale, feedback and information.
12. Superiors to listen to subordinates seeking clarifications, clearing doubts, sharing work experience.
13. To listen to rumours to know the reasons for the spread of rumours.
14. To listen to union messages.
15. To listen in crisis to resolve problems.

WHY PEOPLE ARE POOR LISTENERS?

Some studies on communication indicate that 75 per cent or more of communications are verbal both of speaking and listening, and only 25 per cent are written both writing and reading. On the other hand, only 15 per cent of the information retained in our memories is received through our ears. The other 85 per cent is received through the eyes from the written words, or from the things we see. It is, however, a difficult task to measure precisely.

Studies also reveal that the time spent on communication activities by an average person is broken down as follows:[16]

Listening	45-per cent
Speaking	30 per cent
Reading	16 per cent
Writing	9 per cent

These figures show that people engage in a wide variety of occupation spent more time in listening to other people. Thus, the importance of listening has been greatly and widely recognised in recent years, particularly by those people who are involved in public relations, and a wide variety of occupations day in and day out. In educational institutions, emphasis is given more to training in the skills of writing. This is followed by reading and speaking. The least training they receive is on how to be an effective listener.

Despite the great time one spends in listening, the average person does not listen carefully.

In several of the large companies in the west, considerable weightage is given to a person's skill and ability to listen attentively before he is recruited for a job. The reason: an important responsibility of workers and officers in a business is to listen carefully and intelligently to those with whom they interact. Each day many hours are spent in listening to the instructions of the seniors, customer's orders, views and problems of the staff, discussions on duties and functions and other business-related matters. Better and effective listening habits do contribute towards enhancing chances of business success. A "high listening index" gets you a better rating for securing a job in the US and West European Countries. Training and practice can help improve listening skills.[17]

DIFFERENCE BETWEEN HEARING AND LISTENING

Many people take it for granted that they are effective listeners. One must make a distinction between listening and hearing. Often most people get confused with picking up sound vibrations, whereas listening is concerned with making a sense or meaning out of what people hear. On the other hand hearing is physical and listening is a mental process. The basic principle of effective listening is that unless the listener pays attention, has concentration, and is seriously concerned with the subject, interpreting and remembering the sound stimuli, he cannot understand the message of the speech.

Listening is the use of hearing when one is listening, it does not mean just hearing. It is a process of understanding of what is heard. Listening skills require the use of ears, brain, eyes to understand non-variable cues, with such additional insights like perception, attitudes, participation etc. Listening is with the mind and hearing is with the ears.

Thus, then is a clear distinction between hearing and the listening process. A speech is meant to be heard by the listeners instantly and clearly, as such it should be in a style to catch the ears and the eyes. Hearing is passive, while listening is active. Hearing involves just receiving sound signals or the message in the ears, but listening involves not just receiving stimulate into the ears but into the conscious thought, which requires efforts on the part of the listeners. So listening is a process of making evaluation and judgement of the thought, while hearing is only a simple reception of sound.

Ineffective listening comes from hearing only with the ears, and effective listening comes from listening only with the mind and not with the ears. Listening is more than hearing, but there can be no effective listening without hearing. Hence, effective listening is a coin with two faces, one is hearing and another is listening.

PRINCIPLES FOR GOOD LISTENING

1. Listen Patiently: The speaker is entitled to be heard, even if you feel his approach is wrong. A guide to the listener is to indicate simple acceptance by nodding, lighting your pipe or, perhaps interjecting an occasional 'um-hm' or 'I see.'

2. Understanding Speaker's Feeling: Better to understand the feelings of the speaker expressing his impulses. It is also equally necessary to understand his intellectual account. Effective, listening demand careful attention because most of the people have difficulty in talking clearly about their feelings.

3. Restatment and Summary: Restate the person's feeling, briefly but accurately. At this stage, you simply serve as a minor and encourage the other person to continue talking. Occasionally, make summary responses such as "you think you are in a dead end of your job, or you feel the manager is playing the favourites", but in doing so, keep your tone neutral and try not to lead the person to your pet conclusions.

4. Time for Discussion: It is a good principle to allow time for discussion to continue without interruption. It is also advisable to separate the conversation from mere official communication. In other words, do not make the conversation any more authoritative.

5. Common Cliches: Try to listen for what is not said — evasions for pertinent or perhaps too-ready agreement with common cliches. The omission of this type may be a clue to gather some more facts from the person.

6. Avoid Expressing Views: The sound principle for effective listening — try to limit the expression of your views because these may encourage or repress what the other person says.

7. Less Explanation: In effective communication, better results can be achieved by giving less emphasis to explaining and more emphasis to listening.

8. Rapport: It is a good principle to establish good rapport with the sender.

TYPES OF LISTENING

1. Marginal Listening: A listener has the capacity to listen four times faster than someone can talk. So the listener can use the extra time available to think about other matters than the subject matter given by the speaker. This is known as marginal listening.

2. Evaluating Listening: A listener while listening to a message, spares his time and thinks to judge and evaluate what is said by the speaker, and sometimes, form rebuttals to it. Evaluation of listening does not permit the submission of two opposing ideas.

3. Projective Listening: Projective listening is more commonly used in committee meetings and other types of group communication. It is a process to observe and understand what is said and to assimilate the viewpoint of the speaker. Listeners have to fully grasp the message and the emotional contents of the ideas. In this listening process, judgement-making is not an important aspect but an attempt is made to grasp the message before contradiction or further ideas. Listening to this type is more useful in solving complex problems and in using participative leadership tools.

4. Active Listening: Also called "emphathic listening." Every effective listening is effective or active which will be decided when the receiver understands the message or the subject of communication in the same sense and intention of the sender. It is a very difficult task to become an active listener unless one practices. Listening for feeling content is called active or emphathic listening.[18] Myers and Myers state that active listening consists of listening to a person without passing judgement on what is being said, and to mirror back what has been said to indicate that you understood what feelings that speaker was putting across".[19]

5. Passive Listening: In the case of passive listening, the listener just absorbs the information given like hearing a tape recorder.

6. Deliberate Listening: A listening is said to be deliberate when it is intended to comprehend the content of the message and to understand the feeling and context in which the communication is taking place.[20]

7. Fake Listening: Many listeners mistake silence for listening. They develop the habit of faking attention. They steadfastly fix their eyes on the speaker and try to project themselves as good listeners. They usually miss many important points made by the speaker.

8. Listening by Observation: It is a systematic and deliberate study through the eyes of spontaneous occurrence of feelings and actions of the speaker while talking. The aim of observational listening is to draw meanings from non-verbal cues. The listener observes carefully the facial expressions of the speaker, gestures, body language, nod, smile, and other mannerisms. It includes observation of punctuations like speaker's pattern of breath, sound, pause, cliches, etc. On observation, one may perceive stimuli as they are exihibited by the speaker.

Listening Process

Like communication, listening as one of the elements of communication, is also a process. Because it has some elements, such as:

(1) awareness.

(2) reception.

(3) perception.

Listening is an activity and every active listener and every passive listener is consciously or unconsciously involved. The following is a brief description of these three elements.

1. Awareness: Awareness stage of listening involves getting the attention of the audience so that they will listen. It is the responsibility of the speaker in part to draw the attention of the listeners. L. Brown states that "this responsibility involves using, when appropriate, unexpected stimuli, which will arouse curiosity and expected stimuli which will get agreement."[21]

Lee Thayer developed five basic principles for making people aware so that they will listen. They are:

(1) People will attend to those events (stimuli), external to themselves, which they assume might have some relevance to their personal goals and objectives, immediate or long-range.

(2) People will attend to those external or internal events which serve the unconscious, metabolic needs or "appetites" of the conceptual/ evaluating system itself.

(3) People will therefore, attend to those things which they can, but unattend to those things which are contrary or non-conforming in some way to their own model of the world or of their expectations about the future.

(4) People will attend to the unexpected. This is perhaps one of the few aspects of human and organisational communication for which Information Theory, as such, has relevance.

(5) Finally the relationship which exists between an individual and some object, event, idea or person in his environment will play some part in determining the attention he pays to it (or to the other person).[22]

Effective listening insists on what one perceives and corresponding responses resulting from perceiving. Some people suggested a communication diary to improve awareness. Listeners should follow the undermentioned guidelines:

(i) Look for area of interest.
(ii) Look for benefits, a need fulfilment or an objective,
(iii) Look for new ideas.
(iv) Note non-verbal cues.[23]

2. Receptive and Hearing: Sound waves carry symbols and ears pick-up the symbols, True listening will commence only when listeners are attentive and aware. It is the physical hearing with attention that precedes listening. It is the hearing which catches the sound through the sense of hearing. Sound waves receive the attention of the listener for interpretation and perception. Through the physical sense of hearing, one may put in data about oneself and his universe.

L. Brown has suggested the following responsibilities for the listener to be receptive and to hear.

(a) To Compensate for any physical hearing problem: A person who has hearing problem, it is advisable for him to move closer to the speaker. It is better to sit in the front line. Turn good hearing ear to the speaker's side.

(b) Concentrate on Ideas: Listeners are required to pay attention to the ideas what the speaker says. The guidelines are to keep the mind open, and to avoid skipping over ideas.

(c) Non-Verbal Cues: Message may have content as well as convey feelings. Listeners should not only hear the content of the message, but more with ears for non-verbal cues, such as tone, vice, sounds, body language, gestures, the stance, pause, feelings etc.

(d) Avoid Mind Wandering: The responsibility of the listener is simple. He should avoid mind wandering, avoid expectation of what is going to be said. It is not a sound principle of effective listening to jump to hasty conclusions.

(e) Adjusting Listening Pace: An average person can send the message at the rate of 125 words per minute. But an average person is capable of thinking four times faster. Therefore, the listeners have to adjust their listening pace with the speaker's pace.[24]

3. Perception: Perception is the capacity of physical senses that enlarge the quantity, quality and variety of stimuli that activate the working of mind. Thus, perception is the process of detecting stimuli by inputting data to the human being. The act of perception is the result of interpretation leading to understanding. On the other hand, interpretation is the process of attribution of meanings which requires logical reasoning, analysis and synthesis of data. The act of perception in oral message is also called oral perception like written perception, visual perception and audio-perception. Correct perceiving and understanding the message, depends upon various factors like knowledge, age, emotion, experience, attitudes. values, etc., which enable a person to draw a correct meaning of what one may hear. So perception is a process of physical hearing by sensory organs, sound waves carry the symbols and sensory organs pick up the sound signals.

PACING FOR LISTENING

The word "pacing" applies to the listener in the case of oral communication and to the reader in written communication. The word "pacing" means the rate or speed of movement. The word "pacing" with reference to communication means the rate of speed at which a listener receives and understands more readily the message in the case of oral communication. In a written communication, pacing refers to the rate of speed at which a reader understands more readily to a written message. The communication to be effective requires adjustment of listening or reading pace with the speaker's talking pace. The rate of speed in communication is very important. Speaking slowly and rapid fire talk are the common styles of speech.

Usually, a speaker may take time in the selection of words, formation of sentences and delivery of sentences. The amount of time taken may have much to do with the interest that the speaker may create among the audience. The optimum rate of speed at which a speaker delivers depends upon the situation, ideas or stimulus or the behaviour of the listeners. The average rate of speech is 120 to 150 words per minute. But the mind is faster than the speaker's delivery. The average person is capable of thinking at a rate nearly four times faster. It is, therefore, necessary to avoid being carried away by many thoughts and use extra thinking time to summarise and analyse what is said. But, however, the same rate does not apply to all situations. The speaker may lose audience when he speaks at a rapid fire rate. Similarly, audience cease to listen when the rate of speed is too slow. The listeners feel waste of time and then become uninterested. An optimum rate of speaking is advisable, and it is up to the speaker to decide according to the situation. In the case of written communication, the pacing for the reader may be introduced by adopting short sentences, familiar words, avoiding superfluous words, following unity, coherence, emphasis, clarity, completeness, accuracy, brevity etc.

OBSERVATION IN LISTENING

Observation is the most important and general technique of obtaining information and understanding the speaker. It is a systematic and deliberate study through the eyes of spontaneous occurrence of feelings exihibited by the speaker. The aim of observation is to draw meanings from non-verbal communication or non-verbal cues. Observation method alone is suitable to understand non-verbal cues. The features of observation method are observation of an event through the medium of eyes, definite aim, well planned and organized and noting observations. Uncontrolled observation, uncontrolled non-participant observation, participatory observation, controlled observation are the various methods of observation.

Effective listening requires the listeners to observe the speaker. Listening skills require separate observation. One is to observe carefully the facial expressions of the speaker, gestures, body language, nod, smile, pitch, voice tone and other mannerisms. It is also necessary to observe the punctuations of the speech. The punctuations are the speaker's pattern of breath, sound, pause etc. One should observe what is actually said instead of hearing only what listeners expect.

A speaker is not an expert noticer. To listen effectively, notice certain aspects which are generally overlooked or paid less attention. An effective listener usually searches for internal and external cues that signal:

Who

What

When

Where

Why and

How of the messages.

On observing an event, one may perceive stimuli as they exist in the real world. For instance, one can see a real world computer, hear its key board, monitor, and space bar. But when he reads or he perceives stimuli which stands for, or which represent actual objects or even events.

BARRIERS IN LISTENING

(1) Psychological Ear Muffs: One of the prevalent reasons for poor listening identified, has been the psychological ear-muffs. It is a state of split attention, and half-listening where full attention and clear understanding are necessary. People develop psychological ear-muffs to avoid unnecessary matters or details to be listened to. Psychological ear-muffs protect them from listening enormous amount of talk, manipulative matters, dull, trite, annoying and not interesting matters develop psychological ear-muffs. "But the habit of poor listening which is unconsciously formed for protection is carried over into situations where we really wish to listen but find that we just can't listen attentively and effectively." For instance, while witnessing and listening to a serious feature programme on a television, the television advertisement contributes to the temptation to develop psychological ear-muffs.

(2) Distraction of Mind: When listening to someone, it is sometimes difficult to be attentive because of distractions. The distractions can be external, internal, physical or mental. On such causes like personal mood of the speaker, place of sitting, thinking about a domestic problem, pressed time, hurried or worried noise, atmosphere etc., the concentration is not apt to be very effective. So distraction is yet another barrier to effective listening in the mind of the listeners themselves. While listening to a speaker on a particular subject, thinking on some other irrelevant and unwanted matter is a distraction. .

(3) Lack of Motivation: Lack of motivation is another major reason of poor listening. Listening costs time, physical and mental energy etc. Unless people are motivated, they do not expend energy, time etc. The lack of interest to listen is one of the serious impediments to effective listening. Unfamiliar speaker, unrelated subject, ineffective speech, lack of faith and confidence on the part of the speaker are the motivational factors. An old proverb says," A wise man can learn from a fool; a fool from a wise man — never."

(4) Wandering Mind: A listener may have a great deal of time while listening to a speaker's talk. It has been estimated that most speakers can send the message at 125 to 150 words per minute. Whereas the listening capacity of human organic system for oral communication is nearly 1,000 or more words per minute. Therefore, the listening capacity is more than speaker's capacity nearly by six times. So the listeners may have a lot of spare time and the mind wanders or takes mental excursion.

(5) Emotional Screen: When listeners try to listen to someone, they may find it difficult to concentrate because of emotional screen. Many people ignore the importance of emotional screen in effective listening. It works powerfully, and acts as powerful invisible screen that lets in the pleasant, the familiar, the desirable and shuts out the unpleasant. It develops from some natural tendencies like emotion, experience, beliefs, prejudice, fear, likes, dislikes, desires, bias, apprehension etc. These emotional instincts prevent one from effective listening and act as an impediment to listening.

(6) Rebuttal Instinct: The rebuttal instinct is a destructive invisible weapon and invisible steel walls. Many people in meetings fall into this destructive habit. It is a deadly enemy, most common in the case of interpersonal and small group communication. Rebuttal is a statement proving that something that has been said is wrong and gradually leads to quarrels.

(7) Jumbled and Mumbled Words: Effective listening is not possible when the spoken words are mumbled and jumbled. Some speakers are habituated for known reasons to mumble words. It means to speak in such a way that they find it difficult to hear. The term jumbled words with reference to oral communication refers to confused mixture of words. It is a mixing or throwing together without order.

(8) Self-Evaluation: A basic problem in effective listening is the tendency of the listeners to evaluate in terms of their, rather than, the speaker's frame of reference. The listener's prejudices and beliefs are cured by the words, or the speaker may inhibit transmission of information between the parties.

(9) More Thinking than Listening: Many people can think a great deal faster than a speaker can speak. The mind of the listeners wanders speedily and too far and lose the speaker completely. A good listener does not let his mind drift away from what the speaker has to say.

(10) Listening Only for Words: Another major barrier to effective listening is that some people sometime give importance only to listen to words rather than their meaning or ideas. Some people even attempt to memorise the specific sequence of words used by the speaker.

(11) Taking Notes: It is common habit of the people to take notes of the speaker's message. Thus, people may reduce their listening capacity by taking detailed notes. A good listener's approach is to listen carefully and write down only the points or leading ideas. It is a common experience that a bad listener may rationalise his habits and express some reasons for not listening, but they are often used to soothe the conscience of the lazy listener.

(12) False Listening: Pseudo-listeners make the speaker believe that they are listening or have listened. They appear to be listening but not actually involved in the process of listening, interpretation and understanding the message. They exhibit eagerness and intense look and put a periodic comment or a question, which is the usual technique.

(13) Monologing Attitude: In a real life situation and interpretational communication, we come across people who are ego-centric or self-centred. Such people prefer monologing frequently instead of sharing conversation with others. Monologue is a long speech by one person who always feels to be heard and neglects about hearing others.

(14) Selectivity Listening: Still some people are always selective when they listen to a speaker's talk. They concentrate and pick out only those aspects, which interest them and reject other things. Listening is crucial but still, there are some people who may listen to what they want to hear. For instance, a person may pretend to be listening only to avoid the situation. They listen only to what they want to listen. Similarly, an executive who dislikes to hear a problem exhibits as if he is actually listening.

(15) Listening Defensively: Some other people may be very sensitive. Such type of people take everything as a personal attack. So many people may listen defensively. It is a barrier to effective listening.

(16) Noise: Noise is anything that hangs like a cloud over the entire communication environment. Noise is anything that distracts the listener from understanding a message, clearly as perceived by the sender. Communication noise cannot be ignored as one of the barriers to or problems in effective communication. Distraction of various types prevent concentration in active listening. Physical noise, technical noise, visual noise, cultural noise are examples of communication noises.

(17) Poor Perception: If the message received by the listener is not perceived in the same meaning as perceived and intended by the speaker produces a barrier to active listening. If signals of message are not understandable by the listener, truly effective communication is not possible. Incapacity of listener due to inadequate knowledge of the language used by the speaker is a great problem in the art of successful listening.

(18) Deaf Spots: Emotional block is called "deaf spot" which prevents a person from taking in and retaining certain ideas.

(19) Closed Mindedness: The expression closed mind refers to the thinking tendency of the people that they know everything about the issue and inhibits communication. They do not open their minds to new ideas that are placed before them.

(20) Entering into Arguments: Sometimes, a message perceived and delivered by the speaker may create a desire to enter into a good argument against the speaker's point of view. Such a situation may generally occur when a speaker makes a controversial or sensitive or personal reference or statement which may conflict with the listener's view. A listener may get excited and in great temptation gets involved in arguments.

(21) Wandering Attention: This type of listener while listening, mentally moves quickly from one subject matter to another or from one thing to another and return to the original theme, further jumps to another matter and backtracks. He seems roaming over or across something. He listens without any fixed plan or purpose, without any behaviour about the message to be responded to. A wandering-listener has a mental deviation without any definite destination.

(22) Lack of Interest: Showing lack of interest, the speaker's talk is a barrier to effective listening. Rejecting the speaker, considering a message or impulse dull or boring or lack of new message or little useful matter etc., are the causes for exibiting lack of interest.

BAD LISTENING HABITS

(1) Calling the subject uninteresting: Instead of turning in first and seeing if the speaker has something worthwhile to say, the listener assumes from the start that the topic will be boring.

(2) Tuning the speaker out because of his delivery: The listener allows delivery to take precedence over content.

(3) Getting Overstimulated: The minute the listener hears something with which he or she disagrees, the person stops listening and starts fuming, thereby missing the rest of the message.

(4) Concentrating only on facts, to the exclusion of principles of generalizations: Facts do not always present the whole picture. Principles and generalizations are often necessary to put everything in its proper perspective.

(5) Trying to outline everything: Some speakers are less organised than others, and until the individual gets into the presentation, it can be difficult to follow him or her via an outline. Good listeners are flexible in their note taking.

(6) Faking attentiveness.

(7) Allowing distractions to creep in.

(8) Tuning out difficult or technical presentations.

This often occurs when the managers are listening to financial or quantity oriented reports.

(9) Letting emotional words disrupt the listening process: Any time when a word evokes emotion, there is a good chance that listening will be interrupted.

(10) Washing thought power: Most people speak at the rate of 125 words per minute. However, the brain is capable of handling almost five times that number. If the speaker goes on for more than a few minutes, it presents a temptation to the listener to wander, mentally, returning only periodically to check in and see where the speaker is[25].

Behavioural scientists identify certain factors that are responsible for poor listening habits. Their findings are as follows:

(11) Listening attitudes in early life: Our listening attitudes and behaviours are formed quite in early life. These presuppositions have a long lasting influence on most individuals.

(12) Influence of parental models: Our listening habits are shaped partly by the parental models we have grown up with.

(13) Authoritarian parent: Children who have grown up with authoritarian parents often learn poor listening habits.

(14) Homely atmosphere: Good listeners are largely those children who grow up in homes in which parents are warm and accepting, who explain family rules and invite verbal give-and-take. When parents listen, children feel appreciated and worthwhile. They are more likely to become good listeners' later on.

(15) Negative listening messages: Parents and teachers unknowingly send negative messages about listening. Consider these reactions:

The common refrain of these statements is that listening is something you shall have to do; it becomes a form of compliance.

(16) Powerless and submissive behaviour: When listening becomes a duty, listening is associated with powerless and submissive behaviour. It is natural for this feeling in a child to result in resistance to listening.

(17) Defensive mechanism: The resistance to listening, i.e., the act of not listening, becomes a defensive mechanism, a behavioural pattern of the underlings to assert their power.

(18) Practice of resistance: The resistance becomes a way of safeguarding one's autonomy and self-respect (although, in the long run, the attitude turns self-defeating).[26]

ERRORS IMPEDING UNDERSTANDING

A study of Campbell reveals the following sources of systematic errors which impede understanding:

(1) Length of the Message: The length of the message would result either in loss or retaining of message. Necessarily, the listeners tend to shorten, simplify and eliminate the details of what they listen to a message. Consequently, it may produce a loss of information and accuracy. The longer the message, the greater the loss.

(2) Middle of the Message: Listeners tend to be the best/the first or last part of the message. Usually, the middle of the message is least remembered.

(3) Round-off: Listeners are good tailors who frequently tend to tailor messages according to their own need, requirement or beliefs. Listeners tend to make message perception. The systematic error of round-off as a message often distorts the true content and meaning of the message.

(4) Fast Haunting Imperfectly Transmitted Messages: Generally listeners will perceive all unclear or ambiguous messages either in terms of positiveness or negativeness. If the message has positive things in the past, it will also be perceived to be positive. If the source has said usually negatively on the topic, the message will be judged negative as well.

(5) Reductive Nature of Listening: As observed in the above point, the past message affects listeners' perception in the positiveness or negativeness. So they allow previously expressed ideas to colour their interpretations. Once listeners heard what the speaker has had to say before, they know what the speaker says now. Thus, they are now in reductive nature of listening or simply does not listen.

(6) Hearing What One Expects to Hear: Listeners always tend to hear what they expect to hear. In this situation, the listeners rather than ceasing to listen, continue listening, but this error distorts the message received.

(7) You Agree With Me: The listeners, particularly when confronted with an admired or respected source, often modifies the message so that it more closely coincides with her or his attitudes or beliefs.

(8) Black and White Listening: The listeners in the process of listening tend to polarise the words, seeing things as either good or bad, right or wrong, beautiful or ugly, and to evaluate the message in terms of these extremes.

(9) Filtered Listening: Often we tend to filter the message through the attitudes held by the groups with which we identify. We let the group members tell us what to think or how to interpret the message rather than relying first upon our intelligence.

GUIDELINES FOR EFFECTIVE LISTENING

Listening is a fine art, and everyone should develop effective active listening skills. The success of effective listening depends on the talk worth listening. This is crucial to good oral communication. Delivering a listenable talk will command and hold an audience's attentive listening. This paragraph deals in brief with the subject which is almost the sole content of some listening course, how to develop effective active listening skills. The useful hints given below help how to make one hear, listen and understood by all the listeners in a lecture or meeting room. Common guides and practice drills are covered for improving communication skills. The following guidelines are the techniques to overcome poor listening habits and to accomplish an effective listening and improved listening.

(1) Eye Contact: When one of the audience does not look at the speaker, it means, he is not interested in listening. A listener must exhibit a behaviour of making eye contact. It encourages the speaker.

(2) Bodily Exhibitions: A listener must show himself that he is interested in listening. Non-verbal signs can be used to exhibit affirmative head nods and appropriate facial expressions, eye contact etc., convey certain things to the speaker.

(3) Avoid Distracting Actions or Gestures: Avoiding actions, mental presence etc., are some other measures of exhibiting interest in listening. Looking at one's own watch, shuffle papers, playing with pencil, reading newspaper or letters, and other distracting activities should not be practised.

(4) Ask Questions: An effective listener always asks questions, clarifies doubts, seeks explanations, and ensures clear understanding. This makes the speaker realise that he is really listening.

(5) Paraphrase: Restating in one's own words what the speaker is said is called paraphrasing, for instance, "Do you mean", "What I hear you saying is" etc. There are two important reasons for paraphrasing or restating the same what the speaker has said. Firstly, unless one is listening carefully and attentively, he cannot paraphrase, so it acts as a check or control over listening. Secondly, it ensures accuracy.

(6) Avoid Interpreting Speaker: Good listeners interpret the speaker after completing his speech.

(7) Do Not Overtake: Some people instead of listening to the speaker "till he completes his version", speak their own ideas or points. Listening is the price one has to pay to get the people talk. An effective listener will never overtake the speaker. One cannot talk and listen at the same time.

(8) Put the Speaker at Ease: By your attitude, help the speaker become relaxed and aware of a willing listener. Be not only seen to listen, but felt to listen. And use eye contact.

(9) Listen Patiently: The speaker is entitled to be heard, even if you feel his approach is wrong.

(10) Avoid Premature Arguments: Don't interrupt to question or argue about facts, "That's not so..." "prove it..." and other such interjections only serve to abort the discussion.

(11) Stay Objective: Try to avoid emotional involvement; simply try to understand the feeling, or the 'point of view' of the speaker. Do your evaluation later.

(12) Avoid Mental Rebuttals: Too much time is spent mentally preparing a rebuttal or counter argument, instead of listening. Let the speaker finish before you reach a decision.

(13) Remove Distractions: Don't doodle or play with papers, pencils or anything else. What about shutting a door or window to eliminate extraneous sound, or turning off the radio?

(14) Indicate Acceptance: An occasional 'yes' or 'I see' or even a nod of the head indicates attention. It can also acknowledge what is being said (not necessarily agreement).

(15) Hold your Temper: An angry person almost inevitably gets wrong meanings from words. Anyway, any fool can lose his/her temper. It takes a real person to keep it.

(16) Respect Pauses or Silence: It is all too common for us to "jump in" when the speaker passes. Silence is an embarrassment for too many people. Don't fall victim to this fault.

(17) Redirect a Direct Question: With few expectations, this helps a great deal if the speaker asks, for example, "what do you think I should do?" the reply might be "what do you think you should do?" Be on guard against too much of this, that might be frustrating. It is always better to avoid direct questions and arguments about facts. It is advisable to refrain from saying, "that just is not so", "hold on a minute," "let's look at the facts review" or "prove it." You may want to review evidence later but it is irrelevant to how the person feels now.

(18) Be Honest with Answer: When faced with a genuine request for your opinion, give it honestly (if you have enough information to do so).

(19) Listen between the Lines: What is not said is not important. Be alert to this: attitudes, moods, feelings often convey far more than words. It calls for a strong feeling of empathy on the part of the listener. Try to find the right "wavelength."

(20) Listening Habits: One should be aware of listening habits. Emotions often affect our listening ability. Introspection will tell you that if a speaker says something you like, you hear everything. If the speaker says something to which we are opposed, we become indifferent. Listen and understand the viewpoint of those you disagree with.

(21) Listening a Personal Risk: Active listening involves personal risk. If you hear the person out, you risk being changed yourself. Momentarily, you set aside your beliefs and see the world as he sees it. Have the courage to risk your opinions by listening actively to an opposing point of view. Have an open mind.

(22) Listen to Total Meaning: Listen to the total meaning of the message being communicated. Don't assume and don't pass judgement quickly.

(23) Observe Non-verbal Cues: Search out the main points. Observe the non-verbal cues like tone pitch, physical gesture, etc., which too convey meaning to the message. A listener may note them down as these will help in revealing if the speaker appears to be sincere in his views.

(24) Avoid Fake Attention: Many listeners mistake silence for listening. They develop the habit of faking attention. They steadfastly fix their eyes on the speaker and try to project themselves as good listeners. They usually miss out many important points made by the speaker.

(25) No Personal Bias: It is always desirable to drop personal biases and attitudes about a speaker and his views. Listeners often prematurely dismiss lectures as uninteresting. They assume so and let their mind wander.

INSIGHTS INTO LISTENING

In addition to the various guidelines and suggestions offered above, the following are the additional insights which should be followed for effective listening:

(1) Monopolising Speech: People who continuously speak interrupt effective listening. They obstruct valuable feedback and exchange of information. When everyone talks, none listens but a few hear.

(2) Attitude: Everyone should develop an active and effective listening attitude. It is this attitude that affects one's listening.

(3) Attention: It is suggested to focus attention upon the oral message and the speaker.

(4) Response to Questions: Sometimes, listeners may confront to give answers to questions. It is advisable for effective listening to respond with pertinent and relevant questions or comments concerning the data and their intended interpretation.

(5) Rapport: Effective listening requires to reinforce rapport by listeners' own behaviour. Listening postures, facial expressions, and gestures are parts of feedback languages.

(6) Participation: One can develop listening attitude by active participation in the communication event. If the listeners are inactive in participation, the less informative listening is likely to be. Activeness can be reinforced by responding verbally or in writing or with silence.

On developing one's listening attitude, the listener will become aware of these communication insights also. They are:

(1) Effective listening to data and to the style of presentation acquaints you with interests, needs and values of your associates or customers.
(2) Effective listening provides cues to personalities, biases, abilities and resources.
(3) Effective listening thereby enables you to deal more profitably with co-workers, with customers, and with competitors than you might otherwise do.[27]

It is by appreciating the limits of the listener's perception that communication can be improved:

He sees what he wants to see.

He hears what he wants to hear.

He does what he wants to do.

What he sees, what he hears and what he does are limited by his degree of perception, by his experience, his educational background, his environmental background and his way of life.

TYPES OF LISTENER OR AUDIENCE

The authors like Elizabeth Andersch, Lorin Staats and Robert Bostrom in their works portray eight easily identifiable categories of listeners. They are quite a cast of characters and there are many more types of listeners. Better if a speaker knows them and understands them.

(1) The Sleeper: (*a*) He seeks a restful haven in a relatively quiet hall. (*b*) He has no intention of listening. (*c*) He is irritated if there are disturbances. (*d*) His eyes are closed as he sits, or rather reclines in his seat, (*e*) His blissful repose is reflected in his face.

(2) Eager Beaver: (*a*) He keeps smiling and nodding, (*b*) His eyes have a strange, slightly out-of-focus appearance, (*c*) His energies are directed to impress the speaker with what a good listener he is — a real waste, (*d*) The same energy, if properly channelised, could result in effective listening.

(3) The Tiger: (*a*) He is ready to pounce on everything the speaker says. (*b*) He is occupied with looking for trouble. (*c*) One can see it in his crouching position, leaning forward, eyes flashing with alertness of a big cat. (*d*) He silently snarls as he hears his first bone of contention.

(4) The Shy, Bewildered: (*a*) He has never quite found out what the lecture is all about, (*b*) Pained, quizzical glances from him are a constant reminder to the speaker that he must go slowly, repeating and reinforcing important information.

(5) The Frowner: (*a*) His forehead has a perpetual furrow, (*b*) He seems always on the average of a question, (*c*) His expression is an accurate reflection of his state of mind, but often it is a facade of attention.

(6) The Relaxed: (*a*) He seems to stay awake, but slips down in his chair, rests his head on the back of it. (*b*) He stares fixedly at some object or person. (*c*) There is little tension in him. (*d*) There are no visible means of reading him. (*e*) He never seems to react to anything that is said, either negatively or positively, (*f*) He is a real problem for the speaker.

(7) Busybee: (*a*) He listens and impresses by writing letters, 'buzzing' with neighbours, sneaking glances at magazines, cleaning fingernails, combing hair and so on. (*b*) He is not a listener in the true sense but is a potential auditor in a captive audience, (*c*) He will motivate the speaker causing him to try various devices to capture his attention.

(8) Two-eared Listener: (*a*) He listens with his ears and mind, (*b*) He actively participates, (*c*) He reacts objectively, (*d*) He decodes and evaluates carefully, (*e*) He is a model which all of us should follow, (*f*) His eagerness is reflected in his body tension, standing or sitting postures, (*g*) His face reflects agreement or disagreement, interest, question, approval and other attitudes resulting from thoughtful, objective consideration of messages.[28]

REFERENCES

1. K. Davis, *Human Behaviour at Work,* Tata MacGraw Hill Publishing Co., New Delhi, p. 413.
2. M.T. Myers and G.E. Myers, *Managing by Communication — An Organisational Approach,* McGraw Hill International Book Company, 1982, p. 171.
3. K. R. Balan and C. S. Rayudu, *Effective Communication,* Castle Books Private Ltd., 1994, p. 45.
4. *Ibid.*, p. 45.
5. Myers and Myers, *op. cit.*, p. 168.
6. *Ibid.*, p. 171.
7. K. R. Balan and C.S. Rayudu, *Public Relations in Action,* Castle Books Private Ltd., 1994, p. 13.
8. Leland Brown, *Communicating Facts and Ideas in Business,* Prentice Hall, Inc., Englewood Cliffs, New Jersey, 1982, p. 380.
9. *The Week, Hoi.* 21, 1993, p. 6.
10. *Ibid.*, pp. 8-9.
11. *Ibid.*, pp. 8-9.
12. *Ibid.*, p. 9.
13. *Ibid.*, p.10.
14. C. S. Rayudu, K. R. Balan, *Principles of Public Relations,* Himalaya Publishing House, Mumbai.
15. Glenn J. Cook, *The Art of Making People Listen to You,* Vikas Publishing House, Pvt., Ltd., New Delhi, 1976, p. 5.

16. R. G. Nichols, *Listening: What Price Inefficiency,* pp. 15-22.
17. *The Week,* Nov. 21, 1993, pp. 5-6.
18. Carl Rogers, *Communication: Its Blocking and Facilitating,* North Western University Information, Vol. 20, pp. 9-15, 1952.
19. Myers and Myers, *op. cit.,* p. 171.
20. Charles M. Ķelly, *Empathetic Listening, A Small Group Communication: A Reader,* 1974, pp. 340-348.
21. Leland Brown, *op. cit.,* p. 381.
22. Lee Thayer, *Communication and Communication Systems,* Homewood, III, Irwin, 1969, pp. 51-54.
23. Leland Brown, *op. cit.,* p. 381.
24. *Ibid.,* p. 382.
25. *R.. G.* 1959, PP- I[5’22’]
26. *The Week op. cit.,* pp. 6-7.
27. Wolf Keyser Aurner, *Effective Communication in Business,* South Western Publishing Co., 1979, pp. 26-27.
28. *The Week, op. cit.,* pp. 22-24.

CHAPTER 4

Effective Writing

WRITING IS A CRAFT[1]

If you keep in mind the two principles, clarity and precision, and write simply and naturally, you may disregard the tyranny of small critics. You do not write effectively merely by obeying the rules of grammar and syntax, but before you break the rules, you should know what they are.

Skilled writers study words so that they use those words, fittingly and they consider the most effective way of putting them together. They observe how words affect the thinking and acting of people.

The urge to "write as you speak" can lead to a trap. It can put into letters or print too much racy speech; the resulting prose will be either an enemymaker or something to be laughed at; if one writes as loosely as he talks, his letter or essay or report will command little respect.

In any sort of composition meant to communicate ideas the writer must consider his purpose and the needs of the reader. It is irrational to sit down with a pen and paper to write something that will be worth the effort unless you know: (1) what you wish to say, and (2) to whom you wish to say it.

It may be taken for granted that the person receiving a letter will learn something like this : What is this letter about? How does it concern me? Is this statement true? What does the writer want me to do? Why should I do it?

Creative writing is a bridge between the mind of the writer and that of his reader. Across this bridge, the writer must send information of interest to the reader and ideas which will stir him to thought or action.

The words sent across the bridge have meaning only when they are understood in depth and breadth by the person reading them. A word or a sentence is not merely a bundle of sounds: it is also a bundle of associations. Most of the time, people cannot grasp out points unless they are able to connect it with their own experience.

People respond readily to some words while remaining indifferent to others. Try to use words and language that will affect your correspondent as you wish him to be affected. Take into your account the perception range of your reader: are you sure that he will read out of your letter the thoughts that you mean to inspire him with?

If your subject is difficult, if you must take your reader through swampy land, at least throw him a rope. Give him some help toward reaching solid ground. There are times when persuasiveness consists in saying things that leave the reader believing that is just the way he would have said them himself. But be tactful: Do not remind him that he didn't.

Anyone writing for a wide audience must pay attention to the possible peculiarities and dislikes. An enumerator making his rounds of households before a British general election said; "A number of people can be thrown by being asked what sex their children are. They would look affronted at the word 'sex.' By and by I learned to rephrase the question as "have you got any little boys or little girls"?

Meaning of Written Communication

Another important category of communication is written communication. In the case of written communication, every message is in black and white. It is the best method when the communicator and the recipient are beyond oral communication media. The executives in all organisations can maintain effective inter-departmental and intra-departmental connection through messages by written words. The process of communication involves sending message by written words.

Conveying information by writing, typing, printing or other mechanical means. The words "get in touch with others", which speak something common with someone. This media ensures exchange of facts, ideas, opinions through a written instrument by which the individual or organisation come in touch with each other and share meaning and understanding with another. In other words, it transfers information to others. Written communication has mostly and primarily been used as a medium to pass information and ideas upwards, downwards, communicating with people outside, reviewing and interpreting and to motivate and activate work.

Written communication covers all kinds of subject matter like notices, memos, deeds, resolutions, suits, plaints, affidavits, complaints, pleading, conveyancing, reports, financial statements, appointments, promotions, cost sheets etc., particularly in the function of directing and leadership. This written communication simply means a process of reducing message into writing which is extensively used in organisations. Formal communication, must always be in writing such as rules, orders, manuals, policy matter, resolutions and minutes. In some cases, written communication is the only way out.

Objectives of Written Communication

The systematic filing of written communication is one of the important aspects of communication. Filing along with indexing is necessary because of the limitation of human mind and memory. The object of preserving written messages is to provide necessary information readily and without any delay and when it is needed. However, the following are the main objectives of keeping the messages:

(1) Future Reference: The limitation of human mind and poor memory cannot be overlooked. The change of seats on account of transfer of employees also causes problems. Written messages can be preserved as records and reference source. Various media of communication can be filed for future reference. Thus, keeping records are essential for continuous operation of the business.

(2) Record of Evidence: Words of mouth are not believable and in a number of cases, oral messages have no legal sanction. Written messages have capacity of being stored as record. At times the records can be used as evidence. Papers can be produced as proof in the case of dispute of communication.

(3) Measurement of Progress: Properly-filed messages are useful to know the progress of the concern. The records provide relevant and basic information; from this, it is possible to know the progress of the organisation. It also facilitates comparison with previous years and also comparison with other firms. In other words, filing messages serve as a barometer of progress which supplies information for the purpose of preparation of annual reports and other periodic reviews.

(4) Precedents: Maintenance of communication provides the necessary information on earlier activities and decisions. Best messages are helpful for future decision-making. They may act as a guide or rule in the future. In making decisions, the decision-maker has to follow a precedent set in the organisation earlier.

(5) Avoiding Mistakes: In transmitting messages, earlier records help in reducing mistakes and errors. So there is no need for correction, issue of amended messages, instructions, clarifications and explanations. Effective internal control is possible. So keeping of and maintaining written messages minimise the chances for errors and prevents the occurrence of fraud.

(6) Effective Decision-Making: Old documents help effective decision- making in a great way. Decision-making process becomes easier if old records are available. Because the messages provide the necessary information for decision-making purposes. Decisions may go wrong if the old communications are not followed. Past records may serve as a guide to the decision-making process.

(7) Organisational Efficiency: Organisational efficiency cannot be achieved with confusion and lack of guidance. The records are most useful which guide the employees to take decisions to motivate and for effective internal control. Prepare classification of messages and a suitable filling system. Indexing in this respect would be helpful in making its use towards organisational efficiency.

(8) Legal Requirements: There are certain documents which are required to be preserved compulsorily under the provisions of different legislations. To meet legal requirements, the documents should be preserved and maintained. For instance, the maintenance of certain records and books are compulsory under the Indian Companies Act, 1956 and Banking Regulation Act, 1949 etc.

Essentials of Effective Written Communication

Every written communication has to try to incorporate the basic essentials in every writing. The purpose of writing is to make the recipient to understand the message. Formal communication is mostly written to keep links with officially designed positions in the organisational structure. The inter-departmental, intra-departmental links and links with outside agencies are always in writing. The broad objectives, policies for their accomplishment are transmitted in writing.

As such, written communication occupies an important position in the communication sphere. So the transmitter or sender has to pay adequate attention to certain principles. Necessarily, the essentials of every written communication are principles of units, coherence and emphasis. These principles, along with other essentials of effective communication like language, planning and organisation, make the written communication effective. The essentials are discussed as under

(1) Unity: Unity of writing implies a condition of being one. The principle of unity applies on three levels:

(i) the individual sentences must be unified;

(ii) the individual paragraphs must be unified;

(iii) the totality of the message must be unified.

The first principle calls for each simple sentence to contain a single idea, clearly expressed. All sentences relating to a matter constitute a unified individual paragraph. Each paragraph in a section forms unit of thought. All units of thought structurally constitute the message of an entire communication or a unified message.

Each unified individual sentence conveys only one central idea. It must be direct, simple, brief, clear and vigorous. Too much use of buts, ands, pompousness and technical jargon must be avoided. Prompt and adequate attention of the recipient is the essence of purposeful communication.

Leland Brown states on unity thus: "An orderly arrangement of ideas flowing into other ideas and progressing to conclusions helps achieve unity and is also a major aid to coherence. The relationship between a main idea and a subordinate idea and a lesser idea in the dependent clause and using a conjunction to point out the relationship is indicated by some transitional means. This provides an element of sequence and motion that moves the reader in a definite direction toward accomplishing the purpose of communication.[2]

(2) Coherence: In addition to unity, coherence is also equally essential for good written communication. Clear communication in simple sentences helps the reader to understand rather than misunderstand. Facts and figures must be stated plainly and in an intelligent manner. To achieve clarity in a written communication the principle of coherence should be there. Relation and clarity are the two important aspects of coherence. The principle of coherence applies to sentences, paragraphs and to the message as a whole. It is trying together of several ideas, under one main topic in any paragraph. By interlinking of paragraphs, the whole message is tied together into a meaningful whole. Smooth flow, lucidity, and transition aspects should be given effects and there should not be any scope for the reader to misinterpret, mis-read or mis-spell the message.

A purposeful communication is one that must be *(a)* received *(b)* read; *(c)* understood for taking the necessary action. Coherence is given to a larger paragraph or section of a message. Leland Brown suggested to achieve it in these words: "This relationship can be accomplished by developing the phrases or sentences, relating them, by repetition of ideas and progression of thought, and using topic sentences and topic paragraphs to control ideas and direct the flow of thought. Thus, a message is tied together into a meaningful whole."

(3) Emphasis: The whole message consisting of unity of sentences and unity of paragraphs are of varying degrees of importance. The ideas, facts and figures pertaining to them may have the order of importance or priority. The next important or essential principle of written communication, on which the communicator has to pay adequate attention, is the emphasis on ideas, facts and figures. Under this principles, a certain degree of importance or emphasis is placed upon them, indicating their relative power or values. The principle of emphasis may be incorporated by position, by repetition, by the use of figures, by punctuation, by phrases, by mechanical devices and by skilful arrangement of paragraphs. Thoughts of greatest value or high degree or importance should be placed in the most prominent positions.

A prominent position may be the beginning of a paragraph or section. Position is achieved by keeping ideas, facts or figures at the beginning. The relative importance of thoughts and their placement differ from writing to writing, depending on the objects and type of writing, like business letter writing, official letter writing or personal letter-writing. Similarly, other methods used to achieve emphasis are use of graphs, charts, audio-visual, statistics etc. Above all, the most important thing that the transmitter has to keep in mind is that the principle of emphasis should be used in proper and prominent positions in order to draw the attention of the receiver to the central idea.

The communication of any written communication should repeat by note in the case of any corrections. Notes are needed if there is any:

(i) Inaccuracy denoting

(a) omission or exaggeration of facts;
(b) errors of misrepresentation in the data, citations, etc.
(c) unreliable mathematical treatment; and
(d) discrepancy between the fact and opinion.

(ii) Inadequacy in presentation denoting

(a) omission and incomplete development of the topic;
(b) faulty and improper arrangement of materials to substantiate the thought;
(c) improperly arranged paragraphs; and
(d) inclusion of irrelevant details.

(iii) Weakness in style denoting

(a) long and complicated sentences with incorrect usage of grammar;
(b) lack of clarity and failure to reach to the central point or theme directly;
(c) obstract presentation with the technical jargon; and
(d) failure in presenting the whole subject matter in an impersonal style.

(4) Clarity: Transmitting messages by black and white means to be understood rather than misunderstood. The message should be correctly planned and expressed in a logical way, to see that ideas flow smoothly from beginning to end. Clarity of written message is the first and foremost. So clarity in language is a form of courtesy. It is a good manner not to give unnecessary trouble in finding out the meaning. Clarity therefore, can be achieved in writing by taking pains, by writing to serve the purpose rather than to impress them.

(5) Completeness: Completeness with reference to writing a message means comprehensive coverage of the subject matter to be transmitted. An incomplete message leads to sidetrack, misunderstanding, seeking clarifications and explanations etc. The writer must consider the receiver's capabilities to understand.

(6) Courtesy: Probably, the best principle for writing a report is the quality of courtesy. Courtesy indicates politeness, considerate and respectfulness in writing. While writing it is necessary to evaluate the readers or users of the report. Time is valuable to the readers like the writers. Whether a message is positive, negative, satisfactory, disappointing, it should courteously be conveyed. For instance:

I regret to say — Discourteous

I respectfully regret to say — Courteous

It is to be borne in mind that a report is a record or substitute for speech. This quality in report writing demands genuine awareness of the readers, their needs, purpose, time, attention and cost.

(7) Sequency: The manner and the way in which something presented is more important than something itself. The way a report is represented is also of utmost importance. Material should be arranged so that the reader can pick out the main facts and recommendations easily and quickly. Consistency, continuity, and logical presentation of the message cannot be ignored. And it has to be arranged in a form that will attract the attention of the reader, interest him while he is reading it, and leave him with a desire to do something about it.

(8) Avoid Jargon: As far as possible, the writer should avoid jargon. Jargon is a language which is special to science, commerce, technology, trade or profession. In private language with persons in the field, jargon may be incorporated. In other cases, jargon can be used, but the only thing is that the words used must be clear to others as well.

(9) Conciseness: Conciseness refers to thoughts expressed in a fewest words consistent with writing. It is achieved in writing in definiteness and use of precise words. Unnecessary superlatives, exaggerations, and indirect beginning should be avoided. Care should be taken to use objectives judiciously, avoiding irrelevant details, hackneyed, and mumbling sentences.

(10) Brevity: Like clarity principle, brevity is also a form of courtesy to be maintained. The time of the writer and reader is limited and valuable, and hence time should not be wasted on unnecessary details. A writing should be shorter by using few words for many. Brevity can be achieved by using one word or two from many words. Not only it saves time, but brevity also gives grace to writing. The effective use of language is style. Business communication must be brief and direct. If one takes care to write in short, the style will take care of itself.

(11) Accuracy: The subject matter of communication must be correct or accurate. The manner in which the message is transmitted must be absolutely correct. Accuracy in writing can be achieved by careful checking and editing. Correctness demands in the case of figures, because decisions may go wrong if wrong figures are given. Overwriting, erasures, strikeovers, wrong spellings, faulty grammar, poor sentence construction etc., may distract the readers and lead to misunderstanding. Written communication clearly means to make others to understand.

(12) Strength: "A letter has strength; is forceful and direct, and has language power, the capacity to produce a potent reaction or effect. What gives this power? All the other qualities mentioned contribute to the total effect of the letter." Clarity gives the writing strength, because it ensures the other to understand easily and quickly, and directness is achieved by the principle of conciseness. Other essentials like correctness and completeness, too, add strength.

(13) Readability; Readability of subject matter is important in a written communication. Clarity of writing and understandability of the subject is the purpose of writing. Lack of readability quality in writing leads to not reading the message. So materials should be noted. A number of formulae have been developed for rating materials by measuring their difficulty. Readers do not have time to read involving trouble in understanding. Flesch, Dale and Chall, Farr, Jenkis, and Patterson and Gunning have developed readability formula. Among them, Cunning's method of readability formula is one of the easiest to understand and apply. He advocated seven factors affecting readability. They are:

(1) Average sentence length in words.

(2) Percentage of simple sentences.

(3) Percentage of verbs expressing forceful action.

(4) Proportion of familiar words.

(5) Percentage of personal references.

(6) Proportion of abstract words.

(7) Percentage of long words.

MEDIA OF WRITTEN COMMUNICATION

Media of written communication signify the tools of written communication. In other words, it means the instrument or instruments applied in communicating any message. Written communication has mostly and primarily been adopted as a media for providing information and to get things done through to achieve the goals of the organisation. Without the aid of written communication, it is not possible to inform the organisation's broad activities, policies, programmes, procedures etc. To achieve this, no single medium of communication would serve the purpose. There are several media of written communication. It is the responsibility of the executive to select one or two suitable for specific purposes and particular and peculiar circumstances. Generally, executives, by and large, depend on various media.

The following is the list of written media:

(1) Directives

(2) Forms

(3) News Bulletin

(4) Proposal

(5) Agreements

(6) Handbook

(7) Pamphlets

(8) Brochures

(9) Job Application

(10) Pay Envelope Inserts

(11) Letters

(12) Booklets

(13) Memoranda

(14) Office Orders

(15) Instructions

(16) Manual

(17) Office notes

(18) Explanation

(19) Magazines

(20) Circulars

(21) Newspapers

(22) Posters

(23) Leaflets

(24) Forms

(25) Bulletins

(26) Catalogues

(27) Union Publications

(28) Complaints and Suggestions

(29) House Journals

(30) Handbooks

(31) Hand files

The following is the brief description of various written media:

(1) Directives: Yet another medium of written communication is directives. A directive is a general instruction as to what is to be done, followed etc., issued by a higher authority to subordinates. Directives are issued, pointing out to those to whom it is meant, i.e., guidelines, for the performance of given task and accomplishing given objectives. There are several types of directives like simple, complex, lengthy, short, technical, legal, specific and general. It is a formal medium downwards for the purpose of communicating policies, rules, regulations, procedures, practice etc.

(2) Forms: Forms are written documents of a definite format. Forms, as a versatile medium, serves many purposes like schedule, questionnaire for collection of data, information, attitudes, opinions, recording technical information like production performance, capacity utilisation, legal forms, form of notices, accounting forms, bills etc. Similarly forms may be different types such as long forms, machine rotated forms, financial forms, marketing forms, personal forms and proposal forms. Generally, different coloured forms are meant for different purposes.

(3) News Bulletin: A bulletin is an official written report of news. It is a printed information sheet in the form of a newspaper. Sometimes, a bulletin board is used which is a notice board. News bulletin is a sort of house magazine, in miniature. These are published to include news and notes of current topics. It is the best medium of communication with employees in the organisation.

The advantage of news bulletin is that it is personal and friendly containing up-to- date and latest news which promotes the credibility of the management.

The Editor of a bulletin plays an important role in its quality production to convey policy decisions and fresh news. Like a handbook, it informs the employees about the company's policies, practices, procedures, rules, regulations, plans, future strategies etc. The employecs can know the nature and type of the work to be done from the bulletin. Other items often found in the bulletin are service matters, sports, recreation, transfers, including some paid advertisements. Generally, news bulletins are published weekly or fortnightly.

(4) Proposals: Proposal is also a written medium of communication. Its object is to offer something in writing. It is something proposed or suggested. Proposals may include a plan, alternative for consideration or adoption. A proposal may be legal, technical, financial, short, or long proposal. There are four types of proposal, namely, bids, personnel, organisational and product or service. A bid is offering a quoted price for a product or service deals with customers located outside the company.

On the other hand, personnel proposals relate to members of the organisation dealing with shifts, promotions, hiring, replacements, commitment etc. An application from a candidate in response to a given employment notification is a proposal. Organisational proposals deal with changes in policies, rules, procedures, practices of organisation. Hence, it is called as organisational proposal.

(5) Agreements: Agreement is a written document signifying the state of agreeing. A written arrangement between the persons agreeable to them. It signifies a legal document. A contract is an agreement enforceable by law. Every agreement legally binds the persons, creating and defining of obligations between the parties. An agreement is a very wide term, it may be a social agreement or a local agreement. All contracts are agreements but all agreements are not contracts.

A contract creates a legal tie which imposes upon a definite person or persons the necessity of doing or abstaining from doing a definite act or acts. An agreement which gives rise to a social ligation is not a contract. An agreement not enforceable at the option of the parties is avoidable contract. Thus, agreements impose upon the parties obligations to accept, follow, performance of certain code of conduct etc. Agreements are used to create legal binding to buy, sell, to pay or other negotiable instruments.

(6) Handbook: It is a very useful form of written medium of communication. It provides important information relating to policies, rules, procedures, practices as well as how to do a particular thing, serves particularly newly appointed employees. Companies which are making and issuing handbooks promote organisational image and impression. Big industrial groups use employee's handbooks. A separate page in the handbook is meant for entering the name of the employee, age, token number, department, address, phone numbers etc.

It contains introductory portion, indicating a profile about the company describing its short history, background, growth and development, structure, organisation, policies, practices, rules, procedures, regulations etc. A number of subsidiary handbooks can be prepared such as Recruitment Handbook, Wage and Salary Handbook, Benefits Handbook, Policy Handbook etc.

(7) Pamphlets: Also called "home pamphlets", they serve a very useful mode of written medium of communication. This medium is very interesting and fascinating to the employees and as such pamphlets cover a wide variety of topics such as interior decoration, embroidery, cooking, sports, health, personal and family topics. Big organisations generally publish these pamphlets for distribution among the employees.

Pamphlets which enable the communicator to reach despite the limitation of time and cost are among the most common methods of written communication. Pamphlets give information expressing an opinion on a matter. A small treatise has a fewer pages of sheets, but not in a book form, composed and written or printed, unbound with or without paper or hard cover. It is reporting or describing in a pamphlet. Pamphleteer is a person who writes a pamphlet. Oxford English Dictionary: 'More specifically, a treatise of the size and form described on some subject or question of current or temporary interest, personal, social, political, ecclesiastical or controversial, on which the writer desires to appeal to the public. This is merely a consequential specialisation, arising from the fact that works of this kind are those for which the pamphlet form is now mainly employed'.

(8) Brochures: Brochure is a form of written medium of communication. It is a short booklet generally consisting of printed or cyclostyled pages. Brochures give information on various subjects such as advertising, holidays, products, provident fund, standing orders etc. Brochures deal with a variety of topics disseminating information to the employees generally prepared in a standard format and style.

Big organisations make a more profitable use of the brochure. It may be circulated not only among the employees but also to external market areas or target market audience. Brochures are prepared in different forms and quality, depending on the resources ranging from very simple printed or zeroxed to sophisticated form. Brochures may be brought out in different types like folders, pamphlets, catalogue, house journal, mail covers and enclosures etc. Informing the people concerned to persuade, building image, repetition, impression and to supplement other advertising documents are the important objectives of preparing brochures.

A written document for external communication. It is a short booklet containing information about a particular subject. The examples of brochure are brochure of advertisement, brochure of holidays, brochure of product information etc. It is like a pamphlet on which anything is written or published in a pamphlet form.

(9) Job Application: Job application is also a mode of written medium of communication which contains a resume and a letter of application. Application conveys a message of consent to work in the organisation. The application also contains the requisite qualifications, capacity to accomplish a given task and ability to move; adjust and to get along with others. The resume is prepared by the applicant after examining his own qualifications and his particular aspirations and desires.

(10) Pay Envelope Inserts: The wage payment department prepares pay envelopes every month for payment of wages. Along with cash, a message slip is also included in the envelopes. They are called by different names, such as pay pocket inserts, enclosures in pay slips. They are forms of written media of communication which carry some message to the employees. Pay packet inserts, however are not an important method of conveying information. This medium of written communication serves some useful purpose as they carry some messages about their earnings.

(11) Letters: In the restless world of written communication, letters are business. Letters are used for both internal and external communication. Letters which enable one person to reach another and thus ensures the two-way communication. Writing a letter is an art: it represents a written message sent by post, sometimes, includes an envelope, a post card or an inland letter. A letterhead is a printed heading on a paper used for identity, or publicity etc. Outstation and sometimes local letters are put in a letter box. Through the medium of letter a person reaches to another and as such it is still the most important of all media of mass communication. Total mail load consists of personal, official and commercial correspondence. A letter speaks to wider cross-section like wholesalers, retailers, editors, dealers, pleaders, auditors, employees, students, foreigners, etc. Friendship, business relations and personal relationships depend, to a very large extent, on letters. The quality of the letter written promotes the image of the companies. Wide practical writing for different situations results in perfection and quality in letter-writing. It is easy to write a letter, which is nothing but to put one's ideas in black and white. But to write an impressive and quality letter is difficult. The essential of good letter-writing is to put ideas in a clear manner, convey the message in such a way as understandable by the recipient. Though the principles of writing a letter are uniform, there is a lot of difference between business, personal, and official correspondence. Some views on letters are:

"A letter does not Blush"— Cicero

"Carrier of News and Knowledge,
Instrument of Trade and Industry,
Promotion of Mutual Acquaintance,
Of peace and Goodwill,
Among Men and Nations"— Charles W. Elliot.

"The Letters Are the Soul of Trade"— James Howell.

A letter may be descriptive, narrative, technical, legal, domestic, public, private, foreign, confidential, personal, official, semi-official. The world of letters may be broadly classified as introductory letters, business letters, letters of application, marriage letters, thanking and congratulating letters, letters of condolences and obituary, letter of advice and recommendation. A letter thus must create the first impression and to motivate the reader to respond positively. A good letter must have at least seven main parts like letter-head, inside address, salutation, body, complimentary close, signature and signature identification.

(12) Booklets: The word "booklet" signifies a small, thin book. Companies publish booklets on the history of the concern or a product. They are issued generally for publicity and information purposes. Prime among these objects is to provide an overall picture of the organisation to the visitors, prospective customers, investors, executives, trainees, newly-recruited employees and other specialised audiences. Booklets are distributed to tell the story, background, information quickly and effectively to the interested persons. It may be mentioned here that booklets are only supplementary and secondary, not primary. Personal meet, handshake, face-to-face communication, informal gathering are primary media. A small book is often paper-bound.

Prof. K. R. Balan classified booklets and pamphlets into three types. They are:

(i) Indoctrination booklets welcome the new soldier, employee, association member, student, supplier, or visitor. (Literature for the customer or product-owner, usually emanates from the sales or advertising department). The beginner's booklet helps him to get off on the right foot. It tells him the rules of the game and the benefits of playing according to the rules. It seeks to instill a team spirit — the feeling that he has joined a winning combination.

(ii) Reference guides are the second type of handbook, useful to all members. They concern themselves with the group insurance plan, pension plan, suggestions, systems, hospitalization, profit-sharing, housekeeping and safety, library content, recreation programme and facilitates, contest rules, campus geography, and the like. Handbooks enable members to look up specific information easily. They save time and encourage appreciation of the value of membership. They quickly provide information actually sought by the leader.

(iii) Institutional booklets, books and brochures have subject matter devoted to an idea or a philosophy, total concept or entity. Typical are the messages related to the free enterprise system, national security, educational benefits, or charitable aims. In another category are reports of dedication celebrations, awards, history, success, expansion, and developments on science or the arts.[4]

(13) Memorandum: A written tool of internal communication is used popularly to inform the concerned people about something to be communicated. It is often abbreviated as memo (singular) or memos (plural). A written note which helps the recipient to remember the matter. In other words, a brief written statement about a particular matter which may be served to one particular individual or meant and passed around between colleagues. In all forms of organisation, whether small or large, private or public, memo is an effective tool in maintaining internal communication. The managers at different levels generally adopt memoranda to communicate information. The merit of memorandum is that it provides a record of evidence and proof.

Different colours are used for different purposes and sometimes, forms are printed and standardised. Memos are one-way communication, generally from their top to bottom. It is a matter put into black and white to be remembered, placed at the top subject as the head of a note of something that is to be remembered or a record for future reference. A note to help the memory. In external legal communication it is a writing or document in which the terms of a transaction or contract are embodied. Memorandum of Association is an external informative document required under the Indian Companies Act, 1956, containing certain clauses. A memorandum of a debt between a debtor and a creditor. Memorandum of Agreement of a publishing company, containing the terms of publication communicating to another. In accounting message, it is a brief informal note of a debt of the nature of a due bil!. According to Oxford English Dictionary: "An informal epistolary communication, without signature or formulate of address or subscription, usually written on paper with a printed heading bearing the word 'Memorandum' and the name and address of the sender." Memorandist is one who writes the memoranda.

(14) Office Orders: An official document used for internal communication to give instructions to the employees. Office orders may be usually issued to a particular person or persons. Transfers or promotions, increments sanctioned etc., are normally given effect to by an office order. General messages are conveyed by the office order by way of distribution of copies to all its employees.

The departmental manager and top management are competent to issue office orders. Written in brief covering the core of the subject to be informed, is divided into one or two paragraphs. It is type of office order, in which lower executive issues office order under the authority and direction of the superior authority. Inter and intra-departmental communication can effectively be passed through office order.

Essentials of a good office order are that it should be simple, brief, easily understandable by the recipient. The respective executives will, maintain effective link in the organisation. Without the aid of office order, organisations cannot be run effectively. As such, executives by and large, depend on this medium to inform, instruct and to give introduction.

Official Routine: The language characteristic of official document. An official order is an authoritative direction, injection, mandate or command. Models of official orders:

(i) A decision of a Board that union meetings should not be conducted during office hours in the premises.

(ii) A written direction to pay money or deliver property given by a company legally entitled.

(iii) A direction to make purchases of goods or supply of goods.

(iv) A written direction to the borrower to make, provide or furnish anything as a good security for a loan.

Thus, office order is a written specific command or notice issued by the commanding authority. It is an authoritative direction how to proceed or act in more restrictive application.

(15) Instructions: The ordinary meaning of the word implies to teach or to direct. However, it may be noted in the real world situation that the word is used for giving knowledge or information to others in writing. The originator or sender of instruction or instructions may issue written messages either to individual, or to a group or employees. Instructions are normally found very specific since they aim at achieving a particular purpose. It is, therefore, evident that any such instruction is supposed to move from a higher level of organisation to a lower level. Thus, instructions may be more from executives to the lower level, from top levels to the middle level and so on and so forth. The basic advantage of instruction is that it helps to educate or lengthen on a particular subject. This medium is also one-way communication. It needs to be mentioned that, under all circumstances, it is the primary responsibility of the originator of the instructions, to see that they are, well written and brief, instructive and informative. They should be in a simple language, concise and understandable by the recipient. The basic objective of such instruction is to help the receiver to grasp and understand effectively and instantaneously, without confusion and in a technical manner. The literary and educational background factors also should be taken into consideration by the sender. Some specimen instructions are as under:

(i) Instructions to individuals

(a) Please get ready the agenda and the minutes of the last meeting.

(b) Please pay Rs.... as donation to the flood relief fund and claim deduction.

(c) Please check-up the stock position and place order immediately.

(ii) Instructions to a group

(a) Workers of semi-skilled category are advised to go to Unit II, the management instructs.

(b) Salesmen of Territory II must please get ready to go to field survey.

(iii) Instructions to the employees of the company

(a) Employees of the company are requested not to hold an election meeting during the office hours.

(b) Employees who are desirous of taking festival advance must intimate the accounts section at least one week before to facilitate the office for making necessary arrangement to disburse.

(iv) External instructions

(a) Applicants are advised to write their examination in Hindi or English only.

(b) Inviting tenders.

(16) Manuals: A manual is a compilation of directions and instructions in book or booklet form. Manuals are in popular use both for internal and external communication. It is a medium of exchanging facts, ideas concerned to all people in the organisation. It is usually a one-way communication originating from the top authority on established principles, rules to be followed in the organisation. A small book. It gives information about a particular field of subject. Manual of law, manual of procedure, manual of duties, responsibilities, handbook of planning, handbook of labour relations, handbook of public relations. They speak to them about the rules and the need and benefits following them. They seek to install a team spirit.

A specific information on a particular subject can be obtained easily. They serve as a guide to discharge one's own duties and responsibilities effectively. Organisational or institutional manuals deal with the subject matter devoted to that particular organisation or institution. A small book for handy use, intended to be kept at hand for reference, a concise treatise, an abridgement. Every office may usually have an office manual which contains standard practices, conventions, instructions, or organisational policies based on executive decisions for the guidance to the staff. It is an authoritative guide to office organisation issued for better performance of organisational activities. A manual contains a brief history of the organisation, growth and development, charts, objectives, positions, their functions, duties and responsibilities of each section, general policies, welfare and working facilities. A manual is useful both for new as well as to existing employees.

(17) Office Notes: A tool of internal communication, and hence it is useful in all organisations. A note is a piece of writing to call attention to something. Message written down in a short form. A short explanation of the main subject matter. A subject matter of notes is worth taking notice. Notes are used in all official communications for getting information passed around or up and down. They are one way to communicating instructions, explanations, clarifications etc. It may be mentioned that notes are a widely used technique of communication. They are suitably written communication media in any type of organisation irrespective of the nature and type of business organisation. In the restless and busy organisational activities the executives and their subordinates often adopt notes to pass on the necessary information from one person to another. People are kept correctly and properly informed or instructed. It goes without saying that the basic responsibility of official notes rests on the originator or transmitter of the message. So notes help the recipient to understand quickly catching the central theme. Thus, they avoid delay. They should be short, brief, precise and simple to the receiver.

(18) Explanations: It is an instrument of internal written communication originating from the dealing or concerned authority giving in brief clarifications and explanations, so as to enable the recipient to come to a correct decision. Correct and perfect decision-making is possible when the written subject mailer is fully clarified and explained. This is achieved with the help of explanation. Explanations are communicated to make the main subject matter clear or easy to understand.

It is a written document or statement of facts, figures, opinions explaining the matter. Sometimes, explanatory notes are added at the end of the matter to avoid delay and to get rid of confusion to the reader. They represent queries, views, opinions and decisions about any particular subject. It is the duty of the originator to prepare them most carefully pinpointing the central theme or message. Explanations and clarifications are usually sought on the subject matter which is written in a pompous language, technical jargon, cumbersome approach to the central theme. Explanations should be clear in approach, simple in language, supported with necessary references and information.

(19) Magazine (Periodicals as Media): Magazine is a publication issued regularly containing informations. The periodicity of a magazine may be a week, fortnight, month, quarterly, half-yearly and annually. A magazine contains articles, opinions, findings of studies, advertisement, etc. A magazine is the most important internal communication medium. Magazine is the most important communicating and advertising medium, irrespective of its being monthly, bi-monthly, semi-monthly, weekly, bi-weekly, semi-weekly, and tri-weekly. Next to newspapers, magazine is the best form of a written communication and offers vast scope for product advertisement.

They offer appeals to all kinds of people. Each magazine is long and continuous to live and the matter is fresh for a week, month and even longer. No doubt it is a common medium or national medium. But in a country like India where there are several languages, one language magazine is not suitable. Hence, many regional magazines have come up. The circulation of some regional magazines has always been restricted to a limited area. Consumer magazines are more useful in advertise product information. Farm publications are meant for the rural people. Business publications may be divided into various categories such as industrial publications, merchandising or trade publications and professional publications.

The Magazine Publishers' Association, Marketing Division, U.S. suggests the following reasons why magazines sell:

(i) Authority: Magazine authority dates back to man's very acceptance of the printed word as dependable to his own signature which is accepted by a binding pledge.

(ii) Colour: Magazine colour spreads before the reader a spectrum of exciting visual pleasures. Colour stimulates interest —creates desire, enhances image, identifies the package.

(iii) Believability: Magazines believability builds readers confidence. It influences, affects ideas, opinions and desires. People believe what magazines have to say.

(iv) Performance: Magazines last. People save them aside for future reference, return to them again and again. The permanence of magazines gives your advertising the time it needs for careful consideration, the time that it deserves.

(v) Selectivity: Magazine selectively targets places and people. It reaches your best prospects — wherever they are — while they are most receptive to ideas and information.

(vi) Flexibility: Magazines offer a full range of prospects — with diverse interests — in one or all of the nation's key markets. The degree to which an advertisement stimulates, dramatizes; sells products is entirely at the discretion of the advertiser.

(vii) Efficiency: The ability of a magazine to offer the widest range of incomparable values which can be translated into dollar sales makes magazines the choice of leading advertisers.

(20) Circulars: In order to inform a group of people in the organisation, written matter is issued by way of circulars. It is mostly used for internal communication to intimate or inform the employees. A notice especially advertising something sent to a number of persons. A number of copies of the same matter circulated among the group. To circulate means to go round. Matters of centralised communication relating to all the people concerned, circulated to the whole department. In other words, circulars are letters or notices usually printed, cyclostyled and are addressed to a number of persons in the organisation.

They are normally issued on some infrequent occasions like a change of specimen signature, admission or retirement of a partner, amalgamation, change of address etc. Head office may issue circulars to its regional or branch offices to inform matters for consideration and necessary action. Use of good language, tone, expressing clear intention are the important principles to be followed by the draftsmen. The other considerations are short matter, simple language, selecting appropriate words, drawing attention to the central theme etc.

The following are the models of matter written in circulars:

(i) Circular notifying holidays.

(ii) A rumour circulating that he/she is getting married.

(21) Newspapers: A paper printed daily, or weekly, containing news etc. It is an effective external communication instrument. A newspaper is a daily or weekly publication. It contains news and opinions of current events. The most important communication medium in terms of coverage is daily newspapers. It represents the most important advertising medium. A newspaper may be a local paper, state and national level. There are a number of business publications and editions such as Economics Times, Financial Express etc. The importance of the newspaper as an effective mass medium of communication is indicated by coverage.

Within the newspaper field, there is newspaper supplement as a part of the main edition. Supplements are issued as a special Sunday section. In recent years, colour is also employed in newspaper advertising. In India, the great majority of newspaper advertisements appear in black and white. In metropolitan cities, shopping newspapers are printed exclusively for advertisement. Newspapers are sold mainly by home delivery, on news stands and by mail subscription and hence covers a wide area. The life of communication in daily newspaper is short, rarely longer than a day. But the cost of using this medium has become prohibitive in these days.

(22) Posters: Yet another form of written communication is the poster, generally used for external communication. A poster is a large notice or advertisement for sticking on a wall. A written document, a placard pasted or displayed in public places as an announcement or advertisement. It may include pictorial or picture poster, a placard consisting mainly of a picture of illustration. A poster gives an opportunity to the by-passer to see and read. This form of written communication offers many advantages to the organisation because it draws the attention of many people. A poster is prepared based on planned specialisation and all the activities relating to the poster exhibition are effectively supervised and controlled. A poster in a prominent place attracts a great variety of cross-sections of the people. Posters are generally used for product advertisements. The posters are called as bill books. Poster is used widely for outdoor advertising.

(23) Leaflets: A leaflet is a small printed document containing information. A written medium of external communication to inform people outside the organisation. It is used as an instrument to inform the public about the product, its uses, qualities and characters. The main drawback of a leaflet is that it does not serve as a medium of two-way communication. Oxford English Dictionary: 'A small sized leaf of paper or a sheet folded into two or more leaves, but not stitched, and containing printed matter, chiefly for gratuitous distribution'.

Thus, leaflet is a printed or written folding circular having several unsewed, unstitched pages in one strip. It is a leaflike part.

(24) Forms: A form is a card or a sheet or a continuous strip of paper used for keeping some record. A form has some fixed data which are generally pre- printed on the form and provides space for variable data or information which the user of the form has to fill in. Thus, a form may be defined as a piece of paper containing some information printed or reproduced by any method with blank spaces left for the entry or additional information by the office, staff or/and by the outsiders.

Forms save time and energy. It is a medium by which all messages are supplied and recorded. Forms are generally standardised. Different forms in different colours and sizes facilitate classification and quick reference. Forms are to be controlled. Every organisation must have an effective system of form control to save time and cost. By simplification of work, classification, easy reference and printing delays can be avoided.

(25) Bulletins: Bulletin is an official report of news. It is issued to state about the product, progress results, achievement etc. It is a printed information sheet. The news given out as a bulletin on a very recent matter of attraction. The news bulletins are broadcasted on radio or T.V. in exact terms in which they are written or sometimes may be amended. A bulletin board is a notice board of news. Bulletins are entirely different from posters. It is an arrangement for outdoor advertisements on printed bulletins. Painted display bulletin is the another type of outdoor communication. It is called "painted display." A bulletin may be a permanent bulletin or rotary bulletin. Painted displays are placed on walls in a prominent place. Embellished painted bulletin is another form, such as cut-outs, special illuminations and animations. Buying painted bulletins are more durable than poster paper.

(26) Catalogues: Catalogues are mostly used as a written form of external communication. They contain relevant information about products and educate the public about the prospects to make a purchase. It is a direct medium to draw the attention of the reader. It provides valuable information and can be used as a substitute for the sales information. Catalogue may be issued in loose leaf or folder form and may be released bounded and stitched when there are more number of pages. Special catalogues may be prepared for certain classes of customers, and for certain type of products and for certain occasions.

(27) Union Publications: The place of union publications in communication, particularly in written media, cannot be overemphasised. Unions have equal participation in communication. Union periodicals or set of issues has a channel of communication upon which many employees depend for information.

During the periods of insecurity and uncertainty, union literature gives members of the organisation an outlet to ventilate freely or express their fears, attitudes and thoughts. The collective decisions, opinions, ideas, feelings or actions of the members are transmitted through this medium. Management cannot ignore or eliminate the union activities, for it will survive in spite of everything, and it can make use of the union for effective communication network and can be used to send messages quickly. The management can give some cf its communication to the unions with responsibility. Union's publications in written communication field give confidence to the employees and strengthen the employers. Because of illiteracy among workers, trade union literature plays a very important role in transmitting the message to them. A formal communication with the workers is not effective.

(28) Complaints and Suggestions: In grievance procedure, complaints and suggestions are a method. It is one of the instruments of written communication. Employees individually or in a group lodge complaints or offer suggestions in writing. Generally, a Complaint and suggestion box is installed at a prominent place or places within the premises. The employees who are desirous to make a complaint or any matter like working condition, facilities and on general matters etc., and to offer suggestions put them in complaint and suggestion box. It is a good example of upward communication. The subordinates through this medium can transmit messages to upward channel. Generally, suggestion method is not effective. There are many reasons for failure of the suggestions and complaints box:

(i) Employees are afraid to lodge complaint, *(ii)* Inability to express ideas in black and white, *(iii)* Management may ignore the matters, *(iv)* Lack of full knowledge on the issue, *(v)* There is no interpersonal exchange, *(vi)* The system is impersonal.

(29) House Journals: In-house publication, house magazine or journal, is published to keep employees or customers informed. House journal serves as a useful and common platform to convey the views of management. For instance, the "Brooks News" the employees magazine of the Brook Bond of India Limited, "The Youth News" of the YMCA etc.

(30) Handbooks: A manual. A small book giving information about something. The most important medium of written external communication.

(31) Handouts: A leaflet of information given to the concerned people. It is similar like handbook meant for external communication.

(32) Handfiles: Like leaflets, handfiles are tools of external communication to make the people outside the organisation well informed about something. They do not serve two-way communication.

House Journal

Meaning and Nature

House journal is also called "house magazine", "in-house magazine" or "journal" or "house organs." These magazines are private journals. The word "house" indicates a trading establishment. The term "organ" means a medium of communicating information or opinion. Internal publications, house magazine or journal is published to keep employees, customers, shareholders etc., informed. House journal serves as a useful and common platform to convey the views of management.

It ventilates the opinion or voice of the organisation publishing journal. For instance, the "Brooks News", the employee magazine of the Brook Bond of India Limited, "The Youth News" of the YMCA etc. Big and well-established corporations or trading establishments, industrial houses, public, private, Government agencies, educational and social institutions, voluntary associations generally publish house organs or journals. House journal is, therefore, a tool of internal communication.

In-house or corporate organs or house journals are a new kind of promotional medium. In-house is the name by which they are popularly known. In recent years a large number of companies have been publishing in-house journals. It may be mentioned that not only private companies and establishments but some public sector corporations and establishments too produce in-house magazines.

The production of in-house magazines has picked up in recent years with amazing speed. In-house communication plays an important role in disseminating relevant information to the employees working in various levels within the organisation. They contribute not only to staff benefits and welfare but also help in work place and have significant long-term benefits.

From time to time, a few large organisations have been attempting to produce in-house journals. The in-house journal may handle only one product or may supplement it, usually with a group of much smaller products.

Nature and Characteristics

(1) Ownership: The basic characteristic of house organ is a company magazine distributed to employees, shareholders, dealers, customers etc.

(2) Not Advertising Media: The house organ is not in a true sense an advertising media, in the sense that the term has been used for other publications.

(3) Selling Space: Companies may sell magazine space for advertising to have income which can partially offset costs, make them self-liquidating or actually make the publication a profitable venture.

(4) Sale of Copies: Another method is the sale of copies to the employees to pay for their house journal.

(5) Internal Communication Tool: In-house organs are intended merely to serve as an internal communication tool between the organisation and its internal and external public.

(6) Public Relations: They are primarily public relations vehicles. As such the majority of the house journals are regarded as a part of the public relations programme.

(7) Business Publication: Though most of the house organs do not sell space, in format most of the house organs resemble business publications more than other form of advertising.

(8) Free Circulation: When house organ solicits advertising from manufacturers to defray the cost of production, in such cases the house journal fulfils some of the characteristics of the free circulation business publication.

(9) Internal and External Relations: House organs are designed primarily to help in promoting and maintaining good employer-employee relations or external public relations.

(10) Dealer Promotion: Sometimes, the function of a house organ may be largely in the area of dealer promotion.

(11) Variety of House Organs: A company may publish a number of house organs for each group, for each product, division or each manufacturing plant. For instance, General Motors in the U.S.A. publishes 53 different company magazines, most of which go to separate employee groups.

(12) Publishers: In-house journals, the name by which they are popularly known, are produced not only by the large-scale private sector but also by the public sector corporations, trading establishments, Government agencies, educational and social institutions, voluntary organisations and such other bodies.

(13) Contents: House organs have a specific readership interest. Our modern house organs provide entertainment, information, educational materials so that the reader may relax, escape from fatigue and promotes friendly relations between the management and managed.

(14) Size of Media: A house journal is both of local medium as well as national medium.

(15) Unit of Selling Space: Selling of advertisement space by house journal periodicals is in the form of units such as whole page, half page and quarter page and by the column, half column and so forth.

Classification of House Organs

There may be different ways for classifying types of house organs. There are various classes of house organs. However, the following is the broad classification of house magazines:

(1) Size: The first basis for grouping is on the basis of size. A house journal may be of: (a) Pocket book size (b) Full size or standard size and (c) Large size. In addition there are periodical of various old sizes. A size of a magazine may be 3-column x 140 line page. There are today a very few that represent the older "standard size." Page size may be 2-column x 170 lines (large size). 3-column x 140 lines (flat size), 2-column x 85 lines (small or pocket size).

(2) Readership: The important component as a basis of classification is the type of readership. A company may publish a number of house organs such as for each group, for each product division, or each manufacturing point.

(3) Frequency: As usual, the other basis of classification is on the frequency of publication. They may be dailies, weeklies, bi-weeklies, monthlies, fortnighties, quarterlies, half-yearly etc. Monthly house organs are by far the largest group. Weeklies occupy the second largest group. On the other hand, bi- weeklies, semi-monthlies, quarterlies, or semi-annualies account for a relatively small number of the total.

(4) General and Special: In-house magazines may be broadly classified into special interest magazines.

House Journal Editorial

Meaning and Nature

The editor is a person who edits and prepares the material for house journal by correcting, attending, adding, deletions etc. He censors the materials received for publication. The word "editorial" represents a matter or news in a house journal written by an editor or by persons belonging to the editorial board. In another sense, editorial is the leading article in the house journal. It includes comments, opinions, events, feelings, factors of the organisation collected or expressed by the members of the organisation. It is voice of the sponsor.

Why House Journal Editorials?

The first consideration in a house journal is an editorial policy. The basic question — is it necessary to have a separate house journal editorial? The answer is that it is a must. From the standpoint of both contents and writing level designed to appeal to the various kinds of the readers, professionals editorial is the most important.

A careful observation of several house journals indicates that editorial is indispensable. A good house journal formulates editorial policy. There must be editorial worth the house journal, since the publication is outstanding editorially, it will attract a number of readers.

As a matter of fact the editorial policy will of course determine the readers' selection of the in-house journal. Similarly, the editorial policy will determine the importance of the magazine. If the editorial policy is vigorous and exciting, it surrounds the advertising, when space is sold, with this atmosphere. A journal without an editor is a journal without a soul. Usually a separate standing committee or editorial board for producing house journal is constituted.

The editor may be responsible for working with the editorial policy. The majority of house journals will be regarded as part of the public relations programme. It is the editor who establishes some sort of rapport between the readers and the editors or as in the case of good house journal, the editor and the public relations man.

"The editor should, of course, meet as many of his readers as possible, preferably on their home ground rather than in the editorial office, and he will also be in communication with them by telephone and correspondence, but there should also be something in each issue which is seen to spring directly from the editor or the public relations office."[5]

Merits of House Journals

The importance or merits of making in-house magazines are:

(1) The magazines depict the progress of the firm to the employees and to the shareholders, dealers etc.

(2) They facilitate them to know about the financial position, market potential, foreign collaborations and other activities and future plans.

(3) They educate the investors with a view to inviting more capital for existing and diversified products.

(4) They show the existing and prospective customers of the company to promote confidence.

(5) The magazine probably has the greatest impact on the outside publicity.

(6) In-house magazine is owned outright by the organisation and operates under its direct supervision.

(7) The in-house committee of the magazine or the editorial performs all of the creative and artistic services as provided by the outside publisher.

(8) In-house magazine approach reduces the total cost of advertising. If all the necessary works are done for less money, the difference of benefits goes directly to the company,

(9) Other advantage claimed by the organisations who own and produce house journals is the prospect of saving money by cutting overhead expenses.

(10) Industrial units which run such in-house journals would build good image and goodwill for the organisation and solicits new customers and new business.

(11) It serves as a good platform when the management has something interesting to communicate. They are circulated at the work and office chit chat.

(12) In-house journals promote industrial relations and good mutual understanding between the employees, dealers, shareholders and the management.

(13) Another reason in support of publishing house journal is that it provides an objective news service.

(14) House journal advertisements are good in quality in terms of printing and colour. They are usually printed on good paper that makes for an excellent reproduction of art and colour work. Such magazines give the advertiser an elegant reproduction.

(15) The advantage of house journal is flexibility for the advertiser with a house journal advertisement.

(16) Letters written to the editor promote good two-way communication which is invariably motivated by the spirit of organisational service covering suggestions, advice, complaints, public awareness, grievances and fair criticism. Such letters may appear on merely all subjects like cultural literacy, recreational, information, safety, welfare, promotions, organisational image etc.

Demerits or Limitations of House Journals: In spite of a number of merits emerging from in-house journals, it has its own pitfalls and drawbacks. Critics of the in-house journals offer a number of problems of producing in-house journals. Some of the drawbacks are as follows:

(1) Creative personnel are working on only one product line. The talents tend to become stale. or outdated over time.

(2) Organisational structure indicates hierarchical relationship. As such a certain independency of the thought and creativity is lost.

(3) They may not be effective because outside advertising agencies are more mature professionals, competitive innovators, and see new opportunities, creativity and independence of thought.

(4) From the point of views of receivers of journal, the house journal presents the danger that one will be stuck with it, because they are captive of the in-house journal.

(5) The in-house tends to lack the versatility, experience, and diversity of talents which a large independent outside agency alone can provide.

(6) A house journal may not have an effective internal and external readership.

(7) In number of cases, the house journals could not conform to the highest standard of Indian Industrial Journalism. They are not national newspapers as far as the freedom of the press is concerned. The overall well-being of the management is paramount.

Nevertheless, the in-house journal approach appears to be gaining popularity in recent years among the big organisations. Though criticism has been levelled against in-house journals, there apparently have been some successful in-house journals. Although their number in Indian context has not much in relation to number of industrial units, but still there has been an increasing interest in these type of journals in recent years. History has shown, however, that most in-house journals sooner or later benefited the organisations. In recent years, there has been some increasing trend, leading to the production of in-house journals.

Suggestions for Good House Journal

(1) Every house journal should have the guidelines of definite policies and clearly defined objectives.

(2) A journal without a policy may face problems of waste of money and manpower.

(3) To achieve the objectives of in-house, the publications should meet the needs of both the organisation and its employees.

(4) As to the coverage is concerned, the in-house journal should provide useful and meaningful information.

(5) To some extent, the journal should be distributed externally not only to recover the cost of production by selling space for advertisements but also should go to the group leaders of the community, customers, prospects, researchers etc.

(6) The in-house magazine will be successful only with the joint efforts and interest of management and its editorial board.

(7) To compensate the cost of production and efforts involved, the journal must accomplish something concrete for the sponsor.

(8) Steps should be taken in this direction of making publication two-way by inviting questions and making surveys of attitude and accordingly, then reporting them in print.

(9) The publication should improve good relations not only with one of its principal public, namely, its own employees but also with the other publics like customers, authorities, Government etc.

(10) The editors of the journal should try to conform to the highest standards of ideal journalism of trade, commerce and industry.

(11) A house journal should be informative, instructive, entertaining, stimulating and inspiring occasionally. The employees should consider the journal as a tool of internal communication at all levels, as also being a medium of communication upwards, downwards and horizontal within the organisation.

(12) There should not be any coverage of matter which is provocative and defamatory and to thrive on the exchange of ideas and should give an opportunity to the employees for free expression of their views.

Determinants or Factors

(1) Frequency: The periodicity of in-house organs is an important determinant. The frequency of these organs may also widely vary. These are dailies, weeklies, semi-monthlies, bi-weeklies, monthlies, bi-monthlies, seasonal periodicals, quarterlies, semi-annuals and publications issued at frequent intervals that do not fit any of the other patterns. Among them, monthly magazines, quarterly magazines, fortnightly are by far the largest group. They are most common intervals at which house journals are published. But annuals are generally rare. The other categories account for a relatively small number. Most other costs will be multiplied by the frequency figure, and the number of issues has, therefore, a big bearing on the total cost. So how often will the periodical be published? Publication frequency may be an important consideration.

(2) Size: Regarding size, house journals may vary in size and shape. Size means size of page or format. It includes factors like column and column's width, type setting etc. Generally, a house journal is small containing a few printed or cyclostlyed pages. Though there is no limit on the size, actually they run a few pages. There are four standardised periodical sizes. They are:

(i) Pocket book size;

(ii) Full size or standard size;

(iii) Flat size; and

(iv) Large size;

(v) There are periodicals of various odd sizes.

(3) Selling Advertising Space: The publication of house journals is a costly matter. In a true sense, the house organ is not an advertising medium in the sense that the term has been used for other publications for some organisations may sell space for advertisements to have revenue which meets partially or fully the cost of publishing the house journal or actually make the publication profitable. There are two methods to achieve this objective. The first being the sale of advertisement space, second the sale of copies. Concerns producing large size magazines may have advertisements, while there are no advertisements in small organs. In the case of magazines of educational institutions like colleges and universities, we generally find a large number of advertisements from companies and other advertisements from business establishments. Though such advertisements have no advertising value, but space is sold to collect revenue to offset the cost of production.

(4) Pages: The house organ of a small size may have a limited number of pages, say 6 to 12. There are also large house organs. The number of pages reflect the quantity and weight of the paper. Number of pages is a determining factor to quote printing costs which are usually in multiples of four pages. But the pages have also to be filled and editorial, photographic, art and reproduction costs must be worked out according to the number of pages.

(5) Objectives: House organs are meant to serve as a media of communication or opinion to keep internal and external public to be informed. They communicate in all directions. They are important tools of internal communication to the management, play an important role in communicating the views and desires of the management at various levels within the organisation. They are the media of two-way communication, whereby the employees, subordinates, shareholders, dealers, stockholders etc., can also communicate with the management as well as others on matters of mutual interest.

(6) Black and White or Colour: Colours are an attraction in a house journal; they shine into the eyes of the readers. Good colour combination is largely a matter of arrangement. If an arrangement is to be pleasing, it should be planned around the principles of emphasis and balance to create interest, which reflects the character of the editor. Each colour beyond the first means an extra printing plate and an extra working and cost. There are two classes of colours, (1) chromatic colours; (2) achromatic colours. The chromatic colours are yellow, orange, red, purple, blue, green and intermediate colours called *hues.* The achromatic colours include black, white and intermediate series of grey. They are classified as primary, secondary and tertiary. Yellow, red and blue are primary colours. Orange, purple and green are secondary colours. These colours are obtained by mixing the primary colours. Tertiary colours are mixtures of secondary colours. Full colour requires four colours — yellow, magenta, cyan and black.

(7) Price: The house organs produced and distributed are of two types. They are priced and non-priced, or free copies. The house journals are generally printed and distributed free of cost. They are generally distributed free to all the internal and external public. In colleges and universities, a small magazine fee will be collected from the students. It is also possible for house journals to have income which can partly offset costs, make them self-liquidating or actually make the publication a profitable venture. There are two methods for this. Firstly the sale of advertising space, second, to sell copies to the members.

(8) Method of Distribution: There are two important methods of distribution of house journals. They are:

(i) Handing Out: A very satisfactory and the cheapest method of distribution of house journal is handing out copies to the staff. Under this method, copies are taken round from bench to bench or from office to office.

(ii) Posting Copies: Sending copies through post is yet another important method, which facilitates when the family members wish to read the journal. Dealers, stockholders, and other external public generally require posting. A separate mailing list should be maintained from time to time.

There are two methods of posting copies. One flat method. If the journal is mailed, it becomes more attractive to receive and more inviting to read. A rolled and wrapped magazine can look a mess when unrolled and unwrapped and hence an envelope is usually preferable. The matter of folding should be fixed when planning the page size and choosing the paper.

(9) Editor, Cost etc.: Generally, there may be a separate standing committee or editorial committee to look after its preparation and publication. A chief editor or executive editor, a managing editor is a professional person who is a whole time editor. An editor should conform to the highest standards of Indian Industrial Journalism. The editorial board may contain other members representing workers, clerical staff, officials etc. An editor has to devote his full time and professional expertise to the work of producing journals. Allowance has to be made for salary, allowances to the editor, the cost of layout and design.

(10) Get-up: The get-up of a house journal is fully attractive because it is printed on art paper, good quality paper. They are usually printed on good paper that makes for an excellent reproduction of art and colour work. Such journals also give the advertiser an elegant reproduction.

(11) Art and Photography: If a typographical style is decided for the text and title, the cost can be minimised. The purely photographic material associated with off-set lithography can be both economical and efficient since each character is perfect. As far as possible, obtaining photographs from amateur sources should be avoided.

(12) Paid Contribution: Buying contribution is another aspect of a house journal. Cartoons usually have to be bought and a reproduction fee has to be paid. Big-name contributors are sought. Authors may be approached through literary agents and fees to be settled.

Contents of House Organ

(1) Cover Photo.

(2) Editorial.

(3) Feature articles.

(4) Board of management and official news. News about programmes and visits of the head of the organisation and other top managerial personnel. For instance, the visit of chairman to foreign countries and the programme and visits of managing director etc.

(5) Photographs. Includes photos of various activities taking place in the organisation like literary activities, cultural programmes, recreational activities of staff, workers etc.

(6) Photos and news about the meetings of various types.

(7) Functions, organised and management officers attending the functions such as inauguration of a building, plant, flag hoisting, consecretion of a temple or a place of worship, inauguration of family planning unit, school dispensary etc.

(8) Activities, movements and statements of people who are associated or interested in the organisation like consultants, auditors, business men, entrepreneurs, scientists etc.

(9) News about service and personal matters such as promotion, transfer, retirement etc. It is usual to have a photograph relating to such matters.

(10) Accidents, precautions, accident benefits etc.

(11) Photographs and news of marriages, birthdays, deaths and other social and personal matters.

(12) Suggestions, complaints, allegations etc.

(13) News of literary activities like adult education.

(14) News and social activities of women, children, and their club activities.

(15) News and activities of sports and games, participation in competition along with winning prizes and trophies, tournaments conducted etc.

(16) Letters to the editor.

(17) Quotations, humour, proverb, jokes, quiz, competition, puzzles, riddles, cross-word etc.

(18) Research and development activities.

(19) Results of research as to new method of production and process of production etc.

(20) Speeches, news and messages of chairman, managing director or any occasion like Republic Day, Independence Day, Anniversaries, and other meetings.

MECHANICAL DEVICES IN WRITTEN COMMUNICATION

Modern mechanical equipments and machines play an important role in the efficient and speedy communication. Mechanisation of communication work is fast taking place. Messages are required to be submitted to the inside tall network and flat network as well as to outsiders. It is not an exaggeration to say that there are rapid changes in the communication management because of growing scientific and technological innovations. The present age of communication has brought about many changes in the different fields to keep pace with mass communication and to transmit messages to distant places with considerable speed, accuracy, quantity of message to enable quick and correct decision-making etc. They have necessitated the installation of a number of time and labour saving electrical and electronic mechanical devices in written communication. These machines right from the typewriter to the sophisticated computers and teleprinters are required for transmitting information.

Mechanisation of communication network is for the accurate and speedy communication of messages. Even office work inside the organisation is mostly indoor desk and manual work. The process oi communication is routine, continuous and monotonous in nature. The routine annual work may adversely affect efficient performance. This also equally necessitates the adoption of certain equipment and machines suitable for the efficient writen communication. Therefore, the most appropriate communication work can be done with machines at comparatively minimum possible cost. More accuracy and speed not only improve the general efficiency but also increase the goodwill of the organisation among its visitors and other outsiders.

Today, a wide variety of writing and communicating machines are available in the market. The management has to procure and install suitable machinery depending upon organisational requirements and working staff. There are a number of advantages associated in mechanisation of communication like saving in cost, ensures accuracy and speed in transmission to reduce monotony, achieve uniformity, better appearance and easy record and reference.

The various types of machines which are available for the purpose of written communication are listed below along with a brief description.

(1) Typewriter: Typewriter is a machine with keys for printing letters on a piece of paper. Typewriter is the most popular and commonly used in all types of communication work. Typewriters are now available not only in English but also in regional languages. In every organisation typewriter is seen as a basic requirement now a days. The typed copy is the writing produced by a typewriter. It is called typescript. Different companies make typewriters with different type faces. Type face is a set of letters for printing, cut in a particular style. Typist is a person whose job is to type. Typewriting, i.e., writing produced by a typewriter is a form of written communication.

There are various types of typewriters which are used in typewriting.

(a) Standard Typewriter: It is the most commonly used typewriter in all organisations. It is the most suitable for routine business correspondence and general typing work. Typing work can be done with considerable speed. The typescript is easier to read, more clear and if necessary, a clear carbon copy can be produced.

(b) Portable Typewriter: A machine of comparatively small size, portable typewriter, can be carried or moved easily from place to place. A handy, light- weight machine, it can be used mostly for personal work of limited quantity. It contains all fundamental elements of the standard typewriter. Economically, it is cheaper.

(c) Noiseless Typewriter: This typewriter produces no noise or lesser noise comparable to the standard typewriter. This is generally used in meeting rooms or executive chambers where there is always some disturbance with telephone calls. More number of carbon copies cannot be produced.

(d) Electric Typewriter: Typewriter is operated electrically by the typist. This kind of typewriter is basically in the structure of a standard typewriter but connected with electricity, fitted with an electric motor. It saves the energy of the typist and reduces monotony. Semi-electric machine is another variant form.

(e) Variable Typewriter: There are different types of type faces with various sizes, shapes and styles. Now a days, a machine has been developed by which typing of letters with types of various sizes, shapes and styles is possible. The name itself indicates that it performs variable functions. The machine has differential space justification.

(f) Automatic Typewriter: This type of typewriter functions with the help of punched paper tape or paper roles or cards known as master. An automatic typewriter types an individually typed matter from a punched tape or paper tape of roles, as the case may be. The tape or roles are placed on the machine and the matter punched on the tape is automatically typed on the paper.

(g) Typewriter with Other Devices: The machine facilitates continuous typing of standard and routine work. It is a common standard typewriter with a specially fitted device. Continuous stationery can also be typed provided such stationery can be inserted in the machine.

(h) Teleprinter: Yet another type of typewriter is teleprinter. Teleprinter not only types but transmits electrical signals over wires. It is used for transmitting messages to distant places. Teleprinter is a specialised type of typewriter. A telegraphic system or instrument by which messages are sent out at one place and received at another place in a printed form. The typing machine is connected to a telephone line and the message typed at one place transmits electrical signals over the wire and the same message simultaneously reproduced, printed at a distant place by the machine. It is used at private circuit or through the post office telex service system. The post office gives teleprinters on rent to form a part of private telecommunication.

(i) Stenographic Typewriter: It is not in a strict sense, a typewriter of standard size. Though it appears like a typewriter, not only portable but also less in noise, used by a stenographer to take down shorthand dictation. It reduces monotony and work can be done at a considerable speed.

(j) Continuous Stationery: Stationery of long-run routine forms, a long strip of paper folded in zigzag manner. A separate part called as attachment is fitted to the typewriter. When there is a large quantity of work, continuous stationery is used to cope up of volume of work. It ensures speedy typing with the greatest cleanliness.

(2) Duplicating Machines: Duplicating machines are used in offices which facilitates reproduction of a number of copies of letters, reports, circulars, memos, notices etc., for circulation. Duplicating machines can reproduce promptly, efficiently with secretly. It is a substitute for printing. Usually, these machines are used to produce more number of copies which an ordinary standard typewriter cannot produce. With the help of master impression, a number of copies can be obtained. There are various types of duplicating machines. The important duplicating processor and machines used in the offices are as under:

Electograph:

(a) Flat Bed Type

(b) Rotary Type

(c) Mimeograph

(d) Multigraph (Photographic Film Electronic Stencil)

(e) Offset-Litho Duplication

(f) Copying (Photostatic Process, Diazo Microfilming)

(3) Imprinting Machines: Imprinting machines and its process contribute an addition to the existing copy. They include:

(a) Impression Stamps: Rubber stamp for instance, stamp bearing impression 'paid', 'date', 'numbering' etc.

(b) Addressing Machines: Addressing machines are useful when a number of letters are to be posted. When hundreds of bills, circulars, notices or wrappers are to be addressed, an addressing machine is used. Addressograph machines are used for the printing of the same address. They are of two types: (1) Fibre Stencils and (2) Plates. Metal plates are prepared on special embossing machines called graphotype. These plates when prepared can be preserved for future use and repeatedly used.

(c) Signature Machines: These machines can be used for imprinting signature on cheques, circulars or notices.

(d) Franking'Machines: In order to affix stamps over covers or letters, franking machines are used. These machines are used for imprinting marks of postage in large numbers. The post and telegraph department supplies these machines on hire for use in the business premises. A cover is inserted in the machine and with the help of handle it is possible to mark the letter with the required large quantities of stamps. There is no scope for risk of theft and mutilation in stamping.

(e) Date and Time Recorder: Date and time recorder is used with which all incoming mail is stamped with date and time of its arrival in the office. The mail is inserted in the recorder which automatically prints the time and date. It is used both for incoming and outgoing mail.

(4) Miscellaneous Machines: They include computing, accounting, tabulating machines, mailing scale, folding machines, inserting machines, sorting devices, adding and listing machines, billing machines, book-keeping machines, punchcard machines, and other statistical or tabulating machines.

(5) Telefax: This machine is used for transmitting sketches or drawings. The chart or diagram is originally drawn on a paper. The paper is wrapped round acylinder in the machine. The machine upon switching on transmits the fascimile to the machine at the other end where it is reproduced simultaneously.

(6) Telewriter: Also called Tele-autograph. It also operates similarly on the principle of tele-printer. A message written on a metal plate attached to machine is reproduced electrically on the machine at the other end.

MECHANICAL DEVICES FOR TRANSMITTING WRITTEN COMMUNICATION

The written documents containing messages or subject matter are to be transmitted. The question often arises how to transmit written messages. In use there are two methods of transmitting messages. They are:

(A) By Messengers.

(B) By Mechanical Devices.

Mechanical Devices: Mechanical devices are also introduced for transmission of written messages. Mechanical instruments carry messages from one place to another. Therefore, mechanical devices are broadly categorised into four types for transmission of written communication within the office. They are:

(1) Conveyors: Conveyor is a mechanical device used to convey communication. A moving conveyor with moving belt of rubber, metal is used for carrying papers and documents from one place to another. The messages are put on the conveyor which travels in fixed routes where papers and documents are picked. Conveyors are most useful when a volume of papers and documents are in large quantity. It operates by a motor driven belt under it, moves along its routes and stops at fixed stations. Overhead conveyors, horizontal conveyors, vertical conveyors are the various types of conveyors in use in offices.

(2) Chutes: Chute is a sloping channel for sending the things. A structure of wide diameter pipes or channels running downward from top to bottom or from upper level to lower level. A chute is made of metal or wood. This device can also be used for transmission of papers and documents in larger quantities from one place located in upper level to another place in a lower level.

(3) Pneumatic Tubes: When pneumatic device is desired to be installed, a cylindrical pipe is connected to their various offices. The cylinders containing papers and documents are transmitted by suction from one department to another within the office. Plastic conveyors are also now in popular use. Pneumatic tubes may be of radial type, and continues loop type.

(4) Others: *(a)* Teleprinter *(b)* Telewriter *(c)* Telefax *(d)* Television. Discussion on these devices is covered in this book elsewhere.

Communication Services

External communication is a part of communication system of an organisation. Most of external correspondence is through written communication, it is by post. The Postal Department is the important organisation of the Government of India which has established a wide network of communication services throughout the country.

Communication services provided by the postal department is of immense value not only to the business community but also to all sections of society. External communication is between the organisation and outsiders. In this mail service, the department is very essential for smooth functioning and work. If the mail is delayed, the office work is also delayed. If the communication services are inadequate, it leads not only to late delivery of correspondence but also disrupts office work.

Mail service keeps the work effective and workers with work. Therefore, it can be said that efficient communication services must be provided by the postal department. A business house may receive several letters and may correspond with them. The object of mail service is to carry written messages. The message so transmitted should be interpreted and decision is to be taken to act on that. In order to meet the needs of different businesses, the postal department has been rendering different types of communication services. These services are most useful, particularly for external communication. The important communication services are listed as under:

(1) Prepaid Postage: "Prepaid" means payment in advance to the postal department, It avoids the work of affixing stamps on each letter. It is an arrangement with the post office department to facilitate this work. Under this, the persons or the institution availing of this facility has to pay postage in cash. In case where there are large number of standard letters to be despatched, the postal department provides this facility.

(2) Value Payable Post (V.P.P.): The post office value payable postal service is more useful particularly to mail order business houses or to book publishers and sellers. In this service, post office acts as an agent in collecting money or value from the customers. For instance, a book publisher may despatch a book under V.P.P. service. It means the price of the book is collected by the post office for and on behalf of the publishers or the seller.

(3) Certificate of posting: A mail service, under which the post office gives a certificate of posting. This certificate is an evidence that a particular letter has been actually posted. For this service, post office collects a requisite fee. In all ordinary mail posted, no certificate is issued. It is an additional service of giving a certificate which serves as proof in the case of dispute regarding communication. Company meeting notices, interviews, cards etc., are generally posted under certificate of posting.

(4) Post Box Number: Postal department gives separate post box number. It is also called as post box, letter box or mail box. This service helps to take delivery of post direct from the post office from the post box without waiting for the postman. A business organisation, institution or individual with arrangement with the post office gets the number allotted. Their mail is directly put into the box, provided the post box number is written in the address.

(5) Business Reply Cards: Business houses engaged in mail order business usually use business reply cards. The reply cards help the receiver to place the orders in accordance with the requirements of the business. It is an arrangement with the post under licence. A certain sum of money as fee is payable for this service. The postal department may prescribe certain standards and business reply cards or envelopes should conform to the standards.

(6) Concessional Postage: Concessional rate of postage is another important mail service rendered by the postal department. A company engaged in a large number of letters, bulky, heavy and printed matters can avail of the facility of concessional rate of postage. The department charges a concessional rate of postage in respect of books, samples, patterns, printed magazines and journals, registered newspapers etc. Thus concessional rate is very much helpful to certain business houses.

(7) Registered Post: This service helps security for delivering communication provided a correct address is given. It serves as evidence of sending. Remitting money by money-orders, remittance through bank-drafts, cheques etc., can be done either through registered or insured letters.

(8) Acknowledgment Receipts: When a particular letter is sent by registered post, with acknowledgment due, the post office gives acknowledgment receipt of the addressee. This serves as an evidence in the case of dispute regarding communication.

(9) Telegraphic Address: An abbreviated telegraphic address can be used in transmitting messages by the communicator to the receiver. The telegraphic address is to be registered with the post office. A word containing 10 alphabets or less is to be registered; it serves as a telegraphic address. In case where telegraphic address is used, full address is not required to be written on the telegrams. This facility saves a lot of time and cost.

(10) Cipher Telegrams: This is a fast communication service through telegrams. By this the message is transmitted in a code language and the recipient has to necessarily decode the message. The receiver finds it difficult to decode the message for which he should be acquainted with the code language.

(11) Phonogram: Phonogram is used sending and receiving messages through telegram. The subject matter of the message is dictated over the telephone at either side. The cost of phonogram will be included in the routine telephone bill.

Importance of Written Communication

Lajuna Williams Lee, Saliye Starks Benoit, William Collins and Celeste Stanfield Powers, predict the importance of written communication in the future in the following way:

(1) The direct approach will be used more and more to save time and energy for the busy executive.

(2) The use of visual aids will increase and the amount of text decrease in written reports and oral presentation.

(3) Research will be faster and more economical through technology's expanding data-based systems.

(4) Use of office memorandum for dissemination of information will increase.

(5) Increased data provided by advanced technology will demand skill and competence in handling, storage on microforms will eliminate heavy file cabinets.

(6) Information will be disseminated through computers. Equipment will display information on visual screens, which will enable persons to correct errors before messages are sent. Teletypewriters transmitting electric impulses over telephone systems will reproduce written messages simultaneously on machines in neighbouring or distant offices.

(7) Computers will maintain the major pattern of business records. Primary storage will be in computers and in microfilm equipment.

(8) Business will begin to move closer to a paperless society. There will be electronic delivery rather than postal delivery. Business letters and reports will be read from machines, not just paper.[6]

Merits of Written Communication

Black and white is the most important vehicle used in the communication in all organisations. Information through paper can be transmitted in written form. Written communication as a means of gathering and disseminating information is generally used more extensively, particularly in formal communication. A considerable part of an executive's time is saved. Thus, written communication enjoys certain advantages over verbal communication. Some of the useful merits of written communication are outlined as below:

(1) Work-Relating: There is no scope in written communication to be influenced by self-interest and attitudes. The employees have to care for only their work. The subordinates have to pay great attention to the written matter and the message are formal or official, directly relating to their work.

(2) Reliability: Written communication is more reliable. It has official recognition. Oral communication is not believable but written information is correct and reliable. This principle is equally important; otherwise at times, it tends to reduce effectiveness of the message. Thus, reliability of the communication in the mind of the receiver is a factor of great significance.

(3) No Distortion: The dangers of oral communication are that it may lead to distorted information without any official sanction. Written communication does not suffer from the danger of being distorted. In every tall network where there is organisational distance, written communication is the best medium. But, in the same structure, oral communication may lead to the possibility of distortion which goes up with every increase in the organisation structure.

(4) Long-Distance Communication: Written communication is a formal method of transmitting messages and they are the most suitable for long distance communication. This is the only way out if both the communicator and recipient are located geographically in far-off places beyond the oral communication media or even beyond the mechanical oral device range.

(5) Record of Evidence: Written messages can be preserved as a record and reference source. At times, the records can be used as evidence. Reports, circulars, manuals, and other printed, written or typed documents can be filed for future reference and can be produced as legal evidence.

(6) Suitable for Lengthy Matter: A bulk of message cannot be transmitted fully and clearly by oral media with the minimum cost. But a lengthy message can be effectively circulated in black and white. The problems of missing points, forgetfulness, lack of memory and use of improper words in speaking are the problems which can be avoided in written communication.

(7) Documentary Work: A number of business transactions take place through writing, where oral communication has no place and not believed. Written communication covers all kinds of subject matter like notices, legal documents, proposals, pleading, charts, communication intelligence, memoranda and articles of associations, and many transactions concerning only with paper work.

(8) No Rumour or Gossip: Written communication usually carries no rumours and inaccurate and partial information. It has official sanction and may not even turn into gossip and rumour. It is routine, formal and will continue to exist for all times to come.

(9) Secrecy of Matter: The written media is also useful for dissemination of certain information which cannot be transmitted through the oral channel. There is every possibility that the word of mouth are heard by others. Secrecy can be maintained in written communication.

(10) Time Saving: As pointed out earlier, in a real world situation oral communication does not always save time. Written medium not only saves time, but also the cost. The cost is more in the case of conferences and meetings. In oral medium the time of many people is wasted in conversation, but in a written communication, copies of written messages can be placed on the desks of the employees.

(11) Other Advantages: It has permanent value. It promotes upward communication for clarification, correction of errors and other amendments. It is more orderly and binding on subordinates and superiors.

Demerits of Written Communication

(1) Confusion and Misinterpretation: The purpose of communication is to understand the message by the readers. Written communication may sometimes lead to confusion and misunderstanding. The chances of communication being misunderstood are more. All people may not have the same understanding capacity. Perception differs, educational background varies, interpretation too differs.

(2) Lack of Personal Touch: Written communication is comparatively less effective than oral because there is no instinct of personal contact. Everything is in black and white and a better and immediate impression cannot be created. It takes more time to see clarifications and explanations. There is no scope for exchange of feelings freely, and reaction cannot be understood immediately. Feedback is an important element of communication process. Written communication does not permit instant feedback or interaction.

(3) One-way-channel: One way communication implies giving information in flowing from top to the middle, and from middle to the operating level. Most of the written communication is orders, instructions, memos, rules and regulations issued by the superiors or top management which are imposed and enforced. A communication to be effective must be an effective two-way communication. One-way directs in a definite manner the employees to understand what the management intends them to do. So it is rigid and lacks the quality of flexibility. It is always downward communication. There is no opportunity to the subordinates to communicate upwards; they are reluctant to communicate.

(4) Absence of Grapevine: The importance of informal communication cannot be overlooked. Written communication is purely formal and generally expressed in writing manuals, orders, reports etc. There are many messages which in the general interest of the organisation cannot be put in black and white. In such cases, informal oral medium is more useful. The executives should make effective use of the grapevine for the purpose.

(5) Slow Movement: Written communication moves comparatively with little speed and often no faster than oral communication. Message gets disseminated improperly and impersonally. The element of personal touch is absent.

(6) No Interaction: It does not offer the executive insight into what the subordinates think and feel in the message. The absence of personal interaction makes it difficult to get clues of the reactions of the receivers or readers of the message. The written communication represents no natural desire of the people in the organisation to interact and communicate with each other. It does not grow up spontaneously and lacks flexibility.

(7) No Feedback: Feedback is one of the important essentials of good communication. In written communication, in respect of many matters, like objectives and policy matters, there is no scope for feedback. Feedback provision in the process of communication calls for making it a two-way process. Feedback is an inherent quality in oral communication. The communicator cannot ascertain whether the receiver has accepted or rejected the message. The reaction of the receiver of the message can be assessed effectively in oral communication than through written communication. Getting feedback information is easier in a verbal communication.

(8) Ignores Subordinates: Written communication does not give the subordinates a feeling of belonging and a sense of personal importance. So it does not help to morale building and motivation. In times of insecurity and uncertainty, there is no outlet in written communication to express freely their fears, attitudes and thoughts.

(9) Bureaucratic: The characteristic of bureaucratic administration is another drawback of written communication. It follows with delays and red tapes. Executives act in a bureaucratic way and do things officially, strictly according to the letter than spirit.

(10) Other Disadvantages: Incompleteness of message leads to a chain of clarifications. This delays action and decision-making process. Organisational efficiency is dependent not only on effective writing but on relations and interpretation by the receiver. Due to the problem of the language, the receiver of the message does not interpret it in the same manner as the communicator. Differences in status in formal education, vocabulary and cosmopolitan nature of the organisation etc., make the written communication ineffective.

REFERENCES

1. Baton, K.R. and C.S. Rayudu, *Effective Communication,* Castle Books Pvt. Ltd., New Delhi, 1994, pp. 158-159.
2. Brown L., *Communicating Facts and Ideas in Business,* Prentice-Hall Inc., Englewood Cliffs, New Jersey, 1982, pp. 82-83.
3. *Ibid.*, p. 83.
4. Balan, K.R., *Lectures on Applied Public Relations,* Sultan Chand & Sons 1984, p. 146.
5. *Ibid.*, p. 198.
6. Adapted: Lajuana Williams Lee, Saliye Starks Benoit, Williams Collins, and Celeste Stanfield Powers, *Business Communication* (Chicago; Rand Mcnally College Publishing, 1980) pp. 407-417, as reported in *Communicating Facts and Ideas in Business,* Brown, L., p. 447.

*****

CHAPTER 5

Readability and Readable Writing

Introduction

The purpose of this chapter is to present the subject on readability, principles, techniques and guidelines that will enable the writer to improve his written communication skills. The principles of readability as covered in this chapter will help to evaluate our own writing.

This chapter helps us to understand the principles, concepts to aid, to develop our ability to make writing interesting. Writings are made interesting and readable through the words we use, the vocabulary, language we apply and through our ability to think and express ideas and present them logically.

Every writer should keep in mind that the reader will react favourably and find it interesting by the effect or impression the writer creates. The writing should be familiar and natural. The language should be at the reader's level of understanding and interest which help to read the message quickly and to comprehend it easily.

The personality traits of the writer are reflected in his writing, will secure reciprocal feelings and favourable reactions. A message will promote readability quality when it produces a favourable positive reaction. Techniques that build readable writing includes short and simple sentences, clarity, length and structure, use of familiar words avoiding superfluous words and long sentences, use of simple language, unity etc.

The first basic test for effectiveness of any written message is that it should be understood clearly by the reader. The process of communication is complete with this. So every message should be capable of being readable. Readable quality reflects effective writing. All writen messages have a general and specific purpose to accomplish. Every reader analyses the writing style, so the writer should develop his message content and arrangement of the message to the readers' interest and needs.

In a formal organisation, the management's most frequently used skill in communication, the written media, provides a valuable tool for obtaining and transmitting information used in decision making, problem-solving, planning, co-ordination and creating good inter-personal and group relations.

Readability — Meaning and Nature

"Reading" means eye contact to look at printed or written words or other signs to understand. It involves looking at arbitrary symbols, representing a message. Meaning of words should be drawn to understand the idea correctly. Some words may have multiple meanings. A word when it is used in one sense may be derogatory, but when used in another way, it can be acceptable.

Use of popular words and common symbols would enable the reader to draw the correct meaning to understand the message in its real sense. The writer should keep always in mind the reader's ability, level and understanding capacity.

A response to a message is higher when symbols of the type which the readers prefer to use are used. This is the basic principle behind the idea of readability. Readability indicates that the reader is able to read. In other words, the message should be readable, easy or pleasant to read which seeks to make writing more understandable.

Rudolf Flesch has first popularised the concept of readability in the " Art of Readable Writing." He and others have developed formulae that can be applied to magazines or bulletins in order to determine their level of readability. The ultimate object of a written communication is to enable the readers to understand, so that there is a need to consider while writing the ability of the readers to interpret and finally understand.

K. Davis writes that "Bulletins, magazines, training manuals, employees' handbooks and collective bargaining contracts consistently rate 'difficult' and 'very difficult', beyond the level of statisfactory reading for typical adults."

Many readers can easily understand simple writings than complicated writings, which are very difficult to understand unless all the readers have the same capacity. Readability is the quality that everyone needs to consider when communicating.

"To read" means to look and understand, a process of learning by reading. Reading is to mind, while listening is to ears. By looking at the written or printed words, one is able to get information from it. As such writing would be easy and pleasant. A person who reads a particular matter is a reader. Effective readability indicates the quality as effective writing that creates interest in the readers to read. In other words, readability is the quality of writing, much of the written communication goes generally unread because of the lack of appropriate readability. Some writers do not maintain readability or quality of reading.

Written message is said to have readability quality when the message is easily read and quickly comprehended. Every writer has to understand the level of the reader, ability, educational background, experience etc. Reading is very hard and dry to the eyes. Readability quality of the subject matter is important in written communication. Clarity of writing and understandability of the subject is the purpose of writing. Lack of readability quality in writing leads to ineffective reading of the message.

Characteristics of Writing Style

The readability quality is the style and pattern the writer uses to convey ideas. But the style should be such, that the reader contributes good response. Different writers have different styles of writing. But every style should possess certain characteristics which are essential for understanding. Clarity, conciseness, correctness, strength, coherence, unity and completeness of the matter are the characteristics. Careful arrangement of messages, content, presentation and careful planning are also necessary.

Types of Reading

The following are the different types of reading:

(1) Proof Reading: Reading a proof of the matter which is first pulled in to compare it with the original or manuscript. A proof is a trial or specimen impression from the matter or the block. The object of proof reading is to find out the mistakes by comparing it with the 'copy' or the 'original manuscript.' It is done with a view to carry out mistakes and the copy is printed without mistakes and with absolute accuracy. Proofs are taken at various stages of work like galley proof, page proof, machine proof etc.

Proof reader is a person who corrects the mistakes. A proof reader should possess suitable qualifications to be conversant with all the marks and symbols used in correcting a proof. There are a number of proof-reading marks.

(2) Revisional Reading: "Revisional reading " presupposes reading the subject already read. The reader is already familiar with the subject, so the revisional reading is always rapid or speedy. Revisional reading is meant to confirm knowledge. It is a sort of examination of already read materials to check in order to correct faults and mistakes to make improvement in the knowledge and studying one's previous knowledge in preparation for an examination, or to revise a book for publication.

(3) Reading for Entertainment: Reading a novel is reading for entertainment.

(4) Search Reading: A research reading which is an attempt to find something. It implies to find out the truth by careful examination. It is a process of reading and understanding the subject for examination of material. In other words, it is probing for specific information.

(5) Critical Reading: It is a type of writing undertaken to find or judge good or bad points. In a way, it implies fault-finding. For instance reading a book seriously for review.

(6) Exploratory Reading: Exploratory reading is for the purpose of investigation or exploration. This type of reading helps the reader to get a general view of the subject.

(7) Reading to Master: Some readers are interested in mastering the subject for information. Such a reading is called reading to master the subject. A person who is skilled in careful, slow reading makes repeated readings.

Studying Systematically (SQ3R)

The technique of SQ3R is the most popular technique of systematic study.

SQ3R stands for:

S — Survey

Q — Questions

R — Reading

R — Recite

R — Revise

(1) Survey: According to this technique, the reader is expected to look at or view the book in a general way. In brief, this means that instead of reading a particular part or chapter of a book, one should read or examine carefully in detail the whole book. It means the reader must read not only the main subject but also the object of writing, purpose of a book, preface, acknowledgements, table of contents, index, glossary, abstracts, summary, findings and conclusions.

(2) Questions: This technique requires the reader to read speedily through the chapter and list questions as occur and perceived by the reader. Jotting down such questions encourages, gives purpose and helps to think and master the knowledge.

(3) Reading: The method of reading a novel is quite different from reading a textbook. A textbook should be read carefully, objectively and slowly. The habit of novel reading is generally rapid as it is for entertainment and for general information. A textbook reading requires first and subsequent readings and understanding takes some time. Matters in a textbook are presented systematically divided into paragraphs with headings and sub-headings.

(4) Recitation: The reading of a textbook generally requires to repeat aloud from memory. Slow repetition is needed. Recitation is common in the case of infant school children.

(5) Revision: The last preparatory step in effective reading is revision. It is a process of re-study and re-learn. A revision in reading pre-supposes reading the same subject already read. The reader is familiar, with the subject and having touch, so the revisional reading is always rapid.

Guidelines to Readability

According to R. Flesch, the following list offers some guidelines for more readable writing:

(1) Use Simple Words and Phrases: It is always desirable to use simple words and phrases such as 'improve' instead of 'ameliorate' 'and' 'like' instead of 'in a manner similar to that of.'

(2) Use Short and Familar Words: Readable writing demands using short and familiar words such as "darken" instead of 'obfuscate.

(3) Use Personal Pronouns: A writing is said to have a quality of readability when it uses personal pronouns such as 'you' and 'them' if the style permits.

(4) Use Illustrations, Examples and Charts: These techniques are even better when the things are tied to the reader's experience.

(5) Use Short Sentences and Paragraphs: Big words and thick reports may look impressive to people but the communicator's job is to inform people and not to impress them.

(6) Use Active Words: Such as "the manager said...." rather than "It was said by the manager ...."

(7) Use Only Necessary Words: For example, in the sentence "bad weather condition prevented my trip", the word "condition" is unnecessary. Say "bad weather prevented my trip."

The following are some guidelines for good written communication suggested by several experts on the subject of communications like A. Burack, J. Lindauer etc.

(8) Receiver's Needs: The written message must be drafted with receiver's needs clearly in mind.

(9) Thought Ahead of Time: The facts of the message must be thought ahead of time.

(10) Brief: The message should be as brief as possible. Eliminate all unnecessary words and ideas. Important messages should be prepared in draft form first and then corrected.

(11) Summary: If the message is long, place a summary of the report on the first page. This summary should make the main points clear, with page references for details of each item.

(12) Message should be Carefully Organised: The message should be carefully organised. State your most important point first, then the next most important point and so on. This way, if the receiver reads only the first few points, the main message will get across.

(13) Title: Make the subject clear by giving the message a title.

(14) Short, Clear Sentences: Use simple words. Make the message more readable by using short and clear sentences.[1]

Measuring Readability

Readability Formula: There are number of readability formulae evolved for rating messages by measuring their difficulty. The standard of readability is measured in terms of the general educational level of the readers.

Readability of subject matter is important in written communication. Clarity of writing and understandability of the subject is the purpose of writing. Lack of readability quality in writing leads to not reading the message.

A number of formulae have been developed for rating materials by measuring their difficulty. Readers do not have the time to read involving trouble in understanding. Flesch, Dale, and Chall, Farr, Jenkins and Patterson and Gunning have developed readability formulae. Among them, Gunning's methods of readability formula is one of the easiest to understand and apply. He advocated seven factors affecting readability. They are:

1. Average sentence length in words.
2. Percentage of simple sentences.
3. Percentage of verbs expressing forceful action.

4. Proportion of familiar words.
5. Percentage of personal references.
6. Proportion of abstract words.
7. Percentage of long words.

Gunning's Fog Index: Gunning used two elements in his formula, the percentage of words of three or more syllables in 100 words and the average sentence length in words.

To find the Fog index of a passage, take these three simple steps[2]:

(1) Determine the average sentence length: Count the number of words in the successive sentences. For long pieces of writing, take samples of 100 words. Divide the total number of words by the number of sentences. Do not count the articles 'a', 'an', 'the' as words.

(2) Find the percentage of hard words: Count the number of words of three syllables or more per 100 words. Do not count words that are capitalised, that are a combination of short, easy words (like "bookkeeper" and "Butterfly"), or that are verb forms made into three syllables by adding -ed or-es (like "created" or "trespasses").

(3) Figure the Fog index: Add the two factors (step 1 and 2) and multiply by 0.4.

Impact of Readability Formulae: Readability formulae have been evolved to measure readability which help the writer to organise the material of the message in a readable form. It is also not advisable to write in a style in too many short, simple sentences. Sometimes, use of familiar words and presentation of short and simple sentences is not recommended because most familiar words and short sentences may not convey the idea in clear terms. Writing with a variety vocabulary may solve the problem of monotonous and repetition of the same words.

The formulae evolved may not measure in a particular way for the general reader. They do not prescribe hard and fast principles to be used as rules for writing. The importance of understanding the readers' level background, experience, purpose and many other factors that go into effective writing should not be ignored. The writer should adapt writing to the reader which emphasises the need for clear sentences and understandable words to make the writing readable. Above all, clearness, clarity and brevity should not be ignored.

Clarifying Strategies

Baird has suggested that to avoid misunderstanding, we can employ suitable strategies which promote clear communication. The following are such strategies:[3]

(1) Succinctness: This strategy includes using of only necessary words, speaking as simply and economically as possible.

(2) Definition: It requires to give a definition and explanation of meanings of words and terms used. Every communicator must try to anticipate the scope for misunderstanding and accordingly, it is useful to explain or define clearly our meanings to words used and intended.

(3) Singularity: This strategy considers only one topic at a time, taking things step by step.

(4) Repetition: Key issues, difficult points, ideas usually confusing the receiver should be repeated. Repetition, however, does not mean restatement of ideas, but a rephrasing by which difficult terms or issues are employed to make the same point.

(5) Analogy: It demands drawing an analogy between the situations. Baird states that many ideas and processes may be clarified by comparing them with things the receiver already understands.

(6) Structure: The message should be carefully organised into a clear and coherent structure.

REFERENCES

1. Taken from: A. Burrack, *The Writers' Handbook*, Boston, *The Writer*, 1972; J. Lindauer, *Communicating in Business*, New York: Macmillan, 1974; R. Lesikar, *Business Communication*, Homewood, *IL*; Richard D. Irwin, 1972 as reported in *Management,* Don Hellriegel, John W. Slocum, Jr. pp. 569-570.
2. Gunning, *The Technique of Clear Writing*, pp. 38-41 as reported in *Communicating Facts and Ideas in Business*, L. Brown, p. 89.
3. John E. Baird, Jr., *The Dynamics of Organisational Communication*, Harper and Row Publishers, New York, 1977, pp. 56-58.

*****

CHAPTER 6

Non-Verbal Communication and Skills

Meaning and Nature

One of the multi media of communication is non-verbal communication, also called "communication by implication." Communicating a message without using arbitrary symbols, i.e., words or meaning of words, is termed as "non-verbal communication." In other words, non-verbal communication is word less communication. The communication behaviour of the speaker, as our experience indicates, can be by postures, movements and other cues. A speaker may use many languages of communication, both verbal and non-verbal.

Non-verbal languages consist of hidden messages; it is the cues which convey message. These messages are necessarily wordless or non-verbal, conveyed through without resorting to words or meaning of words, but conveyed through other media like spatial, kinesics, oral cues, objective language action, etc. Kinesics is the most generally used medium of communication. Actions like stroking, hitting, holding, patting and hand-shaking convey meaningful messages. All the forms of non-verbal communication media essentially convey meaning like words in verbal communication.

In simple terms, non-verbal communication includes all messages other than those expressed in oral or written words.

Behavioural expressions or cues that do not rely on words or word symbols are known as "non-verbal communication." Words alone are, in many cases, not adequate to express our feelings and reactions. When someone remarks that he does not know how to express himself in words, it can be concluded that his feelings are too intense and complex to be expressed in words.

Non-verbal messages express true feelings more accurately than the spoken or written language. Both kinds of data can be transmitted intentionally or unintentionally. Even smile symbolises friendliness, in much the same way as cordiality is expressed in words.

Verbal and non-verbal behaviour may be the duplication of one another. If a person says: "Please have a seat" and points towards a chair, they can be complimentary. For example, a person smiles and explains "Come in, I am pleased to see you." The two codes — verbal and non-verbal — can be contradictory. A listener tells the speaker how interested he is in what is being said, while the former is seen staring across the hall with an attractive young woman.

People express their feelings through gestures. In business interactions, the knowledge of body language and non-verbal cues can be of immense use and value.

Words of Caution

It is important to understand very clearly that non-verbal gestures do not necessarily have universal meaning. For example, folded hands (meaning defensiveness) are best understood in relation to the particular situation in which they occur. It has been observed that a hypnotist normally selects only those who are sitting in an informal, relaxed posture, with arms open. Not the people with crossed legs or with folded arms; but they are not necessarily over-inhibited, neurotic people.

Another point to be remembered relates to cultural differences, not situational. In some cultures, girls do not look at the adults in the eye; but this does not mean they should be pronounced guilty if being investigated on some suspicion.

A more accurate understanding of a person's body language is possible if we view it in relation to the particular situation and the person's social and cultural background as well.

Readers may be surprised to know that according to several studies, women are more accurate in sending and receiving non-verbal messages of emotions. Male psychiatrists, psychologists, teachers, actors, artists and designers score as high as women.

Body-language reading is mostly a learned ability. Our sensitivity to non-verbal message increases with experience and age.[1]

Importance

The importance of non-verbal medium of communication cannot be overemphasised. It is necessary that every listener should get himself acquinted with skills of non-verbal communication to observe and understand effectively. Every speaker when talking to us, uses and gives non-verbal signals. According to one study, only seven per cent of a message effect is carried by words and listeners receive the other 93 per cent through non-verbal means.[2]

The question often arises whether silence is a mode of a communication or not. The answer is that one can communicate silently. So silence is a mode of communication. Silence also sometimes speaks louder than words. Actions often speak louder than words. Silence, gestures, handshake, shrug of the shoulders, a smile all have meaning and hence communicate with others.

Forms or Media of Non-Verbal Communication

Different experts and specialists have classified non-verbal communication into various categories. Ruesch and Kees were the first researchers in the field of non-verbal communication. They described three categories of non-verbal communication as three distinct languages.

However, the media of non-verbal communication are discussed in the following paragraphs classified appropriately.

(1) Sign Language: Marks or symbols used to mean something is termed as signs of language. Gestures are used in the place of words, number, or punctuations marks in the sign language. The language system of deaf people and the hitch-hiker's finger is the example of sign language."[3]

(2) Action Language: It is a language of movements. Action is one of non- verbal media of communication, a third type of communication. Action in a particular situation and context is capable of interpretation. By action, one may knowingly or unknowingly be communicating with others. Action speaks louder than words. Some believe in action and some others in words. Some people do what they say they will do, while some others say one thing but do another. The difference between these styles of communication is called a person's "Communication Credibility Gap" and when the credibility gap is large, it signifies loss of confidence or distrust.

(3) Objective Language: (Artifacts) Objective language medium of non- verbal communication indicates display and arrangement of material things. This method may include intentional or unintentional communication of material things like clothing, ornaments, books, buildings, room furniture, interior decorations etc. Objective language speaks something. Objective language with reference to silence or non-verbal communication refers to dress and decoration which communicate a great deal about the speaker's feelings, emotions, attitudes, opinions etc.

Clocks, jewellery, hairstyle interior decorative items communicate something. Their revealing is symbolic, communicating something special about the person. Dress by people of different countries varies. Dress of armymen differs from civilians, land army, airforce and naval personnel according to their rank. Dress of religious heads, political leaders, lawyers, judges, doctors, nurses, sports person and workers, differ from one another. The executive look is different between women and men. Similarly, differences can be noted between professional look, blue collar look etc. Objective language is non-verbal message communicated through appearance of objects.

(4) Spatial or Environmental: It is relating to the place or environment in which the actual process of communication takes place. It may be physical or psychological. The environment for communication must be congenial and conducive to effective communication. It is the responsibility of the leader of the group in the case of a small group, to provide an environment conducive to effective two-way communication. The necessary requirements of environment are lighting, colour, ventilation, temperature, seating arrangement, chalkboard, public address system, audio-visual equipment etc., which would contribute a lot to attract and make listeners more attentive. So environmental factors also have an impact on communication in face-to-face or interpersonal communication.

(5) Silence: In many circumstances, silence also is an effective medium of communication. Through silence, some people evoke response from others. Take for instance, a speaker entering a meeting hall to address a gathering finds the meeting environment unconductive with humming and noise created by the audience. In order to divert the attention of the audience, the speaker climbs up to the stage and takes his position near the mike — a silent posture. The attention of the audience is diverted to the presence of the speaker. It indicates that the audience should be quiet now so that he could commence his speech.

In a number of situations if no response or reply is received within a specific period or happening or non-happening of a situation, the silence on the part of the respondent signifies communication. The practice of silence is usually taken as approved in a number of personal, business and social transactions as practice, custom, tradition or understanding.

Silence as a mode of communication has some legal significance, particularly in the law of contracts. Legal doctrines speak on silence. The acceptance of an offer can neither be implied through silence nor by his failure to answer. Sometimes, silence itself is considered equivalent to speech. In some cases, silence is considered as fraud and in some other cases it is not a fraud. Thus, silence is likely to affect the willingness and consent of another person also. However, silence as a medium of communication is considered as a dangerous mode of communication.

(6) Demonstration: Demonstration is a process of showing how some thing works. It indicates a display or exhibition of how something works. It is a public expression of opinion by holding meetings and processions showing placards. Demonstration is thus yet another effective method of non-verbal words or meaning of words. In this method of non-verbal skills may be shown. Demonstration is made and dramatised as a means of emphasis on the subject under consideration.

Take, for instance, a salesman giving a demonstration to a person or group of persons as to how to operate or use a product. Such demonstrations naturally works out to be more telling and effective than providing written or oral description of the same. Demonstration as to how to use or operate a particular product provides a clear and better understanding of the product.

(7) Inaction: It is opposed to action as discussed above. Inaction also is one of the non-verbal media of communication. Inaction explains with illustration as to how to use or operate a product. A person's inaction in certain circumstances can be a method of communication. Unexplained action often communicates meaning which is not intended.

"Take for instance, some machinery has been removed from the production floor under the orders of the manager, without telling the workers the reasons for the same.

To the workers, this appears an apprehension of a threatened shut down shifting of the plant to another city. Obviously, such unexplained action will communicate a meaning, and a message, the manager has no intention to send".[4]

(8) Proximics: The distance that the people keep themselves between the speaker and the listener is termed as proximics. Generally, people are not conscious and aware about proximics but the distance affect interpersonal communication. Personal space is an invisible factor or rule.

Space between persons indicates relations at the same time and is a dimension of interpersonal communication. Personal space and interpersonal distance are important components of communication. Edward T. Hall in his scholarly work identified three components of interpersonal distance. They are:

(a) Intimate.

(b) Social.

(c) Public.

They govern interpersonal relationship.

(a) Intimate: (i) The intimate distance ranges from very close (3 to 6 inches — for soft whispers; secrets are intimate communication).

(ii) To close (8 to 12 inches — for giving confidential information)

(iii) To near (12 to 20 inches — for speaking in a soft voice).

(b) Social: The social distance ranges from 20 inches to 5 feet.

(c) Public: The public distance from 6 feet to above 100 feet.

Cultural patterns regulate personal space and interpersonal communication. They are unspoken and invisible rules governing personal distance. People who stand too near when they are more intimate. When they are not so close, they should be at a distance.

Interpersonal distance may vary from culture to culture. Different cultures and backgrounds also keep distance. For instance, standoffishness prevails in British culture which tends to widen the gap. On the other hand, closeness to one another prevails in French and Italian culture. The family differences are due to cultural differences.

According to Edward T. Hall, interpersonal distances in different cultures are as follows:

(a) In America, the comfortable distance to stand for social conversation is about 2 to 3 feet.

(b) In France, Mexico, Brazil and Arab countries, it is shorter than 2 feet. M. Patterson's study indicates that people in relatively close proximity are viewed as warmer, friendlier and more understanding than people farther away.[5]

Albert Mehrabian found that physical distance emphasises the status differences and that status is minimised by greater closeness.[6]

(9) Time: Use of time is also as chronemics as an important non-verbal method of communication. Time also conveys the message. Time speaks. Edward T. Hall is the first scholar who has investigated time dimension of interpersonal communication. Time is a mode of interpersonal communication. Time is an important factor which is precise and valuable. In these days of busy living, business and social relations, time can be saved, wasted, given and taken.

Punctuality or delay speaks pleasant or unpleasant feelings and attitudes. Tardiness is considered an insult in some cultures. Late arrival to attend a meeting in time, convey something. Time is very valuable in group activities of many organisations. In certain circumstances, arriving at an appointed place on or before time, communicate something. A telephone call at too early hours or late night conveys, significant message. For instance, a telephone call a 1 A.M. or 2 A.M. communicates something of urgency, unusual message to be attended to on a priority basis.

(10) Paralanguage: Another important dimension of non-verbal communication is paralanguage. Non-verbal things in communication are called paralanguage. Sounds are the basis for paralanguage. Paralanguage include tone of voice, power or emphasis, pitch, rhythm, volume pause or break in sentence, speed of delivery, loudness or softness etc. These languages too influence meaning and convey message. Paralanguage can be divided into four parts.

(1) Voice Qualities: Including such factors as pitch, resonance, volume, rate and rhythm.

(2) Vocal Characterizers: Embracing laughter, coughing, throat clearing and sighing.

(3) Vocal Qualifiers: Referring to variations in pitch and volume.

(4) Vocal Segregates: Including the silent sound such as 'ahs' and 'ers' and pauses. These clues do much to influence meaning."[7]

(11) Kinesics:

1. Facial expressions.
2. Gestures.
3. Body movements.
4. Postures.
5. Eye contact.
6. Tactile (touch).

Sub-categories of Kinesics

Ekman and Friesen have classified body movement or kinesics into the following five sub-categories:[8]

(1) Emblems: Non-verbal cues, which have direct verbal translation. include such gestures as those used to signify "OK" and "Peace" or "Victory".

(2) Illustrators: These cues correspond directly to the spoken words, serving to illustrate the meaning of those words. If you ask for direction and the verbal response is accompanied by pointing in the appropriate direction, that gesture would be considered illustrative. Any movement which accentuates speech, demonstrates a physical characteristic, depicts a spatial relationship, or recreates bodily action belongs to this category.

(3) Affect Displays: Indicators of inner emotions, these behaviours include a clenched fist (hostility), a stooped posture (submissiveness) and a bowed head (depression).

(4) Regulators: Certain non-verbal cues control the flow of conversation between individuals. When one person has finished a statement, she or he may nod in the direction of the other participant as if to say. I'm finished it's your turn to speak. Regulatory movements may also suggest that the individual should speak faster, slow down, repeat, elaborate or in some way modify her or his message transmission.

(5) Adaptors: "Behaviour falling into this category are thought to be fragments of complete behaviours through which people adapt to their environment. Consider the "foot wiggling" behaviour exhibited by nervous or bored individuals. According to the fractional behaviour concept, this foot behaviour actually is a part of the total behaviour the individual would like to perform. Because one is bored or nervous one's true inclination is to get up and leave — to perform the complete foot behaviour. Because of the nature of the situation, however, one is not free to go; thus one adapts to the situation by performing a fractional behaviour, by psychologically running while physically remaining seated.

A detailed discussion of kinesics is presented in the following paragraphs:

(1) Facial Expressions: Facial expressions too communicate message effectively. As a matter of fact, facial expressions as a form of non-verbal communication medium is more effective and communication completes its circle by it. Some expressions are intentional or unintentional, conscious or unconscious. Facial expressions definitely transmit feelings, facts, emotions, ideas, opinions, attitudes etc. It is one of the kinesics media that include smile, frown, narrowed eyes, exhibit friendliness, anger, disbelief etc.

Human face has four important parts. They are:

(i) Upper face — Eyebrows and forehead.

(ii) Middle face — Eyes, eyelids and nose foot.

(iii) Lower face — Mouth and chin.

(iv) The sides of the face — like cheeks.

These parts of human face are capable of conveying wide range of expressions and emotions. Facial expressions convey happiness, anger, surprise, boredom, fear, sadness, disgust, liking, disliking, rejection, love, jealousy, agreement, frustration, ease, pain, pleasure etc.

Smiling at a subordinate communicates meaning. For instance, when a subordinate approaches his superior, with his task assigned, completed to get his approval, the superior expresses his silent approval by a smile. Otherwise, he may frown at to express dissatisfaction or raise an eye-brow to show surprise. The expression or movement to make the forehead wrinkle and the eyebrow moved down are signs of worry, disapproval of deep thought. He frowned at the worker for bad work or behaviour. The way of looking, i.e., long look or short look communicates a great deal about one's feelings, attitudes, emotions, tensed or relaxed mood of the speaker.

Demond W. Evany has listed the following possible components of facial expressions:

(1) "Forehead — upward and downward frowns.

(2) Eyebrows — raising or knitting, furrowing.

(3) Eyelids — Opening, closing narrowing.

(4) Eye pupils — dilating.

(5) Eyes — upwards, downwards, gazing, holding or avoiding eye contact.

(6) Nose — wrinkling, flaring nostrils.

(7) Facial muscles — drawn up or down, for grinning, teeth clenching.

(8) Lips — smiling, pursing, drawn in.

(9) Mouth — wide open, drawn in, half-open.

(10) Tongue — licking lips, moving around inside cheeks, sucking teeth.

(11) Jaw/chin — thrust forward, handing down.

(12) Head — thrown back inclines to one side, hanging down, chin drawn in, inclined upwards".[9]

The following is the list of various range of response from facial expressions as listed by him:

Acceptance	Rejection
Enjoyment	Dislike
Friendship	Hostility
Interest	Disinterest
Anger	Love
Sympathy	Jealousy
Assurance	Nervousness
Agreement	Disagreement
Attention	Boredom
Acceptance	Disbelief
Surprise	Fear
Impatience	Frustration
Envy	Empathy
Ease	Discomfort
Alertness	Stupor
Pain	Pleasure
Ecstasy	Torment
Satisfaction	Displeasure.[10]

Emotions and Facial Expressions: There are important indications of emotions. The positive feelings such as love, happiness, surprise are the easiest to decipher. Negative emotions like anger, sadness, anxiety are usually somewhat difficult to recognise.

There are six basic emotions associated with facial expression:[11]

(i) Anger: Eyebrows furrowed, wrinkles on forehead, eyes squinting, lips pressed together or bared teeth.

(ii) Sadness: Eyebrows drawn together, eyes glazed, with droopping upperlip, mouth closed with outer corners pulled slightly down.

(iii) Surprise: Lifted eyebrows, wide-open eyes, slightly open mouth, parted lips, a strange sparkle in the eyes.

(iv) Fear: Eyebrows raised and drawn together, corners of the mouth drawn back, lips stretched, eyes open wide, drops of perspiration on the face.

(v) Frustration: Lowered eyebrows, wrinkled nose, mouth open or semi-open, eyes fixed in a particular direction, upper lip pushed up by lower lip.

(vi) Happiness: Relaxed eyes, corners of lips raised, usually drawn back, no distinctive eye-brows.

(2) Gestures: A gesture is a movement of the head, hand, body etc., to express an idea, feeling, emotions etc. Speakers sometimes emphasise their words with gestures. Action when exhibited, is intended to show a person's feelings. Gestures were probably one of the first means of communicating even before oral communication came into being.

Gestures convey meaningful messages which either accompany spoken words or stand alone. For instance, nodding head means to say 'yes' and in certain circumstances it also means 'no.' Similarly, shaking of head sideways is to say 'no.' The language of the deaf is a sign language. A blind person has his own sophisticated systems of sign language. A speaker usually in a serious mood, while presenting the text, uses many gestures of hands and head to emphasise certain words.

Gestures play an equally important role as medium of non-verbal communication to convey messages effectively. Some example are:

the shoulder shrug,
thumbs up,
shaking hands,
thumb and finger rub,
hand to face,
mouth guard,
nose lowering,
caller pull,
arm folders,
leg gestures,
head nod,
head shake,
eye signals,
lipstics,
rolling lips,
body lowering,
pointer, including eyes and fingers,
sitting positions,
wink of the eyes etc.
are all various types of gestures of communication.

The following are the commonly used gestures as identified by D.W. Evany:

Head: nodding sideways to urge someone along:
nodding up and down;
shaking sideways;
inclined briefly:
cradled in one or both hands.

Arms and Hands: Widely outstretched;
jammed into trouser pockets;
holding the back of the head with fingers laced;
firmly folded across the chest;
making chopping movements with the side of the hand;
hands pressed together in a 'praying' position;
one or both hand held over mouth;
flat of hand patting desk-top;
hand brushing something away in the air;
both hands placed open upon the chest.

Fingers: running through the hair;
drumming on table-top;
stroking mouth and chin;
stabbing the air with forefinger;
clenched into a fist;
manipulated in an arm-wave;
patting the fingers together with fingers of both hands stretched;
rubbing the thumb and fingers together.

Legs and Feet: Leg and foot making kicking motion;
foot or toes tapping the ground;
moving legs up and down while seated.[12]

"A traffic constable is able to direct traffic on crowded road through gestures of hands and arms, without verbal communication. People reveal their feelings and attitudes by the way they stand or sit and the way they move parts of the body. We feel more comfortable conversing with those who adopt a relaxed posture Here are some interesting findings.

Co-operative Situation: People stand or sit at a right angle to one another.

Stranger or bargaining: Face to face position.

Women often prefer to converse with their partners at a slight angle or side by side especially if they know each other well.

Men often prefer the face-to-face position unless they are in a competitive situation."[13]

(3) Body Movements: Body language is an important mode of non-verbal communication. People communicate in natural way giving meanings to others with their bodies in interpersonal interaction. Ir verbal communication, body language supports in most parts of the words in a speech. Face and head are used for body language mostly along with other body languages like eye-contact, eye-movement, smile, frown, touching, furrowed brow, hip moment, closeness and breathing rate.

Body movements communicate messages effectively. Some movements are intentional, or unintentional, conscious or unconscious. A speaker sometimes may be in upright position but his body moves. Body movement definitely transmits feelings, emotions, ideas, reasons, opinions, attitudes etc.

Myers and Myers on facial expression and body movements state that a person may tend to lean forward when he is involved and interested, and to lean back when not interested. The way of walking often indicates to others whether feeling good, happy and cheerful or sad, gloomy, tired and dejected. They further say that, "You indicate your perception of status by your postures. You tend to relax around people of equal or lower status and tense up around people who you perceive as having of higher status. You sometimes feel that someone is disrespectful simply because he or she talks in a more relaxed manner than you think is appropriate."[14]

Body movements include movements of hands, head, face, eyes and postures which give meaning without using words. One can read others' thoughts by their body movements. They show personal relationships between people, as their body movements speak to others how they feel and think. Unless listeners are aware of and sensitive to others' postures, gestures, facial expressions they cannot understand the message as clearly and effectively as possible.

(4) Tactile Communication (Touch): A gentle touch of a friendly hand on the shoulders communicate encouragement. Feeling of sense communicates something. One can communicate a great deal by touch. Like geature, touch is also one of the earliest methods of communication of human beings. Infants, learn much about their environment by touching, feeling, cuddling and tasting. A pat on the back, shaking hands, or holding hands can express more than a lengthy speech. Lovers know this, and mothers too. Touching is a powerful communicative tool and serves to express a tremendous range of feelings such as fear, love, anxiety, warmth and coldness.[15]

(5) Eye Contact: The language of the eye contact:

(1) "Much of our knowledge is obtained through our visual sense. We are more apt to maintain eye contact with the speaker while discussing pleasant topics.

(2) We are more likely to avoid eye contact while discussing unpleasant or embarrassing topics.

(3) We tend to look more at those whom we admire or with whom we have more intimate relationship.

(4) Women tend to have greater eye contact than men probably because they feel more comfortable with intimacy.

(5) The function of eye gaze or the lack of it is to regulate interaction.

(6) The individuals who engage in high levels of eye gaze are typically seen as more influential and effective in their dealings with others.

(7) Eye contact serves as a signal of readiness to interact and its absence tends to reduce the chances of such interaction."[16]

Small Illustrations

(i) **Touch:** A gentle touch of a friendly hand on the shoulders can communicate encouragement.

(ii) **Taste:** Message may be transmitted by flavour of preparation of food products. They communicate fulfilment of recipes and proper operation of equipment.[17]

(iii) **Smell:**Fragrance, aroma and odour can signify fulfilment of production packing and storage instructions.[18]

(iv) **Hearing:** For instance, typewriter's bell, calling bell indicate the end of the line or calling a person. Bells in schools, colleges indicate commencement or end of the hour.

(v) **Horn:** A horn of a vehicle indicates approach of a vehicle.

(vi) **Calling bells, buzz, beeper etc.** Their sounds indicate calling or attention.

(vii) **Shrug of shoulders:** There is a symbolic meaning in the most ordinary shrug of shoulders.

(viii) **Hand movements:** The standardised hand movements express ideas.

(ix) **Pointed fingers:** Doing skills are exhibited. A pointed finger means that something is to be demonstrated. They convey a whole range of meanings by stylised finger movements. Ticktak men on the race course can convey complex messages to one another.

(x) **Visual aids:** For details see Chapter on Communication Technology.

(6) Vocal expressions: "The tone of one's voice is a valuable clue to the feelings. Para-language is a term denoting the subtle variations in meanings between what is said and how it is said.

The words "wow! how fast you are this time!" could be a compliment. But if the tone of the voice is sarcastic, it symbolises disgust and anger.

Different meanings can be conveyed by the rate, pitch, and volume of the voice.

Speaking fast may indicate nervousness and haste. A soft voice soothes and clams.

A loud, shouting voice foretell danger, urgency, serious problem, joy or anger.

Emphasis on key words indicate the degree of importance you attach to it."[19]

Effects of Non-Verbal Communication

In inter personal communication, every non-verbal cue is an important message. A number of research studies on the subject have disclosed some effects of it. The impact of non-verbal communication is presented under the following paras as disclosed in some of the research studies conducted by the behavioural researchers.

(1) Environment: Maslow and Mintz conducted a study on environment of the three categories like:

(i) An Ugly Room: to appear as a messy janitore' closet.

(ii) An Average Room: a professor's office.

(iii) A Beautiful Room: having carpeting drapes, nice furniture.

The study on these three environments indicates:

Ugly Room: Monotonous, fatiguing, irritating, unpleasant.

Beautiful Room: Pleasure, comfort, importance, enjoyment.

(2) Proximics: The effect of non-verbal communication as revealed by the study of Hall indicates that people want "territories" as their own in any given environment. Such territories include:

(i) Space surrounding one's body artifacts (brief case, books, purses),

(ii) Objects in the environment (chairs, desks, tables).

(iii) Space used by persons such as the area between two conversants, larger territories such as houses or offices.

(3) Para language: Vocal cues have effects, indicating personality characteristics and their emotional status. It is an important dimension of non- verbal communication. Non-verbal things in communication are called para language. Sounds are the basis for para language. Para languages include tone of voice, power or emphasis, pitch, rhythm, volume, pause or break in sentence, speed of delivery, loudness or softness etc. The para language too influences meaning and conveys messages. Para language can be divided into four parts.

(i) Voice Qualities: Including such factors as pitch, resonance, volume, rate and rhythm.

(ii) Vocal Characteristics: Embracing laughter, coughing, throat-clearing and sighing.

(iii) Vocal Qualifiers: Referring to variations in pitch and volume.

(iv) Voice Segregates: Including the silent sounds such as 'ahs' and 'ers' and pauses. These clues do much to influence meaning."[20]

Addington has conducted a study on the effects of vocal cues on perceptions of personality. Some of his findings are as follows:[21]

(i) "Breathiness: Males having this characteristic were rated as younger and more artistic; females prettier, more petite, more effervescent, highly strung and shallow.

(ii) Flatness: Males were rated more masculine, sluggish, cold and withdrawn; females also were rated masculine, sluggish, cold and withdrawn.

(iii) Nasality: Both males and females were attributed a variety of negative characteristics.

(iv) Tenseness: Males were judged older, more stubborn, and more cantankerous; females younger, emotional, feminine, highly strung and less intelligent.

(v) Throatiness: Males were rated older, more realistic, mature, sophisticated, and well-adjusted; females less intelligent, more masculine, lazy, ugly, sickly, careless, naive, neurotic, and a variety of other negative characteristics."

(4) Physical Characteristics: Physical or body characteristics are attentiveness and physique. Attractive people are more persuasive and influential. The study of Singer establish that attractive female students generally are able to obtain higher grades from male instructors than are female rated unattractive.

The research study of Mills and Aronson found that an attractive female speaker could produce more change of attitude in all male audience than an unattractive female could. Physique indicates body shape which too influences the perception of audience.

According to the study of Sheldon, there are three general body shapes. They are:

(i) **Endomorph:** Soft, round and tending to be fat (talkative, warm-hearted, less good looking, sympathetic).

(ii) **Mesomorph:** Bony, muscular and atheletic (stronger, better looking, self-reliant and dominant).

(iii) **Etcomorph:** To be tall, thin and fragile (more ambitious, suspicious of others, tends pessimistic and quiet).

(5) Artifacts: They represent objective language, includes decoration, covering personal decoration of physical bodies with clothing, jewellery and cosmetics. Artifacts, too, communicate messages silently and create an impact and influence the attitude and perception of the people. A person well dressed and decorated would produce significantly more influence than by a person poorly dressed and not decorated. The study of Thornton disclosed that people wearing glasses were rated higher in intelligence and industriousness. Similarly, the research study of McKeachie revealed that females using lipstick were judged frivolous, unworried, less talkative, conscientious and surprisingly, less interested in the opposite sex.

(6) Facial Expressions: The two major parts of facial expression are movements of facial features and movement of eyes. They convey non-verbal messages effectively. Face is the most expressive part of the body, with a facial expression, a large number of complex meanings and inner feelings can be conveyed by all most unnoticed changes in facial expression. There is a close relationship between facial expressions and emotional feelings of the speaker.

The study of Ekman reveals the following:

(i) **Happiness:** Is shown most in the lower face and eye areas.

(ii) **Sadness:** Is shown in the eyes.

(iii) **Surprise:** Is shown in the eyes and lower face.

(iv) **Anger:** Is shown in the lower face and brows, forehead.

(v) **Disgust:** Is shown in the lower face.

(vi) **Fear:** In the eyes.

Thus, eye contact creates behaviour change. An eye contact shows the need for oral communication. Avoiding eye contact indicates avoidance of communication.

(7) Kinesics: Kinesic indicates gestures, body movements, head, hands, feet, limbs. With the help of body orientation, openness and postures, it is quite possible to change attitudes and influence others. According to Mehrabian, the relationship between several postures and positions and interpersonal linking, he found that female communicators used very indirect body orientation when speaking to someone they disliked, and very direct with people towards whom they liked. His study also reveals that persons perceiving to have higher status than the persons they are addressing tend to face them directly, stands with hand on hips, have a greater body relaxation, and maintain a relatively raised head position. On the other hand, persons with lower status tend to face the other more indirectly, have higher body tension and look downward frequently.

(8) Touch: Touch is the easiest and one of the earliest forms of human communication. Stroking, hitting, patting, shaking hands etc., are the important modes and play a role in human behaviour, though many people avoid touch with others. The study of Bardeen classified people involved into three different types and three situations. They are:

- **(i) Verbal Only:** People blind-folded and allowed to talk with one another (distant, artificial, formal, insensitive and non-communicative).
- **(ii) Visual Only:** People allow only to look at one another (artificial, childish, comic, arrogant and cold).
- **(iii) Touch Only:** People allow only to touch and prohibit talking (trustful, sensitive, natural, mature, serious and warm).

Functions of Non-Verbal Communication

There is a close relationship between non-verbal cues and the words accompanied. Non-verbal cues have certain functions to be performed. According to Baird, the functions of non-verbal cues fall into six categories. A brief description of these functions is discussed under the following paragraphs:[22]

(1) Repeating: Repeat or repeating is an important function of non-verbal cues. It implies to say something again which one has heard to someone else. Thus, non-verbal cues are helpful to restate the verbal message.

(2) Contradiction: The function of contradiction in a non-verbal communication is to contract the verbal or spoken message. It is used in a situation where a statement or idea which contains a contradiction. It indicates to saying the opposite of, to argue or disagree with. It is quite often that contradiction/ discrepancy occurs between a person's words and action. For instance, when A is introduced to B by C who says "Happy to meet you." So while giving a limp hand-shake, he looks in another direction. In this situation, one can observe discrepancy or contradiction between his words and action. Therefore, in such circumstances, one must understand the non-verbal message than spoken words.

(3) Substituting: Non-verbal cues also perform the function of substituting. The substituting function implies that a thing or person in or to take the place of someone or something. In other words, they serve as substitutes for spoken words or messages. Non-verbal cues like O.K., peace sign, victory, clenched fist (hostility), a stooped position (submissiveness), a bowed head (depression), obscene etc., serve as substitutes for spoken or verbal messages. Thus, some emblems affect displace, peace signs, gestures, slumping postures, depressed look etc., are substitutes for words.

(4) Complementing: Non-verbal cues help to make up a whole of a message, the words of predict, not including the verb. In other words, the cues invariably complement or elaborate upon verbal message. Baird states that the phrase "I love you", spoken sincerely usually is accompanied by vocal and physical cues that demonstrate the feeling behind the message. When something is said in anger, the feeling is shown not only in the spoken message but in the clenched fists, flashing eyes and strained voice which accompany the words.[23]

(5) Accenting: The function of non-verbal cues from this point of view is to accentuate the verbal message. Non-verbal accenting gives various meanings. While speaking, accenting gives extra force or stress shown to one part of a word, more than one syllable or to certain words in a sentence. Accentuating gives more force or importance to certain words.

So accenting in the non-verbal cues can emphasise the meaning of spoken or verbal message. Accentuating the verbal message appears when increasing the volume of the voice for giving appropriately timed gesture. For instance repeat the phrase " I dislike you" or "I hate you" to yourself alternatively emphasing the first, second and third words, as indicated below:

1. "I dislike you" or "I hate you "— emphasises the person who dislikes or hates.
2. "I dislike you or "I hate you" — emphasises the sentiments like emotion and feelings.
3. "I dislike you" or "I hate you" — emphasises the lucky recipient of the emotion.[24]

Therefore, meaning and intensity varies through non-verbal accenting.

(6) Regulating: Yet another important function of the non-verbal cues is to control the flow of communication. Cues act as regulators. Some non-verbal cues control by means of a system or adjust to obtain the desired results. "A forward lean, a nod, a vocal inflection, or a change in eye behaviour can indicate to the other that you have finished your statement or that you want to interrupt her or his message".[25]

To Sum up: Ray Birdwhistell is a notable authority on non-verbal communication. According to his estimate that in face-to-face interaction the words spoken account for less than 35 per cent of the total meaning produced while the remaining 65 per cent is obtained by non-verbal cues. The sender or speaker transmits messages through appearance, gestures, postures, facial expression, vocal characteristics and words expressed.

A person's behaviour has a message potential. Thus, non-verbal cues perform useful purposes to restate the verbal message, contradicting the spoken messages, complementing verbal messages, accenting and regulating the flow of conversation.

REFERENCES

1. *The Week,* November 21. 1993, pp. 25-26.
2. Albert Mehrabian, "Significance of Posture and Position in the Communication of Attitude and Status Relationship", *Psychological Bulletin,* 71, 1969, pp. 363.
3. J. Ruesch and W. Kees *Non-Verbal Communication, Notes on the Visual Perception of Human Relations,* Los Angeles, University of California Press, 1956.
4. Aggarwala, D.V., *Organisational Communication Management,* Deep and Deep Publications. New Delhi. 1989. pp. 171.

5. Patterson. M "Spatial Factors in the Social Interaction," *Human Factors,* 2.3. 1968. pp. 351-361.
6. Albert Mehrabian, *op. cit.*, p. 363.
7. L. Brown, *Communicating Facts and Ideas in Business,* Prentice-Hall Inc., Englewood Cliffs, New Jersey, 1982, p. 52.
8. Adapted from *The Dynamics of Organisational Communication,* J. E. Baird, Harper & Row Publishers, NewYork, 1991, pp. 44-45.
9. Demond W. Evany, *Peopie, Communication and Organisation,* Pitman Publishing, 128, Long Aere, London, p. 169.
10. *Ibid.*
11. *The Week, op. cit.*, pp. 26-27.
12. Demond W. Evany, *op. cit.*
13. *The Week, op. cit., p.* 28.
14. Myers and Myers, *Managing by Communication — An Organisational Approach,* McGraw Hill International Book Company, 1982., p. 93.
15. *Ibid.*, p. 95.
16. *The Week, op. cit.*, p. 27.
17. Wolf, *et al., Effective Communication in Business,* South Western Publishing Co. 1979, p. 141.
18. *Ibid.*
19. *The Week, op. cit.*, pp. 27-28.
20. Brown, L., *Communicating Facts and Ideas in Business,* 1982, p. 52.
21. Baird, J. E., *op. cit.*, p. 49.
22. *Ibid.*, pp. 46-47.
23. *Ibid,* p. 46.
24. *Ibid.*
25. *Ibid.*, pp. 46-47.

*****

CHAPTER 7

Feedback in Communication

Meaning and Nature

The only real hope of an improvement in our communication system is for the sender to assure himself that his communication has been thoroughly understood by the receiver. All the way through a communication, he must use a control that will ensure the degree of meaning which he has placed on his words is appreciated when received. A piece of message transmitted is said to be effective only when there is a provision for feedback in communication. A communication process is said to have feedback, when the receiver of the message has given his response to the sender's message. On the other hand, the communicator must know how well the message has been received by the receiver, understood, interpreted and acted upon. Feedback helps to determine this process. Sending back the knowledge about the message to the communicator is known as feedback. Thus, feedback is one of the important elements of the communication process. A communication process without a provision for feedback is not an effective communication.

The importance of feedback cannot be overemphasised and needs no special elucidation. Feedback is the yardstick which measures the effectiveness of communication and is used for evaluation and review, and to amend the message in the light of response. Efficient managers have reliable feedback and they succeed in their effective communication.

Leland Brown remarks that, all other things, being equal, the manager who does not allow feedback will be less effective than the manager who receives feedback.[1] The management has to provide an opportunity for feedback for effective decision making. Leland Brown states that, to be effective, feedback takes into account the needs of both the sender and the receiver.[2] "Feedback or response, enables the source to know whether or not the message has been received and interpreted correctly. Feedback can cause the original source to modify future communication according to the way in which the source perceives the reaction of the receiver."[3]

Feedback — A Two-Way Process

Two-way communication is essential in good feedback between the superior and subordinates which promotes good relations between management and employees and motivates people to do their best. Accepting and carrying corrections in messages will create interest and responsibility, recognition in their jobs. Feedback is the means of sub-ordinates getting through to the supervisor and getting approval and encouragement for what they are doing. Management cannot ignore or eliminate the feedback, for, it must exist for effective communication inspite of the channel. Therefore, it is upto the executives to accept it, introduce it, by understanding its importance, and direct efforts to use it for positive good. Feedback is also one of the important factors to be considered while selecting means of communication. The importance of feedback has been well-described by Leland Brown in the following words: "Competent administrators need to become aware of the importance and use of feedback. Most problems with feedback are caused by person's ignoring it or not even being aware of it or by not seeking it when it is not apparent. Adequate feedback should be recognised, sought, and used."[4]

Feedback is one of the important essentials of good communication. In written communication, in respect of many matters, like objectives and policy matters, there is no scope for feedback. Feedback provision in the process of communication calls for making it a two-way process. Feedback is an inherent quality in oral communication. The communicator cannot ascertain whether the receiver has accepted or rejected the message. The reaction of the receiver of the message can be assessed effectively in oral communication than through written communication. Getting feedback information is easier in verbal communication.

Feedback is probably the most important technique of improving communication. Two-way process ensures feedback. The communicator has to obtain feedback from the receiver of communication. Feedback is necessary to understand immediate reaction which would help in a great way in the decision-making process. The formal channel would not serve as an effective feedback system. Similarly, it cannot be used as a testing device. Listening to the feedback response is a good principle of effective communication.

Feedback is necessary in all group activities, irrespective of the type of organisation. An informal communication also helps as a feedback system. So the management can use grapevine as a testing tool. In a feedback, immediate response and reaction can be gained which is more useful in the process of decision-making. Listening to the feedback response is a good principle of communication.

Feedback is, though the last element is the important one in communication process. As it has been explained, communication is an exchange. The exchange to be complete, the information must go back to the communicator. So that he can know the reaction of the receiver. It ensures that the receiver has received the message and understood in the same sense as the sender meant for. Feedback enables the communicator to carry out corrections or amendements or change message to be effective. The principle of feedback promotes a two-way communication. Feedback is a process to ascertain whether or not the receiver properly understood the message, in which the superior has to listen, answer, interpret and amend the message. Interface and interaction are possible in feedback. It avoids errors in the transmission of message and in invoking effective participation of the subordinates. Thus, feedback enables the communicator to take initiative in order to receive feedback regarding the effectiveness of communication.

B. Sigband Writes: "It permits expressive action on the part of one or more persons and the conscious and unconsious perception of such action. Perhaps one of the most important factors in this network is feedback which is vital if the originator and receiver are to secure some level of effectiveness in the communication process."[5]

According to Gellerman, "the hub of the entire communication problem" is the following:

"The sender, to be certain that his message will be accepted by the receiver, must be prepared to let the receiver influence him. He must even be prepared to let the receiver alter or modify the message in ways that make it more acceptable to the receiver. Otherwise, it may not be understood, or it may not be accepted, or it may simply be given lip service and ignored."[6]

Characteristics of Feedback[7]

(1) Intention: Effective feedback is directed towards improving job performance and making the employee a more valuable asset. It is not a personal attack and should not compromise the individual's feeling of self worth or image. Rather, feedback is directed towards aspects of the job.

(2) Specificity: Effective feedback is designed to provide recipients with specific information so that they know what must be done to correct the situation. Ineffective feedback is general and leaves questions in the recipient's mind. For example, telling an employee that he or she is doing a poor job is too general and will leave the recipient frustrated in seeking ways to correct the problem.

(3) Description: Effective feedback can also be characterised as descriptive rather than evaluative. It tells the employee what he or she has done in objective terms, rather than presenting a value judgement.

(4) Usefulness: Effective feedback is information that an employee can use to improve performance. It serves no purpose tolerate employees for their lack of skill if they do not have the ability or training to perform properly. Thus, the guideline is that, if it is not something the employee can correct, it is not worth mentioning.

(5) Timeliness: There are also considerations in timing feedback properly. As a rule, the more immediate the feedback, the better. This way, the employee has a better chance of knowing what the supervisor is talking about and can take corrective action.

(6) Readiness: In order for feedback to be effective, employees must be ready to receive it. When feedback is imposed or forced upon employees, it is much less effective.

(7) Clarity: Effective feedback must be clearly understood by the recipient. A good way of checking this is to ask the recipient to restate the major points of discussion. Also, supervisors can observe non-verbal facial expressions as indicators of understanding and acceptance.

(8) Validity: In order, for feedback, to be effective, it must be reliable and valid. Of course, when the information is incorrect, the employees will feel that the supervisor is unnecessarily biased, or the employee may take corrective action which is inappropriate and only compounds the problem.

The characteristics of feedback for effective and ineffective interpersonal communication in human resource management as suggested by them are as follows:[8]

EFFECTIVE FEEDBACK	INEFFECTIVE FEEDBACK
(1) Intended to help the employee	(1) Intended to belittle the employee
(2) Specific	(2) General
(3) Descriptive	(3) Evaluative
(4) Useful	(4) Inappropriate
(5) Timely	(5) Untimely
(6) Employee readiness for feedback	(6) Makes the employee defensive
(7) Clear	(7) Not understandable
(8) Valid	(8) Inaccurate

Kinds of Feedback

(1) Positive Feedback: A feedback is said to be positive when it is given promptly and with interest in it. Supervisors consider positive feedback in a different way comparing negative feedback. It is received by a positive sense, correctly perceived and accepting the reality. The recipient also does the same thing.

(2) Negative Feedback: In the case of negative feedback, there is always some resistance and some degree of unwillingness in its acceptance. It is not almost always accepted. Managers show resistance because they want to hear always only good news and resist bad and unpleasant news. In some cases, managers accept negative feedback. Some research studies indicate that they may accept negative feedback provided it comes from a credible source.

According to K. Halperin *et al.*, subjective impressions carry weight only when they come from a person with high creditability and status. S.P. Robbins writes thus: "Negative feedback, i.e., subjective can be a meaningful tool for experienced managers, particularly those high in the organisation who have earned the respect of their employees. From less experienced managers, those in the lower ranks of the organisation and whose reputation has not yet been established, negative feedback is not likely to be well received."[9]

Feedback in Oral Communication

The advantage of oral communication is that it can be used for instant feedback. In oral media, feedback is used to improve understanding and avoids faulty communication. It permits subordinates and superiors to interact or ask questions about any points of view that are in doubt to them. Both managers and subordinates directly and personally are involved in the process. Emotions, values, attitudes, perception etc., may lead people to interpret the message in different ways. This is the reason for faulty communication. Multiple meanings for different words causes misunderstanding.

For a word "fast", there are over ten different meanings or definitions given in Webster's Dictionary.

So, oral communication permits instant feedback which helps the speaker or sender to avoid some problems. It checks emotional feelings, values and perceptional impact of the message. Receiver of the message or the listener in oral communication is important in the entire process of communication. Feedback enables the listener's interpretation of his communication and whether he has been specific enough and the words he has used, mean the same thing to the listener. Feedback also helps both the parties in the communication, the sender or speaker, make his message clearer, the listener to interpret the message more accurately.

Fig. 7.1 Feedback in Oral Communication

Feedback — Written Communication

In the case of written communication, the instant feedback is not possible. Robert J. Mockler writes that in written communication: "there is not the same opportunity for instant feedback. A manager must find a way to anticipate the reader's frame of reference gaps in reader's experience and knowledge, reader's levels of intelligence, the emotional connotations of words to the reader and reader's capacity to understand."

There are several media of written communication like letters, pamphlets, booklets, memoranda, instructions, manuals, office notes, circulars, notices, newspapers, posters, leaflets, bulletins, catalogue's, brochures, house journals, union publications, hand files etc.

Effects of Feedback

The effects of feedback should not be ignored. Many people have proved in their research work some effects of feedback. Hellriegel and Slocum have identified four consequences of feedback. The effects are as follows:

(1) The actions of the sender affect the reactions of the receiver. The reactions of the receiver affect the subsequent actions of the sender.

(2) Reactions of the receiver serve as a feedback and tell the sender how well the objectives are being accomplished.

(3) A sender who received feedback that is rewarding will continue to produce the same kind of message; if the feedback is not rewarding, the message will eventually change.

(4) The receiver exerts control over the sender by the kind of feedback he or she gives to the sender.[10]

Fig. 7.2 Feedback in Written Communication

Improving Feedback

The importance of feedback in effective communication has been discussed at length. It occupies such an important place, it is so necessary to introduce it and to derive the benefits from feedback. As such, the system of feedback itself is to be improved. Some experts have suggested some guidelines and recommendations to improve feedback. For instance, Procter and Gamble, Exxon and others, in their training programme, to improve feedback, have given some guidelines. The guidelines are briefly discussed as under:

(1) Help: Feedback should be intended to help the receiver. The object of feedback is to know the receiver's response and to help him in correct understanding, interpreting and to act accordingly. So feedback should help the receiver. So the management should endeavour to improve feedback to achieve this objective.

(2) Descriptive: Feedback should be descriptive rather than evaluative. Descriptive should be in detail to review which must bring some changes.

(3) Specific: A feedback should be specific, rather than general. In specific feedback, the receiver should be provided full information on a particular piece of message under review so as to enable him to understand the message.

(4) Hear: Feedback is to be taken up when the receiver appears ready to hear. It should be well-timed. Feedback should not overwhelm the receiver. It involves to understand the capacity of the receiver to receive feedback load at one time."[11]

Developing Effective Feedback Skills

According to S. P. Robbins, there are six specific suggestions for making effective feedback.[12]

(1) Focus on Specific Behaviour: Feedback should not be general but be specific.

(2) Keep Feedback Impersonal: C. R. Miller says that feedback, particularly the negative feedback, should be descriptive rather than judgement or evaluation. It should always be job-oriented but not personal. Telling people that they are useless, idiots, inefficient, incompetent etc. are not good for the supervisors, as they are unproductive, the subordinates may not co-operate. Even the criticism should be reasonable and related to job but not personal.

(3) Keep Feedback Goal-Oriented: As far as possible, feedback should be positive. It should not be given primarily to dump or unload on the other. The resistance or negative feedback should be directed towards the recipient's goal.

(4) Make Feedback Well-Timely: A timely feedback is more meaningful and useful to the recipients. A well-timed feedback is effective. Delay defeats the objective of feedback. The feedback will be effective when it helps in bringing about the desired change. S. P. Robbins says that "making feedback prompt merely for promptness' sake can backfire, if you have insufficient information, if you are angry, or if you are otherwise emotionally upset. In such instances, *"well-timed"* may mean *"Somewhat delayed."*

(5) Ensure Understanding: The purpose of feedback is to have interaction, to make the recipient understand clearly and fully. It is to be remembered that every piece of effective communication involves passing of information and understanding the meaning. Unless feedback communication is understood by the recipient, it is not an effective communication.

(6) Control: Direct negative feedback towards behaviour that is controllable by the recipient is also an important skill for effective communication. In the case of negative feedback, it should be directed towards behaviour, the recipient can do something about (K. S. Verderber *et al.*).

Feedback Loop

An effective two-way communication occurs when the sender transmits the message and the receiver involves in feedback to the sender. This completes the communication *circuit*. It satisfies process elements like message flow from the sender to the receiver and back to the sender. Douglas G. Curley calls this two-way communication as *feedback loop* or *communication loop*.

The two-way communication can be illustrated with the tennis game, because it has back-forth pattern. The sender sends a message and the receiver's response comes back to the sender. K. Davis writes that "The result is developing play-by-play situation in which the speaker can adjust the message to fit responses of the receiver. This opportunity to adjust to the receiver is the one great advantage of two-way communication compared with the one-way variety. It provides a better understanding for both the parties."

Advantages

(1) It provides better understanding.

(2) Frustration is reduced.

(3) Favaourable feelings are usually generated.

(4) Accuracy is improved.

Disadvantages

1. Strong disagreement may be expressed until a two-way communication is effected.
2. Possibility of separation from each other.
3. Cognitive dissonants may arise.

Feedback performs two important functions for the organisation. They are:

1. Evaluation — the effectiveness of output.
2. Adjustment — allows adjustment of subsequent output to achieve better results.

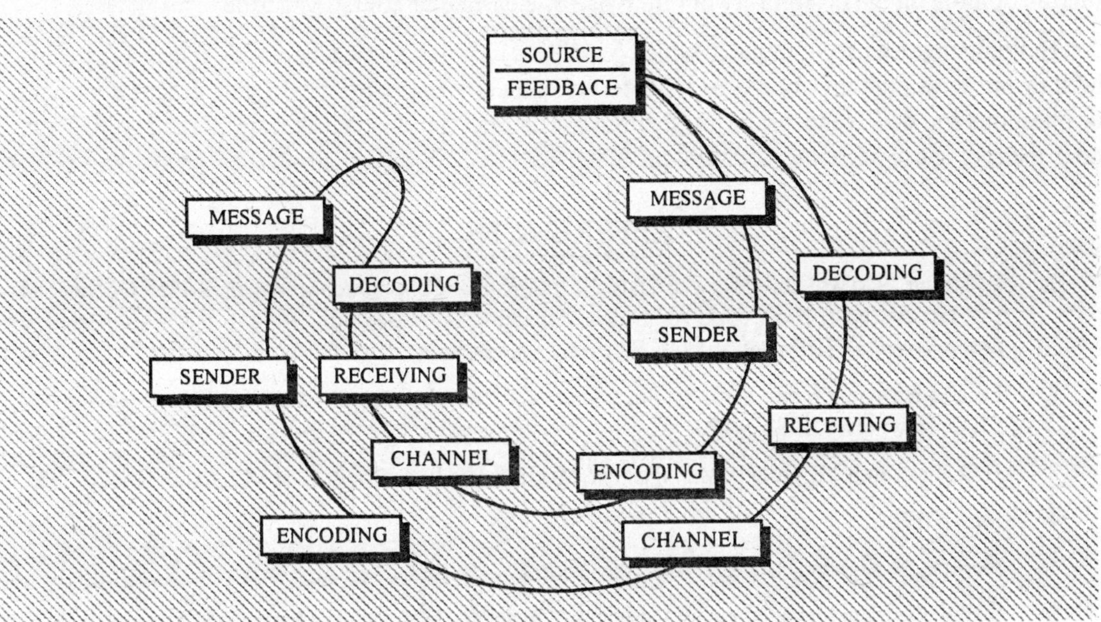

Fig. 7.3 Feedback Chain

Cutlip and Center found that feedback involves a two-step process. They are:

(1) Pre-testing.

(2) Post-testing.

Several media are used to measure the initial state of the environment.

Output Impact

Wright suggests the following four dimensions to be measured in determining communication output impact:

(1) Audience Coverage: What segment of the environment was reached by the message? Were the relevant opinion leaders reached?

(2) Audience Response: How did those receiving the message respond? Did they understand? Were they interested? Was their response favourable?

(3) Communications Impact: Did the message produce observable effects?

(4) Process of Influence: By what process did the message influence the audience? Through what channels did it finally reach each individual? How did influence spread throughout the environment?[13]

To Sum Up

To sum up, effective feedback can be gained by building an organisation free from fear. This is also possible when an organisation whose people are prepared to admit to their senior as well as their equals that they are not sure of the meaning or not clear on the action required. Overall and at its simplest, this assurance can be gained provided that at all times they are prepared and happy to voice an opinion on the desirability or otherwise of a particular course of action.

Building this security-climate in which people are working know where they stand with people and they know where they should be with others in an environment, which encourages comment and questions and which encourage this feeding back sound simple, but in fact is incredibly difficult, and is the root cause of many industrial problems today.

REFERENCES

1. L. Strong, "Do you know How to Listen"? In *Effective Communication on the Job*, J. Dooher and L. Marquis (eds.) New York; American Management Association, 1956, p. 28. As reported in *Management*, D. Hellriegel and J.W. Slocum, Jr., Addison-Wesley Publishing Company, 1982, p. 574.
2. Leland Brown, *Communicating Facts and Ideas in Business*, Prentice Hall, Inc., Englewood Cliffs, New Jersey, 1982, p.19.
3. H.G. Hicks and C.R. Gullett, *Management*, McGraw Hill International Book Company, 1981, p. 513.
4. *Ibid*, p. 19.
5. Norman, B. Sigband, *Management*, New York, 1974, p. 483.
6. S.W. Gellerman, Management by Motivation", American Management Association, New York, p. 46, Quoted in Fred Luthans, *Organisational Behaviour*, McGraw Hill International Book Company, 1981, pp. 350-351.
7. Adopted from Fred Luthans and Mark J. Martinko, *The Practice of Supervision and Management*, McGraw Hill, New York, 1979, pp. 180-182.
8. Fred Luthans and Mark J. Martinko, *The Practice of Supervision and Management*, McGraw Hill, New York, 1979, p. 183. Quoted in Fred Luthan's, *Organisational Behaviour*, McGraw Hill International Book Company, 1981, p. 351.
9. S. P. Robbins, *Organisational Behaviour*, Prentice Hall of India Limited, New Delhi, 1991.
10. D. Hellriegel and J.W. Slocum, Jr., *Management*, Addison-Wesley Publishing Company, 1982, p. 574.

11. J. Aderson, *Giving and Receiving Feedback, Managers and Their Careers: Cases and Readings*, J. Lorsch and L. Barnes (eds.) Homewood, IL, Richard, D. Irwin, 1972, pp. 260-267. As reported in *Management*, D. Hellriegel and J. W. Slocum, Jr. pp. 575.

12. S. P. Robbins, *op.cit.*

13. John E. Baird, J. R., *The Dynamics of Organisational Communication,* Harper & Row Publishers, 1977, p. 311.

*****

CHAPTER 8

Management Communication

Introduction

Some kind of 'communication' must be established before there can be any human activity at all. Man ceased to be merely an animal when he became a talking, sign-making being, who somehow passed from picture-writing to hieroglyphics and then to the alphabets. But, despite endless progress in the techniques of 'communication' and in the speed with which spoken or written ideas are transmitted over oceans and continents, there has been little study of human idea being grasped by the listener.

In most business firms, communication goes down from the top. It seldom moves upward, giving voice to what the lower-level employees are thinking about their jobs and the company. That merely filters up haphazardly — and often too late to stave off trouble. Getting good downward communication is difficult enough, as any executive learns. Upward communication is much more so. Yet management must arrange for upward-communication if it is to be kept informed as to how many employees really know about company policies, and practices and how they feel about them.

There is no substitute for personal contact by means of interviews and informal group meetings. In communication, what is called for is empathy, which is something more than sympathy.

In this chapter, it is proposed to study organisational communication and management aspects of communication.

Need for Organisational Communication

The employee's feeling that he be recognised by others is best built up by a system of communication, participation and teamwork. Communication is a two-way exchange of ideas between, the labour and management. The setting up of such a system is not so simple as it may seem. Modern studies have shown that the old-fashioned method of communication, a one-way handling down of orders from the top, was not always effective in achieving its limited purpose.

There are two major fields of distortion in such a process. The first is implicit in a long line of communication through several layers of authority. Intervening supervisors often unconsciously colour management directives in the light of their own views and temperaments. Secondly, the employees themselves interpret orders against the background of their previous experience and their own psychological make-up. The net result often is a fantastic distortion of the original message.

Management that is sensitive to the reaction of its employees finds that their previous experience with the company, union attitudes, fears of employees about their jobs, inertia and resistance to change all enter into the interpretation of a given policy. Major changes in production policy often require a sales effect comparable with that needed for introduction of a new product to consumers. This may be true even when the changes are to the benefit of employees. Patience, care, and intelligence are required to explain company policies effectively, particularly when they involve a change.

But the very idea of exclusively one-way communication is repugnant to man's desire for the esteem of others; men wish to be consulted about the policies they must execute. Consultation does not necessarily mean that management gives up its authority — a business firm is not a debating society, and management does have the advantage of wider perspective and expert advice in making decisions. But, it overlooks a golden opportunity if it fails to include its employees among its consultants.

Scores of companies have discovered in their employees an untapped source of ideas. They have contributed suggestions for improving the product, bettering production methods, cutting down waste and increasing efficiency. When the workers feel that they are a respected part of the company, they gladly help in furthering its (and their) interests.

Employees first feel a sense of participation when they are continuously informed about a company's policies and problems. They know then why things are being done and why changes may be necessary. They gain a still stronger sense of participation, however when they are told of the problems in advance and asked, either directly or through the representatives, for their views on solving these problems. Their opinions are discussed along with those of others. When the final decision is reached, they know precisely why it was reached. Even though it may be adverse to their original views. They are now aware of the compelling arguments for the final conclusions. Often, they feel that the policy adopted is their policy, even though they did not originally agree with it.

Managements have experimented with various devices to promote communication and participation. Company papers, meetings, notices on blue bulletin boards, suggestion boxes and campaigns, a sound grievance system and careful explanations by supervisors are among the devices used. In this regard, adequate techniques are secondary to sincere management attitudes, supporting whatever techniques are used.

Identical methods may in one situation bring success and in another bring failure. In the latter case, workers may have suspected a variation of the speed up or may have become restive under an apparent paternalism. It is vital that employees feel that the consultation and participation are genuine. Elaborate devices that do not produce such conviction will not succeed.

Importance of Organisational Communication

Effective communication is pivotal and lifeblood of any sound organisation. It is admitted that there can be no organisation without communication. The importance of communication in any organisation is emphasised with reference to the amount of time spent by the members of the organisation at different levels.

According to some studies oral communication accounts at least 80 per cent of the executives' time of the working day. According to Lee and Lee, about 75 per cent of the day is spent in communicating with three-fourth of that time devoted to face to face engagements.

The study of Goetzinger and Valentine suggest that executives speak to groups occasionally but communicates most often in group and interpersonal conflicts. Ulrich and his associate state that 50 to 60 per cent of departmental head's time is devoted to communication with people other than his or her own. Many people at different levels spend considerable organisational time in communicating messages. Directors devote about 70 to 75 per cent of their time to oral communication. This is in addition to time spared to signing letters and files, etc. "Oral means" is the popular medium to learn about policy and procedural changes affecting employees' work.

In many cases oral and written media are complementary and inseparable in the total communication load. Public Relations Officers usually spent more time in active contact with the different groups of public. Therefore, all organisations, irrespective of type, spend a large amount of time, in communication. The distribution of time spent in communication by the supervisors may include telephone, meetings, report writing etc.

A large percentage of time is spent in meetings and with groups. Interviews with customers, clients, telephone conversation, dialogue, oral orders, instructions, advice, training, job assignment, discussion and clarification of rules and regulations, handling letters, informal meetings, conferences, group discussions, problem solving, exchange of information, speeches, dictation, chit-chat, gossip, occasional speech etc., are the various forms of communication.

Communication — A Management Tool

Communication is a tool for management. Communication as transferor of message service to management through its various functions have to employ a number of tools and techniques like other desciplines. It is significant to note that various old tools or media of commnication though in significant use, a number of new tools and techniques have been 'developed either replacing the old ones or in addition to them due to technological advancement which has brought many sophisticated communication technologies. As such, there is no point of surprise that for solving many communication problems, alternative media for transmission of message are available. These modern mechanical devices both the verbal and written communication are meant to remove the drawbacks of traditional media by evolving new tools of superior quality and more scientific in nature and use.

Used appropriately, the tools can be effective and beneficial. However, drawbacks of scientific media, cannot diminish the potential value of tools for doing an effective job of communicating messages. As a tool of management, a system of communication should provide an opportunity for communication within the organisation between various levels. In carrying managerial functions of planning, co-ordination, direction and motivation, management must communicate with managers and operating personnel. An effective tool of communication provides data for effective decision-making. Delegation of authority is to be communicated.

The entire business process may be broadly divided into three areas known as production, finance and marketing. Production is concerned with the making of goods or rendering services. Finance function relates to providing the necessary funds for the activities. Marketing sometimes referred to as "distribution" is concerned with the activities from the point of production to the point of consumption. All these activities necessitate communication between various channels. Marketing involves both internal and external communication.

Sales promotion is concerned with communication and persuasion. Advertisement is a medium of sales promotion. Personal selling, demonstration and demonstration-cum-sale are nothing but oral communication by way of face-to-face conversation. To a considerable extent, production activities involve communication to operating work force as to the methods of production, process of production, safety measures to be taken and similar activities in other organisations. All financial activities revolve around communication, mobilisation of required finance is not possible without providing necessary information to investors. Capital market activities are nothing but communication.

Principles for Effective Organisational Communication

(1) There must be a clear line of authority running from the top to the bottom of the organisation.

(2) No one in the organisation should report to more than one line authority. Everyone in the organisation should know to whom he reports and who reports to him.

(3) The responsibility and authority of each authority should be clearly defined, if necessary, in writing.

(4) Responsibility should always be coupled with corresponding authority.

(5) The responsibility of higher authority for the acts of its subordinates is absolute.

(6) Authority should be delegated as far as down the line as possible.

(7) The number of levels of authority should be kept at a minimum.

(8) The work of every person in the organisation should be confined as far as possible to the performance of a single leading function.

(9) Whenever possible, line-function should be separated from staff- functions, and adequate emphasis should be placed on important staff objectives.

(10) There is a limit to the number of positions that can be co-ordinated by a single executive.

(11) The organisation should be flexible so that it can be adjusted to changing conditions.

(12) The organisation should be kept as simple as possible.

Management Function — A Communication Process

Functions like control, direction, planning, motivation, called "Management Functions", are essentially the functions of the communication process. Data and other information are needed in effective performance of all the managerial functions. Thus, communicating information is the lifeblood of the management in decision-making, action, control, and direction. Information systems are networks like PERT, CPM, simulation, linear programming and other methods of decision-making provide a formal structure for communication of the much needed planning, control, and operating information. But they are the main controlling means.

Under the following paragraphs, how communication applies in the managerial functions is presented:

(1) Planning: Futurity of things thought at present is termed as planning. It is a thinking and creative process. It is deciding in advance what is to be achieved. It is not a task of individual but a group composed of functional heads and other concerned people. Planning involves interviews, discussions, exchange of ideas to finalise a plan. Thus, the planning function of management involves a communication process. A good system of information exchange is indispensable before formulating a plan. Effective system of communication by suitable channel and media will help to accomplish the planning function of the management.

(2) Organisation: Organising things like men, material and machine involves communication. It consists of formal communication, grapevine, downward communication, upward communication, horizontal communication, internal and external communication. Downward communication has its origin from top management by way of orders, instructions, rules, objectives etc. Upward communication flows from lower levels by way of complaints, suggestions, advice, feedback etc.

(3) Controlling: Controlling function of the management is to see that things are going on as per schedule. It is found on planning and organisation function. It is an examination of actual performance and comparing it to standards. It is explaining things and reasons which enable others to do in a better way. Just formulating plans is not enough without performance appraisal. Probably, no management task is more significant than that of communicating the success or failure. Measuring actual performance against set standards, analysing deviations, reasons for deviation and remedial action etc., involve written or oral communication. It is the feedback which is an important last element of communication which ensures effective controlling.

(4) Direction: The directing function of the management applies to communication. Directing involves and imparts instructions, issuing orders to the support staff, communicating rules, objectives, procedures, guidelines, motivating, and supervising them. The act of directing is a process of communication, transferring information and understanding. A successful manager always develops an effective system of communication, so that he may issue instructions, receive the reactions of the receiver of the information, guide and motivate them. It is through effective communication, managers can create a feeling of belongingness on the part of the subordinates. The interaction and exchange of facts, feelings and opinions improve management-subordinate relations by keeping both in contact with each other. Directing function has a leadership role to which communication applies by which a manager guides, helps and influences the work of his subordinates.

(5) Co-ordination: Co-ordinating function of the management requires the communication between various sections and groups. This function of co-ordination affects the manager as a communicator. In a business enterprise, there are a large number of people working in different departments or sections, with different types of authorities and levels. In this, everyone has to contribute towards the accomplishment of the common broad-objectives of the business. It is the co-ordination which is the main tool which makes it possible.

Communication with Employees

Koontz and Donnel state that there are several areas of communication with the employees, right from recruitment to retirement. The following are such areas:

(1) Recruitment: In the recruitment process, the purpose of communication is to persuade potential employees working for the enterprise. Communication is equally necessary to inform prospective recruits about the enterprise to create a goodwill. The prospective recruits also need information about the internal policies and practices, organisation structure, about their suitability in the organisation and the prospects.

(2) Orientation: Orientation to the employees is necessary. The objects of providing orientation is to impart a sense of familiarity and security in their jobs and their alternative careers and growth. It is the communication which serves this purpose. Adequate information is necessary towards making them acquainted with peers, supervisors and subordinates; familiarising them with social and business groups. It is only with communication that explanations are transmitted about procedures, policies and practices.

(3) Operation: The employees in the organisation do not work in vacuum, They have to work in relation to others establishing interpersonal relations. All the employees in the organisation require considerable information. Employees have to respond well to directions and supervision. Every individual needs to know to whom he is responsible and to know his interpersonal relationship and its importance to the overall operation.

(4) Individual Appraisal: It is not just enough to communicate orders, instructions etc. But it needs to evaluate the performance of the employees against the standards set. This is only the best method to know how the employees stand the assessment of the executive about their major attributes; how to improve their skills. Thus, the need for the superior manager to communicate to subordinates arises.

(5) Personal Safety: Safety of the employees working on the job is an important function of the management. It is its responsibility to provide adequate and useful timely information about the safety of the employees on the job. From the viewpoint of employees communication of safety information will establish morale and improve performance. Employees' safety, their lives, welfare are generally of prime importance to the employees. On the other hand, such communication keeps down the human cost of accidents, the problem of compensation, insurance premium and other problems.

(6) Discipline: Discipline is one of the primary duties of every employee in the organisation to practice. The function of communication in discipline is to make the employees know the rules and regulations of the organisation. So, they can adjust themselves with them. The management, with the help of effective internal communication and with appropriate channel and media, has to make the employees acquaint with rules, regulations, working hours, safety regulations, amicable relations etc.

Management by Communication

There are a number of emerging concepts for getting the things done through people like management by exception, management by objectives etc. Similarly, it is possible to get results through people through the concept of Management by Communication. By definition, we have understood communication to mean the process of tramission of information by one person to another. Therefore, managing is getting things done through others. So, the essential requirement is that the manager has to communicate with the members in the organisation.

Managers spend most of their time in communicating either orally or in writing either sending or receiving information. Here one should understand that communication is not a one-way process but two-way process. Two-way process is a continuous and co-ordinated process of transmitting information, listening to subordinates or feedback.

Thus, it is a process of telling, listening, understanding, acting and feedback. The success or failure of all managerial functions would depend on successful and effective communication.

All managers communicate by which information is exchanged between subordinates, subordinates and superiors and between authorities. The functions of the management are carried out by communication process. The functions are planning, organisation, decision-making, controlling, motivation. A good and sound decision cannot be made without proper exchange of information, which is nothing but effective communication.

An ineffective communication system may lead to failure. Eventually, therefore, a suitable organisation structure should be designed suitable to a particular business, so as to enable to communicate job assignments. In simple words, managers have to speak, write, discuss job description for their subordinates. In other words, managers do not work and manage in isolation, but are always involved in carrying out their management functions by communicating with others. A great part of their time is devoted to communicating with others, face-to-face communication with superiors, peers and subordinates. It includes a part of time by telephone calls, meetings, memos, letters, reports, interviews, etc.

Managerial Roles

Managers play three distinct roles:

(1) Interpersonal Roles.

(2) Informational Roles.

(3) Decisional Roles.

(1) Interpersonal Roles: In an interpersonal role, the managers spend about 45 per cent of their time with peers, about 45 per cent with people outside their company and only 10 per cent with superiors. Their duties are mainly concerned with ceremonial and symbolic, legal and social in nature. Generally, managers act in the figure-head role. Every manager has to perform a leadership role. As a leader, he is responsible for the motivation and activating of subordinates. Another role in interpersonal grouping is the liaison role with contact or communication. Mintzberg describes this function as activity of contracting outsiders and informers who provide favours and information.

(2) Informational Roles: In the case of informational role of managers, communication is concerned on obtaining information from subordinates, peers and other concerned persons. It may also include collection of information from organisations and institutions outside. It takes place through print media like newspapers, magazines involving in discussion with others to know changes in the tastes.

Henry Mintzberg describes the informational role of managers as follows:

(1) **Monitor:** It includes to seek and to receive a wide variety of special information.

(2) **Disseminator:** It includes transmission of information received from outsiders or from other subordinates within the organisation to other members.

(3) **Spokesperson:** It includes transmission of information to outsiders on organisation's plans, policies, action, results etc.

(4) **Decisional Roles:** As regards decisional roles, it is the responsibility of the managers to implement the decisions taken. They are all based on information communicated. On the other hand, the managers have to communicate their decisions to others. Henry Mintzberg describes four roles in decisional role, like entrepreneur role, disturbance handler, resource allocator and negotiator.

Management and Communication Interlinked

Managers or managerial group including employees endeavour to bring resources and objectives together. They, therefore, participate in management, which is the process of information transmission, decision, action, feedback etc. This simply means everyone in the organisation participates directly or indirectly in communication process. It involves management through communication.

Both management functions and communication are interlinked and the management objectives and functions, therefore, cannot be accomplished without communication. Therefore, both are inherent and inbuilt in the management process and are inseparable. In every organisational communication, it is the message or subject matter, which is one of the essential elements in the communication process, which influences and changes the behaviour and attitudes of the individuals or group in the organisation.

A communicator, when he writes a letter or communicates through oral or visual symbols, it means, it affects the receivers of the messages. It may be noted that successful managers share useful messages resulting in good actions. A decision may be sound but it may not result in the best action unless the messages are effectively transmitted either by writing or orally, reading and listening or observing and acting and feedback. Thus, functions, broad objectives, procedures etc., are associated with management through communication.

Purposes of Organisational Communication

Lee O. Thayer has classified purposes of functions of communication in an organisation into the following five broad activities:

(1) Becoming Informed or Informing Others: This is the basic purpose of routine, day-to-day communication events. Communication provides a means of affirming the joint-purpose of organisational members so that all the members will work towards complementary objectives. When decisions have been made, they will have to be implemented and reflected in organisation operations only after members involved have been informed.

(2) Evaluating One's own Input or another's Output or Some Ideological Scheme: The dynamic nature of a functioning demands that constant evaluation be made of the activities in order that progress towards the desired objectives can be evaluated. Thus, the complete communication process is necessary, with feedback being particularly important. Feedback tells the effect of communication or action.

(3) Directing Others or Being Directed or Instructed: Manager's function of directing the combinations of persons and materials towards goals requires that communication occur between the manager and the human and physical resources within her/ his authority. Job training depends upon communication. Delegation of authority cannot occur without communication.

(4) Influencing Others or Being Influenced: Motivation must be present as one of the elemental forces in providing for dynamic organisation. Any motivational forces, not inherent, are provided to an individual and then stimulated through communication. The balance between efficiency and inefficiency lies with the ability to persuade or influence.

(5) Several Incidental and Neutral Functions: Many communications within the organisational context have no direct connection with the accomplishment of the objectives of the organisation. However, an auxiliary or contributing communication, may contribute indirectly to organisational objectives and directly to the satisfaction of individual needs that are compatible with organisational goals, providing the social contact within the organisation is an example.

Causes for Poor Organisational Communication

There are some common causes which tend to weaken the communication process in an organisational structure. They are generally of the following types:

(1) Objectives not Clearly Defined: The broad objectives of the organisation aim at expression of purpose of the organisation, either written or oral. For the organisational structure composed of interrelationships between individuals and groups, these objectives should be clearly spelled out and communicated in their completeness. Different media of communication should be adopted so as to be suitable and enable different personnel of an enterprise to be fully aware of these written or oral objectives so that confusion or misunderstanding may not raise their ugly faces to weaken the institutional goals. Creative talent and skills in drafting and transmitting of messages would create prestige for the structure and ultimately tend to strengthen it.

(2) Inadequate Communication Channel: The inadequate communication channel also weakens the organisation structure. The structure of an organisation has to operate in an integrated fashion. This becomes possible when all the divisions of the organisation are/concerned through communication. In fact, inadequate communication channel leads to confusion and chaos and tends to weaken the organisational structure.

(3) Neglecting Informal Communication: The existing informal group within the management cannot be overlooked. The formal structure of an organisation may also contain some informal groups. If the informal communication channels are not allowed to free the flow of communication, the flow presents a front of resistance to the formal group. This results in tension, conflicts, misutilisation of human resources and leads to inhibit growth of the structure. So any disregard for these informal communication group will undermine the co-operation and solidarity of the members. This may ultimately weaken the organisation structure for effective communication.

(4) Absence of Unity of Command: Under the arrangement of unity of command, each individual should receive orders in the organisation and the instructions from a single superior or boss and be accountable to a single superior or boss. Unity of command stimulates orderly action based upon orderly communication. If this principle is not followed, there will be confusion in the discharge of duties of an individual and results in weakening the structure of an organisation.

(5) Activating: Activating requires the communication of what the executives and the workers exactly expected of one another. It involves exchange of facts, feelings etc. Activating requires both verbal, non-verbal media of communication by issuing directions and instructions which have the greatest value when they are clearly written or spoken. This, therefore, requires to communicate not just for the sake of communication of ideas but be able to be understood by the recipient to transform the message and emotions into actions.

(6) Weak Control Mechanism: Control mechanism demands verification or checking whether everything occurs in conformity with the plans and principles adopted. As an effective communicator, the executives have to evaluate the performance in terms of the message transmitted. Feedback or interaction to what has been communicated is the major instrument of control. The managerial functions like planning, organisation, control and transmitting the subject matter alone is not sufficient, it is also necessary to assess the results and revise one's ongoing communication.

(7) Friction and Conflicts: The effective as well as the most important device for achieving harmony is communication skills. The main duty of the superior is to see that his subordinates are working in an efficient manner. He directs them, commands, and controls their efforts. The, staff officers should regard the advice of the staff.

This indirectly averts friction and affects consequent strength.

Types of Organisational Communication Relation

In every organisation, superior-subordinate relationship exists in different activities. Within every organisation, there may exist different types of relationships for communication. Therefore, a clear understanding of these relationships is fundamental for the proper appreciation of the channels of organisational communication. These relationships may be considered under the following paragraphs:

(1) Direct Relationship: A relationship between a superior and his subordinates is a direct relationship. In this, there is a two-way communication and is put into practice by giving directions and instructions by a superior to his subordinates. In turn, the superior has to know the reactions and responses of the subordinates. Thus, the feedback or interaction takes place for appraisal of performance, understanding and exchange of suggestions. When a senior officer hands over his duties and responsibilities to his subordinates it implies the delegation of authority to such subordinates.

Thus, there is a direct communication in all cases where there is a direct relation between the Manager and the Deputy Manager, chief accountant and assistant accountant, foreman and workers. Line-organisation introduces this direct communication-link between the superior and subordinates.

(2) Lateral Relationship: The type of lateral organisational relationship establishes communication channel between the two executives of the same rank and responsibility. This is the work-relation that exists between the executives of a similar capacity. The lateral communication is between two or more assistant accountants or between two Deputy Managers. The working relation may also exist between different functional heads like Sales Managers, Purchase Manager. Personnel Manager etc. This is also an instance of informal communication that arises on account of informal relationship or cross-wise relationship. The existence of such cross-wise relationship provides a better channel of communication. It may also give rise to a complex situation which supplants the formal organisation.

(3) Functional Relationship: Functional relationship is established through the managers or executives with specialised knowledge within a certain field of activities in the organisation. This creates functional communication links. Executives having specialised knowledge play an important role and relations with various people and activities within the organisation. This is an example of functional relationship that provides a useful channel of communication. They assist in the formulation of a social policy, advice at all levels of the organisation on any matter relating to his specialised knowledge and at the same time, answerable to his senior for effective and efficient conduct of his specific and specialised activity.

(4) Personal Staff Relationship: A special type of organisation relationship arises on account of appointment of personal staff. Consequently, this may give rise to another better link of communication. Personal staff is appointed to assist an Executive. The terms of appointment of personal staff may be of general or specific character. But their responsibilities are clearly defined. Generally, they carry no authority. Personal staff in an organisational relationship is just an extension of the personality of a particular Executive whom they serve.

Cross-Culture Communication

"In any organisation, there are the
ropes to skip and the ropes to know."

— *R. Ritti and G. Funkhovser*

Culture plays an important role in the lives of organisation members. In recent years, organisational theorists have begun to emphasise the significance of culture that plays a crucial role. Organisations are institutionalised; it takes on a life of its own, apart from any of its members. Organisations acquire value support and immortality.

Organisational culture refers to a system of shared meaning held by the member that distinguishes the organisation from other organisations. One of the characteristics of organisational culture is the communication-pattern. It is the degree to which organisational communications are restricted to the formal hierarchy of authority. Every organisation may have a dominant culture and a number of sub-cultures. A dominant culture represents the core-value shared by a majority of the members of an organisation. Whenever it is referred to organisation's culture, it means a dominant culture.

A sub-culture, on the other hand, may include core values of the dominant culture plus additional values, particular and peculiar to the members of that sub-group. In large organisations, there are bound to be sub-cultures which reflect the common problems, situations or experiences that members face. Department delegations and geographical separations would give rise to sub-cultures. For instance, a production department may have a sub-culture, i.e., uniquely shared by the members of that department only. Individuals with different backgrounds and levels will tend to describe the organisation's culture in similar terms. Though an organisation culture has common properties, it does not mean without sub-culture.

It is a very difficult task for maintaining effective communication in a situation of prevailing dominant sub-cultures. Cross-culture presents communication problems. According to N. Adler, cross-culture factors clearly create the potential for increased communication problems. Different individuals in the organisations may possess different cultural backgrounds.

Difference in perception, degree of understanding makes a difference in encoding the message by the sender and decoding of the message by the receiver into arbitrary symbols. Because of the difference in cultural backgrounds, the perception or meaning of message is not the same for each person. If the degree of difference in the backgrounds of the members of the organisation is greater between the sender and the receiver, the greater the difference in the meanings attached to particular words or behaviour. S.P. Robbins writes: "People from different cultures see, interpret and evaluate things differently, and consequently act upon them differently."

The results of cross-culture communication are misperception, misinterpretation, misevaluation and misunderstanding.

The following four guidelines can be helpful in improving cross-culture:

(1) Maintaining Similarity: It is always desirable to presume the existence of differences until similarity is established. People always think that others are similar to them. But actually, people working in the organisation with different cultural background, vary from one another. The sound principle is to assume the existence of differences until similarity is proved.

(2) Emphasise Description: Another important rule is to emphasise description rather than interpretation or evaluation. It is advisable to delay the judgement until the observation and interpretation of the situation from different perspectives of all the cultures involved are completed.

(3) Empathy: Empathy is different from sympathy. Empathy is feeling with the other person, not feeling sorry for him which is sympathy. Empathy can be regarded as the primary prerequisite for a satisfying experience in any relationship where a certain degree of depth of understanding is expected. The sender of the message should put himself in the recipient's shoes before sending a message. He has to understand the values, experience and frame of reference of the recipient. He has to see and understand the other person as he is.

(4) Working Hypothesis: Another rule for improving cross-culture communication is to treat interpretation as a hypothesis that needs further testing.

Organisational Image

Impression Management

Image cannot be created out of nothing. It has to have a substance. Over 12 centuries ago, a famous Latin philosopher, LUCRETIUS has aptly said: "Now then learn how tenuous is the nature of an 'image'."

Every organisation is undoubtedly involved in the building of an image. That is "Reputation Building." It is not the exclusive preserve of any one communication skill or department. Impression management is a continuous management function like planning and organisation. Impression creates the idea or effect produced in someone's mind by a person or organisational behaviour.

"Image" is basically a mental representation or a concept. While an image may be clear in a person's mind, reason he/she gives for holding such a view are often hazy and vague generalisations.

The practical way to project a clear persuasive corporate image is by focussing it on the corporation itself. Each phase of a corporation's activity adds meaning to the picture in the public mind. Nothing is perfect; but management and image processing people may have to face up frankly to several internal problems before any face-lifting is effected.

Many people show an ongoing personal interest in how others perceive and evalute them. The impression management is the process by which an individual attempts to control the impression of others; this is particularly so in many advanced countries. For instance, North Americans spend billions of dollars on diet, health, club membership, cosmetics and plastic surgery. All these are intended to make them more attractive to others.

When people perceive positively and evaluate them positively by others, there should be benefits for people in organisations.

It might, for instance, help them initially to get the jobs they want in an organisation and, once hired, to get favourable evaluations, superior salary increases and more rapid promotions. In a political context, it might help to sway the distribution of advantages in their favour.

Impression Management — Corporate Health

Impression management is an age-old concept but unfortunately, many Indian organisations pay scant attention to this important and effective technique. Impression management is a special area or subject of organisational theory that only quite recently has gained the attention of organisational behaviour.

At the individual level, in everyday life, we are careful about how we present ourselves to others. By creating a good impression about our talents, integrity, work ethics and other traits to endeavour to build abundant goodwill that will help us in our advancement.

But such attempts to project better image to the community are not even contemplated at the organisational level. The prevailing conditions of the economy which favour a buyer's market should definitely not make organisations oblivious to the principles of good management of which impression management forms a subject.

Impression Management — A Business Tool

Impression management as an effective business tool is gaining increasing attention even in developed countries, where even successful organisations are particular about building customer, attuned to managing the projection of favourable impression, to the client systems and the public at large.

An organisation's personality and the very core of its philosophy are mirrored in the manner in which it reacts to the environment and interacts with and treats its clients. High professionalism, honesty, and cheerful service to client systems and timely delivery of quality products are some of the aspects the society which are associated with a good organisation, big or small. Projection of such an image should be the goal of all organisations.

Techniques of Impression Management

Impression management techniques basically centre on verbal self-precaution behaviours that individuals use to manipulate information about themselves. Verbal self-presentation skills are the primary but not the only techniques for managing impression. In addition, there are non-verbal behaviours such as proper facial expressions, gestures, body position and tone of voice and artifactual displays such as one's physical appearance. The people in the organisation dress for success, an attempt to convey a proper business-like impression. The following are various impression management techniques in organisations developed by some studies:

(1) Self-Description: A person who makes statements describing personal characteristics like traits, abilities, feelings, opinions, and personal lives.

Example: A job applicant tells an interviewer, I got my Harvard M.B.A. even though I suffer from dyslexia."

(2) Conformity: Conformity with reference to impression implies accepting or behaviour etc., which is the same as most people's. It is agreeing with someone else's opinion. The technique of conformity is intended in order to gain others' approval.

Example: A manager tells his boss, "You are absolutely right on your re-organisation plan for the western regional office. I could not agree with you more."

(3) Accounts: This technique includes excuses, justifications or other explanations of a predicament-creating event aimed at minimising the apparent severity of the predicament.

Example: Sales manager to boss, "We failed to get the ad in the paper on time but no one responds to those ads anyway."

(4) Apologies: The technique of apology centres on verbal self-presentation behaviours that individuals employ to manipulate things. It takes the forms of expression of regret for having done something wrong etc. It admits the responsibility and activates impression. Admitting and expressing responsibility for an undesirable act is a good sign of image building, it simultaneously seeks to get a pardon for the event.

Example: Employee to boss: "I'm sorry, I made a mistake on the report. Please forgive me."

(5) Acclaiming: Explanation of favourable events by someone in order to maximise the desirable implications for that person.

Example: A salesperson informs a peer: "The sales in our division has merely tripled since I was hired."

(6) Flattery: It is praising insincerely, the technique of praising too much to create an impression. It takes the form of, to show, describe etc., someone or something as being better than someone etc., really is. Complimenting others about their virtues in an effort to make oneself appear perceptive and likeable.

Example: New sales trainee to peer: "You handled that client's complaint so tactfully! I could never have handled that as well as you did."

(7) Favours: A kind action adapted to create impression. To do or give something for someone in order to get or gain that person's approval.

Example: Sales person to a prospective client: "I've got two tickets to the theatre for tonight that I can't use. Take them. Consider it 'a thank you' for the time you spend to talk with me."

Strategy: "Image Building" programme needs to be developed in the light of each company's circumstances and business and has to basically cover the WHOs, the WHATs, the WHYs, WHEREs and the WHENs of a company. The question has to be posed as to "Who are you now and what is your present image? "First, the character of the company has to be determined before you sensibly weigh the existing image."

Does the company have corporate objectives? If you can unearth them somewhere in the archives, they are probably out of date. Once you find them, can you truly challenge the *staus quo,* you have to take out insurance against unpreparedness. Over-confidence spells out obsolescence. It is not enough to have well-manicured projections. It is important to determine the abstract values inherent in future growth.

Whether or not corporate image is successfully changed depends, in the long run, upon the daily company-wide effort to sustain the attitude of not achieving by heavy hand, gimmickry, far-out advertising slogans or by corporate window dressing. This is the seed of a new reputation — "Image Building." The job is not that of the public relations executives alone, but it is his job to prime it. Image building does not mean that it is an act of mere glorification where there is more.

Case Studies

Misrepresentation of facts involves high cost. When the image claimed is false, it may be discarded. When one cries 'Wolf once too often, no one is likely to believe when the wolf really comes, therefore, one must be cautious not to be perceived as insincere or manipulative. There may be situations where individuals are more likely to misrepresent themselves, particularly when the situation is characterised by high uncertainty for challenging a fraudulent claim and reduce the risks associated with misrepresentation.

There are many organisations which are noted for their impertinence, unethical behaviour, apathy and slovenliness and insensitivity to consumer needs. A few episodes will illustrate the sorry state of organisational behaviour. These relate to a variety of organisational systems, manufacturing firms, retail firms, hospitals etc.

A manufacturing firm of repute, in its zeal to procure more business from one of its valued clients in a mofussil areas, was promising delivery dates for a sizable order, knowing fully well that it could not honour its commitment. The buyer was making desperate trunk calls every day to ascertain the position and the company officials were giving false assurances stating that the goods had been already shipped. The misrepresentation was explained as necessary to protect the company's interest.

Judging from the numerous trunk calls put through by the client, one could safely presume that the impression management style of the organisation from the short-term as well as long-term perspectives — leaves much to be desired.

A well-known retail cloth store with several branches seems to have given some thought to impression management. It provides ice-cold water even in the days of acute water scarcity. The shop's layout and design are pleasing to the senses and good lighting and air circulation draw crowds to the shop.

Contrast this with the happy but rare experience of being served by the personnel with zeal and where the shop assistant's aim is to clinch the safe with goodwill built through customer satisfaction. Come to think of it, how many of us have seen salespersons and other personnel receive and serve us with a smile? In the ultimate analysis, it is the human touch and adherence to the goal of complete customer-satisfaction that will create a lasting impression. Thus, impression management is a continuing management-function like planning and organisation.

MOTIVATION AND INFLUENCING

Motivation and Communication

Managers are concerned "to get things done through." Next to planning, directing, controlling, motivation is an unspecified yet critical part of managerial function. Motivating function is not something to schedule-work timings, it is a process that requires continuing communication. It is a process to keep employees informed about what is going on in the organisation. Speaking plain English, listening activity, yet to know your staff, involving employees, responding to employees, supportive style etc., contribute a lot to successful motivation.

Motivation, is an internal force at work within the individual person. A communicating model may be the means of triggering a motivating force within a person. This makes a person to act. The ultimate question in institutional management is incentive; what makes men work at a level higher than that of anyone else.

Human resource is the most important and complex factor of production in any organisation. It is the basic function of the manager to utilise human resources to the optimum level. It is easier to achieve the organisational goals by motivating people by effective communication. The success of the manager and his performance would depend to a great extent upon the performance of the subordinates. Performance in most organisations is the usual means for determining how people are informed, how they are encouraged and the extent to which they are participated.

There is perfect positive correlation between performance and motivation. It is because managers constantly face question of how to motivate people to maintain high performance. They are concerned with subordinates' motivation. Efficient and seasoned managers apply communication techniques to motivate them to achieve organisational performance. They keep a two-way communication to motivate and thus enhance their productivity. Through the communication process the manager exerts influence on employees' motivation. There are many factors which motivate people in general.

A thorough understanding of these factors is necessary before examining how managers can influence their employees' motivation.

Motivation Definitions

S.P. Robbins: 'The willingness to exert a high level of effort toward organisational goals, conditioned by the efforts and ability to satisfy some individual need."

Michael J. Jucius: "Motivation is the act of stimulating someone or oneself to get the desired course of action to push the right button to get the desired results."

McFarland: "Motivation refers to the way in which urges, drives, desires, aspirations, strivings or need to direct, control or explain the behaviour of human beings."

Berelson and Steiner: A motive "is an inner state that energises, activates or moves (hence "motivation"), and that directs or channels behaviour towards goals."

Koontz and Donnell: "Motivation is a general term applying to the entire class of drives, desires, needs, wishes and similar courses."

The most popular theory of motivation is Abraham Maslow's hierarchy of needs. He advocates that within every human being, there exists a hierarchy of five needs. They are:

(1) Physiological Needs: They include basic needs which are essential to life. These needs include air, water, food, shelter, sleep, sex and other bodily needs.

(2) Safety Needs: The second level in the Maslow's hierarchy of needs is safety. These needs include desires for safety, protection from danger, physical and emotional harms, threat, deprivations etc. They indicate the desire for security and for steady increase in monetary income.

(3) Social Needs: When physiological and safety needs are statisfied, social needs motivate behaviour. At this level, people feel to have companionship, a sense of belonging, acceptance, friendship and affection.

(4) Esteem Needs: The next level in Maslow's hierarachy of needs is esteem needs. They include the desire for self-confidence, self-respect, feeling of competence, achievements, independence, autonomy and external esteem factors such as status recognition, attention, prestige and appreciation.

(5) Self-Actualisation Needs: These needs include realisation of one's potential, self-fulfilment, growth and creative expression.

When each of these needs become satisfied, the next need becomes dominant. Like this one need after another need motivates behaviour.

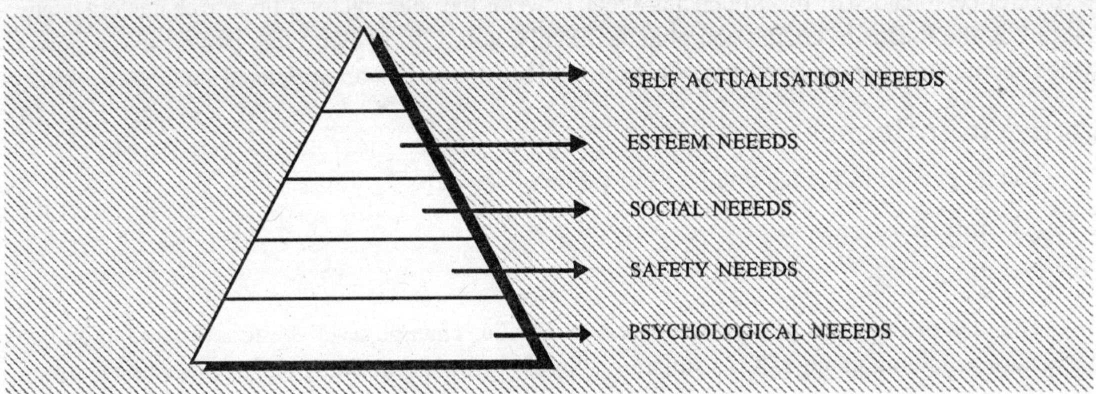

Fig. 8.1 Hierarchical Needs

Communication Implication

In the light of these hierarchical needs, one can infer communication implication in relation to the motivation. The employees make known to the managers what is the priority and importance to them through transactional communication. Managers often get information or message from the employees. This facilitates the managers to determine what are the needs of the employees, what are the importance to them at a given time.

The ultimate question in institutional management is incentive; what makes men work at a level higher than that of anyone else. There are no fixed motivations that we may generalise. People do not want the same thing precisely in the same order or to the same extent. Also what motivates people seems to vary from time to time. So, both the place and time seem to be important variables so far as finding the key to motivation is concerned. In general, all men have the same ultimate need or instinct. The universal desire is to find self-hood or self-fulfilment which is the rounded development of one's capacity.

Communication for Interpersonal Influence

Introduction: The process of communication comprises the influence system in interpersonal communication. Communication system as integral part of an organisational framework attempts to influence behaviour. Influence may be exerted in different ways. The influence may be exercised via upward, downward, laterally in peer-group relationship. There are various specific ways to influence behaviour.

Definition of Influence

Julius Gould and William L. Kolb: "Any changes in behaviour of a person or group due to anticipation of the responses of others."

Katz and Kahn summarise this concept in the following words:

"Influence includes virtually an interpersonal transaction which has psychological and behavioural effects. Control includes those influence at tempts which are successful, that is, which have the effect intended by the influencing agent. Power is the potential for influence characteristically backed by the means to coerce compliance. Finally, authority is legitimate power; it is a power which accrues to a person by virtue of his role and his position in an organised social structure."

Parties in Influence

The process of influence involves two parties. They are:

(1) Influencer.

(2) Influencee.

The idea or impulses of a person causes behaviour change. Even some intimate factor also may cause behaviour change. It is a situation wherein behavioural change takes place as a result of inter-relationships among the people.

Methods of Influencing Behaviour

There are many ways to influence the behaviour of other persons in interpersonal communication. The important of them are as follows:

(1) Emulation: In emulation, there is no direct interpersonal communication between individuals but still it has a powerful influence. According to Kast and Rosenzweig: "Striving to equal or excel; imitating with effort to equal or surpass; approaching or attaining equality."

(2) Suggestion: In the case of suggestion, way of influence, it involves direct and conscious interpersonal communication and interaction between individuals or group. It is an explicit way to communicate to influence behaviour by transmitting a message or suggesting a particular course of action. Kast and Rosenzweig write: "Placing or bringing (an idea, proposition, plan etc.) before a person's mind for consideration or possible action."

(3) Persuasion: In the case of persuasion, the influencer in interpersonal communication uses inducement in order to expect the desired response. Kast and Rosenzweig say that prevailing on a person by advice, urging, reason, or inducements to do something (rather than force).

(4) Coercion: The tool of coercion is also used to influence the behaviour. The threatening or aggressive way of communication is also a powerful influencer. Kast *et al.*, write that: "forcing constant compulsion; physical pressure or compression."

There are four specific kinds of managerial communication for inter-personal influence. They are:

(1) **Directive Style:** To make known to the employees what is expected from them.

(2) **Supportive Style:** Managers to act as a friend, guide, philosopher and maintaining equality.

(3) **Participative Style:** Inviting suggestions and advice.

(4) **Achievement-oriented Style:** To fix goals for employees and performance.

Factors in Interpersonal Influence

Communication for interpersonal influence would succeed provided the accepting managerial influence. Communication applies to path, goal, theory of leadership because the principal task of the managers is to reduce the uncertainties of the job of subordinates. This also applies to their tasks and achievements of personal goals in relation to organisational goals.

There are many communication factors which make a difference in the exercise of interpersonal influence between managers and subordinates. Among the various factors, the most important are as follows:

(1) Trusting
(2) Reducing defensiveness
(3) Listening
(4) Communication style
(5) Span of Management
(6) Ability
(7) Transactional.

(1) Trusting: To have confidence or faith in others and the extent to which, on whom and when are the important factors. According to Rossiter and Pearce, one can only experience trust when your relationship with another person is characterised by contingency, predictability and alternative option. Contingency refers to a situation in which the outcome of another person's action, becomes significantly effective. Predictability refers to the degree of confidence you have in your expectations about the other person's behaviour. Alternative options implies that you are free to do something else besides trusting.

(2) Defensiveness: The type of interaction is important in exercising interpersonal influence. In terms of one's self-esteem, one has to appraise whether the interaction is threatening or non-threatening. The sender of the message should make himself his role to the situation etc., which may conceivably be accepted or rejected to exercise interpersonal influence. Warren and Bannies, in the interpersonal dynamics, state that the problem with defensive strategies is that encourage a ritualistic approach to communication and discourage spontaneous interaction.

(3) Listening: People are poor listeners. Subordinates always complain that their boss do not listen. Effective listening is an important quality of effective communication in interpersonal influence. If there is no listening, there is no influence. So, effective listening is so crucial in order to understand the feelings and ideas of others. Communication for effective interpersonal influence is not possible if the people's listening ability is not effective. Interpersonal influence is possible only when the listeners exhibit conscious efforts of interpreting the sound symbols, grasping symbols and meaning of the words and reacting to the words and reacting to the message.

(4) Styles of Communication: Different people behave in different manner. A manager with a particular manner does not behave the same way all the time and before all the people. Such different characteristics are termed as styles of communication which influence each other. Verginia Satir has identified five basic patterns of communication, namely, blaming or aggressive style, placating or non-assertive style, computing or intellectual style, distracting or manipulative style and levelling or assertive style. These styles influence interpersonal situations.

(5) Span of Management: The principle of span of management is also called "the span of supervision and the span of control." Span of management involves communication for interpersonal influence within the span. The span determines the extent and frequency of superior-subordinate relationships.

(6) Ability: The capacity, effective ability of the managers to communicate instructions, plans, orders clearly and precisely also tend to expand a manager's span of control.

(7) Transactional: Any interaction between individuals may have transactional analysis that has behavioural effects. In the case of power, which is the ability to influence behaviour, more the power an individual has in a given situation, he may exercise more effective influence. In a formal organisation, a person may be dependent on the other at any level. Interpersonal communication influences the behaviour of others in many ways. A person having expertise knowledge and a subordinate can influence their superiors.

How Communication Influences Activities?

(1) Influencing Effective Co-ordination: The modern complex organisations are large in size having a large number of people working in the organisation to achieve common goals. The organisational structure shows many levels of organisational hierarchy — both a tall network and a flat network. This always leads to the problem of co-ordination. An effective system of communication promotes better co-ordination. It helps a lot in co-ordination, which is necessary between groups, channels for the efficient functioning of the entire organisation. It is the communication which influences effective co-ordination.

(2) Influencing Sound Decision-Making: Facts, figures of past and present are to be provided for quick and effective decision-making. The primary basis is communication through which an effective network supplies information, helps in arriving at quick decision. Problem-defining, alternative courses of action, selecting the best course of action are all possible only with the necessary information supplied to the decision-maker. In its absence, it may not be possible even for the top management to formulate broad policies and objectives.

(3) Influencing Uninterrupted Work: Smooth and uninterrupted working of an enterprise is to a great extent, dependent on good communication network. Communication assumes a greater role in this direction. Corrective decision-making and efficiency of the organisation are based on information supply. If the messages are not flowing freely across the levels, smooth functioning is not possible. Herbert G. Hicks writes. "Communication is basic to an organisation's existence from birth of the organisation on through its continuing life."

(4) Influencing Co-operation: Co-operation among workers, collective or joint efforts are possible only with the exchange of information between individuals and groups and between channels etc. Mutual co-operation and understanding between management and the employees promote industrial peace and maximum production. The two-way communication network develops co-operation between people. There can be no mutual understanding and co-operation without communication. The flow of communication would be smooth and receptive with co-operation.

(5) Influencing Managerial Efficiency: George R. Terry writes that communication serves as a lubricant, fostering the smooth operation of the management process. Communication promotes management process, and efficiency. Efficiency lies in the way in which an individual or group is informed about common goals. Managerial functions like planning, control, co-ordination, motivation cannot be discharged without communication. Communication is the tool of the management to convey goals, policies, targets, by issuing orders, instructions orally as well as in written form.

(6) Influencing Increasing Productivity: Communication helps the management in achieving maximum productivity with minimum cost and eliminates wastes. Thus, "The great enemy of communication is the illusion of it." This illusion can be avoided only with effective system of communication. It is through communication that the workers can be well-informed about the process of production, new methods of production and the activities of the workers in similar organisation.

(7) Influencing Job Satisfaction: Communication is essential for achieving job satisfaction. Management conveys messages which promote mutual understanding. Reception and recognition provide job satisfaction to employees. Two-way communication creates confidence which leads to job satisfaction. Efficient managers with good communication skills promote job satisfaction. Openness, frank expression of opinions are necessary in this direction.

(8) Influencing Effective Leadership: Leadership implies the existence of a leader and followers. There is always a continuous process of communication between them. Communication is the basis for direction, motivation, as well as establishment of effective leadership. The followers have to follow him through conveying ideas, opinions, feelings, facts and decisions. It is through the medium of communication, that the followers convey their opinions, feelings, ideas, facts etc., to their leader.

(9) Influencing Morale Building: Morale and good human relations in the organisations are essential to achieve goals and to promote its goodwill in the public. An effective system of communication builds morale and improve human relations. Participatory communication is the best technique of morale building and motivation. S. Khandwala remarks, "Most of the conflicts in business are not basic but are caused by misunderstood motives and ignorance of facts. Proper communication between the interested parties reduce the points of friction and minimize those that inevitably arise. Management at every work-level is primarily charged with the responsibility of seeing that proper procedures are established for sympathetic interchange of information between all parties concerned."

(10) Influencing to Achieving Managerial Roles: Henry Mintzberg has described manager's job and assigned three roles. They are interpersonal roles, informational roles, and decisional roles. Communication plays a vital role in these three types of role. In the case of interpersonal role a manager has to interact always with subordinates. In the informational role, he has to collect information from various people and supply necessary information to others, both inside and outside the organisation. A manager in decisional role has to communicate decisions to others. Thus, it is through oral or written media of communication what managers discharge their interpersonal, informational and decisional roles.

Leadership Styles and Communication

The style of behaviour of a leader towards a group of members is called "Leadership Style." A person as a leader may have many styles or patterns of behaviour and, accordingly, communicate. Leaders often adopt more than one depending upon the circumstance and subject. The pattern of behaviour is called "Leadership Style" which a leader follows in order to influence the behaviour of subordinates in the organisation. Some styles of leadership are more effective than others. It is the behaviour of the leader that decides the effectiveness or ineffectiveness of leadership. It is, therefore, most desirable to search for behaviour indicators of effective leadership than looking at the trait of effective leaders. Researches labelled the leadership styles as autocratic, democratic, bureaucratic, diplomatic, and *laissez faire* styles.

(1) Autocratic Leadership and Communication: One-way communication there is no feedback this leads to misunderstandings, communication breakdowns and mistakes. Autocratic communication involves only issue of orders, direction to subordinates or to the members of the group. The leader of this type makes decisions without obtaining approval, opinions of the group members. Autocratic behaviour is an extreme position. He makes decisions alone, directs his subordinates and expects them to accomplish the results. Downward communication takes place, primarily from the managers to the subordinates. The followers or other group members have to show obedience, and conformity.

(2) Democratic or Participative Leadership and Communication: It allows actively to participate in and help formulate decisions. The leader consistently receives the benefits of the best information, ideas and suggestions. A rich information source is made useful into his decision-making. It is one of the behavioural theories labelled a position, as one extreme, in contrast to autocratic leadership. It is a participative style of behaviour, involves suggestions, accepting criticisms and solicits opinions. Democratic leader always fully shares his ideas in decision-making process with subordinates. Democracy-principle permits a two-way exchange of message, allows each member of the group to carry an equal voice. This style has a positive effect upon the message and the receiver of the message. It is known as participative communication in which participative leadership takes into consideration, the wishes and suggestions of the members. It believes in human relations, public relations, and everyone of the group has an important role to participate in the decision-making. Democratic communication allows an interchange of ideas between all the members of the group.

(3) Bureaucratic Leadership and Communication: Bureaucratic leaders are strict towards policies, procedures and rules. They generally adopt written media of communication.

(4) Diplomatic Leadership and Communication: Diplomatic leader involve in effective communication, by using various media of communication. They take the initiative to explain, persuade subordinates with a degree of co-operation and efforts.

(5) Laissez Faire Leadership and Communication: In this style of communication, the leader furnishes information when asked for. *Laissez faire* leadership allows others to do in a non-interference style. Members of the group have freedom to do. The leader exercises no or little control over its members. Leader in principle is only a group member, giving advice, directing the things. He takes little part in work decisions.

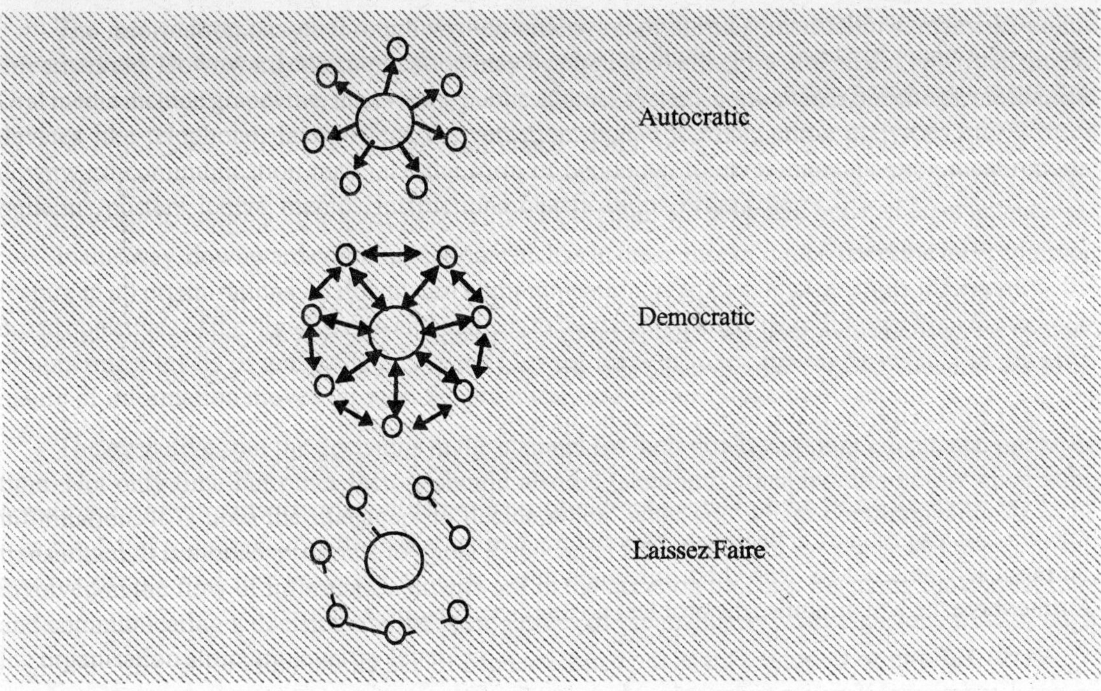

Fig. 8.2 Leadership Styles and Communication

(Source: Adapted from Lewis B. Sappington and C.G. Browne, *The Skills of Creative Leadership)*

Essentials of Effective Leadership Communication

(1) Inspiring Confidence in People: To be a leader, one must have the confidence of the people he is to lead. To inspire confidence requires a number of qualities on the part of the leader. The first is competent knowledge of the technical tools and processes with which his followers work, so that he can instruct and develop them in their use. This does not mean, however, that the leader himself must be an expert.

(2) Persistence in Driving Towards the Goal: The leader must believe firmly in what he is striving to accomplish. He must have the persistence and perseverance to look for methods to attain the goals, trying one after another if necessary, until the right one is reached.

(3) Ability to Communicate Without Misunderstanding: The leader must have the ability to explain the goal to others and make it appealing to them. This neither means that he must be a persuasive orator or a skilled writer, nor that he must have a particular degree of education. It is an ability that can be acquired. It is important to realise the difficulties of communication and to guard against the mistakes of the listeners. Unless the leader can say what he means, there will be misunderstanding.

(4) Willingness to Listen Receptively: This attribute often distinguishes the leader from the commander. There is a difference between listening with a closed mind and listening with a sincere desire to understand and make the best use of the other person's point of view.

(5) Genuine Interest in People: A leader must have a genuine interest in the welfare of the people under his leadership. Such an interest cannot be simulated, a lack of genuiness will sooner or later betray itself.

(6) Understanding People and Their Reactions: A leader must understand people and know why they act as they do. Some people have this faculty intuitively, others must acquire it. It is essential to understand that what the; individual thinks, says, does is the product of many different forces working upon him.

(7) Objectivity: A leader must be careful to be objective and not let the sentiments of other people act upon his own feelings. This is a tough assignment. One way he can practise objectivity is to ask himself, "Why", Why does he say this, and Why does he feel the way he does?

(8) Forthrightness: A leader must be forthright. He cannot let people wonder what he is thinking. He cannot let it be said of him. "He always plays his cards close to his chest."

(9) Keep all Informed: The leader can forge a tremendously effective tool to win the co-operation of his group by appealing to their natural curiosity. He will grow in stature with his men as he purposely sets out to keep them informed about what is going on and how it affects them. Furthermore, he will minimise the problem arising from misinformation.

(10) Talking to People: This is the handle needed to use all the other tools. For, "talking to people" is essential if we are to maintain close and frequent contacts with people, keep all interested parties informed, make sure that all employees receive a fair, impartial and considerable treatment, know what is going on and assume full responsibility for running the job.

(11) Fair Treatment: The quality is that he must make sure that all employees receive fair, impartial, and considerate treatment. Among other things, this includes granting reasonable requests, making proper use of commendations, taking prompt action on all requests, and administrating any grievance procedure properly.

MANAGING AND RESOLVING INTERPERSONAL CONFLICT

Definition of Conflict

Ralph H.L and Kenneth W. Thomas: "Conflict" has been defined as the condition of objective incompatibility between values or goals, as the behaviour of deliberately interfering with another's goal, achievement and emotionally in terms of hostility. Descriptive theorists have explained conflict behaviour in terms of objective conflict of interest, personal styles, reactions to threats and cognitive distortions. Normative recommendations range over the establishment of superordinate goals, consciousness raising, selection of compatible individuals and mediating conflict.

W. Clay Hamner and Dennis W. Organ: On the other hand, stress is defined by a set of circumstances, under it an individual cannot respond adequately or instrumentally to environmental stimuli, or can so respond only at the cost of excessive wear and tear on the organism, for example, chronic fatigue, tension, worry, physical damage, nervous breakdown or loss of self esteem.

Robbins S.: Conflict is the result of disagreement or opposition within one individual or between two or more individuals.

Meaning and Nature: The concept of conflict is being increasingly recognised as an important dimension in the organisation behaviour. Though the word "conflict" is often used interchangeably with stress, in practice, the component of stress is used and treated separately. The concept of stress has been emerging in recent years. Both, stress and conflict have some common characteristics. Stress is more psychological-oriented. Its salient feature is that both stress and conflict are closely associated with intra-individual aspects. The concept of conflict is, on the other hand, closely associated with interpersonal and organisational. But, sometimes, conflict and stress emerge from frustration.

People working in the organisation with different social, economic, political, educational and civilisation background might have hailed from different geographical and distance areas. Because of the different temperaments, it is quite possible that a variety of conflicts often develop in their usual and natural course of interaction. With a variety of backgrounds, different values, varied needs and personalities, people interact. Frequent changes in the organisation play a significant role and contribute to conflict. Some studies show that managers spend an estimated 20 per cent of their time on dealings with conflicts. Though conflict has received greater attention in modern industrial organisation, it has both merits and demerits. Conflicts destroy co-operation, team work, and distrust grows, misunderstandings develop.

Louis R. Pondy lists the following in the terms of conflict which contains four ways:

(i) antecedent conditions of conflictful behaviour, such as scarcity of resources or policy differences;

(ii) effective states of individuals involved, such as stress, tension, hostility, anxiety etc.

(iii) cognitive states of individuals, that is, their perception of awareness of conflictual situation; and

(iv) conflictual behaviour ranges from passive resistance to over-aggression.

TYPES OF CONFLICTS

There are three levels of conflicts. They are:

(1) Intrapersonal Conflicts.

(2) Interpersonal Conflicts.

(3) Organisational Conflicts.

1. Intrapersonal or Individual Level Conflicts

There may be different types of conflicts; source for these various conflicts is the organisational structure only. Hence, here, we propose to discuss the different types of conflicts. The conflicts at individual level is the starting point in the entire process. An organisation is nothing but a group of individuals and most of the conflicts grow at individual level.

Conflicts do not require the presence of two or more people, it may take place within an individual itself. Conflicts at individual level is called intra personal or personal conflicts. Usually in an organisation, a person experiences two types of conflicts within himself. They are:

1. Goal-Conflict.
2. Role-Conflict.

In case of goal-conflict, an individual faces two or more competing goals. In between these two approaches, only one can be satisfied.

In an organisation, role-conflict exists on account of role expectations. There are some factors that determine the role of expectations. They are:

1. Role ambiguity
2. Organisational position
3. Personal characteristics.

Types of Individual Conflicts

Based on these broad conflicts, the following are four intrapersonal conflicts specific.

(1) Approach-Approach Conflict: In this type of conflict, an individual is associated by two goals at the same time. As against these, only one goal can be achieved. And, at the same time, this situation, as we know, has significant impact on organisational behaviour. There would be two alternative goals which are truly to be mutually exclusive. Leon Festinger's Theory of Cognitive Dissonance can be applied to solve the situation like this. According to this theory, dissonance is a psychological condition in which an individual feels discomfort or conflict when he is faced with two or more attractive goals, but only one can be satisfied. Information manipulation is the technique of avoiding dissonance. It takes the form of obtaining favourable information about the selection made and avoiding the information causing dissonance.

(2) Approach-Avoidance Conflict: Yet another important type of conflict of needs is the Approach-Avoidance Conflict. In this conflict, an individual confronts a goal which possesses both attractive and repulsive characteristics. A person while trying to achieve a goal which has both minus and plus are positive and negative points, both attractive and negative characteristics of equal strength. For example, the desire to study and to get a postgraduate degree is a positive feeling, attractive and pleasant feeling, but one must spend two years of hard work to get through, really a painful task. This is a situation of approach- avoidance conflict. Conflict of this type directly or indirectly has an impact on organisational behaviour.

(3) Avoidance-Avoidance Conflict: This is a situation when an individual deals with a conflict where a goal has two attractive options. Both possess attractive qualities but the choice requires selecting, which is the least unattractive. A conflict of this situation cannot be resolved unless favourable alternatives are available. Myers and Myers beautifully explain this situation into thus: "If you absolutely cannot stand your supervisor, but also cannot afford to be without a job, you are experiencing an avoidance-avoidance conflict. Staying in the company means putting up with the unpleasantness of your interpersonal day-to-day transactions with the supervisor; leaving means no job. Neither choice is satisfying, and you may be in a "lesser-of-the two-evils" predicament until the job market looks better.

(4) Double Approach-Avoidance Conflict: This is a situation wherein the individual may persue two goals at a time. But each goal may have positive and negative aspects. The two or more goal objects which faces a person, for each of which the person has atleast one approach and at least one avoidance impulse. For instance, accepting a new job for a high position, prestige and higher pay would involve devoting more time now spent with family.

2. Interpersonal Conflicts

Interpersonal conflict is part and parcel of every organisation. Hence, it should be the philosophy of the management to create favourable atmosphere wherein the conflicts do not grow in destructive manner. Similarly, it would not be possible to understand clearly the dynamics of communication without understanding the notion of interpersonal conflict. It is an established concept that communication is a transaction, so the individual preferences and disagreements should be somehow negotiated to arrive at a common ground of understanding. It is common knowledge that there cannot be disagreement without conflicts.

Conflicts are inevitable in an interpersonal communication. As such, inter-personal conflict has a source or root at different levels in the organisational structure. Interpersonal conflicts do not occur unless two or more individuals are in interaction or interface with each other. Therefore, interpersonal conflicts may arise between two individuals, one individual and a group of individuals and between two groups. The interpersonal aspects of conflicts also have a significant bearing in organisational behaviour. The inter-role conflict certainly has interpersonal implications. An interpersonal conflict is especially concerned with examing the conflicts that arise when two or more persons are involved in interacting by way of transmitting conflicting views.

Joe Kelly remarks: Conflict situations inevitably are made up of at least two individuals who hold polarised points of view, who are somewhat intolerant of ambiguities, who ignore delicate shades of grey and who are quick to jump to conclusions.

In simple terms, conflicts occur in a group setting also, when the members of the group are confronted with a new problem or task. The main reason for the occurrence of conflicts more frequently between the people, is not because they are not agreeing on the subject or an issue but simply because they do not want to accept each other's viewpoint of their relationship. Kelly further states that conflicts occur in a group, when new values are imported from the social environment into the group; or when one member's extra group roles are different from their intergroup roles.

Types of Conflicts

The interpersonal conflict may broadly be classified as follows:

(1) Individual Differences: A conflict does not arise unless there is a disagreement or difference between two or more people. The differences in the degree of perception and attitude may lead to conflict. Myers and Myers remark that differences in age, sex, attitudes, beliefs, values, experiences and training all contribute to people's perpetual set and thus lead to the way they see situations and other people.

(2) Limited Resources: It has been well-recognised and established that limited resources is one of the basic reasons for the occurrence of interpersonal conflict. Every organisation has limited resources like financial resources, human resources, and technical resources. Accordingly, the critical task on the part of management is to make a rational allocation of scarce resources. If the allocation and distribution of scare resources are not made on a judicious basis, people develop antagonism towards others who get more on unjust allocation.

(3) Role Differentiation: Role differentiation plays an important part for interpersonal conflict. This problem arises with disagreement on how relationships should be defined. It has two aspects of inter role and intra role conflicts. It would have undesirable consequences on organisational behaviour. The extent of undesirable effect from role conflict depends upon four major variables such as awareness of role conflict depends upon four major variables, acceptance of conflicting job pressure, ability to tolerate, stress and general personality make up (Alan C. Filley etc.).

Source of Interpersonal Conflicts

Sources of interpersonal conflicts can also be indentified from the levels of organisational structure such as:

(1) Hierarchical Conflicts — between various levels of management.

(2) Functional Conflicts — conflicts between occupational specialists.

(3) Professional *Vs.* — professional conflicts.

Broadly, these conflicts, in turn, can be grouped as vertical and horizontal conflicts.

According to P. A. Bhagwatwar, interpersonal conflicts emerge when:

(1) Situation is ambiguous which provides opportunity for individuals to have different views.

(2) People have different attitudes towards the same phenomenon.

(3) People with different values come together.

(4) People are interested in escalating conflict.

(5) People learn new values.

Vertical Conflicts: Vertical conflicts indicate superior-subordinate relationship. Superiors, by their position, exercise authority over others and subordinates resist. There arises vertical conflict. Sometimes, superiors may behave outside the scope of their authority.

Horizontal Conflicts: Horizontal conflicts arise on account of the typical nature of a person's ego status, value systems, socio-cultural factors, situational variables, interest conflict, role ambiguity etc.

Measures to Avoid Interpersonal Conflicts

The following are the various avoidance measures of interpersonal conflicts:

(i) Avoidance: One of the easiest conflict management strategies is the avoidance style. Interpersonal style for managing conflict involves withdrawal from or remaining neutral in a conflict situation. In other words, it is a situation of non-commital to a conflict. Avoidance as a conflict resolution, action as a method to overcome conflict by the parties involved in a conflict condition was who may either withdraw from the scene or conceal the incompatibility. The logic behind avoidance is the expectation that, somehow, if one does not look, the unpleasant situation is avoided and he may not have to deal with the conflict situation. (See Fig. 8.3).

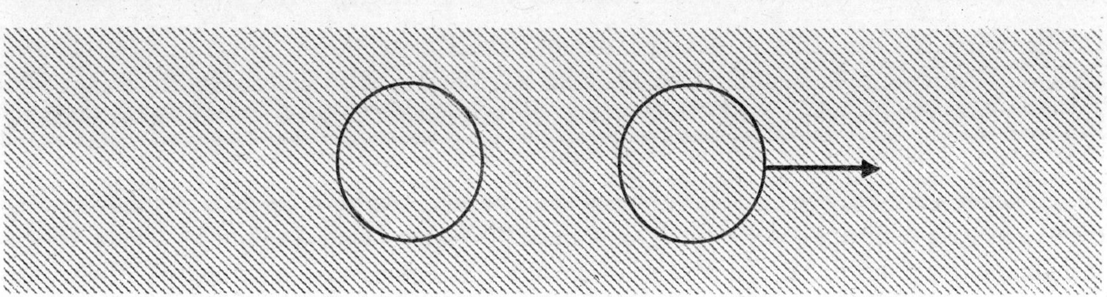

Fig. 8.3 Avoidance Style

(2) Smoothing: The smoothing style as a conflict management strategy is used when a common interest is involved between the people. Smoothing style endeavours to minimise or suppress the conflicting situation while emphasising common interest. Smoothing resolution leads to minimising the differences and similarities accentuated. Smoothing is not a permanent solution but only a variant method of solving conflict. The smooth-prone manager may say that "if you are happy with your point, I try not to amend your view" or " I do not want to say anything that may hurt your feeling." These are the examples of smoothing strategy of conflict resolution. In this style of resolution, the manager or conflicting person seeks the co-operation of all the members concerned. The smoothing style simply encourages to cover up and avoid expression of their feelings. (See Fig. 8.4).

According to Hellriegel, smoothing style is effective on a short-term basis when:

(1) The parties are in a potentially explosive emotional conflict situation, smoothing is used to defuse it;

(2) Keeping harmony and avoiding disruption are especially important; and

(3) The conflicts are based primarily on personality characteristics of the individuals and

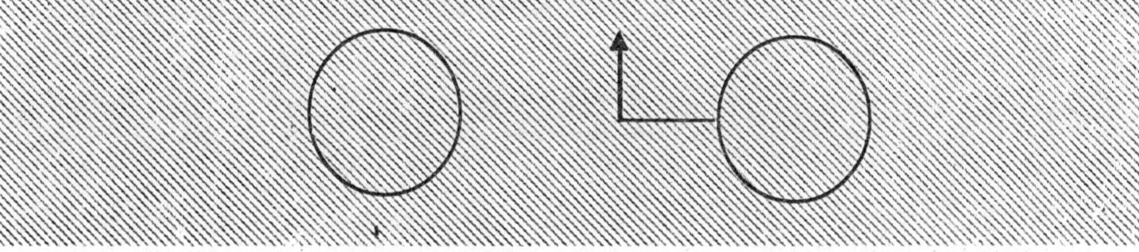

Fig. 8.4 Smoothing Style

(3) Defusion: A measure of conflict resolution adopts a strategy to buy time so as to cool down the tempers of the people involved and to subside the feelings. The issues for discussion are generally classified into two types, minor and major. The parties in a situation may arrive at an agreement on minor issues and sometimes, to solve major issues, some issues are settled and some other remain usettled. It is also a form of an avoidance.

(4) Compromise: The term "compromise" refers to the tendency of settlement of a conflict situation with friendly relations. This method is well accepted for resolving interpersonal conflict. In the compromise state of resolution there would be neither a definite loser or winner. It involves a sacrifice, of one's own position by seeking mediatory ground by splitting the differences in a conflict situation. Compromise method ultimately leads to a settlement of differences in which each side gives up or concedes something which was previously demanded. The scope of compromise includes an amicable settlement of the conflict between the people.

A compromise may be made in various ways. The compromise-prone manager may request them to accept a thing in a conflict. In a compromise process is included a third party intervention including internal members. The process of mediation is termed as "compromise" through the intervention of the third party. When the compromise takes place without the intervention of the external parties, it is known as a bargain. In any case, the conflicting parties would arrive at a common understanding which is purely mutual and give-and-take situation. (See Fig. 8.5).

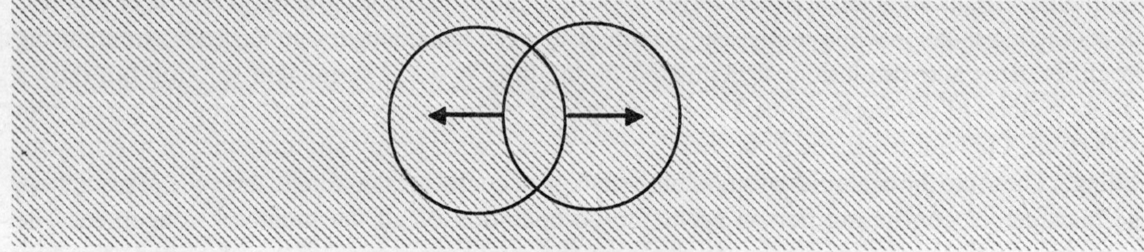

Fig. 8.5 Compromise Style

(5) Forcing Style: The major objective of forcing style of conflict management is to win and dominate, force other person to lose. The forcing strategy is a tendency where winning is often ensured by degrading and overpowering other people so that they are unable to defend themselves. The forcing-prone manager uses coercive and reward power to dominate the other party. In the long run, the consequences of such a strategy can be quite negative. (Fig. 8.6).

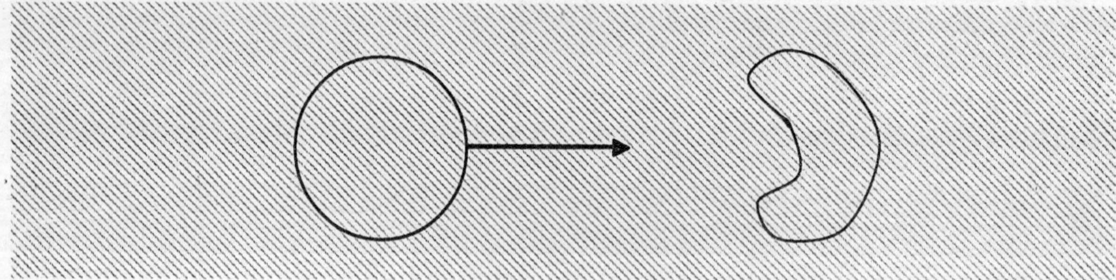

Fig. 8.6 Compromise Style

(6) Collaborate Method: This method of conflict resolution involves identification of the basic causes of conflict, exchange information, open interaction and find out an alternative best course of action mutually beneficial. All the persons concerned and involved are open to recognise conflict and evaluate by all participating voluntarily with bonafide intention of solving a collective problem. A thorough understanding and development of alternatives collectively demands sharing, exchanging, interfacing, analysing the reasons for the conflict to find the best possible solution. The collaborative method gives wider scope for discovering the best possible solution that effectively manages the conflict which is acceptable to all the persons concerned. (See Fig. 8.7).

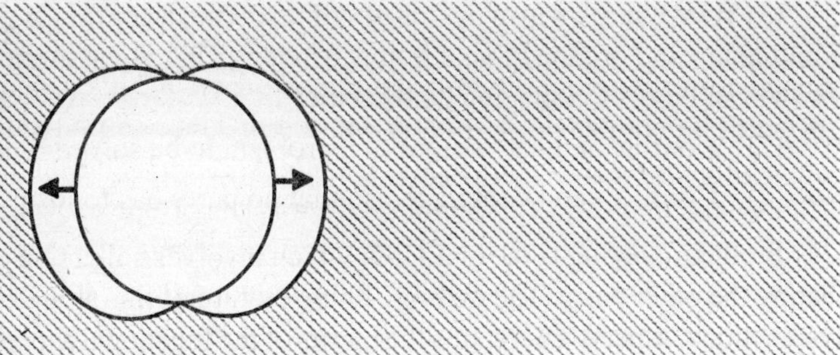

Fig. 8.7 Collaborate Style

(*Source:* D. Hellriegel and J.W. Scocum, *Management*)

(7) Confrontation: In addition to the above strategies and styles to interpersonal conflict resolution, there is another method known as confrontation. Those methods discussed above do not solve some of the conflict-situations if the parties take a rigid stand. Such situations may lead to confrontation in settling the conflicts by the parties themselves. The outcome of confrontation strategy may either result in a win or lose. But actually, there are three basic alternative strategies, such as:

(1) Win-lose.

(2) Lose-lose.

(3) Win-win.

(1) Win-Lose: The parties in a conflicting situation may settle issues based on their power and strength. The principle on which win-lose strategy is based is that one person should win and another should lose. Win-lose style of resolving a conflict is a well-accepted technique. One party in a conflict-situation tries to use his force to win, and the other party loses. The style of resolving is found in superior-subordinate relationship, line-staff confrontation, union management relations. When "win-lose" method is followed, it may have both functional dysfunctional consequences for the organisation. Higher level people in the organisation may resort to confrontation method more frequently than the lower level people.

(2) Lose-Lose: This strategy is also called a compromise strategy. A lose- lose conflict management situation, wherein both parties lose. There are several forms of lose-lose confrontation strategy as identified by Allen G. Filley and his associate.

In one way, the parties agree to settle for a middle ground in a dispute. In the second way, it is to pay-off one of the parties to the conflict. The payment usually takes the form of bribes. In bribery, another lose-lose strategy, one party may pay a high price to get the other to do something very disagreeable. In a third way, the approach is to use an outside third party or intervention of an arbitrator. In a fourth way, lose-lose strategy appears when the parties in a conflict resort to bureaucratic rules or existing regulations to resolve the interpersonal conflict. In all these four types of approaches, both the parties in the conflict lose. The competing parties in an organisation negotiate the allocation of scarce resources on the lose-lose principles. Thus, it is a workable solution to resolve a conflict.

(3) Win-win: A win-win strategy of resolving a conflict is a very common way and desirable from human and organisational points of view. The two assumptions of characteristic features of win-win strategy of managing conflict are:

(1) Conflict is the symptom of a problem to be solved rather than a fight to be won;

(2) Conflict can be managed so that no party has to lose.

Problem-solving is the main task which involves collective energies and creativity rather than beating the other party. The distinguishing feature of this strategy is that it eliminates many of the dysfunctional aspects and retains the merits of the functional aspects of win-lose strategy. Promotion of mutual interest and reward to both the parties are achieved. This indicates favourable organisation, better judgement, experience and more favourable bargains. It reflects the efficiency of the management which is applying this strategy of win-win outcome of an interpersonal conflict, but it is difficult to accomplish.

Johari Window

The Johari window framework is one of the popular tools for examining the dynamics of the interaction between self and others. The model has been developed by Joseph Luft and Harry Ingham, thus derives the name "Johari." This model can be used for anlysing interpersonal conflict situations (Fig. 8.8).

	The person knows about the other	The person does not know about the other
The person knows about him or herself	1 Open Self	2 Hidden self
The person does not know about him or herself	3 Blind Self	4 Undiscovered Self

Fig. 8.8 Johari Window

(*Source:* Adapted from Joseph Luft, "The Johari Window", *Human Relations Training News,* Vol. 5, No. 1, 1961, pp. 6-7.)

The window model would help greatly to pin-point several interpersonal strategies. It also indicates the characteristics and result of these styles. The model also indicates ways of interpreting the conflict that may develop between self and others.

The word "self can be construed as 'me' and 'others' can be thought of as "you" in an interaction of two persons. There are certain things which "X" knows about himself and certain other things not known. On the other hand, "Y", another person knows certain things and does not know certain other things. Similarly, there are certain things which "X" know about the other and certain things that are not known about the other. As such, this model identifies possible interpersonal styles and helps to analyse possible interpersonal conflict situations. The following paras summarise the four cells in the Johari Window:

(1) Open Self: In this form of interaction, person knows about himself or herself and about the other. There would generally be openness compatibility and little reason to be defensive. This type of interpersonal relationship would tend to lead a little, if any interpersonal conflict.

(2) Hidden Self: In this situation, the person understands himself or herself but does not know about the other person. The result is that the person remains hidden from the other because of the fear that other might react. The person may keep himself or herself, into true feelings or attitudes secret and will not open up to the other. There is a potential interpersonal conflict in this situation.

(3) Blind Self: In this situation, the person knows about the other but not about himself or herself. The person may be unintentionally irritating the other. The other could tell the person but may be fearful of hurting the person's feelings. As in the 'hidden self, there is a potential interpersonal conflict in this situation.

(4) Undiscovered Self: This is potentially the most explosive situation. The person does not know about the other. In other words, there is much misunderstanding, and interpersonal conflict is almost sure to result.

Crisis Management and Communication

Crisis management may be defined as the technique of managing/facing crisis situations. Crisis situations are those in the field of management, be it production, marketing, personnel, conflict resolution, interpersonal situations, group dealings etc., when decisions have to be taken without loss of time.

The genesis of crisis situations in any organisation is the failure of the effective planning mechanism for transmission of information to resolve crisis by taking quick and sound decisions without loss of time. The source for delay in taking decisions are lack of message, inappropriate media, channel and inactiveness of communicator and decision-maker.

The crisis may arise in any functional activity like workshop, production, conflict, motivation, influence etc. Similarly, crisis in functional areas would be broadly classified into that of short-term and long-term origin. Both short-term and long-term effective communication arrangement should be made in overcoming such situations. A golden rule to be followed is that crisis situation should be averted/anticipated with effective communication channel and media.

In particular, both written and oral, formal and informal organisation would help to fight crisis sophisticated modern communication technologies may be thought of for accurate and speedy communication. Executives should learn the role of communication to face crisis situations, however limit their resources owning to mechanisation of communication system. The degree of success is not information collection but the number of times and how quickly one transmits information to the required members of the organisation to take decision to solve the crisis.

REFERENCES

1. The discussion is based on *Management — A Systems and Contingency Analysis of Managerial Functions,* Koontz and Donnell, McGraw Hill Kogakasha Ltd., 1976.
2. Henry Mintzberg, *The Nature of Managerial Work.*
3. Lee O. Thayer, *Administrative Communication,* Richard D. Irvin, Homewood, III, 1961, p. 283.
4. Based on *Organisational Behaviour,* S.P. Robbins, Prentice-Hall India, New Delhi, 1991, p. 333.
5. M.R. Leary and R.M. Kowalski, *Impression Management,* 1990, pp. 34-47.
6. Robbins, S.P., *op. cit.*, p. 411.
7. Schlenker,B.R., *Impression Management,* W. L.Gardner and M.J.Martinko, *Impression Management in Organisations.*
   Examples: S.P. Robbin, *op. cit.*
8. Luthans, F., *Organisational Behaviour,* McGraw-Hill International Book Company, 1981, p. 378.

*****

CHAPTER 9

Formal Communication

Introduction

There are different ways of circulating or transmitting communication. Types of communication may be different according to the media and means adopted. Communication is the flow of messages from the communicator to the receiver. In a very tall network and a flat network, information flows in different directions. The organisation is concerned with the flow of communication. As such, it may flow by words, letters, symbols or messages. The positions in the organisation structure must often interact, interface, as a process of exchange of facts, ideas, opinions etc. As such, messages move vertically, upward, downward, horizontally and reciprocally. They may move through formal or informal channel of communication.

Classification of Formal Communication

Thus, the total communication set-up broadly be classified as follows:

I. According to the Organisational Structure and Function

(A) Formal communication.

(B) Informal communication.

II. According to the Direction of Flow

(A) Downward communication.

(B) Upward communication.

(C) Horizontal communication or lateral communication or cross-wise communication.

III. According to the Way of Expression

(A) Oral or Verbal communication.

(B) Written communication or Black and White communication.

The chart given below shows the various types of communication.

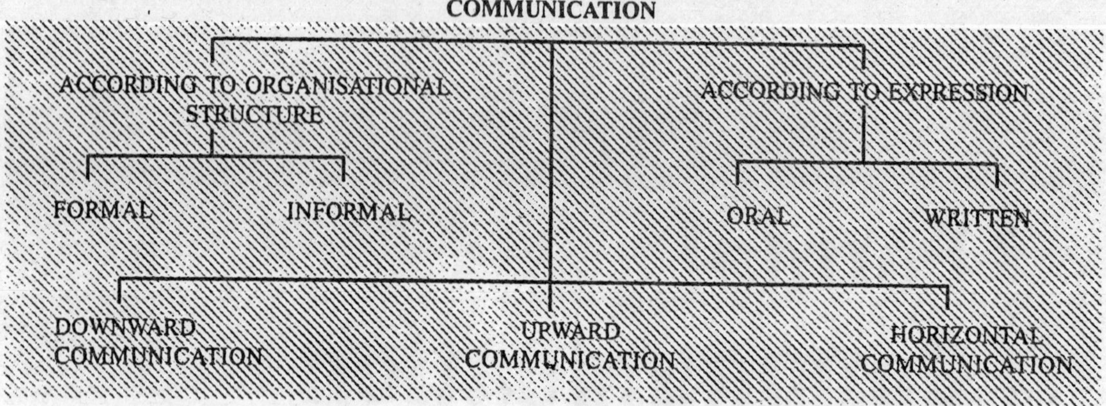

Fig. 9.1

Under the following paragraphs, we will concentrate on the discussion in detail the concepts of the above network which may lead us to understand communication in its completeness.

I. ACCORDING TO ORGANISATIONAL STRUCTURE

A. Formal Communication

Meaning and Nature: An official communication having official backing and sanction. A precise communication channel following a fixed pattern rather than occuring without control. Under formal system of communication, the message flows according to a fixed and prescribed way. Formal communications are both oral and written, but mostly black and white. They originate from the formal organisation structure. They are related to the positions in the organisation. As such, they are linked to all sorts of formalities, rules, procedures etc., opposed to grapevine of informal communication. When information is transmitted by virtue of one's status, placement in the organisation is termed as Formal Communication. It flows through officially prescribed route.

In the route are located officially recognised positions. For example, when an executive instructs his subordinates by virtue of his superior position to do a particular work, it is a formal communication. Formal channel of communication recognises superior and subordinate positions and relationship. In a way, it is a two-way communication. It directs in a prescribed manner, the employees to understand what the management intend them to do. Thus, it does not grow up spontaneously from persons and not flexible. The written formal communication is generally expressed in organisational manuals, handbooks, bulletins, annual reports, handouts etc. With these media, management deliberately seeks to control the flow of communication in the organisation. The object of formal communication is to make it circulate properly and in an orderly way towards organisational efficiency. It also ensures flow of information in a planned route smoothly, accurately and timely.

In all official communications, we come across the words "through the proper channel." It means communication transmitted according to position in the organisational structure. It may be single or multiple channels. In a single channel, there is only one party of communication. The organisational chart indicates the direction or channel of communication.

The structure determines official relations and locations of officially recognised postitions. It also determines the roles and rules which are made and applied accordingly which results in formal flow of information.

Reasons for Rules

Rules are framed and enforced in the formal system. There are a number of causes for formulating formal rules and formal channel of communication. According to Myers and Myers, formal rules and systems of communication exist in an organisation at least for the following reasons:

(1) To control and measure outputs and to articulate the rules themselves.

(2) To co-ordinate complex activities in the system and relate the sub-systems to each other and to the organisation.

(3) To regulate responses to other systems outside to the environment and to competing systems, so that a high level of predictable behaviour may be maintained and consistency encouraged.

(4) To co-ordinate resource allocation of people, money and things.

(5) To create a climate within the organisation so that it can adjust its output as it receives and processes the feedback.[1]

In an organisation where there are a large number of individuals the more difficult is the communication. So, management frames communication rules and message transmitting ways. The rules will be more when there are more groups and activities carrying repetitive and non-repetitive activities. Sometimes, formal rules would be more rigid for effective communication. There would be many rules of communication if there is heavy interdependence, inter-relationship between individuals, groups and between groups, sub-groups and groups. To facilitate communication to be smooth, easy and orderly, the management prepares communication policy manuals, procedures, rules, regulations for their implementation.

Characteristics of Formal Organisation

(1) **Objectives:** Formal organisations grow to achieve the objectives of the organisations.

(2) **Well Defined:** Formal structure is systematically well-defined and controlled.

(3) **Authority:** The structure describes authority, power responsibility and accountability relationships precisely.

(4) **Fixed Channel:** Formal organisations have well-defined route or path and channel for transmission of information.

(5) **Downward flow:** Formal communication in a formal organisation is characterised by vertical downward communication. Messages are usually passed by written media like orders, instructions, rules, procedures and practices.

(6) **Delay:** Formal structure is known for delay in transmitting information because it has to pass through various levels in a tall complex organisation.

(7) **Correct Information:** Only official and correct pieces of information are passed. There is no place for rumours and other unfounded information. Messages are passed with substantial evidence, and official support and backing.

(8) **Job Specification:** The formal organisations assign specific and clearly defined jobs and tasks to the members working to be accomplished.

(9) **Relationships:** In formal structure, hierarchy of relationships are clearly defined. On the other hand, relationships are governed by rules, regulations, procedures and other job instructions.

(10) **Positions and Rewards:** All positions at different levels are defined and rewarded by prestige, rank, status, pay and other perquisites.

(11) **Organisational Chart:** There is a fixed place for formal structure on the organisational chart or structure showing interrelationships.

(12) **Official Backing:** Formal organisations are deliberately created in order to achieve organisational objectives, and as such, they have official backing and support.

(13) **Rigid:** Formal structure is rigid, inflexible and controlled. There is no place for losely defined relationships.

(14) **Applicability:** Universities, big business corporations, State and Central government departments, multinational corporations are the examples of formal organisations.

(15) **Conversion:** Formal organisations can be converted into informal organisations when well defined structure, controls, rigidity, relationships, rules etc., are not enforced.

Formal Channel

Within the network of formal organisational communication structure, there are four types of directional flow. They are:

(1) Downward Channel.

(2) Upward Channel.

(3) Diagonal Channel.

(4) Horizontal Channel.

B. Informal Communication (Grapevine)

II. ACCORDING TO DIRECTION OF FLOW

A.Downward Communication

Meaning and Nature: Another type of communication is according to the direction of the flow. The direction of flow may be downward communication or upward communication. The communication is said to be downward when it flows from the top to the bottom. In the levels of management, from top to bottom means the flow of communication from the superiors to subordinates. When information comes from higher level to a lower level in the organisation structure, it is termed as downward communication.

The information passes through written orders, reports, rules, instructions, manuals, policy directives etc. Downward communication may be circulated either by oral media or written media. Oral media include grapevine, interviews, public address system, conferences, meetings, mechanical devices like telephone, face-to-face conversation, house journal, union activities etc. Written downward communication may take the form of handouts, folders, manuals, periodical reports, bulletins, posters, letters, memos, instructions, clarifications, orders etc.

In this way, downward communication which is in the nature of directives is the most common feature in all organisations. In downward communication, management transmits information, the broad objectives of the organisation and policies to be accomplished. Thus, it flows from the topmost or uppermost levels of management towards lowest level or to the operating level. The directive nature of information moves through the organisation structure stage by stage.

The executives put the decisions in the channel for their downward movement at appropriate time. Not only time but other factors should also be taken into consideration before circulating information. It is upto the managers to decide when, what and where communication is to be transmitted. It is more appropriate to quote Koontz and Donnell: "Timing, scope and means are all involved in the flow of information downward in the decision process. Selecting the correct time and communicating a decision are the prerogatives of the manager. Most decisions flow through the organisation structure level by level."[2]

In downward communication, the written media is mostly followed and is in common use. By this, management can effectively transmit objectives and goals to be accomplished and enforced for implementation. It has official support and backing from the topmost authority. Downward message is not meant for acceptance or ratification from lower levels. It is imposition for implementation. However, there is a scope for better interaction, improving the quality of their response.

Purpose of Downward Communication

To achieve certain objectives, downward communication is imposed. Thus, there are five basic purposes for sending messages from the superiors to subordinates. According to Katz and Khan, the following are the five basic purposes:

(1) To provide specific task directives or instructions on how to do the job.

(2) To provide information which produces an understanding of the task and its relationship to other organisational tasks and, therefore, gives a rationale or reasons for the job.

(3) To provide information about organisational policies, procedures and practices.

(4) To provide feedback on performance to the subordinates.

(5) To provide philosophical information regarding the organisation's mission or orientation towards goals of the organisation.[3]

Downward communication is needed:

(1) To get things done.

(2) To prepare for changes.

(3) To discourage misinformation and suspicion.

(4) To let the people feel the pride of being relatively well-informed.[4]

Usually, downward channel is used by the management for transmitting generally written communication by way of notices, orders, objectives, policies, instructions and through other media to the employees at lower levels in the organisation.

There are five reasons why managers use downward communication which may be summarised as follows:

(1) Job instructions.

(2) Job rationale.

(3) Procedure and policies.

(4) Feedback.

(5) Indoctrination.

Downward Channel

The first type of directional flow is downward channel. The communication from superiors to the subordinates takes place through downward channel. This channel carries formal or official

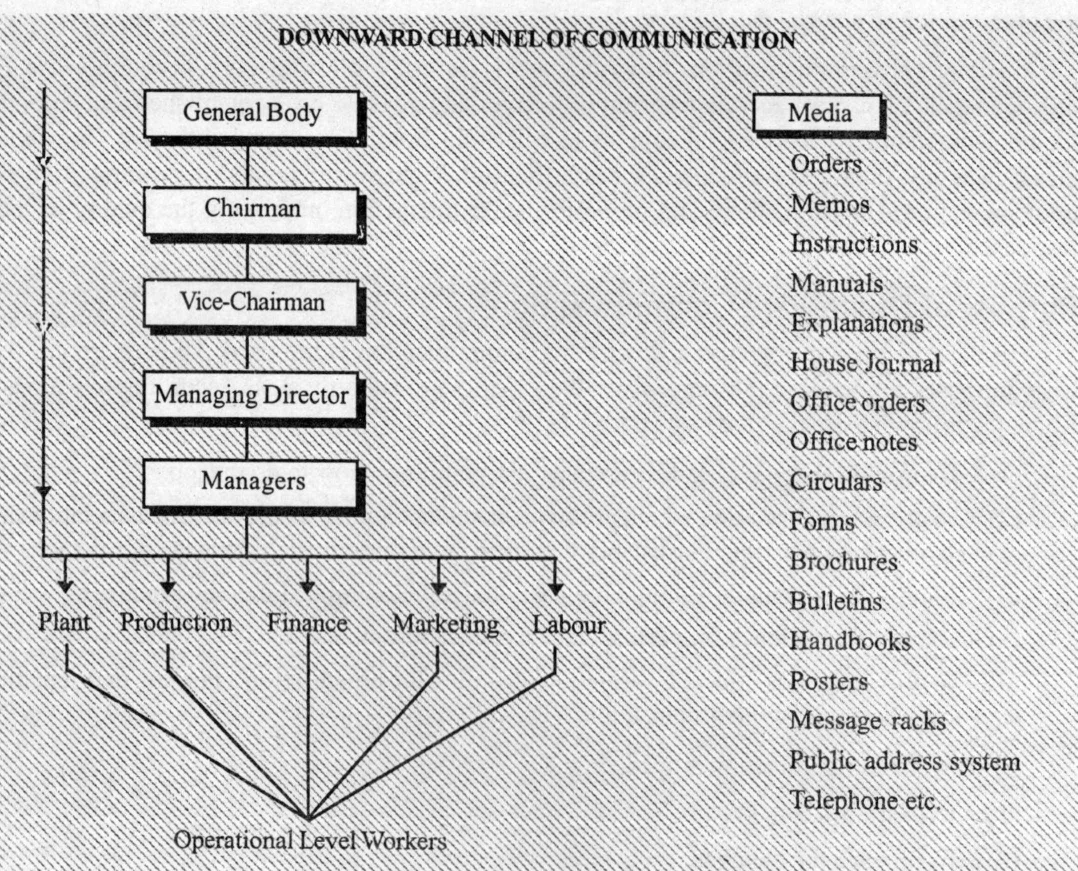

Fig. 9.2 Tactical Strategic Level (Top) (Middle)

communication to the employees. The messages that flow in this channel are orders, memos, rules, practices, procedures, regulations, notices, circulars of day-to-day importance to subordinates. This channel is also called "top-down communication", down in line and through channel.

A well-designed and deliberately planned channel of communication is the formal chain of command. It flows and interlinks organisational hierarchy and official line of authority. Downward channel is a prescribed route or path having official sanction, authority and support. The management's messages are passed from higher to lower levels of management and workers. Formal channel is patterned communication, and is known as downward through the hierarchy.

What Should be Communicated Downward

Downward directional flow of information from superiors to subordinates particularly involves both directional and controlling type of information. It also includes all formal or official information or messages that go to subordinates from superiors in the organisation. There are five categories of downward communication.

(1) Subordinates needs and wants to have: The first category is about information which the subordinates need to have. It also includes the information which the subordinates want to have regarding their jobs. Communication dealing with specific task activities such as instructions, orders, directives etc., mostly relating to the job performance. Other thing is that subordinates also need to know about their jobs relating to the aim of job, job nature, and other activities related information. They want to know that they are making some contribution to the organisation, feeling of security of job, and finally they want to know that their efforts are recognised and appreciated.

(2) Employment Conditions: Communication dealing with subordinates' employment conditions are equally essential information. Subordinates should be informed about their employment particulars like their wages, salary, sick benefit, leave salary, welfare facilities, promotion opportunities, training, complaints, grievances etc.

(3) Organisational Policies: In the context of organisational goals to be achieved by collective efforts, the superiors should also communicate all information concerned with organisational policies, procedures, plans, objectives etc. These are essential which should be informed to subordinates from time to time. The policies, rules, regulations will orient their thoughts and activate them.

(4) Sense of Feeling and Commitment: Communication of specific nature must be communicated to subordinates about organisational members' sense and feeling of commitment to organisational goals. D. V. Agarwal states that "communication derived to motivate organisational members by increasing their awareness and giving them a sense of mission or making them feel commitment to organisational goals.[5]

(6) Feedback: Ideally, a communication is a two-way street. Every manager should know that upward channel is equally important to achieve the object of communication. One of the essential elements of effective communication is to provide feedback. According to Agarwal, "communication that essentially focuses on the subordinate's performance, and provides a feedback to the subordinate concerning his job performance in accordance with performance standards and goals is important to effective communication."[6]

How Downward Affects the Receivers

According to Donald Roberts, the downward flow of information can effect the receivers in the following ways:

(1) People's interpretation of communication follows the path of least resistance.

(2) People are more open to messages which are consonant with their existing image, beliefs, and values.

(3) Messages which are incongruent with values tend to engender more resistance than do messages which are incongruent with rational logic.

(4) To the extent that people positively value need fulfillment, messages which facilitate need-fulfillment are more easily accepted than messages which do not.

(5) As people see the environment changing, they are more open to incoming messages.[7]

Media of Downward Communication

Downward channel is a formal communication route. The objectives, broad policies, guidelines and other directions necessarily have to flow downward. Both written and oral media are used to transmit messages to subordinates. Reports, manuals, procedures and other guidelines come from the top level to the lower level. However, the following are the various media generally used in downward communication.

(1) Written Orders: Superiors issue written orders asking the subordinates to do a particular work or assigning tasks to be performed. Orders are issued by persons in higher authority to the lower level people, directing of what somebody must do. It is a command or instruction.

(2) Bullettin Boards: Bullettin board is the most common medium in all types of organisations. It is a notice board on which are displayed subject matters or messages relating to all the people or section of the people or sometimes relating to an individual.

(3) Bulletin: Bulletins may be distinguished from the bulletin board. Bulletin includes both verbal and written but generally not displayed on the bulletin boards. Bulletin is an official verbal report of news. It is a statement of printed information sheet or newspaper.

(4) Posters: Poster is either handwritten or printed for sticking on a wall at prominent places. Many employees give attention to such posters but a poster is useful as a supplementary device. All the people may not see and do not take care to see them and ignore them. But a poster serves as a round the clock reminder medium. Poster has the quality to catch the eyes but also be concise in its message. It is a large notice or advertisement for sticking on a wall. People see posters advertising or modifying messages.

(5) House Journal: Most of the big companies publish house journals containing a good deal of information. It is a direct medium and meets the needs of both the company and its employees. It covers useful, meaningful information. Management endeavours to spread messages through house journals. Information about the company's policies, products can be disseminated through this medium.

(6) Letters: A written medium to have direct mail contact with the other person. Matters of special interest or personal matters are sent by letters. For instance, letters of appointment, letters of suspension, letters of termination, punishment etc. It is directed personally to an individual. Messages of common interest may sometime, be communicated by letters.

(7) Pay Inserts: Pay inserts are also a form of direct contact. Letters are usually directed to the employee's home address, whereas the use of pay envelope inserts at least ensures exposure to every employee.

(8) Organisational Guides: Organisations issue reference guides useful to all the employees. Guides cover the procedures, forms, pension plan, insurance plan, profit sharing, hospitalisation, welfare and educational facilities, etc.

(9) Booklets, Pamphlets, Handbooks etc.: These media are used by the management when new people are joining the organisation. They are issued welcoming them. They are prepared sometimes specifically for training or orientation programme as an introduction to the organisation. They are often prepared to facilitate understanding organisational set-up and acceptance.

(10) Message Racks: Information racks also supply a great deal of information. Racks contain paperback literature containing company's management techniques, production process, financial results etc.

(11) Public Address System: Loudspeaker system is adopted by the management to disseminate certain matters relating to the organisation which all the employees are expected to know. Gathering of employees of any kind can be informed mechanically to project human voice before a large number of employees for making announcement, sending greetings, emergency events to be communicated.

(12) Grapevine: It is an informal means of communication. Though it is not a formal and official communication medium, yet the management should not ignore the existence of grapevine for providing factual information to counter rumours. It is a powerful medium for sending a message quickly.

(13) Annual Reports: Annual reports should be prepared by the companies as a statutory requirement. They contain a lot of information about the company, its policies, employees etc. Management disseminates information as a part being written for the benefit of the employees.

(14) Union Publication: Union publications contain the voice of the union. They also include the voice of the management to persuade the employees. Union plays an important role in communicating certain matters to the company employees.

(15) Electric and Electronic Media: Telecommunication services and electronic media are now emerging as an important medium of management. Visual media, audio-visual media, other media like video, video cassettes, disc recording, video tape etc., are most commonly used to flow communication downwards.

(16) Other Media: In addition to the above media, there are many other media that are used everyday by the management or superiors in attempting to communicate downward with the subordinates. Other media include personal instructions, lectures, conferences, meetings, interviews, counselling, orders etc.

All media usually may not be useful and may not be adopted by all the organisations. Depending upon the need, requirement and purpose, different managements may adopt different media. Middle level managers may need a quite different media to communicate with subordinates internally. They may adapt different media for external communication using external means like the telephone, press, radio, television to inform the employees as well as the general public. The availability of multi-media imposes responsibility on the part of management to select the appropriate media with the combination of various useful media.

Problems, Hurdles, or Limitations of Downward Communication

(1) Filteration of Messages: Filteration of message is originally put in a channel for downward transmission. When information flows from the top level through the successive lower levels, message loss occurs.

(2) Multi-Levels: There is difficulty in understanding the message rightly, causing confusion when the message passes through various levels.

(3) Lack of Face-to-Face Interaction: The absence of verbal face-to-face interaction is a serious setback in downward communication. Most of the formal communication is in writing or black and white or mechanical media of communication. Delay in feedback is an obstacle in the clear and proper understanding of the subject.

(4) Complexity of Organisation: Downward communication is known for several imperfection in the process like loss of information, delay, negligence, etc., because of complexity of organisational structure through which information has to pass through successive levels in hierarchy. This is particularly so in multi-plant and multi-national corporations.

(5) Misunderstandings and Confusion: Poor perception of the subordinates and ineffective understanding of the message in its real spirit and content. The right understanding of the subject of communication is necessary to act upon it or to take decisions. Sometimes, lower level people get confused.

(6) Reliability of the Source: Credibility and authenticity of the source makes the subordinates to think differently and to understand correctly. A communication received from the higher level receives recipient's better understanding and prompt action than that received from a person with low-level rank. If the subordinates dislike or lacks trust and credibility, they may not give weight to the message.

(7) Overload of Message: If the message load is more than the handling capacity of the subordinates, they may not attend to the communication. They feel saturated, fatigue or boredom. Any information received after the saturation point may not receive their better attention. They ignore all information over and above their handling capacity. For example, many circulation of orders, notes, letters, typing, supervision etc.

(8) Timing: Downward is characterised for delay and slow movement of the messages from higher level to the lower level. Timely passage of information plays a considerable role in accomplishing timely action and timely decisions. Timing of messages is occasionally not appropriate because any information put into transmission may reach at an inappropriate time.

(9) Rely on Written Media: Downward ignores verbal or face-to-face transmission of information. In a formal organisation, for known reasons, it relies heavily upon the written media of communication, including mechanical media in the downward communication. There is no place for personal, verbal or face-to-face transmission except in certain circumstances.

(10) Lack of Trust and Confidence: Downward communication is conspicuous by its absence of mutual trust and confidence between the communicator and the recipients. Filteration of downward information or messages occurs because of lack of trust and confidence between employees, differences among the senders of the message and the existence of large number of links in the communication channel.

(11) Lack of Feedback: Another limitations of downward communication is that it provides no scope for feedback as often as required. It is a one-way traffic. To be effective, a communication which is necessary for successful transmission of downward communication.

(12) Rigidity: In tall network of organisational structure, downward communication must be flexible but, in reality, it is very rigid.

(13) Overlooks Supervisors: It creates communication gap. The system overlooks some hierarchical people in authority. In order to avoid delay and for other reasons, information is sent direct to the concerned authorities, ignoring some levels. It short-circuits the chain.

Suggestions

(1) The sender should be clear in his mind about the subject matter to be communicated; the recipient, the channel and the media to be followed by the sender.

(2) The superiors should have a higher perpetual insight into the recipient's ability, capacity to understand values, background temperaments, etc.

(3) The managers should be clear and use common and familiar words to translate the message to be understandable to the receiver. The language style, manner should be acceptable.

(4) Supervisors must gain mutual confidence, trust, credibility etc.

(5) As far as possible, the communication should be face-to-face, personal and direct, keeping essential matters in writing for record and evidence.

(6) The message load should be within the handling capacity of the subordinates.

(7) The importance of positive communication attitude and feedback cannot be over-emphasised.

(8) The number of levels, as far as possible, should be minimum to avoid tremendous loss of information from successive levels and to save time.

(9) Communication should always flow from higher and responsible authorities which receive the recipients' attention and care.

(10) Listening attitude should be promoted, along with developing trust and confidence between the employees and supervisors and subordinates.

(11) The media and the channel selected for passing information should be suitable and useful to the recipient.

(12) Advance planning participation, active participation in communication process are essential for effective downward communication.

(13) Need for developing of higher perpetual insights, clear, concise and accurate message etc., render the downward communication more effective and productive.

Tripathi, P.C., has offered the following specific suggestions to make downward communication more effective:

(14) A superior must possess more knowledge about facts than what he wants to communicate to his subordinates. His span of knowledge must be greater than his span of communication. Reserve of knowledge is necessary to answer unexpected questions from the subordiantes.

(15) A superior must tell his employees not only what he thinks is good but also what they think is good for them.

(16) There should be a communication plan determining what to tell and how to tell. This advance knowledge about the media and areas of communication reduces anxiety and embarrassment of workers.

(17) The superior should gain the confidence of his subordinates. In fact, confidence and communication are interdependent.

(18) The choice of words and style should fit the language level and ability of the subordinates.

(19) The superior should learn to empathise with his subordinates.[8]

K. Davis has suggested the following prerequisites of effective downward communication:

(20) Being informed, for we cannot communicate what we do not know.

(21) Developing a positive attitude by demonstrating to all employees the importance of sharing relevant information.

(22) Planning for communication by developing policies and procedures by which people will expect to be informed and the effectiveness of downward communication can be monitored.

(23) Gaining subordinates' confidence in superiors and *vice versa* so that messages will flow freely among the organisation levels.

(24) Increased use of face-to-face communication between members of different organisation levels.

(25) Downward channels must be carefully used to avoid problems of message-overload.[9]

Precautions

The following fa^tors on which precautions should be taken to develop available downward communication system:

(1) Need to keep certain types of information confidential.

(2) The timing of a situation.

(3) The amount of information to be sent.

(4) The relationship between sources and receivers; and

(5) The workers' acceptance of the tasks and goals, which the message promotes.[10]

B. Upward Communication

Meaning and Nature: It is opposed to downward communication. A communication is said to be upward when it moves from the bottom to the top. In the organisational structure, from the bottom to top means the flow of communication from subordinates to superiors. Whenever information moves from a lower level to a higher level in the organisation, it is termed "upward communication." Upward communication may be transmitted either by oral media or written media. Oral media consist of face-to-face conversation, informal communication, social groups, union channel of representation etc. Upward written communication may take the form of grapevine, complaints and suggestions, personal letters, explanations and clarifications, reply to memos etc.

So, in an upward communication which is in the nature of suggestive and advisory is the common feature in all organisations. Upward communication system is adopted to submit reports, suggestions, complaints and grievances. Though upward communication is common, but, in practice, it is less favoured by the top management. But still upward communication is a definite chain and formal.

Like reports and suggestions, upward communication includes reactions, proposals for submission to the superiors. But in modern business organisation and complex organisation behaviour of upward communication is considered to be important to achieve organisational goals. It acts as a main source of motivation to employees and to get the things done through them easily.

Upward flow also facilitates the management to know the acceptance or rejection and the extent to which it is accepted or rejected and acted upon. Similarly, executives must, in turn, know the activities and progress achieved by their subordinates. This is possible only through upward communication. For example, a General Manager asks his Assistant Manager to do a certain task.

The General Manager at the same time may be interested to know how efficiently he has performed.

Upward communication has many advantages such as:

(1) It meets a two-way communication.

(2) Feedback on information is possible.

(3) It acts as a check for individual achievements.

(4) Flat networks have sufficient message from the bottom for onward communication upward.

Needs

Upward communication is needed:

(1) To create receptiveness of communication.

(2) To create a feeling of belonging through participation.

(3) To evaluate communication.

(4) To demonstrate a concern for the ideas of each individual.[11]

Upward communication has to do with what the organisation members say

(1) About themselves, their performance and their problems.

(2) About others and their problems.

(3) About organisational practices and policies.

(4) About what needs to be done and how to do it.[12]

Upward Communication Channel

The way or path through which the conceived information, ideas, or message is transferred from the subordinates to their superiors. The upward directional flow of communication is a channel through which the subordinates interact with their bosses. This communication may include seeking clarification, clarifying doubts, participation in decision-making, sharing work experience, etc. Subordinates report to their superiors as to the day-to-day work performance, problems, review etc. P. F. Drucker writes that the good "time users" among managers spend many more hours in their communication up, than on their communication down. This channel includes from the bottom to the top of organisational hierarchy. It is provided through feedback. Superiors obtain information from the subordinates for evaluation, correct it and put it in downward channel. Questions expressing dissatisfaction or disagreement, of complaints to express grievances, giving good ideas, offering suggestions on management policies, procedures etc.

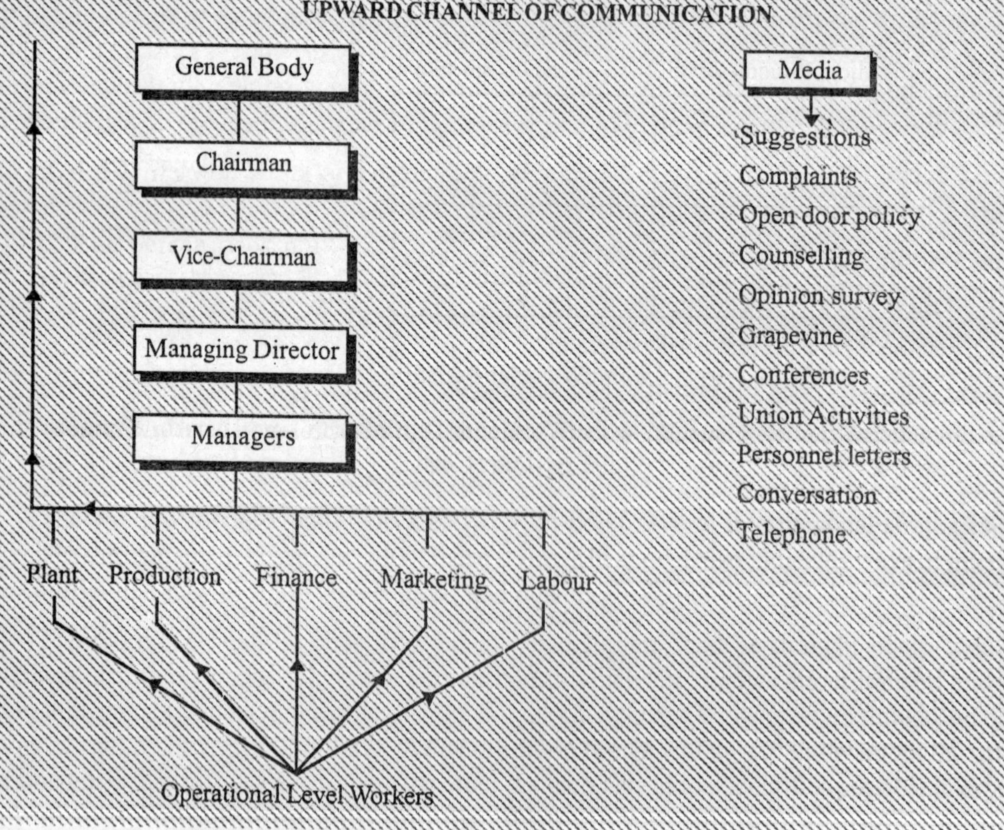

Fig. 9.3 Tactical Strategic Level (Top Middle)

A vertical communication has two ways: one is downward and the other is upward. One of the essential characteristics of effective communication is that it should be two-way. So, upward channel also form the part of the official lines of authority. Upward channel permits to know the rational and emotional reactions of the message passed downward. This kind of formal, structure communication has two channels of both downward and upward. These are two formal channels of communication which are needed to offset the dissatisfaction. Thus, the chain of common channels through which the information is passed up and down the chain in writing or otherwise.

MEDIA OF UPWARD COMMUNICATION

(1) Suggestions: Suggestions by subordinates to superiors ensure a two- way communication. The employees can offer suggestions to the executives or seniors on all matters relating to work for improvement or to rectify errors. Written or verbal media can be adopted to offer suggestions.

(2) Complaints: In addition to suggestions, employees are also entitled to lodge complaints. An efficient organisation generally encourages all types of complaints. It is an upward medium to transmit messages relating to one's displeasures, dissatisfaction to someone, particularly to superiors or top management about the matter. Employees' complaints of working conditions, welfare conditions and general matters of the organisation. Complaint boxes may be established into which an employee can place a written complaint which the management may receive and look into the matter.

(3) Grievance Procedure: A common and best media of upward communication is grievance procedure. It is a window through which messages can be transmitted upward. The workers may present a list of their grievances to the directors or executives. Messages go upward on a number of causes like illness, quarrel, dissatisfaction relating to working conditions and on matters of unfair, unjust or inequitable treatment.

(4) Counselling: It is a verbal upward communication medium. It is a process of giving advice. Executives are expected to give advice on the problems faced by the subordinates. It is the responsibility of the superiors to take up counselling periodically. It ensures a two-way communication. In this, employees have every liberty to express their opinions, facts, feelings etc. Sometimes, counselling with subordinates may fail. Special staff counsellers may be provided to whom employees can have interaction to solve the problem.

(5) Opinion Survey: Management sometimes may conduct opinion surveys to solicit opinion or feelings on a particular matter. Questionnaires may be circulated among the respondents. While giving answers to specific questions the employee can express freely his feelings and opinions.

(6) Open Door Policy: The superiors must have an open door attitude towards subordinates. The open door policy is highly commanded but it has a number of limitations. The policy is workable only in small organisations. The frontline superior may bypass. The management cannot get adequate clues to assess a superior's skill.

(7) Exit Interview: A type of interview which is basically a verbal communication. The interview is convened when an employee is leaving the organisation. It is an opportunity to meet the employee leaving the organization to have interaction and face-to-face conversation to ascertain the employee's opinions, feelings and views about the organisation and knowing the reasons for leaving the organisation. The interview also may sometimes follow filling a questionnaire to solicit information on certain matters. At the time of leaving the organisation, he may not give true and full information.

(8) Grapevine: The management cannot ignore the existence of informal communication. It will survive inspite of many limitations. Informal communication or grapevine is the best channel to transmit messages upward. Management has to listen to it always. Grapevine arises spontaneously out of social relationship and which is always flexible. Through this, management can know the opinions, attitudes, feelings and facts about the organisation from the employees.

(9) Meetings: Participatory communication system achieves a two-way process and sending message upward. Meetings ensure employees to represent their view-points. Periodical meetings with the employees is the best way to achieve natural course of upward communication. It improves communication process.

(10) Union Activities: Labour unions facilitate to ventilate the voice of the union to the management. The office bearers of the labour unions on behalf of the employees convey to management the feelings, attitudes and demands of employees. It is a media of communication for any matter of employer-employee relations.

(11) Participation in Management: Subordinates' participation in managerial decision-making is yet another usual medium of upward communication. It facilitates interaction with superiors.

(12) Collective Bargaining: Collective bargaining also represents a medium of communication which promotes employer-employee relationship.

What Should be Communicated Upward?

The following matters usually figure in the subjects to be communicated upward:

(1) About the employees, whether they are satisfied with their pay in relation to the job.
(2) About their working hours and shifts.
(3) About the distribution of workload among the workers.
(4) About their bosses, whether they observe rules and regulations.
(5) About their promotions, training, and other benefits.
(6) About the policies, plans and actions that affect their work.
(7) About the feelings of their associates like superiors, subordinates or equals.
(8) About their needs and desires, personal or family problems.
(9) About the company's integrity and fairness as an employer.
(10) About the company' s future, reputation, financial soundness, competition and prospects.
(11) About recreational, educational, medical, canteen matters and other welfare issues.
(12) About the work accomplishments, problems, plans, attitudes and feelings of his subordinates.
(13) About the matters of complaints, suggestions, grievances, etc.

Reluctancy to Communicate Upward

Upward communication moves from the bottom to the top. Though the channel is there, upward communication is not effective. But effective upward channel is necessary to achieve a two-way process. Feedback is possible only when there is upward communication to know the responses of the receiver. The measurement of effectiveness of communication is not possible without upward communication. Communication, however, does not simply mean always downward, superiors to subordinates. It involves both transmission and reception.

So upward channel occupies a pivotal role in the process of communication. But, in actual practice, upward communication is not effective and successful. The main reason is that subordinates are reluctant to communicate upward. The managers generally do not wish to know reactions and responses from the subordinates. Subordinates have to take the initiative. There are several circumstances in which a subordinate is reluctant to communicate upward or even manipulates what he tells his boss, as remarked by Harris. The following are the circumstances:

Reasons for Reluctance (Limitations of Upward Communication)

(1) Fear: The subordinate will be hesitant to send upward any messages that may result in the negative, punitive actions against the subordinate by his superiors. The subordinate feels his boss will not be happy about messages and will tend to suppress or slow down. The subordinate will be tempted to distort or rearrange negative information about himself to reduce the probabilities of negative action toward himself.[13]

As Gemmill States

If a subordinate believes that disclosures of his feelings, opinions or personal goal will harm his interest he will conceal or distort it.[14]

(2) Distrust of Superiors: The subordinate who feels that his superior is autocratic, unsympathetic, and task-oriented will develop a distrust of his superior that may cause him to withhold useful information. On the other hand, the more trust and confidence the subordinate has in the superior, the more likely he will be to give the boss messages freely and openly.[15]

(3) Little Use of Messages: The subordinate who feels that his job is of little importance and the information he possesses is probably non-vital will not likely communicate messages to his superior. There appears to be a direct relationship between one's feeling of importance and responsibility and one's willingness to communicate upward.[16]

(4) Lack of Common Sharing: Subordinates keep their superiors better informed when the subordinates know that will be done with their work, when they share common references with their superiors, and when the superior is easily available to the subordinate.[17]

(5) Perception: The subordinate's perception of his boss's attitude toward him (the amount of interest the boss has in him etc.) and the open-mindedness of the boss will affect upward communication. If the superior regularly shows a desire for messages from his subordinates, practices an open door policy and provides feedback on information received, upward communication will be enhanced.[18]

(6) Lack of Ability: Lack of ability to communicate is another barrier to effective upward communication. Most of the subordinates have not developed or cultivated this ability of communicating upward. This means that subordinates must think ahead and visualise the message, plan the message, learn to present and communicate to the superiors. Thus, they are habituated.

(7) Lack of Confidence in Superiors: Yet another block to effective upward communication is the lack of confidence in superiors. The managers hesitate to turn down things presented by the subordinates. Often the situation is by no means so clear-cut, however, the lack of confidence may be subjective and almost unconscious. In many cases, the manager may give lip service or show lip sympathy to the subordinates' ideas or suggestions.

(8) Fear of Criticism: A factor that keeps a man from embracing greater responsibility is the fear of criticism for mistaking. A great deal depends upon the nature of the criticism.

(9) Lack of Self-Confidence and Incentives: Lack of self-confidence and lack of adequate incentives stand in the way of effective upward communication. Finally, there may be inadequate positive incentives which act as a positive inducement for encouraging improved upward communication, like personal recognition, additional incentive for useful advice, approval by respectable members of the company, and other rewards both tangible and intangible. The important point is that the person sending useful information or advice should be provided with a positive incentive that is important to him.

(10) Long Chain of Command: The hierarchical levels cannot be ignored in upward channel. The channel suffers from a more number of levels through which the messages have to flow from bottom to the top. The speedy solution to the problem is not available because it is known for delay and slow process.

People in chairs take their own time to understand before it reaches to the decision-making level. This is followed by filtering, dilution and distortion of the message when messages pass through so many upward levels.

(11) Non-listening Attitude: The executives are not serious on matters coming from the bottom, neither very much attentive, nor inclined to listen. The communicator from the lower level feels discouraged to transmit any information in future, fully and freely. They have the natural bias and prejudices would seldom care to listen with considerable patience.

(12) Status: They feel shame or insult, in listening to subordinates' advice or suggestions. Managers with greater powers and authority feel a sort of complex, feel in terms of their competency.

(13) Self-esteem and Ego: Aggarwala writes that self-esteem and ego is but natural, sometimes influence the subordinates/employees, while communicating any message or information to their bosses. He further states that in order to impress them with the contribution they are making in the achievement of organisational goals, they provide them with information that may not be wholly true but sugar-coated.

(14) Distance: Another reason that keeps the subordinates away from upward communication is distance-factor. There is a long distance between the subordinates and executives in respect of their physical location. The physical distance also hampers upward communication, renders channel and communication tedious and infrequent.

(15) Other Reasons: The social and psychological consideration should not be overlooked in this context. For instance, members have attachment, intimate relationship in the informal organisation which discourages them for the effective communication channel flow upward. It is quite possible that the superiors may withhold any information which they consider unpleasant, and likely to displease or not likely to be acceptable to the boss. The subordinates try to be in the good books of their bosses and pass only such messages which find favour with their superiors.

Upward communication, as we have said, is a two-way relationship. Even then, the boss dares to turn to authority, there may be reasons why superiors shrink from accepting messages.

We see, then a variety of possible reasons why a subordinate may hesitate to communicate upward. These and other points that might be added to the list emphasise the need to think about the individuals involved and the factors that will affect their reactions to any change in the communicated message.

Fortunately, many instances of upward communication encountered none of these obstacles, and in other situations, there may be only one or two points that interfere with effective upward channels. In any case, the list suggests potential reasons to watch for and provide a frame of reference for analysing the Problem.

Measures to Encourage Upward Communication

Superiors should also know the reactions and responses from the receiver on their messages. The message of the sender is of his own initiative. At this end, downward communication moves as a direction or command but upward communication for effective feedback.

O. J. Harris has suggested the following six duties on superiors to encourage upward communication:

(1) The supervisor must make known his need for messages from his subordinates and his interest in hearing from them.

(2) The supervisor should reward his subordinates for their upward communication efforts when this is possible.

(3) The supervisor should cultivate a relationship of mutual understanding and respect between himself and his subordinates. Through his own actions, he can gain the trust and respect, that will also encourage more open-communication.

(4) Superiors should emphasise to subordinates, the positive uses made of their messages as well as the negative uses.

(5) Supervisors can delegate authority and encourage subordinates to feel responsible for specific action performances. The importance of upward communication will normally be felt under these conditions.

(6) If upward is still below desired levels, other steps may be necessary in order to gain needed information. Formal questionnaires, reports and other information sources may be called for.[19]

K. Davis has suggested that in order to improve upward communication, organisation should adopt a policy that employees keep their direct supervisors informed in several areas, such as:

(7) Any matters in which the supervisor may be held accountable by those above him.

(8) Any matters in dispute are likely to cause a controversy between or within units of the organisation.

(9) Any matters requiring advice from the supervisor or his co-ordination, with other persons or units.

(10) Any matters involving recommendations for changes in or variance from established practices or policies.

(11) Any other matters which will enable higher management to improve economic and social performance.[20]

P. C. Tripathi has suggested the following:

(12) The superior should genuinely follow an 'open door' policy. The true test of an open door policy is whether the superior behind the door has an open mind and whether his employees are psychologically free to enter.

(13) There should be a grievance redressal system in the organisation to serve as a means to resolve differences and to redress wrongs, both actual and imaginary.

(14) Informal recreational events like picnics, sports and parties should be arranged to provide an opportunity to the subordinates for unplanned upward communication which is not the primary purpose of these events but which is an important by-product of them.

(15) The superior should speak less and listen more. The nature has given him two ears but only one tongue. Nine commandments for good listening are: stop talking, put the talker at ease (permissive environment), show him that you want to listen (do not read your mail when your subordinate talks), remove distractions (do not doodle, tap or shuffle papers), empathise with him, be patient (do not start for the door and walk away), hold your temper, go easy on argument and criticism, and ask questions.

(16) Subordinates should be encouraged to write letters to the superior. Some space can be reserved in the employees' magazine called "house organ", usually published by many organisations for clearing rumours or for printing letters received from the workers.[21]

Importance of Upward Communication

(1) Upward communication provides useful information, data etc., which are more useful for decision-making.

(2) This channel serves the growth and development of democratic leadership.

(3) It motivates and encourages work spirit to activate workers. The motivation is essential for improved and efficient working of an organisation.

(4) It promotes loyalty, honesty and participative attitude so essential for effective functioning.

(5) Under this system of communication, ideas of the subordinates cannot be obtained without encouraging upward communication.

(6) Effective communication channel flow upward essentially provides the managers with the information of what the subordinates are doing, highlights of their work, achievements, progress and future job plans.

(7) This channel serves as a useful channel because it deals with work-centred matters about which the alert executive normally tries to keep himself well informed.

(8) Effective communication upward channel conveys feelings about the job, feelings about their associates, feelings about the company.

(9) It provides scope which may be valuable to spell out, in detail some of the things an executive should learn through upward channel.

(10) It facilitates an effective inbuilt feedback mechanism particularly feedback in the case of written communication.

(11) It gives an opportunity to present an improved picture of what subordinates think of the willingness of the superiors to discuss policies, plans and actions.

The general objective through strong upward communication is democratic leadership and feedback at work place. Another objective is the development and strengthening of individuals through the satisfaction of the human need for self-expression and participation and the promotion of loyalty and respect for the employer. Thus, for these reasons, managers encourage a free flow of upward communication. There are, in additions, more immediate benefits to the employees, employers and the executives.

Horizontal Communication (Sideways)

Meaning and Nature: Under the third category of communication, horizontal communication is one channel. It is known by various other names like side-ways communication, lateral communication, cross-wise communication, and inter-scalar communication, a third flow of directional communication. A communication is said to be horizontal when it takes place between two subordinates of the same superior.

It is mainly informal and is reflected in meetings, conferences, seminars etc. It occurs between two or more persons who are subordinates of the same person. Cross-wise communication is between functional executives, among a section of officers of a department working under one top superior, the meeting of General Managers of various units of the company, communication between territorial sales managers are the examples of cross-wise communication. It takes place between two or more persons who are linked to each other by equal status or equality of relationship.

The system necessarily relates to the exchange of communication between persons of one level or of one department, with other persons and departments at the same level. Henry Fayol called the horizontal communication a "bridge" or "gangplank" of organisational communication. This permits direct exchange of information between superiors immediately. It takes place among the people of equal status in the organisational structure. The special feature of horizontal channel is that it does not appear on the organisation chart.

In a way, cross-wise communication creates some confusion and practical difficulty. Sometimes, unity of command is affected. In a tall network, there is "gangplank" or bridge. According to Fayol: "Gangplank gives an opportunity to the equal ranks to communicate directly without resorting vertical or up and down the organisation. This refers to informal system. The informal system is generally used when the formal network fails to provide the needed information.

The horizontal or lateral communication encourage to compare inter-departmental activities, performance in the organisation.

Myers and Myers state on lateral communication in these words: When two sub-systems choose to communicate horizontally then, it is altogether possible that they will create a whole set of new messages up both the "legs" of the "high crotch" system just to tell their bosses what they communicate about. Care taking by superiors of the sub-system coalitions, we believe, may, in some instances, add measurably to the message load in the total system.[22]

Oral media for cross-wise communication may be grapevine, gossip, rumour, meeting, lecture, conference, committee, telephone and its various types, union activities, interviews, face-to-face conversation etc. The written media used in horizontal communication are memos, notes, reports, house organs, posters, bulletin boards, handouts, manuals, periodical reports, union publications etc.

Objectives of Lateral Communication

The objectives of this communication are:

(1) To bring about task of co-ordination among peers.

(2) To furnish emotional and social support to the individual on the principle that people in the same boat share the same rate.[23]

(3) Cross-wise relationships exist between personnel in one division.[24]

(4) All the enterprises not only permit but also insist on voluntary cross-wise or horizontal channels of communications at all levels, to speed information and improve understanding.[25]

Functions of Lateral or Horizontal Communication

The following are the important functions of lateral communication:

(1) Department co-ordination is possible by meetings between heads of departments. They can instruct their respective departments in the methods of working in concert.

(2) Problem-solving is possible. Employees generally carry their problems to their superiors who become overloaded with employees' problems. Lateral communication makes possible solving of problems without the intervention of executives. Employees also become more self-reliant, through involvement in the problem-solving process.

(3) Lateral communication enables sharing of information among the departments. This contributes to making the departments effective.

(4) Intra-departmental and inter-departmental disputes can be settled without the intervention of the executives.

(5) The interaction among organisation peers gives emotional and social support to the worker. But if there are no problems to be solved or if there is no need for co-ordination among departments, lateral communication may rise to useless and ideal gossip and rumouring. Hence, if communication forms are irrelevant, they should not be employed as they are destructive of organisation.

(6) Lateral communication may serve as a substitute for upward and downward communication.[26]

Characteristics of Horizontal Communication

(1) Internal: It takes place within an organisation, particularly between line and staff departments. Horizontal communication channel is not necessarily a vertical flow.

(2) Open and Frank among Equals: Horizontal communication permits individuals in the process to exchange messages openly, freely and frankly with the people of equal status in the organisational hierarchy.

(3) Common Understanding: The system essentially relates to communication among the people of equal positions. Hence, communication flows between them very clearly. This solves the problem of any distortion or filtering etc. It is because of the fact of common level of understanding, perception, thinking, decision-making ability and approach to problems.

(4) Co-ordination. Co-ordination between various departments is one of the essential functions of the management. It is the responsibility of the managers, heading various departments to promote co-ordination. Exchange of information among the people of equal status is essentially of co-ordinating function. Downward flow is an authoritative flow of messages, while upward communication provides feedback on operational performance.

(5) Mostly Informal: The basic features of horizontal communication are speed, quick decisions and readiness to accept tasks. This system is more likely to be informal in some respects and formal in respect of some other aspects.

(6) Applicability: The horizontal communication system does not exist in all types of organisations. For instance, the system is almost non-existent in universities and hospitals. But it commonly prevails in big business organisations and multi-national corporations.

Importance of Horizontal Communication

(1) Co-ordination: Co-ordination is one of the primary duties of management to promote effective co-ordination. In a large organisation, there are many departments or divisions, containing large number of people working. It is the responsibility of the people of equal status in the organisational structure to promote co-ordination with effective horizontal communication.

(2) Problem Solving: People of equal status are well-qualified in solving problems. The system of horizontal communication facilitates quick exchange of information, would solve problems of departments or sections or group of persons.

(3) Conflict Resolution: The concept of conflict has been increasingly recognised as an important dimension in the organisational behaviour. Conflict arises as a result of disagreement or opposition between two or more individuals or departments. Horizontal communication is an important channel to resolve interpersonal conflicts, inter-group conflicts among equals. The system facilitates mutual trust and confidence by resolving individual and group's conflicts and rivalries among departments and equals.

(4) Communication by Objectives: The channel gives relief to the superiors by exempting them from certain matters. It avoids referring unnecessary matters to the superiors and facilitates effective co-ordination.

(5) Effective Control: Horizontal communication flow exercises an effective control over things and promotes efficiency of working operations.

(6) Speed Flow: Downward communication is known for delay in passing information because it has to pass through various levels of organisational hierarchy. In the case of upward communication the subordinates are usually reluctant to communicate upward. The advantage of horizontal communication is that the people of equal status in the organisational hierarchy can exchange information more frankly and freely, as such horizontal communication is known for accuracy, quickness and faster passing of information.

(7) Useful to Subordiantes: Subordinates at different levels welcome horizontal communication channel flow. The system allows interaction among organisational peers. As a result, it encourages social and emotional support to workers.

(8) Balances Downward and Upward: Horizontal communication channel flow of downward and upward communication channels. Therefore, it is a good substitute for the upward and the downward channels.

(9) Avoids Vertical Flow: As a special system of communication, it gives an opportunity to the people of equal ranks to communicate directly without resorting to upward and downward channels.

(10) Informal in Nature: Since it short-circuits vertical up and down the organisation, it characterises horizontal communication as informal. The informal system is generally used when the formal network fails to provide the needed information.

Limitations

(1) Creates Confusion: Horizontal communication creates some confusion and difficulty. Sometimes, unit of command is affected. In a tall network, there is a hang plank.

(2) Leads to Disruption: Another shortcoming of horizontal communication is that it leads to disruption in the organisational hierarchy causing problems like conflicts, ignoring levels, message overload etc.

(3) Creates Conflicts: A typical limitation of horizontal communication is that it may give scope for conflicts, misunderstanding and jealousy. This may result in blocking of continuous information flow.

Horizontal Communication Channel

This channel interconnects and is concerned with intra-administrative or external departmental exchange of information or messages with each other. It is better known as horizontal or lateral channel of communication. When the message passes through and across the organisational level it is known as horizontal channel. In this, different flows of the channel communication are between the line and staff centres. The functional heads exchange messages and ask each other's departmental or specialised help. It is a formal channel which functions within the structure of authority-relationship.

Many organisations permit cross or horizontal communication which is horizontal-channel of communication at all levels, to speed transmission of information and improve understandings. Horizontal-channel provides communication that takes place between personnel in one division and personnel of equal, lower or superior status in other divisions. These channels are formalised to the extent that specific contacts which a manager has to maintain to carry out his job and those managers with whom he shares responsibility for specific tasks.

Communication Bridge

Fayol observed this lateral channel or communication form and constructed a bridge of organisational communication. Serial transmission and communication are associated with some of the problems inherent to it, as such lateral communication has been evolved to minimise some of the problems. In a usual flow, a large number of communication links are present. In downward and upward communication, there are problems of filtering, distortion and other difficulties in the transmission of message. Establishing a direct link between the sender and the receiver avoids virtually all these problems.

Fig. 9.4 shows the bridge.

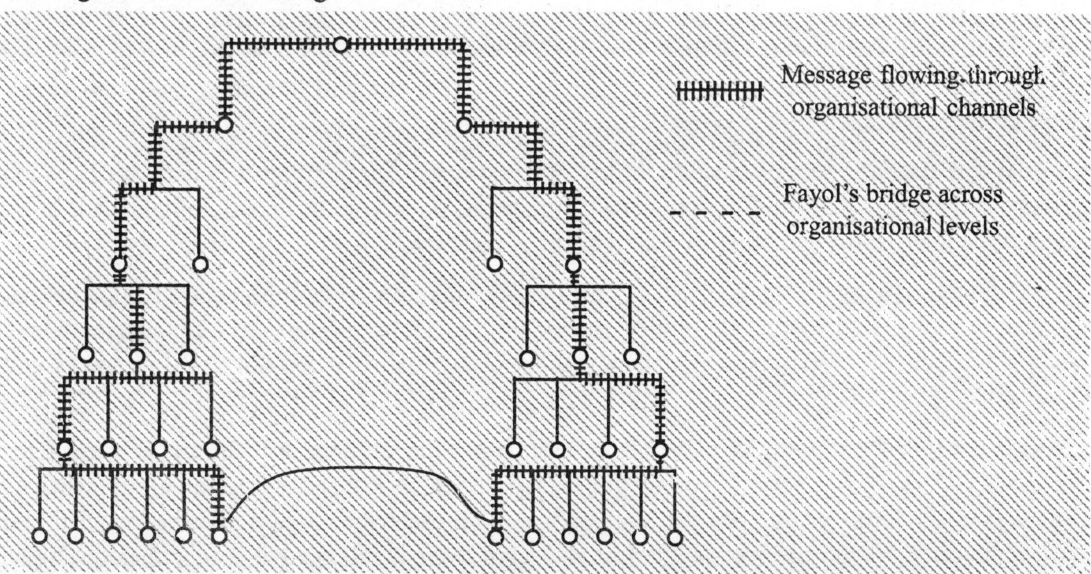

Fig. 9.4 Fayol's Bridge of Organisational Communication

Media of Horizontal Communication

The importance of horizontal or cross-wise communication is being greatly emphasised. Because it is a channel through which messages flow between the sender and receiver or between two subordinates of the same superior. A number of media are used everyday by the Executives in attempting to communicate with others. The positions are usually contacted personally and by such written media. There are many media from which to choose for the horizontal flow of information, feelings and attitudes. Most of the media as covered above may also fall in the horizontal channel. However, some of them are listed below:

(1) Handbooks and Manuals: Handbook signifies a small book containing information on a particular matter. A manual is a compilation of directions and instructions. They are written media mostly used in horizontal communication.

(2) Annual Reports: Firms prepare periodical reports known as annual reports. They contain a detailed information on the activities, performance, progress etc. In support of them, they give statistical figures too.

(3) Bulletin Boards and Posters: A poster is a large notice or advertisement for sticking on a wall. Bulletin Board is a notice board on which are displayed matters of general and particular importance. Posters are called bill boards which may include picture, a play card consisting mainly of a picture of an illustration.

(4) Labour Union Issues: Labour union publications are very helpful in communicating the voice of the employees to the management and to the company employees.

Union publications added to the management voice can be highly persuasive. They convey to the management the collective feelings and attitudes of the employees.

(5) Letters, Memos etc.: Letters, reports, memorandum, office orders, office notes etc. constitute important written media in horizontal communication. They help to communicate and help the recipient to remember the matter. The merit of this medium like other media provide a record of evidence and proof.

(6) Instructions: Communication through the instruction medium often takes place between two subordinates of the same superior. Instruction may be issued by the departmental Heads or by persons who are tied to each other by relationship of equality.

(7) House Organs: House organ is an effective medium of communicating information. Companies publish house organs to inform the employees. House organ is like a magazine which effectively speaks to employees. The management can effectively communicate its views and desires through house organs.

(8) Conferences, Meeting etc.: Like meetings, conferences are the usual media for executives for speaking and making group presentation. Meeting consists of a small group, whereas conference has a large group. The participants have to present their views and the leader of the conference summarises the proceedings. Here also, audience can interact with each other, questions can be put, explanations, clarifications and answers can be sought.

(9) Grapevine: Informal communication between managers.

(10) Telephone: Telecommunication services of various types are used at the horizontal level.

ACCORDING TO THE WAY OF EXPRESSIONS

A. Verbal or Oral Communication

Oral communication is one of the earliest as well as the most widely practised medium of communication. It is through oral words or words of mouth. Oral communication has the advantage of speed, correctness and complete interaction. The communicator and the recipient are the parties. In oral communication, the process is a face-to-face conversation. In oral or verbal communication, mechanical devices can also be used like telecommunication network.

The media of oral communication are the telephone, dictaphone, record, radio, meetings, conference, interview, public address system, grapevine etc. In a face-to-face conversation, doubts, clarifications, explanations and questions can be asked and answered at once. Effective oral communication calls for certain principles for effective communication such as clarity, brevity, precision, conviction, logical sequence, good vocabulary, completeness, etc.

B. Written Communication

In a written communication, every message is in black and white. It is the best method when the communicator and the recipient are beyond oral communication media. This medium ensures exchange of facts, ideas, opinions through a written instrument by which the individual or organisation comes in touch with each other and share meaning and understanding with another. In this type of communication, the words get in touch with those of others.

The process involves sending a message by written words. Formal communication is usually in writing such as rules, orders, manuals etc. There are several media of written communication, such as letters, circulars, notes, explanations, memoranda, leaflets, handbills, reports, forms, questionnaires, handouts, union publications, catalogues, bulletins, magazines, newspapers, posters, brochures, office orders etc.

Diagonal Communication

Meaning and Nature: After having understood the various vertical directional flow of communication like downward, upward and horizontal, let us now come to another direction of communication known as "Diagonal Communication."

Diagonal communication provides a line or route for conveying information in the organisation among the various levels. The communication route under this system takes a line from one department or individuals to different levels. It goes across the organisation. Diagonal communication travels from subordinates to superiors and between persons at different levels.

It takes place among departments or employees of different levels of hierarchy. The functional authorities usually use diagonal communication. It occurs not only among individuals; it also travels among departments. For an effective diagonal communication, it is not necessary that the individuals be on the same hierarchical level.

The system of diagonal communication is not used frequently like upward and downward communication. But, this system facilitates to bring isolated people into the formal chain of communication in the formal structure. All those who are isolated or who are not on regular or horizontal communication now come to the direction of communication flow.

For instance, the Vice-President (Finance) may request to furnish information reports etc., on the sales subject direct to him instead of passing through regular and routine lengthy channels. It is the diagonal flow of communication which necessarily short-circuits the rigid sales chain of command rather than vertical, upward, downward and horizontal. Thus, short-circuiting channel and direct passing of information saves considerable amount of time, money and efforts.

Similarly, the communication is diagonal in the case of special team, task-group, training-group, problem-solving group. These groups have been interested in the execution of special work or task. The members of these groups are neither under the direct control and supervision nor subject to the authority of their functional Heads or hierarchical superiors. The members have direct access to approach top level authorities of various functional areas for any information, data etc.

Diagonal communication channel is an additional one adopted because vertical or horizontal communication channel is not suitable. In such a case, it is the best alternative method available. Similarly, the diagonal communication channel is more appropriate in the case of multi-national, and multi-market corporations which extend their operations to a number of countries.

The word crosswise communication includes both horizontal and diagonal communication. This is what Koontz, Donnell and Weihrich suggest. According to them, the purpose of cross-wise communication is to speed the information-flow, to improve the understanding and to coordinate efforts for accomplishment of common goals of the organisation. So, diagonal communication takes place among individuals or departments who are not on the same line or level of the hierarchy.

Cross-wise communication exists between personnel in one department, and individuals of equal, lower, or superior status in other departments. In this type of communication, there is no need to make a message follow a fixed route or the chain of command. Diagonal communication does not follow the officially designated organisation structure which fixes the hierarchical level. So, it is across the chain of command. Diagonal communication may be verbal or written. Verbal communication has several media like telephone, conference, meetings, oral report, lunch and tea hour meet etc. Written media include newspapers, magazines, bulletins, handouts, manuals and reports etc.

Ways of Communication

Communication has two ways. They are:

(1) One-way communication.

(2) Two-way communication.

(1) One-way Communication: Two types of communication ways are available to the communicator. They are one-way communication and another is two-way communication. In this part, it is proposed to discuss the nature of one-way communication. In other words, it is called as one-way traffic. One-way communication is associated with formal communication. The main characteristic feature of formal communication is one-way communication. It travels simply downward from superior to subordinates. One-way implies only transmission part of the communication. It does not recognise the message from the recipient's point of view.

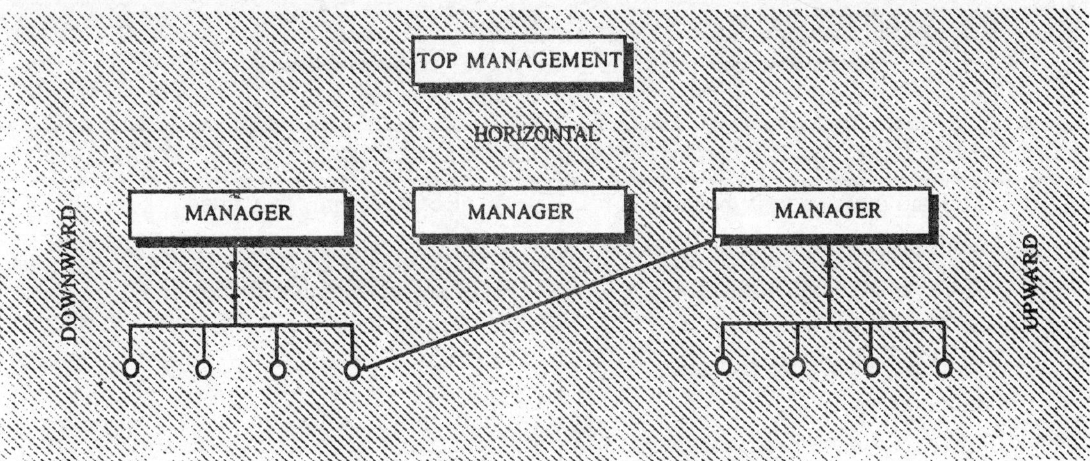

Fig. 9.5 Diagonal Communication

In the early days of communication management, the concept of commúnication was considered merely to the issuing of orders, memos, directions, instructions, circulars etc. At that time, the practice was to give directions, or to tell the subordiantes to do a particular work. The executives under one-way communication did not bother about the subordinates who receive the message, whether they understood the message or not, their responses and reactions. In one sense, in one-way communication, there is no provision for feedback, interaction etc.

One-way communication routes are those established by the organisation's structure. 'Through proper channel', 'going through channels' provide a simple example of what is meant by the expression one-way communication. One way is meant by the expression one-way communication. One way is meant to convey directives from the superior to the subordiantes or from the top to the middle operating level. In this manner, one way communication emerged which implied giving of information.

As generally used, it means giving of information by the management. It travels with message load of orders and instructions downward from the top management through middle level managers. The absence of upward movement of reports, ideas, comments from operating level to top management through intermediary level is the case of one-way communication.

One-way communication provides superiors with a route for conveying information to their subordinates. The main purposes of one-way traffic is to give specific job instructions, to understand organisation structure, interrelationship, to provide procedures and policies etc. The written formal communication is generally expressed in organisational manuals, handbooks, reports etc. The organisational chart indicates the way or direction of communication flow. The formal rules and policies of communication exist in an organisation to achieve some objects like exercising effective control, co-ordinating activity and to regulating of reactions.

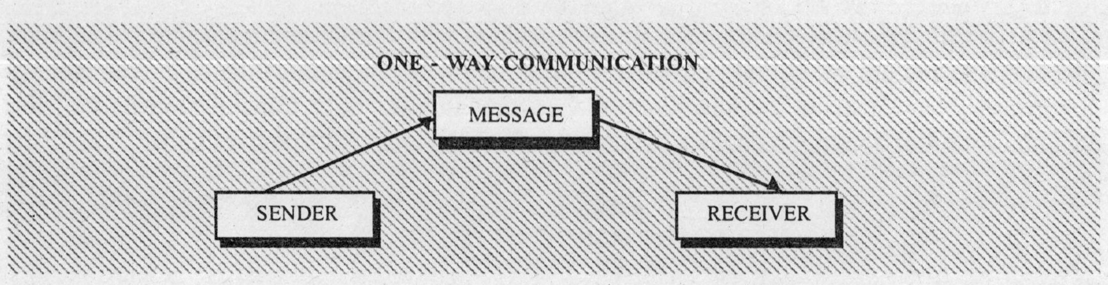

Assets	*Liabilities*
1. Appears quite orderly because sender is not questioned 2. More prestige and authority accrues to sender 3. Sender feels secure and not under attack 4. Fast 5. Cheap	1. Receivers get frustrated 2. Low level accuracy 3. Low confidence about the information

(***Source:*** Myers. M.T., and Myers G.E. *Managing by Communication - An Organisational Approach*, McGraw-Hill International Book Company , 1982, p 68.)

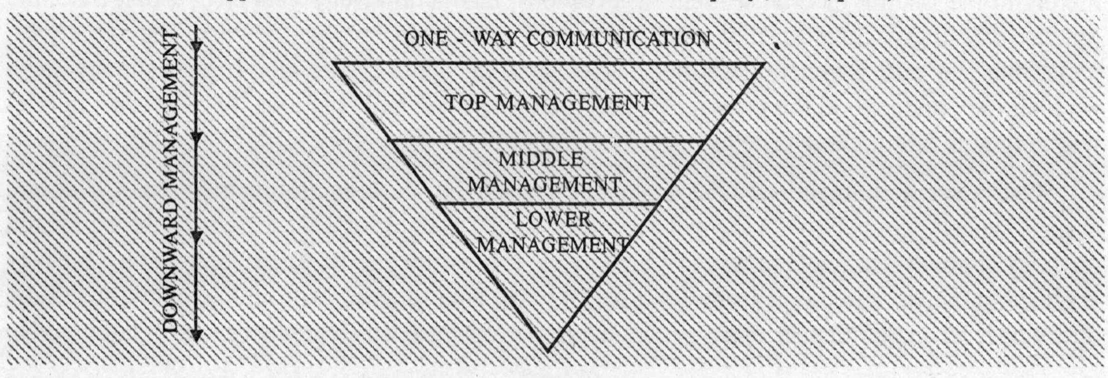

Fig. 9.6

(2) Two-way Communication: Two-way communication implies a two-way traffic. The process of communication is not complete by transmitting downwards. In other words, it does not mean simply downward movement from the superiors to subordinates. In the earlier days, it was considered communication merely to issue orders, instructions etc. Effective communication calls for both transmission and reception. It is not sufficient just to give orders or direct subordinates to do and not to reason why but to follow and to do it. Though the message is transmitted and received by a subordinate he may not understand it, he may not take a decision and may react immediately. It is a case of failure of communication because in such a case, it cannot produce results. The superior when conveying any information should also know its responses, reactions, acceptance or rejection of the message.

It is here that the importance of two-way communication emerges. A manager directs, informs, orders but should also initiate feedback. He must listen, answer, interpret, carry corrections, accept errors and introduce amendments etc. In this way, communication involves a two-way traffic or process from manager to employees and from employees back to manager. It is more appropriate to quote George Terry: "the sender must get through the receiver if the communication is to be complete and satisfactory. It is a great mistake on the part of superior or management to assume that the job of communication is just to transmit message. Thus, it is not complete and effective communication."

The tactical middle management and operative lower level should have an opportunity to participate in communication to question as to the rationale of issued directions and orders, offer suggestions, rectify errors, and defend causes for amendment and all this help in a greater way in the smooth functioning of the organisation. In this way, two-way communication is an important element in a communication process. Two-way traffic calls for both the transmission of the subject matter and reception. It implies giving and receiving, reciprocal of information.

As it has been rightly remarked: "As generally used, a two-way communication meant giving and receiving of information by both management and workers; passing information, orders and instructions downward from the top-management through the intermediate management to the workers and funneling reports and ideas upward from lower organisational levels to higher levels. It includes communication, which originates at any intermediate level as well as worker or top management level because communication is indeed needed by all who work together.[27]

The feedback on the behaviour or behavioural effects of superiors is extremely important. Two hierarchical levels, sometimes three hierarchical levels, are always interested to understand what is the effect of communication transaction. In this triangle system, communication flows between the communicator and the recipient in a chain of command. Two-way communication permits subordinates to speak or express openly and freely. The executives must see themselves for accurate upward movement of information. However, it cannot be ruled out the possibilities of some prevailing supervisors who do not like to hear reports from downward which are not favourable to them. On the contrary, some subordinates do not disclose opinions freely and frankly. Some tactful middle level managers invite accurate reporting, both favourable as well as good information. In such a case, the upward communication can become a reality and effective. But the successful managers should always remember that they should not get frustrated and angry on receiving or hearing unfavourable reports or news. If they lose their temper and balance, the subordinates will. once again begin to screen their comments of unfavourable nature.

As Walter C. Langer, a psychiatrist, noted in a secret wartime report, Hitler burst into a rage whenever bad news was conveyed to him.

It must not be supposed, however, that these rages occur only when he is crossed on major issues. On the contrary, very insignificant matters might call out this reaction. In general, they are brought on whenever anyone contradicts him, when there is unpleasant news about which he might feel responsible, when there is any skepticism concerning his judgement, or when a situation arises in which his infallibility might be challenged or belittled ... among his staff there is a tacit understanding. "For God's sake, don't excite the father — which means do not tell him bad news — do not mention things which are not as he conceives them to be."[28]

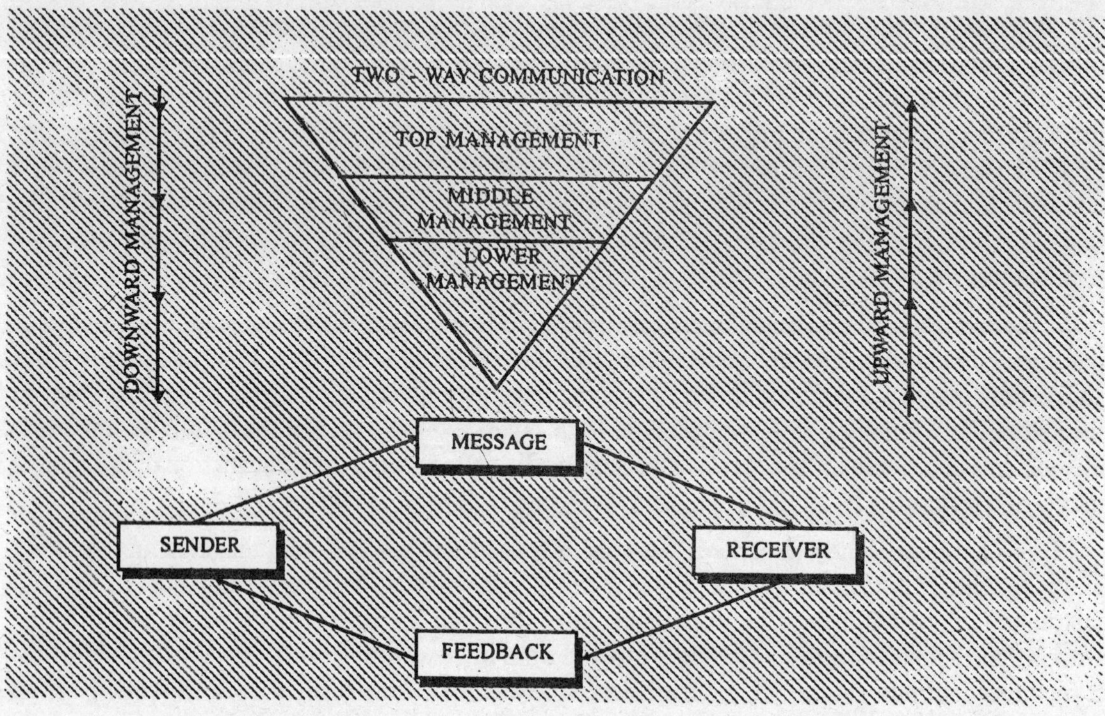

Assets	*Liabilities*
1. More accurate than one way	1. Time consuming
2. Promotes higher feelings of confidence	2. puts pressure on sender
3. Low frustration for receivers	
4. High Morale	

(**Source:** Myers, M.T., and Myers, G.E., *Managing by Communication — An Organisational Approach*, McGraw-Hill International, 1082, p. 68.)

Fig. 9.7

Scalar or Three-Phase Communication

Three-phase communication is referred to as scalar level communication. This is another way of approach to communication. Thus, industrial communication has three phases, namely:

(1) Inter-scalar.

(2) Intra-scalar.

(3) Extra-Organisational.

(1) Inter-scalar Communication: Inter-scalar Communication is nothing but a two-way communication. It implies information flows between different levels of authority. It includes upward communication and downward communication. Management transmits messages to the lower level through middle level management. Upward movement travels from the bottom of the top management through the middle level.

(2) Intra-scalar Communication: It is also called "cross-contact communication" or "horizontal communication." When information travels between two departmental managers or any two or more persons having equal relationship bound to one another, it is termed as "intra-scalar communication." According to S. Khandwale, "intra-scalar communication increases understanding, accentuates group unity, speeds action, aids morale and provides supplementary information. However, if it is over-emphasised and perverted to serve interests of a particular management level rather than the general interest, it tends to weaken the organisation.

(3) Extra-Organisational Communication: A communication that takes place between outside or extra company agencies and the employees within the company, it is termed as "extra organisational communication." It is a way of communication to the workers or the management through union or the workers' families. The union of workers' families are the extra-organisational agencies. The figure given below illustrates the three-phase communication.[29]

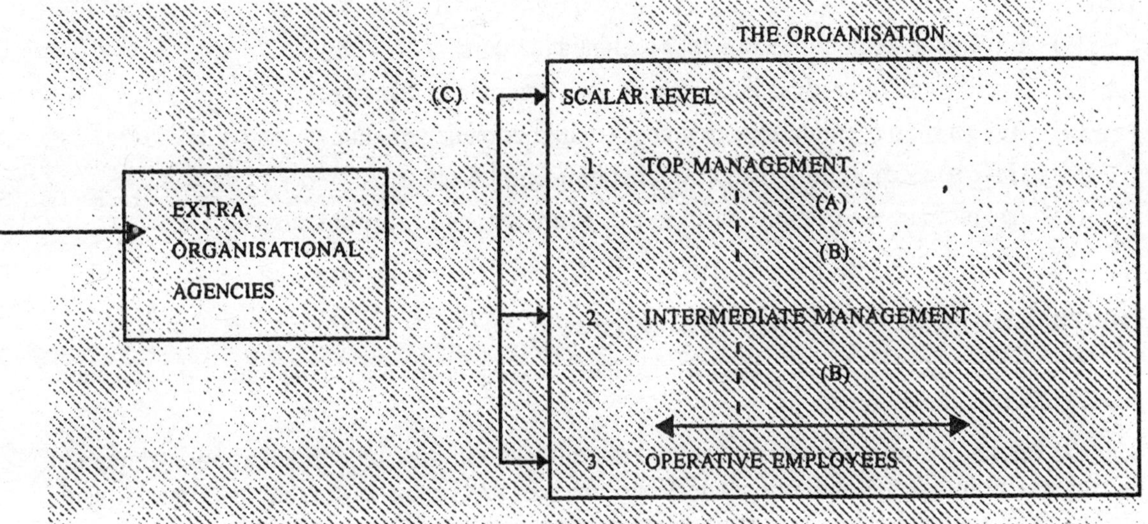

Fig. 9.8 Three-Phase Communication

Communication with Employees' Families

The families of employees will play a major role in effecting employees on the job performance. There are some influences called "off-job-influences" which effect the work. Most of the management's communication, through various media like bulletin-board, are not available to the families of the employees. It is, therefore, more desirable to develop special schemes to include families into the communication system. The members of the families of the employees are more interested to know about their work. House journal plays an important role which carries information to them, so that family members can read and know the things. It is a workable practice to prepare separate handouts or folders to despatch important communication. Information racks and mailing annual reports regularly to the employees' families are the best methods.

Unions and Communication

The role of employees' communication cannot be overemphasised. It ensures a two-way communication. The success of an organisational activity will depend upon the extent to which a union participates in the process of managing organisational communication. As a matter of fact, unions constitute an important channel of communication on which many employees depend. If the channel of the union is ignored, it may have a harmful effect on the organisation. The support of the union on any piece of information of the employer may strengthen employee acceptance of the information and to act.

Communication by Specialist

A researcher, an engineer, an accountant, sales manager etc., are specialists in an organisation. In an organisation of big size and complexity, the groups of such specialists would grow and become complex. They are involved in the communication process which has been mainly assigned to them. K. Davis writes "These specialists play a leading role in communication beyond their own departments." According to him following are the reasons for active specialist communication. They:

(1) Have many communication jobs assigned to them.

(2) Need to sell their ideas because they lack command authority.

(3) Have a shorter communication chain to higher management.

(4) Have a more mobility than most operating employees.

(5) Are more involved in the chain of procedure for handling problems.

(6) Communicate with a number of chains of command.

Internal and External Communication

Communication may broadly be classified into two types. They are (1) Internal communication; and (2) External communication:

(1) Internal Communication: Internal communication may be defined as an exchange of facts, ideas, opinions that individuals or departments of an organisation relating to purely inside matters. Information transmission of various pieces concerns what happens within an organisation rather than its relationship with the others outside the organisation. This implies the concept of internal communication. Thus, internal or inside communication is concerned with and implies the transmission and reception of information clearly, accurately and speedily.

As generally used, inside communication is meant for giving and receiving information by all hierarchical levels. It includes vertical communication, horizontal communication and diagonal communication. It includes communication flowing at any intermediate level as well as at operating level, or top management level, because internal communication is indeed required by all who work together in an organisation to accomplish common goals.

A type of communication is purely of official matters moving with files. It is a communication of indoor management. The outside people who are external to the organisation are not concerned with it. In corporate management, there is a Doctrine of Indoor Management. This allows all those external parties who deal with the company to assume that the provisions of articles in the management of affairs and communication have been observed by the employees of the company. In other words, they are not bound to enquire into the regularity of internal matters. An outsider or the external is not expected to see that the company carries out its internal affairs of management.

In the conduct of office work, internal communication between one person or another is within the premises of the organisation. In a very small organisation as well as large-sized organisation, internal communication does exist as a routine. But in small organisations, internal communication poses no serious problem; for small groups in the office can easily with little effort communicate with each other effectively. Whereas in a modem complex, large-size business organisation with a large group of people, achieving effective communication is a difficult task. But, in those cases, the need for better and effective internal communication cannot be overlooked. Effective internal communication is a real problem which compels a certain amount of care and scientific way of communication, with the increases in the size of organisation, the problems becomes complicated.

Internal communication may either be oral or written. Oral or verbal communication may be face-to-face conversation, telephones, meetings, conferences, group discussions, personal instructions, lectures, interviews, counselling, public address system, grapevine, gossip, rumour, social affairs etc. Written internal communication may be through orders, memos, letters, house organs, bulletin-boards, posters, information-racks, manuals, handbooks, annual reports, grievances, union publications. The main methods of internal communication available in a modern office are messenger service, internal mail service and mechanical devices. Leffin Well and Robinson have suggested three general forms of inter-communication. They are: (1) Notices that certain things have been done; (2) Orders to do certain things, requests for advice and information, notice of happening; (3) Reports of progress on different phases of work.

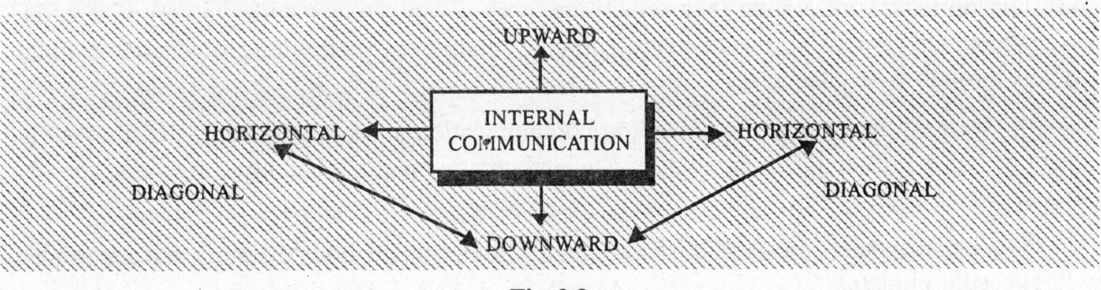

Fig. 9.9

An organisation is a complex organ composed of group of individuals. The individuals and groups communicate and interact within the organisation. It is the responsibility of top management to provide effective internal communication network. In so far as the inside is concerned, the managers communicate with employees and employees with management. Managers also interact with managers. The communication internally should change the behaviour and attitude of the employees and to influence productive activities by keeping them effectively informed.

Organisation is very complex with individuals and groups of individuals. Communication is accepted to change their behaviour in the desired direction. In brief, internal communication is information exchanged among the employees. Within the organisation, top management communicates with the middle level management composed of several functional executives and in turn, middle level management communicates, with the operating level or lower level subordinates. The process permits communication from lower level to top management. Feedback or interaction is a continuous process. Middle level management called "tactical management" interacts with tactical managers. Lower level employees called "operating workers" communicate with themselves. Information exchange flow can be seen diagonally. Informal communication takes place hours together between the people which arises on account of their social relationship, personal contact and other background factors. Information flows downward about the policies, objectives, operations, products etc., which they are bound to know. The organisation structure shows officially designated positions which indicate the described path through which the internal communication should flow.

Requirements for Effective Internal Communication

Lynn Townsend has set forth the following eight requirements for effective internal communication:

(1) "Internal communication must be recognised as an essential tool of management. It is a way to achieve corporate objectives, build teamwork, and motive. It can make managers become better leaders. This requirement recognises that employee attitudes and resulting performance are improved by effective communication.

(2) Employees must be well-informed concerning their mutual interest in company success. Management's position on issues needs to be known, and employees should be persuaded to take actions that will best serve mutual interest and goals.

(3) Individual managers must actively support the corporate communication efforts, managers must develop teamwork among themselves and work co-operatively with the corporate office. Management has responsibilities to create a climate conducive to communication and to maintain the flow through open channels.

(4) Great emphasis must be placed on communication and measurement. Communication cannot be left to chance. There must be a plan who communicates what, how, to whom, for what purpose and to what effect.

(5) Top management must establish a communication climate; other divisions and departments will reflect this climate.

(6) A long-term investment in professional talent and communication programming must be made. Programming and qualified people cost money, but it is well-spent.

(7) Management must recognise its responsibility to listen as well as to speak. If the boss is not a good listener, those who report to him will soon stop trying to communicate with him.

(8) Management must recognise the desire of employees to help their company, and the power of communication to tap this great potential. Employees are willing to help, and communication can turn this desire into action.[30]

External Communication

Channels of communication consist of vertical internal communication like downward communication, upward communication, horizontal communication, diagonal communication, all of which relating to matters within the organisation. There is no denying the fact that every organisation, irrespective of its nature of functioning, has to have communication links or network outside the organisation structure. The bigger the enterprise, the more elaborate the external communication system must be. In such organisations, the greater is the likelihood of expensive and time wasting mistakes caused through lack of external communication.

It would not be out of the way to emphasise that the above channels of communication work within the organisation. But, in the real world situation, every organisation is also linked with the outside parties in the form of suppliers, customers, government departments, financial institutions, holding and subsidiary companies, creditors, debenture-holders, registrar of companies and other body corporates. Under all circumstances, it should be kept in mind that for the effective running of the organisation, an uninterrupted communication channel external to the organisation be maintained to keep the organisation alive and active.

External communication is equally important as internal communication to provide a link between the employees and the shareholders and other third parties. As a matter of fact, external communication is considered as the life blood of modern business. External communication can be arranged by oral or verbal communication as well as through written media. Telex, television, telephone, teleprinter, transmitters, STD, ISTD, and other modern sophisticated communication technologies can be used for external communication.

Written media like letters, circulars, memos, notices, legal notices, newspapers, magazines, manuals, periodical reports, pamphlets etc., are also used towards external communication. External correspondence is mostly in written form except in extraordinary circumstances resorting to telecommunication services.

Communication is characterised as a two-way process, continuing process and a social process. Two or more people are involved in the process. In internal communication, the process is among the employees, may be upward communication, downward communication. A modern business organisation is a complex organisation not only of individuals or group of individuals within the organisation but to interact with outside individuals and groups.

An efficient management need to become aware of the importance of external communication, information exchange and use of feedback. Most problems associated with outside matters are due to lack of adequate communication. Adequate external communication shall be recognised and sought. Problems of pollution, technological unemployment, congestion, housing, medical, crime, family planning, pollution, natural resources, dangerous effects of industrial wastes, fumes, dust, effects of chemical fertilisers, on human health, ecological balance, and a host of many other subject matters fall within the orbit of external matters of social responsibility.

A very important function of the management is to have multi-media approach to communicate with various cross-sections of the society, by maintaining an effective and honest exchange. Within the organisation, employees communicate in different directions. Outside the organisation, a system of communication should keep several people informed. It is utmost necessary to build attitudes, develop rapport, create confidence, win goodwill, moral support and influence, mutual understanding by keeping them well-informed. There are many broad areas outside the organisation about which information should be communicated.

Externally, an organisation has to communicate with customers, shareholders, sister corporations, dealers, government and its departments, general public and entertaining complaints, suggestions, enquiries etc. A brief description about external communication, broadly classified into seven categories, has been presented in the following paragraphs.

(1) Stockholders Communication: The owners of the company are shareholders with whom the company has to communicate always about the matters. Most companies use personal visits, telephone calls, mailing the supplementary reports to keep shareholders informed, interested and satisfied. The communication with them may include reports, matters on corporate meetings, dividend enclosures, magazines, special mailings, notices, resolutions, minutes, periodic correspondence, financial, press release etc. Communication with the shareholders may cover many subject matters such as:

(1) Issue of share certificates.

(2) Share transfer applications and procedure.

(3) Certificate of transfer.

(4) To mobilise funds, pay dividend, interest on fixed deposits received.

(5) To issue dividend warrant, proxy form, dividend coupon.

(6) To issue notice, agenda of the various meetings.

(7) To respond to correspondence received from them.

(8) Correspondence relating to calls, forfeiture, transmission.

(9) Communication on matters relating to statutory requirements etc.

(10) Describing organisational problems and objectives of the company in terms of special current developments in the company's folder and other stockholder communication.

(11) Drafting and circulating to all stockholders a transcript or highlights of the annual progress at the company's annual meetings.

(12) Giving response to each stockholder's inquiry which must be prompt to create goodwill.

(13) Informing by way of circulating or distributing to all shareholders occasional reprints dealing with developments vital to them.

(2) General Public Communication: It is with effective communication and appropriate media that a company maintains contacts with the public. It is the means to create and build goodwill. It also helps as a driving force to reach the public and brings the company and public together, linking with society in general. External communication facilitates through several media of verbal and written contacts with the public in general. It is not possible to build a satisfactory public image for the company without them. The public should be informed about the various products and their uses, comparative advantages, price differentials, product, aftersale services and changes must be communicated promptly. A qualitative communication ensures to promote a positive favourable atmosphere, develops friendly and confident feelings towards the company and its product.

Audio-visual, direct-mail, sales promotion, advertisement, news bulletins, annual reports, posters, hoardings, pamphlets are a few of the many media used to reach public. Public information consists:

(a) Preparing and distributing news releases concerning the company to create public interest.

(b) Public meetings, press conferences between the company and representatives of press, radio and television.

(c) To have a regular and prompt press information service and to answer enquiries from press and radio.

(d) Releasing periodic advertisement in mass media circulating throughout the country and in respect of certain commodities, information to customers directly.

(e) General public communication covers personalised mass mailings, the editors of newspapers, magazines, radio and television directors, educational institutions, religious institutions, public relation offices and officials and other local opinion leaders.

(f) Motion picture is another important medium of public communication which portrays the company's operations and highlighting the economic advantages of the company's areas of operation.

Mass media is the gateway of the company for communication with the public. The public relations department of the company is mainly responsible for promoting goodwill among the outside public.

(3) Customer Communication: An effective system of communication should provide opportunities for customer information. Customer is the ultimate object whose satisfaction and goodwill are of utmost importance for the success of an organisation. In carrying out the sales function of planning, management must communicate with customers. There were times when the customer was not a central figure. But today, customer is the king and sovereign of the market whose needs and satisfaction and winning their goodwill are prime importance in these days of competitive set-up. They must be communicated promptly. It is the communication which establishes the contacts with the customers. Customer-communication helps to establish a relationship with customers who buy and sources of products. The media used for advertisement can be used effectively to reach the customers. It is the responsibility of the communication.

(i) To prepare welcome letters, personally addressed, signed by the chief executive officer to all old as well as to the new customers.

(ii) Customer information should include helpful and desirable information concerning prices, uses, aftersale facilities etc.

(iii) Media like pamphlets, booklets printed in an attractive manner, summarising the company's product etc., are the main purposes of communication.

(iv) Enclosing handouts, progress reports to each bill or to each correspondence mailed to customers. It acts as a repetitive reminder to the customer about the company.

(v) Prompt response to all enquiries made by the customer promotes and builds confidence and goodwill. Effective written communication promotes a friendly understanding of company policies.

(vi) Preparing brochures and other informative folders directed to specific customer group like farmers, small businesses, women, and other special users.

(4) Government Communication: Communication with government and its departments is another important dimension of external communication. Business communication with Government covers several dealings involving many Government departments. A corporate enterprise has to communicate with the Registrar of the Companies, Controller of Capital Issues, finance department and labour department. The relations of a company with Government is many-sided. Correspondence with Government may cover export-import matters, foreign exchange dealings, licensing, registration, taxation matter etc. A company has to file a number of documents to various departments of the Government. Filing of annual returns, tax returns are regular activities. Under the Indian Companies Act, 1956, a corporate enterprise has to take the consent of the government in a number of managerial activities. Government issues its directions, guidelines and other policy matters by way of notification in *Official Gazette* periodically. Business houses have to consider the national objectives, national priorities of economic development as indicated in the Five Year Plans, and other policy statements and resolutions. There is always a routine communication between the Government and the business on several other matters like wage policy, price policy, foreign, industrial policy etc. Government communicates national objectives, priorities, achievements, programmes, through mass media like television, radio, film and through print media like newspapers, magazines, Five Year Plans, budgets, annual reports, special economic survey reports, statistical bulletins, handbooks etc. A firm has to deal with all correspondence in which it is concerned and interested.

(5) Dealer Communication: A communication network should not overlook the importance of dealer communication. Dealer is a trader who carries on the business of buying and selling and other business dealings. A dealer effects substantial turnover involving in buying, selling, supplying or distributing goods directly or indirectly for cash or deferred payment or on commission. Dealer is an important party in external communication. The relation of the company with its dealers like those of other outsiders is said to be dealer communication. A quality of the products, the trading policy, practice, procedure and the image the dealers have to promote are the fundamental factors which must be given major consideration in the subject matter of communication. The way of communicating with dealer will vary depending upon the nature of product, distribution and media of communication. Communication with a dealer is quite different when the distribution is made through agents. Conferences and meetings with the dealers are the usual media of oral communication. Written communication through letters is often the common method. Another medium to maintain close contact with the dealers is in providing all the dealers with regular copies of an external house journal or news sheet. It carries relevant information from the business-house to the dealers, wholesalers, stockist, agents etc. The journal may generally contain messages on display, promotions, uses, benefits, comparative superiority of the product and covering all such matters calculated to improve the dealer's turnover and consequently, mutual profits. Direct mail is also used to have direct contact with the dealers. The public relations officer of the company gives guidance and help to promote sales. He is a liaison between external parties and the company.

(6) Inter-Organisation Communication: No business organisation can exist in isolation without connections and dealings with other sister business organisations. Inter-corporate communication implies a process of information exchange between companies. A company of a particular industry may have links directly or indirectly. Inter-corporate loans, inter-company investment, inter-locking directorship, inter-corporate communication. Information exchange between companies may take place on many matters like cost, process of production, new methods of production etc.

It has been observed that simply a firm cannot exist and survive unless it is related with other firms in the industry. Inter-industry, intra-industry information exchange is necessary to make comparison and to run on smooth and competitive lines. Business houses do much inter-company communication to bridge up the communication gap between the organisation and outside entities. Very often, one may notice that companies resort to inter-corporate and inter-institutional communication. Companies are also involved in information exchange to know the various sophisticated techniques adopted, handling of production method, appraise the people about the organisation's march and social responsibilities discharged and get their employees informed about the movement of the employees in comparable organisation.

In present-day competitive structure, a firm is expected to catch up with the efficiency attained by the competitors and take efforts to reach and exceed item. Communication between the organisation on various functional performance highlights the points of strength and weakness in individual company performance. The inter-firm information exchange facilitates and inter-firm comparison provide an objective and realistic measurement of comparable efficiency of the firms *inter se*. The inter-firm messages on operating performance, financial results, product cost structure, sales trend, market potential etc., in relation to their firms of similar size, capacity nature, industry or trade show vivid picture of comparative strong points and weak points. The firm can improve accordingly their activities. In this, firms supply information reports on their activities in the form of ratios, figures etc.

(7) Complaints Communication: Public relation firmly believes in openness and honest communication. Public complaints and suggestions and responses constitute a complaint communication system. Public is any group of people who share a common interest. An organisation with its effective communication talent has to establish and maintain mutual understanding between an organisation and its public. Complaints made by the public are to be attended to and suggestions offered should be considered. A complaint is really a favour to the company. Correspondence with them is a good means of communication, particularly face-to-face conversation is still effective. Acknowledging any complaint and giving decisions without delay promote goodwill. It is the social responsibility of the business as a way of activity to entertain and be responsive to complaints and suggestions. Social responsibility of a business means obligations which a business owes to the society. Communication sets in all spheres of enquiries, complaints and suggestions.

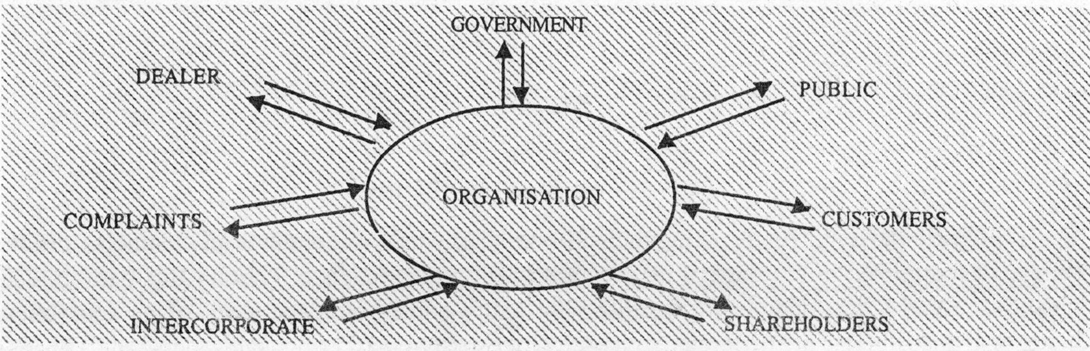

Fig. 9.10 External Communication

COMMUNICATION PATTERNS

The communication pattern has two wings, namely:

(1) Centralised Communication or Star Pattern.

(2) Decentralised Communication or Circle Pattern.

(1) Star Pattern: Star pattern is also called "centralised star pattern" or "wheel." Under this, an organisation may centralise the correspondence section headed by a qualified officer to look after the communication. It deals with the correspondence of all the departments and thereby relieves the burden of handling the communication work of all the functional Heads. Only special or important matters will be communicated by the departmental Heads. The advantages of centralised communication or star pattern are:

(i) Uniformity can be maintained.

(ii) Standard of correspondence is achieved.

(iii) Continuity of policies is achieved.

(iv) Expertise communication creates goodwill.

(v) Specialisation, easy handling, reference etc., are the advantages.

The disadvantges of star pattern of communication are:

(i) The correspondence department has to seek frequent clarifications to a piece of communication.

(ii) It disturbs the work of other functional departments.

(iii) On technical matters the supervisor of the centralised department may not have full knowledge.

(iv) Effective co-ordination is very difficult.

(v) Delay due to each piece of information may have to pass through several times between it and other departments.

In the star pattern, one group member occupies a key role in the transmission of information. Star communication is shown below:

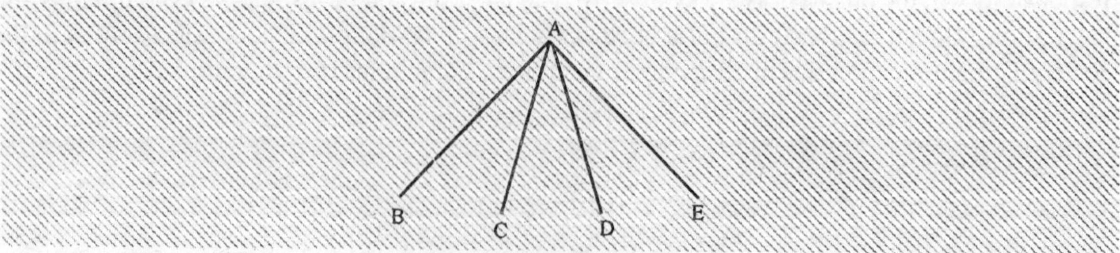

Fig. 9.11 Centralised Star Pattern

(2) Circle Pattern: As the name indicates, the circle pattern connects all channels. It is also called "decentralised circle pattern or decentralised correspondence." Under this pattern, each functional Head is responsible for handling the entire correspondence work of its department. Functional departments are different from each other such as marketing, sales, personnel, finance, production, advertisement etc. Each department may have a separate section headed by an officer to deal with the departmental correspondence with the ultimate signature of the departmental Head. The Executive of the functional department has to necessarily handle the entire message load transmission.

The following are the advantages of the decentralised communication:

(i) The system saves a lot of time as it avoids frequent consultations.

(ii) Systematic filling relating to a department's correspondence can be maintained.

(iii) Communication will be more effective and quality can be achieved.

(iv) Each department is well-acquainted with the matters of its own, so technicalities of a particular work can effectively be dealt.

(v) There is no problem of co-ordination.

The following are the disadvantages in the circle pattern of communication:

(i) Uniformity in correspondence is not possible.

(ii) Message load is limited and there may not be much work.

(iii) The standard of correspondence may differ which may affect adversely the reputation and goodwill of the firm.

(iv) Control will be ineffective over all departments under centralised system.

The following figure shows the circle pattern of communication:

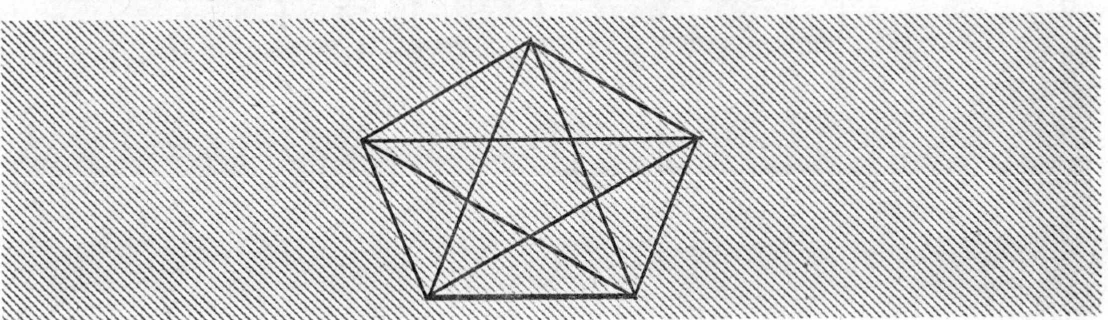

Fig. 9.12 Circle Pattern of Communication

Organisational Hierarchy for Communication

The organisational structure of any concern is depicted on the organisational chart. It indicates clearly different positions, inter-relationships with the organisational hierarchy and their respective responsibilities. The objectives to be accomplished usually decide the nature and hierarchical arrangement of the departments comprising the organisation.

It is the organisational chart which shows the functions, status and interrelationship of each position in the organisation. An organisational chart has two elements, which determine the flow and direction of communication. They are:

(1) Tall Organisation.

(2) Flat Organisation.

(1) Tall Organisation: Delegation determines the tallness of the organisational chart. In a tall organisation, authority tends to be highly centralised. It has all advantages and disadvantages of tall organisation.

(2) Flat Organisation: It indicates spreading or distribution of authority and responsibility across many members in the organisation. In this type, authority tends to be decentralised.

Thus, the organisational structure will determine to a considerable degree, the medium, channel and kinds of communication problems it faces.

Fig. 9.13 shows the two types of organisational hierarchies through which communication flows.

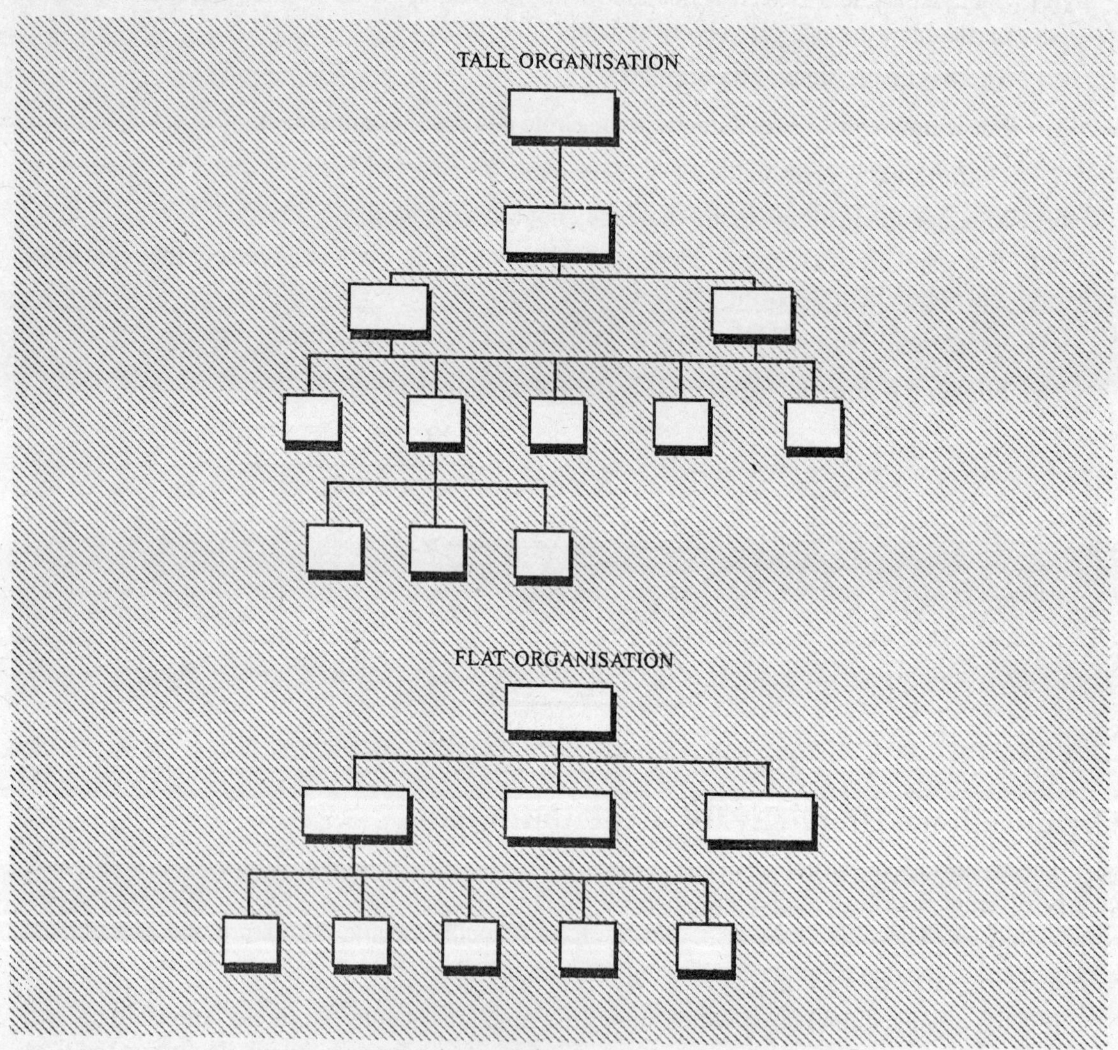

Fig. 9.13 Organisational Hierarchy for Communication

(***Source:*** Adapted from *The Dynamics of Organisational Communication,* John E. Baird, J.R.Harper & Row, 1977, p. 20).

MEDIA CHANNEL AND NETWORKS OF COMMUNICATION

Media

The word "medium" is singular and "media" is plural. The term implies or means something or through which an effect is produced or is made known. Mass media denote those tools of communication that reach a large number of people, such as television, radio, newspaper, cinema, etc. Media in relation to communication implies tools of communication. It means the instrument or instruments adopted or applied to transmit a message, irrespective of its nature and significance.

Media are concerned with the form into which the message is placed, written and oral consist of various forms as used for transmitting the message. In the communication process, the sender of the message forms an idea or ideas which is/are the source of information. He then has to encode ideas or thoughts or feelings. Encoding is the process of translating thoughts and ideas into a message.

It has been rightly remarked that "Anything may count as a communication if a person takes it so."

According to Lee Thayer, communication media refer to "the technological aspects of generating, disseminating, acquiring and consuming message."

The media of communication take the form of symbols, words, action, pictures, numbers, etc. The symbols are used as the media for exchanging information and understanding between different persons. Among them, the words are the most commonly used and are the principal communication instrument of all.

Communication by words may be verbal or oral and written. Both oral and written media have their own advantages and disadvantages. Picture media consist of charts, blueprints, graphs, visuals etc., and are more useful aids. Similarly, action is also a symbol used in communication. It is a form of non-verbal communication. Action or inaction is also an important way of communication. The speaker must also remember that actions speak louder than words. A silence, a nod, a wink, a handshake, grimace themselves speak. A smile has a communicating meaning.

Audio-visuals like television, cinema, electronic media like video, videotape, video-cassette, audio-cassette, computer-assisted instructions, videotext, videodisc, teledon, teletutorials, telephone instructions, telelectures etc., are of the electronic media. There are a number of telecommunication services such as mechanical devices in oral communication like telegraph, telegram, teleprinter, teletype, telex etc.

The main role and responsibility of the media are to transmit messages to inform the receiver of message. Mass media endeavours to send information to the public at large. Mass media not only inform but persuade. Media are used for entertainment and commercial as well as non-commercial. Without mass media, there would be no social, economic and political systems.

(1) Media of Oral Communication

Media of oral communication are:

(1) Face-to-face

(2) Telephoning

(3) Conferences
(4) Press Conferences
(5) Demonstrations
(6) Radio
(7) Recording
(8) Dictaphone
(9) Meetings
(10) Rumours
(11) Grapevine
(12) Public Address System
(13) Group Discussions
(14) Oral Report
(15) Closed circuit television etc.

(2) Media of Written Communication

It signifies the tools of the written communication. In other words, it means the instruments applied in communicating messages. The following is the list of written media:

(1) Letters
(2) Pamphlets
(3) Booklets
(4) Memorandum
(5) Office Orders
(6) Instructions
(7) Manuals
(8) Office Notes
(9) Explanations
(10) Magazines
(11) Circulars
(12) Posters
(13) Leaflets
(14) Forms
(15) Bulletins
(16) Brochures
(17) Union Publications
(18) Complaints and Suggestions
(19) House Journals
(20) Handbooks
(21) Handouts

(22) Handfiles
(23) Annual Reports
(24) News Letters
(25) Directives
(26) Proposals
(27) Agreements
(28) Employees' Handbooks
(29) Pay packet inserts and special circulars etc.

(3) Media of Visual Communication

(1) Visual Aids
(2) Charts
(3) Blue Prints
(4) Models
(5) Posters
(6) Slides
(7) Neon
(8) Hoardings
(9) Pictures
(10) Flannel Boards
(11) Fascimile
(12) Magnetic Boards
(13) Electrowriters
(14) Telelectures
(15) Video-Cassettes
(16) Tables
(17) Maps
(18) Cartoons
(19) Banners
(20) Displays etc.

(4) Action Media of Communication

(1) Handshake
(2) Silence
(3) A Smile
(4) Frown on face
(5) Gestures
(6) A nod

(7) Paralanguages

(8) Body languages etc.

(5) Numerical Media

(1) Figures

(2) Statistical data

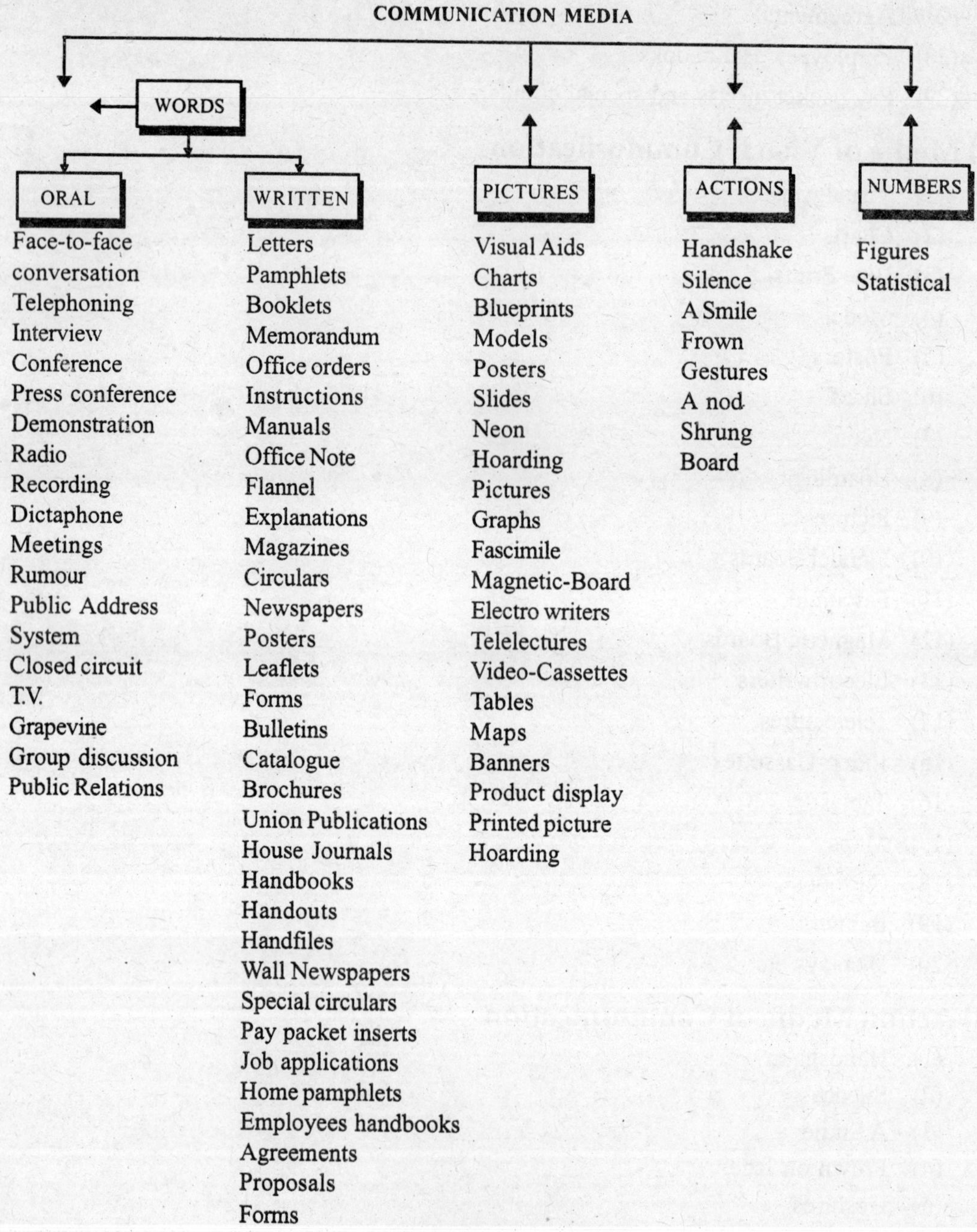

Fig. 9.14 Communication Media

Selection of Media: Selection of media may be oral or written. Any media can be used such as speeches, television, telephone, films, public address system, slides, radio and other varied types of media discussed above. In this context, it may be more appropriate to refer that written communication systems operate rapidly and with maximum validity having official support. However, to meet the requirements of various communicators and recipients, a judicious combination of written, oral and other suitable media is always preferred. Oral and face-to-face presentations at a meeting come out to be more effective. The media for downward communication may be different from upward communication. Meetings involve a two-way communication instantly.

A number of factors may be considered for the selection of media of communication like economics, availability, acceptability, time-saving acceptability cost, speed, resources, accuracy purpose etc.

1. Multi-Media

There are several media, and each has its own merits and demerits. Use of more than one medium in combination of others is termed as multi-media. It uses all media taking into account the utility, and suitability of each medium to a particular situation.

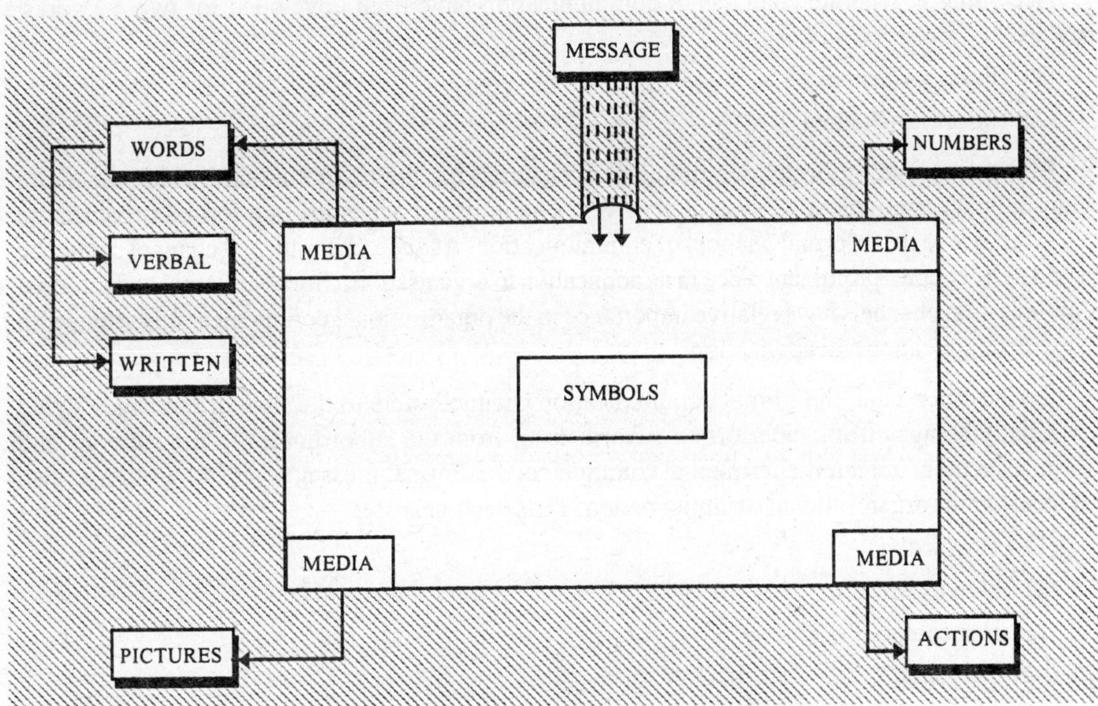

Fig. 9.15 Multi-Media

2. Channel

The word "channel" may be defined as an adoption of various ways and means through which messages can be transmitted by the sender to the recipient. In other words, channels are pathways or routes or media for putting information to be passed to the recipient.

The concept relates to transmission of information or message by the departments, sections or executives or subordinates to the intended users. The transmitter of message has to select an appropriate channel to rely information or messages. There are a variety of channels available to the senders. Channel indicates the direction of flow of communication. The importance of channel in communication process cannot be overemphasised.

The destination to which a message is meant will be reached only when the channel is rightly chosen. Hence, channel plays a vital role. Any media of communication whether of words, numbers, pictures and any other impulse can be transmitted through channels. Channels act as a nervous system within the organisational communication. Channels carry messages from one individual to another individual from one department to another. Jack Halloram explains the nervours system as "the impulses carry the signals from one position of the complex system to another and to a central co-ordination agency through which the entire system is kept in balance and functioning." In any organisation, there are two networks of communication. They are:

(1) Formal Network.

(2) Informal Network.

Accordingly, separate channels of communication have been developed for two networks. They are:

(1) Formal Channel.

(2) Informal Channel.

Both formal and informal communication channels are the pivotal around which the entire organisational communication system revolves. The informal activities in a formal organisation have given rise to the informal channel of communication. As such, the informal channel cannot be ignored as it occupies prominent place in its application to organisations. So, both formal and informal communication channels have relative importance in the organisational communication system with their wider implication and application.

On the other hand, the formal communication channel refers to the flow of messages styled as official messages from superiors to subordiantes, from the subordinates to the superior and intra-management are interdepartmental communication. Formal messages mostly written as also oral form part of organisational communication. Thus, channels are:

(1) Upward.

(2) Downward.

(3) Horizontal.

(4) Diagonal.

3. Network

The word "network" means anything in the form of a net which may have many lines crossing each other. A network in connection with communicating means a widespread connection in the organisation. Communication network is a series of inter-connected points or channels communicating with each other. An inter-connection of organisation structure and/or peripheral devices at distributed locations that transmit communications are necessary to perform the functions of the network.

A network communication structure is a logical structuring information that permits network nodes to be connected in a multi-directional manner. Each node may have one or several communicators and may, in turn, connect any number of other information transmitting centres. A node is an end point of a channel in a network, or a common junction of two or more network channels.

Network in relation to communication reflects the pattern of contacts of employees with decision centres within an organisation. Linking points are constituents connected for the flow of information. As has already been discussed, there are several channels of communication which link various officially designated positions. The interconnections, or the sum total of various channels is known as the communication network. It represents a multiple channel or a multi-channel pattern, but a communication network of an organisation is based upon the number of employees and the nature of channel.

Communication network includes vertical, horizontal, diagonal and grapevine communication. Vertical has downward channel in which information travels downward from superiors to subordinates. Vertical line also shows an upward movement from subordinates; horizontal communication acts as a 'through proper channel' for exchange of information. The formal communication network is based on the organisation structure or a chain of command. Informal communication emerges out of informal relationship which transmits information with surprising speed.

Besides, communication network consists of new sophisticated communication technologies like telecommunication services, electronic media etc. Keeping in view the recent trend of technological inventions and changes, communication network embraces within its fold "Management Information System", "Electronic Data Processing", "Computer Application" and other developments. Thus, a well-netted communication network envisages multichannels. Thus, it represents an integrated operating communication system. A modern complex organisation having many decision-making centres interconnected by various communication channels reflects communication network. This is what is known as a multi-dimensional approach.

Single, Partial and Multiple Network

We cannot suggest a particular line of communication network as universally suitable and applicable to all types of organisations. The building up of a design depends upon the number of factors like, size, nature of channel, number of persons and the complexity of organisation network. The objective that is to be kept in mind in building a network is to achieve the purpose of communication, i.e., prompt and accurate flow of information understandable to the receiver or listener or reader. A simple network may be built up having the constituents, sender and receiver. This is known as circular communication. A partial communication network may be built up that connects only two departments.

The simple and partial network of communication cannot accomodate all aspects of an organisation and may not meet the requirements of all types of organisation. The requirements of a modern complex business organisation having many decisional centres interconnected by channels of communication, should also be considered. Depending on a single chain of command is fraught with many drawbacks and limitations. So, communication network should reflect a multi-dimensional, envisaging multiple channels.

There are various communication networks, as suggested by several research works. One type of network may permit completely free flow of communication and another may suggest a restrictive flow of communication. Accordingly, a network may permit everyone to communicate with one another, another may permit a person to communicate only with his two neighbours. Free flow suggests that everyone can communicate freely with anyone.

Types of Networks

(1) Circle Network: Circle or circular network communication permits, at a time, only two individuals in communication with each other. Under this model, each person can communicate with two persons. These are two neighbours.

(2) Chain Network: In this, neighbours are in communication with each other. The first and the last person have no direct contact to communicate but through a leader.

(3) Y-Type Network: Y-type network is one in which top level strategic management, middle level tactical management involve in communication. Messages travel downward from the Chairman to Managing Directors, to the General Manager, Deputy General Manager and the functional Head.

(4) Wheel Network: In this, only one central person communicates to his boss, through one manager, one person can communicate. Three persons are able to communicate with only a central fourth person. In a variant form of this it permits four individuals to communicate with only a central person. It is called wheel because it allows to communicate through the central person like a connection of hub; spokes of a wheel.

(5) Free-flow Network: As the name indicates, it represents a communication network whereby everyone can communicate with each other. The network figures shown is representative of the free flow concept of communication without restrictions of formal structure.

Distinction between Media and Channel

Media are to be distinguished. Media are concerned with the form or mode into which the message is placed. The channel is the technical transmission of that medium to reach the receiver. Combination of these two put together act as the means of communication. Both are necessary. Selection of media cannot be planned without the channel. In an organisation a channel provides a link between various levels. The link may be between individuals, between individuals and departments and between departments. The organisation structure may create a formal channel from top to bottom. It is an officially fixed route through which the flow of communication is directed. The channel is based on officially designated positions and functions. Formal channel is official and official messages move. Informal channel called a grapevine is an unofficial channel. Thus, communication channel has different directions — flat network, tall network, formal channel, informal channel, upward channel, horizontal channel, internal and external channel.

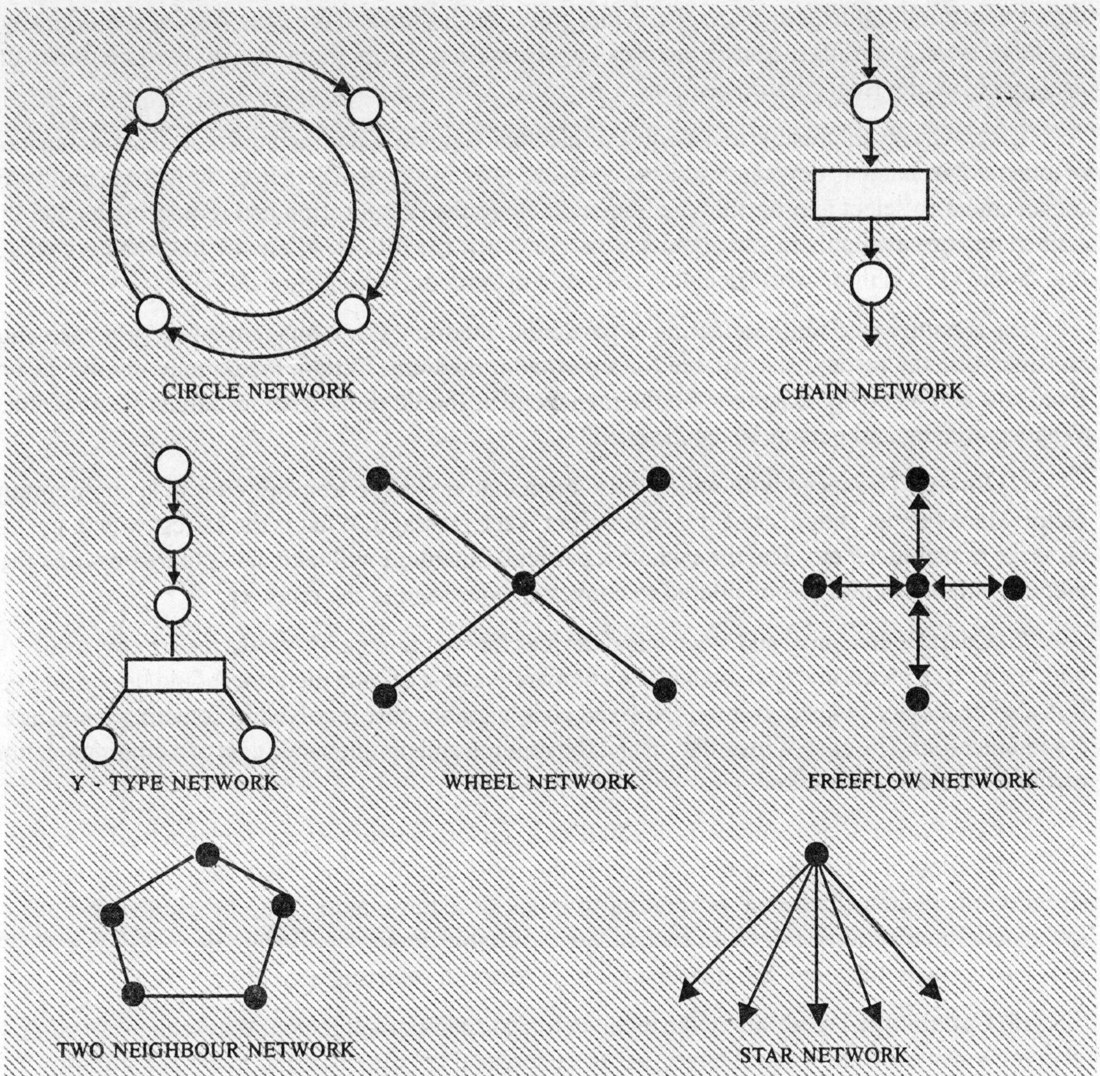

Fig. 9.16 Communication Networks

Factors for Selection of Media

In our comprehensive communication world, we have several media of communication. Written communication has various media of transmission. Similarly, oral communication has also various means of transmission. There are written, oral, visual, audio-visual and combination of any or all of them. Written form of communication are: letters, pamphlets, booklets, memoranda, office-orders, instructions, manuals, office notes, explanations, magazines, circulars, newspapers, posters, leaflets, forms, bulletins, catalogues, brochures, union publications, complaints and suggestions, house journals, handbooks, handouts, and handfiles. Oral media consist of face-to-face conversation, telephone calls, conferences, radio, interviews, closed circuit T.V., oral report, speeches, meetings, dictaphone, discussion, public address system, grapevine, group discussion and rumours. Visual media consist, of slides, neon hoardings, rented pictures etc. Television, short films etc., will come under the category of audiovisual communication.

It is practically impossible to use only one medium. Generally, one medium is used in combination of others. Mechanical devices are also available now in the market. It is the responsibility of management to select appropriate medium suitable to the organisation and requirements and the trained persons available in the organisation. However, the following are the main factors which one should keep in mind while deciding the medium or media of communication,

(1) Resources: While selecting a particular medium the management should take into consideration the resources available for a particular medium. Certain media may involve heavy fixed cost and recurring expenses. So the management should think what resources are available? What equipment and personnel can be used?

(2) Speed: The speed with which the subject matter is to be transmitted is also an important factor. Management should consider how urgent is the message. What is the fastest way to get the message transmitted? etc. The time which a particular medium will take in comparison with other media available should be considered to convey the message to the receiver.

(3) Cost: Both manual and mechanical devices for communication messages are now available both for written media and oral media. The comparative cost of each medium should be considered. It is also necessary to keep in mind the fixed cost, variable cost involved in selecting a means of communication. The cost of installation and the running and maintenance cost of a communication medium should be considered.

(4) Distance: If a receiver is located at a far-off place beyond the reach of a written communication, a mechanical oral device is the most useful. Thus, distance is also a factor in selection of medium. Distance in relation to quick decision-making may necessitate the use of speedy communication devices. In such a case, a suitable device should be selected such as STD, ISTD, teleprinter, telex etc. So, distance is also a factor in selecting a medium.

(5) Capability: The ability of the receiver is also an important factor because the very purpose of communication is to make the receiver to understand the message and to act accordingly. The capacity of the receiver to understand and interpret the message is of utmost importance. The receiver should be capable of understanding the message and to take decisions.

(6) Accuracy: Transmitting the message correctly and receiving it in the same way without filteration is the essential of good communication. The accuracy with which the. message is to be communicated from one place to another, from one person to another will determine the means of communication. In some cases, oral media may achieve the object of accuracy and in some other cases, written media. Mechanical devices may do the work more accurately. It is upto the management to decide the media, considering the various relevant factors.

(7) Secrecy: There are always certain official matters which are confidential and should be kept in secret. The oral medium is not suitable to maintain secrecy of messages. Written communication media may help, to some extent, to achieve the object of secrecy. Some modern electric and electronic mechanical devices will help secrecy to a great extent. In this, a coding device can be used to achieve secrecy. For instance, a cipher telegram transmit messages in code languages and the recipient has necessarily to decode the message.

(8) Impact: The object of communication is not just to transmit the message and say the job of communication is over. The effect of communication on the receiver is to be ascertained. If the impact of message is not effective, alternative steps can be taken to increase the impact. Impact of message is also one of the main factors which the management should keep in mind while selecting a means of communication.

(9) Definite: Reaching of the message should be made certain. Certainty of the message reaching the recipient or not, will also decide the medium of communication to be selected. In the case of written communication media, there are many mail services which assure certainty of reaching. For instance, registered post or recorded delivery and VPP etc., would ensure certainty of reaching the message. In oral communication, mechanical devices should be preferred to words of mouth.

(10) Emphasis: The next important factor to be considered in the selection of medium of communication is the emphasis or impression of the message on the receiver. Under this factor, the degree of impression that means of communication creates in the mind of the recipient will determine the mode of selection. The principle of emphasis may be achieved by using such device which creates better impression on the mind of the recipient. For instance, trunk call, express telegram, STD etc., will definitely create better impression as compared to ordinary letters or words of mouth.

(11) Purpose: What is the purpose to be achieved in transmitting a message will determine the mode of communication. The purpose determines the media to be selected, different purposes may call for different media. For instance, the question of media to inform, to convince, to motivate, to instruct etc., will influence the selection of media. So, the purpose of communication should also be considered while selecting the means of communication.

(12) Effective Handling: The factor of effective handling or convenience in use should be considered. The media of communication should be convenient to use both to the sender and the receiver. For instance, in the case of the use of cipher telegram, the receiver finds it difficult to decode the message, unless he is conversant with the code language.

(13) Training and Education: Sometimes, it may be necessary to impart knowledge to the sender and receiver on the media of communication, their operation, use and handling. Staff training programme is necessary in case of use of mechanical devices for transmission of messages. For instance, training is necessary to operate a switch board, filing communication, transmitting messages, classification of communication etc. So factors like education, need for training staff should also be considered by the management before selecting means of communication.

(14) Safety of Messages: Messages transmitted and received should be preserved as record for future reference. Whether the messages will be preserved will also decide the means of communication to be adapted. Systematic filing of communication, classification of communication and indexing of communication are essential for effective communication. So, the importance of this factor should not be overlooked by the management.

(15) Feedback: Essentials of good communication call for feedback. It is the reciever's response to the sender's message. Communication is a two-way process. The sender must know how well the message has been understood by the receiver, his action, reaction, acceptance or rejection of message. In selection of the mode of communication, the provision of feedback must be incorporated. Communication fails in the absence of feedback.

Merits of Formal Communication

(1) Correct Information: There is no place in formal communication to spread incorrect information as well as rumours. The dangers which arise on account of incorrect information would not take place in formal communication. By definition, formal indicates substantive evidence or facts. It may not be damaging when circulated and acted upon.

(2) Official Backing: The formal communication is always an official communication having official support and sanction. This method may not lead to distracted information because there is official sanction and may not even turn into gossip and rumour.

(3) Existence of Authority: Formal communication through channels and commands promotes respect by subordinates to their superiors. In other words, it maintains authority of the line officers-subordinates. Under this system, there is officially recognised and fixed positions associated with duties and responsibilities. The deliberately created communication rules help in exercising control over subordinates. The superiors can command subordinates to get things done.

(4) Message Handling: Though the management recognises and gives importance to the grapevine, it cannot handle the overload of work. Formal channel of communication is adequate for handling all categories of messages expenditiously with clear understanding. Formal communication can shoulder any communication load.

(5) Absence of Leaders: In formal communication, there is no place to any one person as the key-person or communication leader to spread message like in grapevine. The characters of trustworthy or credibility are not necessary to the communicator because everyone has to follow fixed rules and procedures. There is no place for bias. That is the reason why formal communication is always orderly and systematic.

(6) Efficient Communication: Prompt and accurate flow of information is the function of sound communication. This can be achieved under the formal communication method. It is a sound and proper method of channelising information. There is always direct contact between the parties and relationship is always formal and official.

(7) Support from Top: There is always official support and backing for formal communication. Management endeavours that modified regulations are implemented and enforced. And hence, formal messages would always succeed.

(8) Uniformity in Transmission: In a formal communication, each person transmits the message to another in the order of line. The process continues. There is no place for wrong interpretations, misunderstandings, bias etc. It ensures uniformity or unity in the transmission of message and its understanding.

(9) Organisational Efficiency: Organisational efficiency is indispensable to accomplish organisational goals. The formal communication is inbuilt, inherent and is a part and parcel of organisational process. Management can take suitable steps and action to achieve organisational efficiency.

(10) No Grapevine: In a formal communication, there is always organisational relationship. Though informal communication exists, formal communication endeavours to see that positive and constructive information is circulated for the healthy growth of organisation.

(11) Other Advantages: Besides the above merits of formal communication, there are many advantages that emerge from formal communication. It identifies that communication is a tool of management. Executives get things done through people with effective formal tansmission of common desired goals etc.

Demerits of Formal Communication

(1) Delay: The formal network of communication takes more time to pass information. Thus, formal channel is not spontaneous and flexible and hence, it would take more time in transmitting information.

(2) Internal Means Only: Formal communication represents a natural desire of the management in the organisation to interact and communicate with each other. In this, a superior directs the subordinates. So, it is an effective written internal medium of communication and hence, it is not suitable for external communication.

(3) Information Overload: Information overload represents overload of work with heavy information. In a complex business organisation, there are always many series of messages and information to be tackled. It ultimately leads to work-load on executives. Delay, omission, imperfection and half-execution of information are the evils of information overload.

(4) Absence of Outside Interface: Interface with other sources of information about the organisation is also usually taking place in the real world situation. In a formal communication there is no interface with the outside in any way. Formal communication is transmitted only by virtue of one's position in the organisational structure. It is concerned between the superior and subordinate relationship arising out of officially recognised positions.

(5) Slow Transmission: Formal communication channel operates with the slow movement of transmission. It would not work with considerable speed and is often slower than informal communication. Official channel information gets circulated but not in a prompt way.

(6) Lack of Quick Response: Formal communication is known for delay to get response from information transmitted. Response as to acceptance or rejection from formal communication cannot be interacted immediately. Immediate response for either of the above reactions is necessary to the communicator in the process of decision-making. It is particularly true in the case of a formal written communication. The advantage of immediate response can be obtained from informal communication.

(7) Downward Channel: Formal communication is mostly for downward communication and communication through a chain of command is not suitable for vertically upward. Executive overlook subordinates and may not take active interest in the matter of subordinates.

(8) Lack of General Interest: The formal channel of communication is also not useful for transmitting certain information which in the general interest of the organisation, is necessary. Official channels cannot effectively be used in certain important, urgent matters but which can be satisfactorily transmitted through informal channel.

(9) Absence of Feedback: Feedback is necessary to understand immediate reaction which would help in a great way in the decision-making process. The formal channel would not serve as an effective feedback system. Similarly, it cannot be used as a testing device. Listening to the feedback response is the good principle of effective communication.

(10) No Public Relations: In a modern complex business organisation, responsibility of business to the society, and interdependence of society and industry, the importance of public relations cannot be overemphasised. Formal communication does not promote public relations. Interface with the outside organisation is equally necessary to accomplish both social and organisation goals. For this the formal channel is not effective.

Communication Barriers

"All forms of social progress... physical barriers to communication are rapidly disappearing but the psychological remain. These psychological difficulties are in part a function of the very nature of language; in part, they are due to the emotional characters and mental limitations of human beings."

(— Daniel Katz).

The word "barriers" means hindrances or hurdles or difficulties or problems. Barriers with reference to communication imply hurdles or problems on the way which adversely affect the transmission of information from the sender to the receiver. The way is not smooth and clear. There are many problems on the way leading to misunderstanding or non-reaching the message to the receiver. Sometimes, barriers tend to distort the message and create friction among the organisational members and also adversely affect the morale of the employees as well as are injurious to team-work. Some other reasons may be responsible for the complete breakdown in communication. A large number of organisational problems are the causes of the faulty communication. It is necessary to understand communication barriers so that workable steps can be taken to remove them for effective communication. As Daniel Katz has said, physical barriers to communication are rapidly disappearing. There are several categories of barriers causing breakdown in the communication. The main barriers are organisational, managerial, psychological and language. The barriers are discussed below:

(1) Organisational Barriers

These barriers arise when duties and lines of authority are not clearly defined. They arise on account of distance communication, more layers of communication, lack of instructions, heavy communication load etc. The various types of organisational barriers are as follows:

(a) Policy: Broad objectives and policies of the organisation are laid down by the top management. They are broad guidelines for everyone in the organisation to follow. They change the behaviour of the receiver. Policy is generally in writing. If the policy is not supporting in the free flow of communication vertically and horizontally, it acts as a hurdle in the smooth flow of communication.

(b) Rules and Regulations: Formal communication should follow the path of flow. Organisational rules and regulations sometimes work as obstacles to transmitting a message. They prescribe rigidity in the message to be communicated as well as the channel to be followed and through which alone the communication can move. The rules are so rigid and formal that they restrict the free flow of communication and result in delay in decision-making process and action.

(c) Status and Position: In a tall network and flat network, there are many officially designated positions in the organisation structure. It, by its nature, creates a number of status levels. In the two-way communication, status and position block the flow of communication particularly in upward flow. The reasons are non-listening attitude of the superior, non-answering and interpreting as well as withholding information etc. The superior-subordinate relationship and interaction is not always smooth. Thus, status and position relationship also act as a powerful barrier.

(d) Complex Organisation: Complexity in organisation structure is also an equally serious problem in the smooth flow of communication. Complexity in organisation structure is a common feature in most of the big enterprises. The organisational structure has an important influence on the capacity of the members to communicate. Complexity involves many layers of supervision, long distance, more lines, communication gaps, organisational distance between the workers and the top management. This is also a barrier to effective communication.

(e) Facilities: The management in every organisation must provide minimum facilities to handle message load and to communicate effectively. Facilities like typing pool, media, mechanical instruments, communication carriers, cost etc. Organisational facilities are indispensable for the smooth, proper and timely flow of communication. The purpose of the communication is defeated if minimum facilities for transmitting message are not provided.

(2) Semantic Barriers

Problems of language are called "semantic barriers." Semantic barriers arise on account of linguistic background and ability of the communicator. Linguistic barriers are present both in oral and written communication. Different individuals may have different educational and literacy background. It is always a problem in communication between supervisors, executives, skilled, semi-skilled, unskilled foreman etc. Perception capacity differs from person to person. A message may give a variety of meanings to different people according to their perceptual level. Following are the usual types of semantic barriers:

(a) Badly Expressed Message: The basic essential of an effective communication is clarity and precision. The absence of clarity and precision in the subject matter of communication results in a badly expressed message. The common causes for lack of clarity and precision are using unfamiliar words and complex words, jargon, using superflous words, lack of unity and coherence, use of unnecessary prepositions, adjectives and adverbs, lack of simplicity, longer sentences, poor language, poor construction of sentences etc.

Koontz and Donnell list common faults in the words: "such faults as poorly chosen and empty words and phrases, careless omission, lack of coherence, poor organisation of ideas, awkward sentence structure, inadequate vocabulary, platitudes, numbing repetition, jargon, and failure to clarify implications are common."

(b) Faculty Translations: The message is always an abstract and the intangible requires to use certain symbols. Transmitting and receiving of information is a continuous process of communication in which transmitters and receivers of message function. Encoding process translates ideas, facts, opinions, feelings into words, symbols, action, pictures and audio-visual media. Every communicator receives various types of communication from superiors, peers, subordinates and he must translate the information destined for subordinates, peers, and superiors into a language suitable to each. Hence, the message should be encoded into a set of symbols or words understandable to the receiver. Koontz and Donnell say that it must be put into words appropriate to the framework in which the receiver operates, or it must be accompained by an interpretation which will be understood by the receiver. So, faulty translation is a barrier, in a way to effective communication.

(c) Unclarified Assumptions: Assumptions or propositions are bound to be there in message transmission. Koontz and Donnell observe: often over looked but critically important are the uncommunicated assumption which underline practically all messages. Certain implied things cannot be interpreted by the receiver correctly. Even though a message is specific, the unclarified assumptions may not be clear to the receiver. It may lead to delay in decision- making, loss of goodwill and taking no action.

(d) Jargon Language: All jargon in communication as far as possible should be avoided. Jargon is a language which is special to science, technology, law, commerce, etc. There is for instance, legal jargon, military jargon, technical jargon etc. Special and technical personnel often use technical language of their own. This leads to isolation and limited communication and acts as a communication barrier.

(3) Personal Barriers

I. Barriers to Superiors: Organisational structure creates a number of status and position levels. They may create hurdles in a two-way communication. In downward communication, superiors occupy key positions. The basic barrier arises on account of status and relationship in every organisation. The superior and subrodinate relationship in the formal organisation structure restricts the free flow of information and exchange of ideas, suggestions and questions. Though a two-way communication channel is there, it is ineffective in practice in most of the cases. There are officers or executives who always try to maintain distance and status with the subordinates. Superiors may be reluctant to listen to their subordinates, admit errors etc., as they may reflect adversely on their ability and intelligence. Their hierarchical status and position and relationship with subordinates act as barriers to effective communication. The following are the various ways.

(a) Regard and Attitude: The regard and attitudes of the superiors towards subordinates in connection with communication may affect the flow of message both in vertical and horizontal directions. This in particular adversely affects in the case of oral communication. To mention with face-to-face contacts, it is more serious-non-listening attitude of the superiors, desire to keep or withhold message etc. They feel responding to subordinates will lower their prestige. So, this is a serious barrier.

(b) To Maintain Authority: Fear of challenge of authority is a barrier to the flow of communication. It is the general preference of human beings to maintain prestige and status to satisfy ego and strategy. Managers often underrate the understanding and intelligence of the subordinates. They often resort to withholding information party or wholly coming down the line or downward communication. People generally resist, as frequent passing of information may disclose their weakness.

(c) Self-Satisfaction: Seniors often resist the smooth flow of messages. They ignore anything that conflicts and like messages which confirm their beliefs and ideas. They withhold information and make the subordinates to move round the information and derive satisfaction out of it.

(d) Principle of Proper Channel: They mostly insist on "through proper channel" the essence of formal communication. The officially designated channel for communication is the only path for formal communication. It implies that all communications should flow through the line superior. Superiors always wish to exercise their authority and they do not like their subordinates bypassing them in communication. Sometimes, in order to avoid delay, communication may directly be sent to the concerned but superiors treat this as overlooking them. For this, they often insist through proper channel.

(e) Prejudice: Prejudice among the superiors may stand on the way of free flow of information. Prejudice is a serious problem and a barrier. Prejudice creates a barrier for a proper understanding in the organisation.

(f) Distrust: Distrust of the communicator is a barrier. Superiors often screen or filter the information. They are noted for modifying messages. Distrust of the superior for any reason restricts communication.

(g) 'Yes' Superiors: There are some superiors in all organisations called "Yes" men, who always wish to remain neutral and non-committed. This is because they may sometimes like to be in the good books of the top management. This takes the form of acting to please the boss, not seeking clarification, not expressing opinions which may lead to incur displeasure from boss etc.

(h) Complex: Personal complexity inhibits communication. No superior likes to show his mistakes to someone else, especially to his subordinates. They generally resist the advice given by the lower level people. In their view, they are less competent and less capable; they are not able to advise superiors. Lack of confidence in subordinates complex is a serious barrier to the flow of effective communication.

(i) Lack of Time: "No time", "lack of time" are the terms frequently used by the superiors. They do not spare considerable time to talk to their subordinates. They feel, whether real or not, that they are overburdened with work.

(j) Message Overload: Message overlaod is really a hurdle in the communication process. If message overlead is routine, there is a grave danger to the orderly and smooth flow of communication. The effect of overload may be omission of message, errors, delay, filtering and approximation. They are barriers to communication.

II. Barriers in Subordinates: Subordiantes are also equally responsible for restricting communication flow particularly in upward direction. They act as barriers in a number of ways as indicated below:

(a) They dislike to show mistakes.

(b) People generally resist new ideas.

(c) Unwillingness to communicate upward a message on personal grounds.

(d) Lack of incentives and encouragement.

(e) They slant information relating to their failures.

(4) Psychological Barriers

The psychology of the employees in an organisation is relating to the security of job, dignity, peace of mind etc. Psychological needs and feelings are the prime barriers in organisational communication process. Listening, interpretation or encoding and decoding of a message depends upon the psychological status of both transmitter and the receiver. The following are some of the psychological barriers inhibiting communication:

(a) Distrust of Communication: Roberts and O'Reilly observe distrust of the superior for any reason inhibits communication. It occurs out of ill- considered judgements, decisions not based on logic, screening and infiltration of information etc. Doing these things frequently with these messages, gradually makes the subordinates delay action or act unenthusiastically. Though it amounts to a complete communication process, it is ineffective and serves no purpose and hence a failure.

(b) Inattention: Not giving attention to read bulletins, notices, minutes and reports is a common practice. The simple failure to listen to oral communication, the reason being that, non-listeners are often turned off while they are pre-occupied with other matters, like their family problems. A communication is ineffective and failure, because the receiver is not listening. Koontz and Donnell comment: Unfortunately, non-listening seems to be a chronic human failure. This is illustrated by the common practice of arguing about an agreed matter. The reasons vary from impressing the speaker with one's knowledge to anxiety or plain contempt for another's viewpoint.

(c) Premature Evaluation: it is a barrier which takes the form of prematurely evaluating communication, rather than to keep an uncompromised position during the interchange. Rogers and Roethlisberger in *Barriers and Gateways to Communication*, 1952 identified this barrier. They realised that such evaluation stops the transfer of information, leaving the message sender with a sense of futility.

(d) Failure of Communication: In routine communication work, it may usually happen that managers often fail to transmit the needed messages. There are many reasons for failure such as laziness on the part of the communicator, assumption that "everybody knows", "procrastination", "deliberately", "to embrass" etc. Koontz and Donnell observed to the uninitiated, this "barrier" seems both astonishing and unforgivable, and yet it is a fact that managers fail to transmit the needed messages.

(e) Loss by Transmission and Poor Retention: When a message passes through various levels, it loses its meaning or becomes decreasingly inaccurate. When a subject matter in a communication passes through various levels in the organisation, successive transmissions of the same message are decreasingly inaccurate. Some studies reveal that, in oral communications about thirty per cent of information is lost in each transmission. So, when the word of mouth changes, its meaning also changes. So, in a very tall network or flat network, oral communication is not accurately dependable: Loss by transmission happens even in the case of written communication. Loss of meaning in transmission may arise as far as communication is accompanied by interpretations. Similarly, poor retention of information is also a barrier. Some studies reveal that employees retain about 50 per cent of message and supervisors about 60 per cent of information only.

(f) Emphasis on Written Message: Undue reliance on written message is equally serious in effective communication. So management should not insist on company's viewpoints and policies through slick, easy to read, well-illustrated publications.

Other Barriers

(a) Resistance to Change: It is a common tendency of human being to maintain *status quo*. It is a general preference to resist new ideas. When the matter is transmitted to convey a new idea, the listeners may not listen to it in spirit. They ignore anything that conflicts with the present belief or idea. In case he listens to a new idea, he may filter-in rejecting new ideas or interprets them according to his own convenience. Hence, resistance to change is an important obstacle to effective communication.

(b) Perception: Different people may have different perceptions depending upon their needs, social environment, level of education, and other cultural and personal temperaments. So, everyone perceives things and approach them differently. Everyone interprets, evaluates the information received from his point of view. Lack of uniformity in perception or understanding is a great problem in communication and is a barrier to communication.

(c) Closed Minds: The expression "closed minds" refers to thinking tendency of the people that they know everything about the issue and inhibits communication. They do not open their minds to new ideas that are placed before them.

(d) Fear: Fear is a clear barrier to effective communication. Subordinates fear their superiors who have in turn to depend on subordinates for information. But, there are no hard and fast rules as to the kind, quality of information that the subordinates have to communicate upward. It gives discretion to them in selecting the matter; it is here that fear comes into the picture. Fear creates obstacles, it is out of fear that certain information though available, may not be communicated upward. It may result in sending partial information. They may even think that the matter is not important to communicate. Fear of full disclosure or non-disclosure misleads a superior.

(e) Lack of Ability to Communicate: Communication is an art that can be perfected with continued experience and practice. Lack of ability to communicate is a barrier. All communicators do not have the same skills to communicate. Though the essentials of communication are the same, oral communication needs special skills compared to written communication.

(f) Insufficient Adjustment Period: Changes in positions, status, place of work, group affect the employees till they get adjusted to changes. Shifts in the time, place, type, order of work, skills needed, shift in batch etc., are the common changes in the organisation. Sufficient adjustment time should be given to think and understand the full meaning of a message.

(g) Distance and Time: Distance and time are barriers to effective communication. The case of written communication to far-off places, time and distance inhibit communication. Delayed messages are stale messages.

How to Overcome Communication Barriers?

We have identified many barriers to communication. It is our turn now to discuss on overcoming barriers to communication and how communication can be improved. A thorough understanding of communication barriers is the basic requirement to find out measures to remove or eliminate or overcome them. All types of barriers arise due to wrong organisational structure. Language barrier arises in the organisation where people are of different educational backgrounds and hail from different regions. However, the following are some of the measures for overcoming barriers to communication.

(1) Orientation: All the employees in the organisation should be given orientation. They should be provided with all the necessary information relating to the objectives, policies, procedures, organisational structure etc. This avoids conflicts, communication gap and misunderstanding.

(2) Suitable Language: The proper and appropriate language and tone definitely minimises linguistic barriers to communication. Communication is rejected for a simple reason that it is not understandable. Use of technical terms should be avoided as far as possible and the message should be direct, simple and in meaningful language. Different people perceive the message differently. The manager must use a common language to avoid semantic distortions.

(3) Good Listening: Empathetic listening or improving good listening habits by the receiver should be cultivated. The recipient or receiver of communication has equal responsibility to understand in the same sense as meant by the communicator. If the message is without empathetic listening, response and reaction are not possible. Effective two-way communication is possible with good listening.

(4) Use of Grapevine: Strategic use of informal communication or grapevine is permitted. In the communication network, grapevine has an equal important place. It is an essential part of an organisation's communication. The manager cannot ignore grapevine as it exists inspite of a number of limitations. In a number of occasions, information should be transmitted only through grapevine. Therefore, the strategic use of informal organisation will go a long way in improving effective communication.

(5) Actions and Deeds: Communication through actions and deeds is the principle of effective communication. A message is one to be acted upon. Otherwise it tends to distort the current and also the subsequent messages from the manager. Actions and deeds often speak louder than words. A meaning to a message is achieved only when it is acted upon. Action and words must go together. The acts of the superior should not differ from what he says.

(6) Clarity: As pointed out earlier, effective communication is vital to successful management, every communication should have the skills to have clarity of message. The greater task is on the part of the sender of the message to achieve clarity. The message must be as clear as possible in the mind of the sender what he wants to communicate. Effective communication is possible only if the message is clearly formulated in the mind. The subject matter should be encoded in a direct and simple language. The purpose of communication is to make the recipient understand the message. This is possible with the clarity of communication.

(7) Knowing the Receiver: The importance of understanding the receiver and needs of the receiver cannot be overlooked. The message content is to meet the needs of the receiver. The information should be of value to the receiver in the present needs as well as in the long run. Sender of the message is to have full knowledge about the receiver, his capabilities, background, level of intelligence, social climate, receptiveness, temperament and attitudes etc.

(8) Inter-Personal Relationships: Developing proper inter-personal relations is more helpful in overcoming barriers to communication. In the organisation, there must be good relations between the different people. Lack of co-operation among the people may result in non-accomplishing its goals. The managers should remember that the dignity, individuality of the subordinates shall always be respected. On the other hand, subordinates too should respect the dignity and authority of their superiors. Principles of personal contact, appreciation, recognition, open door policy etc., work effectively in eliminating barriers to communication.

(9) Feedback: The importance of feedback in effective communication has been greatly emphasised in Chapter 7. It improves communication. Feedback is the most important method which identifies the message so received in the same sense in which it was intended. It ensures communication as a two- way process. It enables the communicator to know the emotions, feelings and expressions of the receiver. The acceptance or rejection of a message is easier to know through feedback. In the case of face-to-face conversation the response is quick and immediate while in the case of written medium, feedback may be delayed.

(10) Other Measures: Communication should be based on realistic planning. The message to be communicated must be complete and full, otherwise it may lead to confusion and misunderstanding. It must be timely transmitted. Delay defeats action and decision-making. The pieces of message to be communicated should always be consistent with the objectives, policies and programmes of the organisation.

Sensitivity Analysis

Sensitivity training is a technique used for solving the problem of communication barriers. It helps to break down to communication barrier and acts as an aid for improving leadership skills, motivation and group interaction within the company. It is a laboratory type group training method. The study conducted by Gordon Lippitt indicates that this method includes case studies, informal group discussions, information exchange sessions.

This technique as suggested by Lippitt is quite different from other methods. Sensitivity training is mainly a behaviour learning experience. It is one of the tools of organisational communication management. It is used both for individual development, not only for the job and performance, but also on the job group and improving on the job performance.

Gordon Lippitt has described sensitivity training group as follows:[31]

Sensitivity Training Groups: Here, the participants meet with a professional trainer in groups of eight to fifteen. They have no formal agenda or prior-determined leader. Normally, the groups meet once a day for two hours, but many meet twice a day. They struggle with making decisions about how to spend time profitably and how to provide structure and leadership. They have time to "thrash out" their struggles and examine their group life. As they do, they begin to gain an insight into the forces that are at work — things like the leadership struggle, group structure, group objectives, accommodating individual objectives to group objectives, group standards to guide their conduct, what improves and lessens the appeal of the group, how decisions will be made, how to handle the participation of members, how one's own behaviour is influencing the group, and how the behaviour of other members is influencing one's own behaviour.

As the group pauses to study the parts of their group life in which those have interested them, the trainer helps them to understand the forces at work at that moment. From time to time, an individual member may want to test out with others the effect of his behaviour on them — how they see him — and may ask for reactions and information (feedback) — and the members try to help him see himself as they see him in the life of the group.

Application of the Technique

The technique of sensitivity training can be applied to the following kinds of problems, situations, as identified by Gordon Lippitt:

(1) There is an otherwise effective manager whose attitudes, skills, relationships with his work force, relationships with other persons and sub-units, effectiveness in meetings, and ability to diagnose personal relationship problems in their embryonic stage are seen as inadequate.

(2) The basic face-to-face units of the organisation do not seem to be achieving a level of morale and productivity that is in keeping with their abilities.

(3) The organisation is concerned with public relations, and its staff has enough contacts with outside groups so that the totality of these contacts can materially affect the organisation's image.

(4) It is important for communication to flow as uninhibitedly as possible between peers, between the subordinate and the superior, and between work units, even though they appear as separated elements on the organisational chart.

(5) There is good reason to believe that managers in the organisation are, by organisational practice or climate, discouraged from being inventive or creative, from exercising or receiving appropriate responsibility, from delegating authority, and from exercising initiative in meeting operational problems.

(6) The organisation gets its work done in a large measure through the use of group meetings, conferences and informal group activities.[32]

REFERENCES

1. Myers, M. T., and Myers, G. M., *Managing by Communication — An Organisational Approach,* McGraw Hill International Book Company, 1982, p. 137.
2. Koontz and Donnell: *Management — A Systems and Contingency Analysis of Managerial Functions,* 1976, p. 616.
3. Daniel Katz and Robert Kahn, *The Social Psychology of Organisation,* 1978, Quoted in Myers and Myers, *Managing by Communication —An Organisational Approach,* 1982, p. 135.
4. Ahuja, K.K., *Personnel Management,* Kalyani Publishers, Ludhiana, 1986, p. 445.
5. Aggarwala, D.V., *Organisational Communication Management,* Deep & Deep Publications, New Delhi. 1989, p, 184.
6. *Ibid.*
7. Ronald F. Roberts: *The Nature of Communication Effects,* in Wilbur Schramm and Donald F. Roberts (eds.), *The Process and Effects of Mass Communication,* Rev. Ed., University of Illinois Press, Urbana, III, 1971, pp. 368-371.
8. Tripathi, P.G., *Personnel Management — Theory and Practice,* Sultan Chand & Sons. 1978, p. 84.
9. Davis, K., *Management Communication and Grapevine;* Quoted in *Business Communication,* Pradhan H., and others, Himalaya Publishing House. 1984. p. 33.
10. *Ibid.,* p. 34.
11. Ahuja, K.K., *Personnel Management,* 1986, p. 445.
12. Katz D., and Kahn, R.. *The Social Psychology of Organisation,* J. Wiley and Sons. New York, 1978, p. 428.
13. For a more complete analysis of Upward Communication Problems, see William, M. Pride and O. Jeff Harris, *Psychological Barriers to the Upward Flow of Communication, Atlanta Economic Review,* Volume 21, Number 3 (March 1971), pp. 30-32, quoted in *Managing People At Work; O.* Jeff Harris, Jr., A Wiley Hamilton Publication, John Wiley & Sons, Inc., 1976. p. 261.
14. Gary Gemill, *"Managing Upward Communication," Personnel Journal,* Volume 49, Number 2, February 1970, pp. 107-110, quoted in O. Jeff Harris., Jr., *op. cit.*
15. Pride and Harris, Quoted in *Managing People At Work,* O Jeff Harris Jr., A Wiley Hamilton. Publication, John Wiley & Sons, Inc., 1976, p. 261.
16. O. Jeff Harris, Jr., *Managing People At Work,* A Wiley Hamilton Publications, John Wiley & Sons Inc., 1976 p. 261.
17. Marshall H., Brenner and Norman B. Sigband, *"Organisational Communication — An Analysis Based Upon Empirical Data," The Academy of Management Journal,* Volume 16, Number 2, June, 1973, pp. 323-325, quoted in O. Jeff Harris, Jr., *op. cit.*
18. Pride and Harris; quoted in *Managing People At Work,* 1976. p. 261; and Ronald J. Burke and Douglas S. Wilcox, "Effects of Different Patterns and Degrees of Openness in Superior Subordinate Communication on Subordinate Job Satisfaction", *The Academy of Management Journal,* Volume 12. Number 3, September, 1969, pp. 319-326, quoted in O. Jeff Harris Jr., *op. cit.*
19. O. Jeff Harris Jr., *Managing People At Work,* A Wiiey Hamilton Publication, John Wiley & Sons, Inc., 1976, pp. 261-262, Adapted, courtesy.
20. Davis, K., *Management Communication and the Grapevine:* quoted in *Business Communicator,* Pradhan H. and others, Himalaya Publishing House, 1978 p. 32.

21. Tripathi, P.C., *Personnel Management — Theory and Practice,* 1978. pp. 84-85.

22. Myers and Myers: *Managing By Communication — An Organisational Approach,* 1982 p. 136.

23. Tripathi, P.C., *Personnel Management —Theory and Practice,* 1978. p. 83.

24. Koontz and Donnell: *Management — A Systems and Contingency Analysis of Managerial Functions,* 1976, p. 625.

25. *Ibid.*

26. Pradhan H., and Others: *Business Communication;* Himalaya Publishing House, Bombay. 1978, pp. 34-35.

27. Vide *Industrial Times,* September 1, 1964, p. 11, quoted in *Business Administration and Management,* S.C., Saksena, Sahitya Bhavan, p. 187.

28. Walter C. Langer, *The Mind of Adolf Hitler,* New York, Basic Books 1972, p. 76. Quoted in *Management— Theory, Process and Practice,* Richard M. Hodgetts Hott-Saunders International Editions. 1982, p. 300.

29. J. F. Mee (ed.); *Personnel Handbook,* New York, Ronald Press. 1958. Quoted in *Business Administration and Management;* Dr. S. C. Saksena, p. 189,

30. Adapted; Courtesy, "Chrysler Corporation", Quoted in *Communicating Facts and Ideas in Business,* L. Brown, 1982, pp. 415-416.

31. Gordon, L. Lippitt, *Organisational Renewal,* New York, 1969, p, 218. Quoted in the *Business Management Process,* R.J. Mocker, p. 560.

32. *Ibid.*

*****

CHAPTER 10

Informal Communication

Meaning and Nature of Informal Communication

Informal communication is also called "grapevine." This type of communication arises on account of informal relationship between the persons concerned. Informal communication grows spontaneously from personal and group interest. In such circumstances these types of communication is said to be only informal. Informal communication is characterised and may be conveyed by a simple glance, nod, smile, gesture and even mere silence. Informal channel is the most effective one and transmits information with considerable speed. It can pass both correct information as well as rumours. It all depends upon the group leader and his honesty and credibility. Informal communication network is formed to transmit messages quickly.

Small informal groups are formed on the basis of work and social relationship. In this type, there is no formal organisational hierarchy of superiors and subordinates. They are not formed on the basis of positions and lines of authority. The organisation chart of structure does not determine the informal relation In this type of communication, there are no formalities, procedures, rules etc. It represents the absence of official backing and there is no authority and control. It is called "grapevine" because it denotes informal means of circulating information or gossip. Management can utilise this channel for effective and speedy communication. Certain messages are not suitable to circulate by formal means. According to Koontz and O. H. Donnell: "The most effective communication results when managers utilise the informal organisation to supplement the communication channels of the formal organisation."[1]

It is sometimes used as a substitute for formal communication. Basically, informal relationship arises out of personal friendship, relationship between members of the same group, members of the same club, persons hailing from the same place, common studies and other social factors. It creates a situation where small groups of workers and other groups communicate with each other hours together, working side-by-side. The executives have to informally and personally deal with the subordinates to maintain relations and to get things done through. There are two activities known as programmed activities and non-programmed activities within the formal boundaries of the system. As such communications are very fast, spontaneous and flexible. For the management it is a very active channel of communication. Management can beneficially utilise the communication leaders. In turn, management may create its own grapevine composed of communication leaders.

Characteristic Features of Informal Organisation

(1) Origin: Informal groups are formed out of personal and social needs, working at the same place, with liking and disliking. There are no rules and regulations governing their relationship and there is no official support or backing.

(2) Purpose: Informal groups are growing out of the formal organisation structure. Because, formal groups are not satisfying them in respect of certain social, psychological and personal needs, informal groups are formed.

(3) Size: Informal groups may be small in size which only enable group cohesiveness. Another reason for these small sizes is that, they are created from formal organisation.

(4) Nature of Group: Informal groups by virtue of their nature are not stable; change in the job, leaving organisation are the causes for this instability. The value systems and likes and dislikes may change with the change in the membership.

(5) Conversion: An informal group can be converted into formal by structuring the relationship and establishing interpersonal relations by formal rules and procedures.

(6) Number of Groups: Like formal groups there may be a number of informal groups. A member of one informal group may be a member in other informal groups.

(7) Authority: There is no authority exercised in informal groups and all members are equal. People interact not formally according to rules and procedures but interact for their social, personal and psychological needs.

(8) Rules and Procedures: The behaviour of the members of the informal group is not governed by rigid rules and procedures. But their behaviour is governed largely by the value systems, norms, beliefs, likes and dislikes.

(9) Channel and Media of Communication: The informal channel is multiple in nature. It includes intangible facts, suggestions, suspictions, rumours, that cannot pass through the formal channel. The informal group does not require any formal channel and under this system, the channel of communication system is very wide. It does not follow a fixed route or through proper channel. There is no deliberately created and officially prescribed path for the flow of communication between the members of informal group in a formal organisation.

(10) Abolition: In fact, many of the informal groups are constituted not for any specific purpose but they are formed spontaneously and voluntarily. As such, informal groups cannot be abolished. Any attempt to abolish informal groups may lead to formation of other groups.

How Informal Groups are Formed?

The relationship between the people in the organisation based on personal attractions, emotions, relationship, common studies, place of belonging, membership of the same club, friendship, likes, dislikes, personal and psychological needs. The addition to these, other motives for the formation of informal groups are the common tastes, habits, attitudes, languages, qualification, bias, self-servicing etc. The existing environment is the basic force for their formation and as such they are not pre-planned but develop voluntarily and spontaneously within the formal organisation. Informal communication takes place in the organisation where people work closely together. It also occurs in the cases where the work forces is interfaced with outsiders from whom they get information about the organisation.

H. G. Hicks *et al.*, identifies the following three contributory factors for the formation of informal groups.

Formation of Informal Groups

Physical Location: An important contribution to informal group membership is physical location. Persons who work close to one another, such as in the same department doing the same type of work, are likely to develop social relationships. Everyone in a formal work group may not become a member of the informal groups but, physical closeness often stimulates membership.

Common Interests: Common interests among persons provide another reason for informal group membership. While doing the same sort of work which automatically ensures some commonality, there may be other areas of shared experiences. Educational backgrounds may, for example, be similar. A group of engineers have had similar education. Thus, they are likely to have similar professional interests. These interests tend to create a degree of solidarity among those working as engineers in an organisation.

Common Purposes: Closely related to similar interests are common purposes among group members. To achieve one or more mutually satisfying goals, individuals band together to form a group that supports the goal or goals. For example, workers may agree as a group to keep their production below at a certain level. Reasons may include their desire not to work above a certain level of effort or the fear that management will raise output standards if the workers produce up to their capabilities. They may form a group to seek to keep low production.[2]

Fig. 10.1 Group at Work Place

There are a number of research studies more accurate on group behaviour and communication. It is more interesting that research in group dynamics has multiplied in great proportion in the fields of psychology, sociology, speech-journalism and communication studies. The incidence of group activity involving group process has increased enormously in recent years. People working in the organisation have been spending a great deal of time in communicating informally in groups. According to G. C. Homans, there are three concepts for understanding individual behaviour in social groups. They are:

(1) Activity.

(2) Interaction.

(3) Sentiments.

It is sharing the activity that decides the degree of interaction. The more the people share activities, the more likely they are to interact with one other. Fig. 10.2 indicates the informal leader 'A.' Other individuals are grouped around the leader in various degrees of "Inness," K and L are completely "out of it." G, H, I, and J have fringe status with respect to primary groups.

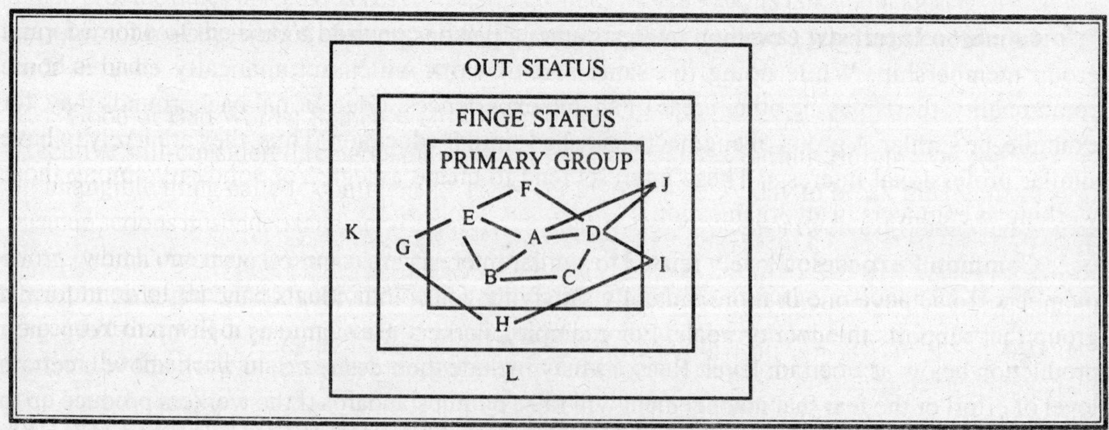

Fig. 10. 2 The Orbit of Small Group Relationship

(*Source:* William G. Scott, *Organisation Theory*, 1976. p. 93)

Causes of Informal Communication

Grapevine co-exists with the formal structure. In every formal organisation, there exists an informal channel for communication. Informal channel cannot be predicted and designed and as a result it cannot be deliberately planned and structured along with the formal organisation. It is because of the fact that grapevine is more a product of the situation than it is of the person. This means that given the proper situation and motivation, any of us tends to become active on grapevine (K. Davis). The informal group is created because the formal structure is not complete and cannot meet their requirements of personal, social and psychological needs. However, the following are the factors responsible for the creation of informal organisation.

(1) Social Needs: Informal organisation is created because the employees want to satisfy their social, personal and psychological needs. After continuous working in a formal structure, they form into informal groups to overcome strain, boredom, fatigue, psychological fatigue and to get relief. K. Davis observed: "Along with man's technical imperative, there is also a social imperative to work together. Man is a social being. He wants to belong, to associate with others rather to work in isolated loneliness. Out of this basic drive of man, the informal organisation arises."

(2) Specialisation: Every field of knowledge has expanded and specialisation has become the order of the day. In an organisation, the entire work is divided into various parts and assigned to different departments and people to accomplish. By this, each employee is expected to do a specific job in a routine manner. More specialisation means more routine and concentrated work which would result in boredom and fatigue. This leads to the realisation of importance of informal organisation to get relieved from boredom and fatigue.

(3) Escaping from Work: When the tasks assigned to the employees are more than their handling capacity, it is natural that employees try to escape from work. This tendency develops because there would be no time for them. Informal organisations have to encourage for informal interaction between the members of informal group.

(4) Hierarchical Structure: The formal organisation structure which is so rigid, durable, objectively structured, imposes defined route of interpersonal relation and chain of command. It establishes designed superior-subordinate relationship, control, span of control, conflict etc. which are factors associated with the day-to-day activities. If the downward channel is not meeting their requirements, the employees may resort to seek information from the informal channel. On the other hand, there are certain matters which can be received or sent through informal channel only.

K, Davis has suggested the following grapevine causes:

(5) Excitement and Insecurity: During the time of excitement and insecurity, the members of the group are overactive in the informal group, for instance lay-off, retrenchment, installing automatic machines and other labour- saving technology, or installation of a computer in the office. David writes that "At times like this, the grapevine is humming with activity, which means that managers need to watch it with extra care and "feed it with true information to keep it from getting out of hand."

(6) Involvement of Friends and Associates: One of the creation of grapevine is involvement of friends and associates. The members of the group are active on the grapevine when their friends and work associates are involved. For instance, if X is to be promoted or demoted, the information in detail must pass to all the employees. They expect to know about day-to-day developments in the organisation.

(7) Recent Information: When there is some information or news, members are more active to know full details about these. If the information is stale, people are not that serious on the grapevine. Davis writes that the greatest spread of information occurs immediately after it is known.

(8) Procedure: The procedure in practice would bring people into contact. These procedures that regularly bring people into contact with one another will encourage them to be active on the grapevine.

(9) Work: The workplace where the people are working, if nearer, would allow conversation. All employees who are near to one another are likely to communicate more than those who are working in distant places or separate buildings.

(10) Nature of Job: The type of job that provides information desired by others is the most powerful cause for the people to be active on the grapevine. The type of job possessed by an employee plays an important role influencing other person's role in the grapevine. Davis writes that some jobs give employees with more news that might be worth communicating. The result is that certain employees are more active on the grapevine, not because of personality but because of their jobs in the organisation.

(11) Personality of Communication: Personality of the communicator is also important in making people more active on the grapevine. Some employees are more active for personality reasons, hence an important grapevine influence. According to Davis: "Perhaps they like to talk about people having a strong interest in what is happening in their organisation or have special communication abilities."

Types of Informal Organisations

Informal organisations are also of various types. Research studies reveal that there are various forms of informal organisation. Mayo and Lambard have classified informal organisations into the following three categories:

(1) Natural: Natural informal groups have a very little structure.

(2) Family Group: Group has regular members who exert influence on the behaviour of the members.

(3) Organised Group: Group has some acknowledged leaders and a more consistent structure.

Sayles has identified the following four types of informal groups:

(4) Apathetic Group: Group of this type shows indifferent attitude towards the formal organisation. The group has special characteristics and qualities like dispersal, unaccepted leadership, lack of cohesiveness, internal disunity and conflict and suppressed dissatisfaction.

(5) Erratic Group: The groups of this type is known for rapid inflammability, poor control, inconsistent behaviour, centralised autocratic leadership and union formal activities.

(6) Strategic Group: Strategic informal groups are subject to antagonism, continuous pressure, well-planned and consistent, grievance activity, high degree of internal unity, sustained union participation and usually good production record in the long run.

(7) Conservative Group: Conservative informal groups are known for usual co-operation, moderate internal unity, limited pressure for highly-specific objectives, self assurance, activity in active cycles in terms of union activities and grievance procedure.

Fig. 10.3 Informal Meet

Informal Leaders

A key person in an informal organisation is the leader in each little group. A person in informal group becomes a leader because he has access to information or in a position to be " in the know" and knows what message and where to pass on. There may be various reasons for a person to become a leader of informal group. The main reasons are:

(a) Age
(b) Seniority
(c) Experience
(d) Work Location
(e) Access to Information
(f) Responsive Personality

The reasons are not conclusive but inclusive and it is not possible to list them because each leader emerges under quite different circumstances. A person who has more influence than others is usually the prime leader. There are several types of informal groups and several persons in the group may be informal leaders of various other groups.

An efficient leader becomes a strong boss and enjoys formal authority. Some persons may fail as successful informal leaders because of the fear of authority and responsibility. Such persons are always critics of management and conservative. In one type or other group, several people of a department may be informal leaders. The leaders of informal groups may render invaluable service to the members, for which they usually enjoy certain rewards and privileges. The managers should know who is the key informal leader in a given group. "When an informal leader is working against an employer, the leader's widespread influence can undermine motivation and job satisfaction." A leader of a group must be trustworthy and must have high credibility.

The manager should follow up grapevine messages with official written messages. This helps to promote mutual trust based on open communication flowing throughout the organisation. People too generally are not daring enough to disclose information because they are afraid of the consequences of disclosure. Leland Brown writes that one of the biggest problems in business and industry today stems from the lack of trust within the organisation and the lack of effective communication. He further suggested that a mutual trust must be created through openness which will be reciprocated, with more credibility. A system of reward of incentives may also be adopted to dispel the fear people have.

Influencing Informal Organisation

Informal organisation grow spontaneously and voluntarily out of personal needs, work needs, common purpose, physical location and other social and psychological reasons. Mostly social factors force the employees in an organisation to form informal groups for personal and social interaction. Therefore, the management neither can create informal organisations nor can they dissolve them. If the management neglects the existence of information organisation, it may face its own natural and adverse consequences. Face-to-face communication, loyalty, interaction, group approach with mutual understanding would work better for the entire organisation. Informal groups work both at the work place as well as outside the formal organisation structure.

Therefore, management cannot afford to ignore or eliminate the grape-vine, for it will exist and survive inspite of everything, else. A sound management, therefore, accepts its existence and endeavours to understand its structure and attitude and direct its efforts to use it in a positive direction.

Every manager has to learn to adjust and live with informal organisations. His style of functioning should not be hard, repressive or autocratic in dealing with the problems arising out of functioning of informal organisations.

K. Davis writes that management's job is:

(1) To accept and understand informal organisation.

(2) To consider the possible effects when taking any action.

(3) To integrate as far as possible the interests of informal groups with those of the formal organisation.

(4) To keep formal activities from unnecessarily threatening from informal organisation in general.

Informal Channel

Informal channel of communication is also called grapevine. It is a channel neither created by official action, rules, procedures, regulations, manuals, nor deliberately planned and designed. It is quite different from the formal channel which is fixed, rigid, officially created, designed and operated as per rules and procedures. The informal channel is created by the operation of persons and social forces at work place. The existence of such channel is to be recognised, though not meant for utilitarian needs of the organisation. The channel is used to carry on non-programmed activities within the formal structure.

Since the formal channel neither meets their requirements nor is it useful for transmission of certain messages. Informal channel is used for passing messages as this channel is inadequate and insufficient. Informal communication has no definite channel and can readily short-circuit any formal chain. Relationship developed between the people in the organisation is based on personal attraction, needs, likes, dislikes, friendship etc. And accordingly, channels too develop for passing information.

Informal Roles of Employees

Task-Oriented: Those who have the role of "getting the job done" and known as those who "deliver the goods."

Technique-Oriented: The masters of procedure and method.

People-Oriented: Those who have the role of patron saint and good Samaritan to people in need.

Nay-Sayers: Those who counterbalance the "yes" persons, who have thick skins and can find fault with anything.

Yes-Sayers: Those who counterbalance the nay-sayers, the "yes" persons who circument opposition.

Rule-Enforcers: The "people of the look" who are stereotype bureaucrats.

Rule-Evaders: The "operators", those who know how to get the job done "irrespective."

Rule-Blinkers: The people who are not against the rules but don't take them seriously.

Involved: Those who are fully immersed in their work and the activities of the organisation.

Detached: Slackers who either "go along for the ride" or "call it quits" at the end of regular hours.

Regulars: Those who are "in", who accept the values of the group and are accepted by the group.

Deviants: Those who depart from the values of the group the "mavericks."

Isolates: The rule "lone wolves", they are further from the group than deviants.

Newcomers: They know little and must be taken care of by others; they are "seen but not heard."

Old-Timers: Those who have been "around" a long time and "know the ropes."

Climbers: Those who are expected to "get ahead", not necessarily on the basis of ability but on the basis of potential.

Stickers: Those who are expected to stay put, who are satisfied with life and their position in it.

Cosmopolitans: Those who see themselves as members of a broader professional, cultural, or political community.

Locals: Those who are rotted to the organisation and local community.

Informal Managerial Roles

Henry Mintzberg, in his study to determine what jobs, these managers do, concluded that managers perform ten different, highly interrelated roles or sets of behaviours attributable to their jobs. These ten roles of managers can broadly be grouped into four roles. They are:

(1) Interpersonal Role
(2) Informational Role
(3) Decisional Role.

(1) Interpersonal Role: All the managers are required to perform roles which arise directly from formal authority concerned with relationship between the managers and others. A manager acts as a figure role by virtue of his position. He has three sub-roles.

(1) Figurehead
(2) Leader
(3) Liaison.

As a figurehead, he is required to perform tasks which are ceremonial, dignified and symbolic in nature. As a leader, he has to recruit, train, motivate and activate his subordinates. A manager has a liaison role. It is the third role within the interpersonal role. According to Mintzberg, this activity includes maintenance of self-developed network of outside contacts and informers which provide favours and information.

(2) Informational Role: All the managers are required to perform, in addition to interpersonal roles flowing from formal authority, an informational role too. Manager collects information from outside organisations and institutions. It would be possible only when he spends a great deal of time to it. Mintzberg calls it as a Monitor Role. The second informational role is that of a disseminator. This activity includes transmission of information collected from outside the organisation to the members of the organisation. In his third role, a manager transmits the information to the outsider and other organisations about its plans, policies, results etc.

(3) Decisional Roles: In the decisional role, he identifies four roles on which a manager has to act upon the information. They are:

(1) Entrepreneur
(2) Disturbance Handler
(3) Resource Allocator
(4) Negotiator.

First Role: A manager initiates the development or improvement projects to bring changes.

Second Role: It is a role like a crisis management.

Third Place: A manager is responsible for allocation of resources of the organisation like Money, Material, Machine.

Fourth Role: A manager is responsible for representing the organisation at major negotiations like grievance settlement negotiation.

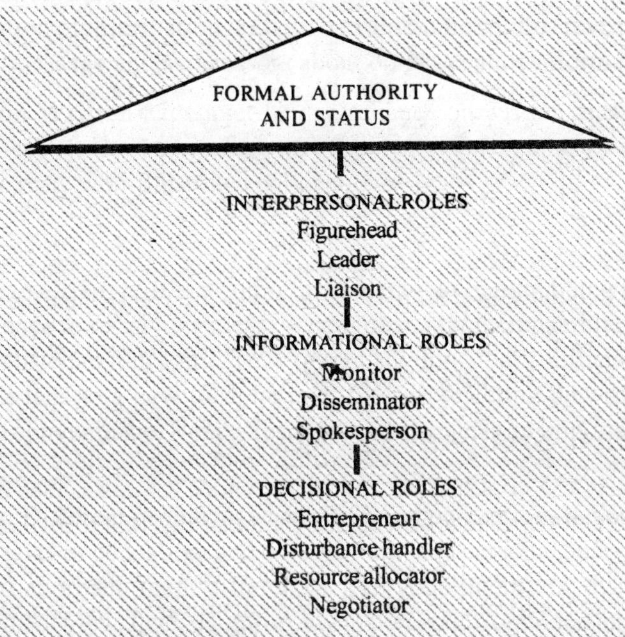

Fig. 10.4 Mintzberg's Managerial Roles

(*Source:* Adapted from Henry Mintzberg, *The Manager's Job: Folklore and Facts, Harvard Business Review*, July-Aug. 1975, pp. 49-61.)

Status, Norms and Roles of Informal Groups

Status, norms and roles in informal groups are important aspects in an informal organisation. Every participant in the group has a status position. Informal groups largely develop from different status positions of the participants. Haimann and his associates say that there are four generally recognised status positions in a group. They are:

(1) Group Leader

(2) Member of the Primary

(3) Fringe Status

(4) Out Status.

Norms and roles are closely related to status in informal groups of modern organisation. Norms and roles are the smallest units of analysis in group dynamics. Norms are "oughts" of behaviour. A role is a position expected and to be acted upon by an individual. A role consists of a pattern of norms. A. P. Bates states: "As a pattern of prescribed behaviour, a role is a bundle of norms. As a pattern of actual behaviour, a role is one side of a set of social relationships." Fig. 10.5 depicts these status positions.

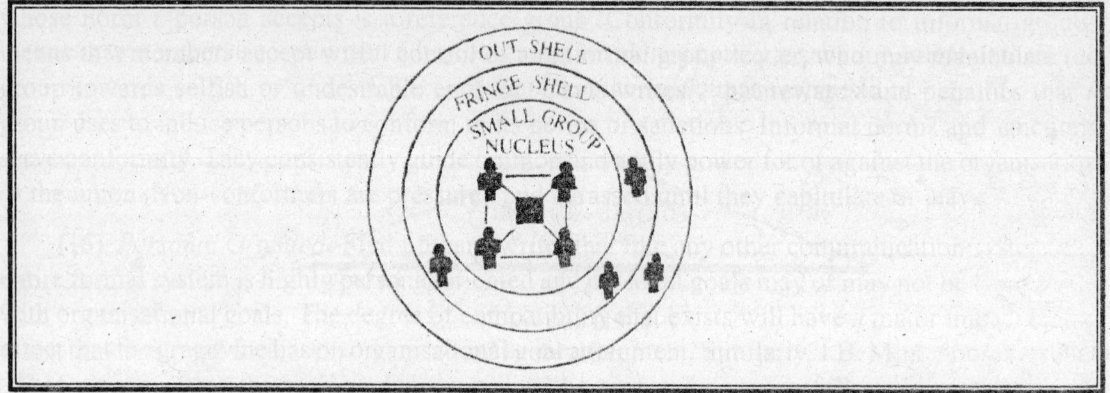

Fig. 10. 5 Relationship of Status Positions in an informal organisation

***(Source:** Theo Haimann and William G. Scott, Management in the Modern Organisation, Houghton Miffin Boston, 1970, p. 433)*

Functions of Informal Groups or Services

Informal groups exist and continue because they render some services or perform certain desired functions of the members. The following are the functions of a formal organisation:

(1) *Social Satisfaction:* This function helps to promote group integrity and social values. The members are co-operative to the formal group and consequently are in the constant association and socialising process. In addition to the formal job satisfaction, the members need social satisfaction also. Informal groups give a member recognision, status and further opportunity to relate to others. This is an important function.

(2) *Group Values and Life Style:* Informal organisations provide group values and life style. Its function definitely is service to the members to maintain group values and life styles. "One function is to maintain and continue the cultural values and life style of the group. In this way, the standards and unity of the group can be continued over a long period of time"[4] (K. Davis).

(3) *Status Recognition:* Informal organisations have evolved from different status, positions of the participants. The formal organisations provide satisfaction by providing status, norms, roles, recognition and future opportunity in the group. There is a relationship of status positions in informal organisations closely related to status.

(4) *Sharing Work Problems:* Another service that informal group renders is solving work problems of the members. The members will come to the rescue of other employees. They collectively take decisions and share job-knowledge. The informal group at work gives personal attention, shares, their common interest and finds a group solution to a problem. Thus, this attitude of sharing work problems of members eliminates redtapism, and short-cuts are evolved and an informal channel of communication is developed to avoid departmental boundaries.

(5) *Operate Communication System:* K. Davis had identified another important function or services of informal group to the members, which is the function of communication. In order to meet the wants and to keep its members influenced about what affects them, the group develops systems and channels of communication.

(6) *Norms of Behaviour:* Oral values and ethical standards should be maintained. Towards this end, informal organisations establish and maintain norms for behaviour of good, bad, moral, immoral, honesty, co-operation etc. Informal groups are the best suited organisation to promote norms for behaviour.

(7) *Social Control:* Research studies reveal that informal organisation "its particularly decisive in achieving social control." It is a service for the members by which the behaviour of others is influenced and regulated. It may operate both internally and externally. Internal control is directed towards persuading members of the group to conform to its way of life. External control is directed towards those outside the group, such as management, union leadership, or other informal groups" (K. Davis).

(8) *Protection from Pressures:* Informal groups arise and persist because they perform a very useful service for their members. One of the important functions is to protect the members from outside pressures or problems. Groups will come to the rescue of other members or group and protect their members against real outside dangers and also from the management.

Distinction between Formal and Informal Organisation

An organisation has been conveniently classified into two broad categories as formal and informal. The label of formal or informal organisation depends much upon the degree and the nature to which they are structured. It is difficult to demarcate completely as formal and informal organisations. Hicks and Gullett rightly remark that "formal and informal define the extremes of continuum of organisational types."

However, the distinctions between the formal and informal organisations can be identified from the following characteristics:

	Formal	*Informal*
(1)	Formal organisations grow purposely to achieve the organisational objectives.	Informal organisations develop spontaneously and voluntarily to achieve members' own and personal objectives.
(2)	Formal structure is well defined and controlled.	There is no informal structure as such not well-defined and controlled.
(3)	It clearly describes authority, power, responsibility and accountability relationships.	Members of informal organisations do not enjoy any described or explicitly specified powers, authority.
(4)	Formal structure has of well-defined route and channel for transmission of information.	In formal relationship, there is only informal communication, as such there is no explicitly prescribed channel for passing information.

(5)	Formal communication is characterised by vertical downward communication. Messages are usually conveyed by written media like orders, instructions	Informal communication is characterised and may be conveyed by a simple glance, nod, smile, gestures, understanding and even mere silence.
(6)	It is known for delay in transmitting information as it has to pass through various levels.	Informal channel is the most effective one and transmits information with considerable speed and quickness. The network is formed to transmit messages quickly.
(7)	Only official and correct pieces of informations are passed.	It can pass both correct information as well as rumours. It is known for spreading messages without substantial evidence.
(8)	It assigns specific jobs to the members to be accomplished.	Informal group does not prescribe any jobs to do by the members. It is formed based on personal and social needs.
(9)	In the formal structure, hierarchy of relationships are clearly defined.	There is no rigidly defined hierarchical relationships between the members of informal groups.
(10)	Relationships are governed by rules, regulations, procedures, instructions.	Relationships of members of informal groups are governed by personal, social and psychological needs of the memBers.
(11)	Positions defined and rewarded by prestige, rank, status, pay and other perquisites.	In informal organisations, there are no positions, recognition, award or reward.
(12)	There is a place for formal structure on the organisational chart or structure showing interrelationships.	There is no organisation chart or structure to determine the informal relationships, their positions and locations.
(13)	Formal organisations are deliberately created, planned having official back ing and support.	Informal groups are formed voluntarily by themselves, as such, they enjoy no official support and backing.
(14)	It is rigid, inflexible and controlled.	It is flexible, loose, ill-defined and uncontrolled.
(15)	Universities, big business corporations, State and Central Government Departments, multi-national corporations are examples of formal organisations.	Clubs, dinner party, friendship, recreation group, literary and cultural groups etc. are examples of informal groups.

(16) Formal organisation can be converted into an informal structure if the well-defined structure, controls, and relationships are not enforced.	An informal organisation can be converted into formal when their relationships, and activities are explicitly defined and controlled.

ORGANISATION

Formals	Informal
1. Well Structure	1. Unstructured
2. Rigidly defined	2. Loosely organised
3. Inflexible	3. Flexible
4. Durable	4. Temporary
5. Strictly Controlled	5. Unplanned
6. Rules, Procedures, Orders and Regulations	6. Voluntary, Spontaneous
7. Pay, rank, status, prestige, and other perquisites	7. Uncontrolled
8. Fixed communication channels and routes	8. Personal, social and psychological objectives
9. Accountability, responsibility, power, authority	9. Not found on organisation chart
10. Located on organisation chart	10. Unconscious
11. Big business organisations, universities, State and Central Government Departments	11. No fixed communication channels and routes
12. Explicit interpersonal relationships	12. Quick and speed in communication.
13. Network, channel and media	13. Rumours and unfounded information
14. Organisation goals	14. No reward, pay, rank, prestige etc.
15. Delay in passing information	15. Smile, gestures, silence communication
16. Conscious	16. No accountability, authority, power etc.
	17. No rules, regulations etc.

Networks and Patterns of Informal Communication

It is assumed that in most organisations, the organisation chart also represents the communication network.

And this is the network used for most communications "up and down the line." There is, however, another communication network which is often ignored but which if understood could often explain some of the seemingly inexplicable actions and reactions of sections of the organisation (Fig. 6).

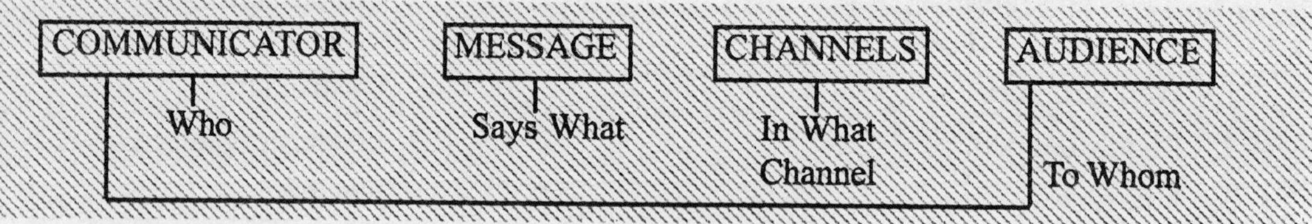

Fig. 10. 6 With What Effect

This is the informal network made up of groups, bound together by friendship, eating-habits; social circumstances or any of the many circumstances that bring people together in the work environment but not directly connected with the work. It is often dangerous to assume that any direct use can be made of this informal network, since any information fed in at end will certainly be so multiplied by the time it reaches the end of the chain as to be unrecognisable.

However, every attempt should be made to plot this network and this will often permit a prior consideration of the effect of certain communications, and will certainly serve to explain in many instances what seems to be a peculiar reaction to certain information. Generally speaking, it is not difficult to plot the informal network. Simple observation of social habits will provide most of the answers. Where, people sit in the canteen, who goes home with whom, membership of sections of the social club, who has girl friends where, and enable the communicator to establish within broad limits the groupings which make up this informal organisation and thus the informal communication network.

Informal communication exists in a formal organisation. As discussed earlier, informal groups within, the formal structure, both co-exist. They can be seen in every organisation, small or big, private or public. There is no scope for the management to establish informal network in a formal structure. A number of research studies have been conducted on the patterns of informal communication. For instance, K. Davis has indicated certain predictable patterns of informal communication. In his paper on communication within a management, he writes:

(1) People talk most when the news is recent.

(2) People talk about things that affect their work.

(3) People talk about people they know.

(4) People working near each other are likely to be on the same grapevine.

(5) People who contact each other in the chain of procedure tend to be on the same grapevine.

Generally, information on the grapevine do not follow a straight-line approach. The messages may be passed along in a much more scattered manner. Some members in an informal group may pass information to several other members of the group. In turn, all the members who have received information may not pass to others, but only a few of them will pass it further. There may be some active and more active members in the group. A member of an informal group is said to be active when he continues to transmit the message to others. The reason for transmission of the same message is its importance and time value. Some members are more active because they are involved in receiving and passing information. The more active people may have easy access to the information source than others. The figure will illustrate how some people repeat the message to several others and while some others do not repeat it at all, a model of H.G. Hicks and C.R. Gullet. They illustrate that: "In this example, some people repeat the message to several others, while some do not repeat it at all. Rather than following a straight-line pattern, informal communications networks are typically cluster chains, resembling the one in this example."

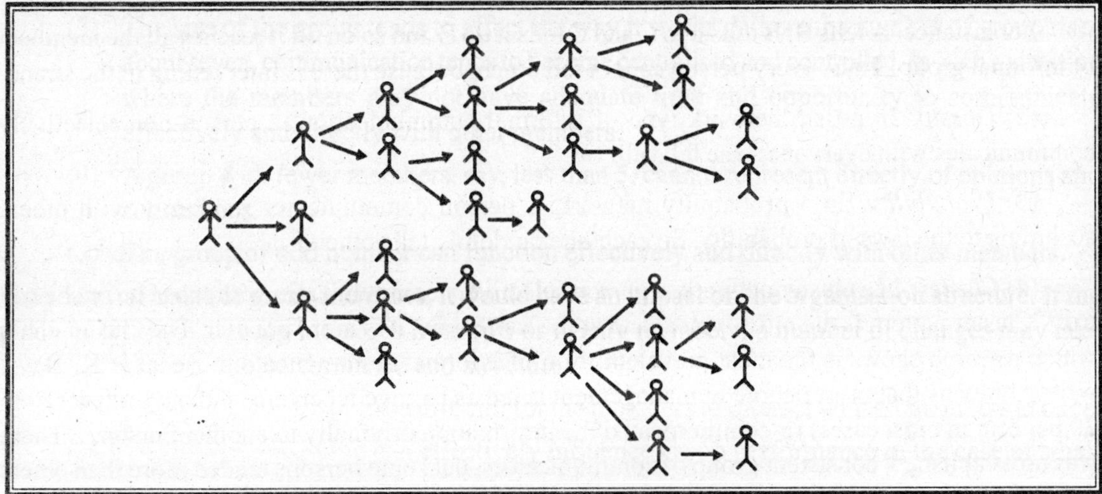

Fig. 10. 7 An Informal Communications Network

Source: *Adapted from Herbert G. Hicks and C. Ray Gullet, Management, McGraw-Hill International Book Company, 1981, p. 522.*

The grapevine consists of a series of small groups of people interconnected to one another until it covers everyone in the organisation. Each group has a person at the centre as a leader who communicates the messages to every member in that group. The members of that group in turn transmit the same message to other member in another group and so on and the process continues. Fig. 8 shows how it operates.

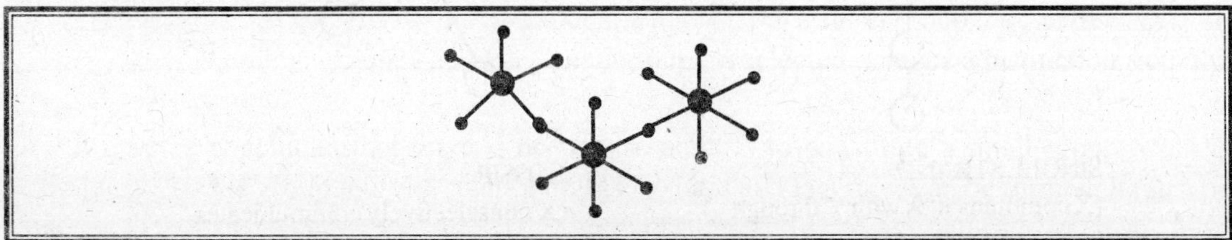

Fig. 10.8

The figure shows that there is a communication leader in each small group who is interlinked to another communication leader located at the centre in another group. The central person is a communication leader because he is in possession of the message to be passed on.

There are four possible ways of informal communication networks as structured by K. Davis. They are:

(1) Single Strand.

(2) Gossip.

(3) Probability.

(4) Cluster.

(1) *Single Strand:* In a single strand network of informal communication, one individual tells others. Each individual communicates with the other individual through the intervening person in the strand.

For instance, A tells B, B tells it to C and C tells it do D and so on till it reaches all the members of informal group. Thus, every person cannot tell others because there is intervening in the strand.

(2) *Gossip:* In gossip network type of informal communication, a person non-selectively communicates with everyone. One tells all.

(3) *Probability:* In a probability network, a person communicates randomly with others according to the laws of probability. So each one randomly tells others.

(4) *Cluster:* In a cluster network, a person selectively communicates with those he or she can trust. Cluster pattern is the most typical and at the same time, it is more popular. The cluster chain which research shows is the most prevalent form of informal communication. Because K. Davis writes: "Means that most people in management acted as passive receivers, and only a few (10 to 30 per cent in most cases) re-communicated the information originally to another person.... There was no established, consistent group of communicators, but some persons tended more than others to be active in communication.

Informal channels, therefore, cannot be designed and predicted and hence are found on a formal structure.

SINGLE STRAND
(X communicates with Y through interviening persons in a strand

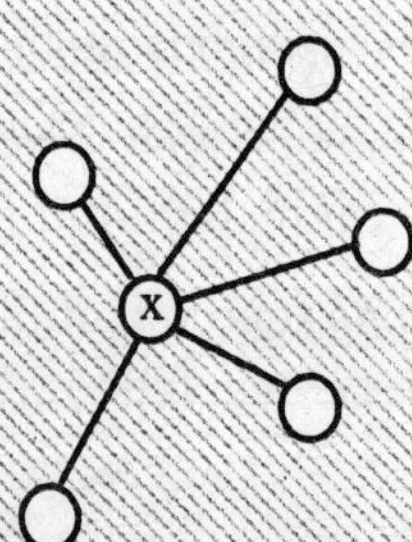

GOSSIP
(X nonselectively communicates with everyone)

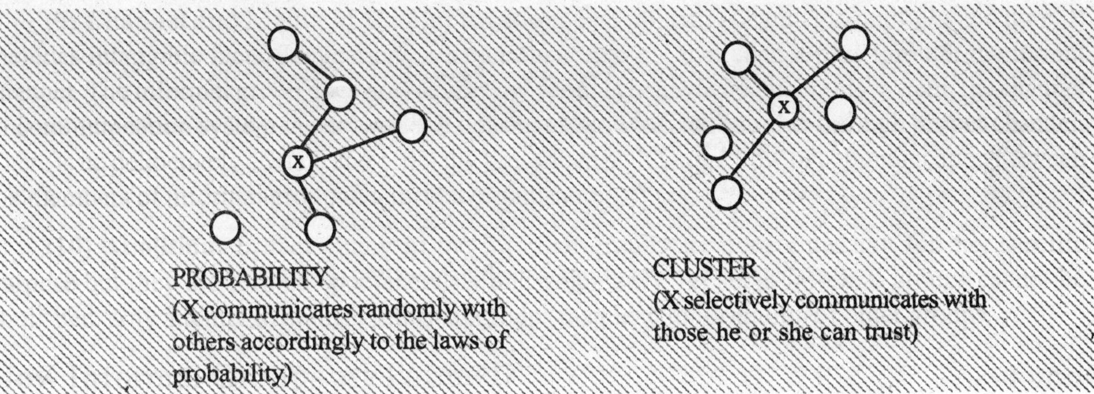

Fig. 10. 9 Informal Communication Network in an Organisation

(***Source:*** *Adapted from Keith Davis, "Management Communication and the Grapevine", Harvard Business Review, Sep-Oct. 1953, p. 45.*)

Informal Communication Channels — Serial and Cluster Transmission

Serial transmission passes the message along a chain running from A to B to C to D. In the case of rumour, it passes through different sorts of structure. Rumour travels through four distinct types of patterns of which cluster network is the most common (Fig. 10). In a group, individuals are called liaisons who transmit messages to different people. Some individuals obtain the same rumour from other sources. Such individuals are termed "social isolates." Social isolates generally participate sparingly in rumour transmission. So in a rumour transmission, there is the possibility of check and cross examine and compare of the message. This enables us to evaluate the validity of the rumour.

Knapp remarked that "in any given group, the amount of rumour being circulated is roughly in an inverse proportion to the degree to which official information is viewed as trustworthy and satisfactory. Festinger et al. have developed the following three principles to account for rumour behaviour:

(1) *Principle of External Control:* That rumours arise when important events are beyond the control of those involved in them.

(2) *Principle of Cognitive Unclarity:* That rumours orginate when situations are unstructured and unpredictable.

(3) *Principle of Integrative Explanation:* The details tend to be distorted to conform to the dominant theme of the rumour.

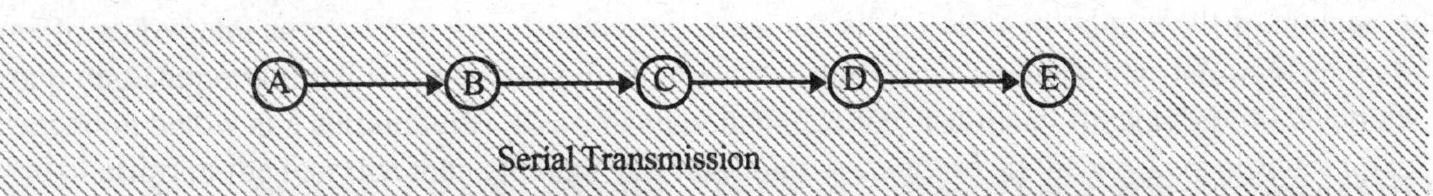

Serial Transmission

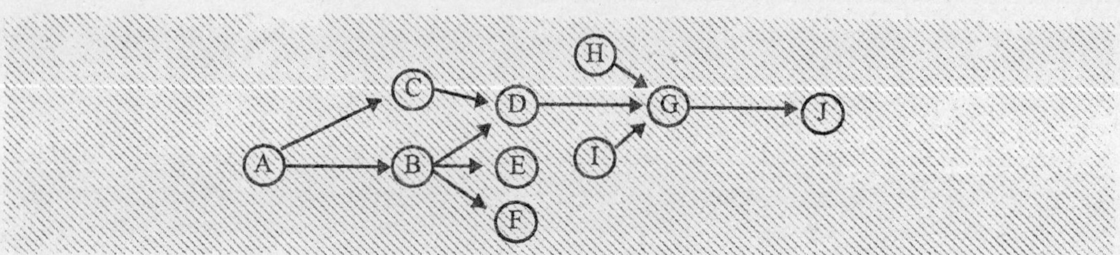

Fig. 10.10 Structures of Informal Communication Networks

(Source: The Dynamics of Organisational Communication, John E. Biard)

Rumours

Meaning and Nature: A rumour is but oral information circulating something. It passes from person to person, sometimes unfounded news. In a rumour communication, a piece of news or story is passed from one person to another which may not be true. This is a verbal general talk or gossip. A loud untrue sound. It is a talk or report of a person or thing in some way noted or distinguished. The fact of being generally talked about reputation and renown. A rumour is a verbal statement or report circulating in a group, the truth of which there is no clear evidence. A rumour once spread is not soon removed. A rumour spreads like wild fire and may create wonders and miracles as a channel of informal communication.

The two persons involved in a rumour are:

(1) rumour spreader

(2) rumour bearer.

The orginator of a rumour is also called rumour monger. In grapevine the leader of a group tell the message to each person in that group. A communication leader recognises rumours. The leader must be trustworthy and hence it gets credibility. The management can make use of them for effective communication. The information can be fed into the informal channel to dispel rumours and to provide quick and easy access to the information. What workers talk about among themselves may be none of the boss's business. But it is very much his business whether the "the word" is good or bad.

Good or Bad Words: Sometimes, in general context of the operations of an organisation, an executive's ill-considered remarks may appear a somewhat trivial affair. But it is, on comparison, an intangible thing called "confidence." He is not involved every day to break the big news or to clear up serious misunderstandings. But every day, only a few, say, ten or twelve different, indefinable ways, which one may say or fail to say. He may even shape and give colour to the contents to suit the opinion of the employees and of the company as a whole. It is the actions and words of an executive that will determine what they talk about among themselves whether the word is good or bad, in the financial analysis, the answer is based upon one's words or action.

Differences between Rumour and Informal Communication

Rumour with reference to the organisational communication is sometimes used a synonym for the whole informal communication. So rumour is a grapevine information communicated without secured standard of evidence. It is an unverified information, report, story, instruction, direction etc. It is a piece of message without a definite source of origin and lack of actual support spreading from one person to another. Again rumour is an unjudicious and untrue part of the grapevine which sometimes distorts correctness of the situation which is an undesirable feature of grapevine.

Manipulation of Information

In the process of rumour dissemination, each person who received a message may subtract or add something to the original message through the process of elaboration and assimilation. When it is passed on sometimes, it damages the reputation. Similarly, sometimes by chance, it may prove to be correct.

Why Rumours are Spread

The reasons for the spread of rumours may be many. Interest and ambiguity are the two elements present in a rumour. To create a rumour, one must have interest in it. When correct facts are known, a person may not have a cause for rumour. If there is ambiguity in a siutation, there is a cause for rumour. A rumour message may change its spirit when it passes from one person to another.

(1) Frustration, emotional tensions, mistrust, misapprehension. These facts create outlets to reflect works feeling.

(2) It satisfies the psychological urge within the people.

The reasons are:

(3) It caters to the needs to make a sense of the world around us — to know how things stand.

(4) Hope, hostility often supply the principal motivational power for passing it on.

(5) Rumour spreads only when the news or story has some importance, both for the rumour-spreader and rumour-bearer.

(6) When the information about the news or story are shrouded in some kind of ambiguity.

(7) When the information about the matters that affect workers' lives is not clearly reported, reaches them in conflicting version.

(8) When news about matters is withheld altogether, which requires some explanation.

(9) Psychological instincts and desires instigate people.

(10) When people are resentful, they will be all the more receptive to ideas that fix the blame on a person or group whom they dislike.

Though the general theme may present in a rumour but not in detail. When the central theme of a rumour has been recognised, it is a natural tendency to distort subsequent news or story with the object of making them agree with central theme. In real life situations the farther the message circulated the rumour, more likely is it to become garbled and twisted. Slowly and steadily, with all speed, it flies and travels around and disseminates the central theme in a different way. Filtering is the nature of spreading a rumour, the story or news becomes worse.

Impact of Rumour

The dysfunctional nature of the grapevine is rumour. It is a serious problem associated with formal organisation. The spreading of rumour is a phenomenon of social communication which lacks substantive evidence of facts. Rumour supplements the transmission of information through the formal communication may be damaging when circulated and acted upon it. It is a preposition for belief passed from one person to another generally by word of mouth without any evidence. What is said is true because there is no further information to support it. Rumour may carry false information sometimes detrimental to organisation functioning. So information spread by rumour is dangerous because it is harmful, serious, and hurting.

K. Davis writes that: "Since rumour generally is incorrect, a major outbreak of it can be a devastating epidemic and sweeps throughout an organisation as fast as a summer storm and usually with as much damage.[5]

Controlling Rumour

One cannot always prevent a fire from breaking out. At the same time, one does no have to stand idly by until it burns down the office. A manager should not ignore to listen what the employee has to say. Listening to subordinates is the best measure to combat rumour. It is the basic responsibility of every manager first to find out what is really on their minds. When an executive talks to an employee face-to-face, establishes his everyday personal relationship, i.e., after a time he expects, understands, and likes him. Then the employee feels free to let the manager know how the manager is getting his ideas.

It is necessary to take immediate steps to get all the facts when a rumour reaches the table of a manager. It may be mentioned that just to tag the story as a rumour does not help. From the real life situations and experience, people know that a rumour may well turnout to be true. When the news or story has implications, it is desirable to say that it is passed on to those who are in a position to take necessary and correct steps to counteract any harm it might do.

The following steps would help to control or handle rumour:

(1) *To listen:* To combat a rumour, it is essential to listen what the employees want to say which indicates the idea prevailing in their minds. This indirectly helps to know the causes of the rumour.

(2) *To have Communication Links:* It is desirable to establish an effective communication system linking all levels to keep all the workers informed about various activities, changes, movements, events etc. This will combat or minimise the harm posed by the rumour.

(3) *Frankness and Honesty:* The managers should be frank, open, honest and trustworthy which promotes confidence and credibility. The attitude of the workers is based on these characteristics of the manager.

(4) *Regular Interactions:* To handle a rumour, it is crucial to adapt a tactful way of frequent interactions with keymen or leaders and discuss with them to know their reactions.

(5) *Accurate Answers:* In the case of handling a rumour, a manager should never put off the answers to any question put by the workers. At the same time, he should not try to evade answering. He should inspire confidence in them and fulfil the promise to get information.

(6) *Rumour Control Centres:* In controlling rumour, generally, some organisations establish formal rumour control centres. To operate that management provides for anonymous reporting of rumours by telephone as well as for prompt correct replies. The official rumour control centre establishes and maintains a high source of credibility.

K. Davis has offered the following ways to combat rumours:

(7) *Remove Causes:* Remove causes in order to prevent it.

(8) *Serious Rumours:* Apply efforts primarily to serious rumours.

(9) *Refute:* Refute rumour with facts.

(10) *Early Effort:* Deal with rumour as soon as possible.

(11) *Face-to-Face Dealings:* Emphasise face-to-face supply of facts, confirmed in writing, if necessary.

(12) *Reliable Source:* Provide facts from reliable source.

(13) *Avoid Repetition:* It is always necessary to refrain from repeating the rumour while refuting it.

(14) Encourage assistance of informal and union leaders if they are cooperative.

(15) Listen to all rumours in order to understand what it may mean.[6]

To Sum up

It gives good results to contact higher levels of supervision. The manager has to ascertain what matters can be made public. Use of actual and correct facts, reduction of causes and use of unions would solve the problems, to some extent. The best measure is to approach the next line of management and fellow managers. Its total stoppage is very difficult, when once started and spread. A tardy corrective approach cannot solve the problem. Here it is more appropriate to refer again to K. Davis, who writes that "When people are emotionally maladjusted or inadequately informed about their environment, they are likely to be rumour-mongers." A manager may have to face a number of questions, a few new questions are also bound to come. He has to be ready with the right answers. When the news or story means that some persons going to be hurt, he has to make sure that everybody understands why the decision is taken. Some rumours may be harmless while some may be serious. Whatever may be it is good on the part of the manager and other to listen to rumours, because they carry the message about the employees.

L. Brown remarks that, "In using the grapevine, management must be able to pinpoint the leaders and work through them, must feed in factual information, listen to the feedback response, and be discerning in not overloading the system and using it inappropriately. It is important that management be sure to follow up grapevine message with official written messages and statement that will verify the accuracy of data obtained from the grapevine. This also helps in building a mutual trust based on open communication followed throughout the organisation or business."[7]

Merits of Informal Communication

(1) *Morale Uniting Force:* Grapevine acts as a driving force to unit the work force in cases of common matters. The grapevine serves as a morale uniting force when there are greater interests in the new policies, innovations in Procedures or personnel, and sufficient data about the organisation without any value judgement.

(2) *Save Time:* The informal communication helps to save time in circulating information. Grapevine is spontaneous and flexible, it would not take more time in circulating the message.

(3) *Speed:* Informal channel of communication operates with a much greater speed. Grapevine is a spontaneous growth and can transmit information with considerate speed. Formal communication network sometimes is not suitable to send message quickly.

(4) *Immediate Response:* Response from informal communication can be interacted immediately. Immediate response from a given information transmitted to the receiver is necessary for the management to take decisions. The advantage of immediate response can be obtained from informal communication.

(5) *Public Relations:* Public relations is another wing of the management function. Informal relations are essential for effective public relations. Public relations fail because lack of informal relations and informal communications. Thus informal communication is the key to the successful public relations.

(6) *Feedback:* Feedback is necessary in all group activities, irrespective of the type of organisation. The informal communication also helps as a feedback system. So the management can use grapevine as a testing tool. In a feedback immediate response and reaction can be gained which is more useful in the process of decision-making. Listening to the feedback response is the good principle of communication.

(7) *Creation of Ideas:* Informal communication generates ideas and offer appropriate suggestions that are proved more helpful. This advantage is not available in the case of formal communication. In a formal setup, interactions must take place according to the prescribed rules, procedure, line and authority.

(8) *Tool of Management:* Informal communication is a tool of management, because it influences the behaviour and attitudes of others. Communication is not just for the sake of communication but to make others respond to decisions. It is only with relations to others to achieve a desired goal. It is because of this that communication is considered a valuable tool of management. It is the responsibility of management to create informal environment conducive for effective communication.

(9) *Accurate Information:* Informal communication fastly transmits accurate information. The communication leader is in a position to know the correct data and when to pass, where to pass and what message to pass. He knows confidential matters and factual information. The accurate information is fed into the grapevine to provide quick and easy access to the message that needs to be known.

(10) *Avoids Misunderstandings:* There can be no mutual understanding without informal relations, which is the core of effective communication. There are a few problems in the real life situation that formal communication cannot resolve. It produces results. In relationships, informal communication produces harmony, resolves problems and dissolves feelings of separateness.

(11) *Other Merits:* It indicates the pulse of the work force. The message circulated is closely and collectively interacted and understood. Informal communication may supplement formal communication. Grapevines are not static but dynamic and non-stable.

K. Davis has suggested the following potential benefits of informal communications.[8]

(12) *Making Effective Total System:* The informal organisations end with the formal organisation to make a more effective total system. Informal groups are flexible and spontaneous, they can be better used to solve some problems because formal plans, or policies cannot solve many problems in a dynamic situation.

(13) *Lightening Work Load:* The informal channel reduces or lightens the work load on management. The employees have a common understanding and working with a spirit of sharing work or job problems. So managers can delegate and decentralise work. "They feel less compelled to check on the workers to be sure everything is ship-shape."

(14) *Helps to get the Work Done:* A significant benefit of informal organisation is that it helps the members to get the work done by way of sharing and supporting.

(15) *Encourages Co-operation:* The most important benefit is the fact that informal organisations tend to encourage co-operation. Informal channel support managers. On the other hand, managers can feel confident but, the employees work in co-operation, when the group supports managers, it would lead to better communication and more productivity.

(16) *Fills Gap in Manager's Abilities:* A manager may not be perfect in all areas of activity. There may be some gaps in his capabilities. In such a situation, an informal group may act to fill the gaps in manager's abilities. If a manager is weak in decision-making, employees may informally help managers with the decision-making process. In this way, decision-making is accomplished, in spite of manager's weakness.

(17) *Satisfaction and Stability:* Yet another merit that informal group brings to the members is satisfaction and stability to work group. Sense of belonging and security can be obtained only when there is work satisfaction and stability in work. Thereby the rate of labour turnover is reduced which is beneficial to the organisation and management in terms of productivity.

(18) *Channel of Communication:* Informal channel of communication is useful to the employees. This eliminates boundaries to communication and people can communicate openly and freely with each others and keep in touch, to know things, to learn things about their environment.

(19) *Safety Valve:* An additional significant advantage that arises from the informal organisation is that it provides a safely valve for employees' emotions, frustration and other personal and psychological problems. The valve provides an opportunity to the members to discuss their emotions friendly, freely and openly and thereby relieved of their emotions.

(20) *Encourages Managers:* The last benefit suggested by Davis is that informal organisation may help to encourage managers to plan and act more carefully. The managers should not neglect the existence and importance of informal organisation. " Managers who understand its power know that it is a check and balance on their unlimited use of authority."

Demerits of Informal Communication

The informal communication is not free from limitations or shortcomings. It has the following disadvantages too:

(1) *Rumours: I*nformal communication sometimes spreads incorrect information as well as rumours. As such, it creates serious repercussions. So it is desirable to use grapevine with certain safeguards. It is really a basic drawback of the system. Koontz and Donnell rightly remarked that this channel is unreliable: "The dysfunctional nature of the grapevine is in fostering rumours, spreading them. Because rumour, by definition, lacks substantive evidence or fact, it may be damaging when circulated and acted on. Usually, full of prejudice, emotion, bias, self-serving issues and partial truths, rumours arise in situations where (1) there is great ambiguity or uncertainty and (2)issues of high interest to group members arise suddenly. Rumour-passers either support the rumour content, add to it, or suggest a counter-rumour."

(2) *Distorts:* Grapevine distorts information. It is without any official sanction. So it is dangerous to the organisation. It may even lead to gossip and rumour.

(3) *Inadequate:* Though the management cannot ignore and eliminate the grapevine this channel is inadequate for handling all categories of messages expeditiously and with understanding. Informal communication cannot shoulder the entire communication load. Only certain matters can be fed into grapevine to circulate.

(4) *Communication Leaders:* The success of informal communication is greatly dependent on the communication leader in each group who circulates information basically. As such, the key persons or communication leaders must be trustworthy and have credibility. But the great problem in the organisation today stems from the lack of trust within the organisation and lack of effective informal communication.

(5) *No Authority:* Informal communication does not help in the maintenance of authority of the line. It is based on free mix up with others and rely upon the informal relationship. There is no place for respect to the superiors by the subordinates. Thus in this way, it does not help to exercise effective control over subordinates. Sometimes, it may fail to enforce the responsibilities fixed and assigned to individuals in respect of tasks to be carried on by the individuals in the organisation.

(6) *Improper Communication:* Prompt and accurate flow of information is the function of sound communication. Informal communication is unsound and improper method of channelising information. Sometimes, in an informal group, it is evident, the absence of superiors mingling with subordinates. There is no direct contact and relationship in informal communication. In a formal face- to-face communication, understanding the attitudes, reactions, levels of intelligent and acceptance and rejection of message are possible.

(7) *No Overload of Work:* Message load is less in an informal communication. In a complex organisation structure and complicated correspondence network, there is always a heavy load of work messages to be communicated. Many messages should be transmitted only through the formal media of communication. As such the informal channel is not suitable to cope with the message load.

(8) *Overlooking Superiors:* Communication through the informal channel leads to overlooking the superiors, sometimes overlooked, by line officers. Grapevine is also not suitable for upward direct communication.

(9) *Interpretation Changes:* In a grapevine, the key person tells the message to each person in a particular group. The members of this group in turn relay the message to someone else in another group. This process continues. This results in wrong interpretations, change of meaning, ideas, half truth. Thus, by keeping an issue thrown open in an informal group or group leads to dilution of the actual information on any given issue.

(10) *Other Drawbacks:* A number of communication barriers like linguistic barriers, managerial barriers act as hurdles to a successful operation of informal communication.

An informal organisation creates problems for the employer. The system has a negative effect on the organisation. The following are the problems associated with it as identified by a number of experts like F. Luthans, K. Davis etc.[9]

(11) *Resistance to Change:* Organisational change is the index of dynamic nature of the structure. Changes introduced may be in the methods of production and other routines. But the informal groups resist changes and want status quo. The informal groups are found by convention, custom and culture and hence they resist change. K. Davis writes that "there is a tendency for the group to become overleap protect of its life style and to stand like a rock in the face of change. What has been is good enough for future."

(12) *Role Conflict:* Differences, disagreements, rivalries are bound to arise where there is a group. The informal organisation produces a role conflict which may become dysfunctional from the organisation point of view. For instance, time for refreshment or tea break is desirable. But, if the employees spend unreasonably more time in socialisation process, it may affect production. It is a disadvantage to the employer. It is clear case of conflict. Therefore, if both the interest of formal and the informal groups can be integrated, higher productivity and satisfaction can be expected. On the other side, much of the role conflict can be avoided by carefully cultivating mutual interest with the formal groups.

(13) *Rumour:* The dysfunctional nature of the grapevine is rumour. It is a serious problem associated with a formal organisation. The spreading of rumour is a phenomenon of social communication which lacks substantive evidence of fact. Rumour supplements the transmission of information though formal communication may be damaging it when circulated and acted upon.

It is a proposition for belief passed from one person to another, generally by word of mouth without any evidence. What is said is true because there is no further information to support it. Rumour may carry false information sometimes detrimental to organisational functioning. So information spread by rumour is dangerous because it is harmful, serious, and hurting. Davis remarks that rumour generally is incorrect; a major outbreak of it can be a devastating epidemic that sweeps through an organisation as fast as a summer storm and usually with much damage.

(14) *Conformity:* One of the important functions of informal communication is social control. The internal groups exert strong pressure on conformity. Informal groups require norms. The group whose norm a person accepts is a reference group. Conformity in relation to informal groups means that members accept wilful control of an informal group leader, who may manipulate the group towards selfish or undesirable ends. K. Davis writes, "that rewards and penalties that a group uses to induce persons to conform to its norms or sanctions. Informal norms and sanctions serve conformity. They consistently guide opinion and apply power for or against the organisation or the union. Non-conformers are pressured and harassed until they capitulate or leave."

(15) *Personal Oriented:* Fred Luthans writes that like any other communication system, the entire formal system is highly personal oriented and personal goals may or may not be compatible with organisational goals. The degree of compatibility that exists will have a major impact on the effect that the grapevine has on organisational goal attainment. Similarly, J.B. Minter observes that "There is very little that can be done to utilise the grapevine purposefully as a means of goal attainment, As a result, rumours probably to at least as much to subvert organisational goals as to foster them. They may well stir up dissension. They are contrary to fact."

(16) *Irresponsibility:* The leaders of informal groups wield group power without official sanction and control. The group thus becomes an instrument of inevitable source of irresponsibility. W.G. Scott remarks that "Since the origin and direction of the flow of information on the grapevine is hard to pinpoint, it is difficult to assign responsibility for false information or morale-lower rumours. speed at which the grapevine is capable of transmitting information makes control of invalid message troublesome".

(17) *Errors:* The informal system carries some degree of error in it. It carries non-factual self-servicing and incomplete information that cause damage to the organisation.

(18) *Communication Leaders:* The success of informal communication is greatly dependent on communication leader in each group who circulates basically. As such the key persons or communication leaders must be trustworthy and have credibility. But the great problem in the organisation today stems from the lack of trust within the organisation and lack of effective informal communication.

(19) *No Authority:* Informal communication does not help in the maintenance of authority of the line. It is based on free mix-up with others and rely upon the informal relationship. There is no place for respect to the superiors by the subordinates. Thus, in this way, it does not help to exercise effective control over subordinates. Sometimes, it may fail to enforce the responsibilities fixed and assigned to individuals in respect of tasks to be carried on by the individuals in the organisation.

(20) *Improper Communication:* Prompt and accurate flow of information is the function of sound communication. Informal communication is an unsound and improper method of channelising information. Sometimes, in an informal group, it is evident, the absence of superiors mingling with subordinates. There is no direct contact and relationship in informal communication. In a formal face- to-face communication, understanding the attitudes, reactions, levels of intelligent and acceptance and rejection of message are possible.

REFERENCES

1. Koontz and Donnell, *Management: A Systems and Contingency Analysis of Managerial Functions*,McGraw Hill, Kogakusha Limited, 1976, p. 623.
2. H. G Hicks & C.R. Gullett, *Management*, McGraw Hill International Book Company, New Delhi, p. 187.
3. Adapted from Bertram M. Gross, *Organisation and their Managing*, Free Press, New York, 1968, pp. 242-248. Quoted in Fred Luthans, *Organisational Behaviour*.
4. Davis, K., *Human Behaviour At Work*, Tata McGraw Hill Publishing Company, New Delhi.
5. Davis, K., *op. cit.*
6. *Ibid., op. cit.*, p. 344.
7. Brown, L., *Communicating Facts and Ideas in Business*, Prentice Hall, Inc., Englewood Cliffs, New Jersey 1982.
8. Davis, K., op. cit.
9. Fred Luthans, *Organisational Behaviour*, and Davis, K., op. cit.

*****

CHAPTER 11

Group Behaviour and Communication

Introduction

The size of a small group may vary from group to group, from time to time, in nature and circumstances of interaction. This is the main reason why there is no single definition uniformly accepted. On the other hand, it is very difficult to define it without a specific purpose or reference. However, the following are some of the definitions of a small group, which may enable us to understand the concept of group clearly.

Fig. 11.1

Definitions

S.B. Robbins: "As two or more individuals interacting and interdependent, who come together to achieve particular objectives."

Smith: "We may define a social group as a unit consisting of a plural number of separate organism (agents) who have a collective perception of their unity and who have the ability to act and/or are acting in a unitary manner towards their environment."

Cattell: "...a group is a collection of organism in which the existence of all (in their given relationships) is necessary to the satisfaction of certain individual needs in each."

Mills: "...they are units composed of two or more persons who come into contact for a purpose and who consider the contact meaningful."

Sherif and Sherif: "A group is a social unit which consists of a number of individuals who stand in (more or less) definite status and role relationships to one another and which possesses a set of values of norms of its own, regulating the behaviour of individual members, at least in matters of consequence for the group."

Fielder: "By this term we generally mean a set of individuals who share a common fact, that is, who are interdependent, in the sense that an event which affects one member is likely to affect all".

Homan: "W mean by a group a number of persons who communicate with one another often over a span of time, and who are few enough so that each person is able to communicate with all the others, not second-hand, through other people, but face-to-face."

Fred Luthans: "Group dynamics is concerned with the interactions and forces among group members in a social situation. When the concept is applied to the study of organisational behaviour, the focus is on the dynamics of members of formal or informal groups in the organisation."

Myers and Myers: "As a collection of two or more people in interaction, with identical goals and established norms, acting in role reactions with each other with a network of interpersonal attraction. Although some scholars in the small group research do not consider a dyad or two people a small group, we prefer to count any number above one as a potential group."

F. E. Kast and J.E. Rosenzweig: "A group is an assemblage, cluster, or aggregation of persons considered to be related in some way or united by common ties or interacts — family recreation, or occupation. For example, in psychology and sociology, the emphasis is on interrelationships among members; a connotation of aggregation is not stressed."

E. H. Schein: "Any number of people who (1) interact with one another, (2) are psychologically aware of one another and (3) perceive themselves to a group."

G. Miller: "A group is usually gathered within a physical space that permits the members to hear and see one another. Each member usually can communicate verbally with every other member. Finally, a group does not have the many hierarchical levels found in an organisation."

Robert Bales: A small group is defined "as any number of persons engaged in interaction with one another in a single face-to-face meeting or series of such meetings in which each member receives some impression or perception of each other member distinctive enough so that he can, either at the time, or in later questioning give some reaction to each of the others as an individual person, even though it be only to recall that the other was present."

Bernard Berelson and Gary A. Steiner: "By this term is meant an aggregate of people, from two upto an unspecified but not too large number, who associate together in face-to-face relationships over an extended period of time, who differentiate themselves in some regard from others around them, who are mutually aware of their membership in a group, and whose personal relations are taken as an end in itself. It is impossible to specify a strict upper limit on the size of the informal group, except for the limitation imposed by the requirement that all the members be able to engage in direct personal relations at one time which means, roughly, an upper limit of around fifteen to twenty. If the aggregate gets much larger than that, it begins to lose some of the quality of small group or, indeed begins to break up into small sub-groups."

Examples of Small Groups

1. Committees
2. Forces
3. Families
4. Team
5. Athletic Team
6. School Cliques
7. Sub-parts
8. Fraternal
9. Workshops
10. Sub-groups.

Size of Small Groups: Small group means an aggregate of people consisting from two to unspecified, but not too large a number. It is difficult to establish any hard and fast rules to be applied to all situations to designate a small group. Different people have suggested different numbers for a small group. Unless the concept of small group with reference to size is understood, it is not possible to go further. The following are several opinions as to the number of members to constitute a small group:

(1) Bernard Berelson and his associate prescribe an upper limit of around 15 to 20.

(2) The most acceptable size according to M. E. Shaw is two or more persons.

(3) Myers and Myers prefer to count any number above one as a potential group.

(4) K. Davis states, in a group there is no such thing as only two people, for no two people can be conceived without their relationship, and that makes three.

(5) Hellriegel opines that a critical point of change seems to be about seven members.

(6) G. Manners suggests that for intensive decision-making, the ideal group size is from above five to twelve members.

(7) Huseman remarks that there does appear to be logical and empirical support for groups of five members as suitable size.

(8) In the Slater study, none of the subjects felt that a group of five was too small or too large to carry out the assigned task, though they objected to other sizes (two, three, four, six and seven). P. Slater in contrasting co-relates of group size concluded that size five emerged clearly as size group which from the subject's point of view was most effective in dealing with an intellectual task involving the collection and exchange of information

about a situation, the co-ordination analysis, and evaluation of this information, and a group decision regarding the appropriate administrative action to be taken in the situation.

(9) D. Foz in his study found that, a group of twelve or thirteen produced higher quality decisions than groups of six, seven or eight. There is no difference among the groups in the smaller size categories of 2 to 7.

(10) In a study of A. Paul Hare, relatively smaller groups of five takes less time to make decision than groups of twelve.

Merits and Demerits of Sizes

(1) The quality of small group and the deliberations of the group are not effective if the number is large.

(2) Many scholars in the field of small group research do not consider dyad — or two people — a small group.

(3) The size of the group tends to affect the way it works. Where the number of group rises about seven, communication tends to become centralised and controlled. In such a situation where the members may not have adequate time and opportunity to communicate effectively and directly with other members.

(4) A group with fewer members, say, less than 5, cannot represent directly of opinions and suggestions.

(5) The group of odd number can function effectively and directly with other members.

(6) If a size of group increases, it would have an impact on the organisation structure. If the size of a group increases from two or twenty members, a number of changes may take place in the performance and structure.

(7) In a large size, it would be difficult for the members to interact with all members at once.

(8) The leader of a group can effectively influence group performance in the case of small size by controlling members and proceedings.

(9) When the group is large, it is advisable for the leader to break into smaller groups. The decisions and ideas of the large group can be conformed in a large group. A large-size group manager should co-ordinate the activities of several sub-groups, which have separate informal leaders.

(10) There are more potential resources available in a large group. These resources could have a negative effect on the overall group performance if each sub-group focuses on looking for its own solution. A large group can be used for the purpose of communicating information, new policies, changes, procedures, plans etc.

(11) The manner of behaviour of a leader or a manager in a small group is quite distinct from that of a large group. The term "small group" is selected to make a distinction from the large group.

It may be concluded that there is no precise number to constitute a small group; what is desirable is that the group must be small. For this, no hard and fast rules can be formed. It must be small for face-to-face interaction, effective communication and everyone in the group should have the opportunity to communicate his view point. Therefore, it may appear that in the case of the problem-solving group, the optimum size is five. To achieve quality, speed, efficiency, and productivity, the size should be small with reference to the subject.

Effects of Group Size

The effect of group size increases as identified by B. Berelson and G. Steiner:

(1) The greater the demands on the leader, the more the leader is differentiated from the membership at large.

(2) The greater the group's tolerance of direction from the leader, the more centralised the proceeding.

(3) The more the ordinary members inhibit their participation, the less exploratory and adventurous the group's discussion.

(4) The less friendly group atmosphere, the more impersonal the actions and the less satisfied are the members as a whole.

(5) The longer it takes to get to the non-routine judgmental decisions.

(6) The more sub-groups (coalition) from within the membership and the more formalised the rules and procedure of the group.[1]

Characteristics of a Group

The concept of group, group information and group activities is not a new concept. But it is as old as family group. Even the epics speak about how people work together in a group. Families are the earliest form of group and group work. Since the birth to funeral, groups are formed and occupy an important place in social activities. A group as defined above is a collection of people with definite ideas, skills and interests, mutually interact and communicate with each other to achieve a definite goal. In every organisation, group meetings occur for the purpose of making decisions, sharing the information etc.

However, the following are the characteristics of groups:

(1) Interface: A basic feature of a group is interaction or interface with other members of the group for which groups occur. The members see and hear one another. They interact and communicate each other orally by paying attention to each other.

(2) Member Role and Leader Role: Members have their own roles. Similarly, the leader of the group has his own role to play. Group decision- making is effective only when there is a distinction between the roles of the members and the leader's role. The respective roles should be defined. Leader has a function of co-ordination of group members and controls the group process. There is no place for personal needs and motives for a leader but collective motives. The leader has to summarise facts, and information, integrate, stimulate thinking, creative awareness of members' problems and agree to a unified solution. A set of roles are identified in the continuous interaction process. The roles are consolidated and the members become differentiated from the leader. The members of a group become actively related to each other in their respective roles.

(3) Principle of Unit: There must be unity of purpose. Unity of purpose in group behaviour implies a condition of being one. A group exists for a purpose. A group without a purpose or causal group is simply a collection of people, say for instance people waiting for a bus or forming a queue at a cinema theatre for a ticket. There must be a common purpose and objectives for the group to transact. In organisations, groups occurs not at any place and at any time voluntarily and spontaneously. Every group has almost new information for the members for discussion and interaction. There is a formal purpose and contents in a formal group information.

(4) Norms: Norms are standards of behaviour formulated and enforced by the members of the group. Norms are developed by the group by interaction which provides an opportunity for codification of norms. The interpersonal relations and activities cannot be controlled and carried on without any norms. They govern the behaviour of the members which decide what the members have to do, or not to do under a given circumstances. Norms are limitations, and boundaries within which their interpersonal relations may be established.

(5) Interpersonal Attraction: Yet another characteristic feature of a group is interpersonal attraction. As long as interaction and interface continues, likes, dislikes, behaviour, temperament of the members are known to each other. It facilitates the development of network of interpersonal attraction on the basis of their likes and dislikes etc. Between them, empathy develops, mutual understanding grows, begin to share the common interest, forming an attitude of mutual help and as such, they share in each others' problems and become involved in risk taking activities.

F. E. Kast and J.E. Rosenzweig have listed the following characteristics of groups:

(6) Naturality: A group may have a high degree of naturalness. They remark that relatively permanent, spontaneous, informal small groups have a high degree of naturalness.

(7) Empathy: Members of the group have the feeling and ability to empathies with other members. A constant interaction over a long period of time gives scope to gain an insight into the value system of other members of the group. It is like putting onself in another's shoes.

(8) Pressure to Conform: Established standards formulated must be enforced and followed. In a group process, there is always an element of pressure to conform to the norms. Small informal groups indicate this evidence of conformity, in a continued face-to-face interaction, which provides an opportunity to make most people's behaviour an open book.

(9) Social Distance: F. E. Kast and his associate remark that one can deal at arm's length with the other members of large social groups or institutions. The idea of distance between interpersonal relations is an important feature of small groups. In a small informal group, social distance is at the minimum. This approach is also possible in dealings with positions in bureaucratic institutions.

(10) Cohesiveness: In a group behaviour, cohesiveness and commitment to the goals of an organisation is the basic characteristic. Cohesiveness is a group condition in which all the members of a group work together for the common goals. Every member in the group has to take the responsibility and initiative. It is quite possible to achieve a high group cohesion with a high degree of interaction between the members of a group. It is equally necessary to have a high degree of agreement and commitment to the organisational goals. Without cohesiveness, it is not possible to provide an opportunity to influence the behaviour.

There are active forces and positive forces at work on each individual. The forces which promote cohesion in the group are in a degree of dependence on the group, size, homogeneity, stable membership, outside pressure, competition etc. Group effectiveness and efficiency would depend upon cohesiveness and commitment to the organisational goals.

Group Co-hesiveness		
	+, − co-ordinated behaviour in dysfunc-tional directions	+, + co-ordinated behaviour in functional directions
	−, − unco-ordinated behaviour in dys-functional directions	−, + co-ordinated behaviour in functional directions
	commitment to the organisational goals.	

Fig. 11.2 Group Cohesiveness

(***Source***: F.E., Kast and J.E. Rosenzweig, *Organisation and Management — A Systems and Contingency Approach*, p. 293).

(11) Participation: The effectiveness and efficiency in the functioning of a group would also depend to a great extent upon the active participation of the members in the activities. Most of the research studies on group dynamics in recent years reveal that more the participation of members, the more is the effective functioning of the group. Some studies indicate that better participation leads to a higher morale or better labour-management relationship in addition to increased production.

(12) Conflict: It is a natural human tendency and social behaviour to develop conflicts with others. A conflict is a difference, disagreement, between the members of the group which often arise during deliberations. The conflict may have both functional and dysfunctional effect on members, group as well as on an organisation. A conflict is inevitably, but partly avoidable; usually develops when alternatives are present. George Simmel rightly states that group require disharmony as well as harmony, disassociation as well as association and conflicts within them are by no means altogether disruptive factors.

(13) Desire to Form a Group: It is a natural tendency that human beings have of strong desire to associate themselves with certain groups for the feelings of prestige and social distinction, i.e., in a way, it is for ego satisfaction. Positively, the groups invariably influence the thoughts and actions of individuals, while individuals achieve a sense of prestige and privilege through their formal and informal association with the group. The individuals become members of the group not only for status, but also for protecting and maintaining various other aspects like tradition, customs, togetherness, rights, responsibilities, technical expertise, faith etc.

(14) Leadership Development: Yet another important characteristic of groups is the need to develop leadership. There is probability for every member to develop leadership qualities by virtue of his association with the group. Generally, a leader develops and encourages others to develop leadership qualities.

(15) Awareness Among Members: It is quite natural that when a group is small, the members are psychologically aware of one another. Strengths, weaknesses, capacities, abilities, accomplishments, talents and needs of each talent and need of each member are known to others in the group. This permits the group to make use of each member according to his abilities and to rise to the occasion to fulfill the aspirations of its members. Every member working in a factory environment may naturally look for companionship, sympathy, appreciation and affection in his work life which solves the problems of monotony, boredom, and fatigue.

(16) Properties of Individuals: The group is alive like an individual. They are born: they grow, they function, they deteriorate and even die. The group has an attitude, approach and behaviour to other groups, individuals and to the organisation at large. Thus, groups maintain the properties of individual human being who are its members.

Theories of Group Formation

(1) Propinquity Theory: Propinquity theory of group formation is one of the popular theories which demonstrates that an individual affiliates himself with another because of spatial or geographical proximity. Closeness to one another in a work place is the basic force for the formation of a group. In an organisation people who are working in proximity are likely to form a group. They work, for instance, in the same room, plant, workshop, etc., for groups than those who are geographically located at a distant place in the same organisation. This theory has greater relevance for explaining group formation. The study of Leon Festinger and his associate revealed and supported the theory of propinquity.[2]

(2) Homan's Theory: George Homan's study of group formation is yet another important one. Activities, interactions and sentiments are the basic components of this theory. These components are directly related to one another and hence, it is more comprehensive theory of group formation. Internal system within an organisation consists of a group's activities and the members of the group are closely interrelated. Any change in one may result in a change in another group. There are both task behaviour and social behaviour in the activities. William G. Scott remarks that persons in a group interact with one another not in just the physical opportunity but also to solve problems, attain goals, facilitate co-ordination, reduce tension and achieve a balance.[3]

(3) Balance Theory: Balance Theory has been proposed by Theodore Newcomb in his *The Acquitance Process*. The basic theme of this theory is that individuals who are attracted more to each other on the basis of similar attitudes towards commonly relevant objects and goals. In a continuous work relations, employees are attracted to one another on the basis of their likes, dislikes and common tastes. Sportsmen will interact and form a relationship or group with other sportsmen because of common activities, tastes and attitudes. If the balance is disturbed due to any reason of conflict, an attempt is made to restore the balance. A group may lead to a dissolution if the balance account cannot be re-built.[4]

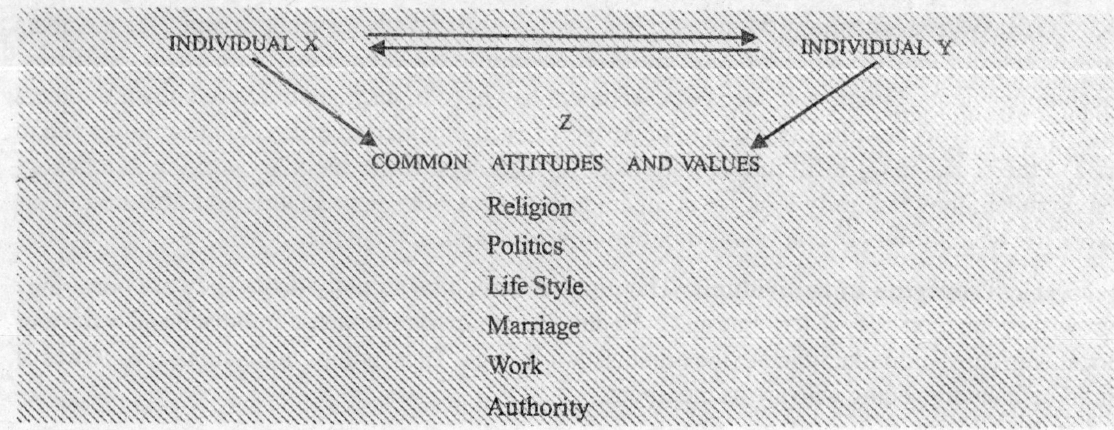

Fig. 11.3 Balance Theory of Group Formation
(*Source*: Adapted from Fred Luthans, *Organisational Behaviour*, p. 320)

(4) Exchange Theory: It is based on the motivation theory. This theory is based on reward-cost outcomes of interactions. This theory is proposed by J.W. Thibaut and his associate. The basic force for attraction or affiliation is reward or cost. The reward should be greater than cost. The cost components include anxiety, frustration, embarrassment, or fatigue while rewards from interactions gratify needs. This theory includes propinquity interaction and common attitudes.

(5) Other Reasons for Group Formation: There are many practical situations which provide reasons for joining or forming a group, for instance social, economic and security reasons.

Types of Groups

There are many types of groups. We propose here to discuss the important groups under the following paragraphs.

(1) Formal Groups: An organisational structure is a formal one, and the group emerging from a formal organisation is called a "formal group." A formal group has official backing and support; it functions under some formal rules and regulations and group becomes more like a small formal organisation. A precise and official group forming out of official requirement which is under control mechanism. Such formal groups follow all sorts of formalities, rules and procedures. Groups are formed through officially prescribed route. Thus, a formal group endeavours to achieve organisational goals, because it is a part of the structure of the organisation. Sections, departments, tasks force, project groups, counselling, enquiry committees, board of directors etc., are the formal groups.

(2) Informal Groups: An informal group is also called "grapevine." An informal group is formed on account of informal relationship between the persons. Small informal groups are formed based on work and social relationship. Such groups do not form part of the organisational structure and as such, their goals and activities do not relate directly to the achievements of stated organisational goals. There would be formally prescribed rules, procedures and regulations governing the behaviour of an informal group. There would be no scope for authority and control to exercise. Basically, informal groups are formed out of personal relationship, friendship, same group, membership of the same club, hailing from the same place, common studies, same qualifications etc.

They create situations where small groups are formed out of day-to-day dealings, working at the same workshop or office, often occur interactions and sentiments of the members. Informal groups are not only the most common in social behaviour but most commonly emerge in an organisational structure. The formal organisation plays an important role for the formation of informal groups. They are formed out of common interest, ranging from sports, friendship, people working in the organisation, from friendship groups in order to satisfy their needs and affiliation because the formal organisation structure does not satisfy some of their important social needs.

(3) Primary Groups: The concept of primary group was first introduced by Charles H. Cooley in his book *Social Organisation* 1909. He says: "By primary groups, I mean those characterised by intimate, face-to-face association and co-operation. They are primary in several senses, but chiefly in that they are fundamental in forming the social nature and ideals of the individuals." While George Homans is the second person to give treatment and refinement to the concept of primary group. According to him, a group is "a number of persons who communicate with one another often over a span of time, and who are few enough so that person is able to communicate with all the others, not at second hand, through other people, but face-to-face."

Though the two terms, primary groups and small groups, are used; interchangeably, truly speaking, there is a difference between them. The prescription of a small size is the basic criterion for a small group. The primary group should possess not only the quality of small size but also to have a feeling of comradeship, loyalty and commonsense of values among its members. Therefore, Fred Luthans remarks that all primary groups but not small groups are primary. Family and peer groups are examples of primary groups. Recent studies on group dynamics reveal that the primary group has no individual behaviour regardless of context or environmental conditions.

Blair J. Kolasa has identified the following four groups:

(4) Membership Groups: The individual members who actually belong to a particular group is called membership group. The organisational participants join a group in order to satisfy their needs and affiliation, for instance, joining a particular trade union.

(5) Reference Groups: The reference group is one with which he identifies or to which he would like to belong.

(6) In-Groups: The in-group represents a clustering of individuals prevailing in a society or at least having a dominant place in social functioning.

(7) Out-Groups: The out-groups are the conglomerates looked upon as subordinates or marginal in the culture.

Barnlund and Haimann identified the following types of groups:

(8) Casual Groups: Casual groups tend to occur by chance, not permanent, not regular and hence called "causal groups." Casual groups are formed without any fixed plan and purpose and emerges voluntarily, spontaneously to the situation. Members of the groups interact orally with ordinary talk, generally contains no new information. As a matter of fact, casual meeting is a foundation for information of informal groups in the organisation. Members of the group are quite established; warm, close relations, pave the way for ground work for more practical communication and overcome or fill silence or ward off loneliness or anonymity (Myers and Myers). There would be no rules, regulations, procedures, timings, control or authority over the process of group discussion. Any topic may figure in for interaction such as politics, sports, trade, hobbies, exchange of experiences, etc.

(9) Cathartic Groups: Cathartic groups can occur among the people who are in close contact and relations. The instances of forming cathartic groups are insinuations like college dormitories, class room, examination period, in industrial locker rooms, around water coolers, television, union meetings etc. The objectives of this group are to provide an opportunity to release feelings, tensions, reduce anger, to understand in a better way one's own motivations.

(10) Learning Groups: Learning groups tend to occur for the purpose of exchange and sharing of information. People come together for the face-to-face transmission of information. Learning groups are formed in educational institutions, conventions, conferences, symposia, seminars, training, orientations courses, lectures, quiz competitions, training groups, executive development programmes, management developing programmes. Thus, learning help the group's participating members to gather and exchange information and gives an opportunity for creative thinking. The learning group reflects:

(a) Expecting more results from members.

(b) Defining the problem clearly.

(c) The objectives to be achieved.

(d) Sharing more information or general knowledge.

(e) More specific preparation for the learning activity.

(f) Statements which are more relevant and better supported by data.

(11) Policy Making Groups: These groups can occur for the purpose of formulation of broad policy matter of objectives. The group frames policy in advance to be followed to avoid the occurrence of wrongs or mistakes. A policy is a written statement of guidelines formulated by the group for the guidance of the people working in the organisation. The members of this group are people empowered to make decisions or recommend the manner and the way of doing things. In other words, policy-making groups are formal, having official sanction, support and backing and function according to certain rules, regulations, procedures and agenda. This type of group is given enough powers to tackle over a task or problem and to take decisions. There are two types of policy- making groups:

(a) **Assigned Group:** Assigned authority and authorised to make a policy over a problem.

(b) **Assumptive Group:** Members themselves constitute a group, go to the situation and exercise control.

Interaction and communication will be characterised by:

(a) A greater sense of responsibility.

(b) Seriousness of purpose.

(c) Controlled and purposive communication.

(d) Critical appraisal of ideas and others.

(e) Attention to external restraints. (Myers and Myers)

(12) Action Groups: Opposed to policy making groups, action group endeavours to put the policy into force or effect. This group is formed to plan when and how to implement the policy. Democracy is defined as Government by committees. Government constitutes the policy-making groups on various subject matters.

(13) Integrating Groups: A special group constituted as one of the measures in managing intergroup conflict. The group may be an integrator department or individual. These groups manage the interdependence of various groups. A special group called integrating group, assumes the task of solving unresolved matters, to achieve tight co-ordination between the conflicting groups. The groups stand in an intermediate or arbitrator position between the conflicting departments which are highly interdependent. When conflicting groups are very different from each other in terms of goals, values, time span, structure etc., they require tight co-ordination. It is the special integrator who may solve intergroup conflicts, manage the interdependence of various groups and solve pending unresolved matters.

(14) Command Group: A group determined by the organisational chart, is a command line, the superior to whom the subordinates have to report directly. A sales manager and his 12 sales clerks and representatives form a command group as to the director, public relations officer and his 10 subordinates.

(15) Task Group: A group is formed for the purpose of accomplishing a given task. A group is formally and organisationally determined, will work together to complete a task. The group need not necessarily report to immediate hierarchical superiors. It can be beyond the structural relationships. Robbins writes, "It should be noted that all command groups are also task groups, but because task groups can cut across the organisation, the reverse need not be true."

(16) Interest Group: A group formed by the people who may or may not be aligned into common command or task groups. These people form a group and affiliate themselves to attain a specific objective with which each is concerned.

(17) Friendship Groups: People having some common characteristics may form a group. Groups often developed and formed are called "friendship groups." Such groups are based on age, hailing from same place, or educational institution, similar views, etc. These are some of the characteristics of friendship groups.

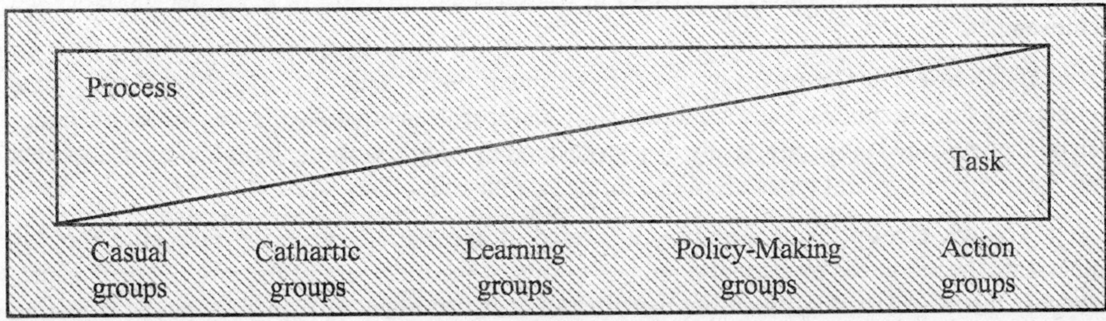

Fig. 11.4 Types of Groups

(***Source***: Adapted from Barnlund and Haimann, *The Dynamics of Discussion*)

(18) Coalitions: Coalitions are also very relevant to organisations. A coalition, as one of the types of groups, has been well-recognised in organisational behaviour. The following are the various characteristics of a coalitions:

(1) Interacting group of individuals.

(2) Deliberately constructed by the members for a specific purpose.

(3) Independent of the formal internal structure.

(4) Lacking a formal internal structure.

(5) Mutual perception of membership.

(6) Issue-oriented to advance the purpose of members.

(7) External forms.

(8) Concerted member action, acts as a group.

(19) T-Group: It is relating to sensitivity training and formation of T-Group. Various "training groups" are formed on the basis of sensitivity training. The main feature of the group is that the members of T-Groups reveal considerable amount of cohesiveness among them. Training groups have regard and respect for their trainers, whom they consider group leaders. The Institute for Applied Behavioural Sciences has recently introduced two training methods. The approach of the marathon group which may meet for an entire weekend without breaking for sleep. The second approach is a combination of spaced and massed approaches in which the initial session may begin with a live-in weekend, continue with weekly meetings and then conclude with a final live-in-weekend. These training methods facilitate the creation of better awareness, better sensitivity, cohesiveness, better identification skill, increased competence, mutual influence and co-ordination.

(20) Peer-Group: Peer-group is another effective form of group making, which cannot be ignored in the context of organisational behaviour. It is a sense of belonging among the workers towards one another, irrespective of their attitudes towards their superiors, on the basis of their membership in a particular work group. High peer-group loyalty is not necessarily associated with high productivity. Some studies reveal that high peer-group loyalty and common goals appear to be effective, in achieving the group goals. Similarly, high peer-group loyalty would reveal more favourable attitudes and approaches on the one hand and less anxiety on matters related to job on the other. High peer-group loyalty results in mutual co-operation and help, resulting in greater solidarity and achievement.

(21) Deliberate Groups: Groups formed intentionally and not by accident are termed deliberately formed groups. They are formed for a purpose in an organisation, so that certain things can be accomplished more effectively by a group than by people working individually. Cartwright and Zander found several types of groups formed deliberately. They are:

(1) Work Group: Work groups are formed to accomplish increased task efficiency by integrating the resources and coordination of efforts of the members of the group. For instance, groups in the case of work of assembly, can produce considerably more than workers endeavouring to produce the entire task.

(2) Social Action Group: An individual by himself cannot change the course of society. But it is possible to bring such changes when more number of people join hands. Small groups may be formed within the organisational changes like policies. Similarly, the entire organisation may form to change society.

(22) Mediating Group: Group conflicts may often arise in any organisation. The dispute or conflict may be between two small groups, departments or two separate organisations. In such a conflicting situation, a mediating group or a third group may be formed to mediate the conflicting group to resolve conflict.

(23) Legislative Group: Legislative groups are entrusted with the task of formulating policies, regulations, procedures and laws. The individuals under their jurisdiction have to follow them. It is like Parliament legislative laws formulated and made applicable to the country. In an organisation, the Board of Director is said to be a legislative group, formulates policies, regulations etc.

(24) Clilent Group: The other deliberate groups formed, as discussed above are concerned outwardly or directly trying to bring changes in their environment. Groups of this develop in response to some common need. Client groups are inwardly, directly trying to change the members themselves. The groups help their members facing a particular common problem. For instance, client groups are formed to solve the problems of alcohol, drug addiction, mental illness, obesity and other problems.

(25) Spontaneous Groups: Baird lists several types of groups formed spontaneously in any organisation. Such groups are formed out of members' own force or drive without any pressure from others. As such they are not created deliberately to solve their own problems or environment. For instance, informal groups like friendship, social clubs, juvenile gangs etc., are formed spontaneously. People join in a group because they are attracted by their certain common characteristics and behaviour. Research studies indicate several factors which are responsible for the formation of spontaneous groups. They are:

(1) Proximity: Geographical proximity, nearness to the workplace will give scope to individuals to form a group. Physical location is also important reason for attraction to each other. People working in the same room, workshop and lab are most likely to become friends than those who are working in a distance, office, room, lab etc. Seated neighbours in a college, class are more likely to become close friends than the students seated at the distant benches or the last benches.

(2) Similarity: Some studies also found that the individuals prefer to be closely attracted who have similar characteristics. So attitudinal similarity is the prime factor responsible for friendship choice. People with divergent opinions are generally less attracted to one another than the individuals having similar attitudes. Other determinates of similarity groups, as revealed by some studies, are:

(1) Individuals having similar personalities tend to be attracted to one another.

(2) Complementary rather than similarity of needs to produce attraction.

(3) Demographic similarity.

(4) Similarity of socio-economic status, race, and sex and promote interpersonal attraction.

(3) Prestige: It is an established fact that people tend to be more attracted to those who have a reputation or influence, rank, position etc. Membership in college activities, organisational governining body, exclusive social club etc., carries with it prestige or reputation.

(4) Group Activities: Authoritative research studies indicate that group or collective activities promote more attraction. Groups are formed spontaneously simply because to engage in those activities. When individuals discover that they all like to play chess, they form a group in order to engage collectively in that activity.

(5) Group Goals: Sherif and Sherif found that providing members of boys' summer camp with attractive group goals reduced intra-group conflicts and generally, increased interpersonal attraction. There is no clear distinction , between group activities and group goals. The study of Sherif and Sherif give scope for considering group goals as one of the factors responsible for spontaneous group formation.

(6) Instrumental Effects: Spontaneous groups are formed to obtain instrumental effects. The study of Rose is a pioneering one in this connection. This principle applies when the members of labour union join to achieve higher wages and greater job security. These are the rewards to be obtained from outside the group or labour union itself. Therefore, group membership is perceived as instrumental in achieving outside goals.

Reasons for Forming Small Groups

A question often arises as to why do people join groups? The reasons for their joining are many and there cannot be a single reason why individuals join groups. An individual may be a member in many groups at the same time. The reason for multi-membership is that different groups may provide different benefits to their members.

Research studies more accurate on group behaviour and communication have been undertaken. The incidence of group formation, group activity involving group process has increased enormously in recent years. Individual behaviour in social groups can be understood in relation with their activity, interaction and sentiments. There may be various factors for group development. However, the following are the most important reasons for formation of group:[6]

DISTINCTION BETWEEN FORMAL AND INFORMAL GROUPS

	Formal		*Informal*
1.	Formal groups grow purposely, deliberately to achieve certain objectives.	1.	Informal groups are formed voluntarily and spontaneously.
2.	Formal group relations are well defined and controlled.	2.	There is no formal structure, and relations. As such, not well defined and controlled.
3.	Authority is given by the organisation. There is delegation of power. There is authority, power, responsibility and accounting relations.	3.	No authority is given to the informal groups. In the organisation, they do not enjoy any described or specified power authority.
4.	Group has well prescribed route and channel for transmission of information. All messages pass through a channel of command.	4.	All messages pass through informal channels. There is only informal communication, as such there is no explicitly prescribed channel for passing messages.

5.	Behaviour of the members is governed by rules, regulations, procedures, manuals and other job instructions.	5.	Behaviour of the members is regulated by norms, values and beliefs. Relationships are governed by personal, psychological and social needs of the members.
6.	There is a status, determined by position or responsibilities of a job. Positions are rewarded by prestige, rank, status, pay and other perquisites.	6.	Status depends on feelings and sentiments of the members. There are no positions, recognition and rewards.
7	Group is rigid, inflexible and controlled.	7.	An informal group is flexible, loose, ill - defined and uncontrolled.
8.	A group can be converted into informal if the well defined structure, control and relationships are not enforced.	8.	An informal group can be converted into formal when their relationships and activities are explicitly defined and controlled.
9.	Formal groups are formed in big corporations, state and central departments etc.	9.	Clubs, dinner party, friendship, recreation groups, cultural and literary groups and other social meets are informal groups.
10.	Formal groups can be abolished as they are subject to management control.	10.	Informal groups cannot be abolished. Abolition of one of such group may lead to formation of several other groups. Formation of such groups are natural human desire to interact.
11.	Message is correct.	11.	Groups spread rumours, and incorect messages.
12.	Delay in message transmission.	12.	Network transmit messages quickly and with considerable speed.

(1) Security: There is a lot of difference for a person to be "'standing alone" and "in a group." Union is strength, group is strength. An individual who cannot achieve individually can do so through group. A group can afford security to the members of a group. A person who does not believe the strength of a group can reduce the insecurity of standing alone. A group gives strength and resistance to threats and feels secure. Individuals who are joining the organisation afresh would be benefited much from the group as they need more information, guidance, advice and support.

(2) Complexity: The complexity and size of society and its problem is a factor for group growth. These are days of specialisation and specialised professionals are being appointed in the organisations to handle a particular area of function. No single manager is expected to manage in all areas of company operations. Thus, there are today specialist in all areas like taxation, personnel, finance, marketing, production, public relations etc. All these people must involve in a group to arrive at a combined decision in some activities to achieve the objectives of the organisation.

(3) Status: A group will give a status and prestige to its members. The success of group efforts demonstrate the role that a group can play in giving prestige. People outside the group recognise and promote the status of their members.

(4) Changed Attitudes: There has been a clear evidence towards changed attitudes of the members of a group towards group participation. Employees started realising that they are loyal and better employees if they are allowed to participate in the activities. They need job satisfaction, information in order to make sound decision. One factor often expected is improved attitude. Some studies revealed the usefulness of group participation as a function of production.

(5) Self-Esteem: By joining a group, it makes the members feel much more important. It is the group which provides the people with feeling of self-worth and conveys status. Robbins states that membership can also give increased feelings of worth to the group members themselves.

(6) Distribution of Knowledge: In an organisation of collective responsibility and common objectives to be achieved with collective efforts in the organisational knowledge should be distributed, there are more people to know it. Group method facilitates exchange, interaction and communication. Multi media composed of written media, non-verbal media may be used for distribution of knowledge. The channels to be selected for transmission of information may be the formal channel vertical, horizontal, downward or upward, depending upon the circumstances of the situation.

(7) Affiliation: One may be individually and independently efficient and wealthy, but may not get any job satisfaction. Besides the work performance, an individual really likes to work with a group. Affiliation with the group makes the people enjoy the regular interaction that comes with only group membership. Interacting with the people working in an organisation can fulfill social needs. Affiliation with the work group contributes to the fulfillment of their needs for friendship and social relations.

(8) Advance of Scientific Method: These are the days of advancement of scientific methods of production process. Every field of knowledge has expanded and specialisation is the order of the day. Technologies are various types like unit or small batch technology, mass production technology and continuous process technology. They influence the relative importance of the group. The degree of group freedom and formation of a group depends upon advancement or otherwise of the scientific method. In some scientific methods there is need for a group and in some types of technology, there is little group freedom. In advanced scientific methods, there is higher interdependence.

(9) Dignity of Individual: In a work place of group of people, dignity of individual refers to the right of every person to be respected. Everyone in the organisation claims the right to know about the activities of the organisation. Every individual, as a matter of right, can ask opinions and bestow data as a resource. In recent years, the trend towards recognition of individual's right to know information has become necessary.

(10) Broadering of Knowledge: Another important factor for group growth is broadening of knowledge and skills in group dynamics which is a process of changing and adjusting. Myers and Myers say that as information about groups has grown, so has the ability to train people in how to improve their group skills.

(11) Awareness: Awareness of breadth of group interaction is a powerful factor in group growth. The group is mainly concerned not only with decisions but beyond formal things. "Groups spend almost half of their time dealing with the relations of members to each other, to the leader and their environmental constraints. The purpose of a group is divided between task and process consideration. Task includes getting a job done and process considerations include making it possible for us to work together as we get the job done.

(12) Power: The significantly contributing factor of group is that it represents power. A person cannot live on work in isolation for long. To achieve certain things, one must be associated with other employees; otherwise, he cannot individually achieve and cannot enjoy job satisfaction. Group is power and strength which protect themselves from management's undesirable activities. Informal relations give more opportunities for this. This is possible through group formation. Groups have power, formal position and authority.

(13) Goal Achievement: Goal achievement is not possible without group affiliation. A single person sometimes in respect of certain tasks cannot achieve the result. Task groups are created to accomplish a goal that cannot be achieved by a single person. Group facilitates to pool talent, knowledge, ideas and to get a task accomplished.

Stages of Group Development

S. P. Robbins has identified the following five stages for group formation. They are:

(1) Forming Stage: At this stage, the members are in search of persons having the same characteristics. Robbins writes that this stage is complete when members have begun to think of themselves as part of a group.

(2) Storming Stage: The second stage of storming is characterised by a great deal of inter-group conflict. The conflict stage is characterised by differences and disagreement over the contact of the group.

(3) Norming Stage: This stage reflects close relationship and cohesiveness. It represents a strong sense of group identity.

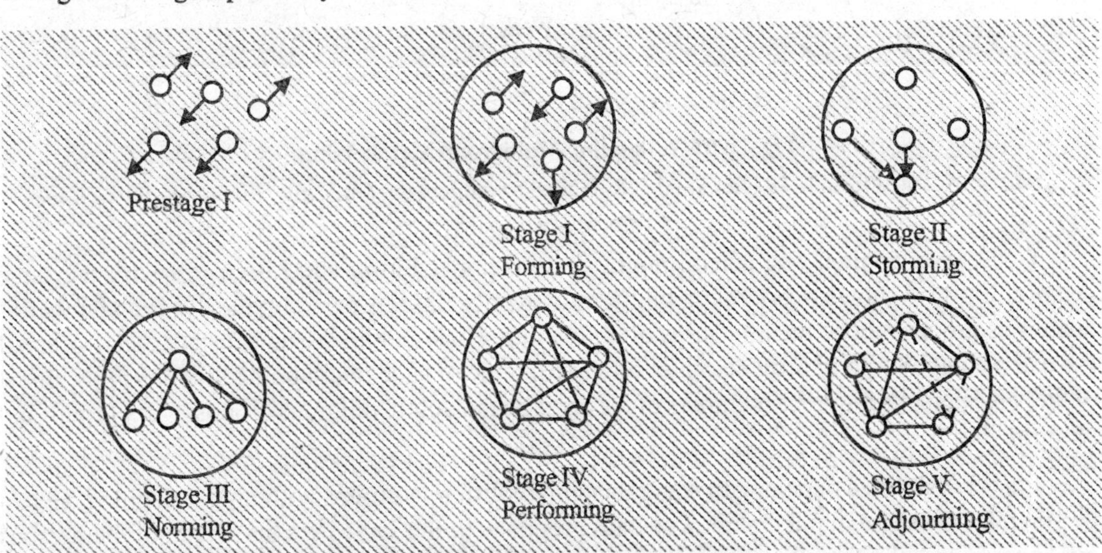

Fig. 11.5 Stages Of Group Development

(***Source***: Adapted from S. P. Robbins, *Organisational Behaviour*, Prentice-Hall of India, 1991, p. 278)

(4) Performing Stage: Robbins writes that "the structure at this point is fully functional and accepted. Group energy has moved from getting to know and understand each other performing the task ahead."

(5) Adjourning Stage: Actually, performing is the last stage in the development of groups. Robbins states that "for temporary committees, task forces, teams, and similar groups that have limited tasks, to perform, there is an adjourning stage. In this stage, the group prepares for its disbandment.

Multigroup Membership: There are two types of multigroup membership:

(1) Overlapping Multigroup Membership

(2) Multigroup Membership without Overlapping.

Hicks and Gullett developed an overlapping multigroup membership. A person may be a member of several groups. Sometimes, he may become a member of twenty or even more. It is common to come across a person to be a member of 8 to 10 groups. In such groups, there is possibility of overlapping multigroup membership and multigroup membership without overlapping.

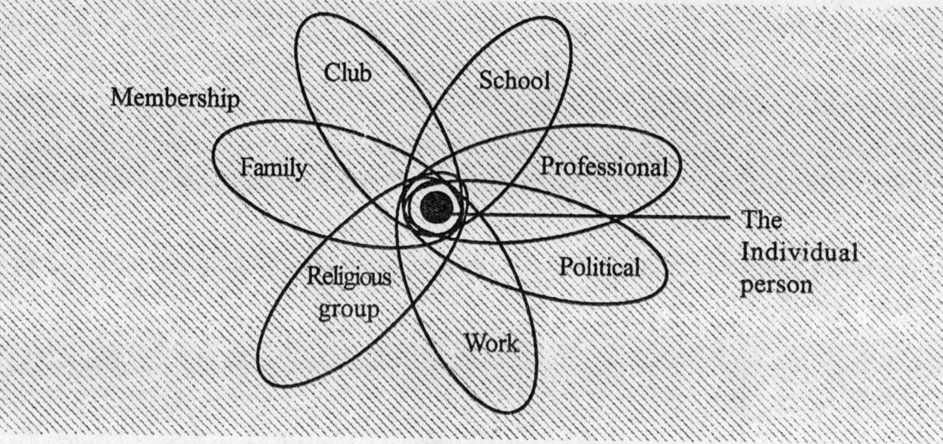

Fig. 11. 6 Overlapping Multigroup Membership

(***Source***: Adapted from H.G. Hicks and C.R. Gullet, *Management*, *McGraw-Hill International Book Company*, 1976, p. 189).

Under overlapping, one person might share membership in several groups with the same persons. Fig.11.6 shows overlapping multigroup membership. A person typically is a member of numerous groups whose memberships often overlap. Hick and his associate state that, "A small town or a neighbourhood provides an excellent example of such overlapping memberships. Some of the same persons might be members of the same school, club, religious groups, work group, and so forth."[8]

Fig. 11.7 shows a person with a membership of different groups without overlapping. Here a person may not share membership in several groups with the same persons. Some of the persons might not be members of the other groups. He may join with members of a new group who are not common members.

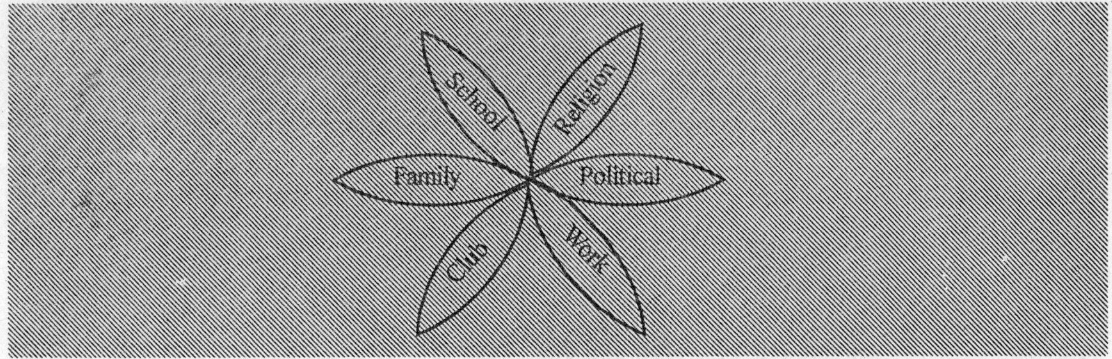

Fig. 11.7 Multigroup Membership Without Overlapping

COMMUNICATION NETWORKS IN GROUP SETTING

Bernard Model:[9] In every organisation, where groups are formed in order to transact some formally designed matters, certain types of communication patterns can be established formally. Formal pattern cannot be ignored where a group is headed by a chairman. Some patterns of network of communication exist not only when a chairperson is appointed but also where the physical arrangement of a layout of meeting hall establish relationship in a particular way.

According to F.E. Kast and his associate, even in these kinds of situation, communication pattern can evolve that support or transcend and subvert the supposedly established pattern. The analysis of communication processes in groups often reveals a communication "centre." In every small and formal group, it is quite possible to develop a variety of communication patterns.

Some of the research studies on communication in small groups reveal countless variations of communication patterns. For instance, take a group of five members, a different typical network arrangements emerge.

Bernard and his associate developed basic communication network in task-oriented small groups. Their network models are as follows:

(1) Wheel Pattern

(2) Y-Pattern

(3) Chain Pattern

(4) Circle Pattern

(5) Freeflow Pattern.

The network models are given below. The numbers given in each model refer to how many times that particular individual has been recognised as a leader. In other words, the numbers refer to the frequency of occurrence of recognised leaders at different positions in the various patterns.

(1) Wheel Pattern: In case of wheel network, the leader seems to emerge at the position of higher centrality. It is the hub of a wheel. In this type of network, communication flows upward to peripheral members (Fig. 11.8).

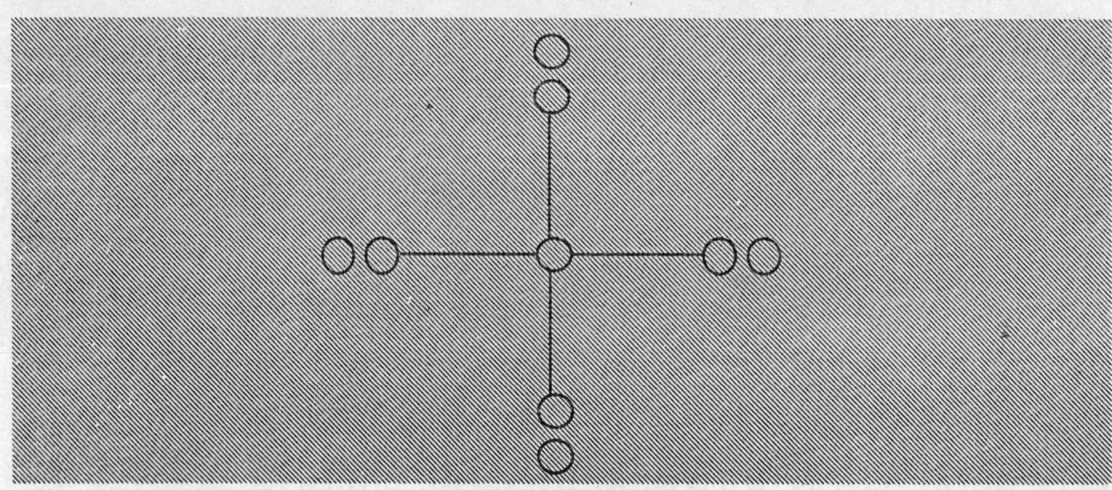

Fig. 11.8 Wheel Pattern

(2) Y-Pattern: Fig. 11.8, 11.9 indicates that a leader of a group seems to emerge at the position of the work. Y-type network is one in which top level strategic management, middle level tactical management involve in communication. In a vertical position, messages travel downward from chairman to the Managing Director, to General Manager, Deputy General Manager and functional head.

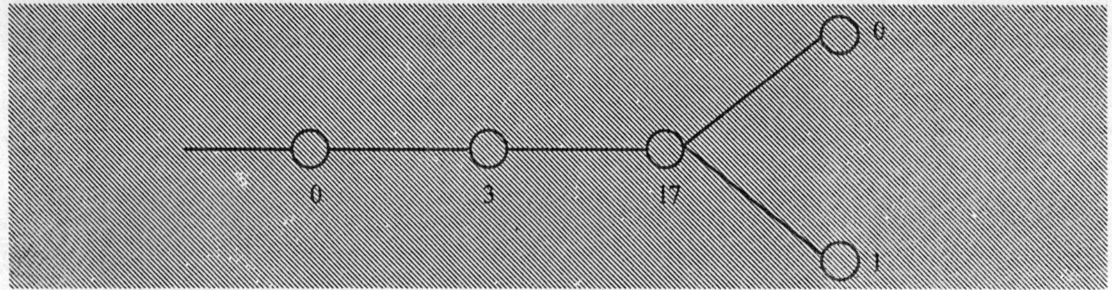

Fig. 11. 9 Y-Pattern

(3) Chain Pattern: In the chain pattern, the leader of a group seems to emerge at the mid-point of the chain. In its vertical position, the neighbours are in communication with each other. The first and the last person have no direct contact, hence cannot communicate, but through a leader (Fig. 11.10).

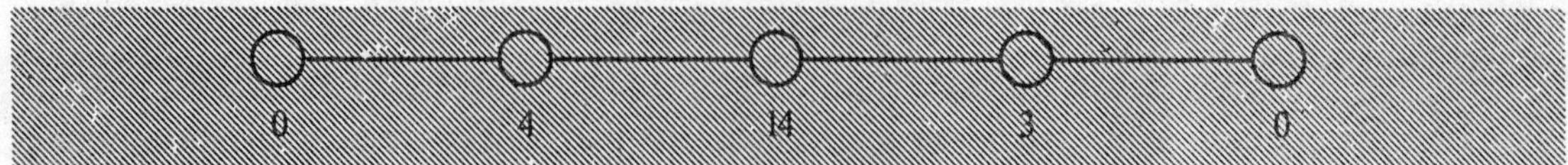

Fig. 11. 10 Chain Pattern

(4) Circle Pattern: Kast and his associate say that, "for the circle, forces other than the communication network obviously become more important in the evolution of the leader in the small group. "Circle or circular network communication permits at a time only two individuals in communication with each other. Under this model, each person can communicate with two persons. These are two neighbours.

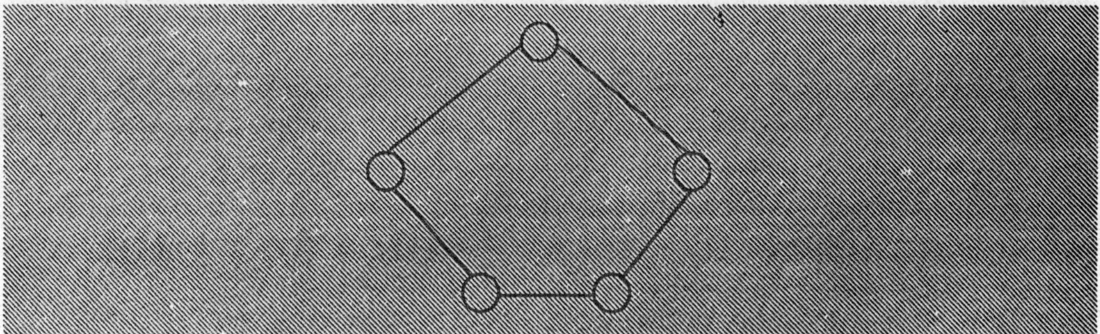

Fig. 11.11 Circle Pattern

(*Source*: Adapted from Bernard Berelson and Gray A. Steiner, *Human Behaviour*, 1964, p. 356).

(5) Freeflow Pattern: As the name indicates, it represents a communication network where everyone communicates with one another.

The communication pattern can be elaborated in a large number of ways. The communication may either be one way or two-way between any two of the individuals of group members. It is also possible that a particular individual may communicate on a two-way basis with members and on one-way basis with another. Thus, there exist combinations of several patterns. In one pattern, there may be combination of some elements of wheel and some circle. The sociometric analysis indicates the existence of a combination of several patterns within the primary group.

A communication in any network will be effective which has two-way communication pattern. The selection of one-way or two-way communication can be related to the decision in the group. For instance, an individual or leader may take a decision and communicate it to the group members. He communicates on the expectation that a particular action be carried out. Generally, what the listeners' hear, coincides with what the speaker says or writes.

In the earlier days, information is used to mean more downwards the hierarchy. But today, more sophisticated communication networks in the organisation have been developed due to the increasing differentiation and the growing need for integration required.

Hage *et al*., state thus: "As the organisational structure becomes more diversified and, in particular, as personal specialisation increases, the volume of communication increases because of the necessity of co-ordinating the diverse occupational specialists. The major direction of this increased flow of information is horizontal, especially cross-departmental communications at the same status level. As organisations become more diversified and more specialised (Personal specialisation not task specialisation) and more differentiated, they have to rely less on a system of programmed interactions to achieve the necessary linkages between parts of the organisation and more on a system of reciprocal information flows to achieve co-ordination. We have also suggested that such organisations would more likely rely on socialisation rather than the use of sanctions as a key mechanism of social control."

Today, communication is not only taking place upwards and downwards, but flowing horizontally and reciprocally between the various departments and sections. For instance, grouping of memoranda and the exchange of minutes of meetings.

Computerised information systems have provided means for more elaborate communication networks. Many organisations have created weekly or monthly newsletters designed to spread the word around concerning major problems, new policies and procedures and other informational items. By developing more effective communication networks, these organisations hope to create more willing and effective co-ordination of diverse activities (F.E. Kast *et al.*)

Traditionally, little importance has been given to communication in organisational theory. However, from 1930s, there has been an increasing emphasis on the vital role of communication. Transmission of image, feedback, control and intrapersonal interactions are the areas that indicate some idea of the broad range of communication concerns in a modern organisation.

Robbins' Model: S.P. Robbins' small group networks consist of the following networks:

(1) Chain Network

(2) Wheel Network

(3) All-Chain Network.

These three networks are given in Fig. 11.12.

Communication Network Structure

Shape indicates the communication network structure. It is the shape which is the basic characteristic of communication networks.

Baird states that these shapes are established through any one of the several processes. They are:

(1) Specification: Where organisational functioning demands that certain persons communicate with one another.

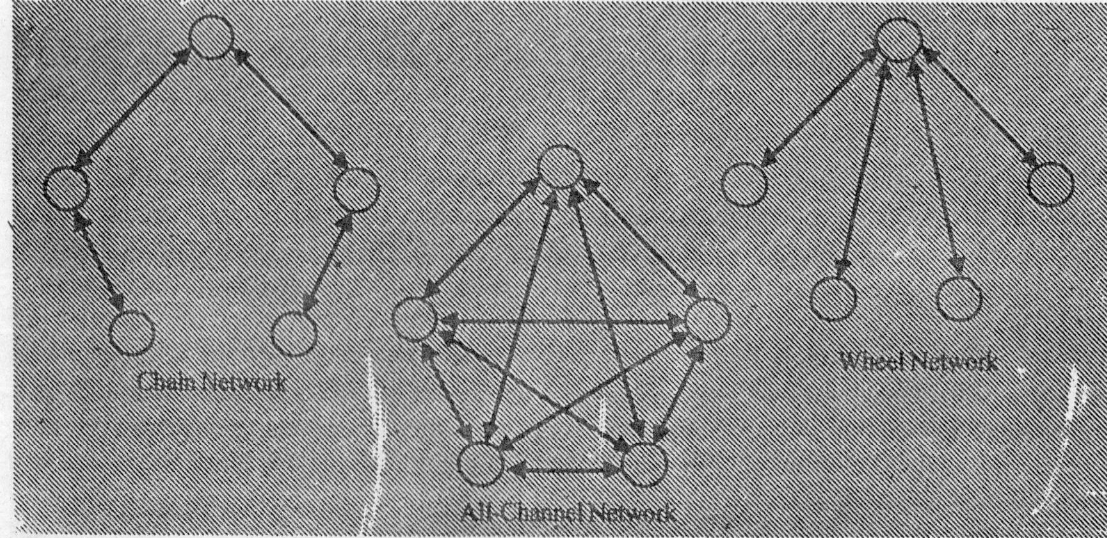

Fig. 11. 12 Small Group Networks

(*Source*: Adapted from S.P. Robbins, *Organisation Behaviour*, Prentice-Hall of India, 1991. p. 321).

(2) Physical Location: Where people in geographically close or proximity communicate with people, further apart do not.

(3) Friendship: Where people seek out certain others for communication, they find enjoyable. Age, sex, qualification etc., are the characteristics for friendship.

Three, Four and Five Persons' Networks: The network configuration for these persons can be established through any process like specification, physical location and friendship.

Fig. 11.13 shows typical network configuration for three persons, four persons and five persons networks.

Three Person Networks

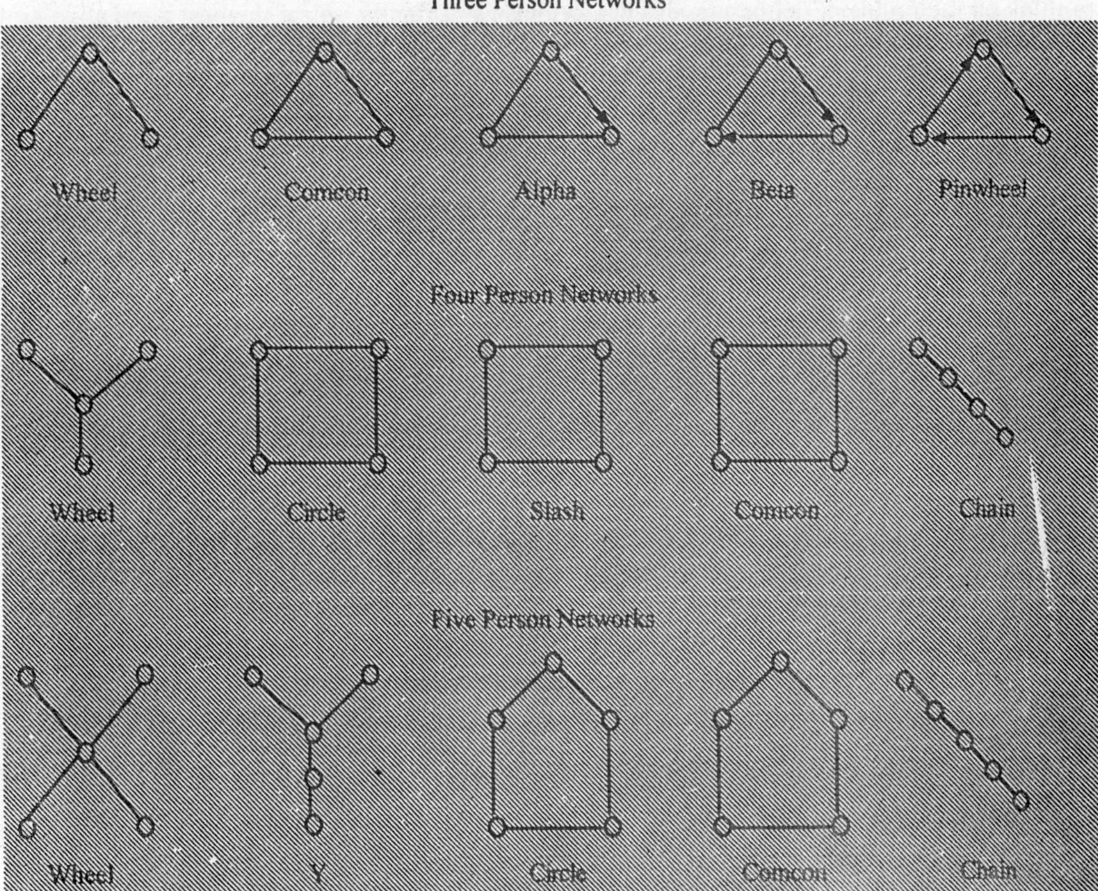

Fig. 11. 13 Typical Communication Networks

(*Source*: Adapted from *The Dynamics of Organisational Communication*, John E. Baird, J.R. 278).

Tree Structures of Wheel Networks

A study of MacKenzie has suggested that organisations generally consist of a 'tree' of wheel structured sub-groups. In this type, only a central person of a group on one level serves as a peripheral person in a group on the next level. It is the most common in any organisation. There are many reasons for the existence of tree structure in organisations.

According to him, there are two reasons:

(1) A wheel has the minimum number of channels necessary to connect the group.

(2) Resources like money and materials are limited and everyone wants to maximise his or her share.

Problem-Solving Group: A group is said to be problem-solving when a group is exclusively formed for the purpose of solving a problem of an organisation. Problems often arise in every organisation at every level and department and for them, solutions are needed. A group of small size is usually formed of five or seven members. The members drawn may have varied and wide experience, knowledge, expertise in different fields of work on a problem. It is the task of the group to think on the problem, deliberate, discuss, criticise and finally, select the best alternative as a solution to the problem.

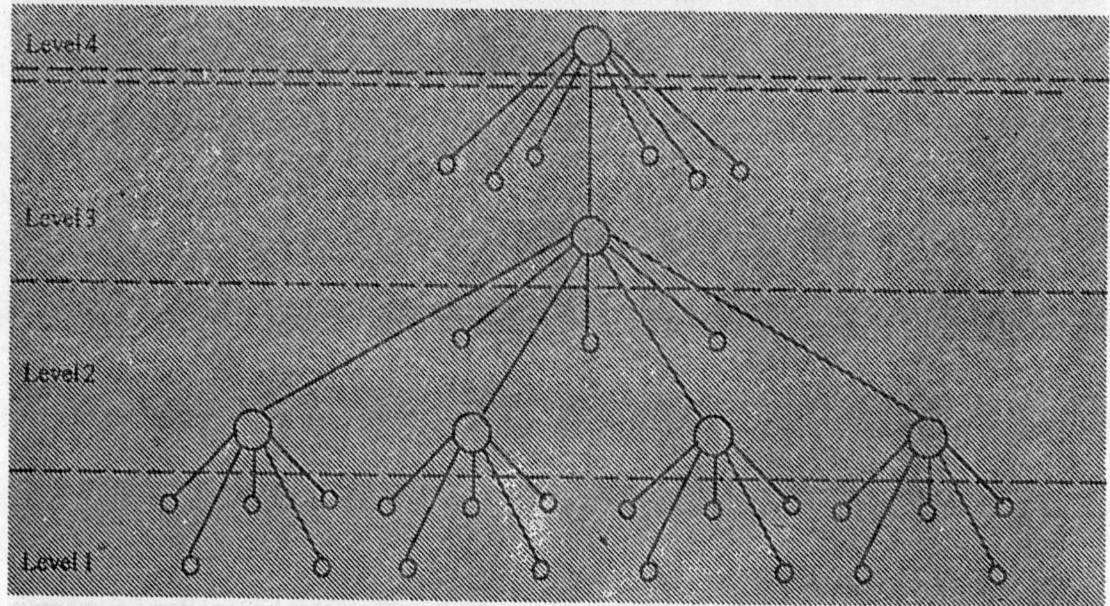

Fig. 11. 14 Tree Structure of Wheel Networks

(***Source***: Adapted from *The Dynamics of Organisational Communication*, John E. Baird, J.R. p. 285).

Groups formed for this purpose may take the form of:

(1) Task Force

(2) Problem-solving Group

(3) Committees.

(1) Task Force: A task group is a small group, consisting of members selected from among the organisational members concerned with the subject matter of the problem. Members may have varied and wide experience, knowledge, expertise etc. The task force after thorough deliberation select the best available alternative to the problem. Within the fixed time period, the task force should accomplish the task of problem-solving. When a task assigned to it on a particular problem, it is a problem-solving group. When something other than a problem is assigned, the members endeavour to work to do the job. The members share duties and responsibilities by breaking the task into various parts, assigned to different members, and finally all results are integrated.

(2) Problem-solving Group: A group of this type is especially formed to find a solution to a given problem. An organisation can operate through problem- solving group for making decisions and solving problems. The group recommends action to be taken for the implementation of the solution. The members of the problem-solving group are drawn from among the members having their work relationship and concerned with the problem. In actual practice and in certain cases, the solution worked out by them may affect the members personally of their work. To solve the problem of vested interest, it is desirable to select such members for the group who have a track record of objectivity and in a position to present different points of view.

(3) Committees: The most popular method is the committee system of organisation to solve the problem. A committee is a formally designated group. Theo Haimann and others define a committee as a group of people who function collectively. The committee after discussion of a problem recommends its suggestions for approval and implementation. A sub-committee or an *ad hoc* committee may be formed. As Urwick remarks, a committee is like a corporation with "neither a soul to be damned nor a body to be kicked." In a committee, minutes are taken but hours are wasted. A committee may be formal or informal. For instance, an accounts committee, marketing committee, finance committee. A committee may perform different functions like service, advisory, co-ordinating, informational, final decision-making, liaison etc. Its functioning is based on the principles that two heads are better than one head.

Group Cohesiveness — Productivity and Performance

The term "cohesiveness" means to stick together in a group situation. It is a group condition or situation in which all the members of the group endeavour to work together to accomplish a common goal. A higher degree of interaction between the members of the group would lead to a high group cohesiveness. Performance and productivity are higher in the case of a cohesive group. Where there is no cohesiveness, there is wide variation in performance. On the other hand, the degree of cohesiveness promotes high control over the level of performance by individual members.

There are many variables which may force to bring about cohesion in the group. They are:

(1) Degree of dependence on the group

(2) The size of group or cohesion

(3) Homogeneity and stable membership

(4) Freedom from outside pressure

(5) Competition between members

The following variables determine cohesiveness:

(1) External Pressure: Cohesiveness is affected to the extent to which external pressure takes place. Some research studies reveal that group cohesive ness increases if the group comes under attack or threat from outside. Under these circumstances, members generally move closer together towards greater cohesiveness when threatened by external agents.

(2) Time Factor: Time spent with members is an important factor for cohesiveness. If the members usually or regularly get an opportunity to meet and interact with each other, they are likely to be attracted. The time spent on interactions with the people in the group promotes cohesiveness. As such, they meet each other, they become more close and friendly.

(3) Size of the Group: The size of the group is also one of the determinants of cohesiveness. It can be affected by the number of the members in the group. It is a natural character that the degree of cohesiveness decreases as group size increases. In a large size group it is a difficult task for all the members to interact with everyone and one cannot spare more time.

(4) Degree of Initiation: Robbins writes that the more difficult it is to get into a group, the more cohesiveness pattern typically put their pledges he is meant to screen out those who do not want to pay the price.

(5) Past Success: Group's cohesiveness tends to increase on account of their previous success. The past relations, previous successes attract and unite members.

(6) Leadership Style: Different leaders exhibit different styles. The different styles of leadership influence the group cohesiveness differently. An effective leader keeps the members of the group close by helping them satisfying their social needs.

(7) Management Behaviour: There is a direct positive correlation between manager's behaviour and cohesiveness. The behaviour of a manager has a direct influence and bearing on the degree of cohesiveness that exists within the group. A close relation is a difficult task, by creating competition among employees and by constantly comprising one employee with another. It is quite easy for a manager to build solidarity by rewarding co-operative behaviour. The task or goal of the organisation can be achieved by utilising group cohesiveness.

(8) Degree of Autonomy: It is a character of a group of individuals who may have dependent or independent function with other groups and thus will have different structure. When each individual of a group has independent and different activities, then the cohesiveness among the members of the group will be less when compared with the group whose members are doing the operations which are dependent upon each other.

(9) Proximity: Geographical proximity or nearness plays an important role to enhance cohesiveness. Therefore, location of the group is to be recognised. On the other hand, isolation from other groups of workers tends to build high cohesiveness. If there is no dividing line between one group and another, cohesion is more difficult to achieve. In case where members of a group are located close together, they will develop greater cohesiveness because of constant face-to-face interaction.

(10) Communication Skills: When the members of a group are located close together and can interact frequently and easily one likely more cohesive. The people tend to develop their own language and symbols and codes to communicate with group members. As a matter of fact, one of the determinants of group cohesiveness is the speed with which messages can be transmitted through the group.

(11) Nature of the Group: Homogeneous membership promotes cohesiveness. Heterogeneous groups, i.e., members who have different interests and backgrounds, are often less effective in promoting their own interests than groups whose members are more homogeneous. Homogeneous groups whose members are alike on factors like age, education, status, experience, background etc., are better. This is particularly in the case of task or goal which requires mutual co-operation and conflict-free behaviour.

There may be disruptive and constructive forces. But there should not be any disruptive forces on group cohesion for effective performance. On the other hand, there are many factors that motivate individuals to performance. H. Bonner writes that:

"Our brief analysis of the role of motivation in productivity reiterates and confirms what the greater bulk of research on motivation in industry has been out: Motivation is not wholly — nor even primarily — an individual variable. Certainly, its force and direction are functions of the social situation in which it arises and is exercised."

It is a behavioural aspect that the effective work groups are always cohesive. Non-cohesion groups are ineffective relatively. If there is an internal disagreement between the members and lacks co-operative spirit, the group may be proved to be not effective. On the other hand, cohesiveness is the degree to which members are attracted to one another and share the group's goals. The performance and productivity of the group is more, provided if the members are attracted more than one another. This may also result in achieving individual goals.

After having understood the variables of cohesiveness, it is easier for us to conclude that group cohesion increases on account of the time spent together, severity of initiative, group size, external pressure and previous success. From productivity and management point of view, increased cohesiveness has an important role.

Effective Group and Performance: Flieshman' s study reveals that higher cohesive groups are more effective than those less cohesive. It may be mentioned that it is true if cohesiveness is more, their relationship becomes complex also. Robbins writes that high cohesiveness is both a cause and outcome of higher productivity. Secondly, relationship is moderated by performance related norms. Norms are established and accepted standards of behaviour which are shared by the group members. They indicate the expected behaviour of the members, by which what the members ought to do or what not to do under certain circumstances.

Norms and Performance: Norms are accepted by all the members of a group, and as such they are binding on all of them; they influence the behaviour of the group, demand no extra external control. Some organisational literature like manuals also contain norms. It means they are formalised. As against several norms, the most popular norm is to deal with performance-related process. Work groups prepare and provide their members clear ideas or hints on how they should work, how to get the job done, level of performance, achievements, suitable communication channels etc. According to Robbins, "These norms are extremely powerful in affecting employee's performance — they are capable of significantly modifying a performance prediction that was based solely on the employee's level of personal performance."

Interrelationship

It is evident that there are some interrelationships between cohesion and productivity. He rightly says that cohesion influences productivity and productivity influences cohesiveness. On the other hand, cohesiveness and productivity depend upon the performance related norms, which are established, binding and accepted by the group. Accomplishment group task is easy when the group is cohesive. If the norms governing group activities are high, the group would be more productive than a group with less cohesiveness. The important rationale requires is that performance related norms should be high. If the norms are not high, productivity will be low, even though cohesiveness is high.

Robbins writes that if the cohesiveness is low and performance norms are positive, productivity increases but less than in the high cohesiveness — high norms situation. Where both cohesiveness and performance-related norms are low, productivity will tend to fall into low-to-moderate range.

Performance Norms	COHESIVENESS: High	COHESIVENESS: Low
High	High Productivity	Moderate Productivity
Low	Low Productivity	Moderate Productivity

Fig. 11. 15 Relationship Between Group Cohesiveness, Performance Norms and Productivity

Factors Affecting Performance

There are many factors which may positively and effectively affect the performance of an individual in a group of given task. Among them, the important are as follows:

(1) Social Factors: One of the variables that affects individual performance in a group is a factor which is social in nature. Such a factor is prestige or recognition.

(2) Working Conditions: The importance of physical working conditions cannot be overemphasised as they are individually-oriented feelings such as safety or monetary rewards.

(3) Competition: Competition is another important factor that affects performance of the individual. Competition may be between one individual and another as well as among others. There are a number of studies on competition and performance of the group of people. The study permits to make comparison of individual normal solitary performance with his performance when other people are present. Allport's study reveals that group situations produce a greater output of energy and achievements.

(4) Ability: The fitness to the job is the major factor for an individual's performance. It influences directly and greatly. The selection process should be good enough for selecting suitable people. The right person to the right job is the guiding principle.

(5) Learning: Imparting knowledge is a powerful factor for changing the behaviour of the persons. Clarifications, explanations, on levels of productivity, quality of work, tools, etc., would give insight into the behaviour.

(6) Role Perception: Verney in his study on Role Perception Congruence Performance, and Satisfaction found that there is a positive relationship between role perception and an employee's performance evaluation. Superiors can judge the effectiveness of the employees. The congruence that exists between them decide the degree of perception.

(7) Norms: The established and accepted standards towards the behaviour show the relationship to performance. If the norms are high, individual performance is higher and *vice versa.* If the cohesiveness and performance related norms are both low, performance tends to fall.

(8) Size: The impact of the size of the group plays an important role in the performance of the employees. Robbins rightly says that "larger groups are more effective in fact finding activities, smaller groups are more effective in action taking tasks." If the management uses larger groups, efforts should be made to provide measures of individual performance within the group.

(9) Personality: Studies on personality reveal personality characteristics which tend to be related to job success.

To Sum Up

It may be concluded that cohesiveness plays an important role in influencing a group's level of performance, whether, it depends on the group's performance-related norms or not. The common factor is the relationship between communication and employee's performance. The distortion that takes place in the process of communication, the more the goals, feedback and other management messages to employees will be received as they were intended. (J.P. Walsh *et al.*)

Thus, group communication improves performance, when a multi-media channel approach is adopted by using downward, upward, lateral and informal channels of communication which reduce uncertainty etc. Some studies reveal that there exist a positive relationship between effective communication and work productivity. Human factors that generate distortions should be eliminated. Selection of the right channel, avoiding jargon as far as possible, and effective utilisation of feedback etc., make communication more effective. The receiver should understand the message in its real spirit which determines performance.

GROUP THINK AND GROUP SHIFT

In group decision-making, there are, two by-products. They are: (1) Groupthink (2) Groupshift.

These two by-products have considerable potential which may affect the group's ability to appraise alternatives whether to make quality and sound decisions.

(1) Groupthink: Groupthink is related to norms. It takes the form of exercising group pressure for conformity. The phenomenon may deter the group from appraising unusual, minority and unpopular views. Groupthink is an epidemic that sweeps like a summer storm that attacks many groups. As we have observed, groupthink hinders performance. In this, the members of the group are the victims of groupthink. Groupthink is the most important decision of formally designed group. The use of groupthink in modern management has been increasing. Small groups have been central to the groupthink decision-making in most meetings. A group can function well when there is cohesiveness.

S.P. Robbins says that you may have been a victim of groupthink, the phenomenon that occurs when group members become so enamoured in seeking concurrence that the norms for consensus overrides the realistic appraisal of alternative courses of action and full expression of deviant, minority are popular use. It describes a deterioration in the individual's mental efficiency, reality, testing and moral judgements as a result of group pressure.[10]

All groups are not vulnerable to groupthink. Highly cohesive groups have more discussions and bring more information. Groups with impartial leaders discuss more alternatives. Leaders should avoid expressing preferential solutions. Insulation of the group leads to alternatives generated and evaluated.

Origin

The book, **Victim of Groupthink**, by Irving Janis (1972) has given, for the first time, a critical treatment on groupthink.

Meaning and Nature

A dysfunction of highly cohesive groups and committees is called groupthink. He defines groupthink as "a deterioration of mental efficiency, reality testing and moral judgement that results from in-group pressures." It thinks groupthink may occur from the pressure on individual members of the group to accept and reach a consensus. Members of a group of committee are forced on reaching a consensus on an agreement on a particular issue. As such, in the process, there would be no scope for the members for a realistic appraisal of alternative course of action before arriving at a decision.

Groupthink usually occurs in group or committees both in Government decision-making and also in business firms or any other type of organisation. A group may make a risky and dangerous decision than individual members would act alone on their own. The members become complacement which may ultimately lead to secure their decisions. Group's collective decision enables them to deny moral responsibilities. Illusion of unanimity creeps into the group, as a result, members do not express and put across their views, points, doubts, opinions. The words like "we and they" which are often used provide for scope for boating practices.

Groupthink, however, does not mean that the members of every cohesive group become victims of groupthink and faulty decisions. It has been rightly remarked "when a hundred clever heads join a group, one big nincompoop is the result."

Thus, the term "groupthink" is used to connote the detrimental aspects of group pressure on the members to arrive at a consesus. Because of the seeming unanimity in the group, the members do not express their doubts on their alternatives chosen. Janis examines the decision-making process in major fiasces at the higher level of U. S. Government. His study is mainly concerned with groupthink in Government decision-making but subsequently he studied the existence of groupthink in business organisations also. He remarks that through the use of vivid details, faulty decisions are reached by highly competent, intelligent people in group decision-making. The concept of group think of Janis has become more popular in various disciplines. The phenomenon of groupthink has thus become more relevant to business organisations. So it is always desirable to eliminate the effect of groupthink in small group decision-making. Groupthink means decisions reached by a group of rational, knowledgeable and experienced individuals which turns out to be irrational and poorly formulated. Groupthink always occur in a cohesive group where the members have positive feeling towards each other and want to remain members of the group. Myers and Myers say that groupthink is a major problem with groups or committees. They remark that a "sense of solidarity encourages the group to seek agreement and prevents it from seriously considering problems which might have consequences that 'rock their boat', the 'boat' being a 'happy ship.' In this way, members of an overly cohesive group fail to use critical thinking."

There are a number of variables which are responsible for group cohesiveness such as friendliness, co-operation, interpersonal attraction etc. Group cohesiveness is characterised by various variables which exert a strong influence on the members of the group. Some studies show that cohesive group members are thus motivated to respond positively to others in the group. (Shaw) Stein's studies indicate that internal cohesion may result from external conflict. The variables which influence cohesiveness are good symptoms in certain cases and beneficial to sound small group decision-making.

Symptoms of Groupthink

The following are the symptoms of groupthink according to Janis:

(1) An illusion of invulnerability, shared by most of the members, creates excessive optimism and encourages taking extreme risks.

(2) Collective efforts to rationalise in order to discount warnings which might lead the members to reconsider their assumptions before they recommit themselves to their past policy decisions.

(3) An unquestioned belief in the group's inherent morality, inclining the members to ignore the ethical or moral consequences of their decisions.

(4) Stereotype views of the enemy (opposition) leaders as too evil to warrant genuine attempts to negotiate, or as too weak and stupid to counter whether risky attempts are made to defeat their purposes.

(5) Direct pressure on any member who after a strong argument against any of the group stereotypes, illusions or commitments, making clear that this type of dissent is contrary to what is expected of all loyal members.

(6) Self-censorship of deviations from the apparent group consensus, reflecting each member's inclination to minimise to himself the importance of his doubts and counter-arguments.

(7) A shared illusion of unanimity concerning judgements conforming to the majority view (partly resulting from self-censorship of deviations, augmented by the false assumption that silence means consent).

(8) The emergence of self-appointed mindguards — members who protect the group from adverse information that might shatter their shared complacency about the effectiveness and morality of their decisions.[11]

The variables of cohesiveness, symptoms of groupthink and defects are indicated in the groupthink model.

Therefore, it is a glaring pervasive phenomenon that the members are reluctant to voice a counter-argument in a cohesive group. This type of attitude on the part of members of the group may lead to groupthink.

"The more actively the leader of a cohesive policy-making group promotes his preferred solution, the greater are the chances of consensus based on groupthink, even when the leader does not want the members to be yes-men and the individual members try to resist conforming.

The work of victims of groupthink suggests that "the more amiability and *esprit de corps* there is among the members of a policy-making group, the greater the danger that independent critical thinking will be replaced by groupthink."[12]

From the above discussion, it is clear that social forces influence individual attitudes and behaviour. Group pressure definitely affects decisions about individual goals. Actions are also affected significantly by pressure.

Overcoming Groupthink

After having examined the phenomenon of groupthink in the decision-making process, let us now process to examine some of the ways to overcome groupthink. The following are some of the suggestions given by Janis for overcoming groupthink.

Janis Measures

(1) The leader of a decision-making group should assign the role of a critical evaluator to each member.

(2) The leaders in an organisation's hierarchy, when assigning a decision- making mission to a group, should be impartial instead of stating preferences at the outset.

(3) Members of the decision-making group should frequently seek advice and counsel from trusted associates in their own department within the organisation.

(4) The consensus - seeking tendency could be thwarted effectively by the use of a devil's advocate at each meeting of the group that deals with decision-making.

(5) After reading a preliminary consensus about what seems to be the best alternative, the decision-making group should hold a "second chance" meeting at which every member is expected to express as vividly as he can all his residual doubts and to rethink the entire issue before making a definite choice.

Other Measures

The potentially disastrous effects of groupthink can also be solved by adopting the following measures:

(1) Free expression.

(2) Recognising minority.

(3) Avoiding minority oppression.

(4) Recognising unpopular viewpoints.

(5) Discussion of each proposed alternative course of action.

(6) Members' viewpoints should be exchanged and encouraged.
(7) Freedom to explore all opinions to all members.
(8) To keep open communication.
(9) To maintain two-way and free flow of communication
(10) Understanding future responsibilities and risks.
(11) To maintain equilibrium in the group interaction process.
(12) Encouraging critical and creative thinking.
(13) Not to persuade consensus while making a decision.
(14) Motivate involvement.

Kasts, *et al.* remark that positive steps can offset the groupthink phenomenon. They offered the following characteristics or features that an effective group should have:

(1) The leader encourages each member to be a critical evaluator.
(2) The leader (and key members) should be impartial in the early stage of deliberations.
(3) The same problem is assigned to outside groups, who put results.
(4) At intervals, before a consensus is reached, each member tests proposals on subordinates and reports the results.
(5) Outside experts are invited in and encouraged to challenge views of key group members. (Daniel S. Greenberg)
(6) At every meeting, someone is assigned the role of the devil's advocate.
(7) There is explicit empathy with rival (nation or organisation) to anticipate consequences of actions.
(8) Sub-groups are used to get more involvement than differences are addressed in the total group.
(9) After a consensus is reached, a follow-up meeting should be held (time permitting) in order to allow second thoughts and residual doubts to be aired. (Janis)

(2) Groupshift: Groupshift is a special case of groupthink. One of the byproducts of group decision-making is groupshift. The concept of groupshift in recent years has received a very important attention in the organisational group communication. It affects the group's ability to appraise alternatives to arrive at quality and sound decisions.

S.P. Robbins states that, "It indicates that in discussing a given set of alternatives and arriving at a solution, group members tend to exaggerate the initial position that they held. In some situations, caution dominates, and there is a conservative shift. More often, however, the evidence indicates that groups tend towards a risky shift."[13]

Differences are bound to be there between group decisions and individual decisions within the group. Some studies indicate that in some cases, the group decisions are more conservative than the individual decisions. According to the study of N. Kogen and his associate, the shift is towards greater risk. In a group meeting discussions may lead to a significant shift in the position of members. The shift is towards a more extreme position in the direction towards which they were already leaning before the decision.

The decision of the group reflects the dominant decision-making norms that develops during the group's discussion, whether the shift in the group's decision is towards greater caution or more risk depends on the dominant prediscussion norms.[14]

On the other hand, R.D.Clark says that the greater occurrence of the shift towards risk has generated several explanations for the phenomenon. The usual tendency is that discussion motivating members to show that they are at least as willing as their peers to take risks. There is always a shift tendency towards risk. A group always diffuses responsibility. "Group decisions free any single member from accountability for the group's final choice. Greater risk can be taken because even if the decision fails, no one member can be held wholly responsible."[15]

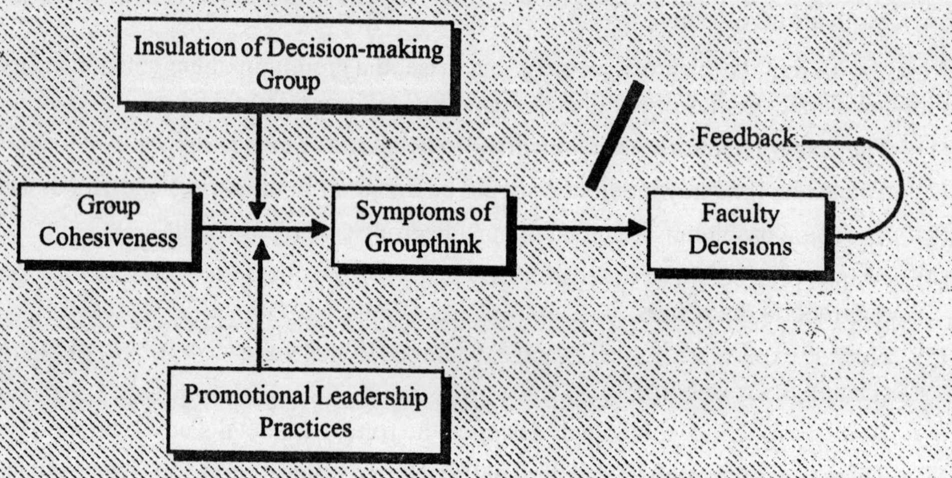

Fig. 11. 16 Groupthink Model

(***Source***: Adapted from R.C. Huseman and A.B. Carroll, *Readings in Organisational Behaviour*, p. 102).

Internal and External Communication within Small Group

(1) Internal: Internal communication within the small group takes the form of transmission of information between the management and small group. In general, in every organisation, there exists a systematic communication with different channels and selected media. The channel of communication may consist of downward, upward, horizontal and diagonal communication. Similarly, in every organisation there exists a pattern of internal communication within the small groups.

The internal system-orientation to the management of communication with reference to small group management inclu les:

(1) Sentiments

(2) Activities

(3) Interactions

(4) Norms.

The external system plays an important role in the development of internal system consisting of sentiments, activities, interactions and norms. The internal system will never develop by itself independently and automatically. The internal system depends on the external system. In fact, the conditions would have existed outside before the internal system came into being. It is the external system which forms the source for the development of internal system which represents the conditions as given.

The external system works as a coaching staff. There exist invariably active interactions between groups, internal and external. Internal groups or informal groups cannot be formed without an external system. The formal organisations have considerable impact on the formal groups. There would be a good amount of power in the internal system — an individual member and his behaviour, which may vary from one situation to another.

The internal system plays a powerful role in the day-to-day behaviour of the members and their interaction. The basic feature is that the internal system influences only among the people who interact. For instance, members who travel with others, members who live together etc.

In every formal organisation, a group is a system within the structure. The internal system pre-supposes the existence of group or groups, and group activities, norms, sentiments and interactions. These variables are positively inter-related. For instance, a change in the behaviour of one of the members could bring about a change in the behaviour of other members. A group is a system which is not just a sum of member behaviour.

An internal system orientation to the management of communication within the small group is given in Fig. 11.17.

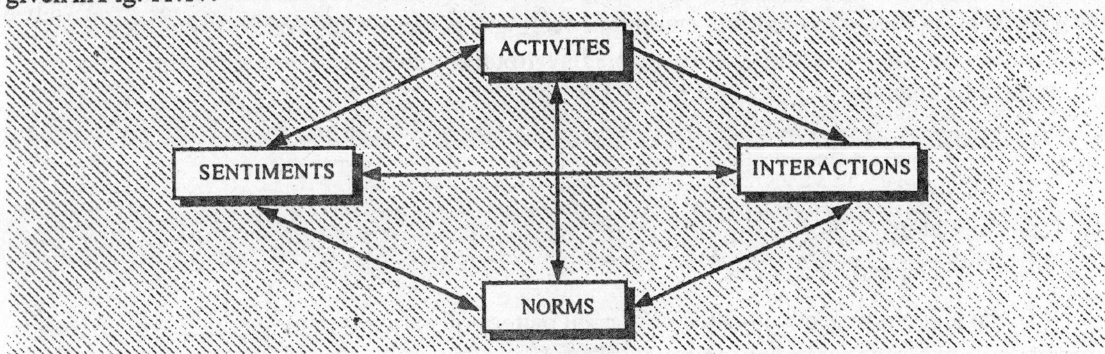

Fig. 11. 17

(***Source***: Adapted from Don Hellriegel and John Slocum, *Management*, p. 600).

The following is a brief description of the components of the internal system.

(1) Activities: Group process involves activities. Every member in the group is expected to do individually or to do with others. Members, in addition to doing things with others, have to do with inanimate objects also such as a machine, tools, materials etc. The activity variables are important which reflect task behaviours like analysing problems, evaluating alternatives and making decisions. The Homans systems Model cover these activity variables. The superiors have to spare a major part of their time primarily on task-oriented activities. For instance, a mechanical engineer is concerned with plant location, site, preparation for installation, construction etc. Little time is usually spent on secondary activities like recreation, entertainment and other social activities.

(2) Interactions: The purpose of interaction is to have interface or face-to-face meeting. Interaction is the process of two or more people who contact or come to affect on each other. The interface of two or more people produce exchange of ideas and information. They include actions and reactions. Interactions give wide scope for communication for generating actions which follow reactions in a small group. It is essential in a group communication as it is a basic element. The process of interactions help as yardstick to evaluate and review the reactions to amend the message in the light of personal interaction.

Hellriegel and his associate remark that interactions occur in task behaviour and social behaviour. By defining job responsibilities and communication channels, the formal organisation strongly affect the interaction patterns of the work group. They suggest that:

(1) "The actions of the sender affect the reactions of the receiver. The reactions of the receiver affect the subsequent actions of the sender.

(2) Reactions of the receiver serve as feedback and tell the sender how well the objectives are being accomplished.

(3) A sender who receives feedback that is rewarded will continue to produce the same kind of message; if the feedback is not rewarding, the message will eventually change.

(4) The receiver exerts control over the sender by the kind of feedback he or she gives to the sender.[16]

(3) Sentiments: Every person has some sentiments. They are tender feelings or emotions. People working in any organisation exhibit sentiments. They are day-to-day in nature, such as feelings like anger, happiness, sadness and deeper feelings like trust, openness and freedom. When the members of the group exhibit emotional feelings, it can be termed as "sentiments." The effectiveness, productivity and performance of the group would depend, to a great extent, upon the four sentiments, namely:

(1) Trust

(2) Openness

(3) Freedom

(4) Felt Dependence.

(4) Norms: Norm is an expected or normal pattern of standard to judge other things. Norms are standards of behaviour widely accepted, shared, binding on all and enforced by the members of the group. It is the interaction variable that determines the norms. They are predetermined standards fixed for members for their behaviour as to what they have to do or should not do under specific circumstances. A work-group may usually define norms as day-to-day routine activities.

— as to how much

— as to how little work should be done

— what type of tools to be used

— where to relax

— what kind of recreation and entertainment activities are acceptable.

— how one should feel towards the management and so on.

A. Athos and his associate write that group norms exist when criteria have been met. They are:

(1) There must be standards of appropriate behaviour for group members.

(2) The members must be aware that the group supports particular norms through the system of reward and punishment. Reward is for compliance and punishment for violation.

To this it may be added that, as K. Davis puts it, the probability that they will be used. A member who deviates from norms is called a deviant member or violator. A deviant member disobeys the standards of behaviour established by the group itself.

There exist a perfect interrelationship among the internal system variables like sentiments, activities, interactions and norms. They may interrelate in a variety of ways. These interrelationships, according to D. Hellriegel and his associate are: [17]

(1) The more frequently individuals interact with one another, the stronger their friendship is apt to be.

(2) Individuals who like one another will express those sentiments in activities over and above the required activities of the external system.

(3) Individuals who interact with one another frequently are more like one another in their activities than they are like other individuals with whom they interact less frequently.

The relationships among sentiments, activities and interactions as observed by Hellriegel and his associate are as follows:

(1) "An individual of a higher social rank more often initiates interaction with another person of lower social rank, than *vice versa*.

(2) The higher an individual's social rank, the wider the range of interactions. A chief in a restaurant usually communicates with more employees than does a waiter or waitress.

(3) The sentiments of the group leader carry greater weight than do those of the followers.

(4) The higher the rank of an individual within the group, the more nearly his or her activities conform to the norms of the group."[18]

(2) External: The other part of Homan's model is the external system of a small group. The external communication system refers to the condition that existed before the group was formed in the organisation. The variables of this system are:

(1) Member Values

(2) Type of Technology

(3) Higher Management Leadership Practices.

These variables would continue even if the group cease to function. The external system of work groups is comparatively explicit. There is a potential impact of different technology on work-group freedom. Technology may be classified as a unit, small batch, mass production or continuous process. Thus, the type of technology greatly influences the relative freedom of the group. The nature of these technologies are as follows:

(1) Unit Technology: Unit production technology is a type of technology installed and exploited for the manufacture of individual items. In other words, products are made to consumer's specifications, and the production process is difficult to standardise.

(2) Mass Production Technology: Under this method, the production process is standardised to produce a large number of similar and identical goods generally meant for stock.

(3) Continuous Process Technology: A type of technology used continuously. Workers do not handle the materials themselves except occasionally.

Highly independent groups are formed in the case of unit technology. The members of a group or groups working at mass is a very little scope for developing their internal systems. The co-workers have little or no opportunity to interact each other mainly because of two factors like noise levels and distance between the workers.

Hellriegel and his associate identify the degree of group freedom in a continuous process technology, i.e., an oil refinery is somewhat greater with this technology. Work-group members are highly interdependent and must communicate with one another on a continuing basis. Continuous process technologies might permit giving the work group considerable control over the allocation of certain basis, including self-selection of members (after initial requirements, established by management have been met), and election of a leader by the group members. For the management who performs the tasks is not so important as encouraging workers to act as a team. It takes team work to keep the process going, prevent break-downs and report production as soon as possible when a break-down occurs (J. Hackman etc.). Here the group leader's role might be limited to co-ordinating assigned tasks, leading discussions on subjects requiring group decisions and serving as the group's spokesperson with management. (G. Susman).

Individuals and Group Roles[19]

(1) Group Task Roles

Contributor-Initiator: He suggests procedures, goals and methods. He puts forward a plan and gets the group moving.

Information-Seeker: He asks for ideas, data, experiences, reports and estimates.

Opinion-Seeker: He asks for briefs, evaluation, feelings relating to what the group is undertaking.

Information-Giver: He offers ideas, data, personal experiences and facts and figures with focus on the group problem.

Opinion-Giver: He states his own beliefs, evaluation, convictions, feelings about a suggestion or its alternatives.

Elaborator: He interprets issues, clarifies ideas expressed by others, gives examples and illustrations on their workability.

Co-ordinator: He demonstrates relationships between ideas, re-states issues, summarises and offers integrated statements for consideration.

Energizer: He inspires and prods the group to greater activity, stimulates others to action.

Evaluator-Critic: He critically examines issues, problems and possible solutions offered and gives an evaluation, supported by arguments.

Procedure-developer: He handles tasks like seating arrangements, operates audio-visual equipment and passes around documents.

Recorder: He keeps written records of meetings, proceedii s and decisions.

(2) Group Maintenance Roles

Against the backdrop of group goals and attitudes, the following are the emerging roles in group building:

Supporter: He praises and encourages. With expressions of warmth and cordiality, he indicates solidarity.

Harmoniser/Compromiser: He acts as a mediator and tries to solve differences through conciliatory moves and gestures. Acts as a sort of a trouble-shooter.

Follower: He listens attentively to others, goes along and accepts group decisions.

Tension-reliever: He introduces humour, lightens the atmosphere, narrates jokes, relaxes others and diverts attention from these situations.

Gatekeeper: He facilitates participation of everyone in the group, brings in members, both active and passive, prevents domination by others and maintains a cordial atmosphere.

(3) Individual Roles

It has been observed that individual traits, habits and attitudes often come into conflict with group building and maintenance roles. The knowledge and keen understanding of various roles are of great assistance to the leader in deciding how to react, how to handle tricky situations and ensure productive exchange of views. The problems of participants do offer a challenge to the leader and his ability and tact are at test while dealing with them. Meet some of these interesting, amusing characters:

Blocker: He constantly raises objections, insists on nothing to be done. He fancies his effort of introducing irrelevant digressions. Tends to be negative.

Aggressor: He is always on a collision course. He deflates the status of others. He expresses disapproval and ill-will.

Recognition-Seeker: He is a perfect example of a self-centred individual who boasts and calls attention to himself. He occasionally seeks sympathy and very often claims credit for ideas.

Self-Confessor: He engages in personal catharsis. He uses the group platform for conceding mistakes.

Clown-Actor: He diverts attention of the group to tangents. Very often, he indulges in horseplay and ridicules. Tries to dispute with cynical comments.

Dominator: He gives directions, orders people. He interrupts and insists on his own way. Tries to assert authority.

Special-Interest Pleader: He supports personal products and interests. He presses others for others, acts as a representative or advocate for other groups like "small businessmen", "factory workers", etc. He cloakes his own prejudices or biases in the stereotype which best fits his individual interests.

Group Decision-Making Techniques

The traditional interacting group is the most common form of group decision. There are some problems inherent in the interacting group or face-to- face group decision-making. It has been observed in some studies that on interacting group members often censure themselves and pressure individual members towards confronting opinions. The following are some of the group decision-making techniques:

(1) Brainstorming: This technique of group decision-making solves the problem of pressure for confronting in the interacting group that retard the development of creative alternatives. Brainstorming means a mental disturbance. Brainstorming with reference to the group or idea-creating groups means mental attention on a subject. One of the uses of group communication is brainstorming. It is an idea-creating group, involved in creative thinking. Creativity in thinking is an important function in the case of idea-creating group. When creativity is an important goal, brainstorming method of decision-making is used.

In this group, people assemble around a table, so as to enable the participants to understand the problem. The leader of the group presents the problem before the members in a very clear-cut manner. The members are free to offer as many alternatives which strike their minds. Ideas are invited and recorded as fast as possible. Everyone in the group will get an opportunity to speak. All ideas are encouraged, better, usual, unusual, and impractical.

The basic principle in brainstorming is to withhold any criticism of these alternatives, but to be discussed and analysed later. It is a popular method of promoting creative thinking. It is essentially a process of generating ideas, with the object of obtaining an advantage of different judgements. Judgement, evaluation, discussions take place after collecting a complete list of ideas from the members. It encourages the participants of the group to speak openly, freely, irrespective of validity or otherwise of ideas. Generally, in a brainstorming session, the group works together for a period from 15 minutes to one hour. There will be no preparation on the problem or subject to be brainstormed. Alex F. Osborn remarks that brainstorming methods have been designed to offset the tendency for groups to be hypercritical of new ideas. All ideas or opinions solicited and recorded may be used at any stage of the problem-solving. The advantages of this method are enthusiasm, broader participation, greatest task-orientation, building upon ideas exchanged and the feeling that the final product is a team solution.

(2) Nominal Group: This technique goes further by offering techniques for actually arriving at a preferred solution. As the name indicates, the group acts in a nominal way. The technique of nominal groups is used for the purpose of decision-making. The word "nominal" indicates that this technique restricts discussions or interpersonal communication during the decision-making process.

The leader of a group presents a problem and on which each member may offer a solution independently. It is nominal because all ideas offered by the members may not figure in for final decision.

As such, the ideas with the highest aggregate ranking is taken for final decision. Though the members have offered their own ideas but may not be considered for final decision. However, the ideas are subject to clarification and evaluation. Each member of the group independently writes down his ideas on the problem. Interaction takes place on the solution offered in a structured format and suggestions are discussed for alternatives, and the best course of action is arrived. Finally, a decision is taken by a majority opinion, either by voting or other methods which indicates the best available alternative. The group decision is called "nominal", because members are only a part of the group nominally. The structural format helps to integrate individual thinking and group interaction. According to A. H. Van de Ven, a typical approach includes:

(i) Silent generation of ideas in writing.

(ii) Recorded round-robin feedback from each member for presentation of ideas to the group, wherein ideas are summarised in terms of phrase and written on a blackboard flip-chart.

(iii) Discussion of recorded ideas to evaluate information.

(iv) Silent individual voting on priorities.

The following are the advantages of the nominal group techniques:

(i) All the members of a group have an equal opportunity to participate, speak, express, oppose freely and frankly.

(ii) No member dominates the scene of discussion.

(iii) It permits tight control of time.

(iv) It is a more time-consuming technique.

(v) The quality of ideas does not suffer.

(3) Delphi Decision-Making: It is a time-consuming and complex technique. This does not require physical or personal presence of the members of a group. There is no scope in this method for the members of the group to meet face-to-face to have direct interaction to discuss on problems, alternatives etc. The earlier two methods are face-to-face, interaction group approach. The Delphi decision-making method is quite opposite to face-to-face, interaction group approach. In this method of decision-making, members do not meet face-to-face for interaction.

When the participants of a group are geographically or physically dispersed or located at different places, the delphi-technique is used. Under this method, there is no opportunity for personal interaction and oral discussion. It is through the written media that all interactions and exchange of communication take place. The ideas and opinions of the members on a particular problem are collected by administering a questionnaire. This is like making a decision in the case of Board of Directors meeting known as "Resolution by Circulation." All collected ideas and opinions are integrated and summarised and the feelings of all the members by way of result of the opinion are sent back to the members for their review.

(4) Electronic Meeting: A latest technique in decision-making is electronic meeting or tele-conferencing. It is the most recent approach to group decision-making which blends the nominal group technique with sophisticated communication technology. It is called "electronic meeting." In this method, people upto fifty sit around a horseshoe-shaped table with a set of computer terminals. The problems or issues are presented to the participants and they type their responses on to their computer screen. Individual comments as well as aggregate votes are displayed on a projection screen in the room. This method helps achieve the advantages like anonymity, honesty and speed. It has been estimated that electronic meetings are as much as fifty-five per cent faster than the traditional face-to-face meetings.

(5) Synectics: The Greek word synectics means the joining together of different and apparently irrelevant elements." The synectics technique is designed to develop creative ideas, attempts to integrate "diverse individuals into problem-stating, and problem-solving." The technique gets people to focus on developing a single insightful solution and includes developing, evaluation, and critiquing ideas. Synectics is based on the assumption that a person is divided into parts. The first part is concerned about safety and is analytical, suspicious, logical, and cautious — and thus, inhibits experimentation and creativity. The second part of a person's thought strives toward learning and is impulsive and sensation-seeking and like to have fun. Because the self-censoring first part inhibits the creativity of the second part, the synectic approach is structured to encourage the impulsive, creative aspect of the individual to override his or her self-censoring tendencies.

Steps

The technique includes the following steps:

(1) Problem Statement and Background Information Stage: The group leader describes a general area of discussion but avoids identifying the specific problem. Creative thinking on the problem is encouraged. The leader presents the background information on the problem and the goals associated with an ideal solution.

(2) Good-wishing Stage: Group members are encouraged to wish for anything that comes to mind that could address the problem. As in brainstorming in this "freewheeling stage", people are encouraged to generate wild ideas and to hitchhike. Exploring ideas and not evaluating them are of utmost importance at this stage.

(3) Excursion Stage: Participants are asked to forget about the specific problem. They are asked to generate ideas about a somewhat unrelated one that eventually might be related to the problem at hand.

(4) Forced-Fit Stage: Participants take ideas from the excursion stage and force them to fit the initial problem. Although, this often appears quite unusual and obscure, it is intended to encourage creativity. In fact, evidence suggests that many great thinkers develop ideas from such experimental thinking.

(5) Itemized Response Stage: The group picks one of the ideas generated during the forced-fit stage and pursues it further. The idea is dissected only in its positive aspects. After all, the positive aspects have been explored, the idea's limitations are assessed. This focuses on the positive aspect and is intended to encourage productivity and creativity.

The outcome of the synectics process is a single unique plan or decision that has undergone considerable evaluation. The process tends to produce innovative ideas. Although the synectics approach can be quite useful for creative planning and decision-making, its cost is high. Furthermore, it produces only one potential solution to a problem. If that solution turns out to be unusable, the problem remains, and the process fails.

The process of obtaining opinions by circulation is continued until consensus is arrived at.

S. P. Robbins characterises the following six steps of Delphi technique:

(1) The problem is identified and members are asked to provide potential solutions through a series of carefully-designed questionnaire.

(2) Each member anonymously and independently completes the first questionnaire.

(3) Results of the first questionnaire are compiled at a central location, transcribed and reproduced.

(4) Each member receives a copy of the results.

(5) After viewing results, members are again asked for their solutions. The results typically trigger new solutions or cause changes in the original position.

(6) Steps four and five are repeated as often as necessary until a consensus is reached.[20]

K. Davis observes that the success of the Delphi process depends on adequate time, participant expertise, communication skills and the motivation of the members to immerse themselves in the task.

Advantages

(1) The Delphi technique insulates group members from the undue pressure or influence of other members.

(2) There is no need to bring geographically-separated members together.

(3) It permits surprising accuracy of decisions in many situations.

(4) It avoids the cost to attend a central place of meeting.

(5) Considerable amount of time and energy are saved.

Disadvantages

(1) It is time-consuming technique.

(2) It is not useful where important and urgent decisions are to be taken.

(3) This method does not permit to have a wide range of alternatives.

Decision-making

A decision is a choice or a resolution on a problem, a selected alternative. Managerial function involves deciding, determination of objectives, policies, programmes, strategies etc. It is the selection of course of action from among alternatives available. A decision is the end result processed by deliberations and reasoning.

Definition of Decision

A. Danish Maxim: "Hear one man before you answer, several before you decide."

R. S. Dawar: "Decision-making can be defined as the selection based on some criteria of one behaviour alternative from two or more possible alternatives. To decide means "to cut off or in a practical content, to "cut off " or in a practical content, to "come to a conclusion."

D.E. McFarland: "A decision is an act of choice wherein an executive forms a conclusion about what must not be done in a given situation. A decision represents a course of behaviour chosen from a number of possible alternatives."

Haynes and Massive: "A decision is a course of action which is consciously chosen for achieving the desired result."

Characteristics of Decision-making

There may be a number of workable alternatives available on a problem. But decision-making is the choice of the best alternative course of action in the accomplishment of a defined objective. The following are the characteristics of the process of decision-making.

(1) Mental Activity: Decision-making is a mental process and exercise. It involves intellectual activity in choosing the best alternative. A mental activity, it is a human and communication process.

(2) End Process: Decision-making is the result in the process, arrived after thorough deliberations and reasoning.

(3) A Selection Process: A decision is a choice of the best course among the alternatives.

(4) Rationality: Rationality means ability to think, from opinions logically on a particular issue. In a decision-making process, rationality is an important characteristic in group deliberations

(5) Commitment: There is an element of commitment in every decision. It is an acceptance to act in a certain manner in a given circumstance A decision once taken is to be acted on it.

(6) Positive, Negative: A decision is a mental resolution, the decision may be negative or positive. It may involve to do or not to do anything. A decision may just be a decision, not to decide.

(7) Situational: A decision is always related to a situation. An executive may take one decision in a particular set of given conditions and another in a different set of circumstances.

(8) Purpose-Oriented: In a decision, there is always a purpose. It is result-oriented. A decision goes with a purpose. It involves time dimension and time lag.

(9) Means to an End: A decision.is always a means to an end but an end itself.

Patterns of Group Problem-solving

Maier, in his research study, found the following assets and liabilities that accrue from the group situation:

Assets are

(1) The greater total of knowledge and information groups possess.

(2) The greater number of approaches to the problem-solving groups available.

(3) The increased commitment to decisions made by the group.

(4) Better comprehension of the decision by the group members.

Liabilities are

(1) Social pressure which causes members to strive for acceptance rather than correctness.

(2) Valence of solutions, or a watering-down effect.

(3) Individual domination so that others are excluded.

(4) Conflicting secondary goals — as and when achieving status or winning an argument becomes more important than the primary group goals.

The following four factors as suggested by Maier which may become assets or liabilities depending upon the skill of the members:

(1) Disagreements

(2) Conflicting interests *versus* mutual interests

(3) Risk-taking

(4) Who changes or which solution prevails.

Decision-making Models

(1) Linear Model: The decision-making in a group situation is a essentially a linear process. It implies that groups move in a straight line from one state to the next until a decision is reached. In other words, according to some studies, groups can revert to the preceding stages. Scheidel and Crowell have suggested with the assumption that if group decision-making are essentially linear, it would be characterised by statements which initiate, extend, modify and synthesise discussion topics. They also observed a *reach-test* cycle in which one participant would reach forward with a new idea.

(2) Spiralling Model: According to this model, decision-making is not essentially a linear process. So the groups would never move in a straight line from one stage to the next stage until a decision is reached. But what actually occurs in the groups is spiralling movement in which the members bounce back and forth. The process is continued and repeated, i.e., bounced back and forth from one idea to another as they move towards consensus.

It is the width of the spiral that decides the progress and movement. There are two spirals in this model. They are:

(1) Narrow Spiral

(2) Wide Spiral.

In the case of narrow spiral, groups may move quickly from one topic to the next. In the case of the wide spiral, they produce by a deliberate, thorough consideration of each topic.

Some studies reveal a tendency for disagreement to be followed relatively closely by changes in topic suggesting that the tension conflict creates may account for changes in the spiral direction. The width of the spiral seems to be a function of two types of groups:

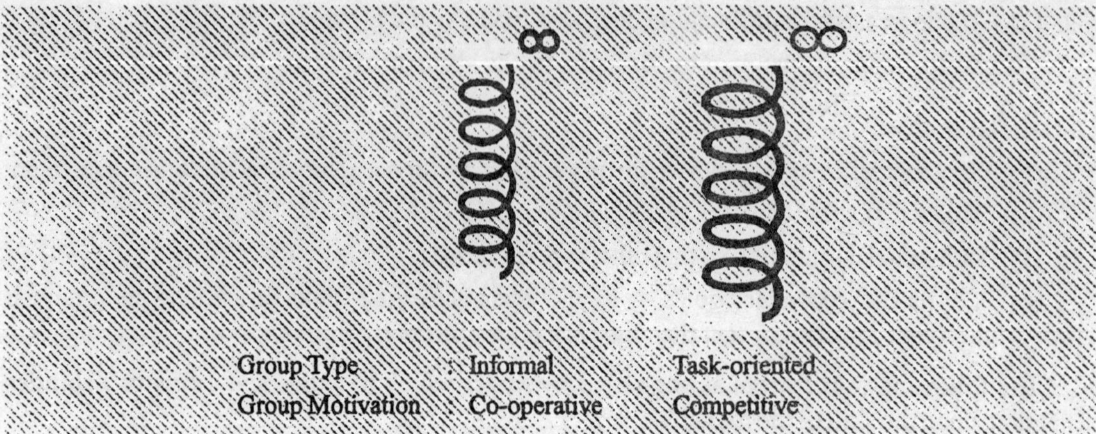

Fig. 11.18 Spiral Models of Group Decision-making

(1) Social groups change topic more quickly than the task-oriented groups when conflict occurred and group motivates.

(2) Co-operative groups change topic more quickly than competitive groups when disagreement arise.

Thus, groups move in a spiral pattern through several stages to achieve their goals.

A Two Stage Process: Burgoon, Heston and others have prescribed and offered a two-stage process through which successful groups progress: They are:

(1) First Stage — Problem solving

(2) Second Stage — Decision-making

The first stage or problem-solving consists of the following three steps, which are called Dewey System:

(1) Problem Identification

(2) Problem Analysis

(3) Discovery of possible solution.

After analysing the problem, the group moves to a second stage, i.e., decision-making stage. It consists of the following eight additional steps:

(1) Recognition of alternative decisions.

(2) Determination of criteria for acceptable decisions.

(3) Rejection of alternative decisions that do not meet criteria.

(4) Evaluation of problem gains and losses from acceptable decisions or return to problem-solving if no acceptable decision emerges.

(5) Selection of best alternative decision or return to problem-solving.

(6) Determination of how decision is to be implemented.

(7) Selection and authorization of people who are to implement the decision.

(8) Action.

Types of Decisions

Decisions are many types and have been classified by various authorities. The main types of decisions are as follows:

(1) Personal and Organisational: The decisions which cannot be delegated in principle to others are termed as "personal decisions." Organisational decisions can be delegated. On personal problems, personal decisions are taken, while organisational decisions relating to organisational issues. Sometimes, it is very difficult to separate both these types of decisions. Both the decisions are necessary in some cases in the attainment of each other's goal. Official capacity decisions are organisational, personal decisions relate to an individual in his personal matters.

(2) Basic and Routine Decisions: There is a clear distinction between basic and routine decisions. Genuine decisions are basic decisions. "Basic" is also called "strategic" decisions like policy matters involving heavy investment, expenditure. These are important decisions taken usually by the top management on such matters. Routine decisions are also called "tactical decisions" which are repetitive and routine in nature. These decisions are taken following certain established rules, procedures and policies.

(3) Programmed and Non-Programmed Decisions: Programmed decisions are those which are routine and repetitive in nature. These are more refined decisions for which the organisation develops specific procedure, extraordinary and non-repetitive. These relate to unstructured problems for which there are easy solution.

(4) Major and Minor Decisions: Classification of major and minor decisions is based on the importance of the subject matter. Decisions relating to buying of heavy machinery, import of machinery, replacement of labour by machines, to shut down, to buy or to make, exports etc., are the major matters. Decisions on these matters are major decisions.

On the other hand, matters of routine which do not involve heavy investment and matters of routine nature which do not require the attention of top management are termed as minor matters and decisions are minor decisions.

(5) Policy and Operating Decisions: Matters require the attention of the top management are policy decisions. Policy decisions are vital and important and taken only by the top management. For instance, a decision to give a bonus to the employees or not is a policy decision. Decisions taken by the lower level management in order to put into effect the policy decisions are called "operating decisions." These are matters relating to routine type of work. For instance, calculating the bonus to the employees is an operating decision.

(6) Individual and Group Decisions: Individual decisions are those decisions which are made by an individual in the organisation. For instance, a decision taken by the owner of the business or by the top executive. These types of decisions are taken in small organisations known for autocratic style of management. When decisions are taken by a group of organisational members collectively they are termed as "group decisions."

(7) Economic and Non-Economic: Decisions relating to financial matters are called economic decisions. For instance, decisions based on economic considerations such as capital, cost, profit, loss etc., are termed economic decisions. On the other hand, decisions relating to moral, ethical, social, technical, behavioural aspects are known as "non-economical decisions."

(8) Long-Term and Short-Term: Decisions can also be classified as long- term and short-term decisions on time or period. The period covered is long in the case of long-term decisions, say 10 or 15 years. In the case of short-term decisions, they relate to matters falling in a short period.

Group Decision-making Procedure

The best sequence described below explain the entire process of decision-making.

(1) Define Problem: It is a very difficult task. If a given problem is not properly grasped, it may lead to making a bad and unsound decision. Perception, clarifying, crystallising and defining the problem is the first and the most important step. It is, therefore, essential for a manager to identify clearly and define the problem before making a decision.

(2) Analysing Problem: Analysing a problem involves diagnosing a problem. It is necessary to have a detailed examination of facts pertaining to a problem. It requires the collection of all relevant and background facts and information. The problem should be classified which may be factors like the nature, impact, periodicity, futurity etc.

(3) Developing Alternatives: The next step is to develop alternative solutions, if not developed one is likely to be caught in a wrong decision. Every problem may have a number of workable alternatives but the group has to consider and select the best alternatives available.

(4) Weighing the Solution: It involves screening the various alternatives worked out earlier. Decision criteria is adopted to judge and evaluate the merits of various alternative solutions. Thus, there are four decision criteria for selecting the best alternatives like the risk involved, cost, economy, timing and limitation of resources.

(5) Selecting the Best Solution: The best possible solution should be selected. It must be a best fit solution in relation to the problem and the need of the group. However, the best solution does not mean the most popular and easiest solution. The past experience of the decision-maker, time, cost and limited resources etc., are the guiding principles in selecting the best solution.

(6) Implementing Decisions: Implementing the decisions taken is the most important part in the entire decision-making process. The aim of taking a decision is to put the decision into effect. Therefore, a decision may not have significance or validity unless it is being implemented.

(7) Feedback: Interacting with the persons concerned in the implementation of a decision is termed as "feedback." Decision-making is not complete and effective without evaluating the result. The circle completes with feedback. Following up decision, though the last step is an important step.

Modes of Decision-making

(1) By Consensus: "Consensus" means general feeling or trend. It is an agreement arrived by the members after stopping arguments and reaching a consensus. It is a genuine agreement and likemindedness. It is a healthy practice in team work if it is reached after honest initial differences.

Consensus is not arrived at simply through agreeing or not agreeing. Contradictory issues are involved in even simple questions. The test of genuine consensus is the freedom to agree or not to agree with the manager or group. This is democracy in action in an industrial setting.

(2) By Majority: Decisions arrived at by a majority of members present in person in a group meeting are called "decisions by majority." In other words, it is the difference between a greater and smaller number of members. It is a majority opinion and the most popular opinion. It may be simple majority representing 51:49. However, some problems may be decided by a vote of the elective membership or specified percentage of the members present say 2/3, or 3/4th majority,

(3) By Minority: A decision is said to be a minority one, when the problem is supported and passed by a smaller number of members of the group. It is generally less than say 49:51. It is a group to be in the smaller of two sections. Decision by minority takes place when a smaller number of the group constitutes coalition. It is formed either before or during the deliberations. The object of coalition is to push continuously and force its solution.

(4) By Persons with Power: It is a bureaucratic and authoritarian style and they do not count the wants and feelings of other members of the group. The decision-maker obtains views and opinions of other members and finally announces his final decisions. This approach is characterised as highly autocratic. The decision by a person with power approach may not be effective in all circumstances. The decision-maker of this type usually may fail to establish close relationship in the long run.

Managing and Resolving Group Conflict

It is not only at the personal level and organisational level where conflicts usually take place, conflicts also may occur at group level. A group may contain a few members who may interface, interact, each person influences and is being influenced by the other. Groups exist in every organisation; naturally conflicts develop, and these conflicts may have both functional as well as dysfunctional effects in persons, groups and the organisation as a whole. Group affects the behaviour of the members: it has an impact on other groups and organisations as well. Group has been an important factor of individual behaviour in the communication process and it is to be studied from various behavioural points of view. Lewis Coser suggests that "the majority of sociologists who dominate contemporary sociology... centre attention predominately upon problems of adjustments rather than upon conflict; upon social status rather than upon dynamics. Of key problematic importance to them has been the maintenance of existing structures and the ways and means of ensuring their smooth functioning. They have focused upon maladjustments and tensions which interfere with consensus."

He illustrates that a person's general orientation has led him to view conflict as dysfunctional and disruptive and to disregard its positive function. He further states that conflict is described as partly avoidable, partly inevitable and endemic form of sickness in the social body. In group deliberation conflicts are bound to occur when there are many alternatives available for a given problem. A scientific way of decision-making would solve the conflict in which both the individual and group must make the best choice.

Group conflict can be divided into the following two types:

(1) Inter group

(2) Intra group.

(1) Inter-Group: A difference or disagreement between the different departments is called intergroup conflict. An official group or informal group may develop a conflict with another in the same organisation. Each group may have its own strategy to undermine the other group, gain power, dominate and to improve its image. Intergroup conflict is a sort of clash or rivalry between groups, departments, sections, divisions within the organisation. Intergroup has its own causes, effects and mechanism for managing intergroup conflict.

There are three levels of conflicts:

(1) Intra-sender role Conflict — incompatible expectations of a manager towards a subordinate.

(2) Inter-personal Conflict — between two or more persons.

(3) Inter-group Conflict — between groups.

Thus, the interrelationship among these three levels of conflict, i.e., indicates the existence of conflicts which are unavoidable.

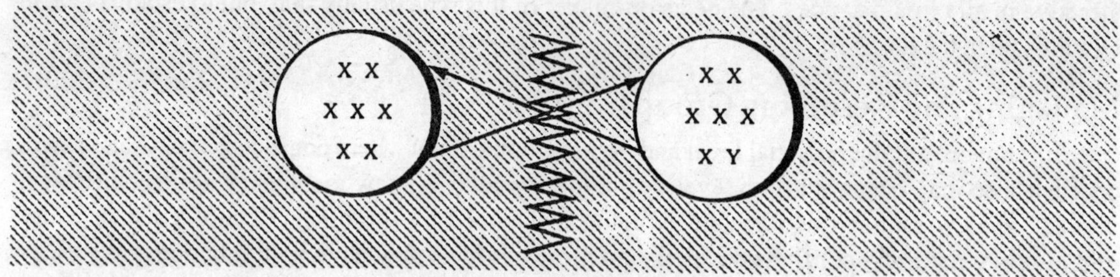

Fig. 11.19 Inter Group Conflict

Differences between groups occur on account of interaction between various groups within the organisation. In a continuous intergroup interrelationship and interaction, some factors can influence relations between two or more groups. The interrelationship between groups are governed by various factors which exist in the organisation. Again, these factors may be positive or negative. Positive factors may not create conflict among the groups while negative factors tend to create conflicts among the groups. Conflict between small groups depend to a considerable extent, on the general environment in the organisation and in particular, among the departments, sections, divisions, as the case may be.

Kast *et al.* state thus: "Manifest conflicts with another small group, or with the large-scale organisation of which it is a part, may foster an increased degree of loyalty and cohesiveness that would not be if its external relationships were conflict-free."

Intergroup conflicts may have a positive impact or creativity, innovation and progress. A conflict-prone organisation is more dynamic, not static and sterile and always with a challenge for group members. The interrelationship between three levels of conflict has a cyclical effect.

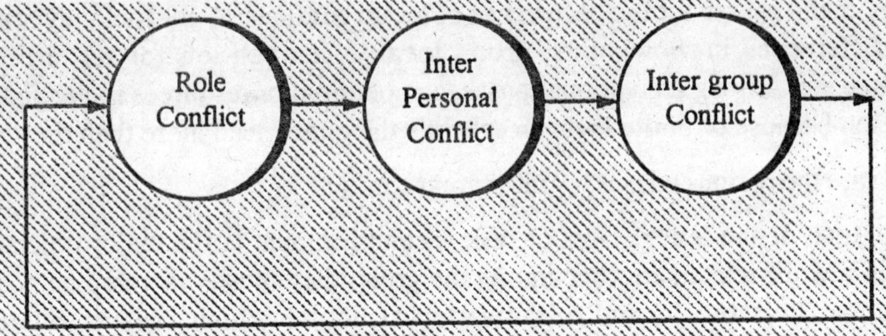

Fig. 11. 20 Interrelationship
(*Source*: Adapted from D. Hellriegel and J.W. Slocum, *Management* p. 662).

Causes for Intergroup Conflicts: Intergroup conflicts may arise in a variety of ways. Inter-group conflicts may lead to role conflict. For instance, conflict may often arise between production and sales department. There would be always a pressure from the sales department on the production department for meeting the demands of delivery dates. On the other hand, the production department may have its own problems. This leads to inter-role conflicts for the members of the production department. Thus, ultimately intergroup conflicts occur due to the role conflict and interpersonal conflicts.

D. Hellriegel and his associate list the following causes for intergroup conflicts:

(1) Task interdependence
(2) Task dependency
(3) Inconsistent performance criteria and reward
(4) Intergroup differences
(5) Sharing scarce common resources.

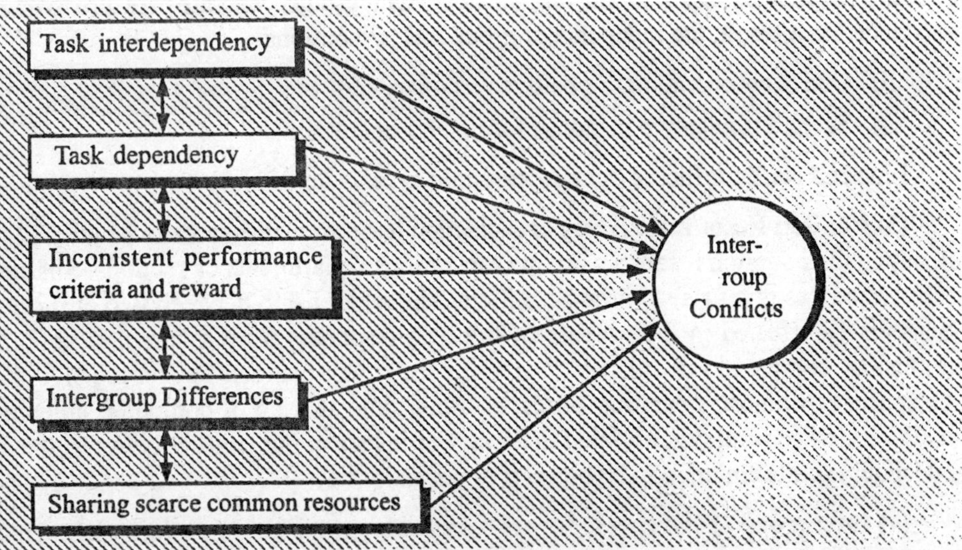

Fig. 11. 21 Causes of Intergroup Conflicts
(*Source*: Adapted from D. Hellriegal and J.W. Slocum, *Management*, p. 663.)

There are many causes for the occurrence of group conflicts. A conflict may arise from such causes like differences in viewpoints, group loyalty, competition for resources, degree of interdependence etc. Among the various causes, competition for resources is a serious problem in any organisation because of limited resources while the group need more than they secure.

The following are the various causes for intergroup conflict:

(1) Task Interdependency: Goal or task accomplishment is the major objective of group functioning. In a work-related conflict among the group they mostly develop an account of task interdependence. It is the formal organisation structure which creates relationship and interdependence between the groups. The organisational process which creates departments or sections for achieving organisational goals. It is quite common for the existence of interdependence task relations when two or more groups co-ordinate and collaborate with another. The work-related conflicts among the group may occur at the peer level, superior level or subordinate level. Task interdependence is a condition in which two groups or individuals rely on each other. The interdependence may be for service, information, goods required for the purpose of accomplishment of their own tasks. It is a case of co-ordination when sub-tasks are allocated to different groups need to be sequenced and agreed upon by the two groups. In case of co-ordination when sub-tasks are allocated to different groups need to be sequenced and agreed upon by the two groups. In case where two groups share responsibility for the accomplishment of certain tasks it is a case of task collaboration.

(2) Task Dependency: In this type of cause for group conflicts there are two variables for interaction. One is dependent variable and another is independent variable. Thus, task dependency is a condition in which one group has necessarily to depend or rely on another group for obtaining service, information for the purpose of accomplishment of goals. The dependent group has to co-operate and maintain good relations with the independent group to obtain services from them, whereas the independent group has less incentive to co-operate with the dependent group. In the process of dependent task relationship, the dependent groups generate pressure to gain the needed assistance. As a result, the independent group has two options:

(i) One is co-operation or positive response; and

(ii) Second is negative response for non co-operation.

Line and staff conflict is the best example of task dependence.

(3) Limited Resources: Every organisation has scarce resources to be utilised judicially by allocating the common resources among the various departments or sections. Sharing process of scarce resources gives rise to group conflicts. The relationship between two or more groups may be adversely affected in the process of drawing resources from a common pool. Thus, group conflicts are common to all organisations where the groups compete for sharing of limited resources like space, equipment, operating funds, printing, time sharing of computer, amenities, working conditions, wages and other related matters. For instance, the conflict between the management and labour is quite common in all types of organisations.

(4) Intergroup Differences: Where a particular group has to perform different tasks and to deal with different departments or sections of the organisation, intergroup differences based conflicts arise on account of differences. Group may vary in their goal orientation, time orientation, formal structure and interpersonal orientation. D. Hellriegel and his associate illustrate these orientations in the following way:

(a) Goal Orientation — Research department, marketing department and production department.

(b) Time Orientation — Time taken to know the result of its action.

(c) Formal Structure — Strictness of rules, span of control, frequency and specificity of supervisory control.

(d) Interpersonal Orientation — Relative openness, sociability, permissiveness in relationship within the department.

(5) Goal Incompatibility: Goal incompatibility is also one of the powerful causes for group conflicts. It operates in such a way that goal attainment by one or more of other groups. This type of conflict often develops, in case of sales department, production department, line and staff department as well as labour management relations. Therefore, the degree to which two or more groups perceive goal incompatibility will affect the degree of conflict.

(6) Inconsistent Performance Criteria: The inconsistent performance criteria as suggested by D. Hellriegel *et al.*, refer to "evaluating and rewarding interdependent groups or individuals on the basis of criteria that motivate them to concentrate on their self (or competing) goals rather than common goals. The greater the interdependency of groups and the more top management emphasises their separate rather than combined performance, the more conflicts there will be between them."

(7) Attitudinal Sets: The attitudes like distrust, competitiveness, secrecy, closed communication, lack of work relations etc., play an important role in creating an intergroup conflict. These are attitudinal variables. When the members of various groups hold these attitudinal variables towards each other, they can become cause and consequence of the nature of their relationship. If these variables operate in group relations, there is a possibility of group relationship being emphasised in a negative way. This ultimately leads to conflicts. A good intergroup relations can be promoted when the members have mutual trust, avoid blaming each other, more open communication and to consider others' point of view.

(8) Sub-Group Competition: Another cause for group conflict is competition between sub-groups within the organisation. Just as a conflict is inevitable in interpersonal relationship, sub-group conflicts are also developed in any organisation.

(9) Absorption of Uncertainty: Groups may face situations, where they are not sure facts or events, correct decisions cannot be made unless things are known fully. Groups sometimes deal with the task of uncertainty and the group which has assigned to deal with it, may absorb uncertainty of other groups. The uncertainty prone group makes decisions for other groups. Thus, absorption of uncertainty may create a visible conflict.

Effects of Intergroup Conflict

From the above analysis of causes for intergroup conflicts, it is clear that no group can be entirely conflict-free, every group faces one form of conflict or the other. Groups require disharmony and disassociation.

After having understood the reasons for conflicts, now it would be beneficial to examine briefly some of the effects of intergroup conflicts. Broadly, inter-group conflicts may create either positive or negative effects, and in some cases, both types of effects. R. Walton and J. Dutton have classified the characteristics of intergroup conflict under five categories, such as:

(1) Competition

(2) Concealment and distortion of information

(3) Appeals to superiors for decisions

(4) Rigidity and formality in decision procedures

(5) Decreased rate of intergroup interaction

(6) Low trust, suspicion and hostility.

The positive and negative effects of these characteristics of inter-group conflict are presented below:

EFFECTS OF INTERGROUP CONFLICT

Characteristics of Intergroup Conflict	Positive Effects	Negative Effects
1. Competition.	Increases motivation, contributes to a system of checks and balances, increases number of new ideas to compete with established ones.	Decreases motivation, may derive higher-level management of information.
2. Concealment and distortion of information.		Lowers quality of decisions.
3. Appeals to superiors for decisions.	Superiors become more informed about operations and subordinate may lead to confrontation with superior as a third party facilitator.	Superiors may become overloaded by referrals, may lead to forcing with superior handing down edicts without full knowledge.
4. Rigidity and formality in decision procedures.	May increase stability in the system.	May lower adaptability to change.
5. Decreases rate of intergroup interaction.	May decrease problem if a group or person is used to provide the necessary liaison.	Hinders co-ordination and implementation of tasks.
6. Low trust, suspicion and hostility.	Increased cohesion within group contributing to co-operation within group.	Psychological strain and turnover of personnel.

(***Source***: Adapted from R. Walton and J. Dutton, *The Management of Interdepartmental Conflicts: A Model and Review*).

Sherif has broadly classified the consequences of intergroup conflict into the following types:

(1) Effects within the group

(2) Effects between groups.

(1) Effects Within the Group

(1) Each group becomes more cohesive. Feelings of solidarity within the group increases.

(2) Morale of each group rises.

(3) Group atmosphere becomes more task-oriented.

(4) Leadership shifts towards an autocratic style.

(5) Group becomes more organised and highly structured.

(6) Group demands more conformity and loyalty from its members in order to present a solid front.

(2) Effects Between Groups

(1) Both groups treat each other as enemies.

(2) Perception of reality is distorted.

(3) Overestimation of oneself and underestimation of others is the consequence.

(4) Communication between groups is minimised.

(5) Ultimately, one of the groups may win and the other may lose.

(6) The enmity continues.

There have been a number of research studies, including Hawthorne, which have implications for organisational behaviour and management. In addition to Hawthorne, there are numerous research studies on group dynamics, more accurate measure of the significance. It is interesting to note that research in group dynamics has multiplied in great profusion in the field of communication. David A. Nadler *et al.*, studies reveal the impact of the groups on organisational and individual effectiveness. The following is the summary of research findings on the impact:

Summary of Research of the Impact that Groups have on Organisational and Individual Effectiveness

	Impact of groups on organisational effectiveness		Impact of groups on individual employee effectiveness
(1)	Accomplishing tasks that could not be done by employees themselves.	(1)	Aiding in learning about the organisation and its environment.
(2)	Bringing a number of skills and talents to bear on complex and difficult tasks.	(2)	Aiding in learning about one's self.
(3)	Providing a vehicle for decision-making that permits multiple and conflicting views to be aired and considered.	(3)	Providing help in gaining new skills.

(4)	Providing an efficient means for organisational control of employee behaviour.	(4)	Obtaining valued rewards that are not accessible by one's self.
(5)	Facilitating changes in organisational policies or procedures.	(5)	Satisfying important personal needs especially needs for social acceptance and affiliation.
(6)	Increasing organisational stability by transmitting shared beliefs and values to new employees.		

(*Source*: Adapted from David A. Nadler, J. Richard Hackman, and Edward E. Lawler, *Managing Organisational Behaviour*).

Managing and Resolving Inter-group Conflict

There are many causes for inter-group conflict. Just as there is no single definition for inter-group conflict, similarly there is no single mechanism for managing and resolving inter-group conflicts. There can be a variety of conflict-resolving methods. There may be minor conflicts or major conflicts, some of them may take more time and some others less time. An effective conflict-resolution mechanism is necessary when there are major differences between the group which need tight co-ordination. However, the following are methods for managing and resolving inter-group conflicts.

(1) Reward System: Usually, every organisation has its own reward system for its employees. In the light of inter-group conflicts and to manage such conflicts, it is desirable that every organisation should change its reward system. Changes in the existing reward system directed towards promotion of motivation to the employees reduces conflict to a considerable extent. Better personnel selection, more effective training, collaboration, group incentives, co-partnership etc. would reduce inter-group conflicts. Group interdependence is the major cause for intergroup conflicts which can be reduced by: (1) reducing dependence on common resources; (2) reducing pressures for consensus; (3) loosening by schedules, establishing inventories or using contingency funds.

(2) Intervention by Superiors: Hierarchical intervention in inter-group conflict may resolve a conflict. To solve the problem, this measure is designed for reference of a conflict to superior's authority. P. Lawrence and his associate suggest that the knowledge needed at the top levels of the organisation. In respect of certain matters the top executives may have the knowledge necessary to understand all the factors of the environment of the organisation. The superiors can keep departments informed of the critical problems which help to ease problem and helps to make sound decisions.

(3) Reduction in Interdependence: Conflict can also be reduced by reducing interdependence. As a matter of fact, task interdependence is one of the principal sources of all conflicts. So with less of such dependence, the less will be the amount of conflicts among the groups. J. D. Thompson classified three types of interdependence such as: (1) pooled, (2) sequential, (3) reciprocal. It is a case of pool interdependence when the various sections or departments in the organisation are relatively self-contained and independent. In sequential interdependence, there is a high degree of interdependence between two or more departments. The departments are more interdependent when the degree of interdependence is reciprocal.

(4) Special Integrating Groups: Creation of separate and special integrators is also used as a technique to manage and resolve conflicts of inter-group. In particular, the most effective interpersonal style for managing inter-group conflict is appointment of special integrators, who may manage the interdependence of various groups. The separately-constituted integrating groups assume the responsibility of solving unresolved matters. The integrator may be of special integrator department or an individual. The group or department or individual may help to resolve conflicts and achieve to maintain co-ordination between conflicting groups. When there are much differences or disagreement between the departments or groups in terms of time span, goal structure and values, the use of special integrator is popular to resolve conflicts. Using a separate integrating group, as a third group, is considered to be the most positive technique for conflict resolution when the conflicting groups are highly independent require tight co-ordination. But the creation of integrating group requires careful judgement by high level managers.

(5) Superordinate Goals: Goals which are shared by the group are superordinate goals. Such goals can be achieved only through the co-operation. The mutual co-operation of the conflicting groups is necessary for the organisation to achieve its objectives. For instance, the conflicting marketing and production departments is the result of superordinate goals. When a conflict pose a common threat, may be a new competitor is competing in the common market. This forces the conflicting group to perceive superordinate goals. Accordingly, the conflicting group may set aside some of their disagreements or differences, co-operate with each other towards solving unresolved pending matters.

(6) Exchange of Personnel: To resolve conflicts, the members of the conflicting groups may be exchanged for a specified period. By this way, inter- group conflict can be managed and resolved. It amounts to the role reversal which helps to greater understanding between the groups, people by forcing each member to present and defend the other person's position. P.R. Lawrence *et al.*, studies reveal that the exchange of people programmes is effective in reducing conflict and speeding agreement.

(7) Standardised Practice: The studies of M. Beer, J. Perry and H. Angel reveal that there are a number of formal procedures and practices that can help in resolving inter-group conflicts. Permanent teams or committees of representatives from the interdependent group should meet periodically which reduce conflict. Procedure may be established for reference to a common superior. Similarly, training sessions in interpersonal and inter-group dynamics are effective. Intervention of a third party is also an effective measure.

(8) Reduction in Shared Resources: Sharing of common resources is causing an inter-group conflict. It refers to groups obtaining services or goods from common source which is not sufficient to meet the requirements of all their needs. Addition to such resources is one of the techniques for reducing such sharing problem. Alternatively, judicious allocation is also a measure towards the reduction of conflict arising from this.

Intra-group Conflicts

Inter-group conflict is within the same group. Conflict within a group depends, to a considerable extent, on the characteristics of group and, to some extent, on an interpersonal conflict. When two or more persons form the same group, interpersonal conflict in intra-group occurs. In a group, an interpersonal conflict is likely to take place to some extent. The causes for interpersonal conflicts in a group are difference in values, beliefs, attitudes and behaviour which create personality conflicts. A group is a collection of few members of common interest whose interactions generate a system of values, norms and sanctions. There are three main causes for the occurrence of intra-group conflicts. They are:

(1) When a group faces a new or novel problem.

(2) When new values are transferred to the group.

(3) When extra group roles come into conflict with his intra-group role.

Intra-group conflict often occurs when the members of a group hail from different socio-economic backgrounds and have different political and religious values and views. The variables like ethics, power exercise, morals, justice, fairness etc., on which disagreements may occur among the members of the group.

Coser states that intra-group conflict can arise in a variety of ways. Disagreement between the members over goals, plans and member roles, etc., has been stronger in the early stage of group development. There is no alternative on the part of the members to resolve the difference of opinions so as to enable the group to function effectively.

Meetings

Introduction: In real world situation, meetings are yet another medium of oral communication. In a democratic set up meetings are a common method. In a restless age of communication, meetings are business. Message is easily and understandably communicated through medium of meetings. Message is carried in family meetings, street gatherings, samiti meetings, panchayat meetings, parishad meetings, municipal meetings, municipal corporation meetings, political meetings, assembly and parliamentary meetings. Meetings may be conveyed regularly and in extra-ordinary circumstances.

In corporate management, we frequently come across company meetings. A company may conduct several types of meetings to convey the matters of the company for the purpose of taking decisions. The usual company meetings are statutory meetings, annual general meetings, extraordinary general meetings, board of directors' meetings, shareholders' meetings of various types, debenture holders' meetings, creditors' meetings etc.

Meetings are gatherings which are groups of persons belonging to a particular interest to whom, as groups, some common matters or issues are entrusted. At this place, information is communicated orally, discussed, deliberated and debated to come to a solution or decision. Meetings are supposed to be of democratic origin.

Sometimes, special invitees such as ex-officio, Government nominees, institutional representatives are invited to have their specialised and technical, legal, administrative advice for consideration. Meetings ensure collective decisions or team decisions. Collective decisions are taken with oral discussion sitting in meetings and hence fear of authority being concentrated in one person is avoided. A meeting may be informational, advisory or problem-solving. In a informational meeting, the object is to present ideas and data to the members.

In an advisory type of meetings, the purpose is to gather and seek advice, information, suggestion relating to a problem. The object of problem-solving meeting is to seek a decision and solution out of collective discussion and mutual understanding of a problem. Thus, in meetings, communication flows both ways. Discussion is an important object of meeting. In this verbal form of communication, the group acts as a team with responsibility since they help in arriving at a collective decision.

An effective group has the following characteristics:

(1) It knows why it exists.

(2) It has guidelines or procedure for making decisions.

(3) It has achieved communication among its members.

(4) Members have learned to receive and give help to another.

(5) Members have learned to deal with conflicts within the group.

(6) Members have learned to diagonise their problems and improve their own functioning. (L. Bradford etc.)

Meeting — Meaning

The word "meeting" denotes an arrangement to come face-to-face with advance plan for a purpose. A meeting is a gathering, assembling or coming together of two or more persons for the purpose of transacting some objective business. It is an act of coming face-to-face. According to shorter Oxford Dictionary, it is an "assembly of number of people for entertainment, discussion or the like." Thus, to constitute a proper meeting, it follows that there must be two or more persons. However, there may be a proper meeting, in the eyes of the law, even if only two or one person is present. There is a law governing the corporate meetings. The proper discharge of duties in group activities requires that the members of the group come together from time to time to discuss matters to arrive at a decision by the majority of opinions. In a view, meetings are common to all organisations where executives, subordinates and other combination of people often interact in a group sitting. Whether referred to as group discussion, board of team, its essential nature is the same, for the meeting is a group of persons to whom is assigned a business.

Meeting is a group. A group tends to have a meeting. A group interaction may be called by many other names such as conferences, seminars, conventions, discussions, associations, teams, boards, etc. Though a variety of special names are used, the nature and object is the same. A meeting is a oral communication tool for the management which facilitates exchange and interaction between concerned group of people. Members of the meeting express their opinions, oppose, offer, suggest ways and means. Free, clear and frank communication is essential for effective decision-making.

Thus, a meeting is an organised activity of communication. It facilitates the transaction of business in an orderly, deliberate, planned and democratic manner for a purpose. Planning physical, procedural and psychological factors greatly governs a meeting. The communication skills endeavour to define a problem, discussion, and finding solutions and resolutions.

Definition: W. H. Newman defines the term thus: "A committee of a group of people specially designated to perform some administrative acts. It functions only as a group and requires the free intercharge of ideas among its members."[21]

Hicks and Gullet: "A committee is a group of people who meet by plan to discuss or make a decision for a particular subject. Because committee meets by plan, we do not include groups that occur spontaneously or informally in the definition of a committee."[22]

Kinds of Meetings: A meeting may be broadly classified into two categories:

(1) Public Meeting.

(2) Private Meeting.

(1) Public Meeting: A meeting is said to be public when admission to the meeting is open to all. Under this, there will be an open invitation to the public at large. Any member of the public who is interested in the subject matter for which such meeting is called can participate and contribute his own matter. A public meeting is convened by individuals or bodies to which there is open participation. Therefore, a public meeting is an assembly or gathering *bonafide* and held in a public place for discussion of any matter of public interest. Matters of public interest may include social, political, cultural, literary, religious and other matters. Public meetings are governed to some extent by the general practice and procedures. For public meetings, there will not be any rigidly framed bye-laws or regulations. But the Government or local authorities may by regulation, impose restrictions or procedures on public meetings. On the other hand, there are, however, a number of general principles applicable to meetings in general.

(2) Private Meeting: A private meeting is one convened by individuals or bodies to which there is no open invitation in general. Invitation to a meeting of this type is extended only to those persons who are concerned or interested in the subject matter. So only a member to whom invitation is extended is entitled to attend the meeting and to participate in the discussions in the subject matter for which such meeting is called. A private meeting may, thus, be defined as any assembly of restricted number of people held in a private place for the furtherance or discussion of any matter of their concern. So a private meeting includes meetings of companies, trade unions, consumer associations, employee's unions, clubs, religious institutions and such other bodies. In brief, the conduct of private meeting or whose business is of interest only to the members of those individuals or those bodies. There are a number of principles applicable to meetings in general. Private meetings are governed, to some extent, by the general law applicable to public meetings. In addition, private meetings are normally governed by bye-laws or regulations relating to the convening and conduct of such meetings and ancillary matters. These bye-laws or regulations may be statutory or they may exist by agreement between the associations concerned.

Corporate Meetings

Meetings of companies incorporated or formed under the Indian Companies Act, 1956 are corporate meetings. A company is an artificial person which has a legal personality of its own and is separate and distinct from its shareholders — the human agency through which decisions are taken. Company meetings are the source of managerial control, powers and function. The shareholders exercise their functional powers and ultimate control over the corporate affairs by exercising their voting rights at company meetings. The ultimate authority is vested in them and hold a vital position in the hierarchy of company administration. However, the company meetings can be classified as under:

(I) Shareholders' Meetings

A. Statutory Meeting.

B. Annual General Meeting.

C. Extraordinary General Meeting.

D. Class Meeting.

(II) Board Meetings

A. Meeting of Board of Directors.

B. Meeting of a Committee of the Board.

C. Passing Resolution By Circulation.

(III) Miscellaneous Meetings

A. Meeting of Debentureholders.

B. Meeting of Creditors (Not in Winding up).

C. Meeting of Creditors in Winding up.

D. Meeting of Contributories in Winding up.

(I) Shareholders Meetings

The company law provides for the holding of sharcholders' meetings. This enables the members to meet and discuss the affairs of the company. The meetings of the shareholders are also called "general meetings." A brief discussion about the various meetings is as follows:

(A) Statutory' Meeting: The first general meeting of the shareholders is called the statutory meeting. Statutory meeting is held once in the life time of a public company. A private company is not required to hold a statutory meeting and not more than six months from the date of commencement of the business of the company. The main purpose of convening this meeting is to provide the members a general idea about the progress made by the company since its formation. It is an opportunity to the members to discuss the various matters relating to the company from its inception. A separate report called "Statutory Report" should be prepared by the Directors and to be forwarded to every member at least 21 days before the date of the meeting.

(B) Annual General Meeting: Every company, private or public, must hold an annual general meeting of the shareholders each year. This is a meeting to be held in addition to any other general meeting of the shareholders. This meeting enables the shareholders to discuss the affairs of the company on the basis of Annual Report of the Directors or the Auditors' Report. In this meeting, the performance of the company during the past one year is reviewed. At this meeting, two types of business are transacted. They are ordinary and special business. Ordinary Business consists of:

(1) Consideration and approval of the annual accounts and balance sheet and the Auditor's Report thereon.

(2) Consideration and approval of the Annual Report of the Directors.
(3) Declaration of dividends, if any.
(4) Appointment of directors in place of those retiring by rotation.
(5) Appointment of auditors and fixing their remuneration. Any other business other than those specified above is considered as special business. A due notice of special business is to be given to all the members. Special business may be transacted by an ordinary resolution or special resolution.

(C) Extraordinary General Meeting: Each general meeting of a company other than the statutory meeting and the annual general is an extraordinary general meeting. This type of meeting is convened for transacting some special or urgent business which cannot be postponed till the next annual general meeting. A meeting of this type may be called at any time when it is found necessary. Generally, all business at an extraordinary meeting is deemed to be special business. It is a meeting usually called by the Board of Directors between the two annual general meetings. The purposes for which extraordinary general meeting is convened are:

(1) Alternation of Memorandum of Association and Articles of Association.
(2) Increase of share capital.
(3) Decrease of share capital.
(4) Removal of Director before the expiry of his term and
(5) For transacting any special or urgent business.

The meeting may be called by —

(i) The Board of Directors.
(ii) The Board of Directors on the requisition of members.
(iii) The requisitionists themselves.
(iv) The Company Law Board.

(D) Class Meetings: It is a meeting of particular group or a particular class of shareholders. Only shareholders belonging to a particular class are entitled to attend such meetings. These meetings are convened for the purpose of making changes such as dividing shares into various classes. Preference shareholders' meetings, equity shareholders' meetings are examples of class meetings. Such meetings are convened for reasons like:

(i) To alter, vary or affect the arrears of dividend on cumulative preference shares.
(ii) To cancel the arrears of dividend on cumulative preference shares.
(iii) To consider redemption of preference shares after they become due for redemption.
(iv) To consider allotment of equity shares in lieu of preference share becoming due for redemption.

(II) Board Meetings

(1) Board of Directors: Directors are the agents of the shareholders who are responsible for the management of the affairs of the company. Company is an artificial and legal person which carries on its business through some human agency. The directors are collectively called the "Board of Directors." It is the body to whom authority is delegated and through whom, the company operates. The management of the company is vested in the board of directors collectively. Meetings of directors are called "Board Meetings." It is at the board meeting that all important matters and policies are discussed and decided. Certain matters are to be decided by the board only. A meeting of Board of Directors must be held at least once in every three months and at least four such meetings shall be held in every year. The Companies Act, 1956 vests several powers which can be exercised only at Board Meetings.

(2) Meetings of Committees of Directors: A committee of directors is a segment of the Board of Directors constituted for a specific purpose. These are called "Meetings of Committee of Directors." They relieve the Board of Directors from attending routine matters of day-to-day administrative work. The Board usually appoints small committees with a membership of a few directors which carry on such activities and report to the Board. Such committees are share transfer, committee, finance committee and disciplinary committee. They may be of temporary or permanent nature. The Articles of Association of a company generally empower the directors to appoint such committees. The Board, therefore, delegates some of its powers to these committees of directors.

(3) Resolution by Circulation: "Resolution by circulation" refers to the Board of Directors Meeting. All decisions are taken by the Board which takes the shape of passing resolutions at the Board Meetings. Their meeting may not be held frequently. In cases where it is not possible to hold board meeting for various reasons like inadequate business to transact, inconveniences, sitting fee, the decision can be taken without a meeting. The law permits that the directors may transact business without meeting also. The Articles of Association normally empower the Board to pass Resolutions by circulation.

Resolution by circulation is passed by sending the necessary papers along with the proposed resolution to individual directors seeking their consent. This is what is known as "Resolution by circulation." No such resolution is deemed to have been passed by Board by circulation unless:

(1) The resolution has been circulated in draft, together with all the necessary papers, to all directors present in India at their usual address.

(2) The number of directors among whom a resolution is circulated is not being less than the quorum fixed for a meeting of the Board.

(3) The resolution has been approved by a majority of the directors entitled to vote on the resolution.

There are certain matters as are required to be passed at Board meetings only which can be transacted by way of resolution by circulation.

(III) Miscellaneous Meetings

(1) Meeting of Debentureholders: It is a class meeting of debenture- holders. A meeting of only debentureholders of a company is called debenture- holders meeting. There may be several purposes of holding debentureholders' meeting. This meeting may be held to discuss the matters connected with them such as (*a*) Variation in the terms of security given for the loan, (*b*) Modification of the rights of debentureholders, (*c*) To mobilise further funds, (*d*) Alternation of the rate of interest payable to them, (*e*) To delete or modify any of the stringent condition.

(2) Meeting of Creditors: These are meetings held by a particular class of creditors. As the name indicates, it is the meeting of those persons who lent money to the company who are called "creditors." This meeting is convened with a view to make compromise with its creditors. The objects may be: (*a*) Compromising with creditors on a dispute. (*b*) Compounding of debt, (*c*) To take up schemes like re-organisation, re-construction or amalgamation with the consent of creditors.

(3) Creditors Meeting in Winding Up: Sometimes, the company in the case of winding up also has to make compromise with its creditors. The court may order a holding of a meeting of creditors or of a class of creditors. An application may be made to the court by the company or any creditor or liquidator of a company. When the company goes into liquidation, a meeting of creditors is held.

(4) Meeting of Contributories in Winding Up: Contributory means every person liable to contribute to the asset of the company in the event of its winding up. When a company goes into liquidation, a meeting of contributories is convened to ascertain certain matters concerning them.

Communication in Ascertaining the Sense of Meeting (Media)

Meetings are held for discussion of specific matters and to take definite decisions on them. Generally, unanimous opinions on all matters are not possible. In such cases of difference of opinion, steps are to be taken to ascertain the sense of the house. An appropriate communication media is to be adapted for ascertaining the sense of the meeting. There are various alternative methods which may be adopted for taking votes, to obtain majority opinion. They are:

(1) By acclamation
(2) By voice
(3) By show of hands
(4) By division
(5) By standing
(6) By pairing
(7) By ballot
(8) By postal ballot
(9) By poll.

(1) By Acclamation: A verbal communication medium. Sometimes, it may take the form of non-verbal communication. Under this method, the members in a meeting express their approval or disapproval on a motion by applause, cheering or clapping of hands. This is known as communication as voting by acclamation. This method is usually adopted when there is unanimity on any matter and this method is not adopted in the case of a proposal on which there is a sharp difference of opinion.

(2) By Voice: Oral communication method of voting to ascertain the sense of the house. This method is adopted when there is unanimity on any matter. The judgement is made on the basis of volume of voice. The chairman reads the motion and explains, "as many as are of that opinion say, 'Aye.' He listens to those who says 'Aye' (yes). Then he exclaims, "as many as are of the contrary opinion, say 'No' and listens to the voices exclaiming 'No.' From the volume of voices, he judges which side has the majority, and then announces the verdict by saying, " I think the 'Ayes' (or 'Noes', as the case may be) have it."

(3) By Show of Hands: In one sense, it is one way communication by words. Under this method, the chairman of the meeting calls upon those in favour of the matter to raise hands and counts their number. Similarly, he calls upon those who are against the matter to raise hands. On a comparison of the hands shown for and against the matter, he announces the judgement. Under Section 177 of the Companies Act, 1956, at any general meeting a resolution put to vote at the meeting shall, unless a poll is demanded, be decided on a show of hands. Proxies are not allowed to vote under this method.

(4) Standing Vote: Standing vote is a variation of voting by show of hands. Under this method, the members are asked in favour of motion and those against the motion in turn stand up in their seats. On a comparison of numbers, he declares the verdict.

(5) By Division: Under this method, the entire house is divided into two blocks. The chairman requests the members present to divide into two divisions. Those in favour walk into one block and those against it in the other block. The teller of the meeting counts the number of persons in each block separately and communicates the numbers to the chairman who declares the result.

(6) By Pairing: A British Parliamentary voting method. Under this method, a member belonging to one party or side agrees with a member of the opposite side, to absent himself if the other member also remains absent. Under this reciprocal agreement, equal number of votes of both sides are neutralised and the relative strength of the two sides can be determined.

(7) By Ballot: A written mode of expressing opinion. Every member who is entitled to vote records his opinion on a ballot or voting papers which are either deposited in the boxes kept for the purpose or are collected by the teller. Expressing opinion by ballot ensures secrecy of opinion. It is adopted in company meetings as well as political election.

(8) By Postal Ballot: In all cases, it may not be possible for all the members to attend. The members who are unable to attend the meeting and cast their votes, postal ballot method enables them to cast their votes. Postal ballot is an arrangement under which ballot papers are supplied to the members. After recording their vote or expressing their opinions, the members send back the ballot papers by post in a sealed cover.

(9) By Poll: The term "poll" literally means 'counting of heads'. This method of voting is adopted in company meeting with a large attendance. Members, under this method, casts a number of votes based on the shares held by them. In other words, the number of votes is proportionate to the shares held by them. The voting power of every member is reckoned with reference to his stake or share in the company. Section 179 of the Indian Companies Act, 1956, provides for a poll to be taken if the chairman or a prescribed number of members are dissatisfied with the results of voting by a show of hands. Each member may cast more than one vote.

Defamatory Speech or Report

The word "defamation" means the act of trying to harm the reputation of someone. Oral or written statements tending to damage someone's reputation. An imputation that directly or indirectly lowers the moral or intellectual character, or lowers the character of someone in respect of his çaste or of his calling, or lowers the credit of that person, or causes it to be believed, that the body of that person is in a loathsome state or in a state generally considered as disgraceful.

Section 499 of the Indian Penal Code defines the term "defamation" in the words that whoever by words either spoken or intended to be read, or by sign or by visible representations, makes or publishes any imputation concerning any person intending to harm or knowing or having reason to believe that such imputation will harm the reputation of such person, is said, except in the cases herein after excepted, to defame that person.

Oral or written statements or reports placed before the meeting is governed with general law relating to defamation. Either in public meeting or private meeting people concerned with meetings are involved in matters arising out of such speeches or reports. Defamation is purely a personal matter. The word "person" includes a company in the eyes of law and can sue and be sued for defamation. Defamation comes within the scope of crime as well as a tort. Tort means civil wrong. The Indian Penal Code provides for the punishment for defamation and makes the printing of defamatory matter and the sale of such matter, a criminal offense. It attracts imprisonment as well as fine or both.

What are Defamation Statements?

All oral or written statements are not defamatory speeches or reports. To constitute a defamtory statement, certain essential ingredients of the offence of defamation should be fulfilled. The essentials incorporated in Section 499 such as making or publishing any imputation, made by words, either spoken or intended to be read or signed, visible representations with the intention of defaming others. The following are the cases where an ordinary defamatory statement does not involve any criminal liability:

(i) It is defamation to impute anything which is true concerning any person, if it be for the public good that the imputation should be made or published. In order to come within this exception, it has to be established that what has been imputed against the complainant (the defamed person) is true and the publication of the imputation is for the "public good." The onus of providing the two ingredients is on the person seeking the benefit of the exception "public good" is a question of fact and "good faith" has also to be established as faith.

(ii) It is not defamation to express in good faith any opinion whatever respecting the conduct of public servant in the discharge of his public functions, or respecting his character, so far as his character appears in that conduct, and no further.

(iii) It is not defamation to express in good faith in any opinion whatever respecting the conduct of any person touching any public question, as far as his character appears in that conduct, and no further.

(iv) It is not defamation to publish a substantially true report of the proceedings of a court of justice, or the result of any such proceedings.

(v) It is not defamation to express in good faith any opinion whatever respecting the merits of any case, civil or criminal, which has been decided by a court of justice, or representing the conduct of any person as a party, witness or agent, in any such case, or representing the character of such person, as far as his character appears in that conduct, and no further.

(vi) It is not defamation to express in good faith any opinion respecting the merit of any performance which its author has submitted to the judgment of the public, or respecting the character of the author so far his character appears in such performance, and no further.

(vii) It is not defamation if a person having any authority, over another either conferred by law or arising out of a lawful contract made with that other, to pass in good faith any censure on the conduct of that other in matters to which such lawful authority relates.

(viii) It is not defamation to prefer in good faith an accusation against any person to any of those who have lawful authority over that person with respect to the subject matter of accusation.

(ix) It is not defamation to make an imputation on the character of another provided that the imputation be made in good faith for the protection of the interest of the person making it, of any other person, or for the public good.

(x) It is not defamation to convey a caution in good faith, to one person against another, provided that such caution is intended for the good of the person to whom it is conveyed, or of some person in whom that person is interested, or for the public good. These are exceptions to Section 499 of the Indian Penal Code.

Privilege in Speeches

The expression "privilege in speech" means a favour or right available to a speaker or a writer in certain circumstances. Oral or written statements are said to be privileged when persons making them are protected from legal action for defamation. Generally, oral or written statements are privileged when they are based on truth, good faith without malice and in a common interest. In the case of meetings while speaking on a matter, a speaker may make critical remarks against a person. The other person may consider it as defamatory. Consequently, he may take legal action for defamation against the speaker who made the critical remark and claim damages for defamatory statements. On the other hand, the law allows a privilege in speech on certain occasions like meetings. This privilege in speech enables the speaker or writer to express opinion, feelings freely and a reasonable criticism. In this, one need not fear of defamation. But protection is available when it is privileged, based on truth, good faith without malice and in the common interest of all. Meeting of directors, shareholders, committee meetings are considered as privileged occasions. Any justified criticism or any statement of critical remark made at such occasions, are not actionable in law and the speaker is protected from legal action for defamation. Following statements are considered to be privileged:

(1) A statement based on justification, truth and for public good.

(2) A statement made for

- (i) Common interest;
- (ii) Discharge of duty;
- (iii) Self defence; and
- (iv) Fair, accurate and impartial reports of parliament, public meetings and judicial proceedings.

Statements of the following persons are said to be privileged:

(1) Statement of directors and shareholders are said to be privileged.

(2) Statement made by the press, parliament, judge etc.

Types of Privilege: The privilege is of two types:

(1) Absolute privilege.

(2) Qualified privilege.

(1) Absolute Privilege: A privilege is said to be absolute where the person making a defamatory statement is free from liability. The speaker is protected from legal action of defamation. Absolute privilege is available where the matter is of such importance, even if the statement is false or defamatory and is made out of malice. Absolute privilege is allowed to:

(a) A statement made by a judge.

(b) A statement made by an advocate or witness in a Court of Law.

(c) Statements made by members of parliament when made within the house.

(d) Statements to newspaper reporters of proceedings in parliament or Court of Law.

(2) Qualified Privilege: In certain cases, the speaker is protected from legal action for defamation. In a qualified privilege, a defamatory statement is also protected from legal action. Qualified privilege is a privileged occasion where the speaker is entitled to make the statement even if it is false, provided that the statement is made in good faith, honestly in the absence of malice and without improper motive. Qualified privilege is allowed in private meetings like meetings of private bodies, corporate meetings and meetings of local authorities. So the meetings of directors and shareholders are considered as privileged occasions and enjoy only qualified privilege. Therefore, in these meetings, a *bonafide* criticism by directors or shareholders or management at a meeting is privileged.

To sum up, in certain circumstances, it is excusable to express freely and publish matter which are both false and defamatory. The reason is that the law recognises that in certain cases, the liability for defamation to be excluded because the interest of the public is more important than the reputation of an individual.

Interruption of Discussions

Interruption of discussions or debate with reference to a meeting means to stop a speaker while he is saying or debating something. In other words, it is making a break in proceedings. When a discussion or debate is going on, it can be interrupted by members. There are various ways of moving motions to interrupt a debate. The methods adopted to interrupt are dilatory tactics followed by members. The object of interrupting proceedings is that a decision on motion is not to be taken. A debate may be interrupted by the introduction of anyone of the following formal motions, which need not be in writing:

(1) The previous question: "That the question be not now put."

(2) To proceed to the next business: "That the meeting now proceed to the next business."

(3) The closure: "That the question be now put to vote."

(4) To adjourn the debate.

(5) To refer back to the committee.

(6) That the question lies on the table.

(7) Points of order.

(8) To adjourn the meeting.

The following is a brief description of these methods.

(1) The previous question: It is a device to prevent further discussion on a matter before a meeting. The mover of the motion wishes to prevent a vote being taken on the proposal. A member rises and moves in the form: "That the question be not now put."

(2) To proceed to the next business: The moving of motion to the next business is intended to solve the matter before the meeting. This is similar to the previous question. Any member intending to interrupt may rise and move it in the following way: "That the meeting now proceed to the next business." It is to be seconded and put to vote.

(3) The closure: Closure is also a method of stopping a discussion. This method is adopted where the object is to close a prolonged and unnecessary discussion on a matter. When a matter has been sufficiently discussed, any member may rise and move the closure. It takes the form of "that the question now be put." This is also known as "Gag." It is to be seconded and put to vote.

(4) To adjourn the debate: "Adjournment" means to defer a discussion to a later date or sine die. Sine die means indefinitely. This motion is put in the form: "That the debate on this subject be adjourned". The meeting continues and will be resumed at a future date but only discussion on the motion is stopped for the time being.

(5) To refer back to the committee: This method is used only when the matter proposed by or recommended by a committee is under discussion.

(6) The question lies on the table: This method is rarely used and has limited application to cases when the communication or document is before the meeting which either calls for no discussion or do not care to deal or come to a decision. The reason is that the discussion is unnecessary or those who present are not competent enough to handle the matter. This motion is put in the following form: "That the question lies on the table." Similarly in the case of a communication or document, it takes the form of "That it be laid on the table."

(7) Point of order: Yet another method to make discussion is the point of order. Under this a question relating to the procedure of meeting is raised. Any member can raise a point of order with a view to draw the attention of the chairman to some irregularities or defects in the procedure or in the constitution of the meeting, thereby causing interruption to debate. The defects may be as to the absence of a quorum or that the proposal is not within the scope of the notice, rules of the meeting or any other irregularity. The decision of the chairman on a point of order is final.

(8) To adjourn the meeting: This method is used at the close of any speech or conclusion of any business.

Proxy (A Representative Spokesman)

A person designated by a stockholder to represent him at the company's annual meeting and vote his shares. Also used for the card that the stockholder uses to appoint his proxy. Written authorisation given by a stockholder to someone else to vote his stock. Under Section 176 of the Companies Act, 1956, every member of the company is entitled to appoint another person as his proxy. A proxy may be a member or non-member. Proxy is entitled to attend a general meeting and vote in certain circumstances. There are two types of proxies.

(a) General Proxy: Under this type, a proxy is entitled to vote on all resolutions in a general meeting.

(b) Special Proxy: A person who is authorised to vote only a specific resolution.

There are two forms of proxies, they are:

(a) One-way proxy: Under this form, the proxy can only cast his vote in the affirmative. This is technically known as one-way proxy.

(b) Two-way proxy: Under this form, a proxy is authorised and given an opportunity to vote in favour of a resolution or against a resolution. This is known as two-way proxy because the proxy can act as he deems fit in the circumstances.

A person who is entitled to attend a meeting and vote has the right to appoint a proxy. A proxy need not be a member of the company. Presence of a proxy is not counted for the purpose of quorum except in the case of a proxy of a body corporate. The Indian Companies Act provides provisions governing proxy. It should be in writing, signed by the appointer filled in a form. Schedule IX to the Companies Act prescribe form of proxy. It is to be lodged with the company at any time within 48 hours before the meeting.

Though a proxy is a representative spokesman of the appointer, he has no right to speak at a meeting. There is no scope for him to face interaction with other members. However, he can communicate adopting written media by putting questions in writing and sending the same to the chairman of the meeting for answers. Similarly, he cannot participate in the discussion. But the private companies through their articles empower the proxies to speak also at the meeting. In the case of a company member, a proxy appointed by any body corporate which is member of the company has a right to speak because a body corporate can speak through a human agency only. A proxy is ordinarily entitled to vote on a poll. A proxy may be revoked at any time by the appointer before the proxy votes.

Notices of Meeting — Written and Oral Media

The word "notice" is derived from a latin word meaning knowledge. The term in relation to a meeting signifies the bringing of knowledge of the meeting to the person concerned. Notices of meetings may be oral, written or in the form of notification issued and published in some news media or in the form of advertisement. A meeting is to be properly held only when notice of meeting is served to the concerned persons. The proper notice of meeting would enable the members to exercise their own judgements as to whether they will attend or not. It should be used by the proper authority. Therefore, a notice must be drafted according to the procedures, practice etc. In the case of company meetings, most of the provisions as to meetings are to be found in the Articles or in the Companies Act. Similarly, in the case of local authorities, there are various rules contained in statutes which govern the holding of meetings. The other institutions may be subject to their own rules as to meetings.

There are a number of general principles relating to the notice of meetings. The following are the general principles or rules to be observed:

(1) Every person concerned and entited to attend the meeting must be summoned or given notice.

(2) The notice must contain all the relevant and material particulars relating to the date, time, place of meeting.

(3) To complete a notice, it must be accompanied by an agenda specifying the nature of business to be transacted.

(4) The notice must be precise, explicit and unambiguous.

(5) The length of notice must be reasonable.

(6) The corporate meetings are governed by the Companies Act and the Articles of Association.

(7) The notice must be served in the prescribed manner and strictly in accordance with the rules, if any, prescribed in that behalf.

(8) A notice may be served orally, i.e., personally or by telephone. Verbal notice must be confirmed by a written notice.

According to Section 171 of the Companies Act, 1956 a general meeting of a company may be called by giving not less than 21 days' notice in writing. Not less than 21 days has been construed as meaning 21 clear days, the day of serving the notice and the day to holding of the meeting are to be excluded. Sometimes, a short notice will be permissible.

A notice may be served

(a) Personally; or

(b) By post at the registered address within India by prepaying the postage;

(c) By registered post or under certificate of posting if a member so desires and a sum sufficient to cover the expenses is received from him in advance.

Resolutions

The word "resolution" means a firm decision or opinion formally expressed by a group of people, unanimously or by simple majority or by substantial majority. The act of resolving a problem. A question on which a vote is about to be taken is called a "motion." When the motion has been placed before the meeting and has been duly voted upon and passed by a majority, it is called a "resolution." Thus, a resolution is a formal expression of the decision of a meeting. A resolution is recorded in a separate book called "minutes." It is an official decision, and the minutes is a record of evidence as to a decision officially taken. The major part of an organisation's work is carried over by passing resolutions at a meeting specially convened from time to time.

There are three types of resolutions. They are:

(1) Ordinary Resolution.

(2) Special Resolution.

(3) Resolutions Requiring Special notice.

A brief description is as under:

Ordinary Resolution: A decision is arrived in a meeting by a simple majority of votes cast by members present in person or by proxy. "Simple majority" means that votes cast in favour of the resolution must at least be 51 per cent. All usual and ordinary business matters for which a special resolution is not required by law may be transacted by an ordinary resolution.

Ordinary resolutions are required to transact the ordinary business such as:

(1) Appointment of auditor and fixation of auditor's remuneration.

(2) Appointment of directors.

(3) Declaration of dividend.

(4) Adoption of annual financial statements like balance sheet, director's report, auditor's report and profit and loss account.

(5) Issue of bonus shares.

(6) Borrowing money.

(7) Adaptation of statutory report.

(8) Removal of director before the expiry of time.

(9) Alteration of share capital.

(10) Issue of shares at discount.

(11) Sale of company's business.

(12) Investment of sale proceeds of the company's business in securities other than trust securities.

Specimen Ordinary Resolutions

(1) "Resolved that the consent of the Company be and is hereby accorded to the Board or Directors under Section 293 (1) (e) of the Companies Act, 1956 for the following:

(i) for making a contribution of Rs. 60,000/- towards the construction of Hostel Building in connection with the Platinum Jubilee Celebration of the said station.

and

(ii) for donating 600 kgs of 3" x 4" of M.S. Pipes 400ft long valued @ Rs. 200/- from the scrap yard of the company for use in the construction of Hanuman Temple at a total not exceeding Rs. 71,500/-".

(2) "Resolved that consent of the company be and is hereby given under Section 293 (1) (e) of the Companies Act, 1956 to the Board of Directors for allotment of 33 acres of land in the farm

book value being Rs. 10,500/- as per the Company's books under the purview of company's free of cost for shifting the hut-dwellers residing on the company's land behind Ram Mandir.

(3) "Resolved that consent of the Company be and is hereby given under Section 293 (i) (e) of the Companies Act, 1956 to the Board of Directors for issue of 35 kgs of free sale sugar during the financial year 1990-91 at levy sugar rate of each of the 35,600 loyal cane-growers as identified by the Company spread over different sugar manufacturing units of the company at total financial incidence not exceeding Rs. 9,50,000".

Special Resolution

The object of this resolution is that every important matter is to be decided after the deliberation and with the consent of a large number of shareholders present at the meeting in person or by proxy. A collective decision is arrived by a large group.

Special resolution requires 3/4th majority to pass. To transact a special business, this resolution is passed. Section 189 of the Companies Act, 1956 provided that a special resolution be passed when:

(a) The intention to propose the resolution as a special resolution has been duly specified in the notice calling the general meeting.

(b) The votes cast in favour of the resolution by members in person or proxies are not less than three times the number of votes cast against the resolution. The following are some of the special business transactions requiring special resolutions :

(1) Alteration of the Memorandum to change the objects clause and to change domicile clauses.

(2) Change the name of the company.

(3) Commencing any new line of business.

(4) Omission of the word 'Limited' or 'Private Limited' from the name of the company.

(5) Alteration of Articles of Association.

(6) Issue of further shares without pre-emptive rights.

(7) Reduction in share capital.

(8) Variation of rights of shareholders.

(9) Payment of interest out of capital.

(10) Fixation of remuneration of director.

(11) Giving permission to a director to hold place of profit in the company.

(12) Applying to the Court for winding up of the company.

(13) Appointing a sole selling agent in the case of companies having paid up share capital of Rs. 50 lakhs or more.

(14) For applying to Central Government for appointing an inspector.

(15) Making the liability of any director or manager unlimited.

(16) Authorising a liquidator in a voluntary winding up to exercise certain powers.

Specimen Special Resolutions

(1) "Resolved that sanction of the company be and is hereby given under the provisions of Sec. 81 (1A) and other applicable provisions, if any, of the Companies Act, 1956 for the issue of 8,20,000 Equity shares of the face value of Rs. 25/- each of the Govt. within the increased Authorised Capital of the Company and the Board of Directors of the Company be and is hereby authorised to offer the said shares to the Government for cash at par payable in full on application and it is hereby expressly provided that the said 8,20,000 Equity shares shall in all respects rank **pari passu** with the existing Equity shares and Board of Directors be and is hereby further authorised to take all such steps for the implementation of this resolution as it may think necessary or expedient."

(2) "Resolved that the existing article 108 of the Articles of Association of the Company be and is hereby substituted by the following Articles as Article 108 of the Articles of Association of the Company with the marginal note "Remuneration of Directors" as under 108. The Directors shall be paid out of the funds of the Company, remuneration for their services, such sum for every meeting of the Board or of Committee attended by each of them as shall from time to time be fixed by the Directors."

(3) "Resolved that the approval be and is hereby accorded for payment of Rs. 1,727.50 to Shri S.P. Prasad Rao, I.A.S., as additional charge pay for discharging the duties of the Chairman and Managing Director of the Company for the period from 5-10-1996 to 10-12-1997."

(4) "Resolved that approval be and is hereby given to the payment of remuneration to Sri Vijay Kumar, I.A.S., Ex-chairman and Managing Director of the Company from the date of appointment, *viz*., from 10-9-1996 to 18-11- 1997 in his grade pay above the time scale pay in the Indian Administration Service under the State Government and the allowances as may be admissible to him from time to time besides leave and pension contribution and perquisites as set out in the terms and conditions of his appointment."

(5) "Resolved that approval be and is hereby given to the payment of remuneration to Shri. P.L. Narsi, I.A.S., Chairman and Managing Director of the Company from the date of his appointment, *viz*, from 10-9-1996 to 11-12-1997 in his grade pay in the super time scale of the Indian Administrative Service and the allowances as may be admissible to him from time to time in the Government besides leave and pension contribution and other perquisites as set out in the terms and conditions of his appointment".

(6) "Resolved that sanction of the Company be and is hereby given under the provision of Section 81 (1 A) and other applicable provisions, if any, of the Companies Act, 1956 for the issue of 5,50,000. Equity shares of the face value of Rs. 30 each to the Government of Andhra Pradesh within the existing authorised capital of the company and the Board of Directors of the company be and is hereby authorised to offer the said shares to the Government of Andhra Pradesh for cash at par payable in full on application and it is hereby expressly provided that the said 5,50,000 equity shares and the Board of Directors be and is hereby authorised to take all such steps for the implementation of this Resolution as it may think necessary or expedient."

Resolution Requiring Special Notice

The Companies Act, 1956, provides for a new type of resolution known as "Resolution Requiring Special Notice: It gives a time sufficient to consider the proposed resolution. A resolution requiring special notice may be passed at the general meeting by a simple majority or three-fourth's majority to the nature of business. There are many matters for which special notices are required.

Certain types of businesses require special notice. The member who wants to move such a resolution, gives special notice to the company at least 14 days before the date of the meeting. The company in turn gives notice to the members at least 7 days before the date of meeting. The resolution require special notice may be an ordinary resolution or special resolution. The business as requiring special notice are:

(1) Removing of a director before the expiry of his term or to appoint another.

(2) Appointment as auditor of a person other than the retiring auditor or that a retiring auditor should not be re-appointed.

(3) Appointment of a person otherwise not eligible as director.

(4) To appoint another person as director in the place of the removed director.

Minutes (Written Media)

A written book or sheet, a record of the proceedings and resolutions passed at a meeting. It contains the date, place, members present, proposals and decisions taken by way of resolution. Minutes furnish evidence as to the proceedings. Minutes means the facial recording of the proceedings of the meetings. Minutes of general body meeting, board meeting, committee meeting and extraordinary general body meeting. A minute book must be in a bound book and signed by the concerned people to be authenticity of the minutes of proceedings. Minutes kept in a loose leaf form is generally not desirable which should not be attached or pasted in the bound book.

A minute book is maintained with a view to preserve a record of business transacted at meetings. They serve, as a permanent record of the decision taken, members present, date, place etc. As the notes taken at a meeting, recording what was decided and resolved duly signed serve as evidence or proof of the proceedings in a court of law. Minutes are written media. For practical purposes, it is desirable to maintain minutes, in all organisations, of the proceedings of every meeting, including committee meetings. They will be prima facie evidence as to meeting duly called and validly held. Thus, organisational practices greatly emphasise the importance of the proper recording and maintenance of minutes of proceedings of meetings. In some concerns, the organisational manuals lay procedure for keeping minutes. As a written medium, they satisfy one of the essential requirements of written communication as to record of message.

The Indian Companies Act, 1956, provides a number of provisions governing minutes as to the maintenance of minutes books, contents of minutes, indexing of minutes, signing of minutes, evidence, inspection and consequences as to the failure to keep minutes.

Types of Minutes

(1) Minutes of narration.

(2) Minutes of Resolution or decision.

A brief description of these two types is presented in the following paragraphs.

Minutes of Narration

Minutes of narration is also a record. They record simply statements of happenings, and events which "do not require any formal resolution. Certain events is do not require to be put to voting. In other words, these are records of events, or items of business which do not require formal expression. They include narration of the introductory part of the minutes, members present recording of apologies for absence, particulars of proposals and seconders of motions etc.

Minutes of Resolutions

Under this type, minutes of resolutions record the formal decisions of the meetings. There are records of decisions or resolutions.. They do not contain narration of the members present, recording of apologies of absence, and details of proposer, and seconders of motions etc.

Methods of Maintaining Minutes

There are two methods generally adopted to maintain minutes.

They are: (1) Bound Book Method. (2) Loose-Leaf Method

(1) Bound Book Minutes: Bound book minutes is a traditional method. The books should be kept under safe custody. Minutes are written in the bound book or typed sheets are affixed in the bound book minutes.

(2) Loose-Leaf Minutes: In order to overcome the limitations of bound book method of minutes, loose-leaf minutes books have emerged. The minutes of each meeting written or typed on sheets are inserted in the loose leaf minutes book which is a special binder with lock and key and kept under safe custody. It can be unlocked to reference and new sheets can be inserted without disturbing earlier minutes. Thus this method is more flexible, elastic and simple to operate. But greater care should be taken to prevent fraud or any falsification of minutes. Adequate steps are to be taken to ensure that no page of the book can be removed or replaced easily. The problems associated with this method can be solved provided certain precautions are taken such as:

(1) The special binder of the loose-leaf book should be provided with a lock and key.

(2) The key should be in the custody of the responsible official.

(3) Each leaf should be consecutively numbered, as issued by the responsible official.

(4) Unused or spare leaves should be under the lock and key under the control of the responsible official.

(5) Similarly, the leaves should be issued under the control of the responsible official.

(6) All the pages in a minute book should be consecutively numbered throughout, without any separate set for each meeting.

(7) Each page should be signed or initialled by the chairman of the meeting.

(8) The last page relating to each minutes of each meeting should be signed by the chairman.

Agenda

Agenda is a written medium which communicates the business to be carried out in a meeting. "Agenda" means a list of things to be done at a meeting. It literally implies things to be done. Agenda is the document or programme of business to be transacted at a meeting. In other words, a paper containing the list of items of business to be considered at a meeting. It states the order and nature of business to be transacted at a meeting. The list of items are usually typed on a foolscap paper leaving sufficient margin at the right hand side to note down remarks.

A copy of the Agenda is normally enclosed to the notice of the meeting and to be sent to all the members concerned to attend a meeting. In the case of company meetings, the Indian Companies Act does not define the word "agenda." But it is required that every notice of a meeting should contain "a statement of the business to be transacted thereat." It is nothing but agenda which is to be included in every notice. The discussions and resolutions passing must be conducted in the same order in which the items are listed in the agenda. In exceptional cases, the order can be changed with the consent of the meeting.

Agenda gives an opportunity to the members to come prepared on the subject to the meeting. Generally, no business should be transacted at a meeting unless it is included in the agenda. Care is, therefore, to be taken to draft it carefully. It is to place routine transactions first on the agenda. The last item in the agenda is usually "any other matter with the permission of the chair." It is prepared in two ways. Firstly, briefly giving the headings of the subject. Secondly, by giving details of the business to be transacted. Agenda is prepared for each meeting separately. The agenda of the Board meeting may contain list of items which are quite different from the agenda of members' meeting. Model agenda for different meetings are given below:

No. 1 : Agenda of the First Meeting of Directors

XY Company Limited,

5, Trunk Road, Mumbai

Agenda of meeting of Directors of the company to be held on the Second June, 1997, at 10 A.M. at 55 Trunk Road, Conference Hall, Mumbai City.

(1) Appointment of the Chairman of the meeting.

(2) Production of formation certificates like Certificate of Incorporation, the Memorandum and the Articles of Association.

(3) To take note of the situation of registered office of the company.

(4) Appointment of the first directors.

(5) Election of the Chairman of the Company.

(6) Appointing of Managing Director.

(7) Appointment of Secretary.

(8) Appointment of solicitors.

(9) Appointment of Auditors.
(10) Appointment of Bankers.
(11) To approve the common seal of the company.
(12) Fixing a quorum for the board meeting.
(13) To approve the share certificate form.
(14) To consider commencement of business.
(15) Fix the date of next Board meeting.
(16) Any other matter with the permission of the chair.

No. 2: Agenda of Subsequent Board Meeting

XY Company Limited,

5, Trunk Road, Mumbai

Agenda of Meeting of Directors of the company to be held on the Fifth August 1997, at 10 A.M. at 55 Trunk Road, Conference Hall, Mumbai City.

(1) To confirm the minutes of the last meeting.
(2) To discuss on matters arising out of minutes.
(3) To consider applications for transfer committee.
(4) To take note of the minutes of transfer committee.
(5) To sanction capital expenditure.
(6) To consider and approve financial statements.
(7) To consider a trading return for the year ending.
(8) To consider and take note of directors retiring by rotation.
(9) Appropriation of profit.
(10) To approve Director's Report to shareholders.
(11) Consideration of auditor's report to shareholders.
(12) Fixing date of the next annual general meeting.
(13) Fixing the date of next Board meeting.
(14) Any other matter with the permission of the chair.

No. 3: Agenda of Statutory Meeting

XY Company Limited,

5, Trunk Road, Bombay

Agenda of Statutory Meeting to be held on the 5th of August, 1997, at 10 A.M. at 55 Trunk Road, Conference Hall, Mumbai City.

(1) To read the notice convening the meeting.
(2) To bring to the notice of the members to the fact that the list of members is open for inspection.

(3) To consider and adopt the statutory report as circulated to be taken as read.

(4) To invite questions, discussions, for the statutory reports.

(5) Speech by chairman relating to formation, progress and trading results.

(6) Discussions on matters arising out of speech.

(7) Any other matter with the permission of the chair.

(8) To be declare the meeting as concluded.

No. 4: Agenda of Fifteenth Annual General Meeting

XY Company Limited,

5, Trunk Road, Mumbai

Agenda of Fifteenth Annual General Meeting to be held on the 5th of August, 1997, at 10 A.M. at 55 Trunk Road, Conference Hall, Mumbai City:

(1) To declare by the chairman that the meeting is in order.

(2) The secretary to read out the notice of the meeting.

(3) To receive and adopt Director's report, and the annual accounts.

(4) The Chairman's speech.

(5) Discussion on matters arising out of speech.

(6) To announce that the Register of Members, Register of Directors, their shareholding etc., are kept open for inspection.

(7) To declare dividend as recommended by the Board.

(8) To appoint two directors in place of S.R. Saxena and N. Mukharji, who retire by rotation and being eligible for re-election.

(9) Appointment of company's auditors for the current year and fix their remuneration.

(10) To pass ordinary resolution regarding the appointment of Shri Joshi.

(11) To pass special resolution regarding the appointment of M/s. Tiger Locks Agency as the sole selling agent of the company.

(12) Any other matter with the permission of the chair.

(13) Vote of thanks and to declare the meeting closed.

COMMITTEES AND MEETINGS OF COMMITTEES

A camel is a horse designed by a committee.

The best committee is a five-person committee with four members absent.

In a committee, minutes are taken but hours are wasted. A committee is collection of the unfit appointed the unwilling to perform the unnecessary.[23]

These remarks are jokes, but they represent the widespread negativism attached to the committee form of organisation.

Meaning and Nature

The word "committee" means a body or group comprising a number of persons selected from a larger body of group constituted with a specific task assigned to deal with to report on specific matter so assigned. It may be referred to as a board, commission, task force, council working group, fact-finding group, teams, batch, by whatever name called, its essential nature and functioning is the same. Committee is an organisation device to take a decision by exchange of information, discussion, deliberation. The members of the committee interact each other as well as with outsiders. Committee has a potential to arrive at a decision through a stimulating communication. It is the most common and widely practiced in organisations. Therefore, a committee may be defined as a group of people pooled together to perform some aspects of the managerial functions like finance, marketing, production, personnel etc., may be advisory or decision-making. In inter-related and inter-dependent group activities, consultation, discussion must be held to take a decision. The functional managers have to meet and discuss inter-related matters to take policy decisions. It is in the meeting that the problems, plans, budgets, issues figure in as to finance, sale, production etc., which facilitate to approach them in an integrated manner. To say a group as a committee, it must be planned in advance. It means meeting spontaneously or informally does not constitute a committee, it must be planned in advance. It means meeting spontaneously or informally does not constitute a committee. A committee meet gives an opportunity to the participating members for excellent and direct transmission of information, ideas, facts, figures, feelings and attitudes to the members. Two heads are better than one is the principle of committee form of organisation than taking a decision by one head.

Definition: According to Hicks, "A committee is a group of people who meet by plan to discuss to make a decision for a particular subject."[24]

In the words of Newmans, "A committee consists of a group of people specifically designated to perform some administrative acts. It functions only as groups and requires the free interchange of ideas among its members."[25]

Allen defines a committee as "a body of persons appointed or elected to meet on an organised basis for the consideration of matters brought before it.[26]

Hicks and Gullet: "A committee is a group of people who meet by plan to discuss or make a decision for a particular subject. Because a committee meets by plan, we do not include groups that occur spontaneously or informally in the definition of a committee."[27]

Types of Committee

(1) Ad hoc Committee: A committee that is constituted for a particular objective and is dissolved soon after the accomplishment of objective. A temporary committee that is appointed for a time being or for a particular purpose. It gives its recommendations or decisions.

(2) Standing Committee: Opposed to *ad hoc* committee, a standing committee is a permanent body which is of a advisory nature.

(3) Plural Executive: The most common example of a plural executive is the board of directors. A line committee performs certain managerial functions. Plural committee works also as a line committee, plural executive or the executive committee. The Board of Directors, high level policy committees, for example, finance, serve in the plural executive capacity. The plural executive enjoys authority to make decisions and manage the offices of the organisation.

(4) Formal Committee: A formal committee is a part of the organisational structure. It is officially designated and with defined duties and authority. The committee is usually required to follow rules and procedures, which are often written.

Besides these, unwritten rules and procedures are also binding on it.

(5) Informal Committee: An informal committee is generally organised temporarily without any specific delegation of authority. Such a committee is described as an informal committee. For instance, the head of an institution desiring to know about group thinking or group decisions on a particular issue may call a meeting of some of the members of the staff. This is an informal committee. Special meeting to seek advice from senior members of the staff or specialists outside their department is also an informal committee. Informal committee also arises on account of the compulsion of splintered authority. An informal committee is usually temporary.

(6) Line Committee: Depending upon the authority enjoyed, a committee may be a line committee. If a committee is assigned a task with a defined power to make decisions and implement them through subordinates, it is described as a line committee or plural executive. In other words, if its power involves decision-making affecting subordinates, it is a plural executive.

(7) Staff Committee: If the relation of a committee to the superior is advisory in nature, it is described as a staff committee. It is so called because its authority relationship to the superior is advisory.

(8) Consultative Management: It is a kind of participation. It will not affect the existing authority responsibility relationships. Under this method, managers consult their employees in order to convey to them to participate on the issues involved, think, discuss, deliberate, and give ideas in the decision-making process.

(9) Democratic Management: Democratic management is also one of the methods of participations to have a group discussion or major problems to employee groups. It is also group dynamics. The principles on which democratic management is based are group participation, group deliberations, group ideas and group influence.

(10) Works Committee: In order to discuss the problem relating to work or job, works committees are formed at different levels. They are also called "production committees." Committees are composed of such members who are directly relating to work to deliberate on job problems. This is the most popular method of small groups in a formal organisation.

(11) Middle Management Committee: It is also called as multiple management which has been in practice in many countries, both unionised and non-unionised. K. Davis writes that its central core is a junior Board of Directors that is giving the opportunity to study any problem and to recommend a course of action. Employers' information is made freely available to the Board and its meetings are unrestricted by the presence of senior executives. Members make their own bye-laws and rotate their membership.

Advantages of Committees

Committees have some important advantages to offer to organisations. The most commonly cited advantages of committees are group decisions, motivation and co-ordination. Besides these, there are many advantages accruing from some of the most important advantages of committees.

(1) Collective Decision: Two are better than one. A committee comprising group of people of more heads have diverse knowledge, experience and judgement. So the decision taken collectively in group deliberation is superior and more efficient than that taken by one person. The solution arrived to a problem is based on the application of a wider range of experience, a greater variety of opinion.

(2) Motivation: The Committee System allows greater representation to important interest groups such as creditors, customers, labour unions and shareholders. The Board of Directors may have representation from financial institutions, Government etc. When subordinates participate in the decision-making process, they feel a sense of belonging and show enthusiasm in implementing decisions in which they are also participants.

(3) Co-ordination: The task of co-ordination in any group activity is more difficult and challenging. The decisions of one functional department influence the other department. The committee system provides an opportunity to promote co-ordination, plans and policies and various activities of an enterprise. Committees help in bringing perfect coordination of interdepartmental activities. Committees composed of many members drawn from different departments can better understand the need for co-ordination.

(4) Creative Ideas: A clearly-defined problem requires creative ideas useful to practically every organisation function. Different members may have different skills and talents. Through brain-storming and other group creative activities, committees can produce creative ideas.

(5) Co-operation: There is a stimulus towards co-operative action in committee organisation. Similarly, it encourages group co-operation and team spirit in the organisation.

(6) Communicating: Committee is a very useful medium for transmitting information. It serves as easier and useful device for exchange of ideas, facts, opinions etc. It is an excellent means of oral communication instrument for transmitting information to interested organisational members. The advantages of face-to-face oral communication, instant interaction, feedback, two-way communication etc., can be obtained.

(7) Democratising: The committee form of organisation in decision- making by allowing subordinates to participate in decision-making process is a democratic process. H.G. Hicks and C.R. Gullett state thus: Where desired, a committee can be used to reduce the "tyranny of an executive" and to permit greater member participation in decision-making.

(8) Consolidating Power and Authority: No single person has concentrated power and authority. A committee system eliminates the fear of too much authority and power in a single person. The main reason for the widespread use of committee is to avoid power, authority and delegation — too much authority to a single person. A committee system ensures consolidating of or collecting the authority of several individual members.

(9) Avoidance of Action: The committee system is the best means to avoid action or delay action. Sometimes, managers constitute a committee if they want to avoid action or delay action on a problem. The problem may be assigned to a committee. According to H.G. Hicks and C.R. Gullett: "With adroit leadership, the committee might quite easily get bogged down in interminable debate and indecision. The chairperson might also delay action by not scheduling meetings, and by injecting 'red herring' issues into the discussion."

(10) Training Ground: Committees serve as a training ground for executives. They help greatly to the executive training and development. Subordinates too have an opportunity to have an insight into the problems faced by the executives. Managers can teach them as to the techniques to solve a problem.

(11) Blurring Responsibility: No individual is singly responsible for decisions taken. But it is the collective decision of all the people known as committee decision. In some circumstances, it is desirable that a committee takes the responsibility for actions for which individuals do not wish to be responsible.

(12) Combining Abilities: Committee organisation effectively leads to the pooling of knowledge and experience. In some cases, committee makes a superior decision that the individual might take. Intricate problems can be effectively solved by the combined abilities of a group of persons. Committee is a means whereby the knowledge and abilities of several person can be brought to bear on a problem.

(13) Advising: A committee can better advice the management. An executive may wish advice and counsel before making a decision. To achieve this, he may convene a meeting to seek required counsel and advice.

(14) Moral Support: There is always available moral support on all risky matters. A collective group has group support. No single person is blamed for any wrong-doings, because the implementing authority acts on the committee advice.

(15) Other Advantages: All kinds of questions are given a hearing before a decision is made. The committee is a forum where differences resolved and compromises are reached. Decisions arrived at are impersonal, leaving the individual free from personal criticism. In an inter-departmental network, all departments know better and have full knowledge of what is going on in the sections so that they can communicate the information.

Disadvantages: Though there are a number of advantages arising out of committee organisations; the system is not free from defects and shortcomings. The operation of the committee is subject to a number of limitations and dangers. A number of disadvantages are also inherent in committee organisation. The following are some of the more important disadvantages of a committee system.

(1) Cost: The committee system is costly in terms of money involved. A committee consumes the time of several persons. Time, expenses of travel, preparation activities involve money. So the financial cost of committee meetings is very high.

(2) Indecisive Action: In committee operation, there exists usually differences of opinions. It is due to the conflicting viewpoints of members or poor membership, a committee is sometimes unable to reach a needed decision in time. So delay in decision destroys the objective of decision-making.

(3) Compromising Attitude: It is the practice to take unanimity of opinion before a decision is made by the committee. In order to avoid the climate of indecision, a compromise method is followed. Such compromise is likely to be the least common denominator of group agreement. Therefore, the decision may not be as strong as effective.

(4) Irresponsible Nature: Everybody's business is nobody's business. Actually, decision of a committee is a collective decision and all the members are jointly responsible for the decision arrived at in a meeting. There is no fixed individual responsibility. So committee system is known for breeding grounds of inefficiency and of evasion of real responsibility. This is perhaps the most serious danger of the committee form.

(5) Tyranny of Minority: A committee generally seeks a consensus of unanimous agreement. It is easily possible for the minority of a committee to thwart committee action by refusing to accept the major viewpoint.

(6) Domination: A strong member of the committee dominates the scene and the decision-making process is influenced according to his own thinking. The possibility is influenced according to his own thinking. The possibility of domination by one strong member or small group of influential members of the committee is a real danger to group decision. Front line executives, a minority group or a powerful member may dominate committee meetings and browbeat it into accepting a decision.

(7) Divided Responsibility: Divided responsibility is thus a serious limitation of committee form. Though the responsibility is joint in practice members do not exhibit a sense of responsibility expected from them. Committee's decision means nobody's decision. Individual members may evade decision- making responsibility.

(8) Suppression of Ideas: In a democratic process, decisions are taken by voting on majority of opinion. This leaves behind a legacy of bitterness, discontent and frustration, new ideas or minority ideas may be supressed.

(9) Political Decisions: The members of the committee are drawn from different departments of the organisations, not on the basis of their merit or qualifications. Committee decisions become an expression of politics rather than based on merits and qualifications.

(10) Absence of Secrecy: The discussions are open in the house. It is being a model of plural executive and lacks secrecy. Maintaining secrecy in respect of certain matters is necessary.

(11) Self-Perpetuation: Hicks and Gullett state on self-perpetuation that committees are usually formed for a specific purpose. It often happens, however, that a committee continues to meet long after it has ceased to serve a useful purpose. The tendency to perpetuate themselves is particularly noticeable in committees which have assembled their own staff of secretaries, research assistants, or attorneys.[28]

Suggestions for Making Better Working of Committees

(1) Size of Committee: Proper size of the committee ensures its successful operations. There should not be too many or too few members. The number of members should be minimum that will function a committee effectively. However, there are no hard and fast rules as to the optimum committee size. A committee size is largely influenced by many committee size. A committee size is largely influenced by many factors like the nature of committee, purpose, abilities of the members etc. Large membership leads to confusion in decision and to inferior decisions.

(2) Degfinig of Scope: The purpose and scope of the committee should be clearly and well defined. The members should know its authority, scope, functions, subject, organisational relationship etc. All these aspects should be clearly defined. Definition of various concepts make a committee a useful agency of management.

(3) Selection of Members: The members of a committee should be carefully selected. The members should have personal abilities, particularly, participative skills, creative thinking, analysing capacity from different points of view. They must be suitable representatives of the interests they are intended to serve. It is always desirable if members of equal status are selected. The subordinates are reluctant to speak, oppose or express freely. Therefore, a successful operation of a committee is largely dependent on the careful selection of members.

(4) Selecting Subject Matter: Only matters relevant to a committee are to be selected. Certain kinds of subjects are to be certainly referred to committee action while other subjects should not be referred to it. Success of the committee devices is based on selecting a limited subject matter that can be effectively handled in group discussion.

(5) Right Chairperson: The importance of the chairperson for the success of a committee cannot be overlooked. A skilled chairman can avoid many wastes and drawbacks of a committee. He has to plan for the meeting in advance and conduct it properly. He should be highly skilled in discussions, have leadership qualities, unbiased, give equal opportunity to all members to express themselves freely and impartially.

(6) Agenda: Agenda is a list of business to be transacted at a meeting. An agenda should be prepared in advance and circulated among the interested members of the committee. Items for discussion should be in the order of items stated in the agenda.

(7) Cost and Time: Committee meetings involve heavy cost and time. The result of deliberations must be worth the cost and time.

(8) Follow up: There should be follow-up of committee decisions. The decisions or recommendations should be strictly enforced and implemented. Mere passing of resolutions alone is not sufficient.

(9) Evaluation: The success of a committee organisation is largely dependent on the evaluation of committee work. It should be in terms of success and quality of its decisions. Judgement of committee work should extend further to determine whether it is worth or not in relation to the cost involved.

Leader of a Meeting

"The term seems to have its origin from the circumstance that in early times the presiding officer alone was furnished with a chair; because he must necessarily sit by himself, apart from the others, who were provided only with benches. Hence in moderns time, the presiding officer frequently dominates himself, and is spoken of by others, as the chair."

The leader of a meeting is called "chairman" of a meeting. A chairman may be designated or elected to preside over and conduct the proceedings of the meeting. To have chairman for a meeting is one of the essential requirements of a valid meeting. A meeting must have a presiding officer entrusted with powers to conduct the affairs of the meeting in an orderly way. In a meeting without a chairman, the proceedings are invalid. Hence, the importance of a leader or chairman at a meeting.

He is the chairperson, a chief authority in the conduct and control of the meeting. He is "the umpire of debate, the judge of advisability and the upholder of order and decorum." The term "chairman" is not possible to define. Even the Indian Companies Act, 1956, does not define the term "chairman." The term ''chairman" is commonly understood to mean a person duly authorised to head, a group or committee duly authorized to control and superintendent the conduct of the meeting. A chairman is usually used to designate the presiding officer. It is more commonly applied to committees and other assemblies of temporary character.

Appointment of a Chairperson: Generally, a chairperson is, in practice a member of the group over which he has to preside. A chairperson may be either appointed or designated in advance to chair the meeting. He may be appointed by the rules, regulations or internal bye-laws or elected at the time of the meeting or according to the practice or custom. The bye-laws of a duly constituted group usually designate a chairperson to preside over the meeting.

In the case of company meetings, statutory provisions are there in Indian Companies Act, 1956, regarding the appointment of chairman of a meeting in accordance with the provisions of the Act. The Articles of a Company generally provide regulations in respect of appointment of a chairman. The chairman of the Board of Directors will preside as chairman at every general meeting. Any director can act as a chairman in the case of absence or unwillingness by the chairman of the Board of Directors to act as chairman of the meeting, one of the directors present at the meeting may be elected as the chairman. It is also a practice that any member can act as chairman in the absence or unwillingness of any of the directors to act as chairman. The Central Government or the Company Law Board may appoint any person as its chairman.

Qualification of a Chairman: There are no hard and fast rules or prescribed qualifications and qualities of a chairman. Even in the case of chairman of company meetings, the Companies Act does not prescribe any qualifications, educational or otherwise, which should be possessed by the chairman of a meeting. Undoubtedly a chairman should possess such qualities and qualifications for the successful conduct of the proceedings of a meeting. He should necessarily possess leadership qualities. Besides, he must be well-educated, having a sense of commonsense, public relations, capacity to understand, listening patiently, the sense of meeting and analyse the complexity of matters that figure in the meeting. He should possess tact, patience and knowledge of general law and procedure of meetings along with his powers and duties. He should be well-conversant with rules, practices, governing and conducting a meeting. He should be a man of judicial mind, impractical and employ democratic principles of proceedings. Other qualities like cool, curteous, humour, command, respect and equalities etc., should not be overlooked.

Duties of a Chairman: (1) To see that the meeting is **property convened and truely considered.**

(2) Bonafide: A chairman should act always *bonafide* in the interest of majority and minority.

(3) To Follow Rules: A chairman can conduct a meeting successfully provided the proceedings of the meeting are conducted according to rules, bye- laws, procedure, custom or practice.

(4) Agenda: A chairman should not violate the agenda. Therefore, the business of the meeting is to be taken up in the order set out in the agenda. The agenda may be varied with the consent of the meeting.

(5) Presiding: It is the duty of the chairman to preside over the meeting. As a matter of fact, he is the presiding officer and chairperson.

(6) Follow Motion: A motion is a proposal placed before the meeting for discussion, consideration. It is a subject for discussion only on the definite proposal before the meeting. The motion should be in writing, signed and generally seconded.

(7) Dignity and Decorum: Chairman has to maintain order, discipline, dignity and decorum in the meeting. He should not allow the members to behave or to use unparliamentary language. He should maintain proper language and orderly behaviour.

(8) Equality: It is his duty to be impartial in discharging his duties. He should give reasonable, sufficient and equal opportunities to all members present in the meeting. He should not show discrimination between majority and minority. He should see the right of the minority members and avoid minority oppression. All members, including the minority, should be given equal opportunity to express their views.

(9) Sense of the Meeting: It is an important duty to obtain the sense of the meeting with respect to any question of law. He should ensure that a sense of meeting is properly ascertained on each proposal. He has to supervise the poll, counting, appoint scrutinizers and declare the results.

(10) Minutes: It is obligatory as well as the practice to prepare minutes of every meeting. It acts as a record of evidence. He should see that minutes are prepared properly and he has to sign in it.

Powers of a Chairman: A chairman cannot discharge his duties properly without powers. For this, a chairman has been endowed with some powers. Usually, he derives his powers from the meeting itself. The members of the group confer on him sufficient authority to regulate the members. The following are the powers of a chairman in a meeting.

(1) To Maintain Order and Decorum: He can exercise his authority to maintain order, decorum at the meeting. This takes the form of promoting the use of proper languages and orderly behaviour. He may even seek the removal of any member whose presence is undesirable and obstructive to the smooth conduct of the proceedings.

(2) Casting Vote: A chairman is empowered to second vote power in certain cases. He can exercise a special vote called casting vote "which is available in addition to the deliberative vote as a member. To break a tie, the chairman can cast this vote. This is a second vote. He can exercise such vote if it is expressly permitted by rules, procedure, practice or bye-laws.

(3) To Decide Point of Order: A point of order is a question relating to the rules, procedure and regulations governing meeting. Members usually can raise a point of order as to the irregularities to draw the attention of the chairman.

(4) To Decide Priority of Speakers: When there are several persons interested to speak on the same proposal, priority of speakers should be decided. The chairman has the power to decide the priority or the order in which the members have to speak.

(5) Minutes: Sometimes, the chairman has the power to direct the inclusion and exclusion of matters in the minutes of the meeting and sign the minutes book.

(6) Regulate Voting Procedure: The chairman has the power to order a poll, appoint, scrutinize, supervise counting and finally declare the results. In other words, he has the power to regulate and declare results.

(7) To Adjourn a Meeting: A chairman is empowered to adjourn a meeting under certain circumstances wherein it is not practicable to proceed further discussion. He can adjourn for some time or *sinedie*. Generally, he may adjourn when the quorum in the meeting is not present or when the motion is adapted for adjournment or when the meeting becomes disorderly.

(8) To Stop Discussions: The chairman has the power to stop discussion on a motion or subject matter which has been fairly and sufficiently debated and put to vote.

(9) Deciding Method of Voting: There are several methods of votings like acclamation, show of hands, voice vote, poll, ballet, division etc. The chairman has the power to decide the order for a vote by show of hands in the first instance. He may also order for poll if he is of the opinion that the sense of the meeting has not been correctly ascertained by show of hand.

(10) To Remove Persons: The chairman has the power to remove a scrutinizer. He can also remove any person for unparliamentary behaviour or using improper or undersirable language.

Planning and Organisation of Meetings

The organisational plan of meeting will depend upon the type and purpose of the meeting. Invariably, the chairman of the meeting will make himself responsible for the conduct and organisation of the meeting, should confirm in advance with the regulations or bye-laws applicable to the meetings.

The planning and organisation of meetings necessarily depend on the object of the proposed meeting. In some big organisations, a permanent body or some definite persons are made responsible for the organisation of meetings. Generally, a small working committee is constituted to look after these affairs.

A private meeting may be called by an individual or association of persons concerned. The organisation of such meetings are either mutually decided upon by the members themselves or by the bye-laws regulations or standing orders. However, the conduct of a private meeting must be consistent with any legal provisions, practice or custom.

The organisational planning relating to meetings may be summarised under the following heads. In organising a meeting, the leader needs:

(1) Fixing and Finalisation: If the date, time and place of meeting are not fixed by the preceding meeting, it is the duty of the leader to fix the same in consultation with the concerned people.

(2) Advertising a Meeting: In case a meeting is one at which the attendance of a group of people is decided, adequate notice should be given. There are several methods of advertising a meeting. The commonly used methods are distribution of handbills, bill postings and newspaper advertisement.

(3) Notice to Members: The leader needs to inform the members about the purpose of the meeting, time and place of meeting. A notice of the meeting along with the agenda should be forwarded in advance before the date of the meeting.

(4) Arrangements: Necessary arrangements should be made with due permission of the appropriate authority. Suitable arrangements may include necessary facilities, seating, stationery, visual aids, equipment, materials and so on. The place of a meeting may include a house, building, tent, vehicle and vessels. In the case of a public meeting, public includes any class of the public or any community. A public meeting is conducted in a public place. The leader has to see to make the necessary seating arrangement for the members attending the meeting and has also to see that the members feel comfortable.

(5) Preparation of Notes and Reports: It is necessary to prepare the required documents, reports, as may be required for the meeting. For this purpose, it requires to obtain the needed facts, data and ideas which may be needed for decision-making or problem-solving. To see that the documents are prepared in conformity with the norms and bye-laws for provisions of some laws.

(6) Agenda for the Meeting: Preparation of an agenda is an important planning activity relating to a meeting. The agenda decides the order of business to be transacted. The agenda is drafted generally in consultation with the concerned authorities like the chairman, or directors and others. Preparation of a detailed agenda is useful to both the chairman and the members to facilitate smooth conduct of business.

(7) Defining Problem: A meeting is a problem-solving group. A precisely defined problem should be prepared to be discussed at the meeting and circulate among other members. It follows to inform the group the stages to be followed in the discussion or problem-solving. It is equally necessary to prepare introductory remarks and plans for group's participation.

(8) Inviting Ex-Officio: If necessary for a particular problem, it is usual to invite outside people or inside people from other departments to participate in the meeting to give their opinion and advice on the problem. It is usual to issue invitation letters to technical consultants, solicitors, accountant, government nominees who are required to attend the meeting as special invitees.

(9) Keep Ready: Before the meeting itself, to have ready the necessary documents and statements likely to be asked at the meeting. It may include to prepare and keep in readiness statements and reports on the organisational problem to be discussed at the proposed meeting.

(10) Minutes Book: To keep ready minutes book for recording the proceedings of the meetings.

(11) Members' Responsibilities: It is the most important duty of the leader who should arrive at a meeting place and make the necessary introduction of participants. The members of the group also have equal responsibilities in preparing and planning for the meeting. Leland Brown has identified the following responsibilities in preparing and planning for the meeting:

(i) To become well-informed and interested in the subject or problem to be worked with and all agenda items.

(ii) To prepare facts, data, and ideas necessary for the meeting (may be records, files, charts, visuals).

(iii) To come to the meeting with an open mind and learning attitude.

(iv) To be on time.

At the Meeting

(i) Signatures: It is to be planned to obtain signatures of the members present at the meeting.

(ii) Deciding Quorum: The leader should ascertain whether quorum is present or not as per the bye-laws, regulations, or practice or custom.

(iii) Reading Notice: The next step is to read the notice convening the meeting, if required or if requested by the leader, the letters of apologies for absence etc. Generally, the notice convening the meeting is taken as read.

(iv) Minutes: In many cases, the minutes of the last meeting has to be read to obtain the signatures to minutes when it is approved by the meeting.

(v) Taking Notes: The proceedings of the meeting should be recorded by taking notes on the agenda paper or on a separate paper including exact terms of the decisions taken on the problem. If the members require any information or explanation, the leader should supply.

(vi) Business as per Agenda: The order of the business to be transacted is included in the agenda. The business of the meeting should be taken up in the order set out in the agenda. The order may be varied in some cases with the consent of the meeting.

(vii) Exchange of Ideas: To achieve an effective and good two-way communication flow and effective exchange of ideas, the leader should see that every member gets ideas of his own. The leader should maintain order, keep discussions on the track, should have the ability to make prompt decisions, patience, listening skills. The leader may have to deal with difficult types of people in a group. He must ensure a free flow of communication to accomplish the purpose of the meeting and also in order to keep everyone in the group listening and contributing ideas, facts to solve the proposed problem.

(viii) Resolving Tie: In the case of an equality of votes, according to the procedure, it may be resolved by the casting vote or second vote of the chairman.

(ix) Adjouring Meeting: A meeting may be adjourned from time to time and from place to place, if the problem is not solved within the meeting time. It may be adjourned temporarily or *sine die*. At any adjourned meeting, the business left unfinished earlier may be continued.

(x) Concluding Meeting: The leader has to conclude the proceedings of the meeting with concluding observations.

(xi) Vote of Thanks: The meeting ends with a vote of thanks.

After the Meeting

(i) Minutes: The first step after the meeting is to prepare the minutes from the notes and enter the same in the minutes book, and keep them ready for approval and get it signed by the concerned people.

(ii) Followings: The next step is to carry out the decision taken to solve the problem. It is of utmost importance to communicate decisions to the concerned persons, departments, or sections. The concerned people have to carry out the intentions of, and execute the decisions taken in the meeting.

(iii) Filing Documents: The necessary documents relating to problem-solving with meeting should be filed, along with the necessary resolutions, and relevant documents.

(iv) Next Meeting: To prepare and collect materials for the next meeting. Accordingly, to make the necessary arrangement to convey any further meeting when necessary.

Meeting, Conference, Techniques[29]

(A) Informational: The purpose is to present ideas, data, techniques, etc., to the people concerned in a minimum possible time.

Methodology: Lectures, guided discussion and demonstrations.

Visuals: Films, charts, slides, posters, stickers, models etc.

Participation Style: Questions, stories, case studies, etc.

Control of Group: Activities rest solely with the leaders.

(B) Advisory: Purpose: To gather and seek advice, information, suggestions, recommendations, etc., relating to a problem.

Methodology: Lectures, role-play, free or guided discussion, case method etc.

Visuals: Charts, slides, reports, catalogues, etc.

Participation Style: Questions, case examples, arguments, demonstrations.

Control of group: Shared by the leader and group, with leader being principally responsible.

(C) Problem-Solving: Purpose: To seek a decision, solution or fundamental understanding of a problem.

Methodology: Lecture demonstrations, role-play, past experience etc.

Visuals: Diagrams, charts, models, films, slides, etc.

Participation: Free discussion, team assignment, buzz groups, brain-storming, fish-bowl, etc.

Control: Shared by leader and group, with group being principally responsible.

Information Meetings: Communication is downward from the leader to the group.

Scientific Objectives: To present facts, to win support, to demonstrate work procedure, to lay out policy, to interpret policy, rule or procedure and to stimulate action.

Advisory Meeting: Communication flows both ways. Discussion plays an important role. The leader draws upon the participants' experience, knowledge and insights to guide him in arriving at a decision. The group acts as consultants since they help in arriving at the decision and are more likely to accept it or give it their whole-hearted co-operation.

Specific Objectives: To gather facts, information and opinions to develop possible solutions, to draw upon knowledge of specialists and to establish a basis for greater acceptance of the decision.

Problem-Solving Meeting: Communication flows both ways. Interaction among members is free. Leadership goes on shifting from person to person, where the participants have the most to contribute in terms of knowledge, experience and leadership skills. The group makes the final decision.

Specific Objectives: To bring the group to bear upon a problem, to suggest possible solutions, to evaluate possible solutions and to arrive at a decision.

Problem-solving Conference

(1) Introducing the meeting: (a) Establish a friendly atmosphere.

(b) Bring everyone up-to-date, summarise events leading up to this session. Sub-Committees' interim reports to be presented at this stage.

(2) Introducing the Problem: (a) Stating the problem — giving the background, asking the group how it affects them and discussing the group's responsibility.

(b) Exploring the problem—to identify the real problem and make certain all are talking about the same thing.

(3) Attacking the problem: (a) Defining the problem — problem to be stated and defined more carefully and divided into sub-problems, if necessary.

(b) Building a conference plan — step by step outline of what the group will do. Decision to be made as to whether the group should analyse symptoms, causes and remedies.

— it should divide sub-groups to consider different aspects of the problem;

— a resource person should be called in;

— available records and reports should be analysed;

— new information should be gathered.

(4) Considering Possible Solutions: (a) Suggesting possible solutions — available data can be analysed and combined in new ways to arrive at tentative solutions. Open-mindededeness is essential — all solutions should be judged objectively and on merits.

(b) Testing possible solutions — carry out preliminary mental tests to weigh the pros and cons of all possible solutions:

(i) How will this work out in practice?
(ii) What is the past experience on similar occasions?
(iii) What new problems are likely to be created?
(iv) What resources are available for their implementation?

(c) Arrive at a decision — Decide upon the best possible solution by consensus voting and decision by majority leaves the minority dissatisfied.

(5) Acting on the Decision: Planning Future Action:

(i) What must be done?
(ii) Who should do it?
(iii) In what sequence?
(iv) Who should be informed of the decision?

Insight Into Conference: Definition: A pooling of thoughts of two or more persons, the purpose of which is to assist in solving a problem.

Criteria

(a) A conference problem should be real.
(b) A conference problem should be specific.
(c) A conference problem should be of common interest to the group.
(d) Phrasing the problem — no value judgements.
(e) Should be stated in concise and understandable words.

Techniques

Group Situation Questioning

Situation	Remedy
Bright, active and responsible	Give it fast, be well-prepared. Ask tough questions, pit them against each other.
Resistant, antagonistic	Find out cause and correct it. Show sympathy. Face issue frankly. Break down bit by bit — don't bulldoze.
Slow, passive	Explain thoroughly — use slide to help understanding. Don't go too fast. Build on their knowledge.
Individual Situation:	
Talks too much	Cut across his talk and summarize direct question to someone else — pit the group against him. Seat him in your blind spot.

Quick, helpful	Cut across tactfully. Ask someone else a question. Thank him for his help. Use him to summarise.
Rambler	When he pauses for breath, thank him, rephrase his statement and pass on. Ask which topic he is discussing.
Arguer	If he is naturally perverse, put him in a blind spot. Pretend not to hear. Take him alone and seek his help. As a last resort, ask him to drop out. Pit group against him.
Obstinate	Does not see the point. Ask others to help you. If he is still obstinate, ask him to see you after the meeting.
Wrong Subject (off-the-beam)	Direct attention to the real subject.
Grips about 'Management'	Tell him the problem. How best to operate under present conditions. Get another reliable person to answer him. Don't waste too much time.
Has personal problem:	It is pertinent; tackle it.
Racial or Political	Frankly, say you cannot discuss.
Side conversationalist	Pause. Let others also listen. Walk down near him — call him and ask his opinion.
Poor voice or choice of words	Help him. Protect him from ridicule. Repeat his ideas in your words.
Definitely wrong	Say "well, that is one way of looking at it..." and proceed further on.
Personalities	Ask him in what personalities he left out.
Ask leader for opinion	When still there is a dispute, cut across with a direct question on the top.
Bored	Redirect question to the group. If no opinion, say so.
Just wants to listen	Find his interest — call on him for his experience.
Shy, hesitant	Use provocative questions to make him come out with his views.
Not disposed to help others:	Ask questions he can answer. Ask for his agreement. Build him in the eyes of the group.
	Tell him how much he can help the group- Draw line out on a few things — thank him.

Purposes

(1) Call attention to a point, an idea, fact, problem or situation.

(2) Evaluate opinions.

(3) Get at causes or facts.

(4) Uncover sources of information.
(5) Control discussion.
(6) Summarise or end a discussion.
(7) Call attention to another phase of the problem or discussion.
(8) Reach a conclusion or agreement.
(9) Control group thinking.
(10) Control group behaviour.
(11) Suggest action, idea or decision.

Techniques — Direction

	Types	Purpose
(1)	Overhead (Directed to the group)	To open discussion. To introduce new phase. To give everyone a chance.
(2)	Direct (address to one)	To call for special information. To involve an inactive person.
(3)	Relay (Refer back to another)	To help avoid giving opinion. To get other's views. To ask someone who knows.
(4)	Reverse (Refer back to the questioner)	To help avoid giving opinion. To bring out opinions. To help questioner think for himself.
1.	Factual	To get information. To open discussion.
2.	Broadening	To broaden discussion. To suggest answer and get group to criticise. To introduce additional facts.
3.	Justifying	To challenge old ideas. To develop new ideas. To get reasoning and proof.
4.	Hypothetical	To develop new ideas. To suggest another, possibly unpopular opinion.
5.	Alternative	To make decision between alternatives. To get agreement.

Meetings are Business

The shape and content of a meeting differ from that of a debating society. Debate is different from discussion. Where healthy discussions take place, the 'know-how' of dealing with men and matters is generated. Then it becomes a meeting with an objective. Where the interests of individuals dominate, then it tends to become a debating society; and no worthwhile decision towards the progress of an organisation emerge. Where the members of the 'board' do not create a situation where it assumes a sort of 'Board Room Battle', then 'do-how' decisions are generated.

(1) No one person can be expert in everything: so to make good decisions, you need the participation of more and more executives who may be anxious to contribute to the form and content of the meetings.

(2) As the number of Central, State and even Local Governments come out with 'regulations', now and then — unlike in the past so too the number of occasions for meetings tend to increase in order to find out correct ways and means of compliance.

(3) We cannot ignore some murmurings in the corridors of executive chambers, 'the core problem with meetings is not so much the amount of time they absorb as the amount of time they waste.' More precisely, many executives may agree that what messes up so many meetings is the inability of a few to perform effectively and efficiently before the audience. No executive can be too smart if he has't learned to communicate.

(4) Once people start arguing and committing themselves to specific policies and actions, you have used up the creativity of the group.

(5) A meeting is really a peer-level review. It's very revealing. You see how someone stands on his feet, how he answers difficult questions, and whether he is an orderly thinker.

(6) Well-run meetings are enjoyable. Any executive worth his salt should enjoy them too.[30]

Speaker-Centred and Audience-Centred Meetings

Historically, the speaker-centred meetings date from before the invention of the printing press and has confined almost unchanged throughout the centuries. It is still a useful instrument of communication in specific situations. Where a number of people must be informed of something that concerns them in common, it is often more useful direct them to a notice on the bulletin board or a memeographed handout.

Experimentation shows that speaker-centred meetings, with exhaustive speeches, occasion a few lasting changes in audience attitudes or ways of acting. The effect at best is temporary production does not rise; sales do not spurt; the tool makers are not more careful.

The very word "audience" comes from the word "audio" which means to hear. But not much of what he hears stays with a listener.

The contents of Communication in Groups what Words get Around

It may be a mistake to equate orderliness with efficiency in group processes.

The irrelevant noise made by people in groups may represent attempts by members to satisfy personal needs. If that noise is forbidden expression, it may not be forthcoming because of barriers in the communication systems.

Some of these barriers may be mechanical, but many of them are psychological, like barriers created by status differences or interpersonal jealousies.

In either case, too much noise or too little, the preferred course would seem to be to promote rather than limit communication, i.e., to accept and deal with information about personal feelings and personal needs as well as information about pertinent facts.

For short-lived groups, the solution to the problem may take top priority. For longer-lived ones, programmes and processes for solving classes of problem deserve precedence.

Advantages of Group Communication

(1) Wide Knowledge: Groups permit to pool more detailed information and knowledge. They constitute crucial impulse for sound decision-making. The aggregation of ideas of several individuals helps to make quality and sound decision.

(2) Diversity of Views: There is no scope in group deliberations for any homogeneity of ideas. Groups permit not only more knowledge and information as input but it can bring heterogeneity in the decision-making process. Several alternatives can be considered and the best possible solutions can be arrived at.

(3) Acceptance: In addition to heterogeneity to the decision-making group, decisions are accepted for implementation. Increased acceptance of solution is possible, people concerned with the decisions will be more likely to accept it and encourage others. There is a support and backing for group decision.

(4) Legitimacy: In a democratic set-up, group decisions are based on the principles of democracy. Group decisions are more consistent with democratic ideas. These are, therefore, legitimate than decisions made by a single person. A single person's decision is known for its autocracy and arbitrariness.

Disadvantages of Group Communication

(1) Time Consuming: A decision by a single person can be made without loss of time than a decision made by a group. Firstly, it takes time to inform the member and then to assemble a group. A group interaction is always inefficient because collective decision is nobody's responsibility. On the other hand, an individual takes an instant and responsible decision.

(2) Pressure: There is always a pressure in group to conform to decisions. The members are forced by the majority or dominant members to accept and to consider the issue. This may result in disagreement.

(3) Domination by Few: Decisions frequently are dominated by one or few members. There would be no choice to the members of a group to oppose, express, suppress and there may not be heterogeneity in idea. This ultimately may affect the overall effectiveness of the organisation.

(4) Ambiguous Responsibility: No one is ultimately held responsible for any decision taken by a group. Group decision is a collective decision and hence there is no person who is singly responsible. Thus, the responsibility of any single member is watered down.

(5) Unproductive: Group meetings are unproductive and one of the employees has to keep production humming. Meetings are not essential and being unproductive part of work of an organisation. If meetings are not conducted properly they may not contribute to the organisational purpose. It is only the name sake participation, integrating interests but in reality things turn out in a quite different way.

(6) Expensive: Group meetings are meant for making certain decisions to find out some solutions to the problems. The cost of conducting a meeting is sometimes high and unproductive. The cost should not be more than the benefits derived from it. As such group meeting should be economical.

(7) Levelling Effect: The strong objection against group meeting is that the members always lead to conformity and compromise. "The tendency of a group to bring individual thinking in line with the average quality of the group's thinking is called the levelling effect or group think. A member of a group may not take much seriousness of the issue and think about the problem but adopts the desires of the other powerful member. The view of dominant, superior person prevails."

(8) Divided Responsibility: This is a known fact that divided responsibility is a problem wherever group decisions are made. It is often said that "actions which are several bodies' responsibility are nobody's responsibility. Collective decisions invariably dilute and thins out the responsibility. This problem can be solved by constituting a proper group structure and optimum group size. Kent Baker suggests guidelines as to how to make meetings more meaningful. They are:

(a) Clarify the objective.
(b) Distribute the agenda in advance.
(c) Encourage the expression of minority viewpoints.
(d) Separate idea generation from evaluation.
(e) Control irrelevant discussions.
(f) Circulate background material in advance.
(g) Legitimize questioning attitudes.
(h) Rotate record-keeping responsibilities.
(i) End on a positive role.
(j) Periodically, evaluate the group process.

REFERENCES

1. Berelson, B. and Steiner, G., *Human Behaviour: An Inventory of Sicentific Findings,* p. 616.
2. For details see: Leon Festinger, Stanley Schachter and Kurt Back, *Social Pressures in Informal Groups: A Study of Human Factor in Housing,* Stanford Calif, 1963, First Published by Harper in 1950.
3. For details see: George C. Homans, *The Human Group,* Harcourt, Brace & World, New York, 1950, pp. 43-44.
4. For details, see Theodore M. Newcomb, *The Acquaintance Process,* Holt, New York, 1961.
5. For details see: John W. Thibaut and Harold H. Kelley, *The Social Psychology of Groups,* Wiley, New York, 1959.

6. The discussion is based on S.P. Robbins, *Orgnisational Behaviour,* pp. 275-276 and the Work of D.C. Barnlund and F. Haimann.

7. The discussion is based on S.P. Robbin's *Organisational Behaviour,* Prentice-Hall of India Pvt. Ltd., New Delhi, 1991, p. 278.

8. Hicks, H.G. and Gullett, C.R., *Management,* McGraw-Hill International Book Company, 1981, p. 189.

9. Bernard Berelson and Gray A. Steiner, *Human Behaviour,* 1964, p. 356.

10. Robbins, *S.P., Oranisational Behaviour,* Prentice Hall of India, New Delhi, 1991, p. 337.

11. Janis. *Victims of Groupthink,* 1972.

12. *Ibid.*

13. Robbins, S.P., *op .cit.,* p. 336.

14. *Ibid.,* p. 338.

15. *Ibid,* p. 338.

16. Hellreigel, D., and Slocum Jr., *Management.*

17. *Ibid.*

18. *Ibid.*

19. Adopted, *The Week,* Nov. 21, 1993, pp. 13-14.

20. Robbins, S.P., *op. cit.,* pp. 339-340.

21. Newman, W.H., *Administrative Action,* p. 270.

22. Herbert G. Hicks and C. R. Gullet, *Management,* McGraw-Hill International Book Company, 1981, p. 360.

23. Luthans, F., *Organisational Behaviour,* McGraw-Hill International Book Company, 1981, p. 326.

24. Hicks, H.G. and Gullett, C.R. *op. cit.,* p. 351.

25. Newman, W.H. *op. cit., p. 217.*

26. Louis A. Allen, *Making Better use of Committees* in Richards and Nielander, *Reading of Management,* p. 320.

27. Hicks, H.G. and Gullett, C.R. *op. cit.,* p. 360.

28. *Ibid.,* p. 362.

29. Balan, K.R., and Rayudu, C.S., *Effective Communication,* Castle Books Pvt. Ltd., New Delhi, 1994, pp. 51-58.

30. *Ibid.,* pp. 58-59.

*****

CHAPTER 12

Report Writing

Introduction

Almost everyone in a management job has to do some report writing. The higher the job, the more reports it usually entails. Report writing can tie a map up in knots. It can ruin evenings and wreck weekends. But it is a chore few people in management can avoid; and higher they go, the more they have to write. There is no way to make report writing easy. But there is a right way to do it — a way that may save time and should result in a better report.

Just as good manners are the evidence of good breeding, so it might be stated that good report writing is the evidence of intelligent. A good report is evidence of the writer's vocabulary, grammar, rhetoric; it shows whether the writer can gather facts, evaluate and analyse them, and then reason logically.

Meaning and Definition

Report means a statement or description of what has been said, seen, done etc. A treatise containing facts, figures, information, analysis, opinions, suggestions, recommendations, maps, graphs, charts, pictures, statistical tables, specially complied for a particular purpose.

C. A. Brown defines a report as a communication from someone, who has to inform someone who wants to use that information. It describes the events or individuals to someone who requires it.

According to the American Marketing Society, the purpose of a report is "to convey the interested persons the whole result of the study in sufficient details and so arranged as to enable each reader to comprehend the data and so determine for himself the validity of conclusions."

Types of Reports

Reports may be classified broadly under the following categories:

I. According to Use

(1) External Reports.

(2) Internal Reports.

II. According to Period

(1) Routine Reports.

(2) Special Reports.

III. Reports According to Levels of Management

(1) Reports to Top Management.

(2) Reports to Functional Management.

(3) Reports to Junior Level Management.

(4) Functional Reports.

IV. Corporate Reports

(1) Statutory Reports.

(2) Directors' Reports.

(3) Auditors' Report.

(4) Non-Statutory Reports.

V. Other Reports

(1) Review Reports.

(2) Cost Audit Reports.

(3) Interim Report.

(4) Oral Reports.

(5) Others.

I. According to Use

(1) External Reports: Shareholders, Government, Stock exchanges, debentureholders, investors, financial institutions, financial analysts, press, researchers etc., are the external parties to a business organisation. Those types of reports which are prepared for the use of external parties are called "external reports." Broadly speaking, a company is not answerable to anyone other than the owners, i.e., shareholders. But still some reports are useful and meant for outside public.

The annual reports are meant to the shareholders which are public documents. Under the Indian Companies Act, 1956, annual reports should be filed with the Registrar of Companies and with the stock exchanges. The annual reports contain auditors' report, and Board of Directors' report, income statement, and the balance sheet. The final statements of acccunts are expected to conform to certain minimum standards of disclosures.

(2) Internal Reports: The reports meant for various persons inside the company are known as "internal reports." They are opposed to external reports. Reports prepared for the use of internal parties to various levels of management. Truly speaking, they are not public documents and as such do not conform to certain minimum standards or statutory standards. As a matter of fact, internal reports are media of written communication to transmit information to the various level of management. Reports for internal use are prepared according to the requirement of the recipient. Different level of organisation like top-level, middle-level and lower-level management need reports for making decisions at their level.

II. According to Period

There are various types of internal reports. They are:

(1) Routine Reports: Such reports are also called "periodic reports." Routine reports are indispensable for the successful operation of control mechanism. Control means to see that things are done according to predetermined standards. It involves a continuous comparison of actuals with standards, to know the deviations and to take remedial measures. This is not possible unless routine reports are sent to various levels of management. The matters mainly cover the day-to-day working aspects of the concern which activate the control function.

Communication through this written medium would act as feedback because the required information has been transmitted which facilitates effective control. The nature and subject of information and details to be reported may vary depending upon the level of management requiring data. Routine reports are prepared periodically like weekly, fortnightly, monthly, quarterly or even daily. When reports are routine, they should not be neglected by the recipient because even slight deviations require great attention. Different colours, formats, or special types of print may be adopted to distinguish priority of the report. Matters which may require routine reports relate to sales, production capacity utilisation, yield, quality, selling cost, research and development, raw materials, market conditions, customer-behaviour, labour problems, public relations etc.

(2) Special Reports: Certain matters may not figure in routine reports for decision-making. Different levels of management may face difficulties because of non-availability of significant and basic data for managerial decision-making. In certain crucial areas of operations or crisis situations, more details of special nature may be required. Therefore, special reports are prepared and supplied for special purposes. Certain long-term decisions like expansion, modernisation, change in method of production, or make decision to replace labour by machine etc., which call for special information. Unless a special study and analysis are taken up, such information cannot be obtained. Therefore, reports prepared with the co-ordinated efforts of various functional departments are known as "special reports."

J. Batty states that special reports should be divided into sections, each covering the main purposes such as reasons for the report, investigation made and findings, conclusions and recommendations. Such reports must highlight the problem, alternative courses, effects, comparison etc. The subject matters which may be covered in special reports are the sales policy, technological change, shut down, further processing, idle capacity, export proposals, decisions like to buy or to make, to lease or own, replacement, capital expenditure decisions, political and economic changes etc

III. Reports to the Different Levels of Management

(1) Report to Top Management: The Board of Directors is considered as the top management, which is mainly concerned with policy formulation, planning and co-ordinating various levels. It acts as a trustee and agent of the company. It requires detailed data and other information for planning and formulation of basic policies of the company. Various functional heads provide information to the Managing Director, who in turn submits reports to the Board of Director. They are concerned mainly with financial statements like profit and loss account, balance sheet, statement of funds flow, cash flow, capacity utilisation, idle capacity, cost of production, sales credit collection, research and development.

(2) Reports to Functional Management: The middle-level management is concerned with the task of implementation of basic goals and objectives formulated by the top management. The nature and matters of reports for treatment would depend upon the extent of centralisation and decentralisation of authority. The following are the various types of reports relating to operational level or functional level.

(1) Production Report: The report of this type deals with:

(a) Installed capacity.
(b) Idle capacity.
(c) Capacity utilisation.
(d) Actual production.
(e) Standard production.
(f) Manpower availability.
(g) Manpower utilisation.
(h) Number of hours worked.
(i) Output.
(j) Cost of production.
(k) Scrap.
(l) Quality aspects etc.

(2) Sales Reports: Sales reports deal with all matters relating to sales operations. The report covers among others, the following important aspects:

(a) Actual sales.
(b) Budgeted sales.
(c) Area-wise and product-wise sales figures and analysis.
(d) Expected sales.
(e) Analysis of difference between actual and expected.
(f) Comparison of sales with the corresponding earlier periods.
(g) Number, value and quantity or orders booked, orders executed and orders not yet executed and reasons thereof.
(h) Credit collection and bad debts would be important aspects which may require careful consideration.
(j) These reports necessarily have to describe the stock position,
(j) The transport, commission, discount, rebate and the cost of selling reports.

(3) Purchase Reports: Reporting on purchases involves periodical reporting on transactions that form part of quality, cost of production and blocking of capital. Preparation of sale reports are very simple and would show:

(a) On value, quantity and the number of purchases made.

(b) The extent to which they are received and not received and reasons for the difference.

(c) Value and quantity of materials used.

(d) Scrap, waste, spoilage, deterioration.

(e) Extent of capital invested and avoid over investment on stores consistent with requirements.

(4) Financial Reports: As the name indicates, these reports are mainly concerned with financial matters other than which form part of the direct cost of production. Interest, taxation sources of finance, cost of capital and number of other items which do not find a place under any other reports.

(5) Reports to Junior Level Management: These reports are also called "supervisory level management reports." Supervisory level management consists of shop foreman, sales area supervisor and other sectional in-charges. The people who are working at this level are mainly concerned with the actual execution of policies. Their reports concerned with day-to-day working performance of their sections. They report to their respective functional or divisional heads.

(6) According to Functions: Classification of management reports is a type of reports which are according to functions. These reports are also categorised as internal reports. According to function, the reports may be classified into broad categories such as:

(1) Operating Report.

(2) Financial Report.

The operating reports may be further classified into:

(a) Control Reports.

(b) Information Reports, and

(c) Venture Measurement Report.

Financial Reports may consists of:

(a) Static Report.

(b) Dynamic Report.

A brief description of these reports is given below:

(a) Control Reports: These reports are prepared where the control mechanism is in operation. They make comparison of the actual with the budgeted one and identify the deviations from the budgeted figures. They are useful to measure performance or results.

(b) Information Reports: The object of preparing information report is to provide information to various authorities. They are not useful to exercise control basically but helps in planning and policy formulation for the future. Trend observation, statistical analysis, graphic presentation techniques are used in the form of trend reports and analytical report.

(c) Venture Measurement Reports: These reports accumulate information about the results of the operations to communicate in summarised form. They may relate to some specific venture or the enterprise as a whole.

(d) Operating Reports: These reports deal with operations of the company at various divisional levels.

(e) Financial Reports: These reports from the subject matter of management. These reports incorporate information about the financial position of a company on specific data or movement in finances.

IV. Corporate Reports

(1) Statutory Reports: Reports which are statutorily required to prepare under law are called "statutory reports." Statutory report, as per Section 165 of the Companies Act, 1956, Auditors' Report, Directors' Report and the Annual Accounts, Reports by the Inspectors appointed to investigate the affairs of the company are some of the important reports required by law.

Statutory report is related to the statutory meeting of the company. The directors have to send a report called "the statutory report" to all the members. The Act specifically lays down the particulars that must be set out in the statutory report to enable the members to get all the necessary information.

(2) Directors' Report (Board's Report): Annul reports of the Directors attached to every balance sheet is called "Directors' Report." These should be attached to every balance sheet laid before a company in a general meeting, a report by its Board of Directors. The report must contain the following information:

(1) The state of affairs of the company.

(2) The amount, if any, which it proposes to carry on to any reserves.

(3) The amount if any which it recommends should be paid by way of dividends.

(4) Material changes and commitments, if any, affecting the financial position of the company which have occurred between the end of the financial year.

(5) Future prospects of the company, changes in the directorate and auditors of the company, i.e., retirement and re-election of old Directors.

(6) The conservation of energy, technology, absorption, foreign exchange earnings and outgoings.

(7) A statement should show the name of every employee of the company who is in receipt of remuneration which in the aggregate was not less than the sum prescribed, if employed throughout the financial year or part of the financial year.

(8) To include whether such employee is a relative of any Director or manager of the company.

(9) The Board is expected to give the fullest information and explanation.

(3) Auditors' Report: Companies may appoint auditors to scrutinise and check the correctness or otherwise of the accounts of the company and submit their reports. The Indian Companies Act, 1956 stipulates to have auditors to audit the books and examine the affairs of the company on behalf of the shareholders and to report to them. The auditor's report should be attached to the balance sheet, including the auditors' separate, special or supplementary reports. The auditors' report must cover all those statements/documents/notes which are annexed to the balance sheet and profit and loss account. Their report may contain a cross reference to any of the attached documents or part thereof.

The auditor is required to make a report to the members of the company on the accounts examined by him on every balance sheet, profit and loss account, and other documents. The report should also state whether in his opinion and to the best of his information and according to explanations given to him by the company. According to the Companies Act, the report must state:

(a) Whether he has obtained all the information and explanation which to the best of his knowledge and belief were necessary for the purposes of his audit;

(b) Whether, in his opinion, proper books of account as required by law have been kept by the company so far as appears from his examination of those books, and proper returns adequate for the purposes of his audit have been received from branches not visited by him;

(c) Whether the report on the accounts of any branch office audited under Section 228 by a person other than the company as auditor has been forwarded to him as required by clause (c) of sub-section (3) of that section and how he has dealt with the same in preparing the auditor's report;

(d) Whether the company's balance sheet and profit and loss account dealt with by the report are in agreement with the books of account and returns.

(4) Non-Statutory Reports: Reports which are not required to be prepared under law are called "non-statutory reports." Such reports may include Reports of Directors to the shareholders on certain special proposals or problems, reports of committees on special matters like finance committee, allotment committee, standing committee and special reports of the company secretary.

V. Other Reports

(1) Review Reports: The management reports must have utility and use for decision-making and policy formulation of plans.

It is, therefore, necessary to consider the facts and events to decide the usefulness of reports. Such reports, are called "review reports." Each executive should examine the reports he has received.

(2) Cost Audit Report: Cost audit report contains the matter about the scrutiny of cost records. Central Government has made cost audit (report) Rules, 1968. These rules shall apply to every company in respect of which an audit of the cost accounting records have been ordered by the Central Government. The cost audit report should contain in detail about:

(i) Cost Accounting system.

(ii) Financial position.

(iii) Capital employed.

(iv) Net worth.

(v) Profit after providing for depreciation, and other expenses.

(vi) Income to be specified.

(vii) Production particulars like licensed capacity, installed capacity, actual production and percentage of production in relation to installed capacity.

(viii) Process of m anufacture.

(ix) Raw-materials consumed both in terms of quantity and value.

(x) Power and fuel in quantity, rate per unit and total cost separately etc.

(xi) Wages and salaries for all categories of employees.

(xii) Stores and spare parts expenditure per unit of output.

(xiii) Depreciation, overhead, royalties, sales, abnormal non-recurring cost, auditors' observations and conclusions.

(3) Interim Report: A committee or a commission may submit an interim report at any time before submitting a final report. This is done in anticipation of the subject matter of the report to be submitted at the period. This is known as an interim report. It is generally submitted after the study has been half way through and the same subject matter is incorporated in the final report

(4) Oral Report: "Oral Report" means presentation of written matter before a group. One must have oral communication skill for report presentation. This method is used in every business activity and at every level. The originator of oral report presents an informational and analytical message. The essentials of good speaking will equally apply to the oral reports. According to L Brown, "The function of an oral report is to furnish the facts necessary to expedite action or to persuade someone or any number of persons to take the action the group decided on or to implement the group's solution."

Like in an oral message, a oral report to be effective must carefully be planned and developed. When a report is orally read before a gathering, it is similar to an oral presentation and should be written in such a manner. An oral report is generally drafted for a particular group of people. For instance, an oral report to a welfare committee, any oral report to the executives of all the departments. Like a speech, oral reports have an introduction, body and ending. With a view to clarify things or to create interest, audio-visual aids may be used.

A successful and effective oral report must follow certain essential principles. Some of the principles are:

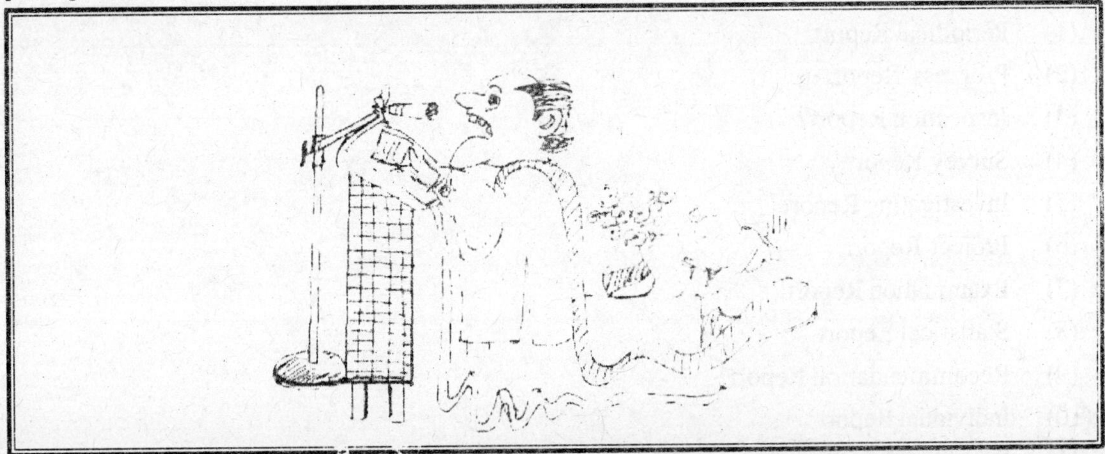

Fig. 12. 1 Oral Report

(1) A report should be complete, clear and short.

(2) To practice report reading by imagining an audience.

(3) To set a gentle style and tone.

(4) To know the audience.

(5) To fix time limit to read.

(6) To divide a report into paragraphs, each paragraph should give a separate central idea.

(7) Other principles of good oral communication and written communication are equally applicable.

Following are the logical steps to acquire self-confidence to present an oral report, suggested by Leland Brown:

(1) "Preparing your talk carefully. Fear of forgetting results in stage fright.

(2) Practicing aloud. You will know your talk better after rehearsing. Practice alone, going over it again and again, imagining your audience before you, or viewing yourself in a mirror.

(3) By not memorising your talk; a tape recorder can be helpful, for it allows you to hear yourself.

(4) Checking your appearance. Dress appropriately for the occasion and your audience.

(5) When you face your group, waiting a few minutes before you start to talk. Think of your audience as your friends. They want you to do well.

(6) Beginning slowly; do not give up once you have begun. Stage fright disappears after you start.

(7) Speaking louder than ordinarily, at least at the outset.

(8) Speaking as often as you can. The more practice you get, 'the easier it is to speak with confidence." (See Fig.12.1).

(5) Others

(1) Periodical Report

(2) Progress Report

(3) Inspection Report

(4) Survey Report

(5) Investigating Report

(6) Project Report

(7) Examination Report

(8) Statistical Report

(9) Recommendation Report

(10) Individual Report

(11) Report of the Committees or Sub-committes, or Commission

(12) Formal Report

(13) Informal Report

(14) Press Report.

Patterns of Reports

(1) Letter Form: This type of report is written in a letter form. It is written in first person, i.e.,

I believe

I am personally of the opinion

I suggest

I recommend etc.,

or

We believe

We are personally of the opinion

We suggest

We recommend

(2) Letter-Text Combination Form: Both letter structure and text form are combined in this type of report.

(3) Memorandum Form: In an organisation, memorandum form of reports are usually adapted, which avoids all formalities to be followed for the purpose of preparation and presentation of report as required in the case of letter form. The printed memorandum reports forms of various types are used in order to ensure uniformity, clarity and simplicity.

Parts Contents Format of Report

The parts of a report can broadly be classified into the following classifications:

(1) Preliminary Section

(2) Report Text or Body of the Report or Report Proper

(3) Supplementary Section.

(1) Preliminary Section: The first section is called "preliminary section", because it contains reference and informal materials. This part reveals identification of the report and the circumstances for which it has been prepared.

(2) Body of the Report: Report text is also called "report proper," or "body of report." This part of the report contains facts, analysis, synthesis, interpretations, findings, conclusions, recommendations etc. This, of course, will vary in accordance with the objectives of each specific case, and the type of the problem involved. It will help to number the major points wished to be covered to group the facts under classifications such as " present procedure", "estimated costs of new procedure", "personnel requirements", etc. Indent, as needed, for emphasis and variety, and to set apart certain groupings of facts or information.

(3) Supplementary Section: Supplementary part of the report is supporting and secondary to the main report which includes materials and information of secondary importance. Though the materials are related to the primary study, they are too cumbersome to include in the body of the report. On the other hand, they are matters of less importance to be included in the report.

Many reports contain materials which though directly concerned with the subject matter, cannot be conveniently included in the body of the report. It is usually best to include this kind of information in an appendix. Typical of the material that might appear in an appendix are computation sheets, showing in detail all the calculations made in arriving at results discussed in the body of the report; graphs and charts, other matters that have bearing on the subject of the report but which is not a basic part of it.

Parts of a Report

Generally, a typical formal report usually incorporates all the parts as discussed below. But such reports are rare. Sometimes, writers of reports are selective and use only some parts to be suitable to the purpose and use.

A report must be divided into paragraphs, sometimes, numbered consecutively and finally signed by the report-writer or group. The subject matter is divided and presented under various sub-heads or sub-divisions. The following are the various contents which are common and incorporated either in a business report or an academic report:

I. Preliminary Section

(1) Cover: It is to put or spread something on the report or in front of the report which protects the report. Cover contains the title of the report, the name of the author, year and month are printed. Sometimes a printed form is filled out and attached.

(2) Flyleaf: Flyleaf is a blank page at the beginning of a report. It precedes the title page.

(3) Title or Title Page: Provides complete identification, which includes the title or the heading, the author, may be an individual or group or chairman, details of the person to whom the report is prepared, year and month of completion etc.

(4) Authorisation or Assignment: Letter of authorisation or assignment becomes a part of the report. Authorisation indicates the authority and terms of reference under which the report is made. It also establishes scope of the subject to be investigated, the powers given etc. It is also called an empowering or authority to undertake a study and to report accordingly. The style of including authorisation or assignment varies according to the situation and it is done in different ways according to the circumstances. It also includes the time limit, the financial grant to make an enquiry. A report may be an individual report, or committee report, or commission report. In the case of company report, the board of directors, managing committee of the chairman may appoint a person or group of persons for preparing a report. In the case of Government, the ministry concerned, or parliament may appoint and authorise to report. The research institutes, or Universities may permit eligible and qualified persons to investigate and report the findings of the study.

(5) Letter of Transmittal: A letter of transmittal which accompanies the report is also called "forwarding", "introductory" or "covering letter." A letter is used to transmit the report from the writer to the recipient. It contains some important items of significance like the date of submission, details of the writer and the name and address of the person or the company to whom the report is to be transmitted.

(6) Acceptance of Message: This is with reference to the authorisation message. A letter or memorandum indicating agreement or acceptance to take up the report work.

(7) Preface: The object of this paragraph is to include the author's opinion on the report. It includes an explanatory statement about the report, objectives, the circumstances that lead to the writing of a report, objectives, the circumstances that lead to the writing of a report etc. It is an introduction to a report which explains the contents, indicating sometimes the limitations in the report. It includes prefatory words before a report is offered to the readers.

(8) Acknowledgments: A separate paragraph is devoted to record acknowledgments. Sometimes, reporters include an acknowledgments portion under the preface portion only. It is greeting someone or to thank in writing who extended their help or support or advice. If the report received help or used published material or owes a special debt to a particular source, they should be acknowledged under the paragraph.

(9) Content Page: Under this paragraph are described in detail the contents of the report. In the case of a lengthy report having voluminous materials, it would contain the chapter titles, synopsis under each chapter, sub-titles and page numbers of each chapter. It is also called "Table of Contents" which should be drawn up and included at the beginning of the report. The contents page should indicate accurately the titles and commencing pages of all chapters, major sub-divisions, appendices, schedules, bibliography, index etc.

(10) Lists of Tables and Figures: A comprehensive and systematically prepared report may contain illustrations or a number of figures and maps. Lists of tables and figures must be listed separately. The list of tables normally precedes that of figures. After the content page a list of tables and a list of figures, diagrams, maps are included. It indicates the chapter of the table or picture or map and page numbers where they can be located.

(11) List of Abbreviations: Where abbreviations are frequently used in the report, a key to these abbreviations should be provided at the beginning of thereport and should be presented in an alphabetical order. Sometimes, certain English and Latin abbreviations are quite often used in bibliographies and footnotes to eliminate tedious repetition. In respect of these abbreviations, expansion and the country of origin of the word, to be given.

II. Report Text or Body of the Report

(1) Introduction: Here the background of the problem and relevant information about the status of the situation up to the time of writing the report should be stated clearly. The introduction, in other words, should set the stage for the main points you want to present.

The purpose of introduction in a report is to introduce the subject to the readers, It includes a brief description of historical background of the subject, scope of study, methodology, definition of problem etc. It should contain a clear statement about the object of the subject of report, i.e., enough background tto make clear to the reader why the problem was considered worth investigating.

(2) Body of the Report: This, of course, will vary in accordance with the objectives of each specific case, and the type of problem involved. It will help a number the major points you wish to cover or to group the acts under classifications such as "present procedure", "present costs", "estimated costs of new procedure", "personnel requirements," etc. Indent, as needed, for emphasis and variety, and to set apart certain groupings or facts or information.

(3) Abstract: This should consist of a quick reading statement of the problem and the important conclusions and recommendations. Abstract is a summary/synopsis of the subject matter of the report. The terms of reference for writing a report may insist in the inclusion of abstracts in the report. The summary of the report is also referred to as a synopsis or abstract of the report. It is a summary of the report which gives substance or core of the report in brief. This abstract most frequently is about 500 words, 1000 words or more depending upon the length of the report and the importance of the summary. The summary should indicate the main points like methodology, findings, identifying the problems, offering suggestions or remedial measures, conclusions and recommendations in brief that emerge during the course of investigation and the conclusions. The abstract is, therefore, extremely useful in case where the report is lengthy.

(4) Discussion: The major part of the body of the report deals with the discussion. This part includes analysis, synthesis and interpretations.

(5) Headings and Sub-headings: The matter is reported usually under the appropriate headings and sub-divisions. The headings and sub-divisions should be precise and in two or three words conveying the unity of the theme of the matter; headings and sub-headings should give a clear indication of content and be as short as possible. Roman numerals and Arabic numerals are used to distinguish the paragraphs.

(6) Findings: This paragraph includes major findings of the study of the report. A popular report is one which gives emphasis in the report on the findings of the most practical and on the implications of these findings. Findings is the life-blood of the report and it is called the "text proper." Findings are arranged and presented in chronological or logical sequence. According to the order of chapters, it may also include pictures, maps, diagrams, tables, charts etc.

(7) Conclusion: At the end of the report, the significant results should be summarised clearly. The conclusion should follow the same lines as the abstract, only in greater detail. To leave the reader with the feeling that he should take action after he has finished reading the report, it is important that the report ends with a punch line. Throughout the body of the report, an effort should be made to lead up to a climax, then hit the reader with the punch line — the need for his immediate action.

Findings are the basis for arriving at the conclusions. A detailed summary of the findings and the policy implications drawn from the results should be explained. The conclusion of a report consist of a summary of the basic points not covered in the study. The report-writer may arrive at a number of conclusions based on an analysis of different facts, observations and experiences. Points of conclusion are generally classified and grouped.

(8) Suggestions and Recommendations: Recommendations consist of a number of statements which have implications for the policy and decision making, some reports may not include recommendations and in some case, regulations usually stipulate its recommendations and suggestions. In some reports, findings, conclusions and recommendations are written separately to indicate the future course of action. Finally, the recommendations are accepted and put in the form of recommendations. All the recommendations may not be accepted or ratified. A good report should clearly indicate suggestions which need implementation by the user.

(9) Signature: Subscribing signature to a report is an essential duty of the person submitting the report to the authority. The Chairman of the committee or commission signs the report, supported by the signatures of all the members of the committee. Signature to the report signifies their acceptance or consent to its contents, and where a member or members disagree with some of the points in the report, the members sign it with a note of dissent.

III. Supplementary Section

All materials and information of secondary importance are included in this part. Though the materials are related to the primary study but are too cumbersome to include in the body of the report. On the other hand, they are matters of less essential to be included in the report.

Many reports contain material which, though directly concerned with the subject matter, cannot be conveniently included in the body of the report. It is usually best to include this kind of information in an appendix. Typical of the material that might appear in an appendix are computation sheets, showing in details all the calculation made in arriving at results discussed in the body of the report, graphs and charts; other matter that has a bearing on the subject of the report but which is not a basic part of it.

However, the following are the contents of supplementary section.

(1) List of References: In the case of a research report, the researcher should give the list of references containing entries of books or works referred in the report. The separate list of reference has not been included at the bottom of the related page or at the end of each chapter, they are listed at the end of the thesis immediately after the appendices. The list is arranged in chronological order.

(2) Appendix: A section in a report usually containing extra information, added at the end of a book, document etc. Appendices may be given for all technical matters relating to the questionnaire, mathematical derivations, elaborations, details on a particular aspect of analysis and the like one. Most detailed information and data on method are presented in the form of appendices. There may be a number of appendices like diagrams, charts, maps, pictures, tables and other materials which support the main body of the report. In brief the appendix is a part of the study whose details are separated from the main body of the report and included in the appendix.

(3) Glossary: Glossary is a list of words etc., with their meanings relating to the subject of the report. It is a list containing entries of jargon words, prepared in alphabetical order. If such words are a few, they are generally explained in the footnotes in the respective pages. The glossary becomes an essential part of the report.

(4) Index: A good quality of report is that an index must be prepared and be given invariably in the report at the end. The Index helps the readers as a good guide. It contains both subject index and author index. The index like bibliography is arranged alphabetically. In the case of a lengthy report, index is essential. It is common to prepare only one index both for names of the authors, subject topics and concepts and the like ones.

(5) Bibliography: The word "bibliography" refers to a list of books by an author (s) on a subject. Preparation of bibliography is one of the major component in a research report and the research study remains incomplete till the bibliography is the next final step almost in the preparation of the report. This list of books is known as bibliography, which is normally appended to the research report also, contains all those works like books, journals, articles, reports etc.

BUSINESS REPORT AND ACADEMIC REPORT

Report in the case of research is considered a major component of the study. The research work is completed only when the findings are reported. C.R. Kothari remarks that even the most brilliant hypothesis, highly well designed and conducted research study, and the most striking generalisations and findings are of little value unless they are effectively communicated to others. Academic reports are well served when they are made known to others. A research study culminates in report writing. A research report is a written medium of communication of various aspects of the study. In respect of a research report, research is first planned and conducted to achieve the objectives formulated. But in respect of business report writing, the report is first planned for this purpose.

Academic reports generally take the form of research reports may be briefly categorised as comprehensive research reports. There may be research report which covers a wide variety of subjects and its coverage is also quite expensive. Another category of research report can also be in the form of a separate research articles or paper or monogram. Business reports act as business communication while the research reports present research findings on a particular subject of study. Therefore, reports are broadly categorised into two types:

(1) Business reports.

(2) Academic/Research Reports.

The format or contents which are to be incorporated in any report as discussed above are applicable to all types of reports. In the case of academic report, in addition to the above contents, the following are special to be included in a research report.

Contents Special to an Academic Report

(i) Statement of the Problem: In the opening paragraph of the research report, the problem to be investigated should be stated clearly and briefly. The key questions and the location of the problem in the theoritical context of the concerned discipline should be specified. The significance of the problem, the contribution which the proposed study is expected to make theory and methodology as well as its practical import, and national relevance should be specifically indicated.

(ii) Overview of Literature: Summarising the current status of research in the area, including major findings, the report should clearly demonstrate the relevance or insufficiency of the findings or approaches for the investigation of the problem at hand.

(iii) The Conceptual Framework: Given the problem and the theoritical perspective for investigating the problem, the proposal should clearly indicate the concepts to be used and demonstrate their relevance for the study. It should further specify the dimensions of empirical reality that need to be explored for investigating the problem.

(iv) Research Questions or Hypothesis: Given the conceptual framework and the specification of dimensions, the specific questions to be answered through the proposed research design specification of variables and posting of relationships among them through specific hypotheses must form a part of the research proposal.

(v) Coverage: If, in the light of the questions raised or the hypotheses proposed to be tested, sampling becomes necessary, full information on the following points should be given:

(1) Universe of study.

(2) Sampling frame.

(3) Sampling procedure.

(4) Units of observation and sampling size.

If the study requires any control groups, these should be specifically mentioned. An explanation of determination of size and type of the sample will also be necessary. Proposals not requiring a sample selection should specify their strategy appropriately and describe the rationale.

(vi) Data Collection: The different type of data proposed to be gathered should be specifically mentioned.

The sources for each type of data and the tools and techniques that will be used for collecting different types of data should be specified.

(vii) Data Processing: The manner in which the different types of data will be processed, the tabulation plan and the types of data that will be processed through the computer should be explained in detail.

Writing is a Craft

On Writing a Report: Most of us find ourselves at some time up against the job of writing a report. It may be a business report or the report of a meeting. It may be our report as secretary of an organisation, or an analysis of a situation in a factory.

Writing a report need not be the ordeal so many of us fear it to be and sometimes, find it. Like so many other things, it is not particularly difficult if we break it down into small jobs. The purpose of this topic is to show step by step how to write a report. All the suggestions will not be appropriate to every report, but the principles will be generally useful.

We should try to make reports constructive. Instead of threshing old straw, or moving in a pedestrian way through an account of some convention or meeting, it is much more interesting to offer vigorous and thought-provoking interpretations and ideas of our own. To prepare a good report, we need to cultivate dependability, resourcefulness and patience and do some hard work.

Kinds of Reports: There are, broadly, two kinds of business reports. They are,

(1) Information Report.

(2) Research Report.

The information report is to keep an executive upto date with events, developments and projects. The research report is the outcome of investigation of phenomena. This may be in any branch of human activity, from politics to labour relations, from some crank's idea about taking electricity out of the air to a plan for extending customer use of the power already developed.

Any report upon which action may be based or which may influence executives in this or that direction is an important piece of work, and deserves our earnest attention. There is no more engrossing job than that of exploring in search of material for such a report.

The work of writing starts long before making a motion that is planned. The writer must be properly briefed, and that is a joint responsibility of the writer and the boss. He must know exactly what is wanted and why it is wanted. Requests for reports should refer to definite and limited problems.

This simple outline will be of help:

(1) Comprehend what you are required to report on.

(2) Ascertain all possible sources of information.

(3) Decide upon what sources to draw.

(4) Gather information and explanations.

(5) Sift the evidence.

(6) Synthesis the acceptable evidence.

(7) Abstract what is to the point and discard the rest.

(8) Throw what is left into report form.

(9) Summarise the findings.

Limitations

There are atleast four limitations upon research for report:

(1) Time

(2) Staff

(3) Money

(4) Data.

It is important that the report-writer should do his best within these limitations and his report should note any shortcoming because of them. If the report is taken from the files' years, it should provide evidence of the difficulties the people encountered, so as to give a realistic starting point for following up or modernising the report.

Economy of efforts will be possible to the report-writer if he keeps a clearly defined purpose in mind, and refuses to allow himself to be drawn away by other things, however attractive they may be.

Objectives

In planning the report, serious thought should be given to the need and temperament of the person for whom it is being prepared. Some persons want great details, others will be content with deductions. Some will want tables and graphs, while others will run a mile from the statistics.

'What' the report writer should ask himself, "is to be done with what data by whom?" The kind of report we are considering now that gives information on the basis of which an executive may take action — is a sort of diagnosis.

It tells us what is wrong, and gives an interpretation which all the executive's guide to the remedy, should one be needed.

There are two occasions when recommendation by the report-writer are in order; when they are requested, and when the writer believes that because of his knowledge, experience and other qualities his voice is worth listening to.

All recommendations are touched with the personality of the writer of the report. The wise man will make a distinction between his conclusions, based upon the facts he has uncovered, and his suggestions based upon these conclusions. The former are actualities, the latter are tinged with the colour of his opinion.

Form of the Report

Writing a report will be much easier if the writer works out a form, or skeleton.

A good plan for the inexperienced report writer is to start with a statement in one sentence setting forth the objective of the study which is being reported upon. This will focus attention upon the primary purpose. Then follow with the main and sub-headings, growing out of the sentence and leading towards the conclusion.

It is surprising how greatly this plan helps to eliminate vagueness, fill in gaps in information and reasoning, and keep the writer on the track of competent thinking.

Although it does not hold true in every case, the success of many reports may be attributed to a well-written introduction or synopsis. If attention of the reader is siezed at this point, he is likely to proceed into the body of the report with an expectant mind. Even when one is sure the report will be read, as when the topic is one of particular interest to an executive, it still is good practice to provide a summary, telling what the report is about and what points it makes. It should be sharp in its diction, sparing of words, and careful to promise no more than is in the report.

When the writer reaches his preliminary outline, it should be drafted so as to give a fairly clear idea of the road ahead, enable him to judge what you should stress, and provide with a test of the adequacy of research.

It is not necessary in this short mention of the form of the report, to go in detail about the appendix, the table of contents, the index and such like. These are features which are required only in exhaustive and lengthy reports, and they fall into place quite naturally when their use is indicated.

Not much need be said about the various kinds of analytic reports except just to name them. The case study, while incomplete in itself because no conclusion can be drawn from one case, is useful as part of a larger project. It can be enlightening, and because of the narrowness of its field, it can be thorough. The genetic study traces the development project.

Much of abiding value may be learned by report-writers and research men who study military "appreciations." These follow a logical sequence:

(1) The object to be attained.

(2) Factors which affect attainment of the object.

(3) Courses open to

(a) our own side.

(b) the enemy.

The factors relevant to a military situation do not apply in industrial or social like, but the thorough analysis of the problem demanded by the military people is suggestive for all those who write reports.

Sources of Information

Collecting information is the foundation of all good reporting. Thomas Edison gave this advice: "The first thing is to find out everything everybody else knows, and then begin where they let off."

After defining a specific problem for decision-making, we come to the problem of data collection. There are two broad sources of numerical data or information. They are primary source or data and secondary data or source.

While every problem will have its peculiar requirements, certain sources of data are common to nearly all. They are observation, experimentation, books, questionnaires, interviews, workshops and accounting records. The successful writer will be resourceful in this research activities, thinking of new approaches and seeking data overlooked hitherto.

Data may be primary or secondary. Just as in law, the evidence of an eye witness is more valuable than that of a person who justifies at second hand, so in business and other reports, the fruits of observation and experimentation rate high marks. He is a wise report-writer who applies, whenever possible, observation and experimentation to check the findings of others; he is likely to remain unremarkable for his work if he merely echoes the opinions of others, believes things because others believe them, and uses only books and papers with which he is in complete accord.

Secondary sources depend for their value upon their accuracy, their acuteness of valuation, the validity of their reasoning, and the applicability of their conclusions to the case being studied.

No statement is more reliable than its source. The report-writer must spend long hours in gathering facts, arranging them, interpreting them, and then as much time again in checking the accuracy and worthwhileness of what he has in his hand. It is useless to quote a writer unless he is known to be competent in his field. It is danagerous to give the opinion of a man unless he is recognised as being unbiased, up-to-date and in all respects reliable.

Different types of problems may have to depend on their concerned source, which is secondary source, includes books, report of surveys, memoirs, autobiographies, life histories, accounts of travels, historical documents, government publications, RBI and other institutions' publications, reactions, attitudes etc. Information can also be gathered as a primary source by adapting methods like interview methods, observation, questionnaire, schedules etc.

Methodology

Yet another important aspect in report writing is the methodology of writing. The methodology to be adopted may vary from report to report to achieve the objects of reporting. This part of the report should give the methodology adopted for the purpose.

It should give the exact meaning of various concepts and terms used. In some studies if it is not possible to study the whole universe and as such, sample method is adopted and the method of drawing out the sample should be indicated giving reasons, if any for adopting a particular sampling procedure. Under the methodology paragraph it should be indicated clearly the particular method adopted giving reasons thereof.

Every report writing has to follow its own methodology. A methodology may be understood to mean as all those methods and techniques that are adopted for collecting information and data to prepare the report. Methodology in a report-writing refers to the methods which the researcher or report-writer use in compiling and presenting a report. In other words, all those methods which are used during the course of study of a problem are termed as "methods of study."

Therefore, a methodology is to be followed in both the reports, i.e., academic and business, which is almost similar in both the types of reports. There may be a slight variation between them, depending upon the type of report, nature of subject/problem and circumstances of each case. As V.P. Michael points out, there is no harm if the research report is used as business report.

PROCEDURE GENERALLY FOLLOWED

(1) The individual or chairman in the case of a committee or commission submits the report to the person or authority appointed.

(2) The report includes details of meetings held by the individuals or the committee for collection of information and data. It also indicates the number of meetings held, date-wise and place-wise.

(3) The committee may constitutes to carry out the objectives of the study.

(4) While entrusting the work to sub-committees, the committee may lay down certain broad guidelines about the objectives and the requirements of the survey. The guidelines are enclosed in the report itself.

(5) The report received from individual or sub-committees should be examined by the committee and summaries of the result of the investigation are prepared and included in the final report.

(6) Along with the terms of reference, the report indicates the composition of the committee giving details of chairman, members, secretary or member-secretary, their names and addresses.

(7) Sometimes the chairman may specially invite other persons connected with the subject. The committee meets with different cross- sections of individuals, institutions, Government departments and other related and interested in the study.

(8) To achieve the objectives of constitution of committee and writing of report, the committee/individual may give wide publicity in the press as to the appointment and terms of reference and attention of the people would be invited to the finalised questionnaire.

(9) Wide publicity would also be given as to the committee's tours, visits, so that all those interested in the enquiry can put across their views personally before the committee. The object of these tours is to obtain first-hand information directly on the subject of investigation. This would facilitate to present a reliable and correct information in the report.

Bibliography

The word "bibliography" refers to a list of books by one author or one subject. It is a list usually arranged at the back of a book. The list of books is known as bibliography which is normally appended to the research report. It is a list usually arranged at the back of a book, of those books which have been mentioned in the text. The bibliography of various sources consulted and included in the book or report. The heading bibliography should be capitalised and centred. The headings of subdivisions (e.g., primary source) should be typed in lower-case from the left margin and underlined. The spaces should separate the division heading and the first entry in the division. Each entry should begin from the left margin but the second and subsequent lines of entry should be intended four or five spaces and single-spaced. Where more than one work by the same author is cited, it is usual to type a line instead of his name repeated in the second and subsequent entries.

On one subject, the list of books usually included at the back of a report or book are the books which have been mentioned in the text. Preparation of bibliography is one of the major components in a research report and the research study remains incomplete till the bibliography is prepared. Preparation of the final bibliography is the next final step in the preparation of the report. The list contains all those works, may be books, journals, articles, reports of the committees and commissions, annual reports, Acts etc., which the researcher has consulted.

Not only in a research report but also in book writing, may be a reference book or textbook a bibliography is appended. The bibliography is prepared by arranging the list alphabetically. Generally, it may be divided into parts such as books, articles in journals, magazines, Acts, Rules, Regulations, Orders. Newspapers, doctoral thesis, monograms, etc. The preparation of bibliography by arranging in this way is considered scientific, convenient and satisfactory from the readers' point of view. It should be remembered that this is not the only method of presenting a bibliography.

All works cited in the text and footnotes are usually included in this list. The practice has been that people prepare a bibliography either as a single alphabetical list or divided into two or more lists. The classification is generally as unpublished, published sources; primary and secondary sources; books and articles. In some cases preparation of bibliography involves the combination of these arrangements. When once it is decided how the bibliography is to be organised, it is usually arranged in source cards accordingly.

The information for making any entries in the bibliography are taken from the very source itself. In all cases where the source fails to supply necessary bibliographical information, the writers/ researcher can collect it on the library catalogue.

Co-author: In the case of works which have been co-authored, i.e., a work which has two or more authors, the abbreviation *et al.* can be used. The word *et al.*, a Latin abbreviation, is quite often used in bibliographies which stands for etc., meaning 'and others' can be used for second and subsequent name.

Pseudonym: In cases where the author writes under a pseudonym, means a false name used by the author, that should be placed first, then the author's real name should be indicated in square brackets.

Anonymous: It is usual to come across situations of some works which are published anonymously. In an anonymous publication, which is an indication of without the name of the author or authors' name is not known. Anonymity is the state of not making one's name known. In such a case, 'Anon' an abbreviation is used.

Initials: On the other hand, in cases where a book or report originally appeared under the initials, the same should be completed in square brackets.

Edited Works: In cases where a work has editors rather than authors, the name (s) should be followed by the abbreviation 'ed.'

There are several ways of presenting bibliography. The entries in the bibliography should be made adopting, such as for books and pamphlets, the order may be the name of the author, last name first; title, underlined to indicate italics; place, of publication, name of the publisher as well as number of volume. Similarly, for magazines, and newspapers, the order may be the name of the author, last name first; title of the article, in quotation marks, name of the periodical, underlined to indicate italics; the volume or volumes and number, month and date of issue and imagination.

The order of writing entries in bibliography as illustrated above are just the samples for bibliography entries may be used. But one should remember that they are not the only accepted forms uniformly applicable in all cases. The order and style of making entries in bibliography may vary from situation to situation and the knowledge of technical expertise on the part of the writer preparing bibliography. But, however, in practice the only thing important is that whatever method one selects, it must remain consistent throughout.

Illustrations

For a Book: Name of the Author/authors/institution. Full title of the book, including subtitles, if any. Title of series, if any, and volume or number in the series. Volume number, if any. Edition, if not original. City of publication. Publisher's name. Date of publication.

For an Article in a Periodical: Name of the author. Title of the article, Name of the periodical, Volume No. (Sometimes issue number), Date, Pages occupied by the article.

Single Author: A personal name must be given in an inverse order, the last name first. Some foreign names are likely to pose problems in the ordering of the names. In such cases alone, the name may be given in the bibliography exactly as it appears on the original works.

Example

Kumar, Ravi J.

Sankar, R.M.

Prasad, Hari B.

Rayudu, C.S., *Media and Communication Management*, Mumbai, Himalaya Publishing House, 1995.

Two or More Authors: Where there are more than one author, only the name of the first is reversed while the following names remain in the original order, not reversed.

Example

Balan, K.R., and Rayudu, C.S.

Gutta, K., and R.K Sharma,

David, Aaker and G. Myers, *Advertising Management* 2nd ed., Prentice-Hall of India Private Limited, New Delhi.

More than Three Authors

Khanna, B.S., *et al.*, *Practical Costing*, S. Chand & Company (Pvt.) Ltd., New Delhi, 1988.

Organisation, Institutions, Associations and Corporations

International Monetary Fund, *Surveys of African Economics*, D.C., Harper and Co., Ltd., Washigton, 1966.

Parts of a Book

Kaiser, Ernest (1995), "The Literature of Harlem." *In Harlem A Community in Transition*, edited by J.H. Clarke, 199-213, New York: Citadel Press.

Date of Publication Unknown: When the book will be published but the date has not been determined at the time it is listed in the bibliography, "Forthcoming " takes the place of the facts of publication.

Mitchell, D.C., *The Historian as Prophet, Forthcoming.*

Articles in Journals

The names of author(s) of journal articles are treated the same as names of book authors. The titles of journals/magazines are italicised and capitalised as titles. They may be abbreviated, provided the abbreviations are clear to the readers and are used consistently.

The following example illustrate the various kinds of journal/magazine entries:

1. Kumar, R.B. and S. Ramesh Kumar (1995), "Changing Trends in Marketing", *Modern Management*, August-January, pp. 18-20.
2. Rayudu, C.S., (1985), "Ratio Analysis and Financial Performance", *Indian Co-operative* Review, July, 54-70.
3. King, Andrew J. (1976) "Law and Land Use in Chicago", Unpublished Doctoral thesis, University of Wisconsin.

Essential Requirements of Good Report-Writing

The report-writer needs to analyse, group, and marshal his facts into order. He must classify and conquer the elements of the chaos around him before he can hope to appeal with any force to the intelligence of other people. In this process of viewing the whole situation and at the same time, seeing its components, the writer will deter incongruities to avoid and discern a path to follow.

These are skills which come only, so far as we know, with practice, but there are some hints about the process of writing which apply in all circumstances. The report must be practical. We have to avoid the loose way of thinking and a think as a realist who not only sees things as they are materially, but acquiesces in them; let us rather, as report-writer, consider ourselves as being realists in the sense that we understand things as we have found them, not as we would find it convenient to believe them.

A report is prepared by a writer which the recipient has to read and, as such, it must be capable of being understood by the readers. The ultimate object of writing or communicating in writing is that the readers must understand the matter in the same spirit as intended by the writer. As such, while preparing the report, the reporter or writer has to keep in mind certain general principles of a good reporting system.

The principles are only general guidelines for effective writing. As a matter of fact, these general principles cannot be applied uniformly as standardised guidelines to all situations. There may be variations or deviations depending upon the type of report and subject matter to be covered in the report.

However, the following are some of the essentials to be taken into consideration while writing a report:

(1) Selection of Title: The nature of contents of a report cannot be known unless a report is suitably titled. Every report should be given an appropriate title which; at a glance, indicates the nature and subject of its contents. A short and suitable title should be selected. It is the title which indicates the object for which the report has been prepared. The title also should indicate the person or the department who needs the report, for instance, 'Sales report', 'Stores report', 'Financial report', 'Investigation report' etc. Thus, these titles indicate that they are concerned with their respective departments.

(2) Clearness: The report must be clear. Only a careful organisation of facts and interpretation will enable the reader to follow what is to the writer a clear-cut line of reasoning, the art of good prose resides not much in the swing and balance of the language as in the marshalling of arguments, the orderly process of ideas, the disposition of parts so that each finds its proper place. The writer misses his target if the idea in his mind is not received with understanding. As Alice said, after reading Jabberwocky: "somehow it seems to fill my head with ideas — only I don't exactly know what they are."

(3) Completeness: The report must be complete. We must have walked all around the matter about which we are reporting, seeing the good and the bad, the perfect and imperfect, the desirable and the undesirable. We must have provided adequate proof for our favourable and our unfavourable findings.

(4) Conciseness: The report must be concise. It may be as along as a rolled towel or short as a meeting message on a postcard. The length is not the criterion. Conciseness does not consist in using a few words, but in covering the subject in the fewest possible words that will express what is in the writer's mind.

(5) Simplicity: Since a report is a written medium of communication, consideration is, therefore, should be given to the simplicity in which the report is to be prepared. An effectively written medium demands that a report should be described in a language which can be understood by the reader. As such, the report should, as far as possible, be in a simple and clear language. The report should be prepared without scientific and technical language but in all cases, it is not possible to avoid scientific and technical language.

(6) Understandable Language: Language is very essential in good communication. He can adopt his own language but should write on the listener's level. This will make the message pleasing and interesting. An individual reader is interested to read anything which satisfies the purpose and desire. A pleasing message not only puts the reader at ease but also relaxes its reader.

(7) Courtesy: Probably, the best principle for writing a report is the quality of courtesy. Courtesy indicates politeness, considerate and respectfulness in writing. While writing, it is necessary to evaluate the reader or user of the report. Time is valuable to the readers as well as to the writers. Whether a message is a positive, negative, satisfactory or disappointing, it should be courteousely conveyed. For instance:

I regret to say — Discourteous.

I respectfully regret to say — Courteous

It is to be borne in mind that a report is a record or substitute for speech. This quality in report writing demands genuine awareness of the readers, their needs, purpose, time attention and cost.

(8) Accuracy: The report writer has to incorporate the quality of accuracy to achieve the purpose of his report. Accuracy involves a valid, reliable, complete format for presenting the matter in a logical arrangement, suitable word selection to convey correct meaning, appropriate grammar, spelling, language and punctuation. The writer has to get all the relevant facts and check them when necessary to ensure accuracy, and he has to analyse the facts logically. In writing the report, he should keep in mind the person to whom the report will be addressed and try to select the right method of presentation, best suited to appeal to the persons. Accuracy is achieved when the materials are arranged in a natural sequence and should lead to the logical conclusions.

(9) Brevity: Brevity is essential in report-writing, though of course, all the important facts must be included. Too often, a report fails to accomplish its purpose because its author presents his material in a long-winded, round-about manner. A good report-writer gets his message across with as few words as possible, avoids repetition and does not use superfluous words when a simple one will do. It is enough if it is brief, consistent, and relevant, which solve the problems of confusion, misunderstanding and sometimes self-contradictory. The thoroughness in the subject excludes what is insignificant. Reading and understanding a brief report gives the readers time and an opportunity to understand, decide and act upon. Using simple, familiar words and avoiding superfluous words are important factors in effective written communication. J. Batty writes that, if the report is quite long, or detailed, a synopsis should be prepared to cover all significant facts and conclusions.

(10) Coherence: In addition to brevity, coherence is also equally essential for good report-writing. Coherence in communication helps the readers to understand rather than misunderstand. Coherence requires message planning, emphasis, linguistic usage, transition, modification and parallelism. To achieve the clarity in communication, their principle of coherence is very much needed. Relation and clarity are the two important aspects of coherence. It is applied to sentence, paragraphs and the message as a whole. It is tying together of several ideas in any paragraph under one main topic.

(11) Honesty: The report must be intellectually honest. The facts must be scrupulously weighed and properly evaluated, and the writer must sincerely attempt to present something that has a judicial quality. He will draw a distinct line between what he has found to be factual, what is his opinion and what he sets up as a hypothesis. Honesty in reporting involves a sense of obligation to one's self, to other people and to the absolute. Rightness is known by intuition in the mind. Respect for it gives one an expertness in living. Honesty is one of the noblest words among the social virtues.

(12) Readable: The report must be readable. We cannot afford to assume that our report will be read because the boss is interested in the subject. We should try to add to the clarity of our presentation something that will lift it above the ordinary. The truth is that nothing written is useful unless it is attractive enough to be read. We are entitled to be as brilliant and interesting as we can be, so long as we observe the requirement and interesting as we can be, so long as we observe the requirement of correctness, relevance and the objective. There may be an ivory-tower disposition towards decorum, leading us to think that research requires a depersonalised manner of writing.

It is well to read the report aloud. If it is easy to read, you may bank its being easy to understand. If you hesitate over a word, a phrase or a sentence, take a second look.

(13) Sequence: The manner and the way in which the something presented is more important than the something itself. The way a report is presented is also of utmost importance. Material should be arranged so that the reader can pick out the main facts and recommendations easily and quickly. Consistency, continuity, and logical presentation of the message cannot be ignored. And it has to be arranged in a form that will attract the attention of the reader, interest him while he is reading it, and leave him with a desire to do something about it.

(14) Unity: Unity means the condition of being one. The principles of unity applies on three levels:

(1) The individual sentences should be unified.

(2) The individual paragraphs must be unified.

(3) The totality of the subject must be unified.

Every sentence must contain a single idea clearly expressed. All such individual sentences relating to a matter constitute a unified individual paragraph. Each paragraph in a section forms a unit of thought. All units of paragraphs structurally constitute the unified message. Unity principle is an aid to coherence.

(15) Emphasis: The whole message consisting of unity of sentences, and unity of paragraphs are of varying degree of importance. The ideas, facts and figures of them may have an order of importance or priority. The next important principle of report-writing is the emphasis on ideas, facts and figures. Under this principle, the degree of importance or emphasis is placed upon them, indicating their relative power or values. It involves positioning, repetitive use of figures, phrases, and by skilful arrangement of paragraphs. The subject of greatest value, or high degree of importance should be placed in the most prominent position. A prominent position may be the beginning of a paragraph or section. Position is achieved by keeping ideas, facts, or figures at the beginning.

(16) Cost: Preparation and presentation of a report involves cost. One of essentials of reporting is the consideration of cost factor. The guiding principle is that the advantage derived from the use of such report should be more than the cost of preparing and presenting the same and it should be within the affording capacity of an organisation. If the cost of preparing a report is expensive and prohibitive, all types of concerns may not go for the reporting system.

(17) Timely Presentation: The matters contained in a report have a time value. The management can take a timely decision when the report is prepared in time and presented timely. Where the control mechanism is in operation, control reports are used as a controlling device. Therefore, the report should be prepared immediately after the happening of an event so that decision may be taken before the wrong is allowed to take a serious turn. If the reports are not submitted timely it would be just a waste of time and money in respect of certain matters. Information and data are more useful when the facts are fresh in the minds of the persons concerned with the reports. As pointed out by Welsch, timeliness is generally more important than a high degree, of accuracy in the figures. The report should be prepared within the time originally fixed. The non-availability of timely information, when needed, may lead to wrong decisions. On the other hand, the time required for preparation as far as possible should be fixed at minimum.

(18) Adaptability: The nature and subject of the report and its coverage should, as far as possible be served and suited to the person using it, to the purposes for which it is required. Steps and remedial actions can be taken when the report contains in precise terms, possible suggestions, solutions and summary of recommendations. The advantage of written communication by reporting lies in various forms and varied presentations to suit the temparament and outlook of different persons at various levels of management.

According to Welsh: "In the design of reports suited to the principal user, consideration must be given to the method of presentation. Those executives, who are going to utilise th reports, have different backgrounds, working methods, personalities and personal preferences. Executives having controller-ship background, prefer tabulated and detailed data, those having engineering background frequently prefer graphic presentrations and highly summarised data.

The style of writing, arrangement, layout, the wordings to be included are to be well - planned and as simple as possible.

(19) Media of Rep ort: There are several media for presentation of a report. For instance, it may be presented in written form or oral form. A good reporting is one which is presented in the form which judiciously blends different media. Thus, the media selected decide the size and shape of the report.

(20) Facilitates Comparison: A good reporting system which facilitates proper flow of information would be more effective and useful when it gives scope for comparison with previous figures, standards set for budget prepared. It is the comparison of actual performance with that of past or budgeted figures will enable the reader or decision-maker to find out the trends or deviations.

Remedial measures can also be taken to improve the performance. When a report provides a basis for comparison, the reports gain considerably in meaning and significance. While making the comparison, it must be true and fair and attention must be drawn to significant points of difference.

(21) Attractiveness: R. B. Lewis has observed, "In meeting this broad requirement in reporting, the accountant assumes the role of an artist. His task is to print a picture that will appeal to the eyes. His report should serve as panorama which is attractive in an artistic sense and, therefore, one that will be regarded and studied by the potential viewer."

To Sum Up

The writer, who achieves distinction of expression, conciseness, directness — and, if the nature of his work permits it, dramatic quality, beauty of rhythm, and some adventurousness of phrase and idea—has not done something miraculous. He has worked hard and intelligently.

None of these suggestions can eliminate the sweat and strain that often go into report-writing. But, if followed, they should streamline the job considerably and make the report more readable and effective.

*****

CHAPTER 13

Letter Writing

Introduction

Letters are the most ancient and the most important of all mass communication media. A selling medium on which the entire modern business structure depends. Letters enable to sell products, to put out ideas, win goodwill and to incite action of various kinds. Envelope-letters permit enclosures like cheques, D.D., L.R., R.R., memos, receipts, returns and others.

In the restless world of business communication, letters are business. Letters are used for both internal and external communication. Letters enable one person to reach another and thus ensure two-way communication. Writing a letter is an art. It represents a written message sent by post, sometimes, including an envelope, a postcard, an inland-letter.

A letterhead is a printed heading on a paper used for identity, or publicity etc. Outstation, and sometimes local, letters are put in a letter box. Through the medium of letter a person reaches another and as such, it is still the most important of all media of communication.

Total mail load consists of personal, official and commercial correspondence. A letter speaks to a wider cross-section like retailers, wholesalers, editors, dealers, pleaders, auditors, consultants, employees, students, foreigners etc. Friendship, business relations and personal relationships depend to a very large extent on letters. The quality of letter written promotes the image of the companies. Wider practical writing for different situations result in perfection and quality in letter writing.

It is easy to write a letter, which is nothing but to put ideas in black and white but to write an impressive and quality letter is difficult. As talking, everybody can write a letter. The essential of good letter writing is to put ideas in a clear-cut manner, conveying the message in such a way as understandable by the recipient. Though the principles of writing a letter are uniform, there is a lot of difference between business, personal, and official correspondence.

Types of Letters

A letter may be:

(1) Descriptive letter
(2) Narrative letter
(3) Technical letter
(4) Legal letter
(5) Domestic letter
(6) Public letter
(7) Private letter
(8) Foreign letter
(9) Confidential letter
(10) Demi-official letter
(11) Personal letter
(12) Official letter

The world of letter may be broadly classified as:

(1) Introductory
(2) Business
(3) Letters of application
(4) Marriage letters
(5) Love letters
(6) Greeting letters
(7) Letters of testimonial
(8) Resignation letters
(9) Thanking letters
(10) Congratulating letters
(11) Letters of condolence and obituary
(12) Letter of advice
(13) Letter of recommendation

A letter thus may create the first impression and to motivate the reader to respond positively. A good letter must have at least seven parts like the letter head, inside address, salutation, body, complimentary close, signature and signature identification.

Views on Letters and Letter Writing

Wren and Martin: "The art of Letter writing is no mere ornamental accomplishment, but something that every educated person must acquire for practical reasons:"

Rustam J. Mehta: "A well-written letter may bring you new friends, collect money for you, help you to achieve your desires; but a poor one may cost you everything you value most.

Cicero: "A letter does not blush."

Charles W. Eliot: "Carriers of news and knowledge, instrument of trade and industry, promoter of mutual acquittance, of peace and goodwill among men and nations."

James Howell

"The letters are the soul of trade."

John B. Opdycke

I am the letter
I am the bearer of the tidings of great joy
I am the cavalier of culture
I am the courier of commerce
I am the ambassador of production
I am the winged Mercury of industry
I am the plenipotentiary of finance
I am the alpha and omega of big business
I am the bearer of tidings of grave import
I am the letter.

Parts of a Letter

The components or parts of a letter in a usual order of appearance in a message are given below:

(1) Head Address: This part is also called "letter head" or simply "heading." Usually, a printed letter head is used by individuals or business firms and hence it is called a "letter head." This indicates the particulars of sender's name, full address including pin code, STD, emblem, gram, telephone numbers, fax, telex, branch location etc. The address is usually printed at the top centre. It is nowaday's fashion to print at the right hand side or top left hand side.

(2) Dale Line: This line is called in different names like message, date, or simply date. Generally, the date is written at the right hand corner of a letter sheet placed two-to-five spaces below the address. Here the date, month and year of the letter are mentioned. This part indicates the time importance of writing. There are several methods of writing the date line. They are:

1-12-1996

10th December, 1996

December 10, 1996

All these various methods of date line styles are in use, but in modern practice, the style of using letters like st, nd and th, are avoided. However, practice varies from country to country. So the exact writing of date line in a logical order is more desirable, i.e., day, month, and year.

(3) Reference: There is a place for writing reference in a letter which is equally important. Reference may be written in one line or two lines. It is generally located in the same line as the date line below the head address at left- hand corner. This part of reference covers such aspects like file number, number of the letter, year, reference numbers of parties etc. In a reply letter, it is necessary to give corresponding reference number against 'our reference.' It is usually written as:

Your reference

Our reference

Reference number

Place quote in reply.... (reference number)

(4) Inside Address: Inside address contains the name, address of the recipient of a letter. It is nothing but the address of the addressee. It is written to give the receiver's name, job, department, designation, address, code, etc. It is written at the left-hand corner above the salutation, generally two to five spaces below the date line. The inside address is exactly the same as found on the envelope. There are various methods of writing inside address like block form, indented form, semi-block, full-block, open or closed punctuations etc.

(5) Attention Line: Attention line is a special part of a letter which is used when the letter is intended to receive the attention of a particular individual (s). It runs:

"For the attention of Mr. N.D. Saxena"

Or "Attention of..."

This line is placed between the inside address and salutation part. Sometimes, it is underlined or kept in quotation marks.

(6) Salutation: Salutation line is written and placed between the inside address, keeping two to five spaces below it. It is a greeting to the receiver of the letter which opens communication with the added essence with honour. It also implies courtesy, politeness or affection. It is a practice and custom to use permissible words to respect the receiver of a letter. Salutation is to be used whether the receiver is an individual, firm, company, co-operative society or any other institutions. It is placed after the inside address, before commencing body of the letter, usually with double line space. At the end of the word "salutation", punctuations like comma, or colon is used. Putting a colon is not popular but comma is frequently used.

Examples

Sir,

Dear sir,

Dear Mr. Saxena,

My Dear Sir,

Dear Sirs,

Dear Gentleman,

Madam

Dear Madam,

Mesdames,

Dear Financial Manager,

Ladies and Gentlemen,

Mr. A. N. Saxena,

There are two methods of using punctuations; they are:

(1) Open Methods.

(2) Mixed Method.

In the open method, punctuations after salutation and complimentary close are omitted. In a mixed method, colon is placed at the end of salutation and comma at the end of complimentary close.

Examples

1. Open Method

Dear sir:

Yours sincerely

sd/-

(A.N. Saxena)

2. Mixed Method

Dear sir:

Yours faithfully,

sd/-

(A.N. Saxena)

(7) Subject Line: Below the salutation line is written the subject line, placed at the centre of the letter sheet. This is an important part of the letter. It indicates the message theme, core-thought of the subject. In one way, it helps to identify the message reference. It may be written as "subject" or simply "sub." The reader of the letter understands the central idea of the letter.

Example

Dear sir:

Subject: Remittance of advance

Body of letter............

Yours faithfully,

Sometimes the subject line is not necessary if the opening sentence gives reference to the subject of the letter.

(8) Reference Line: Like the subject line the reference line is placed below the subject line. It is written to indicate any previous reference to the subject matter of the letter. This facilitates systematic filing of correspondence, reply, sequence etc. The reference line identifies the purpose, earlier communication, to sort out easily, inward letters, file tracing etc. It is written as "reference" or simply "ref" or "re."

Example

Dear Sirs

Sub: Remittance of advance
Ref: Your letter No. 756/III/A-2, dated 10-12-1996.

Body of the letter...

Yours sincerely,

(9) Body of a Letter: Body of a letter or message body is an important part of the letter sheet, located between the salutation line and the complimentary close. This part contains the main text, substance or essence of a letter. Margin is allowed on the left side of a letter. The subject body of a letter is usually divided into three parts:

(1) Opening or introductory paragraph.

(2) Main part or important message.

(3) Closing paragraph deals with conclusions.

The opening paragraph usually deals with reference to earlier correspondence. Second part is the nucleus or main part of a letter or message proper. Closing paragraph is a sort of formality, concludes the message in summary.

(10) Complimentary Close: This part conveys preferable nuances of tone, indicates a polite way of concluding or closing a letter. This special part is compulsorily to be used. As a letter commenced with a respectable salutation, must end with respectable compliments. In an interaction or personal talk, we usually say "Goodbye" or "Good-night", or "Thank You." Similarly, in a written communication of letter writing, use of complimentary expression indicates the quality of letter. The commonly used complimentary closing expressions are as follows:

Yours faithfully
Yours sincerely
Truly yours
Yours very truly
Very truly yours
Sincerely yours
Cordially
Cordially yours
Yours very cordially
Faithfully yours
Yours respectfully
Respectfully
Yours ever
Yours cooly
Yours tastely, etc.

(11) Signature: Signature line written below the complimentary close signifies giving consent to contents or the message of the letter. It is a signed name of the letter - writer. Sufficient space is left, generally five spaces below the complimentary close for signature. The signature should be written in hand by the writer of a letter. The signature should be followed by the name of the signatory in block letters. Writing full name of the signatory in block letters after signature facilitates knowing the name of the signatory because sometimes the signature may be illegible. In some cases, facsimile signature may be used instead of signing personally. There are different methods of putting the signatures.

Signature has legal implications and effects. Signing his own name indicates responsibility for all the contents in a letter.

Per pro (per procurationem) is a type of signature used when a person is signing for and on behalf of original person under power of attorney. It means the signatory is not personally liable for contents or for legal implications but just signed on behalf of an individual, company or firm. The words per pro or p.p. are used before the name of the firm. Some examples are as follows:

1. Yours faithfully
   Soni & Co.
   C.S. Saxena
2. Yours faithfully
   Per pro Soni & Co.
   C.S. Saxena

3. Yours faithfully
   p.p. Soni & Co.
   C.S. Saxena
4. Yours faithfully
   Soni & Co.
   C.S. Saxena
   Manager
5. Yours faithfully
   Per pro Soni & Co.
   C.S. Saxena
   Financial Manager

(12) Reference Initials: This line indicates giving the initial letters of the typist's or transcriber's name.

(13) Enclosures: This special part indicates any other relevant matter in support of the message of a letter which accompanies the letter. All additional papers, documents, tables, charts, etc., enclosed to the letter are listed consecutively under this part. They are annexures or appendices attached. Enclosure part is located below the signature at right side of a letter-sheet. It may be written as "enclosures" or simply "encl."

Example:

Enclosures: Price list
Order form
Application form
DD
Catalogue
Vouchers
Share warrant
L.R. or R.R.

(14) Copy Notation: This line is written at the left-hand corner of a letter sheet below the word enclosure. It indicates the same message, copies sent to the various persons. It is mentioned against "C.C.", which stand for "carbon copy", or "carbon copies" The counter part notation for "photographic copies." is written against "P.C." means "photo copy." For instance:

CC A.N. Saxena

PC A.N. Saxena

It is usual to write like CFWC which stand for "Copy Forwarded with Compliment."

The letters "bcc" are used to indicate for "blind carbon copy" or "bpc" for "blind photo copy", when such a notation appears on a copy but not on the original message."

bcc Welfare Office

bpc Public Relations Department

(15) Postscript or PS: The word postscript is derived from a latin word "postscriptum", means written afterwards. It relates to messages or matters included in a letter at the end which is afterthought. Additional information typed or written after the letter is fully completed is called "postscript." Afterthought writing occurs when the letter writer fails to include some messages in the body of the letter proper. Postscript is written in the case of unplanned and unprepared with hurry and carelessness. It is not the main message but forgotten or afterthought message included after completing the letter.

For instance:

1. Material prices shot up Rs. 5 per tonne.
2. Shipment held up, cheque enclosed for Rs. 20,000.
3. Do not neglect, issue closes on 15th December, 1996.

(16) Superscription: It is writing the address on an envelope. It is written outside or above, which is the same as the inside address.

SPECIMEN FORM OF A LETTER PARTS

(1) Head Address

(3) Reference (2) Date Line

(4) Inside Address

....

....

....

....

(5) Attention Line

(6) Salutation Line

(7) Subject Line

(8) Reference Line

(9) Body of the Letter ....

....

....

(10) Complimentary Close

(11) Signature

(name)

(12) Reference Initial

(13) Enclosures

1.

2.

3.

(14) Copy Notation

(15) Postscript

1. Head Address; 2. Date Line; 3. Reference; 4. Inside Address; 5. Attention Line: 6 Salutation: 7. Subject line; 8. Reference Line; 9. Body of the letter; 10. Complimentary Close; 11. Signature. 12. Reference Initial; 13. Enclosures; 14. Copy Notation: 15. Postscript.

LETTER, STYLES OR LAYOUT

A letter has a number of parts as discussed above. All these parts or components of a letter may be arranged in different forms. It is called "layout" or "letter style." It indicates arrangement parts in such a way as to have a decent and attractive look. The appearance of a letter will add to the image, goodwill and influences opinion creation.

The following are the various forms of a letter layout:

(1) Indented form. (2) Full block form.
(3) Block form. (4) Semi-block form
(5) Hanging indention form. (6) Modified block form.
(7) NOMA form.

(1) Indented Form: It is also called as "stepped-in form." Indented form of writing a letter is not popular today because it is an old-fashioned form. In this type, the inside address, body of the letter and all the first line of each paragraph are indented five to seven spaces from the margin. comma is kept at the end of each line of address and full stop at the end of the last line. The letter of this form looks of uneven appearance and it is not attractive too. It is tedious to the typist to type because it takes much time for space adjustment.

(2) Full Block Form: It is also called "complete block from." Full block form is the modern or fashionable form. It is used by quite a few business houses. In this form, the lines of inside name and address and all the first lines of each paragraph in the body of a letter are not indented from margin. All parts or components of a letter begin from the left margin. In other words, it concentrates too much on the left hand margin rather than the right which is rather blank. All parts like date, line, inside address, salutation, each paragraph, complimentary close, signature, designation, name commence from left margin. But this form gives an imbalance look but it is easier for the typist to type in this form. Because it requires no change of margin and adjustments. Double space is allotted to separate and distinguish each para.

(3) Block Form: In this form date line, complimentary close, signature and designation are written at the right hand side of the letter sheet. The block form is the most popular and is widely used by many concerns. Double space is used to separate and distinguish between paragraphs. The special feature of this form is that every line of inside name and address, each paragraph commences from the left hand corner of a letter sheet.

(4) Semi-Block Form: This form of letter is the outcome of combination of both block form and indented form. It is a sort of compromise between block and indented form. In this type of writing a letter, the address is written in block form. Indented form is used for the first line of every paragraph, usually indented five space. The complimentary close, signature, designation are placed at the right hand corner below the body of letter. In other words, all the parts are more or less blocked. Like blocked form, it is easy for the typist to type. Punctuations are open.

(5) Hanging Indention Form: This is a special form of writing a letter which is quite distinct from block form, full block form or semi-block form. In this form, first line of every paragraph of the body of a letter begins from margin and all other lines of a given paragraph are flushed 5 spaces from the margin. Every starting paragraph is at the margin but all subsequent lines of that paragraph are indented 3 to 5 spaces. This form is not popular but some concerns have been adopting this method for writing sales letters. The head address may be place at the centre or at a corner of left hand side of the letter sheet. The complimentary close, signature and designation are placed at the right corner. Thus, the look and appearance of this form is quite distinct, eye-catching, draws the attention of the readers. The date is placed at the right hand top corner of a letter sheet.

(6) Modified Block Form: The modified form of the letter writing is more popular. It appears like the full block form with mixed punctuations. Block form is used for writing the sender's address, date, complimentary close, and signature at the right hand corner. The body of the letter containing other parts begin from the left hand margin and are fully in block form.

(7) Noma Form: The letters NOMA stand for the National Office Management Association and popularly called as NOMA form of letter writing This form avoids many formalities involved in other forms of letter styles. It looks impressive and has a good appearance because it is a little shorter. The salutation and complimentary lines are considered redundant and so are done away with.

Illustrations

SPECIMEN FORMS OF LETTERS

1. Indented Form:

Head Address
....
....
....
....

Ref. .... Date ....

Inside Address
....
....
....
.... (Salutation)

Body of the letter :..
....
....
....
....
....
....
....

Yours faithfully,

Sd/-

2. Full Block Form

Head Address

....

....

....

Date: ....

Inside Address

....

....

....

.... (Salutation)

Ref. ....

Body of the letter...
....
....
....

....
....
....

....
....

Yours faithfully,

Sd/-

3. Block Form

Head Address

....

....

....

Date: ....

Inside Address

....

....

....

.... (Salutation)

Ref. ....

Body of the letter...

....

....

....

....

....

....

Yours faithfully,

Sd/-

4. Semi-Block Form

Head Address
....
....
....
....

Date ....

Inside Address
....
....
....

.... (Salutation)

Sub: ....

Ref: ....

Body of the letter ....
....
....

....
....

Yours faithfully,

Sd/-

5. Hanging Indentation Form

Head Address
....
....
....

Date: ....

.... (Salutation)

Body of the letter ....
....
....

....
....

Yours faithfully,

Sd/-

ESSENTIALS OF GOOD LETTER WRITING

The following essentials should be observed for effective letter writing:

(1) Stationery
(2) Letter Head
(3) Typing
(4) Neatness
(5) Appealing
(6) Creating Interest
(7) Give Genuine Advice
(8) Courteous
(9) Paragraphs
(10) Appearance and Layout
(11) Folding
(12) Envelope.

(1) Stationery: Paper, envelopes, pen and other articles are the important requirements for writing a letter worthy to be considered. Paper creates goodwill provided if we avoid using cheap, oiled, worn out, mutilated and glossy paper. For writing letter, unruled bond, fairly textured should be used for clear and attractive conveyance of message. Regarding size of the paper, a standard sheet size of 8½ x 11½ inches is popularly found in practice. For a short message, short size sheet measuring 8½ x 5½ inches is used. Letter format sheets measuring the various sizes may be used occasionally for special purposes. Though there are several colours of papers like light yellow, pale blue, green, pink, but using of white bond paper is the most popular for business.

(2) Letter Head: A printed heading on a letter sheet. Letter heads are printed headings. They show the name, address, telephone numbers of the sender. It is called letter head because it shows the name and address printed in an attractive way on letter sheets. It may also contain firm's identifying emblem, symbol, logotype, slogan, motto, code, telex, fax, branch address etc. The essential features of letter, heads are that they should be actually correct, legible, clearly and quickly readable, eye-catching, pleasing with complete address. Fast colours do not enhance legibility of data and should, therefore, be discouraged. Dark red, deep, yellow, green, twinkling blue are not desirable. But light colours remain the most popular for business.

(3) Typing: Hand-written letters are not legible and not attractive. Many of the handwritings are not readable, because of a scribble or a scrawl. Typing letter is a fashion of the day, it gives good look and appearance, and makes reading easy. In typing letters, double space is desirable. In the case of long letter it is the practice to type single space by giving double space between paragraphs.

(4) Neatness: The customers judge the firm's attitude by the way it writes letters. A neat appearance in an attractive way creates a good impression. Neatness of a letter is the first and foremost important step towards winning the esteem of company's customers.

(5) Appeal: The importance of opening with polite and pleasant manner cannot be ignored. Stressing sales appeal is a corporate business-courtesy. The salesman booking orders can make easy sales. The convincing, appealing and attractiveness in a letter would create a desire that makes customers to place orders.

(6) Creating Interest: It is a desirable quality to show interest, the customer buys your full attention when he buys a ticket or service. The appeal should indicate that you are clearly interested in his problem. The undecided buyer is likely to buy more, provided the body of the letter showed interest in his problems.

(7) Give Genuine Advice: The psychology is that the customer turns to you for help, if you give him sound advice you win a friend for your service, may even change a prospect into a customer.

(8) Courteous: Courtesy involves genuine awareness of customer's needs, purposes, attention span and time. Our customers expect courteous and friendly treatment. "Business goes where it is well received and remains where it is well treated." Therefore, the best way for developing courtesy in the correspondence is by empathy and friendliness.

(9) Paragraphs: The whole of the message or body of the letter should be divided into convenient parts. Usually, it is divided into three parts, namely, introductory part, body proper and conclusion part. The skills lie in the logical division and presentation of paragraphs and of those sentences that begin and end.

The principle of unity of sentence, unity of paragraphs and unity of entire subject as a whole should be strictly adhered to. Each paragraph may consist of many sentences conveying a particular theme. Generally, each paragraph may contain three to five lines and each letter may have three to five paragraphs. A multi-page letter may have more than five paragraphs. The introductory paragraph is usually shorter because it is an opening message in one or two sentences. The main body of the letter may have two or three paragraphs. Closing paragraph may be only one to two sentences.

(10) Appearance and Layout: All parts of a letter should be arranged systematically. Date line, salutation, complimentary close should be placed a. their respective places. The appearance may depend on the style of the letter writing like indented form, block form, hanging form, etc. The style gives appearance. The appearance of a letter sheet and message are the important stimuli that the reader of a letter perceives. The factors that influence the appearance are using the type of stationery, letter head, typing neatly, margin, spacing, style and envelope used. Unruled white bond paper gives good appearance. It creates a visual impression before it is read.

(11) Folding: The letter sheet should be folded in such a way to insert into an envelope. Folding according to the respective sizes of envelopes indicates decency, and artistry. Folding is a cautious work to attend, it requires careful attention to fold particularly in the case of a letter accompanying a number of enclosures. In the case of a window envelope, the letter sheet is to be folded in such a way that the inside address can be seen through the window of the envelope.

(12) Envelope: It is a thin flat, wrapper or cover, for inserting a letter. It surrounds a letter completely to achieve secrecy and security. Business envelopes generally match their standard letter sheet or letter head stationery. A business letter may be single page, multi-paged or letter with enclosures. The usual sizes of envelopes are 3½ x 5½ inches for single sheet letter. For sending bulky pages or letter with many enclosures, envelopes of big size and thick cover of size 6 x 9 inches, 9 x 12 inches, 10 x 13 inches or 10 x 15 inches may be used.

Window envelopes have a transparent panel in the place where the address of the receiver is written. The letter sheet is folded in such a way that inside address can be seen through the window of the envelope.

Window envelopes are not advisable for matters of utmost confidence and secrecy. On the top of envelope, the sender's name and address are printed either at left top-corner or top-centre or left-bottom side of the envelope. The name and address printed should appear as eye-catching like as they on the matching letter head. Optical Charter Recognition, a device in new office technology, requires special typing of envelope addresses so that they can be sensed and processed by electronic machine.

LETTERS TO THE EDITOR

Writing letters to the editor of the press may, be it be newspaper, or periodicals, to make known to the public, is called letters to the editor. Some people in the society are motivated by the spirit of public service or civil service. Such people write long letters to the editor. All subjects are covered in writing letters.

Scope: The scope usually covers the following:

(1) Politics
(2) Suggestions
(3) Complaints
(4) Allegations
(5) Notice
(6) Public Awareness
(7) Grievances
(8) Criticism.

Subject: Subject of such letters appears on nearly all matters under the sun, be it on mosquito nuisance or national or international matters. No broad classification is possible, However, the subjects broadly cover the following:

Unemployment
Population
Railway safety
Hygiene
Corruption, nepotism, and favouritism
Civil supplies
Culture and religion
Health and hospitals

Educational institutions

Plans, budgets and policies

Games and sports

Central-State relations

Elections and war

Historical and public policies

National integration etc.

The following are the letters to the editor which appeared in National newspapers in recent years.

Some Letters to the Editor

(1) Train Accidents: Sir, More than 50 people were killed in the accident Sir, involving the Mardras-Kanyakumari Express which collided head-on with a goods train on the Jolarpet-Salem section of the Southern Railway last month.

Of late, incidents of head-on collisions, one train ramming into another etc. have been taking place all over the country with increasing frequency, not to speak of the so-called "freak" mishaps. This is all the more baffling given the tall claims made by the Railways that sophisticated methods such as automatic block signalling systems etc. have been employed to prevent accidents. The Railway Ministry has apparently taken passenger safety for granted.

(2) Coins to Replace Notes: Sir, With reference to the news-item "Coins to replace Rs. 1,2 notes" *(The Hindu,* May 19). While the move of the Reserve Bank to withdraw one and two rupees denomination notes from circulation is to be welcomed and appreciated as soiled notes will be gradually phased out, the following points need serious attention of the authorities concerned:

Now Re.1 coins come in three different sizes (in dimameter). The Re. 1 coins issued during the Janata period (1977-79) have a diameter of 28 mm. Those minted during the Congress rule under Indira Gandhi/Rajiv Gandhi have a diameter of 26mm and the ones minted after 1990 have a diameter of 24 mm. Perhaps this indirectly indicates the decline in the value of the rupee and the erosion in the purchasing power of the people. Further, the Re. 1 coins of 1977-80 and the Rs. 2 coins minted in 1991, are nearly identical, as the diameter is 28 mm in both cases. One, therefore, finds it difficult to distinguish between them, especially during night.

Hence the Reserve Bank may ensure that there is conspicious variation in the size and thickness of coins of different denominations so that the public is able to differentiate between them.

(3) Insecticides and Mosquitoes: Sir, That 966 persons have died of malaria in different parts of India in just five months from September to February *(The Hindu,* May 4), is a sad commentary on the strategies adopted in the war against mosquitos and malaria.

The great myth which prevails is that mosquitoes can be contained by insecticides. Mosquitoes and other vectors can only be contained in the long-term by the adoption of bio-engineering techniques.

The World Resources Institute at Washington has indicated that 50 species of mosquitoes have acquired resistance to a wide range of insecticides. Apart from the fact that mosquitoes develop resistance to insecticides, the widespread use of insecticides may lead to the elimination of the predators, resulting in insecticide-induced-infestation of their prey, which leads to an ecological imbalance. Furthermore, insecticides, due to their non-biodegradable qualities, are hazardous to humans who are at the top of the food chain through their concentration in the lower life forms.

(4) Governor's Role: Sir, While the President assumes the constitutional responsibilities at the centre, he deputes the Governors to look after such responsibilities at the State level. That is why even when a State comes under President's rule, and the elected Government is dissolved, the Governor continues to remain in office.

By passing a resolution demanding the recall of the Governor, has not the Tamil Nadu Assembly challenged the constitutional right of the President, as the Governor holds office at the pleasure of the President and no one else? If this trend continues, can a Judge of a High Court or Supreme Court or other bodies also be removed by passing resolutions in State Assemblies?

According to Abraham Lincoln, democracy is rule by the people, of the people and for the people. Everyone in this country has a responsibility to upholding our democracy and is accountable to the people. If this is not understood clearly and acted upon by everyone, none can save democracy, as it is not the rule by a mute majority.

*****

CHAPTER 14

Recent Trends and Communication Technologies

Introduction

In this 'Age of Communication information and wide access to it' is considered as wealth. One of the keys to such a source lies in the application of information retrieval techniques which have contributed a lot for the emergence of new communication technologies. But the use of the word 'new' is not appropriate; technologies are not new, but remarkable transformations have taken place in their application of communication. They are now available for mass consumption. These technologies have been defined as a micro-electronic system, incorporating computers and telecommunications.[1]

The new technologies are those based on the silicon chip, the laser, fibre optics and the set of technologies known as bio-technology. Over the last two decades, remarkable developments have taken place in communication technology. They constitute an important and inevitable component of written and oral communication media network. Corporate sector in India has also realised the potentialities of information. Many corporations have initiated and installed some of the new technologies in communication. Financial Institutions, Banks, Insurance Companies, Production and Service Corporations have made significant strides in the application of communication technologies. The installation of national level and international connections, the scope of corporate information transmission, based on mechanical communication media, has been further enhanced.

This Chapter's aim is to examine the role of technologies in communication. This has been attempted primarily through two chapters, ''Effective Speaking" and "Effective Writing." They cover in detail the information technolgoies used for oral and written communication, their application, various media of new technologies in these respects. These aspects have been dealt with in separate chapters.

The chapter on "Effective Speaking" broadly emphasises different types of new technologies in communication, their importance, use and their role in transmitting messages and in solving some of the crucial problems of communication. The chapter on "Effective Writting" provides the application of various new technologies in written communication. Their need, scope and the importance of using new technologies within the framework of the organisation are also discussed.

The limitations of old technologies in communication cannot be overemphasised. They have been practised in all organisations, irrespective of private and public organisations, over a fairly long time. The availability of communication technologies calls for an early switch over to new communication technologies. The change is indispensable. This would enable the management to solve the problems relating to the qualitative improvement of transmission of messages and its accesibility to all. It may be more appropriate to mention that new communication devices serve as an aid for speedy transmission, accuracy etc., and not as a replacement of the human element.

New technologies both in written and verbal media have a potential role in distance communication which have emerged as an important channel for external communication. Different technologies, *viz*., telephone, teleprinter, telex, short circuit, T.V., video cassettes, dictaphone, and many other telecommunication devices have been used in India for distance communication. "Modern communication technologies have the potential to bypass several stages and sequences in the process of development encountered in earlier decades."[2]

The use of new communication technology can tackle some of the basic problems, namely, accuracy, cost, speed, quality, quantity in the light of wide corporate business operations. The predominant method of communication in many organisations have been through old and manual methods involving overcost, time, lack of accuracy, inability to shoulder quantity of message loads.

So, the search for alternative methods has become imperative in the modern complex business organisations, where communication has to go to vast georgraphical territory, both inside the country and outside. Overscoring the traditional media, radio, television, computer, audio and video cassettes. video disks, video tex, telephones and many mechanical devices have been successfully used as a means of communication in many organisations. They have also assisted management in decision-making quickly and in discharging many managerial functions like planning, control, direction, motivation etc.,

For all times, business world must adopt new technologies for the cause of communication to serve the community at large as social responsibility or, it will be difficult to survive in the competitive condition. In the light of recent development in telecommunication services, the corporate enterprises can expand their area of operations. The assumptions behind the communication technologies are:

Assumptions

(1) Equality: New media can achieve equality in the provisions of communication reaching, particularly with reference to geographical location.

(2) Quantity: It can lead to cover the quantity of population to whom the messages must reach. Mass media help in a great way in this direction.

(3) Quality: New technologies help to bring an improvement in the quality of the subject matter to be transferred. Accuracy in the quantity of message-load can be better handled by the new technology.

(4) Economics: It can help to reduce the cost of communication.

The problems faced by the Indian corporate sector or other organisations are percisely these four—Equality, Quality, Quantity and Resources. The media which are currently used in all the organisations are face-to-face communicaton and printed materials. The words of communication, or verbal media, have been in vogue for centuries and it is still the most dominant sytem in business organisations because of its cheapness.

However, it is very effective where it is done by the efficient superior, and loses its effectiveness if the speakers or the receivers are of a poor quality. Face-to-face conversation which has served the purpose of communication for a long time has its own limitations.

Print media, composed of several media, no doubt an important technology, is more popular and common. The fact that written medium is a source of great instructional and directional medium in formal communication in all organisations needs no emphasis. Both as downward and upward channel and external communication, the print medium is a very powerful medium and is likely to remain as the core-medium of communication in the days to come inspite of the emergence of new technoigoies in communication. Print-medium have certain advantages over all technoigoies. It is relatively cheap to produce and operate; it needs no special technical skills. Further, they provide a lot of flexibility and are elastic to changes.

The question often arises as to what are the communication technologies which are used presently. Some of the advanced technologies are available in the advanced countries in their purely scientific style of organisations. But many of modern technologies are available in India also. The most important of these technologies which have been extensively used during the last few decades for communication purposes are telephones and its various types like teleprinter, teletype, telex, radio, television etc. The telephone device is more useful to talk to the receiver who is located in far-off places.

Another important mass-medium is the television. Because of visual impression, television transmits messages effectively and creates a greater impact. Computer is another technology gaining importance in recent years. Availability of audio and video cassettes and their importance cannot be overlooked. The audio and video cassettes can be stored as record for future reference and as an evidence like filing of written communication.

Similarly, the video disc, particularly the optical disc has an enormous communication capacity. Recent developments in the electronic media such as video discs and videotex are enhancing the capacity of the television set. Video disc is a system, similar to the long-play-record, except that it carries both audio and video through the conventional television set.

Video Tex allows the home television set to function like a computer terminal and to retrieve information. It is very useful for transmitting information. In all organisations today, telelphones are used both for internal communication and external communication which provide instant interaction between the speaker and the receiver. The organisations must, however, have a telephone system.

In advanced countries, instances are there using audio and video conferencing. Tele-conferencing is being used in Canada.

The new communication technologies that are being used in some organisations and Government Departments cannot blindly be used in all forms of organisation without relevance to the needs of the corporate requirements. In this connection the cost and the need of high quality expertise cannot be ignored.

Further, in addition to the technology being useful more for external communication, it can effectively be used to improve the efficiency of management and administration. In large business organisations in a complex and competitive set-up, new technologies are necessary for the efficient and effective decision-making, control, co-ordination etc. Modern enterprises are large and in matters like sales and marketing management, and in the monitoring of progress, price trend, market position etc., technologies are of great help.

Communication Systems

The subject of communication technology and electronic media, has been discussed in the following paragraphs.

(1) Visual Systems
(2) Audio Systems
(3) Video Systems
(4) Audio-visual Systems
(5) Computer and related Systems.

1. VISUAL SYSTEMS

A Chinese proverb says: "One picture is worth a thousand words." In real life-situation, according to this proverb, a picture speaks about 125 words per minute. There are varieties of audio-visual or other sensory-aids more in use, they are used to make more comprehensible or to supplement in other ways. Every image in audio or visual media requires a spoken word or comment to clarify its meaning. It may be noted that audio-visuals and other sensory-aids are of little value or significance if they are not supported by a talk.

Speakers and instructors or training teachers use them to illustrate in order to make them more comprehensible. In other words, the image and spoken words both are necessary to make the discussion or session lively, effective and more interesting. In a number of cases, presentation of visual-aids need the help of spoken words. In number of cases, spoken words are necessary in support of visual aids to clarify its meaning. Sales, navigational, air, railways, roads and defence would be impossible without maps or other images. Similarly, a doctor, an engineer, a mathematician, a statistician cannot communicate effectively without some aids. Therefore, audio-visuals are complementary to one another.

Sensory aids are the means we use to reinforce verbal explanations in encoding messages, so that they become clear, simple and stimulating. They are only effective if they are well-used and adopted to the group. They can be anything from a gesture or a natural sound, up to a computerised flight stimulator, or a surgical-operation demonstrated on closed circuit television. They help the speaker as much as they help the audience.[3]

Visual aids contain grammar-like language; its own grammar. Visual communication also has similar grammar and other rules of language and visualisation-meanings. It is possible to transmit a visual theme into a forcible communication by giving a structure. They can be used on the emotions to make people laugh or enjoy. Visual aids like pictures, slides etc., can be used to a greater extent to transmit feelings, opinions, messages, themes etc.

"Pictures have been used with speech way back to the designs scratched in the sand by the Greek Philosophers, Egyptian scribes and the prehistoric cave artists, through the magic lantern to all the sophisticated methods of today. Nevertheless, rarely has proper attention been given to the choice of colour, symbols and visual dynamics in layout."[4]

Visual Communication

A visual aid is any visible device that assists an instructor to transmit to a learner facts, skills, understanding, knowledge and appreciation. The visual method is actually an aid to use with other methods of instruction rather than a method in itself. It is particularly useful with the dramatisation and lecture method. In the visual method, instruction is carried on through such devices as film strips, movies, photagraphs, charts, posters, cartoons, models and actual objects. It is used, as far as possible, in a visual sense; it is measured as effective as an avenue of learning. The visual-sense can be increased to a great extent by visual aids. Quick and fast presentation can be achieved, which show a relationship among ideas, facts and can serve as a review device. The aids should be clear, simple, legible, interesting to have positive effect. It is practically possible to use visual media in combination with other media.

Facts, figures etc., can be presented in an early assimilable manner so that information can be spelled out exactly and the same helps to picturise the required matter. In corporate organisation, the executives can substantiate the policies and the goals of the corporation with reference to data properly presented by the pictures. Like other electronic media, visual medium also plays a significant role in bridging up the communication gap. Here, one should remember the recently developed technology, namely, audio-visual. In this technique, visual technology is the key factor as a tool to give effect to audio-visual communication. Visual device is an aid to visual communication that implies opinions, expression, interpretation, explanation and narration of the pictures, photos, slides, etc.

Visual aids cannot make the communication adequate by itself. To be effective, it must be supported by interpretation and narration by the transmitter. In communication, visual aid helps observation. It is also an effective means of communication and developed techniques are widely practised by the business and industrial houses, educational institutions, meetings, conferences etc. It can be used to communicate the communicator's thoughts and ideas through a visual medium.

Presentation of figures, statistical data, can effectively, be presented through visual aid. Visual aids represent a message by symbols. Visual aid is used to combine with the oral message, with a view to clarify, to explain, to convince and even to attract the listeners' attention or interest. A number of factors are responsible to be receptive to visual aids.

Kinds of Visual Aids

Basically, there are whole range and variety of possibilities of presentation by visual aids. The following are such types:

(1) Film strips and slides
(2) Overhead projector
(3) Opaque projector
(4) Flannel board
(5) Facsimile
(6) Magnetic boards
(7) Electrowriters
(8) Telelectute
(9) Audio-visual cassettes
(10) Signs and symbols
(11) Displays
(12) Drawings
(13) Photgraphs
(14) Colours
(15) Trademarks
(16) Design
(17) Layouts
(18) Posters
(19) Hoardings
(20) Exhibits
(21) Pictures
(22) Models and mock-ups
(23) Adhesive boards
(24) Tachistoscope
(25) Flip over chart
(26) Cutting papers
(27) Yellow pencil technique
(28) Arrow gun
(29) Ultra-violet light
(30) Monometre
(31) Boards
(32) Graphs
(33) Diagrams

(34) Maps
(35) Pictograms
(36) Cartograms
(37) Charts
(38) Words
(39) Illustrations
(40) Numbers
(41) Forms and shapes

(1) Film Strips and Slides : In earlier days, lantern, i.e., a case for holding or carrying a light, was more in practice. It is now more closely related to film-strips and slides. These two are the descendents of the magic lantern. Films and slides are projected on a screen, in most cases, in a darkened room or partially lighted room. Strips and slides are in the nature of static in projection. It is also in practice, for some time, that visuals are projected on three or four screens called as multi-media presentation. It is operated in such a way that projections are arranged behind the screen, rather than behind the listeners.

Film-strips or set of slide-strips are visual aids of communication. They are less expensive than the photographic visual aids of 35 mm slides. The strips generally consist of a number of or series of still-pictures with or without caption. Photographed as a slide film of 35 mm and projected through a projector in a sequence. If required, they can be used in conjuction with recorded sound. They provide half-way house between colour slides and fully animated cinema films.

Generally, in cinema houses, slides are displayed for about 10 seconds each. The message on a slide should be concise, bold, clear, familiar and appropriate words should be used. Another variant form of film slide is colour transparency slides which are generally used for commercial advertisements but are costly to produce.

Film-strips can be produced for educational purposes, public importance, to create awarensess without commercial value. Usually, the slides of the categories are projected free of cost; because of public importance, projection of slides of commercial advertisements may be charged. Sometimes, a narration is used to explain the pictures which can be provided in printed form or recorded on tape or disc with music or sound-effect.

For still projection, any form of art work or direct photography of reality can be produced. Film-strips and slides are actually designed to be looked in relation to a caption and the text. In order to solve the problem of projecting them by side down or the wrong way round, generally they contain a code as to how to put into the projector. A hole or other marks are given for identification showing how they should be inserted into the slid carrier or the cassette.

A picture on photographic film is to be slid into a projector and shown on the screen. Film-strips and slides both look the same to many people. But they are different. Slides are a set of pictures and they are identified in sets. Film-strips rented on 35 mm. are produced in two categories.

They are:

(1) Vertical form.
(2) Horizontal form.

Accordingly, projections are designed to show both types.

(1) Vertical: The special feature of the vertical format is that pictures move down on the screen. If the short side of the picture is vertical, it appears as less movement, while observing, the eyes of the viewers fall from upward to downward. Hence, the picture coming from above depicts its new images without distraction.

(2) Horizontal: In a horizontal format, the pictures move horizontally from left to right. When longer pictures move from left to right and the eyes of the viewers follow it; the comments are presented with the same.

Similarly, film-strips and slides are produced in two colour forms. They are:

(1) Black and white.

(2) Colour.

(1) Black and White: Black and white film-strips and slides are more flexible as they can be projected effectively in an auditorium or room partially lighted, on walls, grey chalk board and panel boards.

(2) Colour: On the other hand, colour slides or film-strips require full blackout and good quality screen. Coloured slides or film-strips are more attractive to look; project reality and add interest to the picture.

Film strips and slides can be made in two forms. They are:

(1) Without sound track.

(2) With sound track.

(1) Without Sound Track: Under this method, pictures are projected without sound. In this category of projection of film-strips or set of slides, they are projected without combining the element of sound system. But they are presented in conjunction with comment by the speaker. The speaker or instructor will describe the image completely in conjunction with comment.

(2) With Sound Track: Talkie-strips or film-strips are accompanied with automatic sound. The second category of projection of film-strips are a set of pictures that are prepared with sound track. The message of the slide image is recorded and reproduced with the help of a magnetic tape or disc. The advancement in communication technology in recent years has made it possible to introduce electronic devices which operate the projector and change the frame as predetermined and designed. This is another method which operates to make a bleep or sound a bell to indicate to change the frame. Accordingly, the speaker or the instructor change the frame.

Preparation of Film-Strips and Slides

(1) The exact purpose and scope of the film-strips or set of slides is to be decided. Factors like time, nature of session, discussion etc., should be considered.

(2) The next stage is to write a treatment. It is a narration for film-strips or slides to be projected.

(3) To prepare the script, it is necessary to be made in two-column script. One side is used for visual picture and on the other side, the sound. On the left hand side is given a sketch or visual picture and on the right hand side, sound.

(4) The message should be simple and avoid details.

(5) A few details which help easy reading and comprehension which stimulate memory.

(6) Titles and numbers should be given on individual strip or slide for easy reference and identification.

(7) The main little should be in bold letters and in the case of colour frame, with a distinctive colour. The words "selected" should be very few, appropriate, concise, clear and convey the meaning directly. Adapting fancy type faces and handwriting are desirable in certain cases.

Advantages

(1) As there is no quick movement or change of frame, the picture remains immobile on the screen. The viewer can see the picture leisurely.

(2) They give an opportunity to the viewers to study and find defects and imperfections in them.

(3) They are cheap and easy to make compared to the motion film.

(4) The advantages of flexibility is achieved.

(5) Each still picture depicts a precise image and clearly defined theme.

(6) They permit the speaker or the instructor to adjust the rate of speech.

(7) The speaker can give comments in support of the image and the message simultaneously.

(8) There are electronic devices which operate the projector and change the frame as predetermined and desired.

(9) The merit is that they can be produced with sound track and without sound track.

(10) Film-strips can be made ranging from short to any length in size containing over 100 pictures to be shown.

(11) Economical in space use for storage and easy for transportation, being small in size of 35 mm, they are relatively easy to store and carry from place to place.

(12) Two types of projectors are available. Manually operated projectors and automatic projectors are available to meet the requirements of various users.

(13) Manual projector helps to refer back or to review during the course of a session.

Disadvantages

(1) Unless the speaker or instructor is trained or skilled, they cannot be used for effective presentation and to give uninterrupted message completely.

(2) In the case of a long session, it involves to make film-strips and set of lights too long. Some may even contain hundreds of pictures shown in a short session.

(3) Generally, it is not possible to remeber and recollect the images of individual pictures.

(4) People without the knowledge of their operation are inclined to project them upside down or the wrong way round.

(5) The storage and catalogueing of all sets of slides and film strips is a difficult task; unless scientifically and systematically stored, it may be very embarassing if the correct aids are not available timely.

(6) The choice of suitable projector equipment to the requirement is difficult.

(7) The use of automatic projector does not permit to refer back when the session is going on which is designed to show pictures in a particular sequence and speed.

(8) They confuse and distract the viewers. They are the same often true of photographs and projected for a limited time.

(9) They are not suitable for the projection of all types of themes and pictures.

(10) Just by looking at a visual picture, they cannot understand or grasp the subject without the details of the next. The viewers take more time to look at them, refresh the text to understand. Obviously, this means that very little is remembered of the individual picture when hundred pictures are shown in a short session.

(2) Overhead Projector: Overhead projector is one of the most advanced and efficient visual aid. By tilting the lens-head up and down and adjusting the levelling legs, it is possible to produce uniform pictures. The machine has a light equalising reflector, light intensifying condenser etc., which gives a consistently bright and sharp picture.

There are a number of models of overhead projectors. They are used to project prepared transparencies by the speaker or instructor to the audience. The image can be made to appear on the walls or screen. Horizontal apparatus, mirror, wide-angle lenses, projector, transparencies, cellophane film sheets for tracing, cardboard frame, grease, pencils, special ink, head throws etc., constitute the system of overhead projector.

In this, a powerful light is reflected through the projector-head that throws the image on the screen. The image can be projected only from a short distance. The make of a projector will give four foot square image with a ten inch symbol image at a six feet distance. Transparencies can be made photographically of any material for projection.

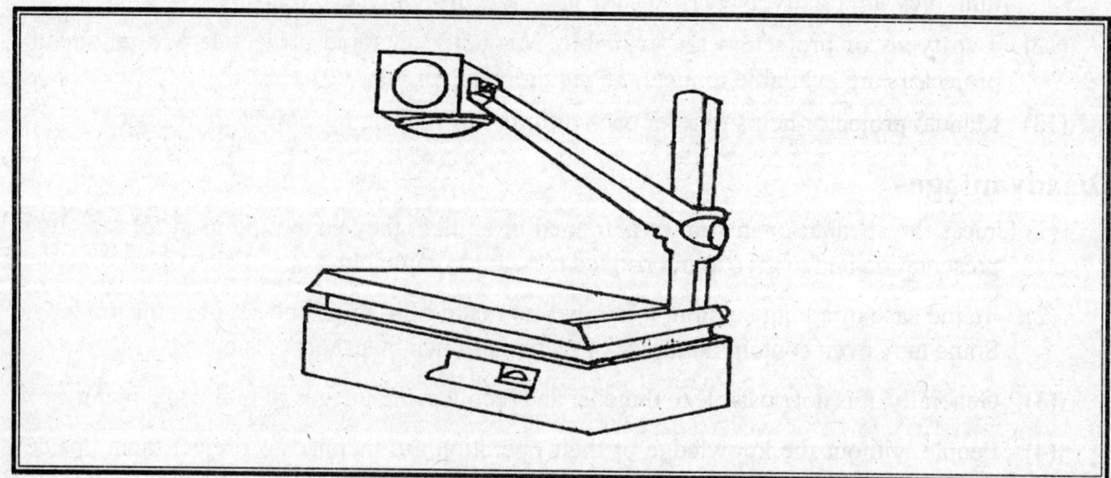

Fig. 14.1 Overhead Projector

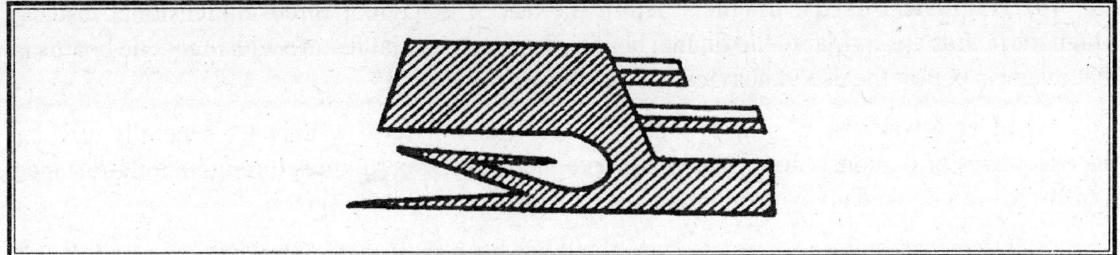

Fig. 14.2 Opaque

Overhead projector is the most effective conveyor of ideas, feelings etc., with an instant transmission. It can be used in a round table conference, small group conferences, seminars, symposia, etc. Advertising agencies also use overhead projector by preparing the pictures in advance. Animated charts can also be made and projected through this device.

(3) Opaque Projector: It is one of visual communication aids in popular use. Opaque is a projection device which does not allow light to pass through or not able to be see through, not transparent. It is called as episcope; can be used to project any non-transparent object on the screen. The device is more useful to project image on the screen like pictures, diagrams, book illustrations, photographs, maps, texts, flat specimens, graphics, material etc.

Advancement in technology has led to the development of modern episcope which can even project three-dimensional objects. They are projected on to suitable sized-card, tracing paper or plastic sheets. The process gives an enlarged copy. This can be further simplified, coloured, modified to meet the requirement of the situation.

A picture to be projected is placed on a tray at the bottom of the projector. The image of the picture is reflected on the screen by lenses by supplying powerful light on to a mirror. In a darked room, opaque projections are made but some opaque models can also be used in semi-light room. Episcope can be used in the management-process at regular meetings at which subordinates and lower management can be informed to widen their outlook and work situation.

(4) Flannel Board: The ordinary meaning of the word implies a piece of material made of cotton or wool. A cotton cloth made in the imitation of flannel. Flannel boards consist of a board covered with felt. Sticky-backed visuals are placed on the surface. It allows the speaker to put some action or movement and flexibility into an otherwise static presentation.

Flannels are used for writing or speaking. Most of the problems of the management can be put in the form of animation which is ideal for flannel board. Animation is a process of giving life and movement to the inanimate objects. In the organisations, they can be used to inform about the changes in the layout of the factory, re-allocation of sales area, change in the process of production etc., can be well explained with action.

(5) Facsimile: Facsimile is a mechanical medium which makes an exact copy. Fascimile transmits through telephone lines, exact copies of blueprints, layouts and other visual materials. It is increasingly used to transmit exact copies between distant places. So, it is not used popularly to send copies between an organisation and communication medium or between the offices of agency and client.

(6) Magnetic Boards: Magnets permit the use of behaviour three- dimensional visuals. Magnetic boards are similar to the flannel boards. The only special feature with magnetic boards is that magnets permit the use of heavier three-dimensional visuals.

(7) Electro-writers: Writing is caused by electricity. Electro-writers are generally used by the executives or demonstrators. They can write their black board notes through a long-distance transmitter unit hooked up by telephone lines with projector unit and screen.

(8) Telelectures: Telelecture as a visual aid has been discussed elesewhere in detail. It is a common tool for making an audio-visual presentation at a distance. It is best technique for making audio/visual presentation at a distance. With the arrangement of telephone department, there is hook up from a speaker's office to a meeting place or class room or conference where visuals can be shown while the speaker is heard.

(9) Audio and Video Cassettes etc: A number of electronic media have emerged in the field of communication. They are highly sophisticated communication technologies produced by devices made according to the principles of eletronics. There are a number of electronic media available and are gaining importance all over the world. They are similar to audio cassettes, video disc, telidon, video tape, videotex, disc recording etc. They are useful in overcoming some of the difficulties associated with conventional media.

(10) Signs and Symbols: Symbolic form of expression includes the use of words, numbers, signs etc. The realistic form of expression includes photography, slides etc. In simple terms, communication in symbolic form includes a collection of signs and symbols that may be put together in an infinite number of ways and the impression created at these symbols is the image. These are working tools of communication. These can be used to make the viewer visualise a sleek product like sports car and as it cannot be sent by itself, it can be encoded into signs and symbols.

A sign is a group of letters, sounds, pictures or other communication elements that stand for something. It may stand for an abstract idea or stand for a product. An advertisement, for instance, is a collection of signs, verbal or non-verbal. These signs usually operate at a sub-conscious level and are not consciously associated with past and present impressions. Signs indicate to the viewer. Trade work is also a symbol- A trademark includes any word, symbol, name, or device or any communication thereof used in the identification of things.

Symbolic presentation of facts or feelings is the fascinating area of visual communication. The more human use of symbolism is more popular in real-life situation also. There is symbolic meaning in every symbol. Some symbolics are more popular as they are established by long usage and understandable to various situations; some other symbols are obscure. The situational-factors play an important role in attributing meanings to symbols.

(11) Displays: "Display" means things set out for show. Fairs, festivals, exhibitions, carnivals etc. would give an opportunity for installing or arranging displays. They are prepared and presented powerfully to attract the attention of the public and create desires and interests on the things displayed at important places like fairs and exhibitions.

Both interior and exterior customers see merchandise and products displayed. Human instinct is used as a basis for building an image that customers like to see new and useful items and that they offer to buy on impulse.

They have the important quality of appealing to the sight trade. Businessmen and manufacturers have come to recognise the intrinsic worth of display at shops, establishments, exhibitions etc. In addition to various physical senses like seeing, tasting, smelling, feeling, weighing, telepathy is also one of the important media of communication.

Items are displayed on showcases called "windo-dressing" and stands. There are various methods of display, namely:

(i) Open display
(ii)) Closed display
(iii) Architectural display
(iv) Platform display
(v) Ledge and Wall display
(vi) Interior display.

On the other hand, display may be interior which follows certain factors of layout, decoration and product display at counters. The objects of display are to sell goods, show the use of product, introduce new groups, demonstration, build image, suggest merchandise, and build goodwill.

(12) Drawings: It is also called "realistic drawings." It is an art of making a picture with the help of pencil, brush, crayon, colours by the use of lines and shades. Drawing made by a professional artist are clearer than photographs. Human intellect is applied to be the filters. Print, illustrations can be made by drawings. There are different drawing techniques available in the vocabulary of an artist.

Drawing work is done with pen, pencil, ink, crayon or dry brush techniques which may result in clear card-lines of solid black and white. "Printing and wash drawings — a black and white brush technique similar to water-colour painting produce varying tonal graduation from black through shades of gray instead of solid black and white."[5]

It is possible to give several tonal effects by using brush and ink with varying amount of water. Tight and loose are the two important treatments which can be given to a wash drawing. In the case of tight drawings, detailed information is given to achieve realism. Impressionistic treatment can be given in the case of loose drawings. Drawings without tonal effects can be produced with line drawing called "pen and ink drawings" or photograph. Illustrations, cartoons etc., are made by the technique of line drawings.

"Scratchboard drawings are made by using stylus to scratch through a surface of black on a white piece of drawing board. The result is a series of white lines on a black background."[6] The advantage of novelty can be obtained when pencil, crayon and charcoal are used. Too much details should be avoided as they are distract-elements.

(13) Photographs: A picture taken by a camera is known as photograph using the action of light on film or plates covered with certain chemicals. Photography, one of the main visual aids, can be the most powerful communication device. Photographs approach reality. It may be considered as art work supported by chemicals and camera. One can see on a photograph things much in the same way the eyes see them. Photographs have the greatest attribute of realism. Every photograph shows the pores in the skin, the gain in wood, texture in cloth in a way few drawings can.

They represent illustrations to life and makes the subject more believable. The great advantage of a photography is that it creates a feeling of immediacy and the viewer feels a sense of being there. Things or people in a photograph are real, it stimulates emotional involvement. The angle and distance affect translation of the three-dimensional objects into a two-dimensional picture. Real object is produced by suitable light and shade. A photograph effectively conveys written or spoken message in a few minutes in an interesting and fascinating way. Screen, contact, matt, glossy, contrasts, double weight, paper of single weight, whole plate etc., constitute the system of photography. Elements like creativity and imagination are also present in a photography; it is an art called "photographic art."

(14) Colours: Like other visuals, colours also speak. Colours have symbolism of their own which have elements of communication process. Colours increase attention value, realism, prestige, emphasis and identification. Colour is a quality which objects or things have and which can be seen more clearly when the light falls on them. Certain colours can be seen without light. Skin has colours which varies with races. Vividness and interesting quality on object can be achieved by colours.

Over the years, the use of colours has increased substantially because of improved colour technology. There are several colours. For instance, they are classified as warm and cool. Blue and green are cool. These two colours are cool and restrained colours. It is because of their association with the sky, sea, trees, and grass.

Red and orange are warm colours, suggesting fire, passion, action and excitement. Yellow is bright, cheerful, indicates warmth without heat. These colours have a symbolic or psychological impact. It is the skill in the vocabulary of the artist to understand the different dimensions of colours. Depending upon the purpose of their use, they should be classified accurately to get the desired impact. All art techniques like drawings, layouts and photography can use colours.

Colours are of two types. They are chromatic colours and achromatic colours. The chromatic colours are yellow, orange, red, purple, blue, green and hues like orange-red. Black, white and intermediate series of grey are achromatic colours.

Chromatic colours may again be classified as:

(a) Primary.

(b) Secondary.

(c) Tertiary.

Red, blue and yellow are primary colours. Green, purple, orange are secondary colours. Tertiary colours are obtained by mixing secondary colours.

The type of electric lamps used has a great deal to do with colour effect. Colours offer the following advantages as suggested by Stanley:

(1) Attracting attention to an advertisement.

(2) Representing objects, scenes and people with complete fidelity.

(3) Emphasizing some special part of the message or of the product.

(4) Suggesting abstract quantities appropriate to the selling appeal.

(5) Creating a pleasant first impression for the advertisement.

(6) Creating prestige for the product, service or advertiser.

(7) Fastening visual impression in memory (partly because of the performance of other functions listed above, and partly because of inherent power to stimulate interest.)[7]

Generally colours have three basic purposes.[8]

(1) Realism: An object can be easily recognised if it is drawn in a simplified way but actual colour should be used. Fields, sea, faces, pillar boxes, traffic signs, signals and other objects can be easily recognised, provided the colours are true to situation. It is quite possible that some objects may have similar colours which may lead to confusion and misunderstanding.

(2) Codes: We come across in practice a number of codes in use. For instance, red colour is used for fire, electric and other dangerous elements. In traffic signals red colour indicates stop, amber colour wait and green go. Piping systems can be identified in distinctive colours; the electric wiring system in contrasting shade. A speaker may use different coloured visuals to help the audience to distinguish one situation from another. In office management, different coloured documents are used to make distinction between one group of documents and another. Different variables in a graph can be in different colours. Similarly, different colours are used on maps to indicate hills, mountains, highlands, lowlands, water, different classes of railway lines, crops and boundaries.

(3) A rtistic Contrast and Mood: The basic purpose of using colour under this method is purely artistic. Colours are not meant for reality. For instance, human figures may be purple, red, green. Here, no emphasis will be given to stick to actual colours. This purpose is not popular, because they lead to confusion or irritation.

(15) Trademark: The term "trademark" is related to marketing governed by the Trademark Act which regulates the registration of identifying marks. A trade mark includes any word, name, symbol or device or any combination thereof adopted by a manufacturer or merchant to identify his goods and distinguish them from those manufactured by the competitors. It is a brand which gives a legal protection, because under the law, it has been appropriated by one seller.

All trademarks or brands include the words, letter or numbers that can be pronounced. Trademark may include a pictorial design. A pictorial design is a brand mark. It appears that some people believe by mistake that the trademark is only the pictorial part of the brand. We can see trademark appearing on every advertisement. When the consumers go shopping, the trademark recalls the advertisement and its features. It is a trademark by which consumers can identify the product which they want to buy.

Identifying marks or trademarks in recent years are more important because mass communication makes it possible to capitalise on identifying marks. The trademark is an important factor in the product's brand-image, the style or graphic approach. Trademark is different from the trade name. These are two different terms which are often confused and misued. Trademark is any device or mark that identifies the origin of a product, telling who manufactured it or who are selling it. On the other hand, trade name is the name that applies to the business as a whole but not to any individual product.

(16) Design: "Design" is a sketch or plan produced before something is finally produced. It is a style or pattern, the way in which something has been made or put together. It may be simple or painted, printed, embroidery pattern. The word "design" has been in popular use but often confused and misunderstood. It can be used as a noun form; it indicates an arrangement of parts and the plan behind the arrangement that produces a desired unit or structure. In verbal form, it means, any human activity relating to organising, arranging, displaying elements in a manner which achieves some specific purpose.[9]

(17) Layout: Composition or layout serves the purpose to convey an exact message. It is a major job of the artist in executing layout of the advertisement. Layout is a format in which the various elements of communication are combined. It is a sort of physical visualisation of the creative idea. It is an advertising colloquialism. It is a simplified way of the element of an advertising within space limitation. It is used with reference to the newspaper, magazine and outdoor advertisements.

There are several forms of layout; each has its own characteristics. They are like thumbhnail sketches, rough layouts, finished layouts, comprehensive layouts and working layouts. The important principles to be followed in making a layout are balance, movement, unity, clarity, simplicity, emphasis etc. There are some aritistic laws for making effective layouts. There are real reasons for having rectangular; tools like chalk-board, flannel board, newsprint, charts and projecting screens. The layout reinforces the importance of the visual.

(18) Posters: Yet another form of written communication is the poster generally used for external communication. A poster is a large notice or advertisement for sticking on a wall. A written document, a playcard pasted or displayed in public places as an announcement or advertisement. It may include pictorial or picture poster, a playcard consisting mainly of a picture of illustration. A poster gives an opportunity to the by-passer to see and read. This form of written communication offer many advantages to the organisation because it draws the attention of many people. A poster is prepared based on planned specialisation; and all the activities relating to the poster exhibition are effectively supervised and controlled. A poster in a prominent place attracts a great variety of cross sections of the people. Posters are generally used for product advertisement. The posters are called bill boards. Posters are used widely for outdoor advertising.

(19) Hoardings: Hoardings are large wooden flat objects on which advertisements and posters are struck. They act as silent salesmen. They are often described as round-the-clock reminder as medium. Generally, they are prepared by a professional artist in an attractive way to catch the eyes of the viewers. Agents engaged in using large hoardings also call it "bill board business."

Some agencies and contractors confine themselves largely to offer special facilities to advertisers. They contact the hoarding owners. It is the responsibility of the contractors to undertake the work to have regular inspection of hoarding size.

They may include cement erected at important places, canvasses and allied materials are used for painting the matter on them.

(20) Exhibits: Exhibits are used to display to the public at a place called exhibition where a large number of people gather. The principle to exhibit is creative thinking to be applied before display.

(21) Pictures: Picture is one of the communication media having much impact and creates an impression. Pictures are used as a medium in support of verbal communication, especially to clarify certain points arising out of a picture. For symbols, blueprints, charts, maps, films, three-dimensional models are used. There is a saying that "a picture can be worth a thousand words." Picture is a painting, image or drawing includes a photograph which clearly describes a theme, any image, that is, scene on a wall, paper etc. Pictorials consist of many pictures.

(22) Models and Mock-ups: A model is a visual aid useful for putting over management technique. It may include a design, type of image, pattern, or system used as a basis for copy or an example for one's action or plans displayed. Mocks are not real substitute model for training or practice. They are not genuine models. Models and mock-ups are used for transmitting information, particularly more suitable for the starting point of discussion. Usually, they are supported by a short explanation which keeps them in touch with what is happening in the training field.

(23) Adhesive Boards: As the name indicates, it is, a substance which is used to make things stick to a board. Most of the problems of the organisation often lend themselves to the type of sticking information on a board. Adhesive boards can be used to display information of any problem. For instance, chemical formula, mechanical proçess, process of prodcution etc., can be shown on adhesive boards. Image or diagrams representing practical problems can be presented, simply made without undue finish.

Presentations are generally used for a few times. They help to present an intelligent simplification into visual terms. Another advantage of this method is that the speaker or the instructor, too, can understand his own subject better. Many work situations, production methods, management situations can most suitably be presented on a flannel board.

(24) Tachistoscope: A visual device by which a text can be made to flash on the screen. This equipment helps quick reading of instructions and other special situations.

(25) Flip-over Chart: Yet another popular visual device is the 'Flip- chart.' It is also called as 'Flip-over Chart.' These charts are effective visual aids that are made professionally or improvised. It is a pad of sheet generally about three by four feet. Under this, a series of charts marked are covered by a blank sheet of paper. The operator can turn or flip over to the back or he may turn from the back to the front.

To flip means to turn over quickly. There are special strands of various complexity to hold a flip chart. They can be mounted on the same or similar easel. Alternatively, the instructor can just prop it up against the front wall facing listeners when he is satisfied.

There is another novel method of mounting the component charts on a series of rings they are turned over. The speaker has to turn over the pages to show visuals and explain in support of these charts. Professionally prepared may be inter-leaved, with blank sheets, the instructor can show them coinciding his comments. Transparent sheets can be used to be flipped over a basic chart. The charts of these types are designed basically to syncronise the visual chart with talk.

Projectors can aslo be used to move up slightly which makes a good impression on the listeners. Good speakers, for effective speaking, invariably use visual aids. Meeting places like hotels, conference halls, colleges, training schools, seminar halls and board rooms may have projectors.

(26) Cutting Papers: Cutting papers of desired shapes and designs constitute a usual visual instrument. Paper-pads are used for this purpose. They can be cut-out windows or flaps. The speaker can lift cuttings of the subject or theme on the sheet behind. The technique of cutting papers gives an opportunity to present by cutting off parts of the paper or sheets progressively. The cut sheets are flipped over from the back of the board to the front.

Each sheet shows a piece more of the total picture. The questioning part of a problem can be put on vertically half-cut sheet on the left-hand side. Perception, imagination, etc., will help to cut sheets, making windows and using adhesive tape.

(27) Yellow Pencil Technique: A visual aid as an aid-memory for speaker's self. Light yellow china graph or wax pencil is used for drawings. The speaker can present more information to the listeners. In the case of certain subjects of speech, where one cannot rely on his memory like accounting, statistics, engineering etc., yellow pencil technique is used.

(28) Arrow Gun: A visual aid either of a battery or mains operated hand projector. The projector on operation flashes an arrow on the screen. It is used with static or moving projection. There are other systems like circles, dots, crosses, tick marks, arrows or pointing things.

(29) Ultra Violet Light: Short or long-wave ultra violet light, fluorescent crayons, chalks, paints projector, ink etc. constitute the system of ultra violet light device. They produce dramatic effect when used on the stage. Fluorescent crayons, chalks, paints, ink, etc., some of them are invisible in ordinary light are exposed to ultra violet light. Flannel board material paints with fluorescent colour can also be used to put on the board to glow brilliantly and startle the participants. Ultra violet projector is the main part of the system.

In Italy, a road safety organisation made posters showing a road scene a few seconds before an accident took place. When an ultra violet light was uncovered, the accident become visible, for it was drawn in invisible fluorescent ink. [10]

(30) Monometer: The 'monometer' is a device used for gathering group participation with a large audience. It is also used for entertainment. Near each seat, a button is arranged, all of which are in circuit with a large dial on the stage. The chairman or speaker explains their operations and uses before the commencement of the meeting. He gets the audience to test the equipment by pressing the button. When all the buttons are pressed, the dial shows 100 per cent, if half-buttons are pressed, it shows 50 per cent and so on. When the speaker asks a question, he gets those agree to press the buttons. The readings on the monometer shows the feelings of the meeting and the speaker reacts as if he had a 'yes' or 'no' answer. [11]

(31) Boards: Blackboard is the oldest and cheapest method pictorial presentation. Though it was used commonly and popularly in earlier days, even today it is used. In earlier days, lantern, i.e., a case for holding or carrying a light, is more closely related to slides and film-strips. Visual aid may be a simple image or a few words on a chalkboard. In earlier days the board was available in black colour only, hence they are called as "blackboard."

But, today they are called "Chalkboard" and are now available in different colours like green, brown, white etc., with a beautiful glass top on them. In modern educational instructions, they are called "chalkboards." They are very pleasant to write and neither make hands dirty nor do the white dust fall on the clothes of an instructor. Developed from a simple chalkboard, advancement in techniques has led to emergence of a variety of boards. The various types of boards which are in use are:

1. Plastic boards
2. Magnetic boards
3. Peg boards
4. Electric boards
5. Hand-worked mechanical boards
6. Miscellaneous boards.

(32) Graphs: Graphical presentation of information, including numerical data, gives an idea. They provide an attractive information in a picture manner. They are symbolic representation of statistical, economic or mathematical data. They communicate in a more accurate manner. For instance, a line on a graph going up is a good sign, while falling down is a bad sign. Study of graphs requires mental efforts to think and interpret a graph. They help to present correctly, provided a scale is to be taken correctly and honestly. Graphs are used now-a-days increasingly in all types of reports which convey message at a glance. A graph may be mathematical graph, statistical graph, diagram, charts, cartograms or pictograms.

(33) Diagrams: Diagrams, explain the message rather than represent. They are drawings used to explain, present numerical data in an understandable manner. It is known as diagramatic presentation of factual information. They are visual media of description which explain, meaning and language to convey message. They are being attractive, eye-catching and interesting.

Diagrams can be used to show the working of a machine, layout, production method, process of production, electric circuits, piping, lubrication systems and organisational chart showing superior-subordinate relationship, chain of authority etc. There are several types of diagrams, such as one-dimensional, two-dimensional, three-dimensional, cartograms, maps etc.

(34) Maps: Map is a visual medium of communication of real life situations. It is drawing or plan in outline of any part of the surface of the earth with various characters. Features like roads, rivers, seas, towns, mountains, boundaries, railway-lines etc., can be shown on a map. Similarly, maps can be made with a similar type of drawing showing the surface of the mocn, the position of the stars in the sky, solar system, planetary movement etc.

Map also permits a number of other ways of conveying information like various projections, conventional signs, contours, etc. Maps can be understood better if we learn navigational charts. They are, therefore, very often more suitable for class room or conference use for effective communication, to support the subject in session, provided they should be as simple as possible.

(35) Pictograms: A picture is a painting or drawing a photograph, i.e., a scene, a small symbol conveys message. With the help of the pictogram, small pictures represent the data. For instance, a car manufacturing company may present the data regarding its sales by means of small pictures each representing say 500 or 1000 cars. Pictorgrams mean pictures, a technique of presenting statistical data. It is a popular and widely used device in practice. It may very well be ascertained that pictograms speak of things much more which can be easily understandable even by a common man without any mathematical background.

(36) Cartograms: Cartoon means drawing making fun of something. Also called "statistical maps" they are used to represent quantitative information. Maps are used to show the facts on a regional or geographical basis. Shades, colours, dots, points, plus marks and other symbols may be used to show quantities on a map. For geographical comparison, pictograms are used. Distribution of rainfall, population, density, etc., can be shown through pictograms. They are best suited and most widely used where geographical comparisons are necessary.

(37) Charts: The term "chart" denotes a map showing some information. It may be a table or diagram giving information, sitautior, possessions etc. Generally, charts are used to depict non-numerical information. It shows the relationship of non-numerical nature systems and activities etc. The organisational chart is the best example to illustrate a chart. A numerical data may also be recognised in the figure. For instance, in an organisation chart, the number of staff against each level can be arranged.

A chart is a pictorial presentation of a table or diagram of information about a particular subject. A chart depicts non-numerical relationship and a graph depicts quantitative relationship and a graph depicts quantative relationship. Information may be presented by charts, graphs etc. They are by far the most popularly used visual aids. May be painted, printed or drawn.

(38) Words: Words are the most familiar tool or type of symbol employed by communicators. Words have power only to the extent the people know their meanings.

Words have flesh, sound and appearance. Words exist for their meanings. Words have to be employed as a means, not as an end. Words are like leaves: Where they most abound, much fruit of sense beneath is rarely found. Words should be used not only to balance a sentence but to balance an idea.

Spoken words are influenced by the quality and volume of voice, pitch, speed of delivery and timing of pauses. When the speaker can be seen, his facial expressions, gestures, movement, manner and appearance are elements of his communicating. In the use of writing words, choice of words and composition of phrases and sentences are important.

(39) Illustrations: Illustrations are used to communicate. Everyone has heard the old claim that "one picture is worth a thousand words."

(40) Numbers: Numbers are a third type of symbol of the communicators use. Just about all numbers are clear and they are commonly used to denote sizes and prices, quantities and values.

(41) Forms and Shapes: Forms and shapes can communicate. They can be abstract or they can be a well-known triangle, star, circle, spiral and rectangle.

Advantages of Visual Aids

The visual media are more extremely useful. The advantages of visual media are as follows:

(1) Quick Communication: Visual aids are known for quicker communication. Speedy communication is necessary in respect of certain subject matters. Where certain important facts or figures need to be highlighted or attractive, observation is necessary.

(2) Understanding At a Glance: Visual techniques like pictures, slides etc., enable the observer to concentrate on them to understand at a glance. This merit is not available in respect of other oral and written communication.

(3) Memorising Effect: Message in a pictorial form may long last in the mind. The observers can carry home on a permanent way and recall and refresh the image whenever he wants. It has more memorising effect. A well-designed aid can project a distinctive image of the situation and hence more memorable.

(4) Comparison: Charts and graphs depicting data for various years, so that they facilitate easy comparison of data by observing trend like having characters of constant or up and down movement. The figurative relationship can be presented pictorially.

(5) Bird's Eyeview: Charts, graphs, slides and other visual aids give a bird's eyeview of a given text of subject matter shown at appropriate time and spot. The information presented on them is easily understood, simple, readily comprehensible and intelligible.

(6) Dynamic: Information transmission is a continuous process routine on different matters. So, the subject matter of communication may continuously be changing based on activities, work and correspondence. Visual aids can be prepared accordingly to changing needs. Therefore, visual aids are not static but dynamic. They carry a greater force through its ability to demonstrate the current message.

(7) More Revealing and Appealing: Visual aids are more revealing and appealing to the eyes. Figures are dry, hard to eyes, but visuals are more attractive, fascinating and impressive to the eyes. Numerical data may not leave a much lasting impression on the minds. Even a layman can understand the nature of pictures.

(8) Stimulating: They can often generate interest by providing a contrast to the written or spoken text of the subject matter.

(9) Saving Time: Visual aids save a lot of time as a very little effort is sufficient to grasp, understand, and draw meaningful inferences. The psychology of the human mind is such that an individual may not like to go through hard- written words.

(10) Audience Participation: The participatory approach in communica tion can be achieved through visual media. It involves audience participation to have effective interaction. The term "participatory" communication refers to the efforts along several lines to develop communication involving recipients of message. In this, audience also affect the communicator. The audience or a part of the audience play an effective role in communication.

Disadvantages

The visual aids also have their limitations and disadvantages which are as follows:

(1) Message Limitation: At a time, one picture, slide, chart, graph etc., can be shown. Only limited subject matter can be accommodated in each medium and only transmit a limited number of communication pieces. A congested or heavy message load may result in the risk of confusion.

(2) Preparation: Preparation of visual pictures takes a lot of time. It requires technical and expert people to draw, print or paint.

(3) Cost: The main limitation of the media is that it is a costly matter. This is the reason for not using visual aids in majority of the cases. It involves not only heavy installation-cost but also recurring revenue-cost. The real criterion for not using by majority is the cost.

(4) Time: The media, though simple and attractive to see, is not so easy in practice because it takes a lot of time, effort in their preparation. The preparation of subject matter of discussion or text or oral report is invariably be quicker to produce than visual aids. It requires lead time to prepare.

(5) Approximation: Approximations and adjustments, rounding of figures are the common features in preparation of chart or graph. Pinpoint accuracy in the presentation of message is not possible in all circumstances. It gives some sort of confusion and communication gap.

(6) Personal Preference: Certain people dislike or are suspicious of graphs, either because they have been conditioned to believe that high technical skills are necessary to their understanding, or because they consider that printed numbers automatically invest them with a degree of authority that is lost immediately if they are displayed in graphical form.

Factors in the Selection of Visual Aids

There are many kinds of visual aids. They include such devices as tables, charts, graphs, photographs, maps, diagrams, pictorial presentation, visual projection, cine, slide, overhead projector etc. All kinds may not be useful for all kinds of messages. It is the responsibility of the efficient communicator to exercise his skill in the selection of appropriate visual aid. As a matter of fact, the choice of suitable visual material depends on several factors such as:

(1) The need and requirements of the organisation.

(2) The nature of subject matter to be transmitted.

(3) The group of people or listeners to whom the subject matter of message is intended to put across.

(4) The selection of appropriate aid among various kinds of visual materials available to meet the purpose.

(5) The object of transmitting a particular piece of message.

(6) The attitude and the capabilities of the listeners to observe visual aid and understand the message.

(7) The nature of the message to be presented in the aid.

(8) The availability of adequate expert people to prepare aids.

(9) The time, cost and labour factors also to be considered.

(10) Any special purpose for which visual method is to be adopted.

(11) The knowledge of the transmitter as to how it is to be operated.

There are various types of charts such as lines, bars, mathematical graphs, cartograms, diagrams, area graphs, bargraphs, grouped bar, sub-divided bar, range bar, stop bar, twin bar, gantt chart, paired bar, deviation bar, sliding bar, column bar, histogram, curve graph, slice graph, matrics graph, multi-scale graph, cumulative graph, cumulative frequency graph or give index graph, - chart, frequency polygon, semi-log graph, log graph, band graph, etc.

Guidelines for Using Visual Aids

(1) The media should enrich or increase the listener's viewer's knowledge as a basis for decision-making.

(2) They must show the most important and significant matters referred to in the oral discussion part.

(3) To prepare charts, diagrams, or transparent paper typed before beginning speech.

(4) Pictures, slides etc., should be attractive and interesting.

(5) They should clearly and precisely clarify or explain a point or to convince and at the same time to attract the attention or interest of the observer at a glance.

(6) Keep the aids in the order and sequence in which oral part of the text follows.

(7) Each aid should bear a caption or label clearly and lucidly.

(8) The observer grasps the pictorial message quickly and correctly.

(9) The captions or titles or labels should be as far as possible in capital letters or written in bold letters. This will help not only the people who are farthest away but also can be read and understood at a glance.

(10) Avoid all distraction activities in the place of display.

(11) Display visual aids with sufficient light or in a dark room, depending upon the type of aid used.

(12) Select the appropriate time and context of text discussion to show aids.

(13) Wherever necessary, footnote explanation should be given at the end of or the bottom of the picture or chart.

(14) Visual aids should be simple and good enough to depict the message to help the observer to comprehend quickly.

(15) It is desirable to use different colours to draw attention to a particular aid.

(16) Accuracy of message incorporated in the aids and which need to be matched with the spoken words is utmost important for smooth transition and discussion.

2. AUDIO SYSTEMS

The following are the audio media of Communication:

(1) Radio: Listening to sound is one of the mechanisms through which one may absorb. Radio is a audio-medium, a theatre of mind. Like television and film the radio is also mass medium. Radio has occupied top position and most important advertising medium, particularly for local advertisers. User's use of radio set is a habit forming and it is much more personal and family medium. It is non-visual, all-communication, reception through a sense of listening; users ears but not the eyes. Radio is a very useful instrument for adult education as well as University education. All India Radio is today fully owned, controlled and run by the Central Government. The AIR service programmes include national service, special audience broadcast, external service, regional service, school broadcast, Vivid Bharati, rural broadcasting and rural radio forums. Radio programmes include news bulletins, radio drama, news-reels, radio features, music, quiz, talks and movie trailors.

Standard broadcasting for radio is 'AM' and 'FM'; they stand for Amplitude Modulation and Frequency Modulation. Broadcast time may be purchased for advertising is called "radio commercial". Live commercial for radio, radio commercial recorded, retail radio commercial are the various forms. Making radio programmes and radio commercial are simple and cheap to make. It is a mobile medium, an instantaneous form of communication.

(2) Audio Cassettes: One of the advanced technology in information technology, which is presently available in the market, is in popular use and gaining importance throughout the world. Among others, the materials used as a tool of self-learnings as a means for executive training, and as an aid for continuing education. "Audio" means sound or hearing. Audio cassette is also used in recent years as the most useful teaching medium. These enable the learner to have control over the learning materials. The learner can listen to the cassettes according to his own convenience. It can be stopped at any time. Another advantage of audio-cassette over radio is re-use over a section of the tape whenever he wants and it can be used again and again for revision or recall. Photograph records and flexidiscs are further developments in this matter.

An obvious advantage of the audio cassette over the radio programmes is that they are under the control of the user. Students can stop the player to take rest, make notes or can replay a difficult section. One more use of the cassette, in the words of a student, is: "I find the tapes very useful, particularly the discussion ones. It is definitely a 'contact' with the staff even though it is removed."[12]

A study of the Distance Teaching at Thailand's Sukhotahi Thammathirta Open University (STOU) gives us an idea of the different purposes the audio cassette can be used for. STOU used the tapes to:

(a) Provide orientation of the course;

(b) Clarify certain complex ideas;

(c) Give feedback to the student's activities and assignments;

(d) Summarise major ideas of each unit; and

(c) Present the views of external experts.

Massey University (New Zealand) tried using caseette tapes for tutorials in History. Groups of learners listened to a lecture on the tape. Then they would discuss the given questions and record the conclusion on the tape. They sent this tape to the university which sent its comments either again on tape or through mail. Gwynn has analysed the result.[13] They would be applicable to all the subjects where "tutorial" forms an essential part and where no single answer is possible for a given question.

(3) Tape Recorder: A tape is a narrow strip used for recording sounds. It is one of the media of audio systems. A magnetic tape is a tape orribbon coated with a magnetic materials on which data and information may be stored in the form of magnetically polarised spots. For this, a plastic ribbon, iron oxide or other magnetisable materials are used for coating. Tape in large reels is used in mini frames. It is called as magnetic tape cassette.

A tape recorder is a mechanical device which records sound on magnetic tape and reproduce when required. Recording is storing process of information of a programme at a particular place. The process of making a record of something like message, talk, news, interviews especially on a record or on a tape. Tape recorder makes it possible to capture sound signals and can be replayed when required before the audience or over a public address system.

Meetings, brain-storming sessions can be edited and played back to show the realities and used to rehearse speeches. It permits to hear our own voice and speech. Many people own their own tape recorders for this purpose. However, listening over voice through a tape recorder does not in itself make the speech better. But it only makes us aware of good or bad points in our voice and speech and in our use of speech, mumbling, hesitation, dullness, repetition etc., are noticeable on a tape recorder.

(4) Record Player: Record player is an electrical instrument which reproduces the sound recorded on records. The information, statements, messages recorded are intended to be reproduced or made public. They are written down or recorded for future reference.

(5) Public Address System: In oral communication, public address system is an important dimension of audio system. It is a system adopted at meetings, shows, carnivals, melas, exhibitions, gatherings of employees or mass audience. Through public address system, it is possible mechanically to project the human voice spread among a large gathering. Mounted on a mini truck, or any other mobile auto, the public address system can be transported from place to place, presenting speakers and programmes as it goes, and reaching a widely- distributed audience. Sound tracks can also be rigged up at stationary locations, providing facilities for meeting and special programmes in lieu of a permanently installed public address system. Portable bull horns afford great mobility wherever amplier sound is needed.[14]

(6) Magnetic Tape: Magnetic tape is a magnetic storage device; it utilises magnetic properties of materials to store data on such device. Such devices are disk tapes and chips. A magnetic tape is a tape or ribbon coated with a magnetic material on which data and information may be stored in the form of magnetically polarised spots. It has been in use for long as an input on storage medium for batch processing.

Even today also, it is used for high-speed large-volume batch application. Its advantages are high data density and fast transfer rate. The magnetic tape input medium is packaged in different ways. On a plastic ribbon, iron-oxide or other magnetizable materials are coated. Tape in large reels is used in mini and mainframe computer systems. Magnetic tape cartridges are used in mini computers. Magnetic tape cassettes are also used in a sound tape recorder. It is plastic ribbon coated on one side with iron oxide or some other material. Both information, data and sound can be retrieved. "Read" or "write" heads are small electromagnets capable of reading, writing or erasing the polarised spots that represent data on the magnetic tape.

3. VIDEO SYSTEMS

Video: A modern technology can greatly enrich oral messages relating to television and radio. The word is applied to all visual aspects of television signals, equipment etc. In common usage, for video recording or for any machine that can be used to record and playback such recordings, such as video cassettes, recorders, video tape recorders etc. Prior to 1966, a good quality black and white video recorder and player had cost any where between 50,000 and 1,00,000 U.S. dollars. A massive breakthrough in this technology has taken place in the mid-1960s and by

1970s good VCRs were available for about 1,000 U.S. dollars. In India today, it is possible to acquire a colour monitor and VCR about twenty thousand rupees and the prices may go down further in the years to come. VCRs have already made mass use in the entertainment field and also made a modest beginning in the educational field. Video-based instruction is already in use in advanced countries.

The experience and facilities in the United States are of some interest. As of 1980, video-taped lectures for 450 courses prepared for a faculty drawn from 22 universities were available to interested users. A National Technological University has been established and it offers on-campus as well as off-campus instructional television courses through video programming, which enable students to work towards a master's degree programme. Video cassettes are available for programmes produced in the studio as well as those produced through recording of candid classroom instruction sessions. [15]

A remarkable development in India has been the production facilities for the preparation of video instructional packages as set up in some universities. There are many advantages in video use for communication. Among its advantages, which one may mention, is the richness of the medium in conveying instructional material using visual images, colour, sound and special effects. A major drawback noted is in terms of the lack of interaction between the teacher and the student. Except for special situations, if one treats video-based instruction, not as a substitute for an existing arrangement of live-instruction, but as an aid, there is little dispute regarding its utility. For many special situations, video based instruction can also successfully serve as a substitute for live-instruction. It is high time, therefore, that engineering education in India begins to explore the potential of this new technology for making instruction more effective and widely accessible. [16]

Video programmes are more extensive than slide programmes. Video programmes are simpler to play back as one does not have to undertake the laborious process of mounting slides. Other advantages are duplication, it is cheaper and are of the two types, namely, studio production and the candid classroom production, which is an impromptu presentation. In the case of studio production, a complete script is to be prepared prior to recording.

A number of video programmes have been produced in India in the educational information field. It has been under the aegis of the Curriculum Development Cell of Civil Engineering Department at IIT, Delhi, using the production facilities at IIT and the Mass Communication Research Centre of Jamia Millia Islamia. The video programmes are: Alterberg's limits, consolidated undrained Traixial Test with pore water pressure Measurement; Dewatering of Sub-soil using wellpoint system, construction of under-Reamed Pile Foundations.

Videotape: It is a recording tape carrying pictures and sound. It is used to record programmes in pictures and sound using videotape. Videotape is a powerful alternative to conventional printing. Videotapes have literally taken over the entertainment world from the Indian Cinema. Videotape store magnetic signals for simultaneous subsequent retrieval of the visual and the audial information components. Lectures by experts, demonstration of processes techniques and field trips of inaccessible/remote regions could be recorded on videotapes for subsequent use. TV series like "Secrets of the Sea" and "The Living Planet" illustrate the numerous possibilities of its use in OLS as well as FLS. Videodiscs have not been as popular as videotape inspite of their obvious advantage.

Compared to video tape, videodisc "... represents the densest storage medium in existence. It is very durable and because of the nature of the system, free from wear... its radial format provides almost instant access to anyone of 55,000 clear, sharp and rocksteady images, instead of having to wind foot after foot of video tape.[17] Compared to videotape, videodisc recording is less cumbersome, though its front-end cost is much higher. It is almost thrice as cheap as a videotape in the long run.[18]

Video tape is a very useful innovation which removes the constraint of viewing TV programmes at a fixed time.

These tapes are like films and have the same impact as the film. The audience for a film is larger than video tapes. Video tapes have the same impact of film but tapes are being seen on a television screen. The audience for video tape is smaller, such as a family, friends and more intimates. Films are costly to make while video tapes are cheaper to make. Tapes are, however, subject to editing but no need to be processed. There are large companies which have their own video studios to produce programmes.

Videotex

The international name for the system originally designated view data but also often taken to mean the broadcast service, generally known as Teletex. Sometimes, the term "broadcast videotex" is used for Teletex.[19] The remarkable development in the electronic media, among others, is the videotex. This technology increases the capacity to the television set to function like a computer terminal and retrieve information and graphics from a remote data base. A videotex system would be very useful in disseminating general information about courses and programmes available through distance education.[20]

Word processors and text processors have made text-editing much less cumbersome and they now provide easy availability of simpler versions of text to suit the competence of individual learner. Electronic publishing could be videotex based. Videotex system comprises a telephone, a television set for monitoring, a computered data base, a key-board controller and a modern unit. "Modem" is an acronym for a modulating-demodulating device because it converts a digital square-wave signal that cannot be processed by a telephone into an analogue signal that can be easily processed by it. It also provides for reverse function, i.e., conversion from the analogue into the digital form. The following figure represents a schematic diagram of a videotex system.

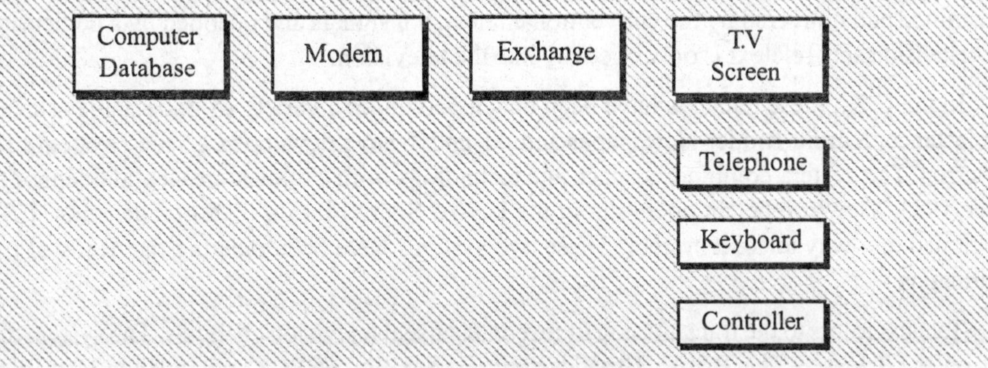

Fig. 14.3 Components of a Cable

The listener/viewer operates the key controller and the oral information is available through modem over the telephone and its visual counterpart is flashed on the T.V. screen. The telephone and modem allow for a two-way interactive system wherein the listener/viewer can ask questions, seek clarifications or get supplementary information.

Prestel (Great Britain), Antipoe (France), Captain (Japan) and Telidon (Canada) are good examples of successful videotex systems. Among these, Prestal was the first to become a world videotex service in 1979. Teletex, on the other hand provides for one-way facility. The listener/viewer cannot seek additional information. Videotex is relatively faster and provides easier access to and more fruitful use of computer database. Videotex thus holds greater promise for Indian Open Learning System.

Information can be stored in large quantities in the database. The Council for Educational Technology of Great Britain provides a good example of a fast developing educational database. Large databases stored on the main-frame computers with multiple access points can put learners in contact with an almost inexhaustible storehouse of information. The American Centre at New Delhi, through its instant access to various database in the U.S., now makes available the latest information on almost any topic to any scholar who is sure of the nature on information that he seeks. Data vendors like DIALOG, MEDILINE, MUXUS can be hooked on to the telecommunication network in the U.S.A. and made available to information-seekers almost all over the globe.[21]

Videotex is a transmission device system. It uses a T.V. set to display text. It helps to use the computer-based information services. Teletext and viewdata are the two kinds of video systems.

Thus, videotex is an electronic device of sophisticated communication technology. It greatly helps as it provides new opportunities for communication with the general public. In videotex; the viewer is directly connected to a central computer by way of home terminal permitting the viewer to call upon or send information. It is a two-way communication system like a telephone.

Teletext

Teletext is an electronic device of communication operates with sophisticated communication technology which provides an opportunity for communication with the general public. This technique of communication offers a limited or narrow choice of information and services. The messages are transmitted and delivered by the conventional television signals and decoded by a device attached to a television set. Teletext is only one-way like the television.

In the U.K., these teletexts have been developed under a variety of trade names since 1979. For instance, Knight Ridder Newspaper and AT and T have developed a video system called as Viewtron. The system combines a space age technology with a television set and telephone lines. Since 1983, Viewtron began operating in the U.S.A. South Florida. Taft broadcasting, USA, has developed one-way teletext system. These two systems have been meeting the needs of lifestyle information.

Teletext refers to the transmission of text on the usual television channels. The system displays text on the T.V. set. The British Broadcasting Corporation (BBC) and Independent Television (ITV) render pages of information when requested by the viewer. Teletext system is more popular in British region. On switching the key pad, within a few seconds, the required page appears on the screen. The system covers many specific topics like stock market, consumer prices, financial matters, weather information, economics, technology etc.

2. Viewdata: Viewdata is another type of videotex system. It is also computer-based information system. The network operates by linking Viewdata terminals to a central computer through telephone lines, like in the case of teletext, on a request by the viewer, page appears on the screen or printer. Originally, information is transmitted on pages.

Video-Cassettes: The technology is available and is gaining importance all over the world. The materials used for radio and television can be supplied in the form of video cassettes. The video cassettes can be stored. In view of the limitations of television, increasing use is being made of video cassettes.

Videodisc: Videodisc is a new development in the electronic media. It increases the capacity of the television set. Videodisc is a system similar to the long conventional television set. It has enormous storage capacity. The glossary of technical terms related to the new technologies gives meaning to the videodisc as a system for recording video information on a disk, similar to a long-playing record, which enables it to be replayed. However, such a system can also be used to record digital data. Such discs can hold very large amount of information, although the data can only be written once and in order to amend data, it has to be re-written on a blank part of the disc.[22]

The optical disc has more enormous storage capacity. The optical disc can store 1,08,000 tracks and 54,000 on each side. The entire Encyclopedia Britannica can be stored on a single disc with a room to spare.[23] Usually called "disc communication" videodiscs are other powerful alternatives to conventional printing.

Videodisc is a rival to videotape. The merits of videodisc: they are cheap to make, less bulky to store and so light and thin that it can be posted in an envelope. Videodisc is used for library catalogue, servicing instruction. To play back through television, a special recorder device is necessary.

Telidon: It is the Canadian Videotex service. It differs in a number of respects from the UK Prestal Service, particularly in that the data are transmitted in the form of "picture description instructions" rather than as serial character stream. As those PDIs occupy more than one byte each, it may be a less efficient method of transmitting data. But this, in fact, is dependent on the data being transmitted. The graphics displayed are of a higher resolution than those possible in alpha-massaic system such as Prestel.[24] A Canadian video system. Technologically advanced countries have developed a useful combination of cable TV, electronic blackboard, fibre optics and telephone that converts a simple television set into a powerful and educational tool called the Telidon.

Cyclops: It is British electronic system. Cyclops is a system devised to overcome the lack of visual support. This allow tutors and students to use a light open to write or draw on an ordinary TV screen. The picture is converted digitally to a second signal and sent down a standard telephone line, where it is decoded and appears on the TV screen at the other end of the line. Prepared visual material (stored on audio cassettes) can also be sent down this line.[25]

It is an audio visual teaching medium. The British Open University has developed an extremely versatile audio-visual teaching called Cyclops which is based on the conventional TV set, standard audio cassettes and micro-computer technology. The Cyclops can also be linked to a telephone and that increases its versatility as a teaching tool.

G. A. Yewdall *et al.*: "Communication of the methods of transmission with the methods of expression yields four basic techniques from which to choose:

(1) Visual-Symbolic; (2) Visual-Realistic;

(3) Audio-symbolic; (4) Audio-Realistic.

However, these four can be 'permed' in a variety of ways to obtain the optimum technique relative to the particular communication context."[26]

The Techniques of Communication
(Some Examples)

Transmission Express	*Visual*	*Audio*	*Audio/Visual*
Symbolic	1. Printed words. 2. Printed numbers. 3. Sings (e.g., a red light) 4. Mathematical symbols 5. Statistical charts.	1. Spoken words and numbers. 2. Sounding of fire alarm Reveille "wolf Whistles." 3. Music (National anth-em & back- ground music etc.).	1. A speech supported by charts. or deliberate use of gestures. 2. Same speech reproduc-ed as a slide/tape pre-sentation with back-ground music and/or sound effect for added emphasis.
Realistic	1. Drawing. 2. Photographs. 3. Silent films of actual event or situation. 4. Working models or ot-her fascimile of direct observation (e.g., sand table model). 5. Demonstration by miming.	1. Reproduced sound (e.g., a speaker's use of vocal mimicry for added effect.)	1. Reproduced sight & sound (e.g., a simulator for training pilots). 2. Also role-playing as an aid to teaching.
Symbolic	1. Printed words.	1. Spoken words & num-bers	1. A speech supported by by charts, or deliberate use of gestures.
Symbolic/Real-	1. Maps. 2. Flow charts. 3. Circuit Diagrams 4. Critical path diagrams 5. Cartoons.	1. A speech supported by a tape recording of an actual event or sit-uation or reproduced sounds (e.g., actor's voices) used to synth-esize the event. 2. Also radio plays & enactments.	1. Business games. 2. Many educational films & strips. 3. Teaching machines tap-pes & records. 4. Also the theatre, ballet and cinema.

Source: Adapted G.A. Yewdal, G.P. Mead and others, *Management Information,*. Pan Book Ltd.

4. AUDIO-VISUAL SYSTEMS

(1) Television: The term "television" is often abbreviated as T.V. The word "television" is divided into two parts such as "tele" and "vision." Televisions is a theatre of home while radio is a theatre of mind. It is a process of sending of pictures on a screen. Broadcast receiving set is an apparatus with a screen for receiving these pictures.

"Television" means to send a picture by television. In other words, it refers to transmission of vision. The system of television broadcast comprises of audio (sound) and video (picture) or image transmission. The audio and video signals are processed separately; the same antenna works to radiate both signals.

Television is a glamour of family medium processing as it does the immediacy of radio with the mobility of cine camera. It can make the best use of other media like printed words, spoken words, motion picture, colour, animation and sound.

There are two sets of channel to operate television. They are Very High Frequency (VHF) called older ones, and more recent ones (Ultra High Frequency (UHF). The picture or video is transmitted by amplitude modulation (AMO) signals and sounds called audio is transmitted by Frequency Modulation (FM) signals. Television combines the elements of sound, sight and action. Camera, scanning, bandwidth, video amplifier, audio amplifier, antenan, video detector and channel, sound channel, cathode ray, picture tube etc., constitute the television system.

In India, the most remarkable and momentous development in television is the Satellite Instructional Television Experiment, inaugurated in 1975. Educational use of television programme is termed Educational Television (ETV) which broadcast curriculum-based lessons on certain subjects. Cable television has become popular in recent years as it is called "Community Antenna." It improves television reception performanec. Colour television transmission commenced in India from 1982 coinciding Asiad 1982.

Television in India has been used for higher education. University Grants Commission has taken the initiative for utilisation of 1NSAT. Country-wide Class-room programme marks a successful beginning. Newscast, quiz programmes, interviews, documentaries, music, and dance, news-programmes, children's programmes, rural programmes are the various types of television programmes.

Advertising part of the broadcast programme is called "television commercial." National broadcast is called "network." Other programmes are spot and local. Commercial advertisements in television may be straight announcement, slides, demonstration, dramatisation or animated commercial. Programmes may be sponsored. This sponsorship is of two types called alternative week sponsorship and co-sponsorship. Television commercial may be live television, filmed commercial and taped commercial.

(2) Cinema and Film: Film is also an effective medium of communication. It is a audio-visual like television. Motion pictures are more useful for instruction, information education and entertainment. Audience can see the film in direct contact with the facts and ideas through sight, hearing and action and thus makes a direct impact on them. Films can be used for a variety of purposes for organisation communication to inform or motivate the employees about the activities, programmes, philosophy, outlook etc. Films can also be used to show about the organisational chart, authority relations, production process, methods of production and other work situation. Films also help for training or for promotion of morale, safety etc. Organisations can sponsor films for external audience or general public. It is the best medium to present work study operations of machines, equipment etc., and topics of social interest. Events like conference, demonstration, experiments, and other events in programmes can be filmed.

Animated films can also be made. The art technique and process involved in giving apparent life and movement to inanimate objects by means of cinematography. Animation in film imparts the impression of life and movement to static images. A film made can be a feature film which means fictionalised film exceeding 2,000 metres long in 35 mm. Feature film means a full length cinematograph film produced wholly or partly with a format and a story woven around a number of characters where the plot is revealed mainly through dialogue.

Cinematograph film includes a soundtrack, telefilm, on which sounds have been recorded for the purpose of their being reproduced in connection with the exhibition of a film. Unauthorised cinematograph films are uncertified and cannot be exhibited. Films for public exhibition are subject to film censorship by the Central Board Film Censors.

Documentary films can be produced which give some information on certain subjects. There is a Film Division under the Jurisdiction of the Ministry of Information & Broadcasting. Children's Film Society was set up in India as an autonomous body to produce films for children. For the purpose of development of film industry, a special financial institution has been established, known as The National Film Development Corporation.

Script writers directors, cameramen, producers, editors, script makers, pushers, film loops, etc. constitute the film system.

(3) Closed Circuit Television: Closed circuit television means live pictures and sounds can be piped from the originating point at one or more receiving locations for viewing by selected audience. The programmes of this TV are not transmitted to stations for broadcasting to general home viewers. TV programme are designed for specifically invited audiences. It is as private as a telephone conversation. Telelectures are being used quite widely in education technique now-a-days as it is less expensive compared to broadcasting.

A medium of oral communication operates by using a television set. The television camera scans the picture to be transmitted. The camera converts the picture into electrical signals, i.e., video signals. The video amplifier applies the range of frequencies. Amplitude modulated picture transmitter is a circuit which places visual information on a career wave. The microphones convert audio signals into electrical signals. The complete process gives us continuous viewing of pictures and hearing of sound.

COMPUTER AND RELATED SYSTEMS

Introduction

It was only from the middle of the last century that rapid transmission of communication by electrical means became possible. Telegraph helped the transmission of written messages, almost instantaneously. Telephony from 1876 onwards facilitated the transmission of speech, enabling the dissemination of information and knowledge very rapidly. Telegraphy and telephony are, however, means of communication from one individual to another, from any place and could be said to be private means of communication. What is transmitted by telegraph or telephone could be known to millions only when it was printed and distributed through newspapers or otherwise.

The next quantum jump occurred with the invention of the radio and its utilisation for broadcasting of information from a central source to any and everywhere equipped with a radio receiving device. This is communication from one to many.

By the beginning of 1930s, almost all over the world, radio broadcasting for information transmission over wide communities and areas had been established. From then onwards, we could say that the information was becoming more and more electronic-based. In the 1950s began the transmission of pictures along with voice for broadcasting. Television increasingly caught on. The black and white pictures were themselves a wonder, but television became an arresting marvel with colour transmissions. It has become increasingly affordable by more and more people because the transistors and the integrated circuits made the mass-produced radios as well as the television sets cheaper every decade. The invention and increased availability of portable recording and replaying devices enabled the capture of events as they were taking place and their near instantaneous broadcasting throughout the world. Communication satellites with the capability of telephony and telex and television helped the worldwide instantaneous transmission of news and views of events. Before the invention of the telegraph, it took weeks and months for news in one country to be known in other countries and continents. But with the radio and the television, both carried over satellites, distance and time has so shrunk that information from one continent to another can be transmitted and known in as little time as it takes goods within a village. In other words, our globe itself has been reduced to a village.

Audio and video cassette recording their multiplication in million is enabling the spread of instruction and training and entertainment and education. One illustration of how an electronic medium involving education spreading system has come up could be useful. India is having the largest unlettered population of over 500 million. The school-going population is also of the order of hundreds of millions. If all of them are, in the traditional fashion to be sent to schools, the amount of expenditure over buildings, textbooks and transportational programmes can be recorded on video cassettes and broadcast over countrywide or regionwide media through the satellite, we can very economically, and rapidly propagate education. What is called 'Projection Television' is a versatile aid. Pictures are reproduced on a very large screen attached to the television monitor, enabling scores of viewers to be instructed with the least expense. Also, instead of libraries of books, if there is a library of video cassettes containing text and illustrated and explained by the best teachers, and if these cassettes can be circulated among the schools, the quality of instruction in the village-level schools, which are poorly-staffed, can be fantastically improved.

Electronics, computers and tele-communication media, are enabling the simultaneous printing of newspapers from several centres. Electronic book publishing is another rapidly growing activity. Personal computers, access data bases over telecom media and print out a mass of information in whatever format it is wanted. They are a great aid for information storage, retrieval and processing.

In modern times, because of the industrial revolution and intensive and economic exploitation of resources and increasing consumption of goods and services, huge companies or corporations and organisations are a necessity. They are also economically efficient. It is very necessary that all these companies and organisations explain to the masses of money-providers and consumers why and how they are performing and how best their services could be utilised by the consumer. This is one of the most important aspects of public information and relations that every corporate organisation has to undertake. While newspapers could be useful only a fraction of the 30 per cent of the lettered people in India, mass communication media like radio and television are the most effective and economical means of mass information. Huge organisations become more and more impersonal and bureaucratised. Customers and may be even the workers, will find helpless in understanding or reacting to these organisations. Various communication media like audio and video cassettes and electronic reproduction methods enable a public instructional and information programme to be carried out easily. They are the means by which the mind can be informed and influenced for the achievement of an organisation's goals and for the transformation of society.

Electronic Media

A wide range of electronic communication technology which can bring about a meaningful revolution and improvement in information transmission are now available. Many of the organisations in developing countries may not be in a position to make use of all the latest innovations. The developing countries in collaboration with large business organisations should chalk out a phased programme for introduction of new communication devices into their organisational structure to make communication effective. Radio, television, audio-cassettes, video-cassettes, video-tape, videodiscs, telidon, video, videoterm, etc., are the important innovations. The most significant new technologies are those based on the silicon chip, the laser, fibre optics and a set of technologies known as biotechnologies. It is necessary to introduce such latest and sophisticated communication technologies in collaboration with other countries. The managements in developing countries must realise the importance of new communication technologies for speedy, quick, correct and low cost-transmission as well as for imparting education to catch up with the advanced countries of the world. The following paragraphs present a brief coverage of electronic media in wide use.

Both television and radio are electronic media, because they are major mass media. On the other hand, they form a second group of advertising commercial media. In this chapter, we present in some depth electronic media other than radio and television as well as films existing in the communication field. Here we shall investigate the unique nature of electronic media in communication.

Geoff Potter points out satellite and its impact on distance education: "In some cases, hermes (the satellite) brought people together in a way that was every bit as emotionally moving as it was intellectually stimulating. In other cases, students became bored, technical problems made effective interaction impossible, information seemed colourless and static." [27]

Griffin points out some basic faults in "mouth to mouth" communication. They refer to the problems of duration, speed, absence of visual clues, unidimension, absence of phatic communication and disembodiment. According to Griffin, the role of the co-ordinator is very crucial and very difficult in a satellite programme.[28]

Mass media assistance is required to communicate development programmes and achievements to the mass. Thus, today seventy per cent of the population in the country is covered by television.[29]

Computer

A large mechanical and electronic contrivance with associated electrochemical equipments are capable of carrying out mathematical functions at high speed and accuracy. Computer is capable of storing and processing huge quantity of information and performing calculations through the data processing machine.

Computer has been defined by the United States of American Institute, as a device capable of solving problems, by accepting data performing described operations on the data and supplying the results of the operations. Calculators, digital computers and analogue computers are the types of computers. It has components like input unit, memory storage, arithmetic unit, output unit etc. Computing processing is done, controlled by a computer programming. It has separate language like Cobol, Fortran etc.

An electronic contrivance which solve problems and does complicated calculations by processing data according to the prescribed, programmed instructions and then produces and/or retains the outcome of these processes; one who computes; a reckoner; a calculator. (New Webster's Dictionary).

According to M.K. Alder, "computer" is a machine for carrying out calculations of several stages automatically. May be the Analogue computer which stimulates, processes and produces results, measured in physical quantities or Digital Computer which carries out mathematical processes by operations based on counting.

Computer is used for not only mathematical purposes, but has important s role of communication, in education, particularly more in engineering education. It is an excellent device that can be fully employed. V.J. Sabharwal has greatly emphasised computers and its role in education. His observations are as follows:

Computers are going to be the "whizz-kids" of our future educational system. Computation, information storage, communication and control are the four major functions of most computers. Super-computers are endowed with artificial intelligence and they are capable of intermediate level reasoning as well. Intricate calculations or multivariate data analysis become almost 'kid-stuff' with their help. Huge amounts of information can be systematically stored in its memory (depending upon its memory size) for subsequent retrieval and use. Computers can provide flexible interaction with learners within the limits of the programme that defines their functional range. Computers can help us exercise extra fine control over various processes like satellite manoeuvring, satellite tracking and rocket launching. A computer memory may be of ROM (read only memory) or RAM (randum access memory) variety. The ROM variety is more widely used and its four sub-types, *viz.*, mask programmed ROMs used for storing programmes during its manufacture, PROMs (Programmable only once at manufacture stage), EPROMs (erasable programmable read only memories that can be programmed many times) and EAROMs (electrically alterable read only memories) have been described in detail by Hankridge and Bradbeer *et al.*

The use of computers in education has resulted in CAL/CAI (Computer Assisted Learning/ Instruction). Arrival of computers in American classrooms has been compared to an avalanche. A variety of computer languages, both low level and high level (algebraic), enables users to work with various computers, e.g., ADA, APL, BASIC, COBOL, FORTRAN, LISP, PASCAL, PL/I, RPG-II, SNOBOL, SPITBOL, WATFOR, WATFIV, LOGO etc. Computers can be immensely useful in providing individualised repetitive or analogous practice to learners, problem-solving exercises as well as activities for developing a variety of skills in a training programme. Project CLASS should prove a catalyst for increasing the use of computers in Indian education.[30]

B. Singh, in his key-note paper presented at the International Conference on New Technologies in Higher Education, New Delhi (1985), explained the use of computer in academic communication. He remarked that the computer is an excellent device that can be usefully employed for evaluating student's assignments. A fully developed computer assisted education system can be used for correction and comments on students' replies to multiple choice questions with carefully selected distractions. In this system, an optical reader "corrects" the students' replies, after which the computer selects the relevant comments and explanations from among a great number of those programmed and stored for the purpose. The computer also checks and refers to the individual student's answer or an unsatisfactory answer elicits different comments from the computer, depending on the way in which the student has misunderstood or wrongly combined items. Sometimes, even correct replies are commented upon to underline something important or to strengthen the motivation of the students. Encouraging and counselling comments based on the overall performance of the students are also provided by the computer. All this is typed by the computer into a personal letter addressed to the individual student. However, this use of the computer is restricted to the objective assignments of the multiple choice type. Therefore, a number of subjects, themes within subjects and general types of learning like free problem-oriented learning would require live tutors. Even in the multiple choice questions which can be marked by the computer are not always suited for all kinds of learning outcomes. The greatest advantage of tutor-marked assignments is that it greatly reduces the average turn-round time of the assignments. The computer also eliminates the chances of erratic making which has become the bane of our examination system. The computer ensures uniformity in evaluation.

Computer Aided Design, Instruction and Learning

The role of computers in engineering cannot be overemphasised and needs no special elucidation. The computer-assisted instruction involves the use of computer to perform instructional functions. In order to update the syllabus and improve the standards and to prepare the students to tackle the problems of the future, the curriculum must compass the latest technological advancement relating to Robotics, Computer Aided Design (CAD) and Computer Aided Manufacturing (CAM). Computer-based instructions include a broad range of application. But they can be divided into two types, namely: (1) Direct instructions (2) Instructional Management. The first types is called "Computer Assisted" or "aided Instruction, and the second type is called "Computer Managed Instruction." Some of the features of these two systems are:[31]

(I) Computer Assisted/Aided Instruction

It covers a number of activities such as drill and practice, simulations, gaming, enquiry, dialogue, information retrieval and problem solving. It is relating to an educational concept which emphasises the student in conversational form with a computer which has the programme formulated in advance. It performs any instructional function presenting materials, problem situations, guiding a student thinking by answering his questions, assessing his performance, managing his path through a course of selecting the material to be presented or by assigning tasks to be performed away from the computer, or any combination of these. Alternatives through instructional units are programmed into the computer. Besides, machine-directed activities as mentioned above, it includes machine-student dialogue, counselling and guidance. In sum, it is the use of computers on time-shared basis to carry out many instructional management functions.

(II) Computer-Managed Instruction

It includes instructional support functions such as testing, prescribing, record-keeping, scheduling, monitoring and time and resource management. The machine discharges the functions to monitor the instructional process. The object in its use is to provide diagnostic and prescriptive information to the instructor to guide him in making instructional decisions. It takes advantage of conventional data processing equipment.

Computer Aided (assisted) Assessment, Examination, Test (CAE/CAT), Computer Aided Design (CAD), Computer Aided Learning (CML) are some of the new developments in education communication. In the days to come the emerging role of computers in Engineering education would be very great.

Types of Computers

Based on the type of data processed computers may be classified into the following categories:

(1) Analog Computer: An analog computer is a device that operates on data by measuring changes in continuous physical variables like voltage, resistance, rotation etc. It operates on data in the mode of continuously variable physical quantities. An analog computer is used when data is processed continuously such as monitoring temperature or pressure. It is opposed to the digital computer.

(2) Digital Computer: A device in contrast with analog computer. A digital computer is used when data are discrete. It manipulates discrete data and performs arithmetical and logical operations on the data. In other words, it operates on digital data.

(3) Hybrid Computer: A type of computer which combines the features of both digital and analog computers. A data processing technique is which utilises both analog and digital representation of data. It handles both discrete and continuous data.

Other Types of Computer

(1) Mini Computer: A small general purpose computer such as desk top size, and four drawer file cabinet. The term "mini" means small which has smaller memory capacity as well as input, output capacities, in comparison with other computers or mini computer. However, the difference between mini computers and micro-computers is very thin. The physical size of the PDP-11 is six feet high and occupies 14 by 18 inches of floor space. This does not include a printer but does include storage devices like the magnetic cassette and the Floppy Disk.[32]

Comparing medium-sized or large-scale computers, minis originally meant low speed, small memory, less software and few peripheral units. The minis are 16-bit machine. There are 32-bit super mini-models. Earlier mini computers were applied to a single purpose specialised such as to monitor instruments or to control a machine tool or general applications in small concerns. But today mini-computers are applied to complex situations. They are the most popular data processing system in business concerns.

(2) Micro-Computer: This the smallest device of a computer. It consists of a micro-processor, storage and input and output elements. A micro-processor is a technique that provides the basic arithmetical, logical and control circuits necessary for processing. A micro-computer, with micro-processors, is given additional memory and input-output capabilities. It is a general purpose processing device. Small in size, a computer on a chip to a small typewriter size. It is easily carried from one place to another and can be placed on a small desk. The usual storage devices like magnetic tape cassettes, floppy disks etc., can be used as external storage medium. It forms an important part of the integrated information system. Today, it is used in all types of organisations, small or big schools, offices, Banks, homes and other office works. Micros can be linked to a big computer. The distinction between a micro-computer and mini-computer is that a mini is originally designed to serve multiple users simultaneously.

(3) Main Frame Computer: These computers have a greater storage capacity and offer faster processing speed compared to other types of computers. In size the main frame computers are ranging from small to very large. The smaller mam frames and super-minis perform on a similar scale. But a main frame is more powerful than a typical mini and hence often called the main frame. In centralised data processing system the main frame computers are used in many organisations. A number of users can work simultaneously as they support a large number of terminals. Word processors are used as terminals. They prepare thousands of paychecks, invoices, making labels etc.

The main part of the computer is usually referred to as the Central Processing Unit. The entire series of a mainframe model of small and large is typically lumped together under a family designation by mainframe manufacturers. It permits to carry programs framed for one machine on other models in the same family. Mainframes have been playing an important and vital role in information processing.

(4) Personal Computer (PC): As the name indicates, a computer originally designed and oriented towards a single use. It denotes the use of computers by individuals; a general purpose computer system. It carries programme instructions to perform a wide variety of tasks which possess all the functional components available in a larger system. They are usually found in the home management, personal productivity. A TV set can be used to display output. It has a limited primary storage capacity. PCs can be used not only for the game programme but enables the user to acquire computer literacy. They give an opportunity to become familiar with computers as to how and when to use it. Today, they come in a variety of configurations side by side using television and cassette player. They are available today in different sizes and shapes like the portable models, notebook-sized, briefcase-sized, desk-top models, transportables etc. They are called single-user-oriented because most of the personal computers are designed to be used by one person at a time. In recent years, another system has emerged, which is multi-user oriented.

(5) Super-Computer: A super-computer is characterised by its very high processing speed, very large size, more storage capacity, powerful and costly. Only a few organisations can afford to use super computers, because of prohibitive cost and processing capacity. They are of national importance and used in big scientific research and development fields like energy, space exploration, medicine and industrial technological areas like aircraft. A super computer holds 64 bits of information; so applied to a complex computation. It is very costly, between 4 million to 15 million dollars. Gray Research and Control Data Corporation (CDC) are the important concerns producing super computers in the USA. So a powerful device applied to making top secret weapons, research calculations, complete calculations for petroleum and recasting problems, earth's atmosphere etc. Data of complex nature are fed into the super-computers.

Human-Machine Communication Process

Human thinking of ideas and artificial intelligence is the relation of human-machine communication process. A computer uses many devices to communicate with human beings. The following are the various system components in a computer towards electronic message transmission.

(1) Input: Input in communication denotes devices, media and techniques used in the process of human-machine communication. Pertaining to the computer, the channel involves the insertion of information into a processing system. There are input devices which permit direct human-machine communication. There are some input devices which require information to be recorded on a magnetisable materials such as floppy disks, magnetic tapes etc. The keyboard, the mouse, input pen, touch screen microphone, central processing unit or components used for communication between a person and computer system.

(2) Processor: "Process means a systematic series of operations to achieve the desired result." Processor is the main component and is the heart of the computer system. A processor unit is capable of performing operations upon information inserted. There are three sections such as the primary storage section, arithmetic log section and control section. In order to solve the limited storage capacity of the primary storage section, a computer may have secondary capabilities known as secondary storage devices which are connected directly to the processor.

(3) Output: Relating to a device or process involved in the transfer of information out of information inserted into a processing system. It is information transferred from the internal storage of a computer to any device outside the computer. The process works for taking information out of the computer. Output devices are instruments of interpretation and communication between a person and the computer. Display screens, desk top printers, magnetic tape output device, printer, graphics plotter, visual display of on line work station, laser printers, micro film are some of the output devices.

Computer Communication Language

A computer has a machine language which is used directly by a computer. Language is a set of rules adopted to convey information. A language used to express programme is termed as programming language. So rules used to convey message or data. It is a system of communication which includes all the symbols, characters, and rules to be followed while communicating with the computer. The machine language of a computer consists of strings of binary numbers by which the processor can directly understand. Assembly language translates the specified operation code symbol into its machine-language. High-level language is a computer programming language which is nearer to the natural language. It is oriented towards a particular class of processing problems. The natural letters, symbols or text can be used than by using the machine language consisting of strings of binary numbers (Os Is).

Most of the programmes are prepared today which are written in high-level language. The following are some of the major high-level in use:

(1) Basic: The word "basic" stands for Beginners' All-Purpose Symbolic Instruction Code (BASIC). It is a major high-level programming language developed at Dartmouth College. It is widely and popularly used programming language with personal computers and in time sharing systems. It is an interactive language, popular because it is easy to use. It allows direct communication between the computer system and the user during the preparation and use of programme. A person with little or no knowledge of computer programming can learn to write basic programmes. Within a short period of time, one can learn. Data entering is easy. It is known for simplicity. Recreational and educational programmes are usually documented in basic. School students, engineers, business managers etc., generally use basic.

(2) Fortran: It stands for Formula Translator. A high level procedure oriented programming language used to perform mathematical computations. It is also widely used to draw programmes that perform mathematical computations for scientific, engineering, statistical and selected business applications. Most of the computers now in service can use fortran, standard language. It consists a series of statements which supply input-output, calculations, logic, comparison and other basic instructions to the machine. A compact language serves the requirements of scientists, engineers and business statistics for business application.

(3) Cobol: The term stands for Common Business Oriented Language (COBOL). A specially designed data processing language. A similar high-level language for business application. This language is now the most widely used language for large business application. Conference of Data Systems Language (CODASYL) is a group of representatives of computer manufactures, government agencies, user organisation, and Universities who develop and maintain the COBOL language. The CODASYL Short Range Committee has prepared the COBOL frame work. It can be used in business data processing and can be used with personal computers. It has four divisions. Such as:

(1) Identification division;

(2) Environment division;

(3) Data division; and

(4) Procedure division.

The advantages of COBOL language are:

(1) It can be written in a quasi-English form.

(2) It can be followed more easily by the non-programmers in business.

(3) It does not require much documentation.

(4) It manipulates alphabetic characters in a better way than Fortran. There are many COBOL business applications modules and packages.

(4) PL/1: Stands for Programming Language/1. A similar high-level general purpose programming language, it is a procedure-oriented language designed to combine features of COBOL, Fortran, Algol etc. It processes both scientific as well as file processing applications. It is best suited to solve a variety of business as well as scientific problems. The American National Standards Institute Committee produced PL/1 standard in 1976 in which are found features which exist in both Fortran and Cobol but is flexible and sophisticated language. The language is more difficult to learn in its totality than Fortran or Cobol.

(5) RPG: The letters stand for Report Programme Generator. A problem- oriented language designed to generate output reports. It uses a generator to construct programme that produce reports and function other data processing activities. A file can be updated periodically. It is specialised with file description, input specifications and calculation output. The language is very easy to learn and use. The formal rules are limited comparable with other languages. It is more useful to generate output reports. It is an important language of small business computer.

(6) Algol: Standards for ALGORITHMIC language. It is widely used in Europe. It was first introduced in 1958. It is an international procedure-oriented language designed by group of international mathematicians and developed by a group of international mathematicians and developed by groups in Europe and the United States. It is designed and intended for use primarily for scientific and mathematical applications.

(7) Pascal: A widely-used high level computer programming language. It is named in honour of Blaise Pascal, a French mathematician, philosopher and an inventor. It is designed for use of structured programming devices. It is an offspring of ALGOL and is similar to the building programme found in other languages.

(8) Ada: A similar high level computer programming language. The language is sponsored by the U.S. Department of Defence (DOD) for use in military services. The language is named in honour of Lady Augusts Ada Lovelase, daughter of Lord Byron.

(9) Logo: An educational language developed by Seymour Papert in 1960s. It is widely used for scientific research. tasks particularly in Universities. It can be used by children to achieve talent, intellectual growth and acquire problem-solving skills. They can communicate with a computer and learn graph, raw, colour and animate images.

Electronic Data Processing (EDP)

The term is applied for processing of data by electronic equipment known as computer. The processing of data through electronic equipment is called data processing. EDP is an acronym for electronic data processing. Electron is a very small particle within the atom having the smallest possible charge of electricity. It is produced by a device built or made according to the principles of electronics. In a similar form, it is a branch of science that deals with the study of the movements and effect of electrons and with their application to machine.

The word "data" means statistical data or quantitative information. They are facts, the raw materials of information. A stored collection of the libraries of data which are needed by organisations and individuals to meet their information processing and retrieval requirements. Data processing is application of one or more operations performed on data to achieve the desired objective. Data are different from information.

It is a process of manipulation of large quantity of data quickly, correctly and economically by an electronic equipment known as computer. This electronic equipment had made it possible to process and to communicate large quantities of data to secure useful information.

The computers used for business purposes are digital computers. They are controlled by a programme of instructions stored in the equipment. The device stores data, performs complete processing routine and prints out final reports automatically without human intervention.

The equipment as the computer operates by passing electronic impulses through complicated circuits to compute calculations like adding, subtractions, multiplication, division and comparison of two or more variables.

Data processing consists of three basic activities.

They are:

(1) Capturing the input data.

(2) Manipulating the data.

(3) Managing output results.

(1) Capturing Data: In some form, the data are to be recorded first or captured before the data can be processed. They are recorded on a source document. Alternatively, they may be captured by a direct machine in a paperless readable form.

(2) Manipulating Data: The data so gathered and documented is subject to the following operations which have to be performed.

(a) Classifying Data: The entire data so gathered should be classified. All similar items should be organised into groups or classes known as classification. Abbreviations, codes which are predetermined will be assigned to the items being arranged to accomplish classification.

The following codes are used;

(i) Numeric.

(ii) Alphabetic.

(iii) Alpha-numeric.

(b) Calculating: Calculating means the process of arithmetical manipulation of the data. It is a usual and common processing activity in electronic data processing.

(c) Sorting: The arrangement of classified data in some sequence is called "sorting." The sorting may be done by several ways such as:

(i) First to the last,

(ii) Biggest to the smallest,

(iii) Oldest to the newest.

(d) Summarising: Summarising is the process of a large amount of quantitative data to more precise and visible form. Graphs generated by the computer like Pie chart, multiple graphs, charts etc., are more frequently produced for this purpose.

(3) Managing Output Results: A number of operations computerly operated may be applied on the data which have been computed and manipulated. Managing output result may include:

(a) Storing: It is retaining data for future reference. This operation is called "storing." Data may be stored on a small magnetisable disc. Large magnetic discs, as well as paper, micro-film, tapes, optical discs and other storage media are commonly used.

(b) Retrieving: This second operation implies recovering the stored data and information.

(c) Communicating: Transmission of data and information for use from one place to another, from one operation to another is called "communication management." It may be either for final use or for further processing.

(d) Reproduction: It implies to copy or duplicate data. The reproduction activity is done by machine. Data may be communicated electronically to other location or they may be reproduced by printers or other machine.

To process the data, computer has four units. They are:

(1) Input Unit: The input unit records the data and translates them into impulses which are transferred to the central unit.

(2) Control Unit: The important component of the computer is control unit of central processing, which is the brain of the computer which controls its operations.

(3) Storage Units: The function of the storage unit is to store instructions, data on which the computer works. Storage is of two types called "internal storage" and "external storage."

(4) Output Unit: This unit supplies the required information desired. It is the end-product which may take the form of results, report or final information. The information can be fed into the line printer which finally prints the information.

Advantages

(1) The computer processes the large data at a very high speed with its data processing system.

(2) Correct, efficient and economical way, the results can be obtained.

(3) EDP is more useful for repetitive work, voluminous work within no time.

(4) The system is more useful to corporations, insurance companies, banks etc.

(5) The operations are very accurate and reliable and there is no risk of errors in calculation.

(6) The system is not rigid but flexible, capable of making adjustments according to requirements.

(7) The clerical labour is saved, to a considerable extent, under the system of electronic data processing.

(8) The cost of operations is cheaper in relation to the quantity of data, cost and accuracy.

Disadvantages

(1) The investment in installing electronic data processing system involves an expenditure of capital nature. The initial expenditure is very high.

(2) Small concerns cannot afford to go in for installing an electronic system.

(3) It involves recurring expenditure by way of paying high salaries to attract people to work in the system.

(4) The installed capacity may not be fully utilised because of lack of sufficient work to take advantage of the computer.

(5) Technical know-how and experts are not available sufficiently.

(6) As the computers do much work than manual labour and may involve retrenchment of employees and may not generate additional employment opportunities.

(7) The cost of servicing and repairs is very high in the case of mechanical breakdown of computers. It is a serious problem everywhere.

(8) A rapid sophisticated technological development and improvement has been taking place in the electronic system. The problem of obsolescence and additional outlay to install new electronic devices cannot be ignored.

Computer Printers

Printers are computer output devices used for preparation of documents for use either for internal purpose or external use. Computer output can be brought out either by way of printed output or filmed output. The following are the various types of printers classified on the basis of how they print and how fast they print.

(1) Low Speed Character Printers: They do low volume printing job. They are one-character-at-a-time devices. They are used with micro-computers, mini computers and teleprinting terminals.

(2) Low Speed Page Printers: Laser beams are used to produce the dots under low speed page printer. Printers of these types have been made more popular in recent years. The laser printers write the output image on a copier drum with a beam of laser light that operates under computer control.

(3) Printer Buffer: This is a device which stores additional information, accepts text to be printed as fast as computer can send it. The buffer releases the text, slowly to match the printer's speed.

(4) High Speed Impact Line Printers: They use impact methods to produce line-at-a-time. A form of print drum is used to print lines of information on a paper. About 300 to over 2,000 lines can be printed per minute depending on the printer used.

(5) High-Speed Page Printers: Printers of these types can produce documents at a speed of 20,000 lines per minute. It indicates that they are fast enough to print about 600 pages in about one minute. Sophisticated technological developments in the field of communication resulted electronics, xerography, lasers and other technologies which have made possible this high-speed printing processing work.

Visual Display Terminals (VDTs)

Visual display terminal is a popular input device used for interactive processing and for the outline entry of data for batch processing. For the purpose of entering data into a processor, a key board is used. A cathode ray tube (CRT) or monitor is used, popularly called as, video display. It is like a television picture tube. It displays the keyed data, to collect messages and process information from the computer. A keyboard and a video display constitute a visual display terminal system. There are hundreds of visual display terminal models. They are broadly divided as:

(1) Dumb.

(2) Smart.

(3) Intelligent.

"Dumb" terminal device transmits keyed data immediately.

"Smart" terminal performs arithmetical, logical, and control functions.

They have a micro-processor chip with circuits which performs this function. Intelligent terminals are used to process small jobs. They combined VDT hardware with built-in micro processor.

Advantages of Computer

(1) Efficiency: Every organisation wants to avoid waste and improve efficiency. For this purpose, public, private and other organisations have been endeavouring to achieve efficiency by installing computers. The benefits derived from the use of computers are more than otherwise would have been. Use of computers improves efficiency and productivity.

(2) Quality Production: Computers help to obtain higher quality products and services. For instance, today micro-computers are used in cars to provide control, the engine's fuel mixture and ignition timings. The device of robots facilitate to assemble products or components with closer tolerance.

(3) Better Services: Computers may also help individuals to receive better benefits or services from Government agencies. Better services may include:

(i) Reduce shorter waiting line at banks.

(ii) Airline ticket offices.

(iii) Reservation counters of hotels.

(iv) Preparation and analysis of medical histories of patients in hospital.

(v) Monitoring.

(vi) Efficient customer services.

(vii) Control of inventory etc.

(4) Recreation: In recent years, computers are being increasingly used for entertainment and amusement of people. For instance, computer game programmes are prepared for this purpose. Computer animation gives life and movement to inanimate objects. We have been observing regularly computer animation in movies and on television.

(5) Benefit to the Handicapped: Computers are also used, particularly micro-computers, to serve the handicapped persons to feed themselves. Persons who suffer from lack of upper limb responses, computer will come to their rescue. Computer system helps to develop more effective and artificial limb for the needy.

(6) Safety: In transport, either by road or by air, computers help safety in their operations. Computers can be used to control breaking system in cars and air-crafts which prevent dangers. In this way, they help to achieve safety in many ways. Similarly, computers can be used to achieve public safety by controlling gas pipeline leaks, road safety and control air and water pollution. The control terminals and better retrieval help to search millions of documents in a few minutes. This is greatly useful in hospitals for searching information needed by a surgeon to perform an emergency blood transfusion.

(7) Help to Government: Computers help the government, its departments, undertaking with regard to planning, decision-making and legal enforcement. In U.S.A., a nation-wide police information network connects national crime information centre. The New York statewide police information network is one of the best examples in this connection.

(8) Education Field: Computers are used in educational and research institutes in various disciplines.

(9) Employment: India is today suffering from educated unemployment and the resultant disparities of income and wealth. Introduction of computers in the light of heavy work load in all organisations provide employment opportunities to certain sections of technically qualified people.

(10) Relief from fatigue: People are working and doing continuously repeated work have so far remained bored, feeling fatigue and monotony. Computers will reduce boredom, provide relief from fatigue by working at computers, offer quality of service.

Management Information System (MIS)

A. Management: There are three basic words in the caption, namely, management, information and system. It is an essential part of the study to understand the meaning of these words. The word "management" means the art of managing things and getting things done through other people. It is an art and a profession. The functions of management are planning, organising, staffing, directing, controlling, coordination. The organisations have managers who plan, set goals and direct to accomplish the goals of the organisation. The functions of the managers differ according to the position occupied, namely, high, middle or low level. Management haves three levels, namely:

(1) Top-level management known as strategic management;

(2) Middle level management called "tactical level"; and

(3) Low level management or supervisory level, also called operating level.

The last level is called as first line managers in charge of the employees. Top managers are responsible for overall operation of the organisation. They are top executives variously called: chief executive officer, president and chairman. They formulate broad policies and objectives of the organisation. Middle level managers are under direct control of the top managers. 'They are functional managers, each function is headed by a manager. The functions are Finance, Accounting, Personnel, Marketing, Production, headed by persons having specialised knowledge of each function. In the organisation structure, they are positioned horizontally. Operating level implement the policies of top management routed to them through middle level managers. The principles of management are:

(1) Division of work
(2) Authority and responsibility
(3) Discipline
(4) Unity of command
(5) Unity of direction
(6) Subordination of individual interests to general interest
(7) Remuneration
(8) Centralisation
(9) Scalar chain
(10) Order
(11) Equity
(12) Stability
(13) Initiative
(14) Esprit de corps.

B. Information: The word "information" implies facts told or knowledge gained or given. Information with reference to management means knowledge which the managers at different levels receive or give at a given time. It is necessary to make a distinction among data, information and communication. The word "data" is the plural of "datum", which means fact. Facts or information given from which other facts may be worked out. The facts are data, the raw materials of information. The facts are by symbols like words spoken or written, visual, action and figures. Information is not data, the data comprise of information. Data are presented by symbols, but they are not information except in a limited sense. As used in data processing in computer, information is data arranged in an order and form useful to the people who receive it. So, information is relevant knowledge, produced, as the output of data processing operations and acquired by people to enhance understanding and to achieve specific purposes.[33] Computer data processing converts raw data into information. All information consists of data, but not all data produce specific and meaningful information.[34] The managerial functions like planning, organisation, control and co-ordination etc.

can be discharged effectively and smoothly only when necessary information is given to the managers, who can make timely and correct decision. A timely supply of information is indispensable to make the best judgement; while communication is a process of transmission of matter by symbols. All communication consists of information, but not all information is capable of communication. Communication is only a piece of information which is very comprehensive in scope. Information is like an enormous umbrella, a broad concept which covers communication as one particular type of information. Information is a global concept referring to any pattern of energy input you are exposed to.[35] Information includes both internal and external information. Today, information is a factor of production like, capital, labour etc.

C. System: The word "system" means an arrangement of many parts that work together. The establishment of arrangement of things relating to management. A system is a group of parts that are integrated to achieve the desired objective. A system has more than one element. The other two important characters of a system are integrated parts and having a common purpose of achieving some objective. It is "a grouping of integrated methods and procedures united to form an organised entity; an organised grouping of people, methods, machines, and materials collected together to accomplish a set of specific objectives."[36]

Computer has a group of integrated parts that have the common purpose of performing the operations.

According to Hussain and Hussain:

(1) group of interrelated or interacting elements.
(2) A group of interrelated components that seeks the attainment of a common goal by accepting inputs and producing outputs in an organised process.
(3) An assembly of methods, procedures or techniques united by regulated interaction to form an organised whole.
(4) An organised collection of people, machine and method required to accomplish a set of specific function.[37] Thus, input, output and processing devices are the three important components of a system.

Definition of MIS

Hussain and Hussain: "An Information system is an organised set of components designed to produce intelligence required for decision-making. In a business context, the information is for management. The system itself has four main components; input, output, computer programmes and the processor."[38]

Jerome Kanter: "A Management information system (MIS) is a system that aids management in making, carrying out, and controlling decisions. Decision making, including the process leading up to the decision can be termed "Planning", and management can be defined as the planning and control of the physical and personnel resources of the company in order to reach the company's objectives."[39]

Donald H. Sanderz: "A management information (MIS) is a network of computer based data processing procedures, developed in an organisation and integrated with manual and other procedures for the purpose of providing timely and effective information to support decision-making and other necessary management functions. We will use a business example to illustrate some of the elements in this definition, but MIS concepts certainly aren't restricted to business."[40]

After having understood the three concepts presented above, the concept of Management Information System becomes clear. It implies a system designed to provide information to different level managers, requires to manage and to accomplish organisational goals through effective decision-making. An organisation is a process of continuous decision-making, a complex, dynamic and interacting. The key factors needed in a decision-making process are the information input. The timely availability of relevant internal information, new and additional and internal information helps to make effective decisions. Therefore, the primary objective in developing a total management information system should be the production of detailed up-to-the-minute summaries of the past data and the use of them to project the future activity.

Different managerial levels need different types of information to take decisions effectively. Alternatively, modern complex business organisations, or on the growth of an organisation, more levels may be needed comparable to a smaller organisation. It is, therefore, necessary to provide different types of information to managers at different levels. Top-level-managers who make major policies, objectives to them is necessary to supply objective information concerning general understanding of the organisation. Middle level managers who implement the top-level plans, need such information to control, co-ordinate, allocate scarce resource and to select a particular course of action among available alternatives and the relative consequences of indifferent alternatives available to them. Operational decisions are made by the lower level managers, need detailed information relating to day-to-day operations. Computer technology is required for the computerised information system.

Computer information enables decision-making more effective. Decision Support System (DSS) are the components of Management Information System. They are stimulation, expert system and information centres. The designing of the information system is based on what type of information is needed, why and for whom. Computer based Management Information System help managers in the decision-making process in a number of business areas. The business areas are raw materials, policy-making, pricing, advertisements, research, accounting policies, investment decisions, product planning, marketing strategies, finance etc. Thus, "an MIS supports the planning and decision-making activities of many managers."[41]

Simulation is a trial and error problem-solving approach that is very useful in planning. Simulation models serving managers at different levels may also be integrated into an overall corporate modelling approach to planning and decision-making. An expert system is a software package that includes:

(1) stored base of knowledge in a specialised area and

(2) the capability to prove this knowledge base and make decisions and recommendations.

An organisation may have established an information centre. The centre gives its users a direct on-line path into the organisation's data bases to retrieve the facts they need.[42]

Electronic Mail (E-Mail) or Electronic Mail Message System

The developments in the field of telecommunication have a long way in making the world a 'Global Village' India is also a part of this miniaturised scenario. It may be admitted that E-Mail came to India rather late. Electronic (E-Mail) as it is popularly known, is the first value-added service to become operational in the service sector. As a part of the liberalisation drive in India, it has been thrown open for private participation. Presently, a few companies are offering the services which have been given licences to operate.

In India, E-Mail started in 1986 with the initiation of Education and Research in Computer Networks Project (ERNET) and UNDP. Subsequently, ERNET has started a small network of its own, reaching out to colleges, research labs and commercial organisations.

Mail Box

In E-Mail, one needs to use PC, a telephone home connection and modem link. After having possessed these, one has to subscribe to the service and send mail electronically. E-Mail is a system of transmission of message electronically. The messages are prepared on a computer and transmitted using telephone circuits. Messages proceed across various computers/gateways till they reach the electronic mail box at the destination. In case the receiver is not available due to a change of address, the message is re-routed, re-transmitted or is bounced back to the sender.

Under this system, there is a separate service called Electronic Data Interchange (EDC) meant for exporters who have their documents made in a standard format. Thus, E-Mail can also be programmed for specific users. The success of these services require effectiveness of the telephone links because all modems invariably have a phone outlet that can be used for normal voice conversation.

Information captured and efficiently transmitted is the key to success. In today's competitive world, organisations both large and small, need to be able to respond quickly to opportunities, threats and needs of their customers. Hence, efficient methods of communication become essential. Unfortunately, most systems fall short of the requirements in terms of convenience, speed, confidence and economy. Electronic mail (E-mail), on the other hand, offers a perfect combination of all these. What began as a simple and fast way for individuals to communicate has evolved into a vital business and personal communication tool.[43]

Presently, messages are forwarded through postal service or sent verbally over telephone lines. The computer systems now avoid the usual postal service. There are many problems associated with postal services such as:

(1) The cost of sending a message through postal service is increasing.

(2) It is known that postal service is relatively slow.

(3) Often messages get lost.

In order to overcome the problems of the usual postal service, the "Electronic Mail/Message Systems" have emerged. The EMMS is also called "Computer Mail/Message Systems." (CMMS). The EMMS or CMMS is a network that can store, transmit and deliver messages by electronic means. Because it has several advantages and overcoming the problems in the case of the usual postal services, the EMMS has gained much popularity in most of the advanced countries. Even using telephone for message transmission, there is no certainty that the message reaches the recipient. The presence of the recipient and willingness to take and interpret the call in the same sense are the problems associated with it. The EMMS network has been developed with a view to solving some of the problems in message distribution system.

The new concept or network facilitates transmission of large message load or information at a high speed. Many devices like telephone lines and hookup devices etc., are used to connect distance locations. An Electronic Computer Originate Mail (E-Com) is a postal service system available in the U.S. Under the electronic means, the terminal or computer of the customer transmits messages with high speed, quickly, economically and accurately. The computer or the receiving post office records the message, where the message is printed on a printer. The printed message is then delivered to the addressee. The advantages of this network are that it saves typing time, addressing, mailing etc.

The mail/message by electronic means provide a number of functions. The system provides services like:

(a) Message distribution system;

(b) Transmission of documents; and pictures;

(c) Computerised conferences.

Advantage of Electronic Mail

(1) The users of the system can reach customers, branch offices, distributors, vendors, suppliers, project teams and sales offices anywhere anytime.

(2) Services of this powerful messaging system gives one immediate access to worldwide contacts.

(3) It permits so as to enable one to do everything to run his business efficiently and profitably.

(4) The system helps to implement marketing programmes with greater accuracy.

(5) Pre-empt the competitiveness with a change in marketing tactics before they can react.

(6) It facilitates to improve responsiveness by revising price change in marketing programmes instantly.

(7) Delays and inefficiencies in reporting systems can cripple effectiveness, E-Mail improves report delivery and distribution both inside and outside the organisation.

(8) Sales people mostly rely heavily on telephone calls for contact with their head offices and customers. E-Mail helps in eliminating the telephone tag.

(9) Sending and receiving messages can be done at convenience without delay linking international representatives and closing sales.

(10) The order entry system under E-Mail package helps in serving instant messages as electronic purchase orders/confirmations and in maintaining inventory levels.

(11) The E-Mail assists to increase the efficiency and effectiveness of public relations programmes.

(12) Maintaining close contact by business organisations with clients or customers is the main object of marketing strategy. In this connection, E-Mail can increase responsiveness.

(13) The using of instant messages helps greatly to exchange with great efficiency in areas of appointment confirmations. Requests for information and follow-up reports.

(14) The Videsh Sanchar Nigam Limited (VSNL) has introduced Global Electronic Messaging Service (GEMS 400). It will enable one to exchange mails and ASCII (American Standard Code for International Information) files to any E-mail subscriber or any of the major international public E-Mail systems.

(15) The system allows to send and receive telexes from the privacy of one's computer terminal and communicate with over 1.7 million telex subscribers the world over.

(16) Fax messages can be sent from personal computer terminals to more than 4.2 million fax machines.

(17) The mail message system by electronic means provide a number of other advantages like message distribution system, transmission of documents, pictures etc.

(18) Most types of personal computers, terminals, word processors, telex machines and electronic typewriters can be used to access GEMS 400. The basic components necessary are just a PC terminal, communication software and standard modern.[44]

Videsh Sanchar Nigam and E-Mail

The Videsh Sanchar Nigam Limited (VSNL) has in 1991 started operating their GEMS 400 service to act as a gateway for international mail from India. In addition to its services, in India, today, there are about ten companies offering

and many more are expected to come up in the near future to offer E-Mail services. Today, there are about 30,000 people using E-Mail in India. The list of E-Mail subscribers has been increasing considerably. ICNET (Madras), Dataline and Research Technologies (Bombay), Business India Information Technology (New Delhi) and Datapro are some of the companies rendering the services.

Uses of E-Mail

(1) It has merit of speed, economy and efficiency.

(2) It can be used to access out-of-town libraries.

(3) Exporters can transfer trade documents to their foreign partners.

(4) Customs officers can send memos to and fro.

(5) Journalists can send their copies across.

(6) Lawyers, doctors, consultants and government departments can just use it to keep in touch with.

(7) Postal services are quite unreliable and known for delay.

(8) Traditional postal services do not guarantee security of delivery, delays, and loss of mail causes personal inconveniences and confusion.

(9) E-Mail can be used to transmit computer programmes, spreadsheets, images in a machine readable form.

(10) It permits to avoid to duplicate data entry.

(11) E-Mail is error-free.

(12) From the cost point of view, E-Mail works out to be much cheaper and convenient.

(13) It allows to send prepared documents and graphics to the recipients.

(14) It is simple and easy to transmit information and query for answer and question.

All that one needs for using E-Mail is a PC, a telephone connection and a modem link.

Hybrid Mail Service in India

Hybrid mail service has been introduced in India for the first time from January 14,1995. The Department of Posts has introduced this hybrid mail service. The service envisages that a message brought to the post office manually can be transmitted electronically to another post office for delivery through postmen to the premises of customers. This hybrid mail service facilitates to reach the message to the destination within 12 hours.

A customer will have the option of presenting the materials — either the manuscript, typed form, or on a floppy diskette. After the message is recorded on the computer, the system will automatically calculate the service charges.

Hybrid mail service is now available in many advanced countries. But in India, it is for the first time, to be introduced. Initially, the hybrid mail service is introduced in India in a network comprising Delhi, Mumbai, Bangalore, Chennai, Patna, Lucknow and Shimla.

Hospital Information System

The Management Information System (MIS) is to meet the requirements of business settings, whereas the Hospital Information System (HIS) has emerged to meet the needs of hospitals or healing settings. It has many common elements as are applied with management information system, a HIS supports the planning and decision-making activities of clinics. The systems provide management and clinical information to administrative and health care professional throughout a hospital. An integrated data base management system is used, and software modules are designed for key administrative and clinical applications.

The administrative areas cover matters like personal, financial, materials, and infrastructure facilities. The areas for HIS are to handle financial matters like patient billing, pay roll etc. The other sub-systems are the employees, occupancy, length of stay, food service, skills etc. The storage of patients' medical records are useful for research. In so far as the clinical side of the systems is concerned, the applications cover:

(1) Data collection and analysis for diagnostic purposes.

(2) Lab testing procedures and the analysis of lab data.

(3) Patient monitoring and intensive care.

(4) Pharmacy control.

(5) Specialised research function associated with such topics as assistance for the handicapped, occupational diseases and preventive and community health programmes.[45]

Teleconferencing

It is also called "video-conferencing." Also known as "telephone conference" discussions in which practically all direct communication between the participants is carried out via the public telephone system. It is an arrangement which facilitates the speakers to communicate each other in different localities using public telephone links. Participants of the conference located in different geographical distance areas can discuss issues by using their terminals that are linked together via the telecommunication network.

It helps them greatly to communicate voices, text and video-signals. It is an electronic linking of geographically scattered people who are participating at the same time. It refers to the meeting or people who are geographically separated, but under this system, all are participating in discussions through the telecommunication system. It uses a two-way voice, text or video communication equipment. Under this system, the participants can interact, interface over wide distance in real time.

Meetings are the lifeblood of every business, whether one is exchanging information, reviewing performance, checking progress, making a presentation or discussing strategy, there is often no substitute for a face-to-face conference. But meetings can be difficult to arrange and expensive, especially when long distance travel is involved.

There is an alternative, however, an alternative that not only cuts cost and wasteful time on travel, but also lets one arrange meetings without the usual dealings. The alternative is video conferencing or tele-conferencing.

In recent years, big business organisations are using teleconferencing method to conduct business meetings with the concerned executives who are geographically scattered all over a region. For instance, a firm having a chain of branch offices offers a network for teleconferencing service. The members or participants can go to their local branch and participate, and interact in discussion with the speaker at other branches. It may be mentioned that an alternative to computer conferencing is teleconferencing. An electronic linkage of geographically scattered people is no doubt an oral communication through a medium but without the presence of persons. The advantages of face-to-face conversation cannot be obtained from teleconferencing which cannot replace them. Body movements, facial expressions which also communicate feelings, attitudes etc., cannot be seen with teleconferencing perfectly. But, on the other hand, teleconferencing offers a number of advantages like:

(1) Time is saved.

(2) Cost and energy are saved.

(3) Travel to distance place to attend conference is avoided.

(4) No monotony or fatigue.

(5) The work arrangements, facilities and accommodation is eliminated.

Participants in the teleconferencing can use facsimile devices, electronic blackboards which give chalk impressions to be reproduced on distance T.V, monitors, picturephone, meeting service, and other communicating technologies to transmit opinions, facts, feelings figures etc., over a wide distance in real time. This system passes papers, back and forth to one another as they talk, argue, debate, exchange and interact the important points.

This development of telecommunication resulted in TV meetings, save travel, cost, time and wearying business trips. It helps in a two-way television system, face-to-face conversation with the people at widely separated locations. The American Telephone and Telegraph (AT & T) Company operates picture phone meeting services. It is possible to link all conference facilities that are part of the picture-phone meeting service operated by AT & T Company. They are located in Atlanta, Boston, Chicago, Dallas, Los Angeles, New York City, Philadelphia, Pittsburgh, Sacramento, San Francisco and Washington.

Sophisticated technologies in satellite communication have been developed and expanded the range of possibilities for meetings, conferences and lectures. Under this system, it operates satellite teleconferencing. It is a program of simultaneous session in several places or at distance locations which are linked electronically with speakers shown on screen television equipment. Thus, it facilitates to avoid the speaker to travel and spend time and to travel to participate in person in sessions.

The saving in travel time and cost of meeting facilitates and boarding of participants can be more than off-set the cost of using the electronic technology of teleconferencing. Many organisations have been using teleconferencing technology to hold national press conferences to answer reporters' questions. The participants can ask questions, seek clarifications and get answers simultaneously in two-way communication with the speakers. Thus, this medium is being increasingly used now-a-days by many organisations.

Across the Table and Across the World

Video-conferencing allows people in different locations to meet face-to-face. It is almost like being in the same room, even though the participants might be hundreds or thousands of miles apart. By looking at combined monitor/ camera unit, a few feet in front, one feels as if his collegues are sitting on the other side of the table. Without thinking about it, one slips into a natural conversation, picking up the nuances of body language and facial expression so crucial to personal communication. And thanks to the open sound system, everyone can say their piece without having to worry about cutting someone else off.

Video-conferencing may sound complicated, but it is not so. Any one who can handle the remote control of a television can master the technique of video-conferencing within a few minutes.

Running Meetings as Normal

The video-conferencing services are designed to make life straight forward and natural. One can use a flip chart or electronic white board, show overhead slides and transparencies, study plans and documents, and look at objects in close-up. One can also play videotapes and display PC graphics. Every one involved can see and hear what is going on and speak whenever they want to.

One of the few things that cannot be done is to pass the coffee pot across the table, to his collegues, otherwise the rule is carry on as normal.[46]

In recent years, big business organisations are using tele-conferencing method to conduct business meetings with the concerned executives who are geographically scattered.

Videsh Sanchar Nigam and Video-Conferencing

In India, Videsh Sanchar Nigam Limited (VSNL) has four public video-conferencing centres at its offices at Mumbai, New Delhi, Kolkata and Chennai. There are more than 450 public video-conference centres in cities throughout Europe, North America, the Far East and Pacific Rim. In addition, thousands of companies around the world now have their own in-house video-conference facilities. All of them are within the reach of VSNL's video-conference centre.

The studio at VSNL allows up to six conference participants to be viewed at the same time on two side by side monitors. Control of the system is by means of the infra-red control key pad. Outgoing pictures are transmitted using the two signal sensor colour CCD cameras which allow the images of six participants to be displayed via the split screen facility or alternatively the three participants image as viewed by either camera. The 10" confidence monitor displays the image currently being transmitted to the remote location. Incoming pictures from the remote location are viewed on two 27" colour monitor mounted side by side.

With either the graphics recall or preview, facilities are selected, one monitor is reserved for the incoming pictures, while the second monitor displays the local requested image. This simultaneous display allows for continuity to be maintained throughout the conference.

The system includes two low profile micro-phones and two built-in loudspeakers. A mute facility is provided to enable private conversation to take place during a conference; there is a volume control which enables incoming sounds to be set at a comfortable level.

The status display informs participants about the current mode of operation and overall system status. The VSNL systems are equipped with a stand by mode. This feature enables both sound and vision to be switched off temporarily to provide full privacy during a transmission. The system supports auxillary video interfaces such as display station, camera and VCR's with selection via the infra-red control key board. Full duplex open sound at wideband frequencies enables interactive conversation to take place. There are auxillary data ports for use with a facsimile machine, electronic whiteboard or general data communication applications.

Multi-Point Conference

The Multi-Point conference unit is an advanced switching system which enables video conferencing meetings to be conducted from up to four locations simultaneously. It is capable of supporting up to two simultaneous multipoint conferences and up to four point-to-point connections. During a conference, the video is switched either by voice or manual selection. Video conferencing prior to one's business trips increases the value of the trips. It also saves certain trips which one really need not make. It also minimises time and productivity losses due to travel and streamline project development time.[47]

Advantages of Tele-Conferencing

Video-conferencing is one of those business tools that becomes more and more useful as one gains first-hand experience of its benefits. There will always be times when one needs to meet in person, but video-conferencing has the potential to play a major role in the overall communication strategy.

Tele-conferencing offers a number of advantages:

(1) Time is saved.

(2) Cost and energy are saved.

(3) Travel to distances to attend the conference is avoided.

(4) No monotony and fatigue.

(5) Conduct highly efficient meetings.

(6) Making meeting arrangement are avoided.

(7) Cost of accommodation and other facilities are avoided.

The most obvious benefit is cost. For example, bringing in three collegues from the U.S. for a meeting in India could easily add upto Rs. 3 lakhs when all the travel and accommodation charges are taken into account. On top of that, there is the time lost in travelling and fatigue. In contrast, hiring a VSNL's video-conference centre and linking cost may cost around half a lakh an hour. Video-conferencing tends to produce highly efficient meetings. Because the facilities are booked for an agreed period, people usually come well-prepared and stick to the business under discussion.

Video-Conferencing Systems

(1) Studio-based: Traditional video-conferencing, typically very plush, boardroom type surroundings with considerable concentration on room lighting and acoustics. Usually, with a dedicated satellite or leased line communication.

(2) Roll-about: The first move to mobility enabled by dial-up communication. Practically, considerations such as the weight of the equipment and fear of damaging it have limited movement in practice. Commonly uses multiple ISNO lines on a dial-up or switched service basis.

(3) Desktop: Comes in two forms:

(i) A compact dedicated video-conferencing system.

(ii) A plug-in option for an existing PC.

Though core standards exist, there is much jockeying for market position in the area of data exchange: annotation, whiteboards, computer conferencing etc. Two digital telephone lines are used.

(4) Videotelephony: Promised so much for so long but has not delivered. Now, perhaps, merging with the desktop market, usually uses a single digital telephone line.

(5) Multimedia: Very considerable overlap with desktop video- conferencing. Multimedia concentrate on creation, storage and reply than interactive meeting.*

Computer Based Conferences

In teleconferencing, it is necessary that all the participants of a conference to be present or to be line at the same time. The system uses audio and video equipment for communication. The requirement of all the participants to be on line at the same time often poses problem. Under

* Jagdish Seth, *The Economic Times*, 30th March, 1995.

computerised teleconferencing, it is not necessary for all the participants to be on line at their terminals or personal computers at the same time.

Similarly, it facilitates that it is not necessary that the participants be physically present at the same place. A computer based teleconferencing permits the participants to attend meetings at their convenience or permits conference to be held at the convenience of the participants.

The electronic mail/message system (EMMS) is a device which can be used to store and deliver by electronic means, messages which otherwise would be sent over telephone lines. An EMMS system is capable of performing a number of functions, among them computerised conferences is one. The computer conference known, as computer based teleconferencing permits, that the conference dialogue can be stored in computers. A participant can sit at a terminal or personal computer at a convenient time and call up any conversation not seen, make comments, if any, reply to questions etc.

The special feature of this system is that many participants can speak at the same time. Thousands of people at different geographical areas can use the system. The system requires that each participant is expected to have access to a computer terminal connected to the conference network. The participant can sit at the terminal or personal computer at a convenient time and call up any conversation and respond to any message.

There is a data base facility in the system possessing a large number of text messages. The conversation or message is entered by a member of the computer conference. The participant can directly write his conversation, messages and comments which will be stored in computers.

It is surprising to note that in developed countries computer-based conferencing has been increasingly used. There are many computer conferencing networks developed for service. For example, the Informedia Corporation of Palo Alto, U.S.A., provides two computer conference facilities known as Planet and Notepad. Similarly, the New Jersey Institute of Technology, U.S.A., offers conference services on their network known as Electronic Information Exchange System.

In order to use these services, any member of a group has to dial local access telephone number, couples the telephone to a terminal. All group members can share a file. Under these systems the subscribers are grouped topic-wise or groups according to their specific topic of interest such as technology, economics etc. A subscriber who is interested in many topics may join more than one group. Group members may belong to corporations, Governments, local authorities, hospitals, educational institutions and other non-profit organisations.

The Stockholm University in Sweden offers another system known as COM in two languages, Swedish and English.

The computer-based conferencing systems offer a number of advantages. A few of them are;

(1) A lot of time is saved.

(2) A person can sit at a terminal according to his convenient time.

(3) It avoids extensive travel and stay to attend a conventional conference.

(4) It saves money and energies of a group of participants.

(5) They can attend on other important works.

(6) It maintains a permanent history of all conference discussions.

(7) The discussions are recorded and stored in a computer.

(8) It permits which message or conversation each participant has already seen.

(9) When operated, it displaces all the conference entries which have not been seen.

(10) A person can directly read and write at a convenient time.

(11) Messages are stored in a computer.

Thus, government and business organisations can use profitably computer conferencing to conduct periodic meetings, transmission of ideas, opinions facts, etc.

Word Processing

The expression "word processing" is pertaining to computer application to text. Like data processing by the computer, it also processes words or text. Word processing is another major application of computer to create, view, edit, store, retrieve and finally print text materials. The modern electronic offices have been using automated and centralised typing, dictation, copying and filing information.

A device which does word processing naturally, such as composing, correspondence in format, editing, revising etc. Optical character recognition or facsimile equipment converts the printed materials into machine readable text. A text can be stored in memory. The keyboard is the typewriter. Text editing process over entering, editing, and deletion of text, and printing process function includes to print and read. Computer technology is now greatly used in modern offices to transmit ideas, facts etc., into written communication. The process avoids laborious typing or to cyclostyle or print the letters.

When a number of letters are to be sent to customers, it is possible to personalise each letter by printing on the word processor printer for each address. The matter can be stored in magnetic storage device and be used to send a similar letter. The advantages of word processing are easy correction, revision, storage of message, easy creation of new documents from stored data, no erasures, overtyping on white paper as it is the case in typewriter, print charts, and figures, it is also faster and efficient than mechanical typewriters, goodwill and satisfaction of the customers.

Processing is a manipulation of words. The input is through keyboard and the output may be produced on either a display screen or a printer. The common types of business communication are repetitive letters, standard documents, special reports and financial reports. The basic function in all business communication are input, processing, storage and output. Keyboard is the input component, processing unit receives instructions, co-ordinates the entire system, storage is a memory component, receives and stores data or text for manipulation.

The output may be obtained either on the screen of video display or a printer. There are many organisations today which have introduced communication technology to reduce cost, avoid delay achieve accuracy and speed. A word processing package is used to create, view, edit, retrieve and print matter. Use of computer in word processing application is more important in electronic office.

Tele-Commuting

Tele-commuting refers to employees work who do their official work at home on computer linking to the office. In advanced countries telecommuting is the most popular method of communication between the home and office. With the help of a computer people are doing work like booking orders over telephone, processing, filling forms and analysing information. Forecasters predict that 10 to 20 million people could be telecommunicating by the year 2000.[48] Tele-commuting in India is at present not widely and popularly used. But it may in the years to come.

Electronic Newspaper

The electronic newspaper is already a reality in the United States of America, it brings the electronic information to the very doorsteps of the subscribers. The Columbia Dispatch became the first newspaper in US to go electronic on 1st July 1980 by making almost all its editorial product available to the house and business computer subscribers.

The subscriber has a television terminal in his house connected to the newspaper office through telephone lines. They call it 'Cable TV', when the subscriber dials the newspaper office and turns on the Video Terminal, the latest edition of the newspaper like sports, entertainment, market report, retail shopping etc., can be called up on the screen by pressing the coded keys. That is the electronic newspaper which has eliminated the printed world.

Several other forms of interactive home electronic information systems have been introduced in America and Europe by newspapers and Press agencies in several cities for transmission of information of all sorts through the Cable TV system.

Electronic telephone directory was introduced in France on an experimental basis in 1981 to provide telephone directory information via video-terminals in lieu of both the yellow and white page directories, more than one quarter million entries, including advertising. If this and other experiments prove successful, all of France's 30 million subscribers will get free videotex terminals instead of the printed telephone directories. One can understand how much traditional printers would be greatly affected by the loss of such huge quantity print-orders.

Paperless Book

A paperless book has been published by a Californian publisher. The entire text of the *Computer Cookbook* is available in a disk and customers can sign on to their own computer terminals for viewing the pages by paying a fee. A US schoolbook publisher estimates that by the end of this decade, about one-third of its books will come from computer related equipments.

Every computer or computerised equipment that is put on the market every day is more powerful than its predecessor and also much smaller in size and cheaper in price. Personal computers, word processors and video terminals may become household items during the current decade. Their capabilities will become hundred-fold. The impact of having a remote terminal in every office and house could be all pervasive. Printers will have to silently witness vast quantities of information bypass the tradition ink-on-paper process to go the route of instantly updatable, random access videopoint. In India, of course, it may take some years to reach this point.

Yet, printers need not lose heart. The need of printed books like popular novels, biographies or travel books for relaxed reading at home and during travel and perhaps even for reading in the bed before sleep, can never be replaced by the electronic terminal. With regard to our great scriptures, great sages have said that as long as life exists on earth, the *Ramayana and the Mahabharata* will exist. As far as India is concerned, we can be confident that as long as the stories of the *Ramayana* and the *Mahabharata* are narrated, so long will the printed word continue to exist and enlighten the human being, leading them from darkness to light.

Transmission of Pictures (Facsimile)

Like messages, pictures can be transmitted by using a special machine known as *Fascimile Machine,* or *Fax Machine.* Under the electronic mail message system, an original document containing photographs, maps, charts and other drawings are transmitted by placing in a sending facsimile machine. The computer-based facsimile systems are more useful in modern offices. The sending machine scans documents containing pictures and the receiving device reproduces the scanned picture or image.

Message Distribution Services

In a message distribution service, a message is transmitted to a recipient who has a device called as "Electronic Mail Box." A written message is keyed into the system, the Video Mail System (VMS) holds recorded voice messages.

Transmission of Text

The telex system has been in use for transmitting messages through teleprinter exchange network. This is an old or conventional method for transmission of text. In this Electronic Mail Message System function, text is transmitted over telecommunication lines. There are two terminals in this system known as teleprinters which appear like typewriters. There are two devices, sending-end-terminal and receiving-end-terminal, the message is keyed into the key board. The receiving-end teleprinter prints the message so transmitted over the lines by the sending-end-terminals.

In this Electronic Mail Service function, the teleprinter terminals are connected to computers. Computer is also used in transmission of text. The text is keyed and appears on the screen. Under this system, it is possible to check the message before transmission.

Disc

The word "disc" refers to the computer system. A revolving device platter on which data and programmes are stored. A file, i.e., an organised collection of connected records, that resides on a magnetic disc. Disc drive is an electronic mechanical device that rotates magnetic disc that writes data and reads data from a floppy disc.

Disc pack is a storage medium having multiple magnetic discs. Magnetic discs are a popularly used device for direct access to secondary storage. It is a metal or plastic platter like a photograph record. There are several types of magnetic discs. But all magnetic discs are round platters coated with iron-oxide or other magnetizable recording materials.

Discs are of different sizes, such as large 14 inches metal disc, same size metal disc packaged in removable cartridge or disc pack. Small 8 inches and 5 1/4 inches rigid disc housed in Winchester disc devices and same size portable floppy (flexible) discs, 4 inches compact floppy and rigid discs.

On a magnetic disc, there are no grooves. Data and information are stored on discs in a number on invisible concentric circles called "pracks." A drive rotates the disc at a constant speed of between 300 and 600 revolutions per minute. Hard discs rotate at a speed from 2400 to 4700 revolutions per minute.

Floppy Discs

It is a computer device used to store data and programmes. It is also called as diskett. A low cost thin flexible disc coated with magnetic particles. A magnetic medium used for storage purpose. Standard discs are eight inches in diameter and the more common mini-discs are about 5 1/4 inches. A mini-disc has a storage capacity around 15 to 20 pages of a book, its special quality is that it is flexible, flat, that magnetically records and provides access to stored data.

Contrast with a floppy disc, it is a hard disc which is rigid metal platter coated with magnetic particles. Optical disc is a device used with laser reading or writing to store huge quantities of data. The source document data to be keyed directly into a floppy magnetic disc. It is called floppy disc because it is made out of flexible plastic materials. The plastic material is coated with iron-oxide recording substance and data are recorded as tiny invisible magnetic spots on this coating. As storage medium, floppy disc is used in word processing.

Telecommunication

As we approach the 21st century, a new level of human activity is emerging as Government, industry, commerce, trade and transport increasingly transcend national frontiers to operate worldwide. The explosion in business and personal travel underscorpes this trend. Globally accessible telecommunication is be-coming an essential part of modern civilisation.

The mix of terrestrial telecom networks and services fixed and mobile, now spanning the earth meets many of the modern needs of communication. But, it is only through the mobile satellite services that the demand for total worldwide mobile communication can be fully met.

It is a device of sending messages, information etc. by telephone, telegraph, radio and television. This term refers to transmission of signals through electromagnetic medium. All India Radio, Doordarshan and INSAT-IB are good examples of telecommunication based transmission/ dissemination of information. Telecommunications convert audio and/or visual information into electromagnetic signals which further modulate radio or microwave carrier signals.

These signals are bounced back by the ionized layers in space satellites and are picked up by radio or television receivers. These receivers demodulate the received signals and separate the audio and visual respectively. The recent decision to provide a separate channel for educational telecast in view of the excellent technical infrastructure provided by Doordarshan which has established more than 100 low and medium power TV transmitters. It is a welcome step and offers tremendous possibilities for strengthening and broadcasting Indian Open Learning System.

Telecommunication Tools

While we are discussing the various communication media, it will be appropriate here to make mention of some of the mechanical, electronic, electrical type of communication media. Covering mechanical communication media under this paragraph will, perhaps, serve as a good information purpose and to achieve full coverage of the subject. Mechanical communication media now-a-days rapidly gaining popularity within all walks of life, more particularly with organisations and business.

The important telecommunication tools are as under:

(a) Telegram: A written message supplied to the department of telecom munication which in turn sends the message by telegram.

(b) Telegraph: A system of sending message by telegraph using either wires and electricity or radio.

(c) Telegraphist: Also called as a telegrapher. He is the person who operates a telegraph and acts as intermediary between the communicator and the recipient.

(d) Telegraphy: With reference to telecommunication, telegraphy is the process of sending message by telegraph. Telegraph wire by which telegraph messages are sent.

(e) Telepathy: A quite different style of communication of ideas, though directly from one's mind without the use of audio or visual. Telepathist is the person who studies or practices telepathy.

(f) Telephone Booth: Other names used are telephone box or call box. It is a small room or compartment established at a prominent public place containing a telephone for public use.

(g) Telephone Directory: Directory is a specially prepared type of book containing the names and addresses of a particular group. Telephone directory is a list of names, addresses and telephone numbers of a group of all the people in a particular area who have telephones. The list is arranged in an alphabetical order.

(h) Telephone Exchange: A centrally-controlled system through which telephone calls are directed. The telephonist, in a telephone exchange, in giving a number connects. The use of telephone exchange is necessary in the case of non-STD and in the absence of direct dialling operation.

(i) Teleprinter: A machine in a communication system. Teleprinter is a specialised type of typewriter. A telegraphic system or instrument by which messages are sent out at one place and received at another place in a printed form. The typing is connected to a telephone line and the messages typed at one place transmits electrical signals over the wire and the message is simultaneously reproduced, printed at a distance place by the machine. It is used as private circuit or through the post-office telex service system. The post office gives teleprinters on rent to form a part of private telecommunication.

A teleprinter is made up of:

(1) A key board for data entry.

(2) A built-in-printer to record typed input and produce computer process output.

Portable Teleprinters

There are many small and portable teleprinters mostly used by salespersons, newspaper reporters, engineers, managers etc. A travelling sales representative can use it for sending sales information to the Head Office over the telephone either for knowing the stock positions, placing orders etc. A portable teleprinter can be carried by them wherever they go. A sales representative can link the terminal to a customer's telephone and dial into a company's computer system. It is possible to obtain immediate information on the terminal printer. Similarly, lawyers, press reporters, etc., can carry a portable teleprinter.

(j) Teletype: An electronic system of transmitting information in typewrit-ten form. Used in operations of the various public relations activities, newswires, as well as by the associated Press and United Press International. A mechanical device of a telegraph system of transmitting messages by means of a typewriter keyboard. Each key of a keyboard produces coded signals which are simultaneously printed at the receiving end called "teleprinter." Teletypes relate to message transmission by teleprinter or teletype. A teletype means teletypewriter. This is also called a "telex" which provides automatic communication through the printed words between the subscribers having telex facilities.

(k) Telex: Sending messages by teleprinters. Detailed discussion is given under Teleprinter paragraph.

(l) Telecom: Telecom signifies inter-communication system used to communicate with one another, especially to talk between two rooms, offices, buildings etc., by means of a telephone or a radio system.

Mobile and Cellular Telephones

Cellular phones, paging and trunking constitute three types of mobile phones. Cellular phones have began to appear recently in the country. Mobile telephone service in India has begun on a limited scale. For the first time, it is introduced in Delhi by the Government owned Mahanagar Telephone Nigam Limited in the early 1980s. Radio paging services and cellular phones both belong to the same technological family of mobile services. They are satellites. Cordless phones are also mobile phones. In advanced countries, mobile telephone services had been introduced much earlier.

To mention the first, Korean mobile telephone service began in 1960s itself with a three cellular system called "mobile telephone service" (MIS). But it served a very limited area of coverage of the Seoul metropolitan areas. Later, the service area has been expanded to cover all cities and major highways.

Conversation from Car

The word "cellular" is derived from a cell or area created around an antenna to transmit and receive telephone messages. A cellular telephone makes it possible for the user to have two-way telephone conversation from a car. The user of a cellular telephone has to dial out and receive any call from the car or from any mobile location to another car having such a phone and telephone at stationary location within or outside the town or city.

In order to provide city-wide coverage, it is necessary that the antennas and cells should be repeated at many places in the city. The cells are interconnected for uninterrupted communication from a moving vehicle. The whole system of operation and communication is linked to the telephone exchanges of the telecommunication authority. This facilitates that the user can talk to any other user in the same city. The user can also make STD/ISD calls from moving vehicles. There are many cellular technologies which are not only more popular but also they have been standardised.

Pan European digital mobile telephone standard is specified by the European Telecommunications Standard Institute. This standard specified has been adapted by many countries.

It has three elements:

(1) Mobile Stations (MS).

(2) Radio Base Station System (RBSS).

(3) Mobile Service Switching Centres (MSSC).

The centres are associated with:

(1) Home Location Register (HLR).

(2) Visitors Location Register (VLR).

The digital cellular, radio mobile system will be accessed through the existing public switched telephone network (PSTN).

Paging Facilities

A question often arises as to What is a Pager?

A pager is one-way wireless message receiving device. It enables a person to receive complete messages, allowing to act upon them. Pager keeps the person constantly in touch. Paging service is a very simple. Telephone the paging company and give the operator our page number and the message. Almost instantly, the pager alerts, press the Read Button and get the message. That is Paging facility.

Fig. 14.4 Mobile Telephone

Need for Pager

Today, we are spending a lot of time on travelling to attend several assignments. It is known that the conventional devices cannot keep us in touch while we are on the move. Some research studies found that 65% of senior executives and businessmen interviewed in an 8-city survey feel the need for a mobile communication device. Therefore, pager is essential to stay connected. As paging service companies get licence to cover more cities. One can use pager across wider geographical areas too.

Fig. 14.5 Pager

It is an internal oral communication system useful when the executives move from one section to another section. Under electric paging system, each executive is given a number. It is a telecommunication facility. In recent years, satellite link is being increasingly used as highly sophisticated communication technology, in the highly specialised age of information and communication. A satellite link all over the country or all over the globe serves an important purpose. Satellite is being used and applied for communication meteorological purpose, research, defence, explorations etc.

In the United States, there is the National Paging Facility. Paging is a telecommunication device which helps to seek or summon the required personnel. The purpose of the paging facility is to establish contact between the organisation and the personnel working away from the organisation, either localised or far away from the organisation. A message or a code is transmitted by the communicator to the person who is required, which serves as an indication to the personnel to establish contact with the organisation. For this purpose, the personnel carry a separate device known as *Beeper* which receives the signals or the message transmitted. The paging facility permits the personnel to move from one place to another. They can be contacted by the paging facility with the help of Beeper wherever they are.

Thus, the system removes all the restrictions on the movement of personnel. In some organisations or professions, the personnel will be moving from one place to another by virtue of their position to discharge their duties. For instance, doctors, police, force, travelling executives, defence, factory and other industrial supervisors etc., are frequently moving personnel. According to the size of the organisation, nature of activities where personnel are working, paging facilities can be localised or extended to far-flung areas. For instance, the Mahanagar Telephone Nigam

Limited (MNTL), New Delhi, has started providing localised paging facilities to organisations in the Union Territory of Delhi. Paging facility can be operated either by using telephone exchanges for the purpose of transmission or satellite links for this purpose may be adopted.

Types of Paging Services

(1) Individual Paging: By this, one can page subscribers wherever they are.

(2) Anytime Paging: One can page any subscriber twenty four hours a day and 365 days a year.

(3) Auto-paging: Auto-paging facilitates one to page any subscriber automatically by dialling a given number.

(4) Group Paging: Group paging helps to page a group of people at the same time. What to do is to dial a number. Group is given a page number. The common message to be conveyed is to be transmitted by the group pager. Within seconds, all the members of the group will receive the same message, whatever the time, wherever they are. Thus, all this makes split-second communication the norm rather than the exception. So paging helps in an urgency in today's world of communication.

Radio Paging Services

Radio paging services belong to the same technological family of mobile telephone services. The radio paging services have been introduced in India in Delhi and Mumbai.

It has been decided to franchise it to private parties. Initially, it was decided that all cities with a population of one million or above or having a telephone capacity of more than 25,000 lines will be covered. On this criteria the service will be introduced in the following urban areas: Delhi, Bombay, Kolkata, Chennai, Ahmedabad, Bangalore, Hyderabad, Pune, Kanpur, Nagpur, Luchnow, Surat, Jaipur, Ernakulam, Coimbatore, Vadodra, Indore, Patna, Madurai, Bhopal, Varanasi, Ludhiana, Vishakapatnam, Chandigarh, Rajkot, Trivandrum and Amritsar. In phase II, it is proposed to cover all territorial circles (other than the 27 cities).[49]

Recent developments in telecommunication are as follows: (1) There are two personal mobile satellite communication services. (2) Portable mobile data. (3) A brief case telephone. (4) Satellite paging, a global paging service to pocket-size data receivers. (5) Global hand-held phone.

Radio paging service would provide alert signals, emergency calls, valuable information, etc. The service will be highly useful for medical professions, business executives, commercial applications, emergency services, in most of the urban and rural areas. For the operating services, All India Radio appoints licences/operators at selected centres where AIR has FM transmitters. FM radio broadcast technology has an advantageous feature.

Radio Paging in India

In communication service, India has made another landmark in recent years. Radio-paging based on modern sophisticated communication technology has been introduced in India for the first time on January 1995 in New Delhi through All India Radio. Use of this technology in India is for the first time, through the Government broadcasting department.

The radio paging service would provide alert signals, emergency calls, valuable information etc. Radio paging service will be more useful for sales persons, sales representatives; medical professionals, business managers, emergency calls, emergency services etc. It is proposed to operate radio paging service in 13 cities in India by the end of March, 1995, including the pilgrim -centre Tirupati in Andhra Pradesh. For this purpose, All India Radio will appoint licencees or operators. The subscribers have to send their data or messages to the control room. The persons to whom the messages have to be transmitted will have a separate device called "receivers." The receivers will give signals in turn as soon as messages are transmitted by the control room. Information can be observed on liquid display of the receiver.

Radio-paging broadcast technology has an advantageous feature. The vacant space of a radio in its allotted frequency band permits to inject additional signals in the form of data on sub-carriers. The data or information can conveniently be utilised to disseminate value-added service like public utility information and educational information etc. This service is in addition to the main programme like stereophonic and monophonic. When the radio is used in broadcast channel, it is called "RDS", whose primary application is radio paging.

All India Radio has announced the availability of FM-Based paging services. This is the first instance of a public broadcaster in Asia adopting paging techniques for public information services using the FM band.

Radio Paging Mechanism*

(1) The person sending the message calls the paging service office with the number of the pager and the message.

(2) The operator who takes the call enters the page number and the message into the computer terminal.

(3) A paging computer encodes the message in Post Office Code Standardisation Advisory Group (POCSAG) protocol.

(4) A rooftop antenna beams out the message using ultra high frequency (UHF) waves in the 425 MHz band width.

(5) Rooftop antennae or drop station relay the message to the pager through very high frequency (VHF) waves, using the unique band width for that company.

(6) Recognising its unique number, the alphanumeric paper picks up the signals, decodes it to digital form, and flashes it on the screen using letters and numbers.

(7) In case the target pager is a numerical one, it receives and displays numerical messages only — usually a number to be called back.

Other Communication Technologies

As discussed above, paging and cellular technologies are household jargon due to the media attention. But in addition to them, there are several other technologies that are now increasingly available in India. Some of these are:

* Anil Garg, *The Economic Times*, 30th March, 1995.

MARR: The Multiple Access Rural Radio (MARR), is a technology providing basic telephone services in rural regions. However, in India, it has not yet well spread.

VSAT: The Very Small Aperture Terminals (VSAT) as the name implies, are portable antenna dishes for communicating with other VSATs or a central hub station via a satellite channel. These are also meant to be inexpensive. But again in India, they tend to be quite expensive not only to buy but to install and use. Also their operation is limited to private networks with no interconnections allowed with the switched telephone network.

Networks such as RABMNm NICNET and the National Stock Exchange network in the country employ this technology for transmitting data between different locations.

CB Radio: CB stands for Citizen's Band. It is a set of radio frequencies that are available free for use to the public at large. While CB radio has been available in the West for decades, it is only recently that its use has been allowed in India. This is intended to give a long overdue boost in the use of radio technologies in low cost communication devices and services. It is expected to provide an inexpensive mechanism for people to communicate. In India, there is a requirement for a licence.

IMMARSAT — Mobile Communication: IMMARSAT stands for International Maritime Sateilite Communication Organisation. It was set up in 1979, its headquarter is located at London. It is an international organisation having 76 member nations. It is an internationally owned co-operative organisation which provides world-wide mobile satellite communication for maritime, aeronautical and leased mobile users. India is not only a member, but has a credit for being a founder member of IMMARSAT. On behalf of India, Videsh Sanchar Nigam Limited (VSNL) is the signatory to the IMMARSAT.

It has public switched network. It permits all direct dial telephone, telex, facsimile, E-Mail and data communications between mobile users and subscribers around the world connected to the international public switched network. However, the following are the objectives of the IMMARSAT:

(1) To serve the maritime community. It has subsequently expanded its services being the sole provider of world-wide mobile satellite communication for commercial and distress and safety applications at sea, on land and in the air.

(2) To render support services.

(3) To serve direct dial telephony, telex, facsimile, E-Mail and data communication between mobile users and subscribers.

(4) To service around the world connected to International Public Switched Network.

(5) It has specialised applications like automatic position reporting and High Speed Data 56/64 kbt/sec.

The INMARSAT System

The three essential components of this system are:

(1) Space Segment: The INMARSAT Space segment, comprising satellite and associated group support facilities.

(2) Land Earth Station: The Land Earth Mation (LES) which provides an interface between the space segment and the nationally and internationally fixed telecommunication network.

(3) Mobile Earth Station: The Mobile Earth Station (MES), the satellite communication terminals located on a ship, truck etc.

Types of Services of INMARSAT: *The mobile communication services offered by the INMARSAT have been classified into the following types:

A, C, B, M and P.

A-Service: It supports two-way direct dial telephone, facsimile, telex, electronic mail and data communication systems from anywhere to anywhere in the world, even in areas where local network and terrestrial communication are unavailable or unreliable.

INMARSAT-A is transportable and is thus a flexible communication tool which can be used for a variety of applications, limited only by the imagination, for instance, from sites of natural catastrophes. The terminal is also used for more general communication from remote sites like those at mineral exploration, construction sites, rural areas, news broadcast, surveyors and explores.

C-Service: INMARSAT-C is an advanced packet data communication system operating at 600 bits/sec, using a small, low cost mobile earth station suitable for installation in any size of vehicle, truck, car, trains or vessel-ship, yacht, fishing boat or at remote data monitoring and control sites, or carrying it in a briefcase by an individual anywhere in the world.

It provides two-way data store and forward telex, electronic mail, one-way position reporting and data reporting, fleet management, polling and distress safety services, to and from virtually anywhere in the globe. Enhanced group call (EGC) broadcast service able to address both groups, specific geographic areas.

B-Service It is an all-digital service that offers very high quality voice and telex communication. It will make very efficient use of the space segment and will offer a wide range of services with a facsimile rate of 9.6 kbit/sec, and a data rate upto 16 kbit/sec, over satellite channels. Optional services like 64 kbps HSD service is also available.

Both Land Mobile and Maritime Mobile users terminals are available for INMARSAT-M and B services. Both these systems have common protocols and signalling equipment, thereby greatly reducing the cost of equipment at fixed common site locations.

M-Service: The system offers all digital telephony, data and facsimile service through light weight, low cost terminate, which can be installed on motor vehicles, ships and small boats. This is also produced in briefcase sized personal version. The services are available for telephony (Digital Voice 6.45 kbts/sec), Group 3 facsimile (2.54 kbt/sec.) and Duplex data (2.4 kbt/sec). The speciality of it is the cost of the mobile terminals and usage charges. The user terminal weigh upto nine and 13 kg with a battery backup for emergency use. The approximate price for basic M terminal is US $ 17,000.

* *The Economic Times*, 30th March, 1995.

Global Pager Service

The world's first truly global personal pager is now under development at IMMARSAT. It is designed to operate via the IMMARSAT satellite system, the pager will be able to receive messages of upto 64 characters in length. It is compact, light weight and pocket portable with a signal strength indicators, saves on power and has sufficient memory to store messages. Services have options like tone only, numeric/alphanumeric message reception, call designation based on priority, protection against message loss and value added applications like market update, weather services and news.

Aero Service

This service provides two-way voice, data and facismile services for aircraft operating virtually anywhere in the world. For Aircraft Earth Station (AES), there are two kinds of antenna specified for use-high gain and low gain. The high gain antenna is used for high-speed data transfer, facsimile and voice communication. The low gain equipment can support low speed (data) packed more services only.

Hand-held Satellite Telephone-P

The advent of the hand-held satellite telephone -INMARSAT-P will be the realisation of one of mankind's ultimate dreams–the ability to communicate instantly and effortlessly to and from any place on earth.

Videsh Sanchar Nigam Limited (VSNL)

The Government-owned VSNL was established in 1986, maintains and provides India's Overseas Communication Services. The liberalised Policy permitted the country's main telecommunication system to be operated by the private sector.

But VSNL has been through its satellite, undersea and terrestrial links providing telecommunication services to its clients. It has been doing so through its four gateways at Mumbai, Kolkata, Chennai and New Delhi. It has leased telecom lines from Department of Telecommunication (DOT) and the gateways are interconnected through three lines.

VSNL is proud to shoulder the responsibility as the nodal point for overseas communications. It is located at the heart of the commercial capital of India, Mumbai. To sustain India's rapid economic growth in the new liberalised economy, reliable communication networks are a pre-requisite.

With its extensive infrastucture of earth stations, state-of-the art digital gateways, optical multimedia submarine cable and data switches, VSNL provides a range of basic and value added services. In the future, it is positioning itself to provide: Bandwidth on demand, Global Virtual Private Networks, ISDN, B-ISDN, VSATs, INMARSAT B/M and hand held Personal Communications.

VSNL's Services at Finger Tips

(1) Telephony with ISD to 237 countries from 2,400 towns and cities.

(2) High Speed leased line services (9.6 - 64 - upto 2 Mbps).

(3) Video-conferencing (Domestic, International).

(4) Packet Switching World Wide.

(5) Electronical Mail (The only company to provide domestic/international E-Mail Services).

(6) INMARSAT - A and C Mobile and Duplex High speed 64 Kbps Data Services.

(7) EDI-Electronic Data Interchange (The only company to provide Paperless Trading from India to destinations world-wide).

Development of Facilities: The first important stage was the establishment of the High Frequency (HF) Radio Station known as Beam Wireless Station in 1927. Dight, near Pune, was the transmitting station; Dhond was the receiving station with control at Mumbai. In 1933, the first radio telephone service was established with the U.K. Radiophoto made its appearance in 1943. During 1944, New Delhi HF Station began operating.

Major development after Independence was the establishment of regular H. F. radio stations at Kolkata (1955), New Delhi (1958) and (1960). Additional services like telex leased services, meterological services etc. began gradually.

The great leap forward commenced in 1970, with the establishment of the Vikram Earth Station in Arut near Pune. Seven years later, our second satellite earth-station began operation in Dehradun.

The wide-band submarine telephone cable system from Chennai to Malaysia over the IOCOM (Indian Ocean Commonwealth) Cable system commenced operation, followed by the troposcatter system in Srinagar, linking India with USSR, 1981.

The Prestigious Gulf Cable System between India and UAE commenced its operation in 1987.

The H.F. radio stations, except at New Delhi and Kolkata, were eventually closed down.

Modes of Operation: All international telecommunication services began in the manual mode of operation. With the establishment of (Penta Conta Typo) Cross Bar Telex (Telephone Exchanges 1972-73), semi-automatic services became possible.

By 1977, fully computerised, stored — Programme controlled telex exchange (GATEX) was established facilitating automatic dialing. Similar gateway systems were established for telephony in 1982.

For telegraph traffic, meanwhile, fully automatic Computerised Message Retranmission Systems (MRS) began by 1980.

Presently, the VSN operates through the four major gateways at Mumbai, New Delhi, Chennai and Kolkata. At Kolkata it is to proposed to have a satellite communication system. We have already fully computerised system for telephone/telex/telegraph operating at Mumbai, New Delhi and Chennai.

International Facilities Offered by the VSN

Telephony: Fully automatic access to over 175 countries/territories/ designations is available to an Indian telephone subscriber, on ISD basis. Other countries/territories are accessible.

Telex Fully automatic access to 183 countries/territories/destinations is available to an Indian telex subscriber on IXSD basis. Other countries/territories are available on manual or semi-automatic mode. We have also provided a store and forward (SFI) facility in telex service to select 24 countries from the metropolitan cities of Mumbai, New Delhi and Chennai. For full details of country code, one has to consult telex directory.

Telegraph: The MRS network facilitates automatic transmission and reception of telegram to and from practically all parts of the globe.

Leased Services: Voice-grade and telegraph type circuits can be leased by any Indian customer to a place anywhere in the world. Extensively used for Data purposes.

Private Message Switching System (PRIMES) is a leased facility available to an Indian customer having two or more international leased telegraph circuits, enabling him to contact national telex parties and foreign counterparts by leasing a 'port' in the system.

A 64 kilo per second (KBPS) INTELSAT Business Service (IBS) is operated by VSN on lease basis at Bangalore.

Television: Transmission and reception of International Television is carried out by VSN in coordination with Doordarshan.

Bureaufax: This service enables an Indian party to send or receive documents or pictures — black and white — to and from selected (27) foreign destinations almost instantaneously.

Radio Photo: The press and the public can either send or receive radio photos to and from Mumbai (to be shortly made available at New Delhi) enabling an Indian party to have simultaneous audio conference with up to 3 foreign parties.

Programme Transaction: This facilitates mostly Press correspondents to book calls to their headquarters abroad and pass on information either recorded or direct.

Multi-address broadcast service: This is used by the External Affairs Ministry to keep India's consular posts informed about India's position on various national and international issues.

Meteorological: This service, run, by the VSN provides data to the Meteorological Department for appropriate use.

Standard time and Frequency (ST & F): ST & F service is used by the National Physical Laboratory.

Press News Cast: Initially, it was leased by PTI for newscast to Tokyo and Kathmandu. Now, it is used for transmission by PTI to Afghanisatan, South East Africa and Burma.

Research Development and Training: The Company has a separate division at Pune for its Research and Development. A training institute provides post-entry and refresher training courses to all the engineering staff at operational level. The company plans to expand the scope of its training facilities shortly so as to include various other connected disciplines.

International Circuits: There are about 1600 telephone circuits, 1200 telex circuits, 47 pubilc telegraph circuits, 200 leased circuits (Voice, IBS and teleprinter type) and 65 Record Bearers in operation at present.

International Traffic (May, 1988): VSN handles daily over 1,50,000 international telephone calls, 60,000 telex calls and 12,000 international telegrams.

Telelecture: In oral communication, telephone is the most popular method. Telecture is an arrangement which enables a speaker or a lecturer or a instructor to communicate with several classes or meetings or conferences in different locations — simultaneously by using public telephone links. The best technique for making audio/visual presentation at a distance. With the arrangement of telephone department, there is hook-up from a speaker's office to a meeting place or class room or conference where visual can be shown while the speaker is heard. Telephone is used in distance communication to have interface between the speaker and the listener.

In many advanced countries, telephones are used in distance education to provide interaction between the tutors and students. In a country like India, where telephones are not within the reach of ordinary man, these cannot be used in all communications. With the help of two-way hook-up facility, members of audience can put questions to the speaker. There are countries which are using audio-conferencing and video-conferencing. For instance, in Canada, teleconferencing is being used in several education programmes, including professional development courses, in medicine, law, teacher education, health science, business and management.[50] In addition to the telephone being useful for teaching purposes, it can be effectively used to improve management and administration not only in educational institutions but also for efficient and effective communication in large business organisations.

It is a major problem for the top management to select the right type of these items, depending upon requirements.

Other Devices

Broadly speaking, mechanical devices used for oral communication which are in popular use are as under:

(1) Calling Bell, Buzzer and Coloured Bulbs: They are signal devices used for calling a person, calling a peon, attender or secretary.

(2) Speaking Tubes: They are used as a medium of internal communication.

(3) Dictating Machine: Dictating machines are used for the dictation of routine correspondence. Detailed discussion is given above.

(4) Telephones: Telephoning as a form of oral communication has been discussed above. Telephone communication has the following systems.

(i) Direct Exchange Line: It is related to receiver and exchange line.

(ii) Direct Exchange Line with Extensions: Big organisations may have extension facilities. Under this, there may be one or two exchange lines and a few extensions within the organisation.

(iii) House Exchange System: The system has a few exchange lines and many extensions. Operated with a row of bottoms. It operates outside calls to be made from the extensions and internal communication takes place between the extensions.

(iv) Private Branch Exchange: It is private branch exchange because there is a private 'switchboard' under the control of an operator. The board is connected with extensions in different rooms. Through the operator, it is possible to extend the call to any other telephone connected to the private switchboard. The same purpose can be achieved with the help of an automatic switchboard. It is called PAX Switchboard or Private Automatic Exchange. There is another method called "Private Automatic Branch Exchange." (PAXB).

(v) Intercom System: Intercom is a system of communication with an organisation by means of microphones and loudspeakers.

It facilitates quick verbal communication. Intercom system is more useful in an organisation having many departments or sections.

(vi) Electric Paging System: It is an internal oral communication system, useful when the executive move from one section to another section. Under the electric paging system, each executive is given a number.

(vii) Executive System: Also called House Telephone, by this system executives can speak to others more easily than through individual telephone numbers. They are connected with loudspeakers.

(viii) S.T.D.: The abbreviation stands for Subscribers Trunk Dialling. A communication system of making telephone calls in which people can call each other without resorting to the telephone exchange or without the help of the telephone operator.

(ix) I.S.T.D.: The abbreviation stands for International Subscribers Trunk Dialling. Technological developments in telecommunications are creating some international subscribers trunk dialling is a recent technological development in telecommunication. It is a communication system to sending messages and information by making telephone calls directly to the other countries without resorting to a telephone exchange. By this means, one can speak to anybody located in distant places like talking by a local telephone call.

Types of telephones: The telephone telecommunication devices as available today are:

1. "Base-free and dust-free telephones": These may be attached to the side of the desk or put in a desk drawer, freeing work space on the desk.

2. Cordless telephones: A box is installed where the telephone is usually placed. The telephone handset is battery operated with an FM transceiver which enables one to carry the handset within 300 feet from the box.

3. Signalling devices: A gong, bells, lights, and chimes replace the usual ring of the phone.

4. Dialling equipment: Makes dialling easier for the handicapped.

5. Privacy control: This enables one to deny access to the line in use on the extension phones. It also can be arranged for listening signals on the expansion.

6. Musical features: Often used with a paying system to provide musical background. A page system uses well-mounted loudspeakers.

7. Touch-a-Matic telephones: Provide automatic dialling.

8. New Switching system: Makes conference calls easier*.

Telephone — A New Education Technology

Telephone has now become a popular new technology in higher education. A telephone can be used as an instrument of two-way communication which provides two-way interaction between the learners and the teachers. Particularly, it is more useful where the students are disbursed or scattered over a vast area. This technique is also most usefully applied where experts in a particular field of subject are short. Two-way interaction is possible with telephone where there is a shortage of specialists. This technology is more popular particularly in developed countries. According to the World Bank Study published in 1982, the telephone has, in recent years, come to be used for direct teaching in the developed countries. The study has listed six different methods in which telephones can be used for teaching.

(1) Tutor-learner: When it is not possible to provide group teaching because of shortage of teachers or insufficient number of students, the learners are allocated to telephone tutors.

(2) Learner-Learner (Self-help): To facilitate interaction among the learners.

(3) Tutor-Learners in a group: In the case of shortage of tutors and long distances involved in reaching the learners, a tutor is linked to a class by means of a loudspeaker telephone in the study centre. The students can also communicate back to the tutor by means of a microphone linked to the study centre telephone. In this way, a tutor can cover several telephones and a tutor can cover several groups of learners consecutively without having to travel.

(4) Tutor-Learners in Several Groups: By this method, the teacher can lecture up to 200 classes or over 40,000 students simultaneously. This system has been successfully tried by the Wisconsin University in the USA for its extension programme.

(5) Conferencing (with tutor): This method can help in arranging telephone seminars without students or tutors having to leave their homes if they have telephones. Seven different numbers can be lined simultaneously with one another and every one can speak to and hear every one else. Alternatively, seven study centres could also be linked together.

(6) Self-help Conference Calls: This method is exactly the same as the above method, except for the absence of a tutor.*

The technological advances in communication affect written and oral communication.**

---

* Brown, L., *Communicating Facts and Ideas in Business*, Prentice-Hall Inc., Englewood Cliffs, New Jersey, 1982, p. 444.

* "New Technology in Higher Education," Association of Indian Universities, 1986, p. 22.

** Brown, L., *Communicating Facts and Ideas in Business*, p. 448.

Electronic Communication Media

A media with reference to communication for data transmission is any way by which information may travel. The data transmitter has to first select the channel to send data. Communication channels indicate media through which the information passes. The channel may be of any technological device.. Channels are hardware media necessary for communication through which data is transferred. Telephone lines, for instance, have been in use as a communication channel. Besides it, there are a number of both conventional and modern types of communication channels.

Bandwidth

The word 'band' relates to radio communication, indicating a range of wavelengths within a specified limit. In other words, the amount of data that can be transferred in a fixed amount of time is called bandwidth. The bandwidth is generally expressed in bite or bytes per second (bps), in case of digital devices. For analog devices, the bandwidth is expressed in cycles per second or hertz (hz). It is measured in mega bits per second (mbps) (10^6 bits per second) and giga bits per second (gbps) (10^9 bits per second). The Gbps is thousand times faster than Mbps and terra bits, therefore, a thousand times of Gbps transmission.

Bandwidth is the measure of the speed of communication operations. It is similar to a pipe's capacity to carry water, gas etc. In IT, it means the capacity to transmit data.

The broader the pipe, the more faster it can transmit or receive data. Similarly, the broader the bandwidth, the more faster it can transmit. Many Net-Savvy nations have over 10 giga bits per second.

Communication highways are data transmission channels. The functions of these channels are to carry data from one place to another. The channels are broadly categorised into the following three types: narrow band, broad band and voice band.

They indicate the rate at which data is transmitted. If the bandwidth of a channel is wider, it means it has more capacity to transmit data.

Bandwidth is a dream where one could have thousand times faster interaction with services available to the internet. They are:

Coaxial cables

Microwave radio

Communication satellites

Trans Atlantic coax

Trans Atlantic cables etc. which constitutes major components of bandwidth technologies.

Guided and Unguided Media

Transmission can be divided into two broad categories:

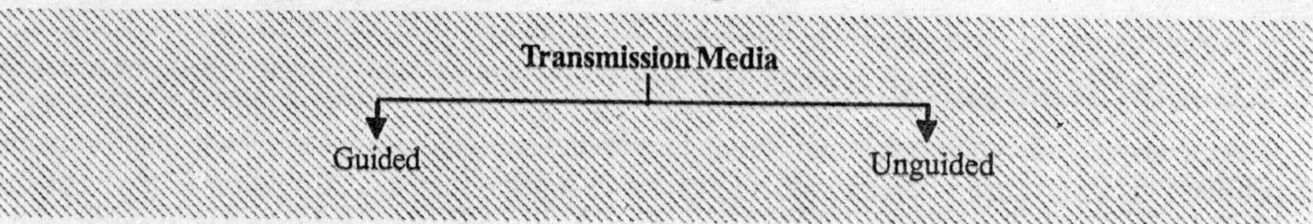

(i) Guided Media

The media that provides a conduit from one device to another is called guided media- It means media which uses the physical conductor for transporting electromagnetic waves. There is a physical limit in this media, because signals travelling always along these media are directed as long as the media stretches. It cannot travel beyond a physical limit.

The media that fall under guided category include: twisted pair cable, coaxial cables and fibre optic cables.

A. TWISTED PAIR CABLES

A cable is a length of thick strong rope made of wire. Pair means two. A set of two insulated wires are turned or twisted to make them into a rope. A turned par cable consists of two insulated conductors that are twisted together. The name suggests that it is a coiled wire of two insulated copper wires twisted together. A wire cable may be open lines or twisted pair cable. The advantage of this cable is that it provides better immunity from spurious noise signals.

Twisted pair cables are available in three forms. They are:

(i) Shielded Twisted Pair Cable: The cable has a metal mesh to cover the encases of each pair of insulated conductors. The case prevents the entering of electromagnetic noise and eliminates cross talks.

(ii) Unshielded Twisted Pair Cable: These cables are mostly used in telephone systems. They are mostly used for both data and voice transmission. A twisted pair contains two conductors each with plastic insulation and distinct colour. Colour is used to identify and distinguish a particular conductor in a cable.

Twisted pair cable is used for short and medium range telephone lines. It is more useful in the LAN system, Both wires pick equal interference. This cable is useful for communicating upto a distance of one kilometre with a transfer rate of one to two megabites per second. It is a low transmission rate applicable to telephone lines and narrow band local network. It is known for its simplicity. In the same cord, two wires are used forming a twisted pair.

(iii) Two Pair Open Lilies: A cable may be a twisted pair cable or two wire open line. It is known for hard wiring and simplicity and it is the simplest of all communication channels. The two wires of metallic form are made of copper or sometimes aluminium and each wire is insulated from the other. The measure is between 0.4 and 1 mm diameter. There are various types of this cable with several pairs of wire enclosed in a single protected cable. It is called a multi-core cable and it is moulded in the form of a flat ribbon. The wire open line is used for communication within a short distance, upto a distance of 50 metres. It's transfer rate is upto 19.200 bits per second. This cable is the oldest and still it is the common channel used throughout the world for both voice and data transmission.

B. COAXIAL CABLES

Open line and twisted pair cables have limited transmission rate and useful for communication upto a maximum distance of one kilometre. But they are not sufficient to meet the modern heavy data load and long distance requirements. In order to solve this problem, a new transmission media has been designed known as coaxial cable.

It is a cable which consists of small cables in a protected cover for protection from physical dangers and from electromagnetic interference. A new cable consists of a solid conductor running coaxially inside a solid outer annular conductor. The various cables are shielded within the cover. Dielectric insulating materials are used to fill the space between the two conductors. If the cable diameter is large, it means lower tranmission loss and assures higher transfer speed.

C. FIBRE OPTIC CABLES

Glass or plastic materials are used to make fibre optic cables. These cables are as thin as human hair. The cable consists of a glass or plastic core surrounded by cladding made with similar material. The glass fibre filaments along which data travels are high speed pulses of light. The light passes through the cable. The cable consists of strands of glass-like thread, each about a diameter of a human hair. Light waves give a much wider bandwidth than the electrical signal. Fibre optic cables are used to carry a great deal more data covering long distance. Its transfer rate is about 1,000 mega-bytes per second and can be used for long and medium distance transmission links. It has a variety of applications and virtually replaces copper wire cables in communication networks.

One or more hair thin filaments of glass fibre are wrapped in a protective jacket. Their feature is to conduct light pulses generated by lasers at a rate of 2 billion bits per second. Their capacity is much greater, it is about 10 times that of coaxial cables and 200 times greater than twisted pair wires. It may be mentioned that 1/2 inch diameter fibre optic cable has the capability to carry upto 50,000 channels, while coaxial cable has only 5,500 channels.

2. Unguided or Wireless Media

As the name indicates, an unguided media covers those that do not provide a conduit from one device to another. A signal travelling through unguided or wireless communication media is not directed and contained by the physical limits of the media like twisted pair cable, coaxial cable and fibre optics cable. The transmission media transmits electromagnetic waves without using a physical conductor. The signals are broadcast through air waves. The signals are openly travelling in the air and thus are available to anyone who has a device capable of capturing or receiving signals like radio.

The unguided media include:

- Radio frequency allocation
- Propagation of radio waves
- Terrestrial micro waves
- Satellite Communication and
- Cellular telephony

1. Terresterial Microwave

The Earth bound microwave systems transmit high speed radio signals in a line of sight path between relay stations. Terrestrial means living on land, on the planet Earth on which terrestrial species live.

A system of communication transmits microwave signals to transmit data without the use of cables. The antennas are usually installed on local peaks such as on the tops of buildings, mountains, hill rocks etc. The antennas transmit microwave signals. Microwave systems transmit high speed radio signals in a line of sight path between relay stations. Their range of transmission is restricted to about 30 miles. So to bounce the microwave signals, a chain of towers are located at intervals of about 30 miles on which dish like antennas are mounted.

The waves cannot bend with the curvature of the Earth, so waves are relayed via antennas placed on top of buildings, towers, hills and mountain peaks. The waves use the upper atmosphere as a reflective surface. The waves travel in straight line through the air, so the towers are located at intervals of about 30 miles distance within the line of sight from one another. The signals pass through the space in a straight line without any material obstructions such as topographical features, tall buildings, hills, mountains etc., and signals are freely received by the other dish antenna located at 30 kilometres away, which receives and amplifies and re-transmits by another antenna. The process is called relay.

2. Satellites

Satellite channels use electromagnetic propagation in open space. The advantage of these channels is that they have the capability to cover larger geographical areas. Satellite links use microwave frequencies in the range of 4-12 Ghz with the satellite as a repeater. Their data transfer rate is about 1,000 Mbps.

Communication satellites passing overhead are placed in stationary objects or bits about 22,300 miles above the Earth's surface. On the Earth, earth station satellite dish antenna transmit and receive data. Telephone signals and microwave signals are relayed to an Earth station for transmission to a communication satellite. In a global overseas communications system, satellites have become an integral part. There are a number of such satellites placed in the geo-orbit.

These satellites in space, orbiting in the Clarke Orbit are also used as microwave relay stations because they rotate at the practice point and speed above the equator which makes them appear stationary to microwave transmitters on the ground.

The International Telecommunications Satellite Consoritum (INTELSAT) has launched many satellites presently orbiting the Earth and handling voice, video and data communication. INTELSAT in 1965 launched Early Bird Satellite (EBS) which now forms a global communication system, meeting the requirements of long distance international communications covering over 100 countries. Communication satellites are like radio relay stations which solve the problems that arise in case of remote and isolated locations surrounded by oceans, mountains and other obstacles of nature.

3. Infrared

Infrared is the invisible and heat giving race below the red in spectra. The transmissions by infrared are optical in nature. They are carried by beams of light invisible to the naked eyes. Its capacity is limited to distances of a few hundred feet. Infrared operates outside the broadcast jurisdiction of the radio spectrum. Infrared application is suitable to local networks, its range is several hundred feet. The other features are line-to-sight, which are affected by weather.

4. Laser

A laser is a communication technology that generates an intense and highly controlled beam of light. Laser is used as a communication device which narrowly focusses beams of light, which are invisible to the naked eyes. There are separate receiving equipments and beams of light relay on these equipments. The normal line of sight transmission is 15 miles. Repeaters or relay stations are employed with a view to increase the transmission distance.

Fibre optic cables conduct light pulses generated by lasers at a transmission rate of about 2 billion bits per second.

This medium of application is suitable to local and area networks, its range extends between 3-15 miles, line to sight.

5. Radar

Radar is a system which detects the pressure, pollution and movement of solid objects within its range of sending out short radio waves which they reflect.

The word radar is the acronym of Radio Detecting and Ranging. High frequency radio waves are transmitted from a powerful device which scan the surrounding space by means and reflected by any object.

The word radar was first coined in 1942 during the Second World War by the US Navy. It is a device designed to gather information about a distance object. The electromagnetic waves are sent to the target and in turn the reflected waves or echo-signals are analysed. The transmission and reception of the high frequency waves are effected in the radar apparatus. The electronic circuits are used to deflect an electronic beam in cathode ray tube.

6. Radio

The word radio as a channel of communication does the work of process of sending and receiving data message etc. by electromagnetic waves without a connecting wire. A radio set is an apparatus used for transmission. Radio uses electromagnetic propagation in open space. Frequencies below 1,000 Mhz are radio frequencies. Radio waves are used normally for voice communication. Radios are more flexible, less expensive and permit portable work stations.

Its disadvantage is limited data transfer rate as well as very low-security.

Standard broadcasting for radios is AM and FM. AM stands for amplitude modulation and FM for frequency modulation. Based on the parameter altered in accordance with the information signal, there are three modulations.

There are eight ranges in which electromagnetic spectrum is divided. They are called as bands. These bands are broadly rates as

- Very low Frequency (VLF)
- Extremely High Frequency (EHF)

Being more precise, they are as follows:

- Very Low Frequency (VLF)
- Low Frequency (LF)
- Middle Frequency (MF)
- High Frequency (HF)
- Very High Frequency (VHF)
- Ultra High Frequency (UHF)
- Super High Frequency (SHFJ and
- Extremely High Frequency (EHF)

Radio waves are propagated. There are five different types of propagations. They are : Surface, troposphere, ionosphere, line of sight and space.

Television

In recent years, television has become the most popular mass transmission media. Radio is theatre of the mind and television is a theatre of home. It is an audio-visual medium. Television, a new technology, is a mass medium of communication having a distinct element of radio or visual characteristic in combination of audio and motion. Today television enjoys world over an unrivalled status as a medium of mass communication.

Experimental television broadcasting was started in United States of America in 1920s. The electric television tube was invented in 1923. Subsequently, picture tube, electronic camera and the television home receivers were invented. In the 1930s, TV stations were set up in New York and London.

Doordarshan, the National Television service of India, devoted to public service broadcasting, is one of the largest terrestrial networks in the world. The first telecast on Doordarshan originated from a makeshift studio of Akashvani Bhavan. New Delhi on 15th September, 1959. The first experiment with satellite technology in India, known as the Satellite Instructional Television Experiment (SITE) was conducted in 1975-76. It has a three-tier service structure namely national, regional and local.

The structure of the television industry is quite distinct from the radio industry. There are two sets of channels to operate television. They are Very High Frequency (VHF), called as older one, and more recent one that is the Ultra High Frequency (UHF). The picture or video is transmitted by amplitude modulation (AM), signals and sound called audio is transmitted by frequency modulation (FM) signals, The structure of the television industry is like the structure of the radio composed of network and individual stations. Thirdly, it is Community Antenna Television (CATV) Transmission. Presently, community antenna television is called cable television.

Integrated Services Digital Network (ISDN)

At present there are different wireless technologies available via satellite connections, T.V. service providers or cellular phone network.

Three new technologies that are gaining popularity world wide, promising faster connectivity are namely DSL, Cable and Wireless.

ISDN, Analog modems, Satellite and leased link technologies have been assumed traditional in this case.

ISDN was developed in 1976. To combine digital telephony and data transport service, a separate protocol is required. The protocol that combines these two components is ISDN. Since it is integrated, it is known as integrated subscribers' digital network. The object of digitalisation of telephone network is to allow the transmission of audio, video and text over the existing telephone lines.

The benefits of ISDN include:

(i) Standardisation of subscriber services

(ii) Provides user network services and

(iii) Facilitates the internet working capabilities of voice and data.

Data Communication (DATA.COMM)

Transmission of knowledge and ideas is the fundamental characteristic feature of a civilised information society. In this context, we are concerned about how information can be communicated, the modes. channels and media used through time and space. This is the objective of information technology-based communication systems to send and receive from one location to another destination (space) so that an activity can be carried on quickly (time).

The electronic-based techniques designed for transmitting data like optical, laser, wireless, radio, microwave, satellite, telephone of various types can be seen as a key element in data communication. Primitive societies used to communicate using drums, smoke signals, gestures etc.

In the information age, information is carried in data communication systems as electronic signals through circuits from anywhere to anywhere at any time, without boundaries.

To understand data communication, one needs to study elements and media, modes, channels, devices and the process of communication. Understanding data communication involves knowing four basic concepts such as data, signal, signalling and transmission. Data communication is the sharing of computational power of a computer along with various devices and channels available in the information technology environment. With the increasing awareness and need in exchange of information across the globe, the demand for data communication has increased in many folds. Information highways and information super highways have been laid down to facilitate data communication. Intranet, extranet, LAN, WAN, MAN, techniques are contributing to substantial global access to information and potential business opportunities. Fibre optics as the most advanced medium offers the potential of low cost, higher speed and greater capacity of data communication.

Elements of Data Communication

Digital and Analog Communication

In telecommunications, anything can be represented in one of the two methods. It means there are two categories of data transmission: Digital and Analog.

Whatever may be the original form of message, the actual transmission of signals may be either digital or analog. They indicate transmission of signals. In data communication one of the concepts that should be understood is the nature and difference between digital and analog signal and communication.

Digital

The digital representation of data consists of values measured at discreet intervals. The digital signals are discreet electric units transmitted in extremely rapid succession. It is like ultrafast telegraphy. The signals may take on only a discreet set of values within a given range.

The word digital means any system that depends upon discontinuous data or events. To transmit digital signals, digital transmission uses special equipment which transmits data directly into binary form i.e., binary code, binary number or binary digits. The digits are Is and Os or off and on.

Analog

Data transmission by analog is termed as analog communication. An analog signal is one which is continuous with respect to time. Its feature is that it may take on any value within a given range of value. Analog signals are produced by using separate devices. Human voice, video and music when converted into electrical signals produce the analog signal.

The analog method represents data which is continuous. In the early days, attempts were made to make computers using analog techniques.

An analog signal consists of continuous but variable electrical waves. For instance, telephone circuits and some scientific equipments are analog. The common use of communication channels like telephone lines are used in the analog mode. Telephone line serve as communication channels and the modes as the data communication device.

Analog Data and Digital Data

Data can also be either analog or digital.

(i) Analog Data: Human voice is analog data. The speech of a person is continuous wave in the air. A microphone captures waves and converts into analog signals.

(ii) Digital Data: A digital data is stored in the memory of a computer in binary numbers like Os and Is. A digital data is converted into digital signals when it is transferred from one workstation or computer to another computer.

Analog and Digital Signals

Signals can be either analog or digital.

(i) Analog Signals: In this, a signal is in continuous wave form which changes smoothly over time. When a wave moves from one value to another, it passes through and includes an infinite number of values along its path.

(ii) Digital Signals: The digital signal is discreet. It means it can have only a limited number of defined values say zeroes and ones. It is like a light being switched on and off.

Transmission Modes

Transmission of binary data across a link can be accomplished either in:

(i) Parallel mode—where multiple bits are sent with each clock pulse and

(ii) Serial mode—were one bit is sent with each clock pulse.

Where there is only one way to send parallel data, there are two subclasses of serial transmission. They are: Synchronous and Asynchronous.

Parallel Transmission

Computers can understand data in digital mode such as ones and zeros. The binary data can be organised into groups of 'n' bits each. When we send data 'n' bits at a time instead of one, this is called parallel transmission. It means use of n' wires to send 'n' bits at one time. Each bit has its own 'n' wire and all 'n' bits of one group can be transmitted. For instance, 8 wires are bundled in a cable with a connector at each end. The advantage of parallel transmission is speed. Its demerit is that it is limited to short distance. It is also expensive.

Serial Transmission

In this method of transmission, one bit follows another. In this method, one needs only one communication channel rather than 'n' to transmit data between two communication devices.

Communication within devices is parallel. Conversion devices are used at the interface between the sender and the line (parallel-to-serial) and between the line and the receiver (serial-to-parallel).

Serial transmission occurs in one of the following two ways:

(i) Synchronous transmission and

(ii) Asynchronous transmission

In serial communication, data is transferred in bits. Bits are sent one after another in a series along with the same wire. It means each bit is transmitted sequentially one after another. So this type of transmission requires only one pair of wire conductors for connecting and receiving and transmitting units. Serial transmission is slower than parallel transmission. It is primarily used for transmitting data between devices at the same site. For instance, any communication between computers is almost always serial in nature.

Synchronous Transmission

The bit stream is combined into larger frames which may contain multiple bytes without any gap between it and each byte is introduced to the transmission link. The receiver can separate the bit stream into bytes for decoding purpose. Simply the data is transferred as an unbroken string of ones and zeros and the receiver can separate into characters or bytes.

Each byte consists of 10 bits, of which 8 bits are data and 1 bit is for start and another is for stop. The transmission of each byte may be followed by a gap of direction of flow. This gap can be represented either by an idle channel or stop bit.

In synchronous communication, the mode of transmission of data characters are transmitted as groups. The data bytes are transmitted one after the other at regular intervals. The time interval between transmission and receiving each bit are precisely timed. The group of bits are made as identifiable characters.

Asynchronous Transmission

In asynchronous transmission, timing is not important. Data is transmitted and received by the agreed upon pattern. If patterns are not followed, the receiving device cannot retrieve the information. Patterns are based on grouping the bit stream into bytes. A group of 8 bits is a unit sent along the link.

Start bit is '0s' and stop bit is '1s'.

Start bit alerts the receiver about the arrival of a new group. The stop bit lets the receiver know that the byte is finished.

Therefore, one or more additional bits are used to start and to stop indication.

In this mode of transmission of data, each character is transmitted separately and at a time.

Transmission Modes

The word transmission mode means the direction of signal flow between two linked devices. There are three principal modes of transmission. The next step is the selection of direction in which the data should move. The user has to consider and select the direction of communication lines. The direction in which information flows over the transmission path is determined by the properties of both the transmitting and receiving devices.

They are: (i) Simplex (ii) Half-duplex and (iii) Full-duplex.

Their features are mentioned below:

(i) Simplex. The communication is unidirectional, as in a one way street. Only one of the two stations is on a link to transmit, and the other station can only receive.

Simplex mode of transmission permits communication only in one direction. In other words, the terminal may receive data but it cannot transmit or *vice versa*. The receiver device at one end receives the signals from the sending device only. It means the receiver can only listen but cannot talk back. This mode is not widely used for data communication. Its typical use is to the other data from monitoring device.

(ii) Half-duplex. In this mode of transmission, one station can both transmit and receive but not at the same time. When one device is transmitting, the other station can only receive signals and *vice versa*.

While vehicles are moving in one direction, vehicles going the other way must wait. In simple terms, in this mode of transmission, the entire capacity of a channel is taken over by one of the two devices sending signals at that time. Walky-talky and citizens band radio are the examples of half-duplex.

In half-duplex mode, the communication channel is used in both the directions, but only one direction at a time. It means only one party can speak at a time. This mode demands the receiving and transmitting devices to switch between send and receive modes after each transmission. There will be a change in the direction from one speaker to another speaker. For example, when one speaker completes his message, he says 'over', then the other speaker takes the turn to speak. It may take sometime to change directions from 1/20 to 1/4 seconds. It is similar to the citizen's band radio.

(iii) Full-duplex. It is a mode in which both the stations can transmit and receive signals simultaneously. It is like a two-way street with traffic flowing in both the directions at the same time. The signals share capability of the link in either direction. There are two methods for sharing transmission capacity.

- Link containing two physically separated transmission paths, one for sending and other for receiving and
- Dividing the channel between signal travelling in opposite directions.

Voice Communication over Analog Networks

Basically telecommunications networking is analog involved for the transmission of analog information in the form of voice.

Voice Data Communication over Analog Networks

In this, modems are used in all digital exchange over existing analog lines. The user can exchange both voice and data.

Analog and Digital Services to Subscribers

It is a stage of service to add the digital technique while continuing analog services.

Accordingly customers are classified into three categories. They are:

- Conventional customers using local loops for analog purpose.
- Customers using analog facilities to transmit digital information via modem and
- Customers using digital services to transmit digital information.

Integrated Digital Network (IDN)

The telephone authorities create Integrated Digital Networks to provide customers a variety of services such as Packet Switched Networks and Circuit Switched Networks.

ISDN

It integrates customer services with IDN. In this digital network, it is possible to send data, voice, image, facsimile etc., on over any digital network. Thus, the customers of ISDN will become digital wholly rather than analog.

The digital services are more efficient and have more variety and flexibility than analog services.

Encoding and Modulation

The data first must be transformed into signals before it can be transported across communication media. To begin, the data must be translated into digits namely zeros and ones using the American Standard Code for Information Interchange (ASCII).

There are four methods of conversion of data. They are:

(i) Digital-to-Digital Conversion. It is a process of encoding digital data into digital signals. The information in a computer is stored in the form of Os and Is. If it is to be transferred from one place to another, the data first must be converted into digital signals. This process is called digital-to-digital conversion or a process of encoding digits into digital signals.

(ii) Analog-to-Digital Conversion. It is a process of digitising an analog signal. The process of conversion of analog signals into digital signals is called encoding of analog-to-digital.

(iii) Digital-to-Analog Conversion. It is a process of modulating a digital signal. The digital signals produced by a computer is converted into analog signals. This is called digital-to-analog-converstion. Sending messages through telephone lines is an example of digital-to-analog-conversion.

(iv) Analog-to-Analog Conversion. It is a process of modulating an analog signal. Voice or music from a radio is analog signal. It is transmitted through the air. High frequencies are required to carry the signals. The process is called analog-to-analog conversion.

Communication Software

To facilitate communication between the equipments, a separate communication software known as communication software or package is used. Like other softwares namely graphics, word processing, spreadsheet, time management etc., communication software facilitates to speed up the flow of data from one place to another. It is a software that transmits data through the network of computers and workstations.

The data stored in one computer at one station can be transmitted electronically to other stations. The receiver need not be present at the computer to receive the data, the user can retrieve messages anytime at his convenience. The package also facilitates easier access to data stored in large online libraries.

Communication Protocols/Standards

The individual equipment or networking equipments have to follow protocols or standards in order to achieve the objects of data communication. Protocols are the accepted practice or procedure in the communication field. It is necessary to follow a set of rules laid down which is known as communication protocol or standard. It defines and sets a set of standards/rules which all the equipments of various brands want to involve in data communication.

There are several manufacturers of communication equipments, computer hardware and software, both inside and outside the country. Data therefore cannot successfully be communicated unless these equipments are compatible with each other. They should confirm to certain rules to work effectively. These rules are predetermined standard set rules codified in protocols. The set of rules is known as communication protocol or communication standards.

Communication Devices

There are several types of communication devices or interfaces in data communication. These devices facilitate exchange of data between equipments. They are connecting between sender and receiver hardware involved in data communication.

A micro computer is connected to the telephone lines by two devices. They are : (i) Adapter and (ii) Modem.

(i) Adapter.

There are two ways by which bits of information flow between computers. They are:

Serial. In this, bits flow in series. It is a common method used to send bits in a continuous stream.

Parallel. In this, each of the 8 bits make up a character which travels in a separate wire simultaneously. In order to handle the transfer of data between the computers and telephone lines an adapter is used. Adapter is a circuit board which handles the transfer of data between a computer and telephone lines.

A communication adapter may be used in two different forms namely: a built-into computer system and optional circuit board. The adapter connects to the outside world via a 25 pin connection.

(ii) Modem.

We also hear computer professionals referring to modem. The acronym MODEM is a short form of Modulator and Demodulator. It is a device used in computer relay communication system. Modem is, therefore, a piece of equipment of the computer and it therefore, comes under the category of computer peripheral family. It is an intermediary equipment capable of computer information to be transmitted to another computer. To transmit information, it is necessary to connect terminals to a computer via telephone lines. The digital signals of the terminal and computer are to be converted into analog form, which helps to transmit along with telephone lines. The modem device helps to achieve this.

In data communication system, there is a special device which is known as an interface element. 'It converts the discreet stream of digital 'on-off electrical pulses used by computing equipment into the type of continuously variable analog wave patterns used to transmit the human voice over many existing telephone lines. *(D.H.Sanders)*

In the voice communication system, the voice cannot be carried over a distant place over lines by digital pulses. The device Modem is used to modulate or convert digital pulses into analog signals. At the destination or the receiving end, another modem is used to a demodulate digital data which subsequently bridges the two locations.

Teleprinter

Teleprinter is a machine in communication system which is a specialised type of typewriter. It is a telegraphic system or instrument by which messages are sent out at one place and received at another place in printed form. The typing is connected to a telephone line and the messages typed at one place transmit electrical signals over the wire and the message is simultaneously reproduced, printed at a distant place by the machine. It is used as private circuit or through the post-office telex service system. The post office gives teleprinters on rent to form a part of private telecommunication.

A teleprinter is made up of a keyboard for data entry and a built in printer to record typed input produced by computer process output.

Portable Teleprinter

There are many small and portable teleprinters mostly used by:

- Salespersons
- Newspaper Reporters
- Engineers
- Managers
- Doctors and
- Lawyers and others on the move.

Small portable teleprinters have been widely used in recent years. These are mostly being used by sales' persons, engineers, reporters, managers, medical professionals and others who are always on move on their duties. For instance, the sales representatives can send sales orders to the head office. The terminal can be attached to the telephone and they can transmit information to the computer system by the company. It is the most convenient, easy in application and a time saving device to ascertain the stock availability and orders of the customers can be booked instantly.

If there is no stock, it is an alarming signal for the production manager to produce quickly according to time schedule. Thus, teleprinters facilitate communication from any remote location to the company's computer system by the sales representatives moving in the field. The battery operated portable terminals are also available which can be placed on the palm of a hand used to send information of sales to the computer. The small battery operated terminals have limited capacity and capability to receive data.

Fax or Facsimile (Transmission of Documents and Pictures)

Like messages, pictures can be transmitted by using a special machine known as Facsimile machine or Fax Machine. Under the electronic mail message system, an original document containing photographs, maps, charts and other drawings is transmitted by placing it in the fax machine. The computer-based facsimile systems are more useful in modern offices. The machine scans documents containing pictures and the receiving device reproduces the scanned picture or image.

Fax is a short form of facsimile. It is yet another public service device which has been more popular in recent years and as much its use within a short period has been widespread. Its importance has grown beyond expectation. It can be used for transmitting pictures, diagrams and images from place to place within a few minutes from anywhere to anywhere. A fax terminal appears like a small desktop electro-static photocopier. Its main function is to scan and print pictures, images, diagrams etc., on the same principle of the photocopier.

Fax has the facility of both transmitting and receiving documents. Some makers of fax machines have introduced the facility of automatic dialling, multiple polling, call reservation and transmission of documents of various standard sizes. This public service has grown in importance because images, pictures and diagrams can be transmitted from one place to another destination with terminals connected to a standard telephone line.

Transmission of documents and pictures instantly is now possible to any distant place electronically through a special computer related machine called Fax or Facsimile. A document or picture to be transmitted is to be placed in a separate fax machine. At the destination, there will be another machine called the receiving fax device. They maintain a communication link-up between both these fax machines located at two ends.

The function of the sending fax machine is to scan the document or a page and picture, while the receiving device produces the scanned document, picture or any image on the document. The transmission may be picture or text. The process is the result of the receiving device to produce a duplicate page or facsimile of the original document placed in a sending fax machine. There are low speed and high speed fax services. It looks like a photocopy of the xerox machine which reproduces the duplicate copy of an original document. The facsimile system enables a precise reproduction of the original document.

The difference between a xerox machine and a fax machine and their processes is that fax facilitates to transmit documents and pictures to any distant place including other countries within a few seconds. Thus, fax is one of the automatic machines which forms part of the automated offices particularly in large business organisations, service institutions like universities etc. A xerox machine reproduces duplicate copy at a stationary place, but cannot transmit to other places.

Though the use of fax machine has been there, in recent years efforts are being made to improve the working system by way of enhancing transmission speed and reduction in the cost of transmission speed. So facsimile system is designed to facilitate the user to transmit and receive documents and pictures.

Both the machines adopt synchronized scanning at the sending or transmitting end and receiving or receiver device end. The original document inserted into the sending facsimile means placement of document around a drum inside the facsimile machine. The transmitter or sending machine scans line by line. It is more fascinating to note how documents or pictures are transmitted at the receiving end. While scanning line by line, the resulting electrical signals are transmitted over telecommunication link to distant receiving stations. The duplication can be either on a paper or document.

There are two forms of facsimile systems. They are: Analog and Digital - which is faster than analog.

The process is a sort of electronic mail message service.

Presently in India, the telecom department is offering public fax service to the users to send a printed, written, cyclostyled page or pages of documents or pictures and images from anywhere to anywhere in India or even outside for a charge.

Fax Broadcasting

It is a special technology of a computer based faxing application that lets the user send the document(s) to many recipients or destinations automatically. In case of an ordinary fax operation machine if a document(s) of one or two pages is to be sent to 200 destinations or recipients, it requires to dial 200 different numbers and to feed the same document into the fax machine.

Uses and Advantages

The following are some of the business situations where fax broadcasting is useful.

(i) Stock Market. For fast and uniform delivery of time-sensitive and essential information like share prices, quotes and company results.

(ii) Sales. To communicate price changes, spreadsheet revisions, product introductions etc., immediately to all dealers and company offices.

(iii) Business Communications: Transmitting documents (like memos, circulars, requests for proposals or invoices) to branch offices, company representatives or vendors in diverse locations quickly and efficiently.

(iv) Advertising and Marketing: Distributing time-sensitive information like press releases, special offers and focussed marketing campaigns to a large audience.

(v) Crisis Communications: Where immediate dissemination of information can help save lives and prevent injury (drug recall or defective product alert, for instance).

Telephone Communication

The Printed Word and The Electronic Invasion

It was the invention of the "movable type" cast in a mould, using an alloy of lead-tin-antimony, by Gutenburg, a German, in 1554, that created a revolution in the medium of mass communication and introduced the term "printed word" which has become the most potent weapon in the fight against illiteracy and superstition and in spreading knowledge to every nook and corner of the entire world.

The traditional method of printing termed the letterpress, started by Gutenburg, using the metal type through the printed message, remained almost unaltered for over 500 years. Any changes that were introduced in the methods or techniques of composing were only in the mechanisation and automation of the type-setting process but not in the basic process of printing by the letterpress method. With the spread of books, journals and newspapers in the Western countries, after the industrial revolution, which required faster typesetting and printing; mechanisation of the typesetting process became an absolute necessity. From hand composing, an entirely manual process of setting individual types, the transition was to mechanical composition, that is, setting types with the help of machines.

Several inventors came into this field of typesetting machines between 1820 and 1889 but many of them could not stand the test of time. Only two machines — Linotype (1886) and Monotype (1887), both American, survived the test for fully automatic text-setting. With several improvements made constantly, they were serving the printers, particularly the newspaper printer, all over the world, setting types in all the languages in use. But with the invasion of the electronics on the communication media, during the 50s, these hot metal typesetting machines have become completely outmoded and in the advanced countries, they have been entirely displaced by computerised photo-typesetting machines. This technological revolution in the form of photo typesetting has entered the Indian scene also.

Let us examine briefly the origin of this electronic revolution in the field of communication and its impact on the printed world. After the World War II, there has been enormous growth in the amount of recorded information, especially in science and technology, which is often referred to as "information explosion." This is created the need for information for information storage and retrieval systems vastly different from the traditional method of the printed book which was too slow to keep pace with the information explosion.

One of the effects of this greatly expanded quantity of information is development of specialisation. There is so much to know about so many things that nobody can encompass everything known about a major field. Therefore, one tries to segment the field, learn it in summary or outline form and concentrate on a sub-field in detail, which is specialisation. As the information of every major field increases enormously and the areas of specialisation widen in greater proportion the traditional methods of storing the information in printed books becomes uneconomical and the stored information much laborious.

Thus, arose the obvious need for a new way of processing the information at a fast pace, which will also permit subsequent location and retrieval as quickly as possible. This was how electronics came into the field of information processing. Though originally the systems were developed with scientific and technical communication specifically in mind, these were further developed to accommodate other kinds of scholarly and professional information transfer. It is a new technology and a technological revolution, much of it electronic or related to electronics and computers. A whole range of new equipments, methods and techniques have been developed in the past few years for every segment of our system of communication through the printed word.

Though initially these changes were more technological than conceptual, the sweeping technological changes have already started encouraging new concepts and new modes of communication. Some of new methods and techniques are listed below:

(1) Electronic document creation and editing which includes word processing and computerised text editing.

(2) Photo typesetting with a wide variety of direct entry, on-line and offline computerised systems.

(3) New imaging and reprographic techniques such as electronic printing, microform publication and laser electrographic printing.

(4) Electronic communication, including electronic mail, electronic publication and electronic journals.

(5) New recording, storage and retrieval system like holographic storage, bubble memories and so on.

What is the impact of these electronic media on the printed word and what changes have they introduced in the traditional method of producing the printed product? The first of these has been to alter the nature of the basic product. In the traditional technology the printed word was the one and only product. But, with the introduction of the computer and the electronic media, the fundamental product was now a data-base. It was no longer the printed word but a precise, manipulatable, compact record which could be used with considerable flexibility or various applications, including that of the printed product.

The first impact is then the development of an electronic literature, a term used very loosely. The new technology makes possible ways of presenting information that were previously unthinkable — creating enormous user-searchable bibliographic and numeric data-bases stored in interactive computer system as well as electronic message systems. Publications such as dictionaries, telephone directories and trade journals can now be revised, updated, sub-divided and raised with a degree of flexibility never before known. Only the computers which drive the photo typesetters today make all this practical.

It is also now possible for the text or data-bases created on a word processor or computer in one location to be transmitted electronically to a compatible device in another location simply through the conventional telephone lines. An author, for example, can sit at home, use his word processor to create a machine readable record in the form of a magnetic disc, transfer, thus, text-data to the printing press located far away through the telephone lines and the printer, using an interface, can transfer these data to the photo-typesetter which produces the author's copy in the form of final page proofs. By this means, the publishers and the typesetting operator are both eliminated and the author directly produces the printed word and the printer carries out only the platemaking and printing in the press.

Phototypesetters and the Printed Word

Though the entry of electronics has vastly changed the printing machinery, processes and techniques, in a general way, its greatest impact is in the area of typesetting only. In fact, photo typesetters have not only revolutionised the typesetting process but have changed the very structure of the printing industry as such.

With the introduction of photo-typesetters of the first generation, in the beginning of 50s, we have come to the fourth generation of photo-typesetters in the beginning of the 80s. These are electronic marvels, very highly sophisticated and capable of things beyond the common man's comprehension. Many factors outside the printing industry have played a dominant role in bringing out these third and fourth generation photosetters. They include: computers, micro-computers, micro-processors, lasers, digitization of information, screen-based technology, including television and telecommunicaton.

What is a photo typesetter? To define in simple language, photo-typesetters are machine which produce images on photographic film or paper as negative or positive, in the design required for the printed page. They have suitable devices to store the characters, to select and expose them in the required size, form and measure on the film or paper.

The first generation machines (1946-50) were just the replica of the hot metal machines and the operation was mechanical.

The second generation machines hold negative film masters of characters in a disc or drum and use the optical system, such as zoom lense or turrent lens, to vary the type size. They were partly mechanical, partly electronic. The third generation machines are wholly electronic and use cathode ray tube (CRT) for the projection of characters. The characters are digitised and stored in magnetic discs. They can be electronically enlarged, reduced, slanted and emboldened. Digitization also provides the potential of producing pictures as well as text.

The fourth generation typesetter use lasers for imaging. Revolution is 1000 dots per inch and output speeds of about 1000 newspaper lines per minute can be achieved.

Today, we have a proliferation of these photo-typesetters that are manufactured with a system and modular approach so that a buyer can install a simple system according to his present needs and expand it periodically to suit his growing needs. The direct entry photo-setter is the simplest of these machines and an Indian firm has started manufacturing this in India in collaboration with the foreign manufacturer. Then we have the on-line systems, off-line systems and page make-up systems.

The common feature of all photo-typesetting machines is the input system to capture the author's words in the form of digital data, which can be manipulated and fed into a photosetters to produce the printed word. Keyboards are still the principal means of capturing the text, which are based on the 'Qwerty' standard typewriter layout, with a number of additional functional and command keys besides the usual alphabet, punctuation marks and numerals. In the off-line systems, the key-boards, which are attached to a central computer, directly or indirectly, are termed the front-end system.

Most of these systems were developed initially for use in newspapers as they have been mainly responsible for taking the initiative in changing over to the new technology. Today, the photo-typesetters have become the mainstay of the general printers too.

Future of the Printed Word

Will the printed word survive the onslaught of electronic invasion? There are skeptics who believe that there is no future for the printed word, produced in the traditional way for over 500 years. They predict that there will be a worldwide paper shortage in the next century and printing of books will be extremely costly and electronic publishing of both books and newspapers will be very much cheaper. Though the actual events based on the experience of the past may disprove this belief, it is still anyone's guess.

Some damage has already been done, displacing the printed word in several areas. Here are some of these.

Microform publication or Micropublishing and Microlibraries are the dreams of the future which may completely displace the printed book. The dream is of a library, housed in a catalogue cabinet. The ''microfiche book" is a development that has come to stay and the computer output of microfiche has enlarged its scope. As an indication of the space saving capacity of micropublications, a library in the UK contains some 58,000 pages of data on 880 microfiches, each 105x 148 mm. filled in a cabinet 7 in. by the printed issues could ever be. Hence, where continuous updating of information is essential, such as in legal, professional practice and financial compilation, microform publication has become an established competitively priced medium. Synoptic publishing and simultaneous publishing are two recent developments in periodical and learned journal publishing using microfiche.

Teaching and Learning without the Printed Word

With the phenomenal advance already made in the micro-computers and further dramatic developments expected, which will increase their capacity for information storage and retrieval at a much reduced cost, the micro-computer is potentially a teaching device and may become the teaching machine of the future. In educational settings, it will be used for information retrieval, information of different experiments and so on. Using programmed learning techniques and with its capacity for interaction with the learner, the microcomputer could eliminate the paper-based text or the traditional printed book, when all the students are enabled to have easy access to it.

For home-based education too, data transmission systems already developed and in use in the Western countries, like PERSTEL of the British Government Post Office, CEEFAX, ORACLE, BBC and ITV data systems would be used. When these are developed further as high power interactive systems, they will have many more possible implications for interactive systems, they will have many more possible implications for educational use. It is likely that correspondence courses of the future run by universities-institutes would switch over to such a system at the expense of need for the printed word since they can supply the texts, diagrams and equations on the video terminal and also offer an inter-active element with information storage and retrieval facilities.

Information and Communication Network[51]

A National Conference on Distance Education in India was held in November 1986, at Ahmedabad. Prof. Ram Takwale in his paper presented at the conference, covered information Communication Network. It states: "New communication technologies are helping in building up national and international Information Communication Networks and a new information order is getting developed. The Network has great capacity of storing, processing and transmitting information electronically, and anyone having access to the network can receive any information from anywhere stored in the network. Versatility and capabilities of the network are expanding with unimaginable rapidity. With the fifth generation computers round the corner, and such technological change in the offing, in which TV electronic tube may be replaced by liquid crystal screens, thereby reducing the size and cost of the television and increasing its portability and convenience, and the availability of more versatile satellites that would offer a large number of channels and would link any two locations on the surface on the earth, the stage is well set for revolutionary changes, which even the best experts in the field fear to forecast. The new information technologies have, on the whole, very specialised and centralised needs for the development of their hardwared. However, its mass production has made the product very economical. Further, the software developments, appropriate to local situations and requirements, necessary to use new technologies have given the technologies the common features of being economically versatile, having wider accessibility and decentralised nature.[52]

The new communication technologies, with the above characteristics, will generate creative processes and activities at various localities and will effectively contribute to the creation of knowledge, which itself will become decentralised in future.

Broadcasting (radio, television) and non-broadcasting (audio and video cassettes, computers, etc.) channels of communication network offer an excellent opportunity of creating an Educational Network. The educational network will essentially consist of storage of learning material in audio-visual and textual forms with linkages through terminals with the receiver.

Information Technology[53]

The recent information technology revolution has transformed a communication-conscious human society into, metaphorically speaking, an information-obsessed global village in the short span of just two decades. The course of development for the developing and the underdeveloped countries is no longer linear-sequential; it is increasingly characterised by leap-frogging wherein one or more stages are bypassed in order to arrive at the state-of-art stage of information technology. Today, our traditional concepts of 'knowledge' and information' call for re-examination. "Knowledge is power" is the slogan of 'this decade. Distance has been wished away, thanks largely to information technology. Sitting in our parlors, we joined million spectators at Atlanta during the grand spectacle of the Olympic Games. This was made possible by the video recording camera lens that extended the range of our eye. For the first time in human history, people from different parts of this planet can talk and see one another and be simultaneously watched by millions of viewers all over the world. Tele-conferencing no longer belongs to the world of science fiction; it is reality on our national TV network. At present, our children face an incessant "information blitzkrieg." India never had such generation of knowledgeable youngsters who quite often know a lot more than their parents. Information technology has come to stay whether we want it or not and its implications in terms of accelerated socialisation and learning are quite fascinating, sometimes even ominous.

The only opinion available to us is to ride this tigress of information technology and our skill lies in riding it to our advantage. "Knowledge and information" constitute the meeting point between education and information technology. If we understand the range of possibilities available to us through information technology, we may be able to understand better some of the constraints that have characterised educational endeavour throughout human history and which have circumscribed its range as well as effectiveness.

Like its mother 'science', "information technology" may prove a "faithful servant or a fiendish master" depending on how judiciously and to what purpose we successfully master it. Consequently, there is a need greater than ever before to perceive the entire gamut of possible/relationship between information and technology and education so that the former is made subservient to our needs.

Information, Education and Information Technology

Information experts now make a distinction between information and knowledge. Knowledge, consequently, is no longer the same as information. Information comprises data transmitted into a meaningful guide for specific action. Knowledge, on the other hand, is an organised body of information that facilitates insights and judgements.

To quote Stonier, "What is information at one level may be data at the next.[54]" Thus facts, data, information and knowledge constitute a hierarchical order. One of the imperceptible shifts in our social order relates to the fact that political power is increasingly becoming information-based, till the recent past, it was capital-based. Hence, information and knowledge are the grist common to the mills of education as well as to information technology.

Information Technology (IT) has meant different things to different persons. However, the consensus of opinion is more inclined to define IT as the technology that deals with "the collection, storage, processing, dissemination and use of information"[55] or "new ways of storing, processing, and transmitting information brought about by rapid developments in electronics, computing and telecommunication."[56]

UNESCO has defined IT as comprising "the scientific, technological and engineering disciplines and the management of techniques used in information handling and processing, their application; computers and their interaction with men and machines; and associated social, economic and cultural matters."[57]

This IT is not entirely concerned with information processing hardware and software. It is equally concerned with the fall-out that it generates in man's social, economic and cultural left. Distinguishing among terms like technology (i.e., total body machines and systems), artifacts (i.e., the interface between their native insufficiencies and demanding and complex millieu, coping (i.e., the manipulation of three essential resources—matter, energy and information) and manipulation (i.e., various processes encompassing, producing, processing, storing, transmitting and counting) as various aspects of IT.

Hamelink defines IT as "the aggregate of scientific/technical disciplines basic to the production of devices/tools/machines) and systems for the capture, transportation, storage, processing and retrieval of voice, text, numerical and pictorial information."[58]

The following survey of operations[59] related to IT as illustrated in the following figure should help us to understand its range, Contrary to popular belief, IT has three forms, *viz.*: Primitive; Intermediate and Super.

They are also called –

Low IT.

Mid IT.

Hi-IT.

IT provides the essential infrastructure for an unprecedented variety of human activities due to increased significance of resource information in various fields. Its effects are not limited to a section of society; it influences all people at all times. It has been hypothesized that "the most advanced stage of information society will be high mass knowledge creation society. The spirit of information society will be the spirit of globalism, a symbiosis in which man and nature can live together in harmony, consisting, ethically of strict self-discipline and social contribution."[60]

Education has all along been an activity related to a very sensitive area of human relationship, the development of children. Transmission of knowledge and information have been central to educational endeavour throughout its history. Expert and lay opinion might have different views about other purposes of education but so far as transmission of knowledge and information is concerned, they have been expected to enable its consumer learners to acquire maximum knowledge and information in the minimum time to promote the simultaneous progress of the individual and society. Education has occasionally been described as the knowledge industry.

Figure Operation x Devices Spectrum of IT

Operations	*IT Devices/Systems*
Capture	(a) Remote resource — sensing satellites
	(b) Radar systems
	(c) Electronic camera
	(d) VCR systems
	(e) Video discs
	(g) Optical character recognition
Transportation	(a) Coaxial cable
	(b) Optical fibre cable
	(c) Microwave link
	(d) Communication satellite
	(e) Cellular mobile radio

	(f) Fascimile transceivers
	(g) Videophone
	(h) Electronic teleprinters
	(i) Modems
	(k) Multiplexors
Storage	(a) Memory chips
	(b) Magnetic film/tape/drum
	(c) Holography
	(d) Inter emulsion
	(f) Microfilm
Processing	(a) Integrated circuits
	(b) Computer software
	(c) Peripheral equipment
Retrieval	(a) High definition television
	(b) Teletext
	(c) Videotex
	(d) Pay television system
	(e) On-line database/databanks

Source: *Studies in Distance Education*, Association of Indian Universities, and IGNOU, 1988, p. 93..

DEVELOPMENT OF INFORMATION TECHNOLOGY

TIME CHART

Pre-3500 BC	Signs and Speech
c 3500 BC	Earliest known writting (cuneiform);Mesopotamia
63 BC	Tiro, Rome invents a shorthand which is taught and used to record speeches
100 AD	Paper invented in China
C 300	First Parchment book
c 1450	Paper Mills in England, Invention of movable type in Europe
1476	W. Caxton, book printed in English
c 1590	Invention of Lead Pencil
1714	Henry Mill, Patent for a typewriter
1837	Samuel Morse (USA) produces first telegraph
1839	First British commercial use of electricity: Cooke and Wheatstone's telegraph lines open in London
1843	Principles of facsimile transmission patented by A. Bain

1852	B. Dancer, invention of microfilm
1867	James Maxwell proves the existence of radio waves
1868	Scholes develops his typewriter, forerunner of the modern typewriter
1874	Remington Corporation (USA) markets the developed Scholes typewriter
1876	First words transmitted on a telephone by Alexander Bell
1878	Bell predicts the current telephone network
1882	Vertical filing systems introduced
1897	First Cathode Ray Tube (CRT) invented by K. F. Braun
1901	Gugltelmo Marconi sends radio signals from Cornwall to Newfoundland
1913	Vaccum Tube Amplifier (The Value) Produced by H. D. Arnold. First Long-distance telephone cable laid
1920	First electric typewriter in commercial use
1925	John Logie Baird produces the first real television
1928	Baird demonstrates the first colour television pictures
1931	Page-printing teleprinter introduced by Creed
1936	British Broadcasting Corporation (BBC) starts the first public television service in the world
1946	ENIAC-Electronic Numerical Indicator and Calculator a the first modern electrically powered computer demonstrated, Pennsylvania, USA
1947	The transistor is invented by Britain and Barden
1949	First computer (EDSAC) with stored memory is demonstrated in Cambridge, England
1950s	Start of long-distance direct dialling of telephone calls. Photocopying devices on general sale.
1956	IBM Corporation develops computer disc drive
1958	First satellite radio message
1960	Laser light beam developed by T. H. Maiman (initials standing for: Light Amplification by Stimulated Emission of Radiation)
1964	IBM Corporation markets its Electric Typewriter with memory function — forerunner of word processing equipment
1966	ITT Corporation (USA) develops fibre-optics technology
1967	British Post Office introduces its Data Processing Service

1971	Intel Corporation (USA) produces first commercially applicable microprocessor. Floppy disc drive introduced for computer programmings.
1970s	Rapid development of microcomputer based equipment and systems-microcomputer, stand-alone word processor, optical scanner, etc.
1974	Xerox Corporation introduces the 'daisy' print wheel
1979	British Post Office transmits its Prestel viewdata service
1980	British Post Office begins to introduce its 'System X' Computerised telephone network
1981	British Telecommunications Act: Establishes British Telecom as public corporation separated from the Post Office. Also permits the introduction of private enterprise into telecommunications.
1980s	Developments in Information technology proceed space- more powerful microprocessors, area networking for electronic mail, experimental work on voice input into computer, 'wristwatch TV', improved 'bubble' memory for microcomputers, fibreoptic transmission of messages, work with electronics at "faster than light speeds", widening of information technology education in Great Britain from primary schools upwards."

Factors in Selection of Technology

The various types of technologies and mechanisation of communication system etc. have been discussed in the subsequent chapters. There are several media of oral and written communication. It is the responsibility of the management to select appropriate technology to suit its own requirements depending upon circumstances. Each technology has its own advantages and disadvantages.

Therefore, no one technology is useful for all types of organisations. A combination of technologies can be used depending upon the circumstances. One technology supported by the other would help in a great way in effective communication process. The management has to consider a number of factors for selecting the media suitable to its own requirements as against various technologies as available. The following factors may be considered for the selection of the technology.

(1) Availability: The technology is to be available with qualified and trained manpower.

(2) Accessibility: The media selected should be available both to the sender and receiver. Ready access to the technology is necessary.

(3) Acceptability: The success of technology is dependent upon the users. There must be favourable attitude on the part of senders and receivers of messages.

(4) Economics: The technology cost should be low. If it is very expensive, all organisations may not install it. The technology so selected must be appropriate for transmitting messages.

(5) Elasticity: Flexibility of use of technology to meet the changing needs and use for various types of work in offices govern the choice. It is to adjust to the requirements, while the work cannot be adjusted according to the technology too.

(6) Saving Time: The objective of installing machines is to reduce labour time. Saving of time is a more important factor. Machines have more capacity, speed and can do work of more than an individual labour. The extent to which a machine can save time is the principal question before management.

(7) Services: Repairs and maintenance of a particular technology, its recurring cost and availability of expertise people to render service to the machine criteria to be borne in mind. The problem of repairs particularly in respect of imported technology is more serious.

(8) Drudgery: Communication is a continuous process. It is a very hard and humble work. The persons drudge just all the days for remuneration. The work is monotonous and repetitive. The communication technology should reduce the monotony and drudgery of the employees.

(9) Continuity: Consistency in communication is necessary. The principle of continuous utilisation of technology is to be considered. It should be capable of being used in all departments of its being used continuously.

(10) Accuracy: The purpose of communication is to make the receivers to understand the matter. The correctness of transmission and reception are indispensable for effective communication. The feature of accuracy is expected from technology. To err is human, but not so with a machine. So, information technology must promote accuracy.

A brief account of various media of new communication technologies in verbal and written form has been presented in the second and the third chapters.

Advantages of Mechanisation of Communication

(1) Time Saving: New communication technologies avoid errors, duplication, resulting in saving of time. They have more speed with accuracy and can transmit quickly. The message load which the machine can do is definitely more, resulting in saving of time of superiors and subordinates in the organisation.

(2) Saving Labour Cost: Message transmitting machines not only save time but also cost. They are labour-saving technologies and they save the payroll cost.

(3) Labour Saving: New communication technologies are labour saving devices. They save labour. Use of labour-saving devices is possible under new technologies. Less number of workers are sufficient with the installation of devices. The workers thereby released can be utilised for alternative work.

(4) Speed: A large quantity of information can be fed into the machines which in turn transmit with considerable speed. In respect of certain matters, speed and quickness are necessary to take quick decisions. The handling of transmission if assigned to electrically or electronically or radio-wave operated machines, which are known for greater speed of despatch, will help speedy and quick decision-making.

(5) Reduce Monotony: Routine repetitive work may lead to fatigue or monotor Mechanisation of communication reduces fatigue of the employees, resulting in improving t efficiency and quality of the work. For instance, the use of visual and audio-visual aids will redu fatigue and improve the quality of work.

(6) Standardisation: Standardisation of work can be achieved through machines. They ensu consistency, uniformity in the quantity and quality of work. The principle of standardisation is s important that no one can afford to ignore its advantages. The office records become uniform wi the use of machines and give better appearance and promote goodwill outside.

(7) Minimises Fraud: In mechanisation, there is no scope for fraud, misrepresentation an infiltration of information. Use of new technologies, therefore, eliminates the chances of fraud. A machine can be readily trusted on its installation. Franking machines, dictaphones, cablegrams an other telecommunication services, etc., the use of which can avoid fraud.

(8) Quick Reference: Machines supply the management with the required informatio promptly and quickly. This is a great help and enables one to make quick decisions, control and co-ordination.

(9) Accuracy: Correctness of message transmission is necessary to enable the receiver to understand in the same spirit and to act accordingly. The systematic and automatic technologies promote accuracy. Human errors are bound to be there in non-mechanical routine communication.

(10) Other Merits: Employees may welcome mechanisation of communication system. Machines in general increase in communication efficiency. The installed rated capacities can be fully utilised with the increase in message load. In simple words, machines are used in problem-solving matters, communication intelligence and for processing of statistical data.

Disadvantages of Mechanisation of Communication

There is no doubt that mechanisation of communication ensures the speed, accurate transmission and message load handling potential. Communication mechanisation and automation has disadvantages too. The following are some of the disadvantages associated with mechanisation:

(1) Cost: The cost factor cannot be ignored in mechanisation of communication. It involves both prohibitive installation cost as well as recurring maintenance cost. Hence, small offices may find it difficult to afford.

(2) Under Utilisation: Installation of machines and their use may not be economical. The rated or installed capacity may not be utilised to the fullest possible extent. Sometimes, certain machines are used in one department only for a limited or fraction of the working time. So, a machine installed should be useful to all the departments and utilised by all the departments. As far as possible, idle capacity of machines should be avoided.

(3) Less Flexible: The disadvantages identified is that by introduction of machines, the office systems will become less flexible. So, to utilise its capacity to the fullest extent, the office systems should be adjusted to suit the machine because mechanisation once commenced cannot be adjusted without cost according to system.

(4) Need of Operators: Some of the machines require expertise for operation. The work will suffer, machine will remain idle if the operator is absent.

(5) Expensive: Besides cost of installation and maintenance cost, use of office machines involves additional expenditure. Use of machines means standardisation of correspondence. Additional expenditure is towards special type of stationery, printing, training, high salaries etc.

(6) Do Not Work Without Intelligence: Machine is only an artificial intelligence or mechanical intelligence. Machines cannot work without human intelligence. For instance, a counting machine still requires an accountant.

(7) Replacement: Modernisation, renovation and replacement of machines often take place due to technological innovations. By the passing of time, machines may become obsolete and the machines and their methods may be outdated.

(8) Noise: Some machines may create and may disturb routine office work.

(9) Unemployment: Automation and mechanisation may create unemployment which the employees may oppose. This is the main cause for their resistance for automation of office work.

(10) Other Problems: Occurrence of errors in transmission of messages cannot completely be overlooked. The problems of transferring, educating and training cost are other factors. Work load cannot be forecast with considerable degree of accuracy before installation. The monotony of doing routine work will set in. Chances of fraud cannot be found because of technicalities.

REFERENCES

1. Gillman, J.A., *Information Technology and the School Resource Centre* (London Council for Education Technology, 1983) p. 11.
2. "National Policy on Education", 1986, Government of India, Ministry of Human Resource Development, p. 22.
3. Longton, Gould and Marks, *Management Communication Through Audio- Visual Aids*, Leonord Hill, London, 1966, p. 29.
4. *Ibid.*, p. 33.
5. John, S. Wright *et al.*, Advertising, McGraw-Hill Book Company, New York, 1977, p. 450.
6. Maurice I. Mandell, *Advertising*, Prentice-Hall Inc., Englewood Cliffs, New Jersey, 1974, p. 489.
7. Thomas Blaine Stanley, *The Technique of Advertising Production*, 2nd ed. (Englewood Cliffs, N.J., Prentice-Hall, Inc., 1954), p. 50.
8. Longton, Gould and Marks, *Management Communication Through Audio- Visual Aids, op. cit.*, p. 40.
9. Draper Daniels, *Giants, Pigmies and other Advertising People*, Crain Communications, Chicago, 1974.
10. Longton, Gould and Marks, *op. cit.*, p. 171.
11. *Ibid.*
12. Gough, J. E., and R. J. McDonald (1981), "Audio Cassettes as an Educational Medium in Distance Education", Paper presented to RSDTA, Penang (Malaysia

13. Gwynn, Robin (1981), 'Tutorials Without a Tutor: Encouraging Student- Student Contact at a Distance", a Sena Forum Papers. As quoted in Studies in Distance Education, *op. cit.*, p.103.
14. Balan, K. R., *Lectures on Applied Public Relations*, Sultan Chand & Company, New Delhi, 1984, p. 351.
15. *New Technologies in Higher Education*, Association of Indian Universities, 1986, p. 51.
16. *Ibid.*, pp. 50-51.
17. Grove Michael, 1984, "The Interactive videodisc in Education and Technology," 1984-85, London, Kogan, page, As reported in *Studies in Distance Education,* Association of Indian Universities p. 97.
18. Zorkoczy, P., *Information Technology, An Introduction,* London, Croom Helm, 1982.
19. "Studies in Distance Education", *Association of Indian Universities.* 1988, p. 106.
20. Antoni, *Learning at a Distance, A World Perspective,* p. 290.
21. *Studies in Distance Education, op.cit.*, pp. 95-96.
22. *Ibid.*, pp. 105-106.
23. Antoni, SGD, *Learning at a Distance, A World Perspective, p.* 287.
24. "New Technologies in Higher Education," *op.cit.*, p. 105.
25. *Ibid.*, p. 104.
26. Yewdall, G.A. and others, *Management Information,* Pan Books Ltd., London, 1971, p.188.
27. Potter, Geoff, "Satellite-Based Distance Education: Problems and Solutions," Paper Presented to RSDTA, Penang (Malaysia), 1981.
28. Griffin, C.C.M., "Moral Ties and Satellite Networks: Creating Community for Distance Learning Across Cultures of the South Pacific," Paper Presented to RSDTA, Penang, (Malaysia), 1981.
29. "New Technologies in Higher Education", *Association of Indian Universities,* AIU House, 16, Kotla Marg, New Delhi, 1986, p. 27.
30. "Studies in Distance Education, *"Association of Indian Universities,* 1988, pp. 97-98.
31. "New Technologies in Higher Education", *op.cit.*, pp. 40-48.
32. Hussain & Hussain: *Information Processing Systems for Management,* Richard D. Irwin, Inc., Homewood, Illinois, Irwin-Dorsey, Ltd.,Geogetown, Ontario, 1981, p. 3.
33. Donald H. Sanders, *Computer Concepts and Applications,* Mc-Graw-HiU International Edition, Computer Science Series, 1987, p. 14.
34. *Ibid.*, p. 114.
35. Myers and Myers, *Managing by Communication: An Organisational Approach,* McGraw-Hill International Book Company, 1982, p. 15.
36. Donald H. Sanders, *op.cit.*, p. 533.
37. Hussain & Hussain, *op.cit.*, p. 584.
38. *Ibid,* p. 16.
39. Jerome Kanter, *Management Information Systems,* Prentice-Hall of India, Private Limited, New Delhi, 1987, p. 1.
40. Donald H. Sanders, *Computer Concepts and Applications,* 1987, p. 372.
41. *Ibid.*, p. 376.

42. *Ibid.*, pp. 375-376.
43. *The Hindu,* 29th August, 1994.
44. *Ibid.*
45. Donald H. Sanders, *op.cit.*, p. 378.
46. *The Hindu,* 29th August, 1994.
47. *Ibid*
48. Robbins, S.P., *Orgnisational Behaviour,* Prentice-Hall of India Private Limited, New Delhi, 1991, p. 255.
49. Sandeep Dikshit, *Waiting for Cellular Connection, The Hindu,* 29th August, 1994.
50. New Technologies in Higher Education, *op. cit.*, p. 15.
51. Association of Indian Universities and Indira Gandhi National Open University, New Delhi, 1988, p. 28.
52. Ram Takwale, *INSAT-IB and Higher Education,* University News, Vol. XXn, March, 1984, pp. 1-4.
53. Paper presented at National Conference on Distance Education in India, 1986, Ahmedabad, by Prof. Ram Takwale, Published in Studies in Distance Education. Association of Indian Universities and Indira Gandhi National Open University, New Delhi, 1986. pp. 91-94.
54. Stonier, T., *The Wealth of Information.* London. Thames Methuen. 1983, p. 19.
55. Chartrand, R.L., and Morentz, J.W., *Information Technology Serving Society,* London, Pergamon, 1979.
56. *New Society,* Dec. 1982, p. 2.
57. "Further Education Unit, Information Technology in Further Education," *Occasional Paper,* London, FEU, 1984.
58. Hamelink, C.J., *Information Technology and The Third World,* A paper presented at XV IAMCR Conference on 26th Aug. 1986, at New Delhi, p.2.
59. *Ibid.*, p. 3.
60. Masuda, Yoneji, *The Information Society As Post-Industrial Society,* Tokyo, Institute for Information Society, 1980, p. 33.
61. Demond W. Evany, People, Communication and Organisation, Pitman Publishing London.

*****

CHAPTER 15

Networking Communication

Nature and Evolution

Internet is the most efficient platform for accessing information and the potential marketplace today. It allows the customers to place an order simply by logging on to buy and sell things and placing the it..ns they need in an electronic based medium without leaving their chair. E-commerce has opened up new communication pathways for promoting brands, supporting sales of products processing and generating responses from users.

Since the cost of selling up in an e-commerce e-store is considerably less than the real world equivalents, small and medium-sized companies are in a position to compete effectively with larger organisations. The Internet has relatively low cost of information delivery and can be revised and updated with new pricing and enabling users to access information within minutes with the click of the mouse.

Customers are appreciating the security of the Internet which ensures further increase in the growth of sales. The Web is at the crossroads in its evolution, moving towards making the world a global village, spreading information like lighting. Web merchants who experiment with contemporary and new technologies have the opportunity to grow with the web and become business giants with a global presence. Web information technology (WIT) offers a variety of e-commerce sites for small businesses all the way to the large retailers. It provides facilities like shopping cart, security, cyber cash processing, on-line catalogue and customer database.

Internet is the borderless medium, offering awesome potential to organisations and individuals to do business on-line. Technology has allowed companies to automate many day-to-day business practices. Strategies to use the new technology should be exploited on the website for substantial financial returns.

A significant change is being initiated in the global business arena, with the internet as the catalyst for various domains ranging from various internet applications to multimedia and in the process, unearthing tremendous potential for development services for the *'forces'* of the information age.

The global canvas of the Internet and the growing speed and importance of computers have developed a global village comprising of customers and the business fraternity. Today, the most revolutionary development is of the world wide web and the Internet, enabling millions around the world to access the Internet. The growth statistics show extension of the Internet at school, at work, as well as in the home where the personal computers reign supreme.

The number of Internet users are multiplying and mushrooming at a fast pace. The total number of internet users is roughly doubling every year. The trend shows that the rate of growth seems to be actually increasing exponentially. There is almost a gold rush environment as far as the internet application is concerned.

Towards the end of the 1990s, the Internet was dominated by academics, students and other university subjects, especially science and engineering.

Things have fast changed, and as late as 1994, the word Internet drew blank stares from most people. By 1997, business people are investing substantially in the application world wide web.

Thus, the Internet is a worldwide mega network of smaller and larger interconnected computer networks.

The Internet represents a genuine revolution in global communication and substantial data exchange. The new revolution has opened unique and exciting opportunities to maximise marketing efforts of business firms and merchants both internally and externally. It provides an access to the vast wealth of information and services available online. It has left an impact on all industrial companies, products or services. Though the technology may be new, the fundamental goals remain the same — that is to effectively expand the marketing and customer areas profitably and in a cost effective way. Today's interactive technologies permit various businesses to achieve goals and objectives in the global business environment.

According to NASSCOM, the number of Internet connections in India stands at 2,80,000 as in the year 1999. The number of people using it stands at 8,00,000.

The Internet economy is creating new sets of dynamic design points yielding new challenges and potential opportunities. In tune with the changes, IT has also been evolving new digital business designs which go beyond the image of selling products on the Net. Businesses are making money with potential online business.

The Net is emerging as a leading business information channel. The number of worldwide web users is fast approaching the 200 million mark.

Today, major corporations are rethinking their business strategies in terms of the Net and its new culture and capabilities. Companies are using the Web by buying parts and supplies from other companies to collaborate on sales promotions and to do joint research. Exploiting commerce, availability and appreciation of the Net by global business, has enabled many companies to discover potential strategies to use the Net successfully.

The emergence of new technological innovations in industry and trade usually occurs first in developed countries and moves to the developing countries. The technology transfer continues to be from the first world to the third world countries. Some technologies move fast and some others move slowly. Thus, if we consider the trends in e-commerce development and the predictions of these developments in the advanced countries, we can expect its arrival in the third world country only later. E-commerce developments are expected to be only evolutionary and not revolutionary in nature. This means that no path-breaking or potential innovations that will revolutionise the economic world are likely to take place. To enable such innovations, companies will have to work out potential business strategies.

E-commerce activities have made more progress in the recent years. Trade net, EDI, Nicnet and many other networking organisations have been established. The national economic and telecommunication agencies like VSNL are offering access to the international community by dedicated lines. More and more advanced facilities are equipped to identify the potential foreign markets and interchange appropriate business data electronically. In the beginning of electronic trade, the existing communication network, fax, telegram, telephone, e-mail and WAN are widely used. The Net has become the fastest growing communication and advertising method in the recent years.

CONCEPT OF NETWORK—MEANING AND NATURE

The word 'Network" means anything in the form of a Net which may have many lines crossing each other. A network in connection with the computer environment means 'link' between a number of computers within the organisation and outside. Computer network is a series of interconnected points or channels communicating with each other. An interconnection of a number of computers and/or peripheral devices at distributed locations that transmit information necessarily to perform the functions of the network are potential business standards.

The interconnections are the sum total of various channels and is known as the computer communication network. Thus, a well knitted computer network envisages multi-channels. So, it represents an integrated operating system. A modern complex organisation may have many disseminating centres interconnected by various centres and reflects a potential network.

Computer Networking

Computer network is a mechanism of a collection of a set of computers and network components which are interconnected by communication lines. When they are connected, the system permits network computers and components to communicate and work together. The individual computers in a network system may be distributed within a small office, building, premises or distributed over a large geographical area. There are two separate systems of networking depending upon the location of computers. When the computers are located in a private and limited compact area, it is a local area network (LAN) and when computers are located over a wide geographical area, it is a case of wide area network (WAN).

In recent years, networking has increasingly become common. A computer network is a complex process having two or more computers interconnected. A networking is the capability of the computer which permits to link computers together. The object of this linking is to facilitate communication between computers and information can be exchanged between this interlinking. This interlinking of computers is more useful when the information is to be altered and updated for strategic decision making, control etc., where the computers are at separate locations and they can be interconnected and used simultaneously. The electronic means help the data being sent to and from between the computers and this is known as networking system. In other words, it is also called as point to point data transmission. Thus, any number of computers can be interconnected to constitute a processing complex in such a way that they can exchange messages or relevant business data. Thus, the linked computers in a network function by sending and receiving messages to each other. Thus, a set of two or more computers interconnected strategically work together as a single unit. From the viewpoint of the users, it is only a single computer unit but not a set of more computers, though there is more than one individual computer in the network. It is a sort of interconnected and interrelated set of independent and individual computers.

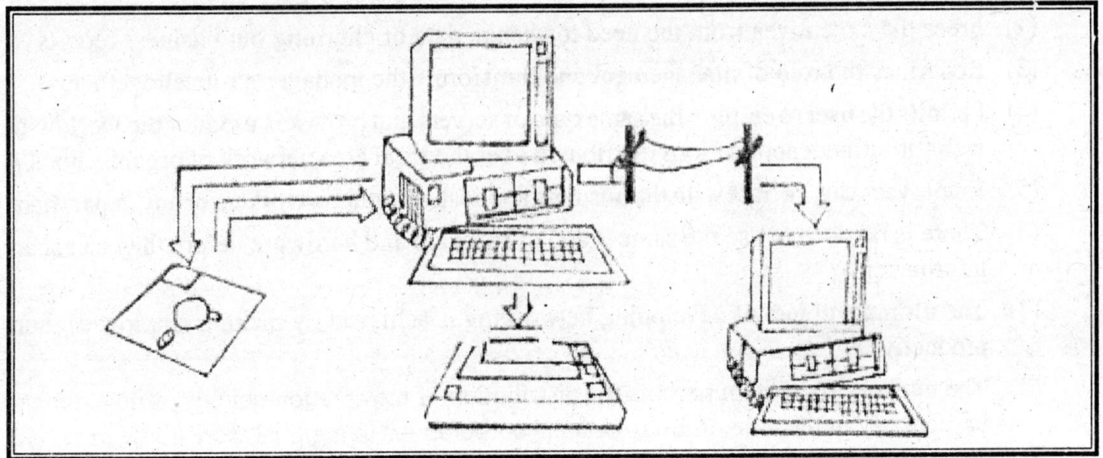

Fig. 15.1 A Network with Communication Links

It is a system having sub-systems linked with several computers. It is an interface between the computers which are linked. The network facility gives an opportunity to get the computer to talk to another computer. It is the cable with the help of which computers are interconnected.

Modern communication technology permits building up local, national and international networks for effective information communication. The network has great capacity of storing, processing and transmitting information electronically, and anyone having access to the network can receive any information from anywhere in the network.

Origin of Networking

It was approximately in the 1960s that intensive research works were undertaken with linking computers to one another and to people through telephone hook-ups. As a result, computers in different locations can be linked using new technology known as *packet switching*.

In the 1970s, a number of developments took place, witnessed the development of rules or protocol for transmitting data between computers and networks. These facilitated the development of the world wide web. Thus, all computers have links in terms of LAN and WAN. By the end of 1970s, these links were developed between counterparts throughout the world. Today, the world is tied together in a worldwide web.

In the 1980s, the group of networks collectively became to be known as the Internet. As a result, a number of individuals, organisations, companies, research institutes, universities and other educational institutions, government departments, agencies, consultants etc., started investing to have a presence on the world wide net. Under this system, anyone with a computer and a modem can tap into the potential online business opportunities.

The 1980s is said to be the decade of networking in the history of information technology with both LANs as well WANs working successfully. Thus, there are two types of industries namely LAN manufacturers and WAN manufacturers. In the 1990s, it witnessed a period of progress, a generic marketplace and overlapping product sets. It is a decade of enterprise-wise management.

Features of Networking

(1) It facilitates to have external communication with outside organisations.

(2) Frees the executives from the need to change data or churning out business reports.

(3) Redefines the role of management and transforms the manager's role altogether.

(4) Permits the user to employ the same type of servers and browsers used for the worldwide web for intranet applications distributed over the local area network of organisations.

(5) Employees can interact with the business applications and co-workers of any department.

(6) There is no need to use the same brand of software and hardware before they can share information.

(7) The ultimate object of developing networking is achieved by making employees more productive.

(8) The networking system permits the distribution of information quickly, efficiently and particularly in the case of multi-national corporations to a global work-force in several countries.

(9) Web-based intranet helps to reach the goal of simplification of information sharing,

(10) Makes global work-force of transnational organisations more cohesive.

(11) The information is always online, it is real time and constantly improving the quality of data.

(12) It connects more computers or terminals and makes communication possible between the groups of networks and individual networks.

Advantages of Networking

They read as follows :

(1) File transfer between computers is easy and convenient.

(2) Mail transfer by electronic data means eliminating delay and permits quick decision by potential business organisations.

(3) It performs functions of web browsing as it performs by the Net.

(4) Easy and quick access, immediate availability information of permits increased production.

(5) It reduces the labour cost of doing paperwork. The maintenance of paper as used in the conventional organisations can be saved in terms of cost.

(6) It will enable the company to process the internal telephone listing by all relevant users.

(7) It saves lot of time and efforts of the employees as the technology permits face to face interaction.

(8) All the employees within the organisation have access to network and can exchange data easily among themselves.

(9) The electronic document, text, audio, video, graphics, animation at any one site of the Net can be circulated over the entire organisation.

(10) The products used on the Net like the web server and power browsers can equally be used on the Net too.

(11) Quick transactions across its manufacturing units.

(12) Business concerns and other institutions which are still using paper-based forms can benefit themselves by making transactions through the Internet.

(13) The system can ultimately reduce paper, printing and distribution cost.

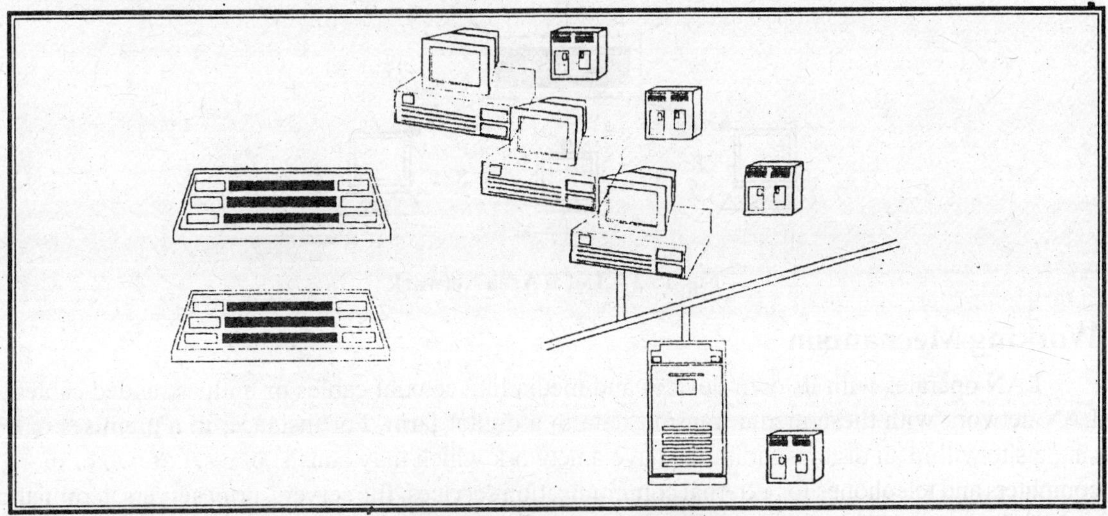

Fig. 15.2 Net work Connections

CLASSIFICATION OF NETWORKS

The entire computer network can be classified into the following five broad categories. They are LAN, WAN, Internet, Extranet and the Intranet.

The nature and working of these categories is discussed in the following paragraphs :

Local Area Network (LAN)

Local Area Network (LAN) means communication system designed to link neighbouring computers that are located within a compact area such as an office, building or a campus. LAN is an independent and privately owned and organised communication system most effective within a particular premises.

The individual computers or group of computers may be located within the same building or in several closed or individual buildings owned by a private organisation, department, company or university etc.

When a set of two or more computers are interconnected in a single room or rooms within a building or buildings on a premises or a site, the system is usually known as the LAN.

A single PC is a stand alone set on a desktop with the facility to share the data stored in one or more. The individual PC is a work station, which lets several users to use the same computer programs, equipment and share relevant information. LAN is designed as a multi-user environment to facilitate the sharing of vast computer resources like printer, disk, central processing unit etc.

For instance, an organisation having several mini-computers located far apart can be interconnected. But it is to be noted that the LAN system is different from the mainframe computer system. LAN may cover a limited geographical area and may be ranging about 8 to 10 kms or more.

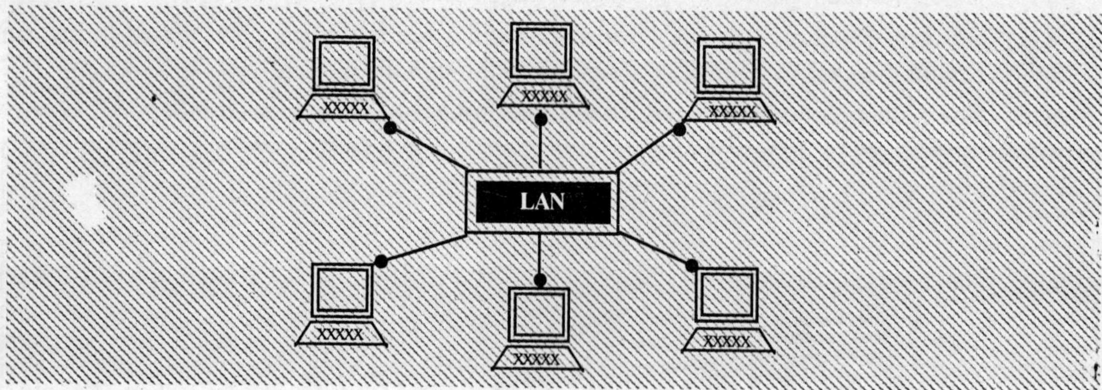

Fig. 15.3 A Local Area Network

Working Mechanism

LAN operates with its own devices and media like coaxial cables or multi-stranded cables. LAN network with these media transmit data in a digital farm. For instance, in a premises or a single site within an organisation may have a network which may consist of a set of two or more computers and telephones for external communication services, file servers, print servers, terminals and work stations. The terminals and workstations are connected to by the computer. The file server is a special equipment of the computer network which acts as a potential storage medium.

Any independent computer in the network can use stored data from the file server of the network. Similarly, the print server also is a similar one which functions to print it. The network may have an external communications server having a set of two or more telephones on the LANs. LAN with the help of the external communication server can communicate between equipments on the networks and receiving system outside LAN. In the local area network, the electronic mail is a popular facility available. In some LANs however, one computer may be shared in handling the electronic mail called the mail server. So, on a LAN, the user can communicate with the mail server when dealing with the mail.

It is basically a digital communication network which interconnects various computers located in a well described locality. A LAN is known for high speed data transmission rates. The rate may range from a few hundred kilobytes per second to a few megabytes per second.

Network Speed

Based on the rate of speed, the networks have been categorised into the following types :

High Speed Networks: Local area networks have designed to provide links between large main frames. They permit over twenty million bytes per second (MBps) to be transmitted.

Medium Speed Networks: The networks have been designed to link with smaller mainframe and mini computers. The rate of speed of these LANs ranges from one MBps and 20 MBps.

Low Speed Networks: The bytes that can be transferred in case of low speed personal computer network is very much restricted. About one MBps can be transmitted over the low speed personal computer networks. They are developed to provide a link between personal computers and various brands of personal computers grouped together.

Factors for Designing LAN

The following are the various reasons for designing LAN. Until the introduction of LAN, computing facilities were mostly contrasted, and each computing place was independent of other computers working in the same organisation. They have become isolated and individual sets and are not shared by others. With the recent advancement in the field of electronic technology, hardware and software, digital electronics has substantially contributed for designing the LAN system. However, there are a number of factors necessitated for developing such a networking. The following factors underline the importance of interconnection of various computer system in locality and bring the local area networks into the picture.

(1) Centralised System: Until the advent of LAN, computing facilities in all organisations were mostly centralised. Recently, the computing requirements of an organisation have increased significantly between the computers and accordingly, interconnecting has become necessitated.

(2) Many Small Computers: It is also increasingly recognised that the utility of a large number of small computing facilities throughout the organisation can be increased in many ways, if there can be an interconnection between the computers. The important consideration is that the effective communication between computers is indispensable for management information systems, decision making etc.

(3) Recognising Capability: Many organisations and institutions and other end users greatly recognised that the microcomputers have much or more capabilities than the most commonly used mainframes.

(4) Non-Sharing PCs: One of the primary reasons for personal computers having a significant appeal is that they are a personal, individual tool and not shared by many others. Thus, PCs have become individual, and to a certain extent, underutilised.

(5) Individual Productive Tool: It is the objective of any organisation to make their staff more productive. One of the best ways is to make the human resources in any organisation more productive and provide them with computers, particularly for managerial, personnel and other levels. One of the major machines providing information and communication of the present day is the personal computer.

(6) Unlinked Individual Computer: The driving force behind the use of the PC is to give each user an independent computing power. Thus, each centre has become unconcerned and unlinked with other computers. This prevents equal distribution of resources and access to all types of information.

(7) No Communication Between Computers: Decision making on sound lines requires information from different computing centres. If different functional departmental computers are interconnected, then there is an easy access to varied information. Thus, the lack of communication between computers has led to developing a networking system. Computers need to communicate to reach the users in the organisations. A communication implies the generic process of transferring information from one individual to another.

Today, micro-computers or personal computers have as much as capability than the most commonly used mainframe computers. This is the reason why large organisations acquired and installed large number of small computers. Thus, all these factors underline the importance of interconnection of various computer systems in a premises and thus bring the local area network into the picture.

LAN Hardware

The hardware components of LAN may include the following:

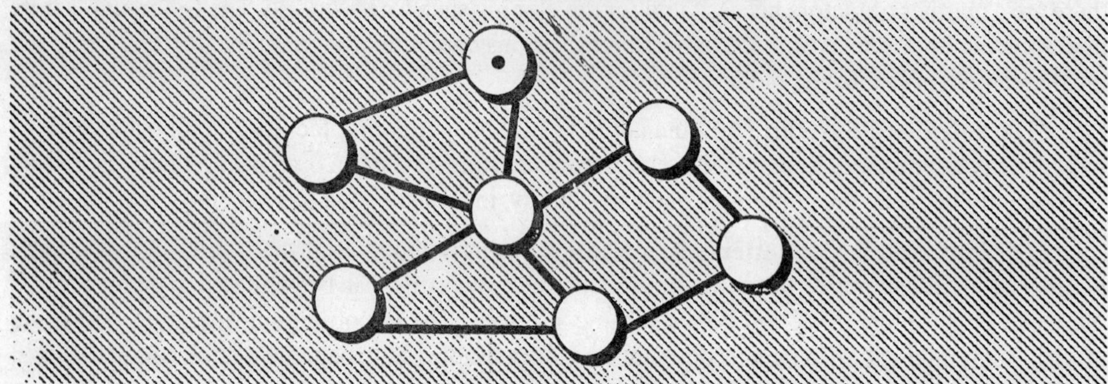

Fig. 15.4 Multi-LANLinks

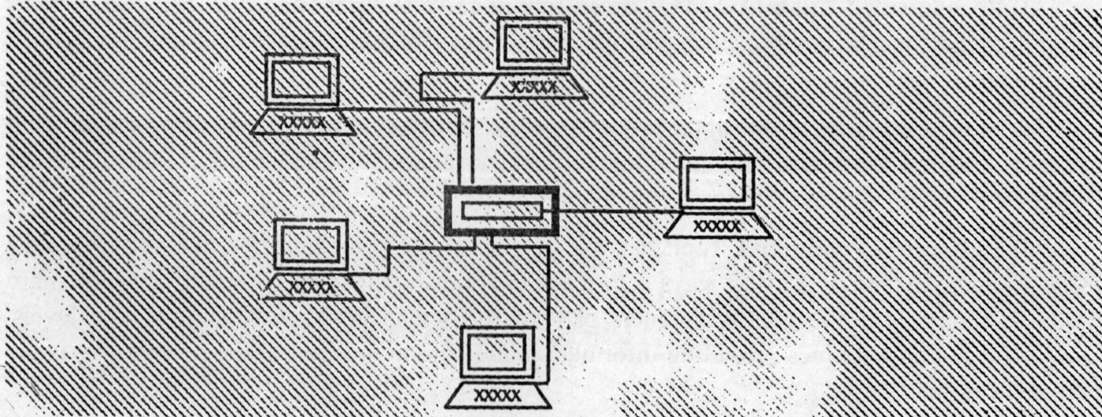

Fig. 15. 5 Multi-LAN

Transmission Channel

LAN uses the following types of channels for data communication:

(1) Twisted Pair Cable: It is made up of two insulate copper wires, twisted together. They are protected from spurious noise signals. This type of cable is used for short. distance and the cable of transferring one-two megabytes per second.

(2) Coaxial Cables: These cables are used for data transfer over a long distance. They are solid cables. Lower transfer loss and higher transfer are the features of the larger cable diameter. There are two types of coaxial cables namely 75 ohm and 50 ohm.

(3) Fibre Optic Cable: A glass or plastic fibre is used in the fibre optics cable. They carry signals in the form of fluctuating light. The glass or plastic is thick as human hair. The data is transferred through the cable as pulses of light.

(4) Radio Waves: Radio waves are used for voice communication. Waves cover a large area, are inexpensive and permits portable workstations but its drawbacks are insecurity and low rate of transfer.

(5) Network Interface Unit (NIU): It is used to implement LAN protocol. All devices in the LAN are connected by network interface units.

(6) Servers: The types of servers used in LAN include print server, file server and modem server.

LAN Software

LAN has a separate operating system which permits the sharing of resources like the printer, storage space etc. There are various types of operating systems—namely Novell Netware, LAN Server, Omninet, PC Net, IBM PC LAN and Etherlink Plus.

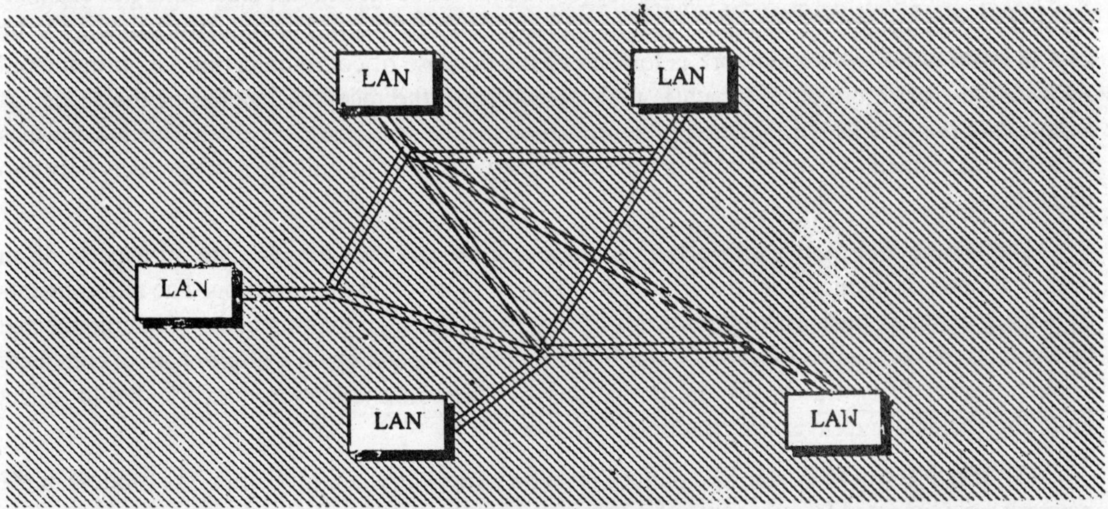

Fig. 15.6 Interconnecting LANs

Hub in Networking

Hub is one of the common components of the devices used in a network. It is called the networking hub. It is a centralised distribution point for all traffic on network. It acts like liason or centre for distribution. It means that it receives messages from the senders and stores once they are transmitted. The in-bound traffic arrives at the hub which receives and reproduces data to the computer connected to the same hub.

Network Topologies

Network topology consists of a lay-out or pattern of connection between the computers. In this type of structure, a single computer under the system acts as a server. It is also called as control computer whose responsibility operates as supervisor or act as a liason which directs and maintains the network. In case of some other network structures, there will be no control computer or server. We now look into various types of network which seem possible to construct.

Any number of standard networks can be designed and developed to meet the requirements of the organisation. In case of LAN, there is the star or chain network structure which connects computers as per suitability. There may be several designs of LANs namely ring, bus, circle, mesh, tree etc., or physical configuration. For instance, in case of a star LAN, it has a central controller and all network centres hook up to it. Similarly, in case of a bus LAN, a single cable is run and routed touching various centres on its route to provide a network linkage. In case of ring or circle LAN, each station having the equipment is hooked up together.

Types of Networks

We cannot suggest a particular line of communication network topology as universally suitable and applicable to all types of organisations.

The building up of a design depends upon the number of factors like size, nature of channel, number of persons and the complexity of an organisation's network. The objectives that are to be kept in mind in building a network is to achieve the purpose of communication i.e., prompt and accurate flow of information which is understandable to the receiver, listener or the reader. A simple network may be built up having the constituents, the sender and receiver. This is known as circular communication. A partial communication network may be built up that connects only two departments.

The simple and partial network of communication cannot accommodate all aspects of an organisation and may not meet the requirements of all types of an organisation. The requirements of modern complex business organisations having many decision making centres, interconnected by channels of communication, should also be considered. Depending on a single chain of command is fraught with many drawbacks and limitations. So, the communication network should reflect multi-dimensional and envisaging multiple channels.

(1) Star Network: A star like picture is made to appear when all computers (nodes) in the network are connected to a central node. The central node is an intelligent switch which can only provide a data connection for various nodes, like a digital PABX. Exchange of information takes place via a central point. This structure is called the start of origin. It is similar to that of telephone central switch. The computer located at the centre, in a star network acts as a server, through which all communication must go through, any message must first be sent to the server which in turn retransmits the message to the destination. The problem in this star structure is that if the control computer fails the entire network suffers.

A star LAN has a central controller that provides interface by the network stations.

(2) Circle or Ring: In the ring configuration, it forms a complete ring, wherein in nodes are connected in series. As a result, data flows from one node to the other until it is picked up by the appropriate target node. In order to control network access, a number of devices have been designed.

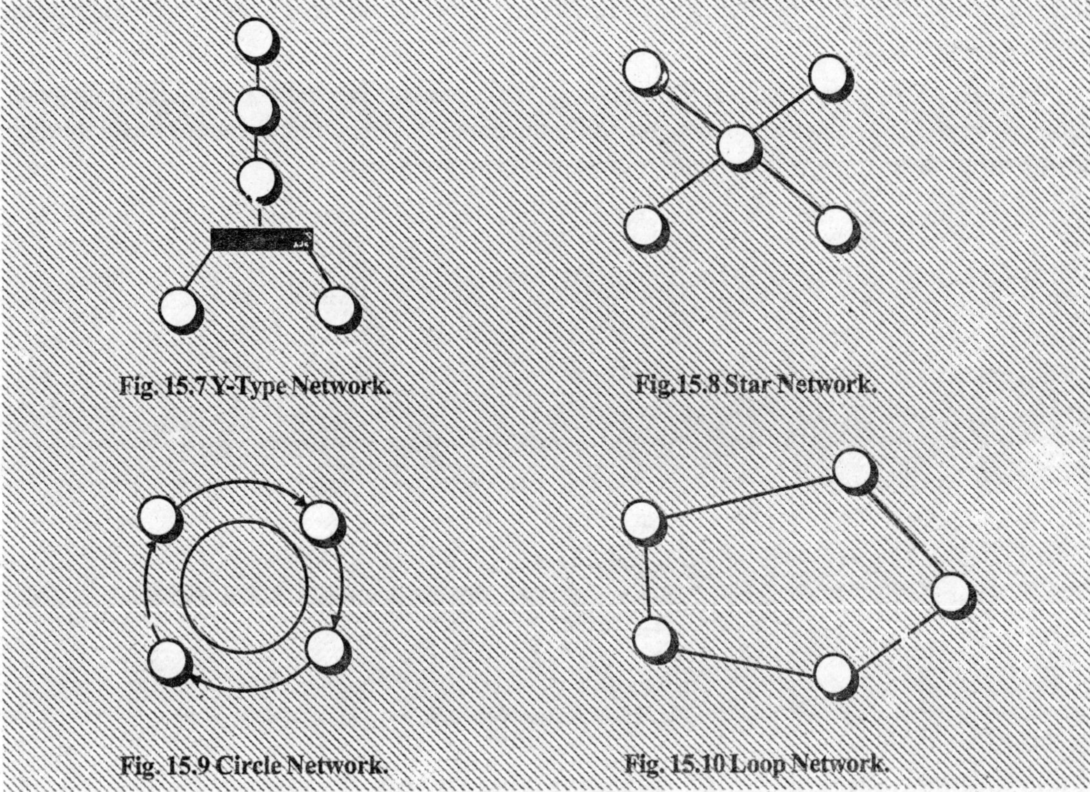

Fig. 15.7 Y-Type Network.

Fig.15.8 Star Network.

Fig. 15.9 Circle Network.

Fig. 15.10 Loop Network.

In this network, each computer is hooked together to form a circle or ring configuration. Further, all workstations are linked to form a continuous circle. The data flows around the circle and the electrical signals pass around the ring from one centre to another.

In circle topology, the computers are arranged in such a way that all computers connected look like a ring. In this network, all communication can be sent by any computer to another around the ring. The messages go through round the ring. The cable takes the form to make a complete loop.

(3) Bus Network: In the bus configuration, the technique of the node is not used. There is no central node to connect all the computers. Here, all the computers operating in a network share the same medium i.e. the cable. A number of devices have been designed to control the access of the network. There is a single cable to which all computers are connected. It is also called as the broadcast bus.

One computer broadcasts the message and all other individual computers in the system have to accept the message. We call this topology as bus network. The bus is the cable to which the computers are connected. All communications must go along the bus. The reliability and efficiency of bus topology depends on the length and quality of the connecting cable.

Any number of computers can be added, removed from the network. The failure of the individual computer in the route does not affect the working of the network.

In the case of a bus local network area, a single cable is channelled from one work station to another work station, thus facilitating network linkage. There is no central controller and each network component must be equipped to handle interface situations. The bus LAN appears as shown in Figure15.11.

(4) Y-Type Network: In the Y-Type topology, the computers located at strategic management, middle level and tactical level are involved in communication. All communications travel through downward from the top level computer to the lowest operating level.

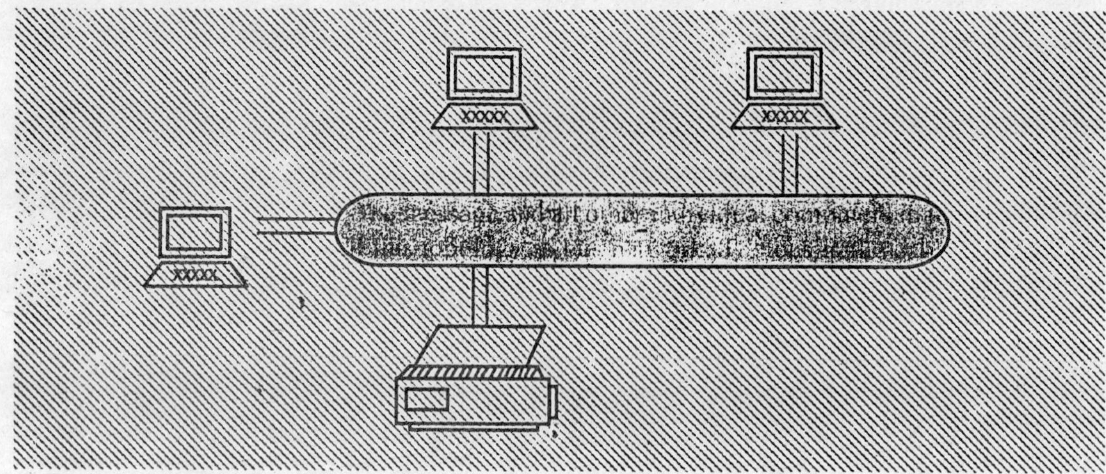

Fig. 15.11 A Bus Network.

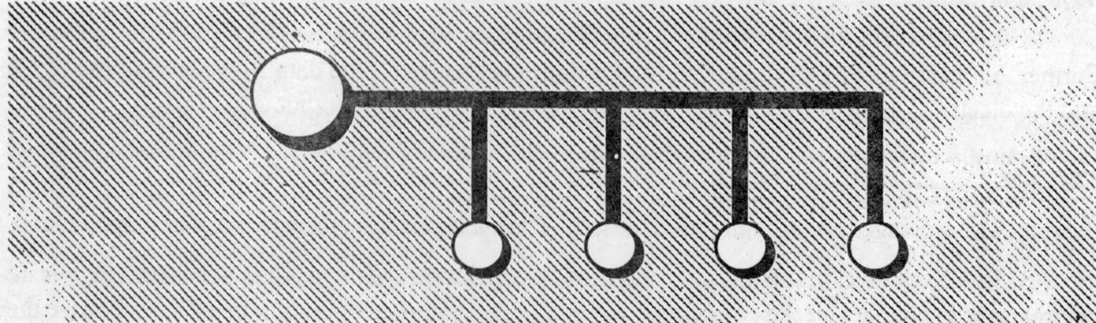

Fig. 15.12 Multi-drop Network.

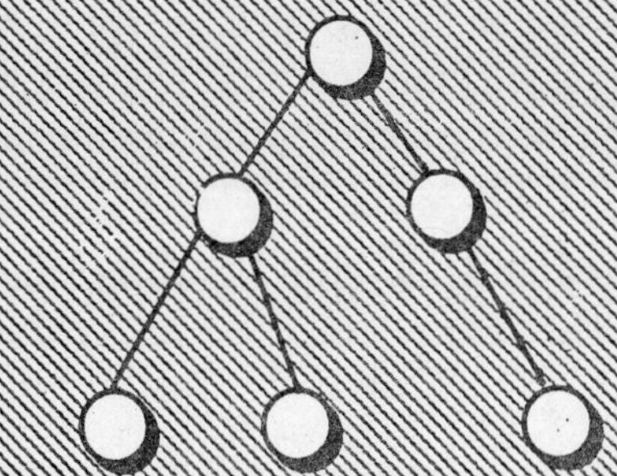

Fig. 15.13 Tree Network.

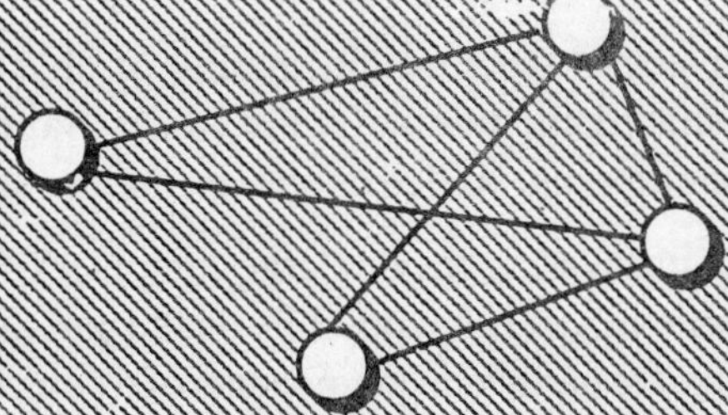

Fig. 15.14 Mesh Network.

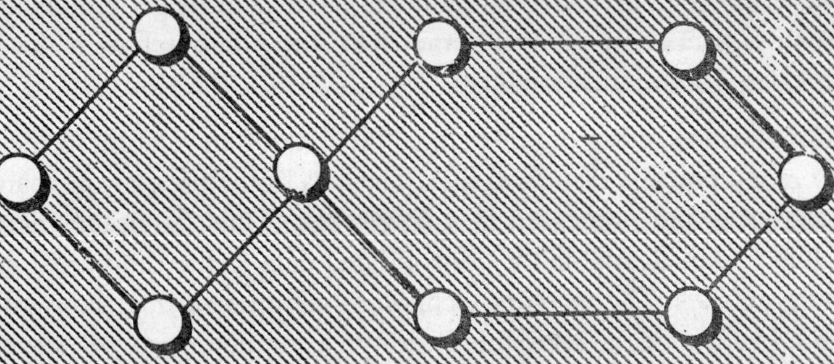

Fig. 15.15 Interconnected Rings.

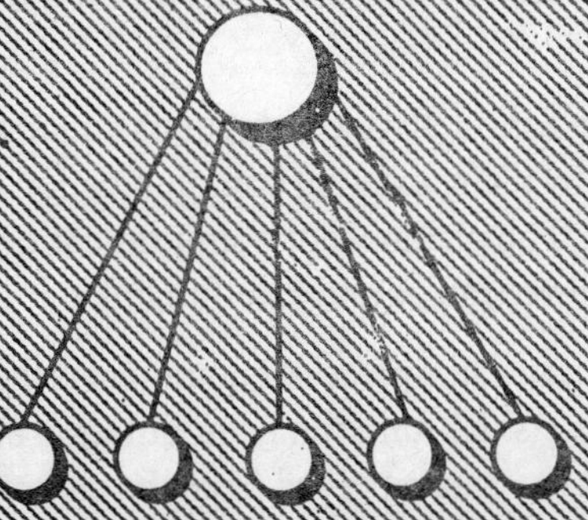

Fig. 15.16 A Variant of Star Network.

(5) Free Flow Network: As the name indicated, it represents a potential communication structure, wherein every computer can communicate effectively with each other. The network figure shown is representative of the free flow concept of communication without restriction of the formal structure.

The other channels comprise of the Multi-drop Network, Tree Network, Mesh Network and Interconnected rings.

Advantages of LAN

In a network system of computer working, the users are located in their geographical distributed areas. The networking permits these users to obtain some benefits. The significance of computer networks will now be dealt with in considering the future trends in business details.

(1) Sharing of Resources: Networks permit the sharing of physical resources. Computer physical resources that can be shared include software, discs, tapes, processors, memory, uninterrupted power supply, air conditioning, skilled operators, maintenance staff etc.

All these will add to the cost of installation besides large computers not only big in size but also costing several crores of rupees. Generally, it is not possible on the part of any single user who may not be able to fully utilise all the separate hardware components of a computer. Even if it is possible, he may not be able to utilise all the time. Network system permits full scale computing facilities a number of sites. It is often more economical and reliable to provide them at one or at most a few sites and provide only terminals with data communications links to its geographically distributed remote users. The remote users can easily interact with the computer with the help of these terminals and authentic data communication links.

(2) Sharing Information: In big organisations, the data often relating to the same general subject is generated at geographically dispersed sites. The data from different sites can be connected and systematically analysed and processed at a single site. Thus, computer networks permit information sharing that makes available the consolidated data to the individual geographically distributed users at remote sites. The network technology permits vertical flow information i.e., upward and downward. In addition, it is possible to design a computer network structure to permit hierarchical flow of data. With the help of the computer network, data can be transmitted to a larger computer as well as retrieve data from the larger computer through the network. Sitting at a terminal, the users can exchange and share information and queries and responses are conveyed through the network.

(3) Communication Links: Terminals and computers are important components in the network to establish communication links by using existing communication channels for sending data between computers or between terminals. The channels of communication presently existing are telephone lines, microwave radio, optical fibre, cables and satellite links.

In communication, the most important piece of equipment is the modem which modifies electrical characteristics to suit these channels. Its function is modulation and demodulation. At another end channel, another modem changes the data received from the channel back into the original computer recognisable form.

Today, communication is supported by computer related support systems. LAN facilitates faster, wide and accurate communication which are indispensable in any decision making process. Managers spend quantity time in communication either orally or written form. The LAN concept of communication lets them expedite this communication among several levels and groups for exchanging data, sending messages and sharing information. LAN facilitates inhouse computer to computer communication reliably and speedily because of easy access to remote resources.

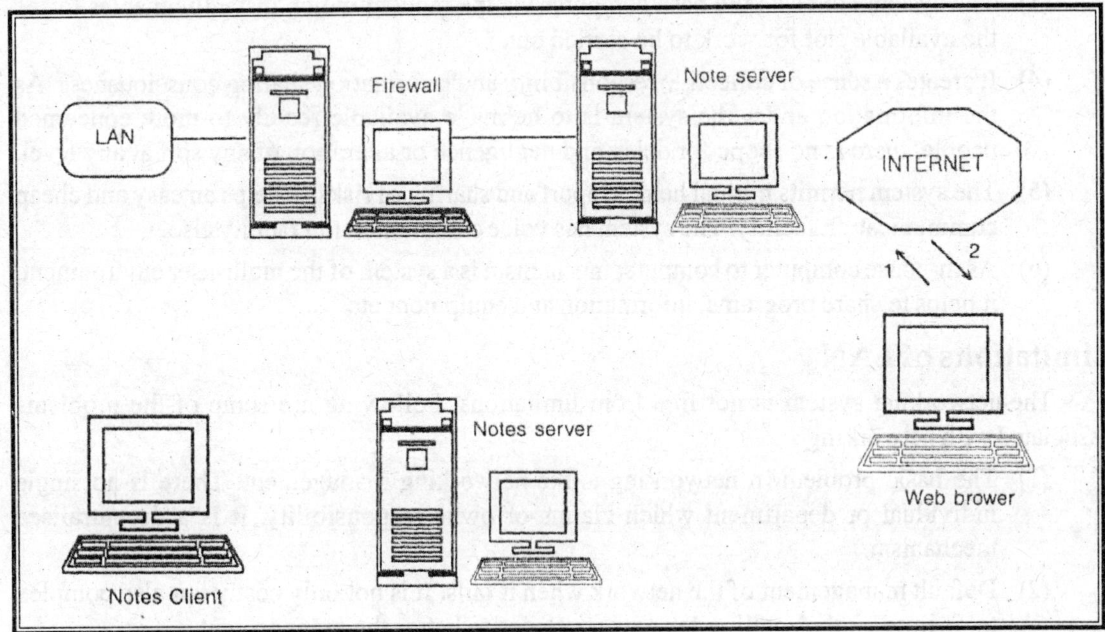

Fig. 15.17 Connecting LAN to the Internet.

(4) Time: It is commonly seen that a lot of time is wasted in the preparation of final draft of any report or text document. Similarly, heavy amount of stationery is wasted in offices to prepare several drafts of documents before the final version is approved. Networking helps greatly to solve these two major problems. So, networking can be applied in the field of desk top publishing. All the computers within an office or an entire building are linked and texts and documents are passed around the office or building for review and improvement and subsequently seeing to it that the final version of the report/ document can be printed.

(5) Management Tools: LAN is a management tool of getting the things done through people effectively and efficiently. In these days of changing needs of working conditions and organisations, the information technology oriented LAN lets the management to solve its basic problems. LAN acts as the monitoring and management control system which improves the performance of repetitive nature, relieving the worker from fatigue, boredom and introducing the elements of variety and novelty in routine work.

The other advantages continue below :

(1) There is no need to use large mainframe computers. It permits to employ a network of servers on desktop machines to do the same function. It operates at lower prices and higher flexibility.

(2) The networking system is of great help for services, businesses and small contracting business.

(3) The system connects the base computer via the modem which instantly enables to see the available slot for work to be carried out.

(4) It creates a sense of collective responsibility and information sharing consciousness. As the information under the system is to be made available readily to more concerned people, there is no scope for delay and negligence or alteration of any sort at any level.

(5) The system permits mutual help, support and sharing of risks, It helps an easy and cheap communication facility. The system has voice communication facility also.

(6) As in-house computer to computer mechanism is a system of the multi-user environment, it helps to share programs, information and equipment etc.

Limitations of LAN

The networking system is not free from limitations. Following are some of the problems associated with networking :

(1) The basic problem in networking is the networking management. There is no single individual or department which claims or owns responsibility. It is a decentralised mechanism.

(2) Default management of the network when it fails. It is not only costly but also complex to operate — thus calling for new strategies to better the management.

(3) Preservation of integrity of networking at all costs and levels is a difficult task unless automatic connections are provided.

(4) Configuration management problem which includes monitoring and controlling total networking from any point on the network.

(5) Any minor breakdown in the networking component may affect the operation of the whole networking. The day-to day maintenance of the network is a costly affair, and it is time consuming and requires expertise to manage it.

(6) Its working is complex, i.e., complex multi-vendor, multi-protocol, multimedia and so the technology requires global know-how.

(7) Design, procurement, project management and installation of cable and infrastructure will take a considerable amount of time. Small organizations therefore cannot afford to go for the installation of LAN or WAN.

(8) Problems like frequent technological changes, indigenous host suppliers can be usurped by the new cost competitive start-up, other modifications and alteration costs to the existing information technology cannot be ignored.

(9) There is a problem of password.

(10) Virus and software bugs problem may destroy the entire networking system.

Distributed Computing

In systems approach, there are two types of computing systems. They are Integrated Information-System and Distributed Systems.

An integrated information system has several practical problems. The failure of the system may adversely affect the entire system.

In order to solve this problem, the concept of distributed system or distributed computing has emerged as an alternative to the integrated system which also has sub-systems.

The network computing is called as distributed computing as distinct from monolithic centralised mainframe computing. But this distinction is also largely disappearing as mainframe computers are being networked to PCs and mainframe computers acting as potential servers.

Network File Server

In case of LAN, the users store files on a file server which is a computer in the network and which is the central node. The file server can access data files. In a network, there are peripherals like printers, printer queues and modem etc. Among them, the file server in a LAN acts as a central hub to share the peripherals.

The purpose of a file server is to store files for application but the server does not involve in the processing of an application. The file server sends all or part of the data. When a file is saved, it copies the data file back to the file server across the network.

Limitations of the Network File Server

They read as follows :

(1) The drawback of this system does not permit simultaneous access to a single data set by multiple users. It means that it does not serve the data concurrently.

(2) Because of heavy traffic, the network can quickly become saturated.

(3) File server operates in files which are large database sets.

(4) The system prevents the user from sharing a file when another user is locked out.

Client/Server System (C/S)

The limitations and practical (operation) problems associated with the file server system led to the genesis of the client server system. It has the advantages of the network computing model along with the stored data access. Any local area network can be considered as client/serve. system.

Origin: The client/server computing system was first used in the late 1970s and started becoming popular and is being used regularly since the early 1980s.

Meaning: Client/server computing is a group of two or more computer systems connected via the network with associated software. The system is the main driving force of the growth of computing in economically potential areas, particularly in various businesses, banking and the Net. Both the server and the client have hardware and software components and packages. C/S computing is an architecture in which a system's, functionality and processing are divided between the client and a server.

Meaning and Nature of Server: The serve is a computer and its software provides relevant services for other computers connected to it via the network. The server is called the Back End. The big computer that your modem dials to access the Net is the server or host on the internet which often has information available to those accessing the Internet. A server (back-end) gives stress on efficiently managing resources such as databases of information. Its main job is to manage resources optimally among various clients. The server manages the database among various clients.

For instance, in a banking application, a large computer is placed in a separate room as opposed to the personal computer on the desktop of the computer clerk, which is a client or the location is the server in which all the transactions and customer details are stored. The server with its software searches the information and sends it to the clients on a regular basis.

Meaning and Nature of Client: The client is the computer with its software requesting for some services from the server. The client is called Front End. You are the client. People use 'Client' software to access information available on servers.

Netscape is a web client giving access to information on a web server. The work-stations are clients who request services such as data, program files or printing from the server. A Client application (the front end) is the part of the system that users apply to interact with the data. The clients send requests and analyse the data that they received from the server.

For instance, in a banking application, the personal computer on the desk of the counter clerk is the client.

Whenever an enquiry is made, the client sends a request to the server giving particular details.

Benefits of Client / Server System: There are many benefits in the case of client/server model which solves all problems associated with the network/file server system. The following are some of the benefits of this system :

(1) The client and the server are the parts of the system generally run on separate computers. The server can store voluminous data and meet the requirements of the client's requests.

(2) The system is less expensive, with minimum disk storage and the memory is sufficient.

(3) Any number of users can be accommodated with productive, easy to use tools to enter and analyse the data.

(4) Client/server system satisfies the principles of flexibility. It is not rigid and allows all the inevitable types of hardware and software changes. This flexibility tends to take out that old server and plug in new servers without disturbing its functionality.

(5) Scalability feature is another benefit of this system. It permits scalability easily to accommodate changes in a work group. When many new workers are formed, it permits to plug into the network systems with the new client workstation.

(6) This system also focusses on the areas of system development. It means that each functional component can specialise to do something in the best possible way.

(7) Another benefit of this system is towards cost saving.

(8) It provides instant access to information for decision making, facilitate communication and reduce time efforts and cost for accomplishing the task.

(9) The system displays information on the users' requests, even though all data and information may be distributed in multi servers.

(10) The system can be integrated with other technologies like e-mail, document, imaging etc.

(11) It uses object-oriented technology in designing tools, enabling quicker development of applications.

(12) It permits integration of applications developed on different types of hardware and software, cutting down the software development project cost.

(13) The great problem is software maintenance particularly in the mainframe system.

(14) The functional departments of an organisation can be computerised and integrated.For instance, production, design, planning, finance and other departments can be integrated.

(15) With the internet technology being easily available, the order despatch to vendors, receipt of customers' orders, and tracking of shipments can be integrated with other functions like purchase, sales, shipping etc. The treasury function is to be integrad with the banking function and connected to the bankers.

Components of Client/Server

A client server system has four distinct components. Each focusses on a specific job. They are: database server, mail server, application server and network.

Based on the services rendered by the server, they are designated as the components mentioned above.

(1) Database Server: A file or a database server stores all the data and information in an efficient way and provides the same to the client on request. The database server mainly deals on the following:

(a) To deal with a single database of information among many concurrent users.

(b) Controlling database access and other security requirements.

(c) Protecting database.

(d) Centrally enforcing global data.

(2) Mail Server: A mail server receives, sends and stores the mail received for the clients connected to it. An internet service provider will have a mail server and a web browsing server including an internet user using the PC.

The e-mail software and web user are the software residing with the client and get connected to other of the servors based on the user's request. It is possible that on the same computer, both the server's software and hardware may reside with the same computer doing dual functions.

(3) Client Application: A client application is called the Front End. It is a part of the network system that users apply to interact with the available data. Based on the requirements and design of the system, the business logic of the application may be shared between the front and back end. The client application's tasks are requesting and receiving information, validating data entry and performing application logic etc.

(4) Network: Another component of the client server system is the network. The physical network may be twisted cable, ethernet cables or optical fibres. A large network widely dispersed may also consist of other components like hubs, routers and bridges etc.

The network and communication software are the vehicles that transmit data between the clients and the server in a system. Both the clients and the server run communication software effectively that allows them to talk across a network.

Network Software

The available network software are Microsoft NT, Novell Net ware and Unix.

(1) Name Server: Name server contains databases of internet host addresses which translate word address into numeric equivalents.

(2) Host: The individual machines at a particular location are generally called as hosts. The resource of a host machine is usually shared and can be utilised by any user on the Net.

Wide Area Networks (WANs)

Originally, the system of Wide Area Network (WAN) originated in the later part of 1960s mainly for research purposes. A number of autonomous computers located over a large remote geographical area is called the Wide Area Network. Opposed to LAN, WANs are used to transmit data over a long distance but not within a complex. They objectively connect a set of two or more computers on different and separate sites, separate cities or even located in other countries. The WAN system transmits data using separate devices like optical fibre media and satellite transmissions.

Accordingly, WAN uses packet switching methods or message switching methods. The special characteristic features of WAN are that different computers are located at different geographical areas and each have their own interconnections to the main network. The point of intersection of concentration is called the gateway. Thus, several computers are linked over a large distance in the WAN system. For instance, railway networking, airlines, intercity and intercontinental network are the categories of WAN.

Modem is one of the computer equipments which help to transfer data from one place to another and which are located at distance places. It allows sending information to a distant place by using personal portable computers with a modem. So, these can be transmitted from a distance field of business to the office computer via the telephone. For instance, it pertains to connecting office computers with that of salesmen who are away from the office. A networking system facilitates salesmen, dealers and others to have direct access to inventory files to know about the stock levels available. Recording is carried on instantly without delay.

Wide Area Network can be used to communicate, send and receive information within an office. between its branches, distributors, factory, salesmen etc., anywhere in an instant, it is a computer-based electronic network messaging system for corporate requirements and conditions.

It has revolutionised the communication between offices, branches, warehouses, dealers and distributors etc. Businesses can receive reports in time or send instructions from where they can communicate to their branches, distributors or vendors located across the country. Thus, when a number of autonomous computers are located over large remote geographical areas, it is called WAN.

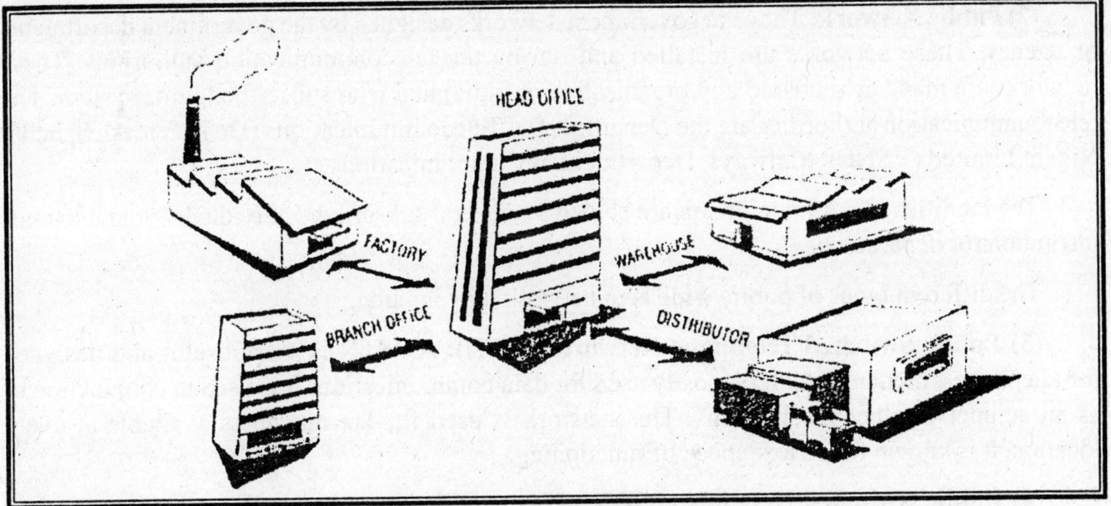

Fig. 15.18 Wide Area Network.

Objectives of WAN

They read as follows :

(1) To provide an effective communication between scattered sites.

(2) To share hardware and software by several users.

(3) To make accessible computer facilities available on sites to a larger community of users.

(4) To replace mail, cable and telex transmission and

(5) To enhance handling capacity.

The existing telephone networks are used to establish WAN to reach remote databases for the public bulletin board. Network services are leased from the vendor.

Types of Wide Area Network (WAN)

There are two types of wide area networks: private network and public network.

(1) Private: A network designed and developed by one organisation is a private network wherin leased circuits (i.e., telephone lines) are to be used for installing WAN. Private WANs have a limited capacity to data and communication transmission. The first private net is ARPANET(Advanced Research project Agency), an United States Network. Its creation was funded in 1969 as ARPANET and was designed to develop a geographically dispersed and reliable communication network for military use. The basic feature in case of all private WANs is to use private circuits to link the location which is to be served by the network. Another distinctive feature is that the user or the owner of the network has complete freedom to use the circuits in any manner they want. The owners of the network can utilise their circuits either to carry large quantities of data or for high speed transmission. They have every freedom to use any level of standard of technology available. But private networks generally have to notify telecommunication authorities by way of furnishing some particulars like location, circuits, modem, multiplexers and other ways of communication used.

(2) Public Network: They are government networks designed by the government departments or agency. These networks are installed and run by the telecommunication authorities. These networks are made available to any organisation or individual who subscribe to this system. The telecommunication authorities are the Department of Telecommunications (DoT), Videsh Sanchar Nigam Limited (VSNL), Railways, Department of Communications etc.

The facilities of communication are shared by several subscriber individuals, organisations, institutions or departments.

The different types of public wide area network may include :

(3) Public Switched Telephone Network (PSTN): A PSTN is more useful and designed for telephones, modems etc. It is mostly used for data communication. It is used in conjunction or as an adjunct to other mechanisms. This network is used for fax machines available at every location. It is known for its low speed of functioning.

(4) Public Switched Network (PSDN): It is used in the case of public packet switched network available to the public. They are known for high speed also. Reliability and quality are the features of PSDN. It is designed in such a way so as to link the computer system and networks of one institution to many other institutions. It is commonly used for electronic mail services.

(5) Value Added Services (VADs): In this service, there is the service provider who processes, stores and manipulates the data which is carried to the network for transmission. This service adds value to the data. The best example of VADs is electronic data interchange. This service permits trading partners to exchange trading and business documents like invoices, transportation and purchase orders. The VSNL is the provider of value added services in India.

In this, the owners of the Net and its users are put into separate categories. The users take network service on a rental basis by way of subscription. On the other hand, the owner designs and maintains this network. The subscribers link their equipment to the networks' facility offered by an external agency. It is a distinct mechanism of organised data communication network wherein the owner leases communication facilities and computers to manage communication link such as microwave station, communication satellite, trans-oceanic cables and other computer-supported communication systems. A network becomes value added on grounds as to what a computer adds to provide capability between the devices.

(6) Integrated Services Digital Network (ISDN): This digital network is also a networking concept which uses digital transmission media.It integrates both circuits and the packet switching technique. The telephone networks have been utilizing digital transmission facilities. Today, the trend is towards global application of the IASDN technology which offers fast digital connectivity. ISDN has the capability of providing for the integration of voice, video, data, tax and other advanced services.

This is a new service from US-West that allows you to connect to computers at speeds of 56 or 64 kbps. To use ISNDN , you must have it installed by US-West and have the ISDN device on each end of the connection. ISDN devices can bridge over two 'B Channel' for 12/128 kbps bandwidth.

Features and Advantages of ISDN

They read as follows:

(1) It is based on digital communication technology

(2) No voice interference

(3) High reliability

(4) Reduces retransmission

(5) Transmits data at the rate of 64 kbps per channel

(6) Data rates are higher

(7) Reduces waiting time for users because the latency of data transmission is smaller

(8) It carries both voice and data

(9) Offers flexibility to the users

(10) The operating cost is less hence it is cost-effective

(11) It works with two nodes namely, Basic Rate Access (BRA) and Primary Rate Access (PRA).

(12) The speed of ISDN connection makes the graphics rich. Permits to access websites and is usable. Performance of PCs at home is improved. The integration networks and services provide advantages for all those involved in the overall communication.

(13) Reduces cost in the offices as well as in the home environment.

(14) Two different networks are run to provide services such as telephones and data communication.

(15) ISDN accelerates the flow of information which not only increases the transmission speed but also multiplies it.

(16) Convenient features which increased its practical value are:

- (a) Call waiting
- (b) Diversion of calls
- (c) Automatic call-back
- (d) Logging of incoming calls
- (e) Calling number indication
- (f) Do not disturb
- (g) Conference calls
- (h) Call charge indication and Transferred change calls and
- (i) Packet Switched Network.

Packets switched Network: A packet is a block of data whose maximum length is fixed like a letter and the packet of information is sent from one place to another. A packet switched network is designed to meet the specific needs of subscribers requiring terminal-to-terminal, terminal-to-host and host-to-host communication. In the packet switched network, a sender's data is divided into blocks of data called the packet. Each packet includes an address along with headers and control information for the routing purposes. A packet switched network uses time flow and protocol network management throughout each data transmission sequence.

Packets are routed individually via the most efficient art from the point of origination to their destination where they are reassembled into their correct order. Packet assembler and disassembler (PAD) converts the data into packets then transmits the packets over the network to another PAD at its destination where it is converted back to its original form. In public packets network, packets travel over shared network facilities, eliminating the cost of a dedicated line between the sender and the receiver. The sender and the receiver just require an access line to the closest network access points.

Gateway Packet Switched Service (GPSS): Gateway Packet Switched Services is India's public Switched Packet Data Networks (PSPDN), and is the gateway to another international PSPDN. Gateway Packet Switched Network of VSNL connects Packet Switching Exchanges at Mumbai, New Delhi, Kolkata and other switches. The GPSS network is expressly provided for data transmission, whereas PSTN is basically designed carrying speech.

WAN Devices/Hardware

Business information is the availability of raw material, inventory and process products. On the other hand, networking for e-commerce is the production line and distribution system. It is also a retail point of sale for the available information products.

The networks may be inter, intra, may function as local, regional international systems for e-commerce. Substantial data is required to be moved on at a distance greater than 3,000 feet. The advancement in sophisticated communication technology resulted in developing several new techniques for linking local area networks.

Paths are specified and the traffic has to necessarily pass through these paths. There are several devices which offer different degrees of discrimination and data capability. A network has several components like bridges, routers, hub, gateways, repeaters and switches etc.

A brief description of these components is as follows :

(1) Router: A router is a complex and expensive device that is linked with personal computers. It is also like a bridge and a stand alone device on the LAN. The router has a module that is a part of the writing hub. A router is used to connect networks which are dissimilar. It provides connectivity between two LANs or WANs over a large geographical distance. It operates at the network layer three of the OSI model. Every router has to participate in a routing protocol to access the network topology. This helps the router tc computer the best route from a sender to the receiver.

It is a device that can decide which of the several paths the network traffic will follow based on some optimality metric supreme and thus reduce traffic congestion on the LAN. Routers do the job of forwarding packets from one network to another based cn network layer information.[1]

1. Computers Today, 16-31, August, 1999, p. 80.

Functions and Features of the Router

The functions of the router are :

(1) To dig deeper into the envelope surrounding the data to find the destination for the data packet.

(2) To record the information contained in each packet or frame.

(3) It uses complex network addressing procedures to determine the appropriate network destinations.

(4) It discards the outer packet or frame and then repackages and retirements the data using these compressions.

(5) There are available sophisticated multi-protocol routers.

(6) It reads and examines the destination address contained in the Netware and IPX Protocol Router. It strips off the ethernet packet or token ring frame information and sends only the IPX packet and its encapsulated data.

(2) Bridge: The bridge is a complex and expensive device that can be found within a personal computer. Bridge is a hand alone device on the LAN and as a module that is a part of the writing hub. It is a device used to connect two LANs operating under an identical LAN protocol over a wide area.

Functions and Features of Bridge

(1) To read the station address of each ethernet packet or of a token ring frame which is the outer most envelope around the data.

(2) To read and determine the destination of the message. ? To connect and pass packets between two network segments.

(3) A bridge does not look inside the packet or frame.

(4) To examine the address of each ethernet packet and to send across LAN to LAN circuits, only those packets addressed to nodes on the other sides.

(5) It is the object of the bridge to reduce the number of packets on the expensive long distance circuits.

(6) To pick up packets from one LAN and filter addresses which are meant for a destination on another LAN.

(7) Bridge passes the packets on the network. It operates at the data line layer two of OSI model.

(8) The amount of processing required is minimum.

(3) Repeaters: It is a component of a network, a device which connects two segments of the networks cable. It retimes and regenerates the digital signals on the cable and sends them on their way again. In order to regenerate and propagate electrical signals, the repeater is used between two distinct network segments. This device is not popular in recent years.

(4) Hub: In a network, the hub device is used to serve as the centre of a star topology network. A hub may be active or passive. It is active when it repeats signals sent through the network. It is passive when it does not repeat, but simply splits signals sent through this network.

(5) Switch: A switch is used to reroute data to its destination, and is popularly found in switching networks. In switching networks, data is grouped and routed on the basis of pre-determined criteria.

(6) Gateway: When two LANs are dissimilar, the component of gateway is used. Gateway operates on the application layer seven of the OSI model. Its main function is to convert data packets from one protocol format to another before forwarding it, as it connects two dissimilar networks.

It is a special purpose device that performs an application layer conversion of information from one protocol stack to another like TCP/IP.

Network Interface Card

The Network interface card is a board in a personal computer. At the manufacturing stage only, the card is installed before it is released into the market. Its function is to strategically network communication to and from that computer system.

X. 25

X.25 is a protocol for interfacing to a public packet switched network, but does not support the implementing of a network. As per the international Telegraph and Telephone Consultative Committee, one of its recommendations is that the most famous is X.25, which defines an interface into a particular data network, and also pertain to that of a packet switched network.

Intranet

Concept, Meaning and Nature: A micro internet is known as intranet. It is also referred to a system with restricted audience. Through the intranet system, a well managed and structured information flow is arranged to select individuals within the organisation. This is the family of internet services. The Intranet has access to internet but the internet has no access to the Intranet. The intranet has limited (private) accessibility. Intra means within and with reference to the computer network, it refers to private networking within an organisation.

Intranet simply means a network of computers which function within an organisation mainly to share data with each other. It uses the existing standardised WWW protocol.

In this system, there is the internal web server where substantial information can be stored. Anyone on the Intranet with a computer on network can view information documents located in the intranet server.

The browser software like Internet Explorer or Netscape can be used. For this system, Macintosh, Windows or Unix application can be used. Internal networks use TCP/IP protocol for data transmission. As a web server, it helps to share and dispense information within an organisation. The mechanism of intranet greatly helps the way in which information is shared, dispersed and broadcast over the network (LAN/WAN) within a company.

One of the essential ingredients in these days of fast growing competitive environment is an easy, fast, accurate and inexpensive distribution of internal information documents.

The intranet is an internal website used in an organisation to disseminate business related information and data to employees. In recent years, many business organisations have been searching for ways and means to improve employee communication. The application and usage of the intranet is a practical solution for distribution of materials more efficiently and thus reduce overhead costs. Documents, reports or a database are the sources in which all information generated is stored. The information is either generated on the LAN or WAN wide systems. With the increasing use of computing in organisations, more and more electronic documents are being generated—thus enabling easy and fast dispersal of information to potential net users.

Documents created in a LAN/WAN are linked with files or the source of information from various databanks and files within an organisation. More multi-tiered level sharing of documents on an inter and intra departmental level is possible to a large extent.

In the conventional method, several application methods are used, compared to using a specific document format.

Intranet facilitates solving all potential problems. In intranet, there is no problem pertaining to the multiple operating system, document's format, tiered level sharing and LAN/WAN.

A browser can be used as the front end which can tie everything from the back end to the front end. Inter and intra-departmental documents can be linked and shared seamlessly. There can be total control over documents, flow, sharing of data, creation, deletion, achieving and also resource centralisation.

Intranet Applications

The mechanism of intranet permits wide application. The following are the important intranet application areas:

(1) Broadcasting news
(2) Document management
(3) Inventory, purchase, orders, travel, library
(4) Linking internet sites
(5) E-mail for inter-office and intra-office communication
(6) Internal circulars called electronic circulation
(7) Bulletin boards
(8) Electronic chat
(9) Daily work assignments
(10) Executive information system
(11) Flow diagram and graphical contents
(12) Product and service literature on the intranet for quick access
(13) Shared database access

(14) Electronic meetings

(15) Collective writings

(16) In-house form requests

(17) Report filing and

(18) Sharing information by electronically generated documents, linking files or sources, information from various databanks placed elsewhere on the network.

Requirements

To design an intranet, it is essential to possess LAN and WAN, a web server up and running and clients using a browsing software to access Intranet.

Thus, intranets are internal TCP/IP based networks that allow information to be shared effectively within an organisation.

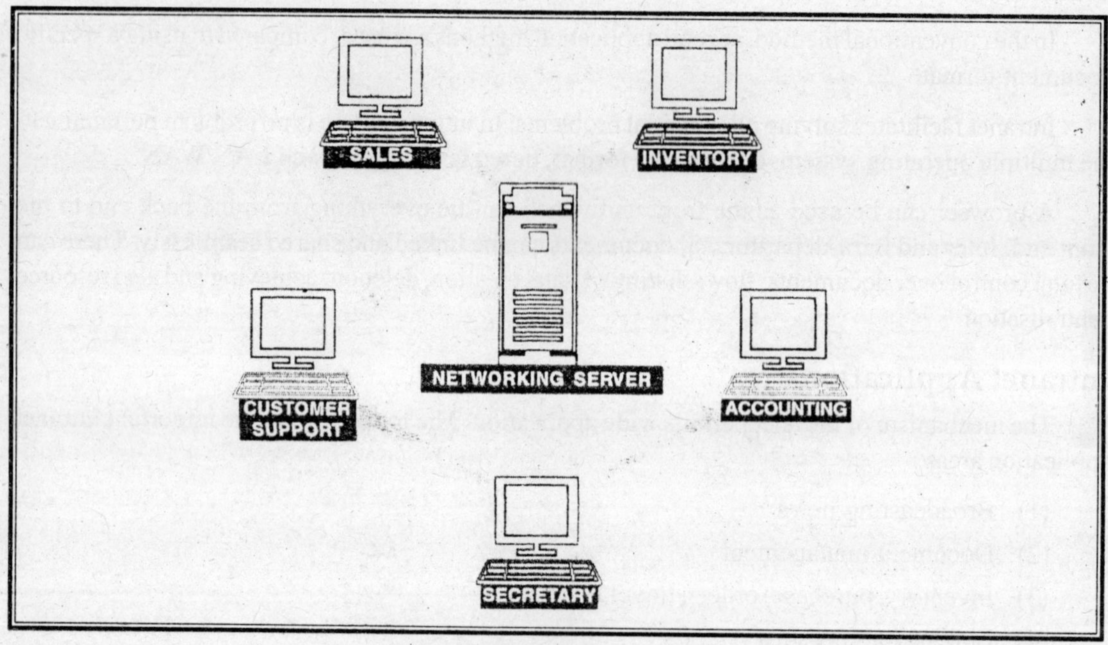

Fig. 15.19 An Office Network

Uses of Intranet

The system of intranet can be used as follows :

(1) Communication: It facilitates to centralise corporate communication. Materials that become outdated on a periodical basis as on a monthly basis, are as follows: phone list, product/ service process, presentation contracts, proposals, requisition forms, marketing materials etc., can be placed on the intranet and will save manpower, wear and tear on covers and printers and they will be cheaper than a print shop.

(2) Facilitating Employees: Intranet gives employees easy access to clients, products and relevant departmental information such as project reports and summaries, updates, catalogues and sales figures. Productivity increases as employees do not have to wait for co-workers to get back to them with job related information.

(3) Interaction: Intranet fosters interaction with departments or offices which are normally isolated from each other and this is done through online newsletters and internal task forces.

(4) Train Employee: Training a small group of employees on an intranet is far less expensive than sending them to a class or using CDROMs. Internet training allows companies to update/ modify information instantaneously and the employees can schedule their training during the not so active business times.

The other uses related to Intranet are: inexpensive distribution, fast movement of data, no need to run to the file room to pick up a form, no need to put in a call to customer services, everyone on this network can access information and it ensures effective monitoring and strategic control of functions.

Features: They are as follows :

(1) Collects information at some central server or a distributed environment.

(2) Sharing resources in an efficient manner.

(3) Improves onward employee speed.

(4) Increases productivity.

(5) Congregates thoughts, ideas, comments, progress and discussions and

(6) Provides contacts which are easier and friendlier.

Groupware in Intranet

In intranet operations, groupware is used. Groupware means programs that help people work together collectively though they are located remotely from each other. Groupware services may include the sharing of calendar, collective writings, e-mail handling, shared database, electronic meetings with each person and be able to see and display information to others and other activities.

There are several resource's solutions for intranets allowing easy use of the intranet and other applications etc. They are very useful towards a better understanding of this emerging technology.

Advantages of Intranet

As per the advantages, Intranet:

(1) Cuts corporate communication cost up to 70 percent.

(2) Increases productivity and efficiency levels.

(3) Meets one or more specific needs better.

(4) Addressing communication issues and

(5) Corporate intranet can provide information in a way that is :

   (a) Immediate

(b) Cost effective and inexpensive

(c) Easy accessibly and usability

(d) Rich in format

(e) Versatile and

(f) Freedom of choice.

(6) Intranet security and safety protects information, SSL technology encrypts packets of information so that it is transferred securely.

(7) It is easy to use and there is no need to learn multiple software packages. The Internet Explorer is used to access all internal and external resources.

(8) It provides a way for people to easily retrieve the information they need.

(9) Intranet removes barriers to free flow of communication within the organisation and allowing groups to communicate and share knowledge.

(10) Intranet automates processing and eliminates the possibility of loss of paper and stationary.

(11) Intranet also provides the publishers who are spending a significant amount of time in producing different versions for the various client-platforms after preparing the content of news letter.

(12) Intranet ensures faster and more effective and increased productivity. It reduces paperwork to establish a paperless office.

(13) Intranet converts the conventional paper office into an electronic office by creating electronic documents for potential business communication.

(14) The intranet functions in such a way that it permits users on the intranet to access data from anywhere to anywhere on the network.

(15) It permits the user to create a personalised home page.

(16) Any member of an organisation has an opportunity to access the technology of intranet and to have access to information within the organisation irrespective of their hardware technology.

(17) All the facilities available on the web are also available on the intranet, browsing, hyperlinking and homepage.

(18) Computer makers are providing intranet products and services which will be easy to install.

(19) Conventional services take 2-3 weeks nearly to reach international customers when the documents are mailed. Intranet solves the problem by transferring the messages electronically.

(20) Web based intranet helps to reach the goal of simplification of information sharing.

(21) It saves valuable office time.

(22) This is by digitising all data and information.

(23) Keeps in touch with dealers, agents, brokers, customers etc.

Extranet

Meaning, Nature and Concept: The extranet is an extension of corporate intranet connecting internal networks of one company with the intranets of its customers, suppliers etc. The mechanism facilitates to create e-commerce application that links all aspect of a business relationship right from ordering to payment of the service.

Like intranet, extranet is also password protected, so that only approved people can get access to it. One way e-commerce is used with extranets for a large sales team that needs to order sales materials and brochures or products to be shipped while they are on the road.

All intranet is designed to facilitate internal communication, while extranets are created for communicating business related information to a particular vendor, distributor or customer. Therefore, extranets are generally more secure and password protected.

Several business organisations, particularly large corporations have been using extranets to improve customer services by making information and orders available within twenty four hours a day, seven days a week and 365 days a year.

Clients/customers in the extranet system can access real time information about project status, costs and development.

Dealers or vendors visiting the extranets can order products or service, check balances, review account information and history, look at pricing agreements and access database information.

Lucent Technologies and AT&T have commissioned World Internet Resources (WIR) to create an extranet. They have proved their metal in this project of communication.

As lines of communication are expanded, productivity improves between teams and departments. Project costs decrease while customer services increase leading to customer loyalty and satisfaction.

Definition of Extranet

Extranets are semi-private networks located outside the corporate firewalls which provide selected internal information to business partners such as clients, customers and suppliers as well as to remote employees. This expansive network supports activities such as sales and marketing, supply chain management, customer/product support, employee support, office equipment and ensuring supply procurement.*

Besides, it expands intranet technology by selectively making the information available to an organisation's business partners, customers and suppliers. This network is key to e-commerce as they combine the privacy and security of intranet with the global reach of the Internet. They are an ideal environment for implementing e-commerce business solutions, build potential business traffic on the Web far above what has been possible with various websites, search engines and banner advertising. So, extranet is the platform of choice for bulk business-to- business e-commerce extranet transactions.

---

* Netscape, Feb. 15, 1999, p. 150

Extranet — A Business Tool

Extranet is an important business tool and has great advantage of the internet technology.

The tool helps to achieve real cost savings and faster responses to changing business condition. There are many reasons that makes extranet an important business tool. Consider the reasons mentioned below:

(1) IP-Based B2B: Extranet is the future of IP-based business to business e-commerce. It is expected of this level of business transactions processing to increase several times. Its business is many times greater than the much publicised business to consumer transactions such as buying books and cars over the Net.

(2) Reducing Costs: Extranet lowers cost by eliminating costly overheads and operation costs. In addition to eliminating the cost of proprietary EDI system, Extranet reduces resources that go into activities like order processing. So, many companies have achieved major costs and recorded costs savings by using Extranet.

(3) Saving Time: This is a potential quality of the application of Extranet.

(4) Partner Relationship: Extranet permits companies to establish stronger relationship with their various business partners by allowing them to share machines and related critical information with each other. A company's business is deeply intertwined with that of its business partner. So, by mutually forming beneficial relationships with their partners, the companies can increase their chances of success.

(5) Feedback: Extranet provides instantaneous feedback on the existing market trends by monitoring of the information accessed on the site. It also provides the following benefits :

(1) Instantaneous feedback on product sales.

(2) Customer, supplier requirement.

(3) Giving companies the ability to keep their timings on the pulse of their business on a day-to-day basis and responses and communication with online clients and customers.

(4) Initiating quick and appropriate.

(6) Decision Making: The launching of a successful extranet allows the companies to make effective and sound decisions quickly which they may not have had to make before. Thus, the extranet brings together organisations with divergent interests enabling them to experience a profound and profitable impact on how a company does business and how it appears to its customers and suppliers.

(7) Goals and Plans: The extranet clearly predefines a company's goals and the means by which they will achieve them.

(8) Forecasting: A well defined extranet network will enable companies to anticipate business problems. Creating a potential business practice requires dynamism and expertise. The mechanism of forecasting makes the companies to think about the issues, practicality those involving business solutions that will come up before they actually implement a system. Identifying these potential problems in advance enables the companies to develop solutions for future problems which inevitably arise.

Extranet Strategy

Maximum benefits can be derived from the extranet provided the strategy developed for this type of network must satisfy the following factors:

(1) Company Needs: This defines the specific company needs, goals and problems that the extranet is going to address both in the short and long - term.

(2) Partner's Needs: Determine business partners' needs and long-term strategies by consulting a large cross section of the partners.

(3) Business Unit and Functional Managers: Get the business unit and functional managers to best understand the business issues, leading them to benefit most from the extranet system involved in strategy development process from the very beginning.

(4) Smaller Partners' Needs: Extranet should work towards adopting business strategies to meet small business partners' needs.

(5) Trusted Partners: Select a wide range of trusted business partners to participate in the pilot programme.

(6) Competitors' Strategies: Analyse major competitors' strategies.*

Internet

Introduction: Focussing on the Internet here is a follow-up of the preliminary material after we understood LAN, WAN, Intranet and Extranet. This subject of Internet briefly and in non-technical terms, explains the internet concept in simple terms to the readers with little or no previous knowledge of computers. It also covers the nature of the subject, uses, application, operations etc., pertaining to the Net. The topic on Internet is included here with the primary object of giving the readers some idea about the principles and concepts of networking to help them succeed in using the Net for success as an entrepreneur, a manager or for other business purposes. While a good idea about computers is essential today, it would be more beneficial in learning the various areas of information technology with expertise and the related aspects of computers.

We frequently come across people talking about the Net in these days. Some business people, research institutions, educational institutions and a group of individuals know and use the internet to the maximum whereas some other people don't really know what it is. With the information technology opening up, people have moulded themselves in the computer culture in a big way, becoming potential IT professionals.

Internet — A Brief History: The Internet has its origin in military operations for defence purposes whereby virtue of its operations, the military personnel are scattered geographically in different distant places. To facilitate reliable, accurate and timely communication network, the Internet was designed for military use so that it is protected from disruption in case of destruction from a nuclear attack.

---

* Dataquest, Feb. 15,1999, p.151.

In 1959, the Pentagon's Advanced Research Project Agency (PARPA) created a network called the PARPA Net which permitted engineers, scientists and others working on military work all over America. In the early days, the initial object of the network was to share computers and information technology. It permitted the exchange of messages as per the system developed.

The PARPA Net subsequently was merged with another network called the Usenet News in 1979. This new organisation is a non-governmental parallel academic network.

Usenet news began to grow slowly and steadily and subsequently it became known as the Internet. The PARPA Net was relating to US organisations having US government associations.

In the global exchange of message, a new development in vogue today is the electronic mail (e-mail).

In the latter part of 1960s, the US government established five super computer centres. These centres acted as the main nodes of the Internet. To this network, all other networks of universities and research institutions were connected.

The designing of personal computers and their widespread use, because of its flexibility, market another important landmark relating to the Internet around 1980s. Till then, the mainframe computers with more speed, storage and memory, have dominated the technology field. Individual users, business organisations, educational institutions etc., went in a very big way to use micro computers. The distinguishing feature of personal computers is that they do not have the capacity of sharing data and resources as they are stand alone machines. In order to solve the problem and to link computers together, the concept of LAN was designed which practically became more popular. Wide Area Network (WAN) was also designed which became widespread particularly with large companies.

Personal computers became more popular and widespread partly due to drastic reduction in the prices. Accordingly, online services like Telnet and CompuServe came into being. The concept of Bulletin Board Services (BBS) came into being, which greatly facilitated to connect individual computers, up to another computer in their vicinity for exchange and potential sharing of information. These are private networks which worked on different hardware and software platforms but could not talk to each other. TCP/IP, as an acronym stands for Transmission Control Protocol/Internet Protocol which are the procedures developed for interconnecting computers and exchanging the data.

Internet technology composed of TCP/IP, which gave birth to the Net helped interconnection of these networks, BBS communities and individual PCs of both home and office.

For exchanging information what is required is to connect any network or computer with the Net by using TCP/IP. Thus, the Internet became the network of all networks.

Yet another development in the history of Internet was recorded in 1990. In Geneva, physicists designed and developed a software for publishing, searching and accessing information on the Net. It was designed as a means to enable scientists to share documents with their colleagues. This is how the World Wide Web (WWW) became popular.

The development of the graphical browser called Mosaic facilitated to access information from the WWW. Thus, WWW has been growing exponentially, dominating the Internet. Thus, the Net came to the mainstream of life.

Internet — A Brief Indian History: Strangely, in India, the Internet is the product of educational and research undertakings. The expression "Internet in India" flashes many images upon the canvas of the mind. In India, the Internet has been for many years in the form of Educational Research Network (ERNET), which was once available only to educational and research committees. In the early period, the Internet facility was not available on a large scale enabling people to get access to it. This is because of the policy laid down by the American Internet Manager, National Science Foundation (NSF), an agency of the American government at that time in the late 1980s. The US government set up five super computer centres which are primarily the nodes of the Internet to which the university and research labs networks were connected.

Internet in India was established in the late 1980s, which was a joint undertaking of the department of electronics of the Government of India and the United Nations Development Programme (UNDP), which used to extend technical assistance to developing nations. Many academic and research and development groups exchanged e-mails with each other using the ERNET. Thousands of scientists and technologists benefit with access to the ERNET facility, which is International in essence.

The Videsh Sanchar Nigam Limited (VSNL), a Government of India enterprise, is India's international telecom carrier, has also contributed its might giving to the expansion of internet technology in India. This backbone network in India is known as VSNL's Gateway Internet Access Network (GIAS). On August 15th, 1995, VSNL launched GIAS for the first time on a commercial basis in the country. It has also set up seven nodes at Mumbai, Delhi, Chennai, Kolkata, Bangalore, Pune, Ahmedabad including access nodes at Ernakulam, Cochin and Keonics. It has also launched intranet services at Lucknow, Hyderabad, Kanpur, Chandigarh and Dehradun.

A full range of internet services are now available. There are the remote internet access nodes which are connected to the main internet access node at Mumbai.

Present Position

In the early days the Internet facility was available to the government particularly for defence, research and development, laboratories, universities and computer science departments etc. In those days, getting connection to the Net itself was a difficult task for various known reasons. In the 1980s, the use of the Internet remained with the above mentioned authorities.

Now, the greatly publicised information super highway is accessible to anyone with time, interest and curiosity. The last fifteen years have witnessed an explosion of the internet activity. The use of the Internet is moving away from pure educational research to a network connecting millions of computers, many of which belong to companies using the Net for commercial purpose.

Concept and Meaning

Net is the short form of Internet, a new name given to the world wide network. The expression stands for inter-network. Computer is a network by itself. In simple words, the Internet is a conglomeration of a number of smaller networks and other smaller inter-connected machines distributed over the entire globe. Internet is a window to the global superhighway and to the cyberspace. So, it is a global system of connected independent groups of computers. It is the world's greatest democracy in terms of getting the information you as a net user require — which is available at your discretion.

These are the days of wonders and the potential of electronics. Among the modern wonders, the Net is one. It is the communication age, and Internet is a network of networks and a mother of all networks. It is a global network created by connecting these smaller networks with telephone lines.

The world network acts as a potential method of communication. Internet is a large repository of information available to the users. The Internet helps to get in touch with anybody around the world at the cost of a telephone call, proving to be economically viable.

It is an arrangement of a link between smaller networks and other individual computers all over the globe. Internet is the world's biggest software library, having opened doors to the vast amount of information available on the space information platform just by the click of a mouse.

Thousands of systems have been connected to the internet which have thousands of files, libraries and documents accessible to the public. Much of this consists of free or low cost shareware programs for virtually every make of computer. There are libraries of documents as well.

The Internet is a two-way communication method. Exploring internet potential brings the world on the screen of the users' computers. The basic principle of the Net is that the sender and the receiver are on the same line of the system.

To explain simply the internet is like the telephone system which is an instrument of global contact. There are many variant ways to connect to the Net. Similarly, there are different types of programs to run. Internet really is a way or path for various computers to communicate.

It is now the easiest thing through the internet to get computers talking to each other. We can communicate within the office, cross the city or even the globe.

Most of the organisations having LANs are now interconnecting. They have crossed the threshold of LANS and enterprise wise networking, internet working or LAN to LAN connectivity is the trend of the hour.

The LAN can be inter-connected with the wide area networks. The routed technology is used to interact with other networks and VSATs (Very Small Aperture Terminal) to integrate remote locations.

The way to merge the world economy with the rest of the world has been paved, thus giving global body corporates potential opportunities to interact with manufacturers world over, to seek technologies and products world wide. Underdeveloped countries face stiff competition in terms of global recognition to multinationals equipped with advanced technologies and strategic marketing tools.

The success of a product in the market depends upon its quality and capacity to compete and sell in the world market. In a global marketing set up, there is a need to inform the potential global customer about the availability of a particular product with certain specifications, price, utility and other features.

The Internet connects computers and terminals often separately by way of boundaries to each other. Simply put, it is a global network and everybody has access to it with a PC connection. Thus, the Internet is accessible to all, but intranet is not freely available to all.

The main objective of the Internet is to facilitate the participating users to have mutual exchange of data-between the computers. To take advantage of these computers are a part of the Internet. The subject or data for mutual exchange may be numerical, alphabetical or a combination of both numerical and alphabetical pictures, movies, any text and anything that a computer is capable of accepting and storing. Graphic Users' Interface facilitates to see pictures also.

Internet — A Global Village

The world is a small place, a global village following the advancements in thc information technology. It means that human potential technology has worked together, leading to globalisation. These words never used to be nor were more true than now. It means that with globalisation, one can sit in parlours or at home and join about millions of spectators watching the Olympics, the Asian Games and other international and national events taking place. The recent information technology revolution has transformed a communication conscious human society into an information-obsessed global village.

The distance between countries has been whisked away, thanks largely to IT. This revolution has been made possible by video recording and camera lenses that extended the range of cur eyes. The new technology in human history permitted people from different parts of this planet to talk, see and communicate with one another electronically.

Earlier, the term global village was considered limited to the world of science fiction, but it is no longer a science fiction. Today, it has become a reality. Today, nothing is too far, or too remote. This is why we say that we live in a global village. In a village, every one knows what is happening in their vicinity. Every one in the village has easy accessibility to information of the village. Similarly, information technology enables us to know what is happening around us and information is freely available with the benefit of easy accessibility to information related to various issues concerned with our lives.

Thus, there is tremendous interaction and inter-dependence which has become true of the whole world. Warious levels of improvement in communication and technological advancement have made this possible. The only thing is to ride this tigress of information technology and our skills lie in riding it to our advantage. There are a very wide range of possibilities available to us through this information technology. This technology may prove a faithful servant depending on how judiciously and to what purpose do we successfully master. Thus, there is a need greater than ever before to perceive the entire gamut of possible substantial relationships between information technology and business so that the former is made subservent to our needs.

Internet — A Woven Global Village

Internet is the global information highway. The networks/computers operating in different environments are knitted to the Net by a common protocol suite and has evolved into one of technology's greatest democracies, permitting the package of all kinds of information criss-crossing with full freedom among the Net users. Through this single channel, scholars, scientists, businessmen, librarians, journalists, artists and software developers are woven into a 'global village', information is vital in today's world. The problem of dealing with the accelerating glut of information is becoming acute and has eased to be within the ability of human beings, leaving them saturated. The human saturated interaction level, the urge to know the latest and in the fastest way has reached such new heights that its realisation through a global information highway of the likes of the Net was but imperative.

Information Highways

Communication highways are data transmission channels. The functions of these channels are to carry data from one placc to another. The channels broadly categorised into three types are narrow band, voice band and broad band.

These bands indicate the rate at which data is transmitted. If the bandwidth of a channel is wider, it means it has more capacity to transmit data. For instance, telegraph lines are narrow band channels. They have the capacity to transmit about 5 to 30 characters per second (cps) voice.

The country has been eneavouring to build the global information highway. It is so essential for the sustenance of fast industrial knowledge and international economics.

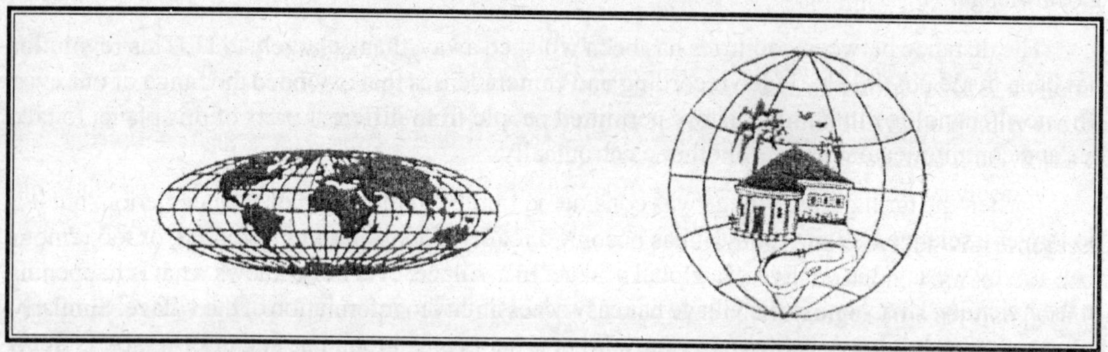

Fig. 15.20 Global Village **Fig. 15.21 Global Village**

Historically, telephone broadcasting and cable television are potential information transmitting media. Developments in technology namely micro-electronics, digital application, optical fibres, satellites, radio frequency range, micro and main frame computing has brought tremendous changes in information exchange. As such, long distance has become so cheap, quick and accurate.

Government of India approved in the year 1997, the creation of National Information highway at a cost of Rs. 700 crore, with plans to create the infrastructure for a national wide transmission of voice and data transmission. A national infrastructure is necessary by pooling in the transmission capacity existing in the country with three different departments, the Department of Telecommunications, Railways and the power sector. It takes place by integrating available communication facilities of these departments as a network. The department of telecommunications has its own transmission facilities. The Ministry of power and Railways has its own communication network. All these can be integrated to utilise the common facility and create national infrastructure, to constitute the potential national information highway. Initially, it was proposed to have a capacity of 8 megabytes per second with a facility to increase as and when demand requires.

Information Superhighways

In recent years, there has been sudden emphasis on international recognition about the information revolution. This revolution is popularly known as the information superhighways. But it needs a well co-ordinated and comprehensive information infrastructure which will cover the use of computers, telecommunications and office systems technologies. This information infrastructure facilitates collection, processing, storage packaging and dissemination of information which may be in the form of voice, data, text and image. Vast amount of information is available on database world wide which must be explored.

Superhighways connect large cities and countries and from these large cities, they come to smaller freeways and pathways to link together small towns whose residents travel or move on slowly with narrow residential ways. The super highway is the high speed net. Information super highways involve the availability of information on-line at all levels—schools, homes, offices and so on. We often hear about superhighways in computer telecommunications in recent years.

Superhighways are very much a part of the communications. Americans call it National Information Infrastructure. In India, the National Informatics Centre (NIC) dedicated national information highways to the nation in the year 1994.

Information superhighways is an advanced version of the already existing information highway, it is a satellite-computer optical fibre communication system which facilitates the transfer of massive data along with audio, video and graphic information at high speed.

Information Superhighways (ISH) have been commissioned by the National Information Centre (NIC) which provides free exchange of information among software and databases, educational institutions and hospitals etc. A large number of networks already operating in India such as Educational and Research Network (ERNET) of the Department of Electronics and the Remote Area Business Message Network (RABMN) of the Department of Telecommunications are part of the ISH which is super-imposed on the giant National Informatics Centre Network (NICNET), India's largest satellite-based computer communication network. NICNET already has about 700 satellite earth stations in 500 cities and towns around the globe.

Applications of ISH

With a large database, ISH enables organizations, public or private and individuals to have access to substantial specific information in various dimensions :

(1) Video conferencing by the ISH would enable business organizations or others to conference simultaneously from different cities.

(2) The database of ISH containing around 15,000 journals including 1,000 full text journals would enable users to have access to all these journals, by cutting costs of subscriptions considerably.

(3) ISH has an impact on the media too. The user can select from the newspapers only those news items which would be of interest to them.

(4) Books fed into the computer database could be read on the computer monitor, with pages being turned over with the click of a button.

(5) ISH offers latest services such as transmission of laser videos over the computer network from which users can select the movies of their choice from thousands of titles stored in the computer databases.

Number of Networks that Constitute the Internet

It is to be understood that the Internet does not necessarily mean collection and connection of a large number of networks. Sometimes, a single computer can form part of the Net. in this, a single computer is connected to a network or service provider which is mainly linked to the Net. Thus, transmitting information or data from one network to another network is done. So LANs, WANs as well as the large commercial online application is also not of the Net character but through gateways, they can be connected to the Net.

So, as regarding the number of computers or networks that make up the Internet, there is no fixed number to constitute the Net system. There is no limit to the number, for this may be in thousands or millions. Globally, lakhs of computers and networks form a major part of the Net.

So, any number of computers can be connected to the Net. The system is so fast, convenient and flexible, making it the only method best suitable to connect universities, educational institutions, labs and research institutes around the world. The academic users can use the Net with different software packages to participate in subject related discussions over the network. It facilitates to create documents and software libraries on the Net making them accessible to all the net users. What is required to connect any network or the net computer up with the internet is the ability to use TCP/IP for exchanging this information.

Size of Internet

How many people are using the Internet is an important aspect to know. According to some studies, ending January 2000, there were about 250 million users. The following is the break :

Canada 4 USA	131.1	million
Europe	64.23	million
Asia Pacific	42.6	million
South America	7.10	million
Africa	2.36	million
Middle East	1.29	million

The figures indicate that the number of net users is growing at a staggering rate. The number of web pages on the Internet recently swept past the one billion mark. They are growing in number over the years.

For example, one billion hours amounts to 1,14,155 years and one billion minutes make 1,902 years. If you got in your car and drove 100 kms per hour, it would take you 1,141 years to drive one billion kms. Even one billion seconds is beyond thirteen years' worth of time.*

* Computers Today, 16-31 March. 2000, pp. 72-73.

Who Owns and Manages the Internet

The world is getting networked in a big way. Today, there are millions of internet users the world over to whom it has become a means of cross border transfer of information, it facilitates direct contact between the individuals, groups and institutions from different countries. Voluminous information available on the Internet becomes available instantaneously, which can be accessible to millions of individuals.

It may be mentioned that the Net is not owned by any single individual or organisation. The management and control of the Internet is completely decentralised and it is entirely managed by individual and organisational volunteers. Every user pays for his part. Each network meets the expenditure for the installation and operating costs as well as those connecting up with the other networks. The Internet is a co-operative environment and as a social as well as technical in essence-catering to all segments of the society. It is the responsibility of the users to ensure the trust and loyalty of the community.

Glorious Dreams — Realms of Reality

The Internet has brought a revolutionary change in computing and communication. It works towards strategies to interact with everyone, thus satisfying the world's growing inclination towards global communication — who are eager to seek information at all levels.

It is supported by satellites that will gird the planet at low altitude like a rotating system of chain mail, transmitting signals from any one point on the planet to any other with speed and capacity of fibre optics cable.

Internet provides a range of facilities and information to computer users. Access to the Net has opened up a whole world of information to the subscribers by using the latest stored program control (SPC) as well a satellite and fibre optics technology to provide global connectivity to these subscribers. This has greatly moved towards facilitating international trade, commerce and industry which needs reliable, fast, accurate and heavy load carrying communication links. The telecommunications network is universal in application and India is connected with communication links to the rest of the world to meet the requirements both in terms of quality, quantity and variety of information.

Global communication systems are providing a multitude of services-voice, data, accessibility and a variety of communication media- copper, fibre, microwave and satellite links. The technological advances in miniaturisation, signal processing, compression, fibre and satellites are shrinking the distinction between different types of services. These communication services *viz.*, voice, fax, date, e-mail, video conferencing, television, radio etc. ensure instant access to information, people and machines throughout the globe. The informatics revolution brought in by the technological advances in the field of satellites, cables, switching, computer, devices, etc., is influencing radically the way the economic activities are being carried throughout the globe, making it virtually one gigantic market place a global village.

The development in sophisticated communication technologies giving overseas communication services has shrunk the world, thus making the world one big family. Nearly 150 countries can be contracted from India, by using satellite and sophisticated gateways exchange and the concept of global village has now become a reality. Distances between countries have been bridged and people have been brought closer to each other. Across the globe, corporations, individuals, business houses etc., have been reaping the benefits of the Internet in a big way.

The Internet has moved towards eliminating the barriers to free and fast communication and allowing groups within the companies and groups outside to communicate and share knowledge. The internet technology is applied to the network of components i.e., making navigating, tracing and making information retrieval far simpler than ever before.

It offers many advantages, most notably is of the use and communication to any hardware platform that supports the web browser. The internet users can download data from the websites.

Information is available on the Net on any topics of study and the data traffic has been increasing considerably in the recent years. Higher the capacity of the Net, more is the speed with which data can be accessed by net users. New technologies have enabled the network towards enabling access to the global village and offered the world opportunity for distributed computing possible. The technologies include :

(1) Network File System (NFS) and
(2) Network Information Service (NIS).

The Net is all set to revolutionise the information. The internet technology is based upon accepted standards which is an unanimously accepted norm and widely used. The internet is based on the following three main standards :

(1) TCP/IP — (Transmission Control Protocol/ Internet Protocol) for connectivity.
(2) HTTP — (Hypertext Transfer Protocol) for interfacing with data.
(3) SMTP — (Simple Mail Transfer Protocol) for electronic mail.

Information Available on the Net

Information on various subjects are available on the internet which can be accessed by any one. For instance, the following are the themes, a few to mention, available on the internet as broadly classified :

(1) Agriculture (international food and nutrition database, agricultural weather statistics, market news, drought information, newsletters.)
(2) Archaeology (thousands of databases of archaeological investments.)
(3) Bulletin Boards System (huge amounts of scientific, technical, non- technical information, environmental protection and hundreds of files on a wide range of subject areas.)
(4) Business and finance (business, finance, research databases.)
(5) Computers-literature (weekly news bulletins on topics like workstations, supercomputers, interviews, news etc.)

(6) Education (covers colleges, universities relating to information on scholarships, ranks, fellowships, research, faculty development etc.)

(7) Environment (information relating to environment data in text, graphics and table form.)

(8) Games (game server permits interesting online games including bucks, moria, tetris sokoban and other adventure games.)

(9) Geography (access to countries, cities, regions and to access their information like population, latitude, longitude etc.)

(10) Health (health information including AIDS, its statistics, risks, treatment, research news etc.)

(11) History (databases of American and European historical topics.)

(12) Internet and resources (information about people, organisations and resources on the Net and related online services and resources.)

(13) Language (choose from online Webster's Dictionary and spelling references, pronunciation, definitions etc.)

(14) Libraries (include databases like library, catalogues, current articles, information databases, other library systems, library and system news.)

(15) News (articles from USA today.)

(16) Physics (nuclear physics, statistical measurements, radiation levels and other information for the US.)

(17) Space (NASA Space link history, current events, projects and plans at NASA.)

(18) Sports and Athletics

(19) Technology (information technology articles.)

(20) Travel and

(21) Weather

What to Do on the Internet ?

Users of the internet can do anything as per their areas of interest which are available on the Net. However, the following are some of the important things which can be done through the Internet:

(1) Online news services

(2) Daily news can be read

(3) Listen to music

(4) Playing sounds

(5) Electronic fund transfer

(6) Cybershow room

(7) Cyber payments

(8) Consumer durable services

(9) Credit collections

(10) Credit ratings
(11) Distance education
(12) Cultural information
(13) Educational research
(14) Foreign exchange
(15) Travel and tourism
(16) Medical health
(17) Publications and journals
(18) Libraries
(19) Legal services
(20) NRI services
(21) Photography
(22) Advertisements
(23) Stock market
(24) Student related higher education information
(25) Yellow pages
(26) Histories
(27) Court judgements
(28) Consultancy
(29) Banking
(30) Shopping
(31) Commodity pricing information
(32) Electronic bulletin boards
(33) Reading, asking questions, answering questions, participation in discussions and other news groups
(34) Teaching and marketing and
(35) Payments etc.

Features of Internet

They read as follows

(1) Computers have the capability to communicate with each other. If connectivity is given, information can be exchanged between computers.

(2) The communication function between computers facilitates access to information residing in one computer from another computer.

(3) A group of computers in a net system are connected with the help of wires, cables or the wireless.

(4) The interconnected computers can communicate with each other with the help of software.

(5) It is the software which constitutes the network.

(6) The device of the modem is to be used on both the sides connected to a telephone line which facilitates that the two networks can communicate with each other by using the modem.

(7) A network may be a simple network of two computers, an office network of more than two computers, network of networks, larger network and networks around the world.

(8) Information can also be obtained through commercial network packages like bulletin board packages etc.

User Groups of Internet

The internet is used widely as a valuable information source on several different subjects which are available to the public. Presently, the user group of internet services are :

(1) Corporations
(2) Commercial organisations
(3) Universities
(4) Government institutions
(5) Research institutions
(6) Commercial users
(7) Individuals
(8) Entertainment users
(9) Homes for pleasure and
(10) Medical groups etc.

The Internet comprises of the world wide network of computers, and it is increasingly being commercialised. Its importance and uses have been greatly recognised by a wide cross section of public and the use of internet is moving away from pure academic and research communities to networks connecting millions of computers, many of which belong to companies and other organisations using the internet for commercial purposes. On the other hand, the service providers on the Net are also undergoing a sea change from contributions by government funded agencies to private operators as well as major telecommunications carriers. These commercial operators have interconnected their network to form Commercial Internet Exchange (CIX).

Thus, information on the internet and opportunities to use it are rapidly growing and the last 15 years have witnessed an explosion of internet activities.

The internet is changing the way people communicate world over. This new technological innovation is gaining popularity faster than any other communication media today with the fast expanding universe of the internet, every one can have access to information on the internet. It can be used both for communicating with others, fun, business, games, movies etc. The experiences of the Net users reveal that internet-based resources and businesses are identifying new ways for promoting and selling their products or services on the Net, thereby mustering new customers, increasing their turnover and ensuring increased profits.

In the early days, the internet was made available only to the government, academic and research institutes. But today, it is used extensively and the number of users connecting to it from home continues to grow dramatically. The primary uses of internet are shifted from research to commercial application, moving to customers and business application has been increasing by lakh of users annually.

Gateway

It is a generic term used as a name for computers that forward and route data between two and more networks. Gate is a short form of gateway. Technically, it means a computer that transmits files or e-mail from one network, which is a window of a country to another window of another country. With the help of interface machines, the networks are connected when more than one data network is connected, this called the gateway.

The network of a building, premises or office is a gateway to the Net. For instance, sending an e-mail by one office network to another office network or by one country's net to another country's net is a case of sending messages online. Gateway is a computer or the program running on the internet which transfers files or e-mail messages or commands from one network to another (C. Crumlish).

India's Gateway to the Internet

The Videsh Sanchar Nigam Limited (VSNL) is the sole overseas communication organisation in India and India's only international communications carrier. It has opened a window or gateway to Global Information Services (GIAS). Thus, India has one backbone network that operates at a very high speed and carries the bulk of the online traffic. All other smaller networks are connected to this backbone.

VSNL has contributed substantially to the expansion of the GIAS network in India. It has been providing access services to the Internet on all India basis. It has its main internet access node at Mumbai, connecting other internodes in other countries. In view of the ever growing internet access needs, the system uses satellite media, submarine cable etc., to cater to the potential Net users.

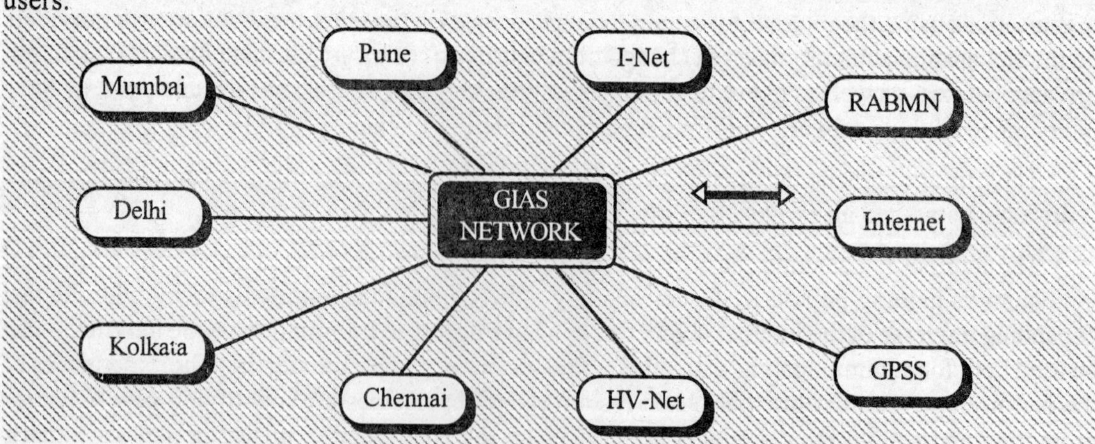

Fig. 15.22 Videsh Sanchar Nigam's Gateway Internet Access Services

Working of the World Wide Net

Small local or regional networks are connected to the World Wide Net (WWN) which is a complex web of various networks. It is like a modern road network of transcontinental super highways connecting large cities. This follows the coming of smaller freeways and pathways to link together small towns, whose residents travel on slower and narrower residential ways. The net super highway is high-speed internet. A computer is connected to this super highway that uses a particular system of transferring data at high speed.

In the US, the major internet 'backbone' can really move data at rates of 45 million bits per second. Smaller computers of particular geographical regions are connected to the internet which transmits data. Individual computers or smaller networks constitute a source of feeding data to these regions. In the system, there is no one central computer running the internet. The resources of the internet are to be found among thousands of individual computers.

Upload/ Download

This refers to transferring files via, 'ftp' Uploading is moving a file from your computer to a remote host on the Net. Downloading is moving a file from the Internet to your computer. It is a 'to and fro' system.

Importance of Internet

The most remarkable facet of the emerging digital economy is electronic commerce. E-commerce is radically changing not only the way businesses serve and communicate with their customers, but also the way they manage their relations with both suppliers and partners. Both the new internet based companies and traditional producers and services are transforming their business processes into e-commerce processes. In an effort to lower the costs, improved customer service and increased productivity, the value of e-commerce transactions world wide is growing exponentially. Many developed countries and some developing countries consider the Net as a unique opportunity leap-frogging whole stages of industrial development.

The Net, apart from enabling potential e-commerce, is also contributing to the rapid internationalisation of the services sector. It makes it possible to unbundle the production and consumption of information-intensive service activities. These activities e.g., computing, accounting, role of personnel, marketing and distribution play a fundamental role not only in service industries but also in manufacturing and primary industries.

More and more people are gaining access to the Net and more and more of them are shopping on-line, because it provides a level of convenience to merchants and customers. The Net is fast becoming the method of choice for transacting businesses globally. In the days to come, all business persons will conduct an ever increasing number of business transactions online. There are several internet access application solutions available in various forms — this is being used by net users in a big way.

They provide cost effective and easy functioning, thus allowing up to the minute flow of information. The network of computers around the world is growing substantially. There are many sources and providers of information on the Net, and almost as many ways to access them are available to the Net users.

The net users are increasing and net business booming, with millions getting to it world wide. The marvellous internet technology is offering ample opportunities and interacting with others from any where to any where at any time. It is a sort of mixing of anonymity and adventure, which most businesses exploit to develop their business. There are no barriers to online entry. Merchants, customers and others can easily access to the Net with initial investments.

Networking is a fortunate business segment that has assumed the role of potential infrastructure industry. Internet and the growth of the world wide web have accelerated the growth of e-commerce and created opportunities. Internet is the medium for e-commerce and the single biggest agent of business. It is changing the way we pay, create, communicate and invest in smooth business transactions. Not only does it open up whole a host of new business opportunities, it also allows and enables traditional business to :

(1) Streamline their business operations.

(2) Reach newer markets.

(3) Reduce costs.

(4) Improve business cycle time.

(5) Improve customer service levels.

(6) Increase efficiency and

(7) Build potential ties with business partners scattered worldwide.

Businessmen have viewed the internet to be an important business application tool of the future. People are moving to take advantages of opportunities created by the internet at a fast pace. Internet-based orders reaching out to the customers is a valuable business tool.

The internet revolution has established itself in India. With the advent of suitable infrastructure and favourable online business policy, there is likely to be an exponential growth in Net applications for e-commerce. The last one year has seen a sharp increase in the number of internet users and an improvement in the overall quality and prices of online services offered. Easy access to the Net is also triggering a boom in computer sales and websites for the global extension of marketing. Major companies have either set up or are in the process of setting up their websites for global recognition.

Shopping and Shopsite over the Internet

The popular area of selling and buying goods in the international niche market has expanded to online shopping websites. There are reasonable sites for rare, classically conventional and modern goods. The more comprehensive the e-commerce solutions, the more sophisticated online shopping services can occur. There are more opportunities to the people to spend money on internet shopping which is a convenient method of buying desired products.

The Internet has completely revolutionised the way we shop. The buyers need not rush home after a frantic spree around the stores and supermarkets shopping for day to day products. Buying and selling transactions online take place in a quite different manner. In conventional shopping, people go to the stores and supermarkets. We are nearer to the online virtual supermarket, final vision screen, where we make a selection by clicking on the products desired to buy, witness a shopping basket graphics file up with graphics indicating your purchases and finally find credit card details to pay and settle for the online purchase. Credit card is an important pre-requisite for online shopping.

A shopsite with reference to e-commerce is an online store creation system. The site allows merchants to bill the user on the basis of the catalogue of products to sell on the Net. It also deals with tools for site creation and management, sales and purchase statistics secure encrypted transactions and online order fulfilment.

Cyberstore - front on Internet

Cyberstore-front Inc. offers storefront creation, order processing, business administration and management tools with unlimited lasting capability and the most comfortable shopping, It handles all aspects-designing websites from logo creations to credit card merchant account, so that the business can accept real time credit transactions. It has great capability, functioning 24 hours a day and seven days a week.

Internet for Small Businesses

E-commerce solutions are available for both small and medium sized businesses. There are developers of integrated e-commerce applications for both these categories of business.

E-commerce builders is one such solution, which brings e-commerce to small businesses with potential online resources and articles about e-commerce marketing, promotion of websites, with software programming and designing tools, for these small businesses ensure their global recognition.

The EC- builder is the first product to bring the power of e-commerce into the hands of small business users. This is known as simplicity — a simple point with the click software application.

Software EC-builder Pro 4.5 is an enhanced credit card transaction processing gateways. With the EC-builder and EC-software one can:

(1) Easily create an e-commerce website for small business.

(2) Automatically promote small businesses to search engines.

(3) Customise online store with any image or video.

(4) Add media files and banners to the website.

(5) Host online business with any internet service provider.

(6) Accept credit cards and complete e-commerce transaction and

(7) Accept multiple product orders with a built-in shopping card.

Feature of EC-builder

EC-builder helps to get small businesses online enabling sale transaction in hour. Multiactive Software Inc is the leading world wide development and market of innovative sales, customer management and internet commerce solutions.

Internet commerce solutions form Multi Active Software (MOS) Inc. include EC-builder, Maximiser Enterprise, Maximiser, tracker and sharkware.

Maximiser Enterprise 5.0 is the leading sales and customer management solutions for small to medium sized businesses world wide. The products are used by organisations and individuals within the financial services, telecommunications, insurance technology and manufacturing companies.

With the availability of IT enabled e-commerce solutions, its acceptability is growing rapidly among small, medium and home based business and people poised to capitalise upon this retail market. Many solutions providers are offering e-commerce capable web sites, online promotion and work on strategies to upgrade facilities, thus allowing potential customer relationships, build customer base and ensure long-term customer commitment to their business. There are many products which brought the power of e-commerce into the hands of small retail business users. The simplicity and sophistication and affordable price software are both far beyond expensive site creation tools.

Thus, the application of the world wide web and Net for e-commerce is no longer a luxury and confined to large businesses, they are not for priviliged businesses, government and home users but all have access to it. Even small businesses can have their own website and do potential global business. It has produced a revolutionary new way for small businesses to communicate and interact with customers and new potential customers. This will be possible by assuring customers online security and providing services at the earliest.

Personalising the Net

Until now; the Net has been a vast repository of freely available information. One of the greatest joys of surfing is the ability to go off on a bizarre tangent, with new sites just a click away. However, the era of personalisation is fast approaching and the **Web is at crossroads in its evolution.**

Will it finally fulfil Marshall McLuhan's prophecy that lighting communication will create a global village where any important news and information spreads through the community like wildfire or will people withdraw into themselves, focussing more and more on their own narrow interests.

Howard Rheingold, author of The Virtual Community, believes in sociability. "There is a hunger for community that grows in the breasts of people, especially as more and more informal public spaces disappear from our lives," he says. Stanford University's Norman Nie takes the opposite view, believing that "the more time people spend using the Net, the more they lose contact with their social environment".

Will the internet bring us together in virtual communities or will it tear us apart as we filter our view of the world so effectively and personally that we lose the shared experience that is at the heart of any real community? This leaves those who hope to provide the Net with its news coverage in a quandary whether to concentrate on the community or on the special interests? Walter Bender, principal investigator of Massachusetts Institute of Technology's News in the Future Consortium, believes personalisation is the key. "Modern telecommunications are leading inevitably to the smallest news product imaginable: the personal newspaper, or Daily Me," he explains.

This would have content culled from all over the Web, personalised just for you. It could take into account your diary and include travel directions, and follow your football teams's progress — perhaps the only way we 're going to see a sports section not dominated by Premiership clubs.

What makes the question of personalisation versus community so fraught is that the Internet is ideally suited to either approach. Chat rooms and increasingly advanced messaging and conference services let people contact each other whatever their geographical location, and huge portals such as Yahoo! and MSN can provide news as one aspect of very general community service.

On the other hand, esoteric groups with little funding or experience can tailor sites to their own specific interest — think of the frightening number of Star Trek sites on the Web. The increased accuracy of search engines lets surfers home in on what they want quickly, leaving everything else by the wayside. Content providers are trapped between the Scylla of people wanting to know something about every thing and the Charybdis of people wanting to know everything about something.

One thing everyone agrees has to be avoided is simply transferring content wholesale from the old media - websites differ from print as much as print differs from broadcast. Its a ludicrously obvious point, but reading from a screen is not nearly as enjoyable as reading from a page. Wired, the technology culture magazine, once received a guilt-stricken e-mail from a reader who had ploughed through an entire issue online and wanted to pay for it. The publisher replied : "If you can read that much from a screen, you deserve to have it free." New media barons have to focus on what differentiates the Internet from old media, and so far, few seem to exploit its strength and understand its weaknesses.

For instance, the simplicity of publishing material on websites means they can be constantly updated. The magical click ability of hypertext means readers can follow their own path through the material, delving into areas more deeply than would be possible using offline publication. Similarly, the online reader can easily browse vast archives for specific information.

David Card, senior analyst at Jupiter Communications, believes there is a market for content online. "At the moment we're seeing errors in scope. Too many sites have eyes bigger than their markets," he explains.

David Shenk, the author of two books on information overload, believes personalised news is inevitable, but thinks it is "very dangerous". He fears that people not exposed to general news will become blinkered.

E-transaction: Handle with Care

Electronic commerce like any other business involves the exchange of some form of money for soft or hard goods and services. But for many, payment processing on the Internet is a major problem. The whole process seems unnecessarily complicated and can be a nightmare to set up. In an interview with Indiatimes. com, Jayanta Chatterjee, chief knowledge officer, Venture Infotek Global, explains how online payment processing works and points out some of the pitfalls that businesses should try to avoid.

Excerpts from the interview :

How prepared are we to use electronic payment systems for e-commerce?

Implementation of electronic payment systems for e-commerce is in its infancy and still evolving. The technical, economic and legal components of electronic payment systems are yet to be comprehended to the desirable extent.

As a result, there are a number of competing proposals and implementations of electronic payment systems. One thing is clear to everyone involved in electronic payments. Electronic payments ultimately are far cheaper than mailing out paper invoices and then later processing received payments. It is convenient for customers and it saves the company a lot of money. Estimates indicate that the cost of billing one person varies between Rs. 50 and Rs. 70. Sending bills and receiving payments over the Internet promises to drop the billing paying cost to an average of Rs.5 per bill. The total savings is huge when you multiply the unit cost times the number of customers that could use electronic payment.

What are the most preferred ways of payment for an e-commerce transactions?

There are many basic ways to pay for an e-commerce transaction ranging from cash on delivery (e.g. VPP), wire transfers (Inter-bank, Intra-bank-Net Banking), payments cards such as credit and debit cards, stored value card and Cyber Currency.

But the most preferred means of e-payment has been payment cards (credit and charge cards), which online shoppers use for a majority of their Internet purchase. Payment cards provide built-in security for merchants because they provide greater assurance that they will be paid through payment card issuing companies than through the sometimes slow direct invoicing process.

The elaborate series of actions associated with using a payment card are often transparent to the consumer. Several groups and individuals are involved: the merchant, the merchant's bank, the customer, the customer's bank and the payment card company that issued the customer's payment card. All of these entities must work together in order for customers' charges to be credited to the merchant's accounts (and *vice versa* when a customer receives a payment card credit for returned goods).

How different is the use of payment cards on the Internet ?

Most people are familiar with the use of payment cards. When you purchase one or more items, the clerk runs your card through the online payment card terminal and your card account is charged immediately. The process is slightly different on the Internet, though the purchase and charge process follow the same rules.

Laws prohibit merchants from accepting payment cards credits to their account until the products are shipped. That is, an Internet stores cannot charge your payment card until the day that they pack and ship your merchandise to you.

Payment card transactions follow these general steps once the merchant receives a consumer's payment card information, which is sent via a Secure Socket Layer-protected Web page.

(1) The merchant must authenticate the payment card to ensure it is both valid and not stolen.

(2) The merchant can check with the consumer's payment card issuer to ensure that funds are available and put a hold on the funds needed to satisfy the current charge.

(3) Often a few days, following the consumer's request for purchase, settlement occurs which means that funds travel through the banking system into the merchant's account after the purchase has been shipped.

When customers arrive at a stores electronic check-out counter, merchants want to offer them payment options that are safe, convenient and widely accepted. The key is to figure out which choices work the best for your company and for your customers. You will have to make some choice and choose the best one or two solutions for your situation and budget.

But payments in e-commerce represents some challenges and several risks.

What are these challenges and risks involved in e-commerce transactions ?

The cyber world is different. The identity of both buyers and sellers is a challenge. On many occasions, the consumer is not genuine and may be using some one else's card, which was lost or stolen. There are also times when you may be dealing with a fraud merchant, who may deliver sub-standard goods to you. And above all, there is considerable risk of leakage and tampering with credit card information flow on the Internet.

How can e-transactions be insured from such a problem?

Electronic payment technologies and services providers will have to develop a secure online payment gateway uniquely designed for regional ground realities taking care of infrastructure bottlenecks yet creating a fairly secure payment system.

As such, Internet business will typically require a separate account and the cost is likely to be higher because the risk is greater. In a retail store, the merchant sees the card and the customer and can compare signature, obtain ID or other means of verifying authenticity. There is greater risk of fraud when the card is not physically presented such as telephone or Internet orders. Therefore these transactions typically carry a higher processing fee, which is another challenge for those working on e-payment technologies.

E-payments: A new way of life

As the Internet continues to transform commerce as we know it, the method of payment is one component which is critical to successfully conducting business across a network. An intense battle is on between the conventional and electronic modes of payments for value-exchange on the Internet. While it is unlikely that cash payments will die out because of their robustness in the face of technical difficulties, a few ungainly documentary methods may quickly disappear. because some electronic payments systems that address the same appear to be much more effective, says Piyush Khaitan, founder of Venture Infotek Global Ltd. He further focusses on the electronic payments system and questions related to it,

What does an electronic payments system mean?

E-payments system is a mechanism wherein payments take place electronically without actual exchange of cash or cheque. Banks are the backbone of the payments systems as they act as a guarantor to the seller and recover money from the buyer. Some of the popular e-payment products are :

(1) Card-based products-credit card, debit card and stored value card.

(2) Electronic Clearing Services (ECS).

(3) Web banking, Internet commerce and other related products.

Why do we need e-payment systems?

The total personal consumption expenditure in India is $ 225 billion (Rs. 10,00,000 crore) out of which only $ 2.5 billion (Rs. 12,000 crore) happens electronically. Compare this with the US economy in which out of $ 6 trillion personnel consumption expenditure, $ 2 trillion happens just using credit/debit cards. Thus we rely for practically all our transaction needs on cash. This increases the amount of currency in the economy. This high amount of cash in circulation has its own disadvantages:

(1) The cost of printing and maintaining the currency is a very expensive affair, especially in low denomination notes.

(2) A high demand for currency results in shortage of currency.

(3) The high incidence of cash transactions has an undesirable effect of tracking these transactions very difficult and leading to loss of revenue in the form of taxes like sales tax etc.

All these factors points to the immediate need for developing a strong e-payments system.

What are the key drivers for e-payments?

Growth of e-payments systems in India will depend on certain key factors such as:

(1) Regulatory: The government is taking a serious note of this issue. The Saraf Committee, set up by the Reserve Bank of India (RBI) in 1994, has identified and suggested a road map to address the technology issues related to e-payments. As a follow up to the various recommendations, we now have legislation in place to recognise and deal with electronic transactions. Likewise, guidelines have been announced for the formation of a consumer credit bureau, issuance of debit cards and stored value cards and also technical standards for the same are now in place.

(2) Competition: With the advent of the new non-PSU banks like HDFC Bank, ICICI Bank, UTI Bank etc, MNC banks are forced to innovate and compete vigorously by offering enhanced value propositions to consumers. We have seen a suite of new payment products unfold. Also, PSU banks and now even the smaller ones are in the market with a variety of offerings. All this means more and more e-payment products and systems.

(3) Consumer Preference: Increased middle income affluence, opening of the economy, awareness and sophistication in urban and semi-urban households due to the reach of cable television have all contributed to the Indian consumer demanding and using e-payment systems that provide convenience, security and status.

(4) Infrastructure and Technology: The telecommunications infrastructure in most metros and mini-metros is now world class. Also, bandwidth and international gateways are easily available at affordable cost. Trends in mobile commerce online transaction processing and knowledge management demonstrate that e-payments will grow at a very fast pace.

What do you think should be done to increase the number of electronic transactions in India?

The government has already announced guidelines and defined a clear-cut regulatory framework, whereby it has become easy for banks to introduce e-payment products. What is perhaps missing is a definitive road map, which agreed to targets and a tracking and feedback system.

The second need is to bring down the cost of the transaction. For example, each point of sale terminal costs about Rs. 25,000, ATM machine Rs. 8,00,000, magnetic stripe card about Rs. 10-25 and smart card about Rs. 100.

These costs are abnormally high by international standards because of the very high customs and other duties. If all such duties are abolished, we will see an immediate affordability of such technology and consequent reduction in the use of cash.

I remember a Rs. 5 note actually costs more than 5 rupees to produce and had a life of only 30-35 days. A payment card, on the other hand, typically lasts 2-3 years. This will encourage the use of cards and result in more transactions.

The third thing is that utility companies should come forward to accept e-payment instruments as an official payment tool and should provide consumers the convenience to go for such payments.

Job Hunting on the Web

When Ajit Joglekar's job as systems analyst in an Andheri based unit became victim of a downsizing operation, he decided to go to the web for professional help. Discarding the traditional route of job consultants and placement services, he began scouting India's leading job sites — the likes of jobstreet. com, naukri.com — jobsahead.com — posting his resume on these online job joints.

Three days following his cyber roamings, he had signed the dotted line with a leading Mumbai-based software house, at a salary atleast 40 per cent higher than his earlier assignment. Roughly translated, that meant a 13 per cent jump for each day he was ironically 'out of work'.

A search on WWW.google.com led Mr. Joglekar to some of these jobs, following which he was besieged with phone calls from organisations looking for someone "just like him." The fact of the matter is when it comes to jobs and careers now, self help, using the Net as a tool is in.

Potential job aspirants say this sure beats chasing after headhunters and agencies that may or may not open the right doors. I feel that both can co-exist. However, looking for a job online allows applicants to take control of their job search. With just a few mouse clicks, they can post their biodatas, pick and choose the companies they prefer to work with and even monitor the safe passage of their curriculum vitaes into the relevant hands.

There are of course the odd instances when people putting out their resumes in the hope of attracting some big fish have found themselves instead hooked and cooked when they received responses from their own companies' HR departments for posts that sounded suspiciously like their own.

Oops! The occasional embarrassment aside, job seekers are finding the Web a virtual storehouse of bigger opportunities and broader career horizons. There's also the all-important perk of by-passing files of snail mail crowding the desks of hiring managers.

Today, most leading companies (both Indian and global) post job listings on their own sites. A regular tapping of these could lead you into a unexpected pastures and a juicy job, well before some other contenders opting for the good old Mumbai postal department path.

In most job searches, speed and access to information are key. On the Web, one can reach thousands of companies by simply leading the cursor up the right cyber alley. You can also access the job listings that appear in hundreds of newspapers. Typically, classified advertisements run only on Wednesdays or Sundays and appear a few days after being submitted to a newspaper. The same advertisement, however, will get online within 24 hours of submission and even stay there until the post is filled. Therefore, if you're looking for a job and you're in a hurry, the Web might be your best bet. If you're willing to go to a different city to work — that is happily move home lock, stock and barrel — from your existing base, you stand an even better chance of getting picked up. The Web's global reach will provide you with access to jobs in places you only read of in exotic travel brochures.

Therefore, if you want to be a keeper of a game park in Kenya, you know what to do if you're very worried about confidentiality, the good news is a number of sites today after ways in which privacy is guaranteed. Meanwhile, there are a few tips you can follow to ensure your web search for jobs does not lead you to a dead end.

TIP 1 : Gearing to move on: If you're fine about relocating, you will probably find the world an open field. Infact, the more open you are to change, the more positive your chances of hitting upon a job that satisfies your wander lust.

TIP 2: Narrow your search: A bit of spadework always helps. Do your homework on companies and fix your sites only on the ones you really want to work with.

TIP 3 : While creating resumers, keep hiring managers in mind. Your resume should be short, crisp descriptions of who you are and what you do best are perfect for the on-line world. Infact, make sure you highlight your skill sets. These will probably show up if an HR chief somewhere does a keyword search. Also, make sure your resume is in tune with the profile of the company you are applying for. Talk the 'language' of the company, you might find yourself getting heard !

TIP 4 : Choose your website carefully, discriminate, act snobbish. Just remember, only the best site is suitable for you, settle for the leading names in the business and only post your resume when you're absolutely sure the site is credible and effective.

Is the Emphasis on IT Justified ?

Yes, IT can Change Lines and Our Country: The economy of a country is no longer measured by the strength of traditional industries but by its technological advancement. Information Technology should be looked upon not as an end by itself but as a means for achieving overall development.

The IT sector is perhaps the last opportunity in regaining competitive advantage for the country, to develop rapidly, to improve the standards of living of our people and to grow out of poverty.

Unlike traditional industries, the IT sector is people intensive and creates vast employment opportunities. This implies a very low capital output ratio and an opportunity for all of us grow quickly. Presently, it is estimated that over 300,000 software professionals are working in the country. According to the NASSCOM report, India will be able to export software, worth over $ 50 billion by the year 2008. The domestic market is likely to expand to $37 billion at the same time. This growth is expected to create an additional 22 lakh jobs in India.

Some feel that this kind of growth in IT will benefit only the elite. I do not subscribe to this view. I think IT will primarily be responsible for eradicating poverty as well strengthening democracy. I believe that IT will be useful as a tool for every poor citizen to demand and secure his right to information. The Government of Karnataka has already taken several initiatives primarily to take the administration to the doorsteps of the common man.

We have plans to set up 7,500 Mahithi Centres (IT kiosks) all over Karnataka. Presently, the state has land records of 60 lakh farmers in the computers. We plan to make this information available on the Net. The same Mahiti Centres will be able to provide many other value added services like e-mail, internet information, birth and death certification, panchayat taxes, information on government schemes etc. These kisosks will also provide the details of different government schemes and the amount spent in each and every village.

IT can make land registration simple and easy. People go to sub registrar offices for registering sale deeds, mortage deeds etc. as well as for an encumbrance certificate. This process is extremely cumbersome. To simplify the procedures for citizens, my government has already initiated computerisation of the department. So far, over 100,000 documents have been registered in a computerised environment. This will give relief to Bangalore citizens. Later, the project will be extended to the entire state.

The Government is using IT to protect the state's natural environment. The forest department has already implemented computerised systems to track poaching and other forest offences, improve wildlife management system as well as manage rare species under the Western Ghats programme.

The new technology can be used to effectively eradicate poverty and empower women. The latest technology in eradicating poverty is via self help groups for women. These women groups are encouraged to save money. The government steps in with revolving fund as well as bank credit. This method is found to be the most effective in delivering rural credit as well as eradicating poverty.

IT can use e-governance as a tool and deliver a government that is more proactive and responsive to its citizens. It'll play a vital role in coordinating with the government departments as well as undertake a few critical projects that are likely to be used in more than one department.

Since most decisions in our system of democracy are taken at the village and district levels, IT provides an exchange database at a single point made available to all decision makers. You can also analyse the data in an intelligent manner and provide a sophisticated decision support system for the use of all decision makers. These are but a few aspects where IT can change our lives. There are of course many more ways.

The Masses get no Benefit from It

Laloo Yadav, Rashtriya Janta Dal Leader said that the impression that I am against Information Technology (IT) is completely wrong. When I said, 'Yeh IT, YT Kya Hota Hai, what I meant was that It is not all that important. But some BJP leaders, wanting a bit of fun at my cost, made it appear that I had mistaken IT for income tax, It was deliberate and mischievous".

Let me set the record straight — I' am not anti-IT. I do realise that IT has relevance in some fields and does provide job avenues. But IT cannot be the main thrust area of a nation like ours. For a country like India and a state like Bihar, the priority has to be agriculture and rural and economic development.

The use of IT is confined to the hi-fi log. The masses have no access to it and get no benefit from it. Agar yeh such nahi hai to Chandrababu Naidu ke highly successful IT pradesh mein kisan atmahatya kyon kar rahe hain? Bijli ke rates kyon high hain? (Why are farmers forced to commit suicide in Andhra Pradesh? Why is the power tariff being hiked?)

To those who harp on IT, my question is — Can IT plough the fields and provide electricity to farmers? Besides, how do you expect people to make use of IT in places where there is no power most of the time? It might be a priority with the urban elite but for the common man, the priority is still drinking water, health, education and power. Without these, Internet and e-mail make no sense.

Indeed, if IT is as important as it is made out to be, why are they having to resort to manual counting of votes in the US? Where are all their super computers? What good are they? The American presidential election has exposed the tall claims of blind IT devotees.

It is obvious that IT cannot provide solutions to our problems. Take Bihar, for instance, farmers here have produced more than 80 metric tonnes of paddy this year. But they are not able to sell it in the market because they are getting less than Rs. 200 a tonne, which is lower than the cost of cultivation. The Union government is not able to purchase their produce at the minimum support price. Why? Because it has made a commitment to the World Trade Organisation (WTO) to purchase a certain amount of agricultural produce from the world market. So our own stuff is rotting unsold. What will be the result? Farmers will stop cultivating their fields and our agriculture will suffer. Does IT have as solution to this problem? it needs common sense, not IT wizardry, to realise the implications of this ruinous policy.

People should know that India is being treated as a huge market. Our shops are being flooded with multinational goods — butter, milk, tomato sauce, you name it. Imagine, even salt might be imported from foreign countries! And all this being done with the help of the IT-backed electronic media. In the process, our dairies and indigenous industry are being harmed. Do you need IT to tell you these simple things?

That's why I do not attach much importance to IT. It can never be our sole thrust area. Too much reliance on IT is an alien approach. It does not cater to 90 per cent of our population. A more indigenous approach is needed to solve our problems.

Online Market Place

In recent years, there has been a drastic shift in the buying patterns of consumers, which is leading in the direction of simplicity. Buying at the online market place is very easy, simple, fast and secure. Business partners who know the potential features of online market place are turning Net to the to buy goods or services. Products are ordered online and payments are made online. Customers are attracted to merchants' websites considering them to be cost-effective online transactions. Shopping is convenient in an online market place, as it is free of hassles, no pressure with instant approval—subsequently increasing online purchases.

Buyers the world over are appreciating the convenience of shopping online. The online market place and online shopping features have gone from science fiction to reality within a very short period. The Net is the force behind its revolution. It is a virtual store online. Online storefronts and sites are usually supported by a database that allows for easy updating and search ability. The sites have the capability to process online orders using credit cards. Online market places are opened for business without any restriction, from anywhere to anywhere at any time, 365 days year with round the clock services.

Shopping online is an online market place which has taken over the internet world by storm. It has enabled businesses to reach a vast audience which earlier was inaccessible. Now, technology has allowed all businesses large and small, to powerfully present electronic storefronts and shopping online. Both the online marketplace and shopping transactions are rapidly becoming common sites on the Net.

Virtual Private Networks (VPNs)

The VPN is a network that uses a public network service as its wider area network backbone. These are more popular now not only in India but worldwide. In India too, the use of VPNs is gaining popularity. It is a sort of public network for private use, assuring maximum online security and speed. But the fact is that the VPNs market in India is still in its infant stage, but because of the favourable information technology policy, the telecommunication policy moved forward towards liberalisation and its accessibility.

This network mostly provides what is being called Internet Protocol Security (IPSEC), an emerging standard among the security protocol. Typically, the VPN software is run so that communication to and from a remote terminal like a hand-held notebook computer is securely provided to the user's office base. The recent release of Windows 2000 means that for the first time, such a security protocol comes built in with the operating software and need to be separately implemented.

There are three types of VPNs :

Intranet: Intranet is also called as site to site or LAN to LAN. It extends secure private networks across the Net or other public network services.

Extranet: The Extranet VPNs are an extension of the Intranet with the addition of firewalls to protect the internal networks. They are ideal for e-commerce. They allow secure connections with business partners, suppliers and customers.

Remote Access VPNs: They are called as Dial VPNs. They allow individual dial-up users to connect it to a central site across the Net or other public network services in a secure way.

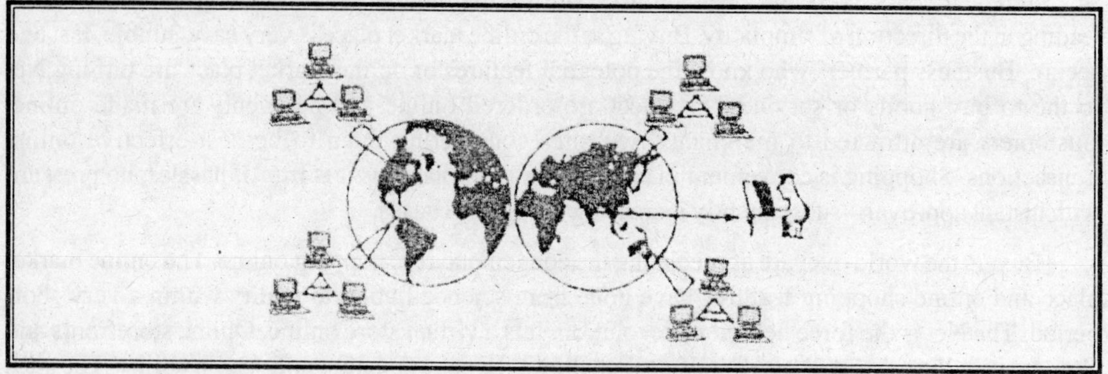

Fig. 15.23 A Global Network

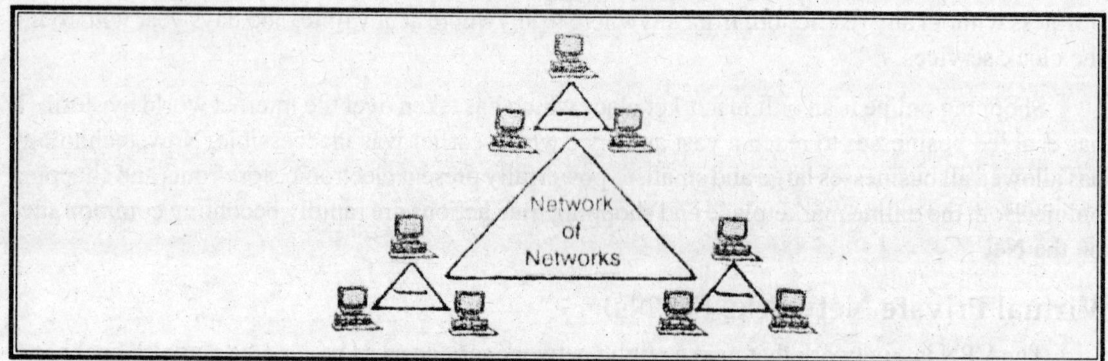

Fig. 15.24 Network within a Network

Protection to VPNs

They are as follows :

(1) The most promising is the Internet Protocol Security (IPS), an open internet Engineering Task Force (IETF) which chaoses standards that provide secure communication transparency.

(2) Point-to-Point Tunnelling protocol (PPTP) developed by Microsoft.

(3) Layer 2 Forwarding (L2F) developed by CISCO for remote access also.

Uses

(1) They help companies by reducing the overall operational cost of WAN through reduced telecom cost.

(2) It replaces dial up connection to remote users and leased line or frame relay connection to remote sites with local connections to an internet service provider.

(3) VPNs permit to increase the span of the corporate network and boost the efficiency of the organisation.

(4) Permits employees who are on move or travelling employees to access the network from any place and respond to messages faster and answer queries quickly.

(5) Offers e-maH facilities, internet access and control database services to users in remote offices.

(6) VPN uses the Net as the transport backbone to establish secure links with business partners. They extend communication to both regional and isolated offices.

(7) They significantly decrease the cost of communication for an increasingly mobile work force with potential sales by businesses.

(8) Product development can be accelerated. Strategic partnerships can be strengthened in a potential way.

(9) Eliminates the use of expensive lease lines or frame relay circuits. It is a secure way to access corporate network resources over the Net or other public or private networks.

(10) They include a number of security features including encryption, authentication and tunnelling. It replaces traditional dial up connections to provide access to remote users and telecommunications.

(11) Helps to connect LANs in different sites instead of using the public switched telephone network or dedicated leased lines. They can be used to give customers, clients and consultants access to potential corporate resources.

(12) VPNs cut long distance telephone charges because a user typically dials a local call to an ISP. They provide flexibility and cost savings as corporations extend their network to include remote employees and business partners.

(13) They save telecommunications cost by using the Net to carry traffic (rather than paying long distance phone charges).

(14) They minimise operational costs by outsourcing the management of remote access equipment to a service provider.

Problems

They are :

(1) Many users worry about security whether the data over these networks are safe or not. Customer security needs to be maintained at all costs.

(2) Lines may be clogged up resulting in delay, lack of sophisticated bandwidth causes problems of prioritising the usage.

(3) Poor infrastructure is another problem.

(4) Failure of networks and the Net itself can play havoc to online business.

Cyberspace

The term 'cyberspace' which was often used in science fictions, has become a common use. It is used in prefix for many terms like cybercash, cybertrade, cyberpayments, cyberlaundering, cybercrimes etc. The expression was used in 1985 by William Gibson, an American author, in his science fiction book titled 'Neuromancer'. The book popularised the term 'cyberspace'.

It continues to be used in today's business language. It denotes information superhighways or 'infobahan'. It means a combination of computer, communication, telecommunications and the entertainment industries.

It stands for the shared imaginary and potential reality of various networks. The term is used synonymously for internet, and it includes talk, computing payments, shopping and other activities via computers and working through the computer network.

Cyberspace links are global in essence and the combination of five industrial segments like computers, communication, tele comprises of communication, electronics and entertainment which are required by consumers.

It is a new terminology in common use, indicating things happening in society leading to advances in technology in the areas of telematics and micro-informatics.

The virtual world is created when people exchange or organise information electronically, To communicate via cyberspace, an individual can send and receive e-mail, post views to a new group or set up a personal home page.

The Open Buying on the Internet (OBI) Consortium

In the year 1996, a round table was formed composing of buying and selling organisations. The object of this forum was to create an open vendor neutral scalable and secure inter-operable standard for business to business electronic commerce. This finally led to the formation of the consortium.

It is a non-profit organisation, dedicated to developing an open standard for business to business internet commerce. It is being managed by Commerce Net as it is an independent collaborative firm. Buying and selling organisations, technology providers, financial institutions and other interested parties on an annual fee basis are eligible to become members of the consortium.

The object of the OBI specification is to facilitate the rapid implementation of internet-based economic solutions by utilising inter-operable standard based internet purchasing systems. The characteristics of this system are universal high speed access, inexpensive paperless information and transaction and platform independent software services.

Thus, this will benefit buying orgainsations, supplier organisations and technology and service providers including marketing and trading hubs.

Objectives

The objectives of the OBI are to provide :

(1) An open vendor and platform neutral architecture for internet purchasing to allow companies to fit these solutions into their information technology infrastructure.

(2) Consumer choice, to allow the creation of buying and selling partnership for high volumes, and low dollar commodity goods.

(3) Inter-operability among purchasing systems to conduct business to business electronic purchasing, independent of technology providers.

(4) Healthy competition to allow buying organisations to select suppliers and technology providers based on their own criteria and not on the basis of proprietary technology.

(5) Standard solutions meeting the common means of organisations to conduct business to business electronic commerce.

(6) Public documents (requirement, architecture, specifications and guidelines) to allow all interested parties to implement OBI- based solutions.

National Informatics Centre Net

National Informatics Centre Net (NICNET) is a premier organisation in the field of information technology in India. It provides state-of-the-art solutions to information management and decision support requirements of the government and the corporate sector. The Centre set up a satellite-based nation wide computer communication network with over 750 nodes connecting the national capital, the state capitals and district headquarters to one and another. NICNET is a very viable gateway to the Net at the national level.

NICNET maintains its leading edge with the incorporation of a powerful Ku-band based national info-highway as an overlay network on the existing structure. It is connected with over 200 international networks in 160 countries through Gateway Packet Switched Service (GPSS) and has dedicated internet access through direct high speed link to SPRINTNET, USA, with more than 700 micro-earth station nodes in all state capitals, district headquarters and selected commercial centres. NICNET has the widest reach among online users in the country.

NICNET, in its present configuration, connects all central government departments, state government, secretariats, district administration headquarters and some public sector organisations in a single intergrated network. In parallel with setting up of its massive infrastructure, NIC has developed a large number of informatics services for almost all sectors of the government such as economy, industry etc. Any of these services make extensive use of NICNET, resulting in timely, efficient and reliable flow of information at different levels in the government hierarchy.

There is also court information system on NICNET. Access to NICNET for the national and internet e-mail will be provided from any of the nearest satellite earth stations of NIC spread over 500 cities and towns in the country. Connectivity will be provided on dial basis. The high cost of data circuits over STD or intercity dial up is not required.

Access to NICNET for other Net services will be provided from any of the major state capitals and important commercial towns.

NICNET—Internet Services

Its internet services include :

(1) Global electronic mail

(2) Views and News — Usenet

(3) Remote log-in (telenet)

(4) File Transfer Protocol (FTP)

(5) Information servers-navigators

(6) Interactive access
(7) Remote database access
(8) Emergency message communication facility
(9) International mail facility
(10) Electronic data interchange
(11) International remote access and
(12) Internet access.

NICNET—National Info Highways

NIC was constituted in March 1975 and entrusted with the responsibility of bringing about a revolution in the work ethos. NIC's satellite-based computer communication network, NICNET went into operation in 1988. The reach of NICNET users went beyond the Indian borders as the network connected them to other international networks to provide access to all information on a global level..

Info Highway Services

The Info Highways provide a wide range of modalities of connectivity to its customers, who can access the network through the low speed VAST network or through PSTN of the Department of Telecommunications (DoT) or through internet working. As each of the remote stations as well as at the hub, facilitates connectivity and is created for providing WAN transit networks in the world, Info Highway services bring to users a host of services including :

(1) Inter-personal communication
(2) Emergency message communication
(3) Access to more than 200 networks in 160 countries
(4) File transfer
(5) Electronic data interchange
(6) Integrated nation wide banking service
(7) 400 e-mail services
(8) Multimedia communication
(9) Tele-conferencing
(10) Full text and bibliographic retrieval
(11) Hytelnet, WAIS services
(12) VLDS access services
(13) Distributed GIS
(14) Large scale data broadcast services
(15) NICNET Info Highway also offers special value added services like EDI, image transmission, multimedia transmission, teleconferencing and directory services.

Info Highway Features

They read as follows :

(1) The network supports high communication at variable data rates beginning up to 2.2 mbps through KU-band SC PC data pipes, at each of the remote sites! Modular design enables the upper limit to be pushed by multiples of 2.2 mbps to cope with the growing demand of these services.

(2) NICNET info Highway implemented as an IP-backbone network to facilitate creation of intranets and easy internet connectivity.

(3) The Network Control Centre (NCC) has a seven metre antenna. This antenna has automatic tracking facility and has all its major modules duplicated for high reliability and availability.

(4) The NCC has a Star Network Management System (SNMS) to monitor the network.

(5) The network has the capacity to increase the speed at selected nodes upto 2.2 mbps without any major investments.

(6) Each remote station uses a 1.8 /2.4 metre antenna equipped tracking facility to work with inclined or bit satellites.

(7) To overcome rain attenuation in the KU-band, the master station is designed with the automatic uplink power control.

(8) Remote stations have the necessary interfaces to support both synchronous and asynchronous circuits.

(9) Remote stations can be configured locally or from the Master Earth Station (MES). These remote stations will provide both operational as well as monitoring information to the network control centre.

(10) The highway incorporates a cost-effective data broadcast facility which uses the same RF portion of the MES but has separate sets of digital equipment. The data broadcast network will initially support 32 data magazines. This can be extended subsequently to support data magazines in the multiple of 32.

(11) Multiple gateways of 266 kbps each set up at Bangalore, Mumbai, Kolkata, Chennai and Delhi (to be upgraded to 2 mbps at Delhi).

How to Connect to the Net?

Any person who is desirous to get connected to the Internet, necessarily has to obtain an account from VSNL. The interested Net users can participate through the VSNL by paying a prescribed amount to the latter.

There are two different rates to get connected depending upon the status like students, professionals, individuals, commercial orgainsations etc. There are two options of dial up account available to use the gateway internet access services. They are terminal dial-up or leased services and TCP/IP dial-up service.

The procedure involved in getting either the terminal account or a TCP/IP account is similar. To get this account, the following two steps are involved :

(1) To get a modem form the computer suitable for use on telephone ines.

(2) To contact the VSNL to obtain the application form and fulfil formalities to initial the Internet connection.

After a careful scrutiny of application, if it is found satisfactory in all respects, the subscriber will be given a login name and password. The subscriber is subsequently ready to log on to the VSNL terminal account to go on to the Internet.

How to Get on to the Internet?

Getting on to the Internet is a very easy procedure. One is required to fulfil the following criteria to get on to the Internet:

(1) To have a compatible personal computer

(2) To use internet software, to possess a modem

(3) To get online via service provider i.e., VSNL in India, which will give the e-mail address after opening an account

(4) To get the personal computer hooked onto the internet

(5) To get an internet account from the internet access provider

(6) To connect the telephone lines to the modem and the computer

(7) To load the window operating system

(8) To connect to the internet using dial-up networking of windows

(9) To launch a web browser i.e., the microsoft internet explorer or netscape navigator.

TCP/IP

The acronym TCP/IP stands for Transmission Control Protocol Internet Protocol. It relates to the internet account and deals with procedures developed for interconnecting net computers and communicating data. Internet is called network, because of the use of TCP/IP. Actually, TCP/IP has given birth to the Internet. The TCP/IP account facilitates to connect any network or computer with the internet. Today, it is possible to initiate interconnection of all types of networks, private BBS communities and individual PCs in both home and offices. Internet works because they follow a simple procedure of the TCP/IP account.

An individual computer or networking computers have to use protocol in order to achieve the object of messaging across a network. It is the practice under the internet management to follow a set of rules laid down which is known as the protocol. It defines and sets certain standard rules which all computers want to link with each other to confirm to these pre-determined standard set of rules codified in the networking protocol. Different computers maybe running on different types of operating systems. Though they are running on different operating systems, the protocol enables them to communicate effectively. Thus, TCP/IP helps the user to transfer data from one computer to another computer.

The TCP/IP account is must for an internet connection-without it, one cannot approach the Net. When once the user connects to the Net, it means he is making connection to any other computer on the internet.

VSNL, as the second level of access, provides a direct TCP/IP account. The subscriber can use transmission control protocol / internet protocol software to connect on a dial-up or leased basis to the GIAS system and access online services available on the Net. In this mode of access, the users will be required to use software for e-mail, file transfer, remote login, mosaic, WWW etc.

Computers talk to one another via the Internet. This communication is possible through a common mutually agreed set of forms and procedures, which is the protocol used for potential information exchange. The technique is designed to ensure up to date transmission of data between the two computers. IP stands for Internet Protocol which receives the data from TCP and trasmits to its destination. As such, any kind of information can be sent over the Net.

It is a feature of the Net computer that every computer linked to the Net has a unique Internet Protocol (IP) address which distinguishes it from other computers on the Net. The address is four sets of digits separated by dots. The INTERNIC, i.e., the Internet Network Information Centre is the one which gives IP address to those getting connected to the Net.

Some Internet Concepts

I-Net: India's domestic Public Switched Packet Data Network (PSPDN), I-Net is provided by the Department of Telecommunications (DoT). I-Net, in its first phase of operations, has nodes at eight locations. I-Net is inter-connected to Gateway Packet Switched Service (GPSS).

I-Net is a domestic switched network which is connected to the GPSS, and subscribers of these networks would also have an access easily to cities of India and they would also be able to avail advantages of I-Net in addition to subscribing to GIAS.

NUI: The acronym NUI stands for Network Users Identification. Subscriber's access to Gateway Packet Switched Service (GPSS) is permitted through a confidential user access code called Network User Identification. The subscriber can use same NUI from Mumbai, New Delhi and Kolkata for accessing GPSS using local dial-up numbers.

RABM: This acronym for Remote Area Business Message Network (RABM) is a data network of the Department of Telecommunications, exclusively developed for communications from remote locations of India. It is inter-connected to Gateway Packet Switched Service in Mumbai.

Easynet: The Videsh Sanchar Nigam has an agreement for database access through EASYNET—the knowledge Gateway system of M/S Telebase Philadelphia, USA. This provides an easy access to over 850 databases around the world. EASYNET system can also be accessed through the gateway packet switched service if the user obtains a password from VSNL by paying prescribed annual password fee.

Free-Net: This is a community bulletin board system which provides free access to local residents. There are many free nets, which extends to all, initiating full internet access. The National Public Telecommunications network support freenet based in Cleveland, Ohio.

HV-Net: It is a high speed VSAT Network of the Department of Telecommunications and it is interconnected with the Gateway Packet Switched Service (GPSS).

Ether Net: It is a local area network technology. The technology has created an ethereal universe and user to become an internaut.

Point-to-Point Protocol (PPP): The PPP software allows a Macintosh or PC to act an internet host. You can use Mac or PC applications to read news, send/receive e-mail, transfer file etc. The only hardware requirements are the modem and telephone line. CS DC uses PPP instead of SLIP because it is a newer and more robust protocol. It is also faster when properly configured. The Serial Line Internet protocol (SLIP) is similar to PPP in functionality. It is older and not as flexible as the PPP.

Netiquette: These are seen as a few unwritten rules of conduct on the internet. A set of guidelines on legitimate behaviour on the Net has been implemented. It covers net using abuse or libel over the Net users.

Kilobytes Per Second (Kbps): It is a standard for measuring data transmission speed. Another standard is cps-characters per second, which is generally V_6 the kpbs rating. A 56 kbps connection transmits 56,000 bits per second. A page of text is about 2,000 bytes or 16,000 bits.

V. 32 Bytes: This is a modem protocol that allows modems to communicate online speeds of up to 14,400 bps (bytes per second), and up to 57,600 bps when the data is compressible. Realistic data transfer rates average at about 1,500 characters (bytes) per second using the Zmodem or . PPP.

Internet Service provider (ISP): The Internet Service Provider has made internet access avaiiable to the private person. Commercial services charges people either a flat fee or an hourly rate, and they inculude America Online, CompuServe, Netcom and Prodigy. There are more and more local providers emerging in large cities as well. Internet access service is provided by designated service providers. In most parts of the world, this access is provided by the service providers for a fixed charge.

In India, the sole provider is the Videsh Sanchar Nigam Limited (VSNL), the Government of India's designed external service provider. It has two types of services. For Rs. 15,000 a year plus registration charges, it provides 500 hours for one year whichever is exhausted earlier via the TCP/IP protocol. It means the subscriber can receive text, picture, sound clips, movie clips — whatever is available on the worldwide net.

Another method is that VSNL provides a shell account or text only without graphics or sound service for Rs. 5000. The *bona fide* students get this service at concessional rates. The VSNL holds monopoly in association with the telephone department as the Internet Service Provider.

Those who opt for the text only service need not invest in a standard browser like Netscape Navigator or Internet Explorer. VSNL provides a menu where users can directly access websites through their URLs or one of the half a dozen internationally known search engines such as Yahoo, Infoseek or Lycos.

The modem is the most popular internet access device which connects a computer to a telephone line, which in turn connects to the modem at the host computer. This is known as a dial-up account because the computer takes route through a process similar to dialling a phone number to gain access to the concerned person.

Access to internet is connected or provided by an Internet Access Provider (IAP). The provider may be a small local operator or one of the large commercial online services. In India, VSNL is the only internet access provider, with its scheme — the Gateway Internet Access Services (GIAS) which enables subscribers to log onto databases, send e-mails, read news, download files, remotely running programs on distant hosts and a range of other applications.

The VSNL has the following options for enabling gateway internet access services :

Shell Account: By using the dial-up access linked to the GIAS Host, the primary level of access for internet users is using this service set up by the VSNL at each of the nodes. By connecting to the host computer, the users would be able to use all internet services. In this node, the users would be using a simple terminal emulation from their PCs and will not require any special software on their machine. The limitation of this access node is that access is primarily limited to text based services.

TCP/IP Account: VSNL as the second level of access, provides a direct TCP/IP Account. The subscriber can use the TCP/IP software to connect with a dial up or leased basis to the GIAS system and access online all services on the Net. In this node of access, the users will be required to use software for e-mail, file transfer, remote login, mosaic, world wide web etc.

Packet Switched Network Access: This third level of access provides access via packet switched network i.e., I-Net, Remote Area Business Message Network (RABMN), Gateway Packet Switched Services (GPSS) and HV Net. Subscribers of these networks would be able to avail full range of internet services using the Shell Account and TCP/IP Account.

Internet Agents

The expression 'Agents on the Net' is commonly used in search engines. Agents are programs that intensively search the Net to give specific results in the Net users. Agents can also be customised and scheduled according to a user's need.

So, agents simply mean programs that will enable users to do bidding automatically. Agents are run over the Net on an individual computer everyday. Agents can find the following for the net users:

(1) The latest news

(2) Download it to the computer

(3) Monitor internet traffic

(4) Report on its total usage

(5) Find the best deal on the CD one wants to buy

(6) Perform important web maintenance task and

(7) Perform jobs cooperatively.

On the Internet, agents are called 'spiders', 'robots' (simply bots) and knowbots.The popular search tools such as Lycos, Infoseek and Altavista use spiders.

The user first has to select the needed task and the agents automatically go off and perform the required tasks. A variety of several languages can be used to write agents' programs.

Working of Agents

(1) Gathering News: A simple internet agent is one who gathers news from a variety of sources while you are not using your computer or while you are using the computer for another task. Newsagents can work in several ways. In the simplest example, you fill out a form saying what kind of news you are interested in and at what schedule do you want your news delivered. Based on that information, at present intervals, the news agent enters news sites on the Net and downloads news stories to your computer where you can read them as HTML pages.

(2) Best Bargains: Shopping agents will let you search through the Internet for the best bargains. On the Web, you fill out a form detailing the product you want to buy. When you send the form, the shopping agent launches programs that search through a variety of shopping sites and databases on the Net. The agent looks into the databases of those sites and finds the best prices. It then sends back to you the links to the sites so that you can visit the sites with the best prices and order the products from there.

(3) Web Maintenance: Web robots or web maintenance spiders can perform important chores related to web maintenance. On websites, particularly large ones, very often HTML pages include links that become outdated. In other words, the objects being linked to have been taken off the Net. Whenever a user clicks on the link, an error message is sent. A web maintenance spider can look at every link on every HTML page on a website and trace each link to see if the linked object still exists. It then generates a report of dead links. Based on that report, the system administrator can rewrite the HTML code, getting rid of the non-existing links.

(4) Extra Load: When robots and spiders do their work on a remote internet site from where they were launched, they tend to put an extra load on the sites' system resources, for example, by swamping the server with too may requests in too short a time. Because of this, some system administrators are interested in ways of excluding robots in certain circumstances by not allowing robots into certain web directories. A variety of ways have been devised to limit robot access including creating a file called Robots, txt. that describes the areas of limits to the robots, which the robots would automatically adhere to and not visit the sites.*

Some Network Security Measures

Presently, internet security measures are not adequately available. Many people believe that it is not an application technology. In addition to the above, appropriate measures may be adopted:

(1) This will retain customer loyalty to a great extent. Physical access to the servers may be controlled.

(2) Total security is almost impossible, so strategies must be worked out to enable people to detect breaches of security.

(3) To create an awareness and develop a culture among the members of the groups.

(4) It is also necessary to identity levels of protection for various aspects of information transmission.

---

* Computers Today, 1-15. April, 2000, pp. 76-77.

(5) It is more safe to use a separate password to run servers.

(6) In tune with the advancement and the emergence sophisticated technology, the outdated hardware and software programs and communication devices must be replaced from time to time.

(7) To adopt network auditing facilities.

(8) Use of fibre optic cables are more desirable as they cannot be easily trapped. In case of twisted pair cables and coaxial cables, they should be concealed to prevent easy access to information.

(9) Use of encryption coding in business messages and data communication ensures security.

(10) Even passwords can be encrypted. It is also desirable to avoid passwords embodied in communication access scripts.

(11) See through devices will also help to a great extent, (for details, see the chapter on e-commerce security).

Advantages of Internet

The use of the Net has grown among people considering the advantages of being online and accessing sites on individual discretion. To mention, it is of publishing and propagating information, the ability to provide continuously up to-date information, freedom from the time zone and other constraints etc. Following are the advantages of being on the Net:

(1) For Operations

(1) It is cost effective

(2) A great equaliser

(3) By establishing relationships with merchants and customers to exchange products and services

(4) Business can gain contracts with strategic online planning

(5) Flexibility

(6) Automation of operations

(7) Saves time

(8) Unlimited transactions not limited by their human factors and

(9) The entire process is automated.

(2) For Pleasure

The Internet can be used at home :

(1) To exchange electronic mail instantly with college friends or family members.

(2) To participate in group discussions on topics that interest you, through the public newsgroup or bulletin boards.

(3) To find educational tools. Universities around the world, book stores, libraries and school systems are sharing online information, enabling students to register online for registering in these universities. Here, qualification matters to a large extent.

(4) To entertain — it is fun and easy to spend an hour surfing from one topic to another and one site to another.

(5) To shop-commercial electronic storefronts are growing in number. You can now order flowers, music and computer equipment over the Net.

(6) To read about interesting sports and leisure events and choice topics.

(3) For Business

From the business point of view, the Net can be invaluable. It can be used to :

(1) Get technical support for products being used by consumers who are new net users.

(2) Distribute software.

(3) Provide technical support, bug fixes and product information to the customer.

(4) Publish information such as technical or marketing literature to the net users.

(5) Communication or collaboration on various projects.

(6) Market and sell products online and

(7) Boost your business while away from the office with a global online recognition at the click of a button.

(4) Others

They are as following :

(1) It facilitates the ways to share information.

(2) Send, retrieve and receive e-mails needed

(3) The user can send mail to others on the Net.

(4) Just typing the correct e-mail address facilitates online communication fast.

(5) Internet can be explored as a form of pleasure, entertainment or fun or for personal communication — its main application being access to information in a big way.

(6) ISD is cheaper in terms of charges.

(7) It is no matter for the internet as to what kind of computer to use.

(8) Daily, millions of messages are sent by individuals, corporations, organisations and government etc.

(9) It enables the people all over the planet to communicate within seconds.

(10) Internet acts as a international computer which is connected through a network at the user end.

(11) The widespread deployment and universal acceptance of internet technologies have created an opportunity for new class of low cost clients who focus on accessing internet based information services. The client primarily runs the internet application such as browsers and e-mail.

Internet-Uses, Services and Applications

The subscribers of the Net can obtain benefits from the existing potentials of the Internet device. It is a global information super highway to the cyberspace and can be used both for pleasure, business generation and commercial purposes. The user of the Net can log onto the databank, send e-mails, read news, download files and remotely run programs on a distant host. The range of other applications or uses to which internet connection can be put to is continuously getting enhanced with the availability of hypertext information, world wide web, video and audio files.

The growth of the Net i.e. the window to global information superhighway has revolutionised the way global network is related for international access to global information.

There are several services or uses available for which the Net can be put to. The wide variety of uses of internet available is expanding slowly. It is recognised today, as a single global unparalleled technique for most of the problems. It is a superpower along the highway which offers solutions to all sorts of global problems.

One cannot explore the vast potential of the Net and the resources offered by the computer, unless some electronic tools are used.

The important uses or applications of internet are as follows :

(1) E-mail

(2) Usenet

(3) Telnet

(4) File transfer protocol

(5) Archie

(6) Gopher

(7) Veronica

(8) Mosaic

(9) WAIS and

(10) Real Time Chatting

E-mail

The basic use to which the Internet is put is e-mail or electronic mail which abolishes the distance between the countries, friends, business associates etc. The essence of networking, i.e., the e-mail, permits to send messages quickly and easily. They travel almost instantly over the network to location around the world. E-mail is the most widely used Internet service. Messages given by e-mail may include text, graphics, voice and video.

The internet is the most suitable global medium for sending e-mail. Corporations, individuals, educational institutions and research institutions are using the internet for transmitting data through electronic mail. Electronic transmission is greatly facilitated by the internet wherein the user types the message and it travels instantly over the network to the receiver. It permits to send messages to a specific person or group. Network information allows the user to send messages on an electronic bulletin board for all to access it.

UseNet, News Groups, News

The concept of UseNet pertains mainly to the Net. The members of UseNet operate with an understanding of the other members of UseNet to share and exchange news between the user groups. It is a way to share information and discussions organised into thousand topics (from celebrity matters and fan clubs to academic discourses). Similar to list servers, this forum is very public, open to anyone on the Net.

News groups are composed of articles posted by readers and contributors on particular topics. A post is called an article which is nothing but messages to a news group. There is a separate program known as news reader which is operated to read UseNet news. It facilitates to establish a link with the news group or the subscriber to the news group, read articles or post articles on the news group. Thus, the UseNet is a public forum.

UseNet is a quite distinct and different system of global communication network, and it is not exactly similar to the Net. The news group is the basic block of UseNet, composing of a collection of messages with related themes. On the other hand, the network groups are referred to as conferences, forums, bulletin boards or special interest groups. It is news internet, which is one of the useful internet applications. There are thousands of these news groups available online in different languages.

It is also called as Net-News. It is one of the important segments of the Net. As a popular online application, NetNews (NN) is a system of interactive communication composing of various topics. There are several thousand groups ranging from recreational to scientific matters. The quantity of information we receive is approximately equal to a 500 page book per minute. The quality of information varies from excellent to not so good information.

The UseNet is a distributed bulletin board system strategically spread over to hosts throughout the entire world. There are discussion groups on almost any topic which can access in an instant by typing 'NN'. The entire news feed uses up to 500 megabytes per week.

A group of people using the Net is called the user group. Under this service, the users can communicate with a group of people at the same time by sending messages to all the people in the group. This is called news group e-mail. One can leave information on the electronic bulletin board where the user can invite responses.

There are seven major categories of news group. They are :

(1) Computer science and related topics.

(2) Group concerned with news network and news software.

(3) Group discussing recreational activities, hobbies and art.

(4) Group discussing scientific research applications.

(5) Group that addresses social issues.

(6) Talk groups or a forum for debate on controversial topics and

(7) Miscellaneous activity that does not fit in any of the above categories.

A part of the internet computer space is devoted to news groups, electronic notice boards, bulletin board service (BBS) and other areas of special interest. It is a program which presents these discussions, enabling users to ask questions, circulate opinions and get help etc.

How UseNet Works

Global Bulletin Boards: UseNet is a global bulletin board and discussion area. It collects messages pertaining to different topics into newsgroups which are freewheeling discussion areas in which anyone can participate. Newsgroups can be found on many host computers. There are thousand newsgroups that cover just about every topic you have ever imagined and many of you probably have not thought of and would like to enter into a discussion.

Posting: To participate, people send and read messages that are posted on the newsgroup. There are two kinds of newsgroups: moderated newsgroups and unmoderated newsgroups.

In a moderated newsgroup, a human moderator receives and reads all the messages for the newsgroups. The moderator then decides which messages should be posted. The messages to be posted are subsequently put on a newsgroup server and other messages are discarded. In unmoderated newsgroups, all the messages are directly put on the server. Newsgroups and all their messages are stored on a UseNet server. They are organised by broad categories and then broken down into specific topics for target discussions by Net users.

Duplication of Messages: UseNet servers communicate with one another so that all messages posted on one server are duplicated on other servers. While there are many UseNet servers, not all servers carry all newsgroups. Each site decides which newsgroups to carry to ensure quality topics and discussions.

Pictures, Multimedia: Pictures and multimedia files and even executable programs can be posted in newsgroups for other people to see and use. However, because of the technology used in newsgroups, these files must be specially encoded to be posted. To view, play or use files, you will have to first transfer them to your own computer and then decode them with a special software package. A common encoding scheme used on newsgroups is called unencode. There are versions of this encoding and decoding program that works on the PC, Macintosh and Unix Computers. Mime is another encoding scheme.

Reading and Responding: Newsgroups reader software lets you read messages and respond to newsgroups. The software gives you ways to manage your newsgroups besides enabling you to subscribe to these newsgroups, which means that new messages will automatically be delivered to you when you check the server. You will also be able to cancel your subscription.*

TelNet

Yet another important segment of the Net is TelNet, which enables the Net user to log on from one computer to another computer via the Internet. Thus, it refers to both the protocol and the terminal emulator that allows Net users to log onto other Unix hosts. TelNet permits to access other computers via the internet by using TelNet. As a protocol, it allows the users to be on one computer system and do work on another host computer which may be located very near or it may be a distance communication. Thus, TelNet allows the user to log onto a remote system. It is an internet program that gives the user power of the internet to connect to database library, catalogue

* Computers Today, 16-30, April, 2000, pp. 30-31.

and other information resources around the world. There are several sites dealing with different areas of interest around the world, which can be searched. on the Net. They are agriculture, bulletin board systems, business and finance, computers, education, environment, games, geography, geology, and the government.

Cyberspace has its libraries, in which TelNet is one of the keys to these libraries. TelNet application strategically permits users to log on to another system to avail and access the services available on the host systems. The user can use the TelNet by grouping data into voluminous database across the Internet network.

File Transfer Protocol (FTP)

This is the most important service available on the Internet. It is a protocol for transferring files on the Net. A Unix system that has files will enable the user to access the FTP program by logging onto those hosts, using a username of 'anonymous' and your address as a password. On Unix system, the program that does this is named 'FTP'. Zip files, (used on PCs) require binary mode transfers, and the user will just type 'bin' at the ftp prompt once he is connected. It is a client server protocol which permits the user on one computer system to transfer files to and from another computer system. The user knows the addresses of the host computer at the remote site.

FT.P is a method or tool as the name suggests, to copy files from the remote host to the main host and viceversa. It is the best method of transferring files from one computer to another computer over the telephone-lines.

Anything available on the Internet can be obtained by way of copying the data/documents available. on the Net. There are libraries of documents. As such, one can also get a copy of the recent US Supreme Court judgement from the Net, besides obtaining FTP copies of historical documents. The users can get songs, lyrics, poems, credit collection, credit rating, distance education, fashion design, shopping, journals, photography, virtual gallery, yellow pages etc., from the Net.

Archie

This is a program that allows the user to search for information stored on anonymous and large FTP sites on the Net. TelNet can be used to access Archie servers. It can be accessed by e-mail. It is in other words called as the search program.

This program helps to look through several anonymous file transfer protocol sites. It indicates the location of all these files required by anyone. There would be many anonymous file transfer protocol sites. It is the function of the internet application of the Archie server to collect services, and as such, each of these services is responsible for keeping track of file locations in these anonymous FTP sites.

Archie servers have the capability to communicate with each other and gather and combine their information into a huge global database. There is also a facility of periodical updating database. A file can be searched and located in the database just by giving a keywork to search for. So the Archie server tells us where the files are located. The Archie catalogue subscription maintains a list of about 1,200 internet file transfer protocol archive sites of approximately 2.5 million files containing 200 gigabytes of information. The current catalogue requires about 400 megabytes of disk storage.

Gopher

Gopher is part of the Internet. It has the capability to 'Go For' textual information from a huge public database. Simply put, it is a potential file finder one can see on the computer screen the rest of files presented by Gopher.

This is a menu-based information retrieval system that allows the user to locate and retrieve information on the Internet. There are a list of government gopher services available in/pub/govt. text.

This use of the Net would permit the user to hop around the Net looking for information in various information libraries or servers, without having to struggle hard to know where the materials are specially located. We often hear net users talking about gopher space In the Internet, there are several hundreds of inter-connected libraries called gopher libraries. So, all gopher libraries make up Gopher space.

The distinctive feature of gopher is that it practically goes around and collects the potential information required by the user and displays it on the computer screen. This is the fundamental difference between Archie and Gopher. The inter-connected menus of Gopher allow the user to burrow deeper and deeper into the database until he gets the information needed for which he is looking for. The gopher service of the internet was developed at the University of Minnesota.

It searches information from a large database. It is a file tracer or finder which displays on the computer screen lists of files and drab text documents. It is a menu-based program that enables the user to look for information without the knowledge where the material is specially located.

So, gopher space is another wed used to describe the entire gopher network spanning the Net.

Veronica

Veronica, an acronym popularly known, stands for Very Easy, Rodent Oriented Network Index to Computer Archives. This technique of internet application helps to find neat files in the gopher space more quickly. It is a search tool that would permit the user to quickly scan the gopher space for a particular file or essential directories. As precursors to search engines, these 'client programs' will search the Internet in various ways and return either lists of sites or actual data to the Net users.

"Veronica is a program that can be accessed through gopher. It requires the user to enter a keyboard. It searches quickly through a database of over 5,500 servers and over 10 million gopher items of files and directories.

Veronica is both fun and amazing because it not only finds files but also gets all these files and directores. It is a big database of information that is available through gopher space. This program helps to track all the gopher menus that can be accessed by the user.

Mosaic

It is popular graphical interface for accessing the world wide web gopher and other services. Version 2 is still being tested and is buggy but has more options. Performance under PPP has much improved and proves satisfactory to those preferring desirable image downloading.

Mosaic brings the way we use the internet into the new era. Its feature is that it is an easy way to reach audio, video-text and graphics.

WAIS

The acronym WAIS Stands for Wide Area Information System. Its task is to search or scan internet libraries as soon as the user types in the word or specific topic. WAIS, as a result, returns a master index providing links to all the sites relating to the user's request. There are WAIS programs designed to work independently of the Web with the help of special gateways software, and the user can reach these programs. It is a distributed database protocol for sophisticated searches over the Net.

Real Time Chatting

This is a program available to users across the Net to talk to each other in real time. Internet Relay Chat (IRC) supports a channel metaphor; where each channel is on a unique topic and can have a number of simultaneous users. IRC tends to be full of immature people flaming each other. Flaming is the posting of offensive remarks to newsgroups. What happens when someone does something controversial or stupid in mail, news or IRS ? It is a nasty or unpleasant response to a message that someone has sent out. If you get flamed by a stranger, do not take it personally. It is best to stop any further communication in this online chat programme.

Chatting interactively in real time is also one of the most widely used services on the Net. It permits the user to exchange messages or voice in real time on the Net, but the user has to use a suitable kind of software. There are several factors which influence the quality of exchange of voice like application, the capacity of the computer and the compression method adopted etc.

Limitations of Internet

Though there are potential uses of the Internet, shortcomings also follow with this global technological link. The following are some of the important problems associated with the Net:

(1) Ethics: As the internet is growing fast, so is a host of ethical concerns about its application ethics and norms. Researchers, scholars and the early users of the Net would like to protect the internet from censorship. But law enforcing agencies particularly in those countries where the Net is widely used and has intermingled in the threads of the social fabric are considering means to curb impersonators, pirates and other improper users. At present, censorship is mainly intended to protect children against gaining access to indecent data on the Net.

(2) Pay-Service: In the beginning, everything that was available on the Net was free. It was intended to provide help to researchers around the world. But as the popularity of the Net grew over the years and is growing, a number of pay-service networks are appearing.

(3) Copyright: Problems of copyright and security have already surfaced.

(4) Disinfestation: The existence of the Internet as a democratic information infrastructure, seems threatened by the notorious web-based terrorists who attempt to spread disinformation and the software giants who are trying to define webonomics are working towards. preventing the detrimental rates of cyber crime.

(5) No Owner: Some people think that the Net may eventually end up in being a medium of ideological propaganda. But at the moment, such concerns do not seem to be well founded because unlike other technologies of the past, the Net is a diversifying rather than a centralising force. It is not owned by anyone.

A Network Computer (NC) is a stateless system designed for accessing network information and services. It is the network server on which all software, data and configuration information rests. A network computer runs specialised software known as network computer operating system which is special to its server vendor. There exists no option, and the hard drive exists for the enhancement or local storage of private documents.

(6) Traffic Jam: The rising popularity of the Net is creating traffic jams and at certain times of the day, the networks are so crowded that it is practically impossible to connect with certain servers and go online.

(7) Lack of Autonomy: Though there are advantages, the NC model is not without its limitations. The end users lose their autonomy to run their own software, create and keep their own data and to configure their own systems.

(8) Crimes: Internet theft and cyber crimes are on the increase. Today, there is no safe strategy for the information put on the Internet. It is a public network. The mechanism of internet must ensure unwanted access to this information and ensures security to customer to customers. A number of cyber crimes came to light in recent years which have been identified and investigations were also conducted throughout the world. They are mostly taking place in companies, banks, private organisations, government departments and public sector organisations.

There are two types of cyber crimes. They are :

(1) Data related crimes and

(2) System related crimes

Data related crimes include tampering with the data, unorganised locking of data, entering into various databases etc. System related crimes include tampering with programs, change in program logic, trozan horse program, trap doors and super japping etc.

(9) Cyberlaundering: Cyberlaundering is yet another new internet crime. It provides facility for the transactional transfer of financial value through the Net. It facilitates an unprecedented anonymity and security for users involved in financial transactions. Consumer articles are taking online. There is no technological breakthrough that can bring cyber based transactions within the preview of law. Laws of most of the countries do not cover cyberlaundering as it has not been anticipated as a futuristic online exercise. The technology makes it difficult to unravel the names of the persons involved in cyberlaundering because it traverses countries and their laws. A transaction passes through and the problem is which country has the right to impose tax has the right to take action against the violators of the law.

(10) Security and Privacy: Online communication requires that the security and privacy of information given by customers be ensured and these are the two most important issues today.

The fact is that privacy and security are generally used synonymously and interchangeably. But both are different problems. They are used in the same breath because of technical reasons, but these two problems need separate solutions.

The security factor involves inclusion into the private network connected to the Net. The privacy factor is concerned with the information that goes out over the internet itself. Snooping into the contents of a message is the most important privacy problem: The users need protection.

(11) Language: Internet use is associated with English language and with urbanisation in a multi-cultural and multi-lingual global world, the benefits of internet technology are available only to few people. Language is the biggest problem to computer literacy. The social impact of computerised english language should not be ignored. In a multi-cultural and multi-lingual country, using the computer for vulnerable business is insignificant. Alternative languages are to be worked out to meet the requirements of the different countries and regions within the country. Thus, the majority of the Indian population has no access to the Net.

CHAPTER 16

Language Skills

English Language

Language is an expression of human activity.

The word 'English' is the name both of a language and of a nationality and is linked with the name of a country, England; but there is the important difference that since England is not a political entity (as a part of Great Britain or the United Kingdom), "English" corresponds only to the genetic situation.

There is no copyright in the use of English and England cannot demand users in other countries that they pay royalties of obeisance as though the language carried a British patent.

English has become one of the most important world languages. The rapidly growing interest in English cut- across political and ideological lines because of the convenience of a LINGUA FRANCA increasingly used as a second language in important areas of the world.

The uses to which English is put are as various as the people and societies that use it. The particular purpose, the conduct of "business" actually calls into being one extreme and remotely related form of English, Pidgin, and has given it its very name.

Dr. Samual Johnson says that "*Language is the dress of thought*" and it has become common place to quote this in support of the view that thought is behind all languages and that language is primarily used to "dress up and send thoughts on their way; give substance for thoughts." "Language", we are often told, exists for the expression of thoughts or ideas.

The uses of language can be as follows:

(1) To dissipate superfluous nervous energy.

(2) To direct motion in others, both men and animals.

(3) To communicate ideas.

(4) As a means of expression.

(5) For the purpose of record.

(6) To set matter in motion (as in charms and incantations).

(7) As an instrument of thinking.

(8) To give delight merely as sound.

Language can be considered to operate three types of organization and on two separate planes: vocabulary and grammar on one plane, means of transmission on the other plane. The part that usually seems most obvious, even most important, is word-stock also known as the "vocabulary." We may think of this as our total collection of names for things; the names of actions, objectives, qualities, and so on.

Everyone should revise his language-habits, from time to time, in accordance with changing life and custom. As mentioned earlier, language is an expression of human activity, and because human activity is constantly changing, language also changes along with it.

Language means the words and way of speaking, writing, usually connected with a particular group of people. It is a manner of the style of speaking or writing. It implies the method of using symbols like words giving expression to facts and feelings. Human speech, the speech of a particular nation, the speaker or writer can adopt but should speak or write on the level of listeners or readers. This alone will make the message pleasing and interesting. An individual listener is interested in listening anything which satisfies his purpose and desire. It is the style of writing or speaking.

In communication, every communicator must know the significance of language which is essential for effective communication.

Grammar: Words are so predominant in language, and a dictionary is so much regarded as the entire register of a language, that we are sometimes tempted to think that there is nothing else to consider. *"Man's word is God in man."* But a language cannot work our words alone. A group of words like 'Arrived, "Girl," "Man", "Say", cannot tell us much until we have added a second dimension, grammar. Grammar contributes features like articles, prepositions, tense, number, and the conventions of arrangement — which word goes before which. With grammar added, the four words we selected can be made to tell us something. *The man said that the girls had arrived."*

Grammar has done three things here; it has arranged the words in a particular order, making clear who did the saying and who the arriving. It has contributed TENSE by the alteration of SAY to SAID, and number by the addition of "s" to "girl." Thirdly, grammar has added some additional words: the, that, and had. This third point raises a difficulty. We have already said that first dimension of language as "vocabulary", the stock of words; now, it is being suggested that grammar also consists in part of words. At first sight, it may be confusing to find the same words, "words", applied to the part of grammar as well to the whole of the vocabulary. English has, in fact, two kinds of words, lexical words and grammatical words, and this basic distinction is important to learn.

Vocabulary

Knowing the meaning of a word is knowing how to use it. It must lead us to take warning in one important respect. Vocabulary is the *"open end"* of language. We spend our lives enlarging our knowledge of words. The more we can do to enlarge that knowledge, the more we can attain the satisfaction of knowing precisely what we are enjoying and of being able to share that knowledge with those around us. But, words are thought of to be rather as tools than as metals and ornaments.

Enlarged vocabulary is equally a ridiculous acquisition without the corresponding knowledge of how the words we have learnt are in fact used and of where they serve a useful purpose.

We do not inherit words and the tales they tell. Many times, as the story of Aladdin and his Wonderful Lamp has told, it must be told again for every child as the new generation comes upon the stages.

When building a vocabulary fit to express all our thoughts, hopes and emotions, we need to remember that words are symbols, standing for things. If we did not have words, we should be condemned to carrying around large bundles of things instead, like the professors.

When you improve your vocabulary, it will be larger and broader, but it will also have greater *depth* and *precision* enabling us to use the word-symbol which most closely calls up the things symbolised. It will enable you to express purposefully facts, ideas, feelings and experiences. A word fittingly chosen is like an electric switch: something that turns on the light.

Our stock of words is enlarged when experiences are woven into our lives. Our writing is effective, vivid and interesting when we put this stuff of our lives into it.

Semantics

The word "semantics" has been defined as "the study of the meanings of speech forms, especially of the development and changes in meanings of words and word group." In other words, it is a systematic study of meanings of the words.

The science of semantic is the science of meaning. It may be noted that "semantic" is not related to phonetics which deals with the science of sounds. Communication is symbolic using of certain arbitrary symbols that give meaning to the words. Meaning to a message is transferred by way of symbolic transfer. Arbitrary words are only a map that describes a territory but not a real territory itself. It is because of the fact that the words should be interpreted. The word "cow" does not look like a cow, sound like a cow, or smell like a cow, but it means a cow, because we have made it a symbol for a cow. The difficult process in communication is a symbolic transfer of meanings. It is purely a personal process.

Age, experience, perception, attitudes, etc., play a major role in drawing the meaning of the words by the receiver. But one can make effective communication understandable to the receiver provided the transfer of meaning is improved.

Semantic is one of the major barriers to effective communication. They occur from limitations in the symbols which the sender communicates. Sometimes, the semantic barrier may lead to emotional barrier and communication may be further blocked. When a communication selects a meaning for a word which is no factual, one has to make an inference.

The First 'Word' = "Maheswara Sutrani"= Vedic Background

"Information, i.e., "Kantras" is the key to enlightenment?" = vedas. Rig, Yajur, Sama and Atharvana vedas communicate through symbols. In fact, the vedic symbolism is telescopic, i.e., symbolism within symbolism. There are three modes of comprehension of the Vedas: The literal or physical, natural and spiritual. The communicating of them is patterned accordingly. Vedas signify the power of a word as well as the power of the meaning of a word. Example: at the end, the Rig Veda says "Let us go together and talk you and I" (Samgachadevam Samvadadhwam).

Probe into 'Maheswara Sutrani' describes 'Mahesware" — Lord Shiva— by playing the minidrum in his left hand, released the alphabets, *viz*., "Ka cha ta tha paa..." for us to communicate with each other by word of mouth. This was followed by our venerable sages writing on palm leaves.

Words

A set of arbitrary symbols used in communicating ideas are called words. Because words are accepted for use and applied uniformly by all the people attributing something to convey. The word "cow" is used to represent the words which have some meaning on account of their being used by large number of people, but all will not attach exactly the same meaning to the same words. It is because words have multiple meanings.

A person may project meaning, depending on his own acquaintance, experience and context with the speaker and the object. Calling a person dishonest or indisciplined or disobedient does not necessarily mean that he is actually so. Another person may call the same person as honest, obedient, or disciplined. Both are right. The situation, circumstances and the context also attribute meanings. Thus, meanings are not in words but in people. Words have no meaning, meanings have words, meanings are in people.

Words are the most familiar tool or type of symbol employed by communication. *Words* have power only to the extent the people know their *Words* have flesh, weight, sound and appearance. Words exist for their meanings. Words have to be employed as a means, not as an end. Words are like leaves; where they most abound, much fruit of sense beneath is rarely found. Words should be used not only to balance a sentence but to balance an idea.

Words are Symbols

A word is the smallest unit of language whether written, spoken or read which can be used independently. An impulse or idea is encoded into symbols, to express in written or spoken language. Encoding is the process of converting the message in wording which implies die manner of expressing something in words. Words are arbitrary symbols used in communication which are not the same as any object they represent.

Words are arbitrary symbols of the object which they represent. The importance of understanding the concept that words are symbols of communication cannot be overemphasised. Generally, people, time and time again consider words as if they have some natural inherent meaning. Words merely represent things. Though they represent things, they represent them imperfectly and incompletely. It is because of the fact that some of the characteristics have been necessarily let out.

Words merely represent things as abstracting. Abstracting means referring to something which exists as an idea which is not physically real. Therefore, words are applied to objects as things only after several steps of abstracting. Yet as a discussion, the word cannot be the event, which would be necessary if the word had meaning in itself. For instance, a pinch on the arm may provoke one to utter words. These words are not the same things as the sensations felt at the non-verbal level.

C. K. Ogden etc developed a simple device to illustrate how a word only represents something in a non-verbal world. They developed "triangle of reference" as given below:

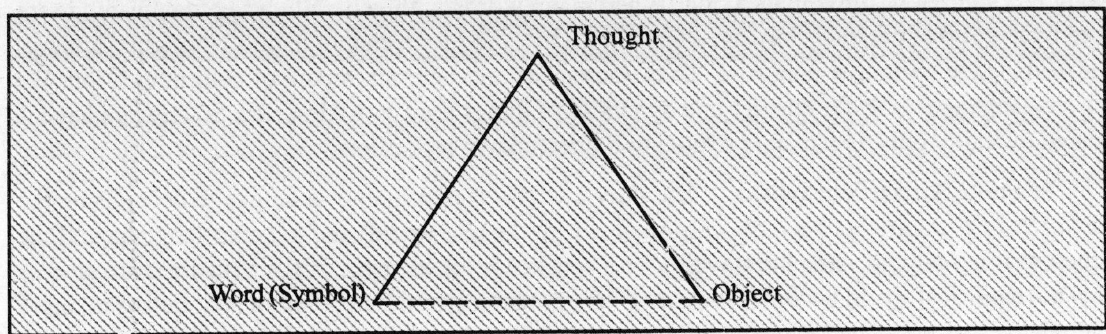

Fig. 15.1

The figure given above has two thick lines or sides and a broken line horizontally to represent the relationship that exist between objects and words that represent objects. The right-hand corner is the object to which a word refers. The left-hand corner represents the word relating to the object. The top corner relating to thought refers to the word and object. Thus, there is a direct relationship between thought and object, that thick side and the direct relationship between thought and word that expresses the thought, left thick line. A word either spoken, symbol bears an indirect relationship to the object, broken line.

The two thick sides indicate a two-sided relationship. The right side line represents the direct relationship between the object and the thought. The words used to denote the object is to represent the relationship between the thought and the word, left side line. The relationship is the most direct between the word and the object. The basic feature is that a word, for instance, "business" is only a symbol for something.

The object may be any concept, i.e., existing for the personal communication. Concept is only an idea or theory or something conceived or imagined but concepts are much more encompassing than physical things. There may be some concepts which may exist in mythical literature, say, for instance "Mermaids." The word "mermaid" means an imaginary sea-creature with a human body down to the waist and a fish's tail.

So people can communicate about mermaids. Similarly, people can communicate about turtles which physically exist. Turtle is a kind of large tortoise, living in water. Therefore, a communication about mermaids which do not physically exist can be as accurate as communication about turtles which actually and physically exist. It is the person who conceives a concept and attaches word attributing to the concept about something. Thus the words or symbols, a person can communicate symbolically using arbitrary symbols about the concept by using symbols or words or signals.

Words are necessary to communicate the perceived ideas. The fields of logic and mathematics too offer wide scope for us to substantiate our argument that words are only symbols, where communication takes place with precision. In these, no physical things exist. Thus, the communicators involved in message exchange use words or symbols to which they attach meanings.

Language is a human speech. It is speech of a particular nation. It also denotes the words and way of speaking, writing, usually concerned with a particular group of people. A manner of expressing thought, a style of writing or speaking. When many words with generally accepted meanings are used by a group of persons, they have language. One, therefore, cannot express thoughts, feelings and knowledge without a language. Thus, languages are the main media of communication. We can say languages lack complexity and dynamics of things they try to describe. So any language is related to reality only as a map is related to the territory it represents.

To quote Alfred Korzybski: " The only usefulness of a map or a language depends on the *similarity of structure* between the empirical world (the real world) and the map-languages. If the structure is not similar, then the traveller or a speaker is led astray.... If the structures are *similar then* the empirical world becomes "rational" to a potentially rational being, which means no more than that verbal, or map-predicted characteristics... are applicable to the empirical world."

The symbolic nature of the words and languages was summarised by Korzybski in the following three premises:

(1) Words which made up our store of knowledge are not the things they represent. (A map is not the territory).

(2) Words can never say everything about anything, for there are always certain characteristics about something which cannot be included in or described by words. (A map does not represent all of a territory).

(3) Thus, an ideal map would have to include a map of the map of the map, and so on. With language, it is possible to speak words about words, words about words about words, and so on to an infinite level of abstraction. (A map is self-reflexive).

Communication requires a source that has some thoughts, ideas or information to transmit. A human source translates mental perceptions into "code that represents the meaning which the sender wishes to transmit. It is only through language which represents as the most popular code used to express mental perceptions of the source. Source is also an encoder of the original message. Receiver also encodes in symbols. Military messages are encoded into a secret code. A business message is encoded into a computer language.

Words Have Multiple Meanings

The method of communication is word. Many people spare more time on the word communication. Many of common words have several meanings. K. Davis states that multiple meanings are necessary because we are trying to talk about an infinite complex word by using only a limited number of words. A word, when it is used in one sense, may be derogatory but, when used another way, it can be acceptable. For example, the word "dummy" in an argument at the office may be uncomplimentary but its use to refer to a person serving as a dummy in a game is acceptable.

One may surprise to know that there are certain words which have a variety of meanings. For instance, the word "round", it seems has 79 different meanings. This definitely gives trouble to communicate in exactly a similar way and effectively.

The word 'round' has 79 different meanings, adjectives 18, nouns 19, verbs 26, prepositions 9 and special 7. For example, round hundred, round trip, go round, go round off etc.

On the other hand, a question often arises when words have no meaning, it is not possible to make a sense with them. Then, how can one communicate with people? The answer to such a crucial question is context or environment. As common words have several meanings or multiple meanings. They have meanings when they are put into context, otherwise they become meaningless. So the effective communication is *idea-centred* rather than *word-centred.* We must remember that words do not mean, but people. As K. Davis rightly remarks that language with inadequate context is a *semantic smog* like *a real smog,* it irritates our senses and interferes with our perception.

In most of message of non-factual meanings, inferences are bound to be there in all circumstances.

A number of factors will influence to draw the meaning of the words in a message such as:

(1) *Recognition* and acceptance by the sender and receiver.

(2) The *context* in which the message takes place.

(3) The *perception and understanding* ability.

(4) Facts, *opinions and feelings* used in communication.

(5) The extent of *abstractness* of arbitrary words used.

Semantics act as barriers to effective communication. These words have universal recognition and popularity for their use as way of life. These words are symbols used by people to express ideas having similarity of experiences and accepting the words. Word meanings have different things to different people. It is appropriate to quote that according to Charles C. Fries and Thorn-Dike Word Book, 500 most-used words in English Dictionary have 14,070 separate meanings in the Oxford Dictionary. Therefore, a correct or effective communication may not be possible in some cases between the sender and the receiver because both of them may not be familiar with the dictionary meanings of more than 6 lakh words in English language. In addition to them, differences in perception, experiences etc., render difference in meaning in exchange.

Words Have Width and Depth

One may be a good workman in writing who uses the implements of his craft of writing with care and skill. He chooses words as a skilled mechanist chooses the tools that will do particular jobs in the finest way.

Words are picked up by the conscious minds and made into pictures in the subconscious. When you write, you are writing a constant, the ratio of the circumference of a circle to its diameter; when you write formula 'NaCl you are indicating the chemical substance sodium chloride and it always means that substance and nothing else. Few words in common use have such limited denotations as these. Consider "mother" and "father." They are extended into multiple new areas of use such as "mother" of parliaments, mother earth, mother wit; the child is father of the man, father to that thought.

Interpretations we give words is bound up with the images they evoke. "Informer" and "informant" may be said to mean, roughly, the same thing, but note the difference that they may be read into them. 'Informer' makes us think of stool pigeons and talebearers; 'Informant' has no such nasty frill attached to it.

Nearly every writer is tempted at times to embellish his work by using qualifying words; others are dead set against the use of words that modify words. Without doubt, adjectives and adverbs can weaken a statement or blur the meaning.

One cannot measure a writer's genius by the length of his words. Some enjoy use of big words without paying attention to their meaning; others use gigantic words on the microscopic topic, like pinning a white beard on the face of a child and yet others think that their dignity demands that they use many-syllabled words. When Dr. Johnson was asked about a comedy, he said: "It has not wit enough to keep it sweet." Then realising that this sentence was not up to the standard of his sonorous prose, he hastened to give a more full-toned sentence: "It has not vitality enough to preserve it from putrefaction."

Choice of Words

Clarity in message is achieved by word-choice. Clarity can be reinforced by stating all of a comparison. Wolf *et. al., state* that clarity of a business message can be attained through word-choice involving (1) empathy, (2) definition, (3) explanation, and (4) description.

(1) Word Choice by Empathy: Even the most commonly used words do not give exactly the same meaning, an idea or feelings in various minds or in one mind at various times. The knowledge of the communicator as well as the knowledge and perception of the receiver would influence the word choice.

(2) Word Choice by Definition: Using unfamiliar words which are unusual to the receiver, the communicator should state that what he means by using and should not state what the term means. Some common terms require definition in messages. Precise definition or what he means by using a particular familiar term in an information way. A statistical or mathematical term may be common terms to a statistician or mathematician but needs definition in messages to a non- statistician or non-mathematician. And the term 'debit' signifies one thing to an accountant but something else to a non-accountant.

(3) Word Choice by Explanation: To satisfy logical needs, choose words, that help your receiver understand, identify, compare, contrast, remember or apply what your message represents.

(4) Word-Choice by Description: The description of a communication event, that clarifies messages to the receiver to understand. "To satisfy psychological needs, choose words that help your receiver experience the *feelings* of seeing, hearing, tasting, touching, smelling, enjoying or profiting from what your message conveys."

In an oral message or oral report, all necessary words for understanding the sentences or ideas are to be included. Omitted words may result in conveying an inaccurate message. Complete wording is more important for understanding and, at the same time, avoid using incomplete wordings.

Words have no Meaning

Words have no meaning; meanings have the words; meanings are in the minds of the people.

Examples

Incomplete Wording	*Complete Wording*
1. The registered office is at 225 Chandni Chowk.	1. The registered office is at 225, Second Main Cross, Chandni Chowk.
2. The bus reservation has been confirmed for 11-30 tomorrow.	2. The bus reservation has been confirmed for 11-45 A.M. tomorrow.
3. Just sign the enclosed pay bill.	3. Just sign and return the enclosed pay bill.

Lessons on communication refer to problems of semantics, which basically mean that words and other symbols of language are attributed different meanings by different people, and therefore, what is said is not what is understood. The problem is easily appreciated when discussed academically; yet, in real life, all of us behave as if every word has a precise meaning and connotation.

Many uproars in Parliament and Legislatures arise out of particular words being objected to. The word "deshadrohi" created a major crisis in July 1991, almost threatening the Government. A few years ago, when President Zia of Pakistan referred to the Prime Minister as that " Woman", it was construed as an insult. Was the "insult" in the word or in the minds of the people? Suppose, if President Zia had intended an insult, and he chose the word "woman" to convey the same. But the word "Woman" in no dictionary is described as an expression of abuse or ridicule. It is as value-free as "Man" or "Child." The word "Woman" does not have the connotation insult. But the meaning of insult was introduced into it, in the context in which the minds of men saw its usage. When two friends are discussing a controversial issue for some time and one says, "My Dear Friend", before beginning his argument, he is not reaffirming friendship.

Consider the situation when a subordinate has presented his original work to his senior and the senior looks up to him and smiles. Is that smile an expression of pleasure, of satisfaction, of appreciation, of sarcasm, of criticism, or something else? The meaning is not in the smile but in the mind of the subordinate, who sees the smile. He draws the conclusion on the basis of the present data (smile plus body position plus eye movement etc.) plus a lot of past data stored in his mind relating to the nature and behaviour of this particular senior and of seniors in general.

If there has to be an agreement between the two about what was intended and what was understood, it is necessary to assess the past data also, which have contributed to the meaning. This is rarely attempted and clarifications are sought and given, if at all, only on the present tansaction will not fully explain the difference in meaning. But even the recall is generally far from accurate, leading to disputes about what exactly was said, and further to assertions of the other person telling lies or twisting facts.

Very often, an idea or a thought cannot be conveyed in a word or two. Several words are used to explain the thought. The listener, however, responds to the words as he hears them. Every word evokes a meaning and several meanings ultimately create a pattern that is identical to the thought intended by the speaker. What happens often, is that the listener get stuck to some words and the meaning drawn from them, misses some other words and as a result forms a different pattern of thought. This difference is then attributed to the speaker himself. The words cited in support would be correct and the meanings, not deniable. It is in such a situation that the speaker complaints of being "quoted out of context." He will admit to mouthing the words and still insist that, that is not what he meant. The listener will say that he is now having second thoughts, or that he is making up.

This situation is similar to making a sketch or a drawing, where the meaning has to come from the totality of lines after completion, and not from certain emphasised lines in part of the picture. The painter completes the picture by drawing the lines, one at a time, and shading the areas one by one. The viewer waits and sees it in its totality at the end. If he were to stand by, watching the creation of the picture and reaching to the parts as they were developing, the understanding could never be proper. In the case of verbal efforts, the total view is possible only after the listener himself draws the lines and shades in his mind from the words that he is listening to, one at a time. He has to draw the lines himself, in exactly the way as the speaker does, with the same quickness, and the same curves. The listener, however, decides emphasis from the words, the tone and the facial expressions plus his own recorded impressions from the past. Congruence meaning being identical in all respects may suffer in the process. Naturally, what he 'sees' is not what was being shown.

If any one has a problem in understanding the above paragraph, it only proves the point that is being made. Written communication is advantageous as it is possible to go back and check to ensure congruence. Non-verbal has the advantage that the listener's participation, in the creation of the final picture, is minimal. These problems occur mostly in feeble transactions. They are encountered repeatedly by insurance salesmanship in their contact with prospects. All literature on insurance salesmanship in their contacts with prospects. All literature on insurance salesmanship warn salesman not to react to the words of the prospects, but to the real meaning; to listen to not what he is saying but what be wants to say. It is emphasised that when an objection is raised or a 'No' is said to a proposal, the real meaning may be that the salesman has not explained enough.

Etymology

The study of the origin and development of words and their meaning is called etymology. The subject deals with the root of a word in the history of its origin. The study of origin of words is called etymology. It has its roots in the Greek word *Etymon* and *logia.* "Etymon" means true or original meaning. "Logia" means science or study. Therefore, etymology deals with the science or study of true or original meaning.

Communication Factors

There are various ways in which verbal intelligence conveys attitudes, tacts, feelings etc. The communication factors are as follows:

(1) Denotation: Literally "denotation" means to be the sign of or to mean things. It is a direct statement of meaning. It refers, point outs with words but not with physical things.

(2) Connotation: Connotation with reference to communication implies what is suggested by a word, in addition to its simple meaning. It is a suggested meaning. To connote is to simply hint about but not to state directly. It refers to what one thinks and feels.

(3) Context: It is what causes before and after a word, phrase, statement which help to fix meaning. it is a communicative environment, a setting of words and symbols. It is the context in which denotation and connotation function.

Puntuations

The use of punctuation marks. It is a process of division of sentences by commas, full stops, colon and other marks. With the help of punctuation marks, a sentence is divided into various meaningful parts. Some types of marks, symbols, signs have been evolved and practised for joining or separating words, phrases, clauses, and sentences. In a written communication, punctuations are very important for achieving clarity in a message and to avoid vague or confusion to a reader.

Punctuations are also used for integration, emphasis, prevention of alteration of message, avoidance or misunderstanding. These are cues which constitute a sub-system of language. The effective writing is not possible unless punctuations are used. These cues or marks' used are called *punctuation marks.* This paragraph is meant to make the reader conversant with various punctuations for application to write skillfully. The following are the punctuations which have been briefly explained below:

(1) Comma
(2) Question mark
(3) Exclamation mark
(4) Semi-colon
(5) Colon
(6) Apostrophes
(7) Quotation mark
(8) Hyphen
(9) Dash
(10) Parenthesis
(11) Bracket
(12) Ellipses
(13) Double comma
(14) Caret
(15) Full stop.

(1) Comma (,): The punctuation mark "comma" is used to show a slight or shorter pause. It is used for several purposes as indicated .below:

Dear Sir,

Yours faithfully,

e.g.,

20th October, 1995

He said,

Mr. Rama said,

Acceptable, However,

Therefore.

Please note that,

Viz.,

etc.,

f.o.b.,

(2) Question Mark (?): In a sentence that says something which is said, written etc., which asks for an answer from someone. Question mark may be put at the end of a word, phrase, sentence. The question words are:

Why

What

When

Where

How

Whose

Whom

What is your name?

How are You?

Why didn't yon come?

Who asked?

Where are you put up?

When is he expected?

Whose book is it?

(3) Exclamation Mark (!): The object of using exclamation mark is to draw the attention of the reader with personal feeling. Exclamation means with personal feeling. Exclamation means an expression of feeling of surprise, wonder or other sudden, unexpected and unheard feelings. The mark (!) shows exclamation. It is generally used in an urgent command, extraordinary emotion, anger and exceptional emphasis. For example,

Stop!

Look!

Listen!

Oh!

Ah!

What a wonder!

How wonderful!

Alas!

Hurray!

Hurrah!

Hoorah!

Hooray!

(4) Semi-colon (;): To complete a sentence, the mark of semi-colon is used. A punctuation mark is used to separate parts of a sentence which have more independence than clauses separated by a comma. It is used to separate a compound sentence transition and items of a series. The words like:

However

Therefore

Hence

Thus

Besides

are used after a sentence.

Examples

(i) Verbal speech has many aspects; for example, facial expressions, body movements, gestures, postures etc.

(ii) There was an earthquake; however no loss of life.

(iii) Idle man's mind is a devil's workshop; but hard work fetches.

(iv) Invitations were short sent to three people; Rama, Murali, Ravi.

(v) **Colon** (;).Punctation indicates a closing of a sentence. It is used to separate sentences like units within a sentence or before a list, a series of changes etc. It is also of a memo etc.

Examples

Ex

Encl

Dear Sir

To:

C C:

From:

Date:

Subject:

Ref:

(6) Apostrophe ('): It is used to punctuate a position to indicate omitted letters of contraction and to show plural abbreviation. The mark is used to show that a letter or letters has or have been omitted from a word.

Examples

(a) Possessive Apostrophe:

Teacher's table

Company's name

Officer's chamber

Dealer's ccmplaint

Director's report

P. M.'s visit

(b) Apostrophe is placed after the letter 's' in case noun is a plural.

Workers' problems

Students' research

Customers' demand

Companies' annual report

Firms' goodwill

Weeks' leave

(c) Apostrophe is used before the letter's' in the case of plural nouns which do not have 's.' For instance:

Children's problems

Women's University

Men's hostel

(d) Omitted letters: In the case of omitted letters, apostrophe is used to indicate omission. When letters are omitted, the words are combined into one word.

Examples

She will	— She'll
did not	— did't
would not	— wouldn't
we are	— we're
I am	— I'm
Was not	— wasn't
were not	— weren't
It is	— It's
I should, would	— I'd

(7) Quotation marks (" " '): These punctuation marks are used to indicate the exact words of the writer or speaker. Punctuation mark (s) are used to show the person's exact words are being repeated by someone. Quotation marks are also called "inverted commas". It is popularly used in practice — both double and single quotation and there is not much difference between them. Full stop is kept inside the inverted comma. Quotation marks are used like to enclose direct quotation.

Examples

(i) I asked, "Who is the class teacher of your class."

(ii) "Who", I asked, "Is your boss"?

(iii) The inspector asked, "Who is your employer? What is his name"?

Inverted commas are also used to enclose title of books, chapters, magazine articles, newspaper items. For instance:

Have you seen "Economic Indicator" in financial journal of March?

Quotation marks are also used to enclose certain special words tike slang terms, unusual words, word for special effect, technical words and other jargon.

(8) Hyphen (-): A short stroke. It is used to join two parts of a word or phrase particularly a compound non. Hyphen is used to divide a word, follow prefixes between two adjectives, compound number and to clarify the meaning.

Examples

co-exist

sleeping-bag

well-thought-out-plan

first-in-first-out

co-operation

co-ordination

co-terminus

co-education

to-morrow

to-day

anti-government

ex-employer

self-centred.

(9) Dash(—): It is used to break a sentence, to show a sudden interruption in thinking or writing to convey momentary suspense for emphasis or apposite and to replace commas for emphasis.

Examples

(1) The chief guest should arrive at 5PM — better make to 5-30 PM to be sure.

(2) Congratulations, Doctor Saxena—you have been conferred a doctoral degree.

(10) Parentheses ( ): The punctuation mark is used to separate the words or group of words within a sentence from the rest of a sentence. Semi-round shaped bracket.

(11) Bracket [ ]: The bracket mark is used in writing or printing to enclose or group together one or more words, symbols. It is also used to enclose figures or words or group of words already in parenthesis. Such marks are:

[[] [()] { } < >]

(12) Ellipses (....): Punctuation marks indicate omission of words or figures. It is called as omission mark it indicates deletion from the already quoted material. A figure of speech in which word or words needed for the sense or grammar are omitted. But understood. Generally, ellipses consist of three dots with intervening space. It is used for a period, question mark, exclamation when ellipses end a sentence. For instance:

The purchase price is Rs. 20 lakhs — original.

The purchase price is Rs.... ellipses.

1995 — original ... 95 ellipses

Any law, for the time being in force, will apply — original

Any law ... will apply (ellipses)

(13) Double Comma ("): The mark is used to indicate "ditto" or the same. Examples

(a) January 10 1995
"15 1995
"20 1995

(b) Media and Communication Management by C. S. Rayudu
Principles of Public Relations by "
Mass Media Laws and Regulations by "

(14) Caret (^): It is a mark used in printing or typing to canny out a correction to show where to insert word or words, phrase, figure etc., missed originally.

Examples

(i) His hand writing is very illegible to read.

(ii) The assessment year, 1995 relating to income from house property.

(15) Fullstop (.): A mark of written or printed point indicating the end of a sentence, period, or abbreviation to separate sentences.

Prefix and Suffix

(1) Prefix: Prefix is a syllable or syllables put at the beginning of another word to change its meaning. It is placed in front of a word to add to or change its meaning or function. Prefixes are of several kinds. They are:

(1) Prefixes that change the meaning

(2) Prefixes relating to numbers.

(3) Prefixes which change the part of speech.

The prefixes which change the meaning of the base of reverse or negate the meaning, degree, size, time, order, attitude. They are anti-, ex-, pro-, self- vice-, contra-, etc.

Examples

a	:	atheist, asymmetry
contra	:	Contra-Entry; Contra-suggestible
de	:	decode, devaluation
dis	:	dishonest; disallow; discharge
im	:	impossible
in	:	inability

Examples

-eer	:	Engineer
-er	:	two-wheeler
-ship	:	membership
-ful	:	fruitful
-list	:	capitalist
-ism	:	socialism
-er	:	writer
-ee	:	drawee
-ment	:	agreement
-ness	:	hardness, happiness
-ity	:	activity
-ful	:	helpful, beautiful
-less	:	childless
-ing	:	printing, jumping

Parts of a Speech

Every sentence has a subject part and a predicate part There are eight parts of speech which should be learnt by every communicator to be effective in writing or speaking. They are:

(1) Noun
(2) Pronoun
(3) Adjective
(4) Verb
(5) Adverb
(6) Prepositions
(7) Conjunctions
(8) Interjection

(1) Noun: Noun is a word as the name of a person, animal, place, state, or thing. Noun is a naming word.

(2) Pronoun: Pronoun is used as a substitute of a noun. It is a word used instead of the noun or phrase containing a noun.

Examples

he

I

she

they

Rare	:	infrequent, scarce
Rear	:	back, backdoor, reverse
Recover	:	regain, disclose, confess
Sage	:	saint, yogi, guru, wise man
Salary	:	payment, remuneration, money
Wit	:	humour, joke, amusement
Wrong	:	error, mistake
Yearly	:	annually
Yield	:	surrender, give, produce
Zenith	:	top
Zest	:	enthusiasm

Antonyms

Ability x Inability
Able x Unable
Abnormal x Normal
Above x Below
Absent x Present
Absolute x Limited
Abundance x Insufficiency
Accord x Discord
Accurate x Inaccurate
Agree x Differ
Arrogant x Humble
Badness x Goodness
Ban x Freedom
Bankrupt x Wealthy
Beautiful x Ugly
Beginning x Ending
Big x Small
Bold x Timid
Bright x Dull
Care x Neglect
Cold x Hot
Crime x Innocence
Cheap x Dear
Clean x Dirty

me

him

you

them

it

we

their

whom

(3) Adjective: Adjective is a word which describes a noun or qualifies a noun.

Examples

White jasmine.

Red flower or rose.

Water which is cool.

The hockey team played a thrilling game.

A huge crowd attended.

He became very old.

Water is overflowing.

Adjective may be of positive, comparative or superlative degree.

(4) Verb: Verb is a part of speech, a word or phrase that gives action or asserts something in a sentence or change. Verb indicates action or state of being. It represents the subject like does, did, done etc.

Examples

I *saw* it.

He *ran* away.

I *have* a feeling,

What *is* that?

He *teaches* speaking skills.

The baby *broke* the glass.

The aircrafts *fly*.

A verb may be auxiliary, ordinary, main or intransitive linking verb.

(5) Adverb: Adverb is used to modify verbs, adjectives and other adverbs. So, adverb is a word used before or after a verb, before an adjective or preposition or with another adverb to show time, manner, place or degree.

Examples

He ran away *very fast.*

I am *dam* tired and I need rest.

Doctor comes to see me *daily.*

Yesterday he exclaimed *more* carefully.

(6) Preposition: A word put before a noun or pronoun to show how it is related to another word. It takes a position before a noun which governs the noun.

Examples

I have seen *through* their window.

Children are playing *in* the garden.

The lesson is written *by* me.

Children lay down *on* the floor.

I shall go to school *after* 10 o'clock.

We have to *cross* the river to reach the town.

(7) Conjunction: It is word that connects or joints sentences, changes or words. It is also called as connectors.

Examples

so that	if
and	although
as	since
that	thus
with	of
but	either of
neither-nor	not only but also
yet	still
while	though
in case	as soon as
lest	as if

X *and* Y danced.

It will go *if you* want.

Give me *either* coffee *or* tea.

I take *neither* coffee *nor* tea.

He is *not only* industrious *but also* intelligent.

He is very good at speaking *as well as* in writing.

(10) Interjection: Interjections are sounds of such words expressed a strong or sudden feeling, surprise, joy, fear, sadness, emotions etc. Interjections are dramatically connected with the rest of the sentence and independent of other words or word group.

Examples

Ah!

hurrah!

Alas!

O!

Oh!

ho!

ha!

Articles: The words a, *an* and *the* are called articles. *The* is called definite article and *a* and *an* are called indefinite articles.

Sentence Structure

There are four types of sentence-structure making. They are:

(1) Simple sentence
(2) Compound sentence
(3) Complex sentence
(4) Compound-complex sentence

(1) Simple Sentence: A sentence is said to be simple when it has a subject and one verb in the predicate part. In other words, it has one independent clause but no dependent clause.

Examples

It is very hot.

He worked hard.

He became a doctor.

It is not easy to pass.

(2) Compound Sentence: A sentence is said to be a compound sentence when it has at least two independent clauses but one dependent clause. The words like the following are used in constructing a compound sentence:

either... or

neither... nor

but

yet

still

for

so

not only — but also

therefore

I went to a theatre several times, but I was unable to get a ticket.

He is very intelligent, yet he is not happy.

There was no notice, so I could not attend the meeting.

He was absent from duties, therefore, he was terminated from the service.

(3) Complex Sentence: A sentence is said to be complex when it contains not more than one independent clause but one dependent clause.

Example

As soon as the meeting began, a shareholder said that he wanted to raise a point of order.

(4) Compound-Complex Sentence: A compound sentence and at least one additional independent clause constitutes a compound-complex sentence.

Synonyms and Antonyms

Synonyms: The word "synonyms" means words that have the same meaning or very merely the same meanings as another is called a synonym. But, sometimes, even the synonym will mean different meanings, depending upon the context. According to Laurence Well, there is no such thing as true synonym. Synonym words are always interchangeable because language functions at different levels, some more formal and others less formal. The user of the words must be careful in selecting a synonym for a word because it must be appropriate to the context and the kind of writing or speaking.

Antonyms: Words that have opposite meanings are called antonyms. Antonyms are also formed by adding prefixes like un, dis, in, im, non, ir, etc. For instance:

Un : Unimportant, unkind, unknown

Dis : Disgree, disappear, dislike

In : Inefficiency, insufficiency, incorrect

Im : Important, improvement

Ir : Irreparable, irregular, irrelevant

Non : Non-semester, non-verbal, non-violence

Selected Synonyms

Abandon : desert, leave, foresake

Able : capable, competent, efficient, skilled, ability, faculty, talent, know-how, efficiency

Abnormal : irregular, eccentric, aberrant

Absence : missing, lost, omitted, wanting

Abstain : refrain, withhold, forebear

Abundance : plenty, fulness, wealth, sufficiency

Ancient	:	aged, antique, hoary
Answer	:	reply, disclosure, clue, response
Bankrupt	:	insolvent, broke, ruin
Beauty	:	attraction, loveliness, bloom, cosmetics
Begin	:	commence, start, rise, starting point
Calm	:	quite,s tranquil, peaceful
Careful	:	meticulous, scrupulous
Category	:	class, division
Complete	:	finish, conclude, over
Curiosity	:	interest, thirst, sear
Confusion	:	disorder, disarray
Clever	:	Intelligent, skilled
Casual	:	chance, uncertain
Comprehend	:	understand, apprehend
Danger	:	peril, risk, hazard
Darkness	:	blackness, dusk, shade, eclipse
Decide	:	determine, resolve, settle
Decay	:	decline, wither, fade
Death	:	expire, deceased, cessation
Disease	:	sickness, ailment, disorder
Efficient	:	able, capable, competent
Eager	:	anxious, earnest, keen
Each	:	every, apiece
Error	:	mistake, blunder, slip, laxity
Fair	:	just, equitable, impartial
Failure	:	unsuccessful, miscarriage, vain
Fictitious	:	false, untrue, imaginary
Flimsy	:	slight, small, thin
Fatal	:	deadly, critical, cutthroat
Forbid	:	ban, prohibit, abolished
Foolish	:	silly, stupid
Godly	:	divine, pious, devout
Greedy	:	avaricious, covetous
Gratitude	:	gratefulness, indebtedness, acknowledgment
Habit	:	custom, practice, precedence
Hasty	:	hurry, rash, speed

Hate	:	disfavour, enmity, hostility
Humble	:	modesty, lowly
Heaven	:	God, Eden, glory, paradise
Idle	:	lazy, unoccupied sluggish
Identity	:	oneness, individuality, same
Join	:	connect, unite, combine
Junction	:	connection, union, blend, merge
Joy	:	delight, happiness, merry, pleasure
Junior	:	inferior, minority, inadequate
Kill	:	death, murder, assassinate
Knowledge	:	idea, cognizance, familiarity
Kind	:	please, mercy, soft
Land	:	earth, desert, ground, wet land
Labour	:	work, toil, energy, hard work
Limit	:	boundary, compound, confine
Loyal	:	faithful, devoted, honest
Luxuriance	:	wealthy, opulence, affluence
Loyal	:	duty, devotion, homage
Length	:	distance, range, span, measurement
Mad	:	insane, lunacy, deranged
Method	:	manner, way, mode
Money	:	finance, fund, treasure, sum
Meagre	:	small, little, insufficient
Name	:	importance, prominence, fame
Negligent	:	careless, thoughtlessness, laxity,
New	:	fresh, modern, novel
Obscene	:	indecent, filthy, unparliamentary
Occasion	:	opportunity, circumstance, offer, tender
Odd	:	strange, peculiar
Offend	:	annoy, outrage
Only	:	solely, singly, one
Onerous	:	burdensome
Opening	:	entrance, doorway, entry
Perform	:	accomplish, discharge, execute
Price	:	cost, wealth, worth, value
Quarrel	:	dispute, difference, feud, attack

ir	:	irresponsible
Non	:	Non-vegetarian; Non-committal; Non-party
Un	:	Unimportant
Extra	:	Extraordinary
Semi	:	Semi circle
Super	:	Super Market
Sub	:	Subdivision
Ultra	:	Ultra violet
hyper	:	hypertension
Mini	:	Mini car; Mini theatre; Mini bus
Under	:	Undercover; Understand; Under-estimate
Fore	:	foretell; forecast
Pre	:	pre-paid; pre-phone; pre-war
Post	:	Post-war; post-independence
ex	:	ex-principal; ex-employer
re	:	rewrite; remind; rewind
Vice	:	Vice president;Vice chancellor
Co	:	Co-operation; Co-ordination; Co-terminus
Counter	:	Counterfoil; Counteract
ante	:	ante government; ante party; ante nation
multi	:	multinational; multicorner; multimillionnaire; multimedia
en	:	endanger
em	:	empower

(2) Suffix: A small part added to the end of a word or stem that changes the meaning and often grammatical function like:

-ness
-ly
-able
-ty
-wish
-it
-er
-ee
-ment
-y
-full

It is a word or syllable placed after a word to add or change its meaning or function.

Caustic x Courteous
Curiosity x Indifference
Danger x Safety
Decrease x Increase
Deep x Shallow
Difficult x Easy
Diligent x Idle
Distance x Near
Dry x Wet
Early x Late
Economical x Extravagant
Emigrant x Immigrant
Encourage x Discourage
Explicit x Implicit
Exist x Entrance
Fact x Fiction
Failure x Success
Fair x Foul
Fashion x Vulgar
Fast x Slow
Fatal x Fortunate
Female x Mate
Flattery x Distraction
Flexible x Rigid
Foolish x Wise
Fresh x Stale
Gain x Loss
Gentle x Rough
Genuine x Spurious
Godly x Impious
Growth x Decline
Guilty x Innocent
Hard x Soft
Haste x Delay
Heaven x Hell
Heavy x Light

High x Low
Hope x Despair
Host x Guest
Humble x Proud
Idle x Busy
Import x Export
Inferior x Superior
Innocent x Guilty
Input x Output
Junior x Senior
Justice x Injustice
Long x Short
Loose x Tight
Loud x Low
Mad x Sane
Major x Minor
Many x Few
Meager x Plentiful
Merit x Demerit
Minimum x Maximum
Narrow x Broad
Native x Foreign
Natural x Artificial
Neatly x Untidy
New x Old
Normal x Abnormal
Omission x Commission
Oral x Written
Original x Duplicate
Outward x Inward
Peace x War
Permanent x Temporary
Pleasure x Pain
Quick x Slow
Quiet x Noisy
Real x False
Rear x Front

Receive x Give

Remember x Forget

Rich x Poor

Safe x Risk

Sane x Insane

Simple x Complex

Smart x Pull

Strong x Weak

Tense x Relax

Thick x Thin

Vertical x Horizontal

Virtue x Vice

Visible x Invisible

Warm x Cool

Wealth x Poverty

Wrong x Right

Tenses

Tense is a form of a verb that shows the time of its action in relation to the time of speaking. In other words, it is action in the *past,* in *the future* and in the *present.* These forms are called the tense form of the verb. There are four forms of tenses, like:

(1) Simple Present

(2) Simple Past

(3) The Past Participle

(4) (a) Present Continuous

(b) Past Continuous

Every communicator should know them to make effective communication. The following are some selected tenses:

Present	**Past**	**Past Participle**
Abide	Abode	Abode
Arise	Arose	Arisen
Awake	Awake/Awaken	Awoke/Awaken
Bear	Bore	Bore/Bome
Beat	Beat	Beaten
Become	Became	Become
Begin	Began	Begun
Bend	Bent	Bent

Bet	Bel/Betted	Bet/Betted
Bid	Bid/Bode	Bid/Bidden
Bind	Bound	Bound
Bite	Bite	Bitten
Blow	Blew	Blown
Break	Broke	Broken
Breed	Bred	Bred
Bring	Brought	Brought
Burn	Burnt/Burned	Burnt/Burned
Buy	Bought	Bought
Catch	Caught	Caught
Come	Came	Come
Cost	Cost	Cost
Creep	Crept	Crept
Cut	Cut	Cut
Choose	Chose	Chosen
Deal	Dealt	Dealt
Dig	Dug	Dug
Do	Did	Done
Draw	Drew	Drawn
Dream	Dreamt	Dreamt
Drink	Drank	Drunk
Eat	Ate	Eaten
Feel	Felt	Felt
Fight	Fought	Fought
Find	Found	Found
Flee	Fled	Fled
Fly	Flew	Flown
Fall	Fell	Fallen
Spit	Spat	Spat
Stick	Stuck	Stuck
Strike	Struck	Struck
Swim	Swam	Swum
Take	Took	Taken
Teach	Taught	Taught
Tell	Told	Told
Think	Thought	Thought

Understand	Understood	Understood
Wear	Wore	Worn
Weep	Wept	Wept
Win	Won	Won
Wind	Wound	Wound
Work	Worked	Worked
Wring	Wrung	Wrung
Write	Wrote	Written '
Get	Got	Gotten
Give	Gave	Given
Go	Went	Gone
Grow	Grew	Grown
Hang	Hanged/Hung	Hanged/Hung
Have	Had	Had
Hit	Hit	Hit
Keep	Kept	Kept
Know	Knew	Known
Lay	Laid	Laid
Lead	Led	Led
Learnt	Learnt	Learnt
Leave	Left	Left
Let	Let	Let
Lend	Lent	Lent
Lose	Lost	Lost
Run	Ran	Run
See	Saw	Seen
Sell	Sold	Sold
Set	Set	Set
Sink	Sank	Sunk
Sit	Sat	Sat
Sleep	Slept	Slept
Smell	Smelt	Smelt
Speak	Spoke	Spoken

REFERENCE

1. Wolf, Keyser and Aumer, *Effective Communication in Business,* South-Western Pubtislnng Co, 1979, pp. 44-45.

*****